MATTHEW

AN EXPOSITIONAL COMMENTARY

MATTHEW

AN EXPOSITIONAL COMMENTARY

R.C. SPROUL

Matthew: An Expositional Commentary

Published by Ligonier Ministries
421 Ligonier Court, Sanford, FL 32771
Ligonier.org

Printed in China
RR Donnelley
0000522
First edition 2013
Ligonier Ministries edition, fifth printing

ISBN 978-1-64289-176-8 (Hardcover)
ISBN 978-1-64289-177-5 (ePub)
ISBN 978-1-64289-178-2 (Kindle)

Cover design: Ligonier Creative
Interior typeset: Katherine Lloyd, The DESK

All emphases in Scripture quotations have been added by the author.

The Library of Congress has cataloged the Reformation Trust edition as follows:

Names: Sproul, R.C. (Robert Charles), 1939-2017, author.
Title: Matthew : an expositional commentary / R.C. Sproul.
Description: Orlando : Reformation Trust, 2019. | Originally published: Wheaton, Illinois : Crossway, 2013. | Includes bibliographical references and index.
Identifiers: LCCN 2019000105 | ISBN 9781642891768 (hardcover) | ISBN 9781642891775 (epub) | ISBN 9781642891782 (kindle)
Subjects: LCSH: Bible. Matthew--Commentaries. | Bible. Matthew--Sermons.
Classification: LCC BS2575.53 .S67 2019 | DDC 226.2/077--dc23
LC record available at https://lccn.loc.gov/2019000105

CONTENTS

SERIES PREFACE

When God called me into full-time Christian ministry, He called me to the academy. I was trained and ordained to a ministry of teaching, and the majority of my adult life has been devoted to preparing young men for the Christian ministry and to trying to bridge the gap between seminary and Sunday school through various means under the aegis of Ligonier Ministries.

Then, in 1997, God did something I never anticipated: He placed me in the position of preaching weekly as a leader of a congregation of His people—St. Andrew's in Sanford, Florida. Over the past twelve years, as I have opened the Word of God on a weekly basis for these dear saints, I have come to love the task of the local minister. Though my role as a teacher continues, I am eternally grateful to God that He saw fit to place me in this new ministry, the ministry of a preacher.

Very early in my tenure with St. Andrew's, I determined that I should adopt the ancient Christian practice of *lectio continua*, "continuous expositions," in my preaching. This method of preaching verse-by-verse through books of the Bible (rather than choosing a new topic each week) has been attested throughout church history as the one approach that ensures believers hear the full counsel of God. Therefore, I began preaching lengthy series of messages at St. Andrew's, eventually working my way through several biblical books in a practice that continues to the present day.

Previously, I had taught through books of the Bible in various settings, including Sunday school classes, Bible studies, and audio and video teaching series for Ligonier Ministries. But now I found myself appealing not so much to the minds of my hearers but to both their minds and their hearts. I knew that I was responsible as a preacher to clearly explain God's Word *and* to show how we ought to live in light of it. I sought to fulfill both tasks as I ascended the St. Andrew's pulpit each week.

What you hold in your hand, then, is a written record of my preaching labors amidst my beloved Sanford congregation. The dear saints who sit under my preaching encouraged me to give my sermons a broader hearing. To that end, the chapters that follow were adapted from a sermon series I preached at St. Andrew's.

Please be aware that this book is part of a broader series of books containing adaptations of my St. Andrew's sermons. This book, like all the others in the series, will *not* give you the fullest possible insight into each and every verse in this biblical book. Though I sought to at least touch on each verse, I focused on the key themes and ideas that comprised the "big picture" of each passage I covered. Therefore, I urge you to use this book as an overview and introduction.

I pray that you will be as blessed in reading this material as I was in preaching it.

—R.C. Sproul
Lake Mary, Florida
April 2009

1

A JEWISH LOOK AT JESUS

Matthew 1:1–17

The book of the genealogy of Jesus Christ, the Son of David, the Son of Abraham: Abraham begot Isaac, Isaac begot Jacob, and Jacob begot Judah and his brothers. Judah begot Perez and Zerah by Tamar, Perez begot Hezron, and Hezron begot Ram. Ram begot Amminadab, Amminadab begot Nahshon, and Nahshon begot Salmon. Salmon begot Boaz by Rahab, Boaz begot Obed by Ruth, Obed begot Jesse, and Jesse begot David the king. David the king begot Solomon by her who had been the wife of Uriah. Solomon begot Rehoboam, Rehoboam begot Abijah, and Abijah begot Asa. Asa begot Jehoshaphat, Jehoshaphat begot Joram, and Joram begot Uzziah. Uzziah begot Jotham, Jotham begot Ahaz, and Ahaz begot Hezekiah. Hezekiah begot Manasseh, Manasseh begot Amon, and Amon begot Josiah. Josiah begot Jeconiah and his brothers about the time they were carried away to Babylon. And after they were brought to Babylon, Jeconiah begot Shealtiel, and Shealtiel begot Zerubbabel. Zerubbabel begot Abiud, Abiud begot Eliakim, and Eliakim begot Azor. Azor begot Zadok, Zadok begot Achim, and Achim begot Eliud. Eliud begot Eleazar, Eleazar begot Matthan, and Matthan begot Jacob. And Jacob begot Joseph the husband of Mary, of whom was born Jesus who is called Christ. So all the generations from Abraham to David are fourteen generations, from David until the captivity in Babylon are fourteen generations, and from the captivity in Babylon until the Christ are fourteen generations.

We do not definitively know who wrote the Gospel of Matthew, but the universal testimony of the early church is that it was penned by Matthew, one of the twelve disciples. Matthew was called from his labor as a tax collector, which was one of the most despised vocations any Jew could hold, yet because of his training as a tax collector, Matthew was acquainted with lists and genealogies from the public registry, so he would know the family history of the people being taxed. He was also, obviously, literate and probably spoke two or three languages. Therefore, his work as a tax collector, under the providence of God, was the Lord's preparation for Matthew to begin his most important and celebrated task. This book has been called, even by critics of historic Christianity, the greatest book ever written.

The Genealogy

Matthew begins his Gospel with these words: **The book of the genealogy of Jesus Christ** (v. 1). Here is a Jew writing principally for Jews, and his first assertion is that he is writing about Jesus Messiah. *Christ* is not the name of Jesus. His name is Jesus bar Joseph or Jesus of Nazareth. The term *Christ* is His title, and it means "Jesus the Anointed One" or "Jesus the promised Messiah." Matthew mentions another important title that would resonate with his Jewish audience: **the Son of David** (v. 1). This title for Jesus, Son of David, is used more by Matthew than by any other Gospel writer, because the Messiah was to come from the loins of the greatest king of the Old Testament; He would be of the seed and lineage of David. So from the very beginning of his Gospel Matthew calls Jesus "Christ, the Son of David."

Matthew then adds, **the Son of Abraham** (v. 1). One of the great difficulties of harmonization in sacred Scripture is the relationship between the genealogy presented by Matthew and that presented by Luke in his Gospel. There are many places where these two genealogies do not agree. The first point of difference is that Luke traces the genealogy of Christ back to Adam, indicating that this Christ is not simply the Savior of the Jews but that the scope of Jesus' redemptive activity is universal. He is the new Adam, who recovers the promise that God made originally to Adam and Eve in the garden. Matthew, on the other hand, goes only as far back as Abraham because he is writing to a Jewish audience, to people who would want to know about the ancestry of Jesus as well as that of Matthew. It is important that His ancestry can be taken back to Abraham.

Ancestry was important to Jewish people, as it has been to people of all cultures throughout history. Probably the culture that is least concerned about ancestry is our own, which is why we often fail to understand the import of lists such as this.

When I enrolled as a student at the Free University of Amsterdam, I had to fill out a form with personal information. One of the questions on the form asked, "What was your father's station in life?" The university wanted to know my cultural class standing. That was also important for the Jew, which is why Matthew begins by giving us Jesus' ancestry. Additionally, the ancestry was important to demonstrate that Matthew's Gospel did not pertain to a mythical character or hero. To the Jew, the ancestry testified to historical reality.

Several years ago a friend of mine, a missionary with Wycliffe Bible Translators, worked among a people who had never heard the gospel in their language. The people could not write or read, so all their communication was oral. The missionary's first task was to learn the language of the tribe. Then she had to change that oral language into written form and teach the people to read and write it. It was a laborious task that took many years. Only after all that was accomplished could she undertake the task of translating the Bible into this language. She began with the Gospel of Matthew. To expedite the project she skipped the genealogy to get to the meat and substance of the story of Christ, and then she sent her translation work off to be printed by a publisher in a distant city. She waited months for the first copies of Matthew to arrive at the compound, and when the trucks came in with the Bibles, or, at least, the Gospel of Matthew, the people were much more interested in the trucks than they were in the translation. After having spent ten years on the project, she was crushed when she saw that the people didn't care at all. Nevertheless, she persevered in her task, and in the second edition of Matthew she included the genealogy. When that arrived the missionary explained the genealogy to the tribal chief, and he said, "Are you trying to say that this Jesus you've been telling us about for ten years was a real person?"

She replied, "Yes, of course."

He said, "I thought you were telling us a story about some mythical character."

Once he understood that this Christ was real in space and time, the chief came to Christ, and shortly thereafter the whole tribe came to Christ.

There are three sections in the genealogy, and Matthew divides these three sections into three groups, each of which has fourteen names. The significance of that has puzzled New Testament scholars. The Hebrew language uses a *gematria*, which is a kind of numerological symbolism. We find an example of this in the book of Revelation, where we read that the number of the beast is 666 (Rev. 13:18). Those numbers can be applied to real persons to identify the beast. If you look at this same kind of structure in the genealogical table, you will see that the number fourteen is the number of David. David is the central character of the ancestry, and Matthew is taking great pains to show that Jesus is from the line and lineage of David and that He has come to restore the fallen booth of the great king of the Old Testament.

Another difference between the genealogy in Matthew and the genealogy in Luke is that Matthew lists the father of Joseph as Jacob; in Luke's Gospel it is Eli. However, Luke does not use the term *begat*; he uses simply *of* someone. If you look through the genealogies, you will see that both the lists are selective, and that Matthew and Luke do not select the same people. The most notable difference is that in Matthew, the list moves from David to Solomon, whereas in Luke, it moves from David to Nathan. Solomon and Nathan were both sons of David, and, actually, the elder son was Nathan, not Solomon. Nevertheless, the kingship passed from David to Solomon rather than to Nathan. This gives us a clue as to why these genealogies are different.

What scholars tend to agree on is that Matthew's genealogy is the royal lineage of the kings of David. When Matthew gets to the sons of Jacob, he lists not the firstborn, Reuben, but Judah. The tribe of Judah was given the kingdom: "The scepter shall not depart from Judah . . . until Shiloh comes" (Gen. 49:10). In Matthew's genealogy the heirs to the throne of David come down finally to the father of Joseph, whose name is Jacob. In Luke's Gospel the genealogy does not come through the lines of the kings but from the son of Nathan.

The genealogies differ past David, and we do not know why. Suggested repeatedly throughout church history is that Matthew is giving us the genealogy of Joseph, and Luke is giving us the genealogy of Mary. This suggestion is highly disputed, but I am inclined to think it is the right solution. We have every reason to believe that Mary also was descended from David, and Jesus, of course, gets His human nature not from Joseph but from Mary. However, in Jewish society the fatherhood of Joseph, even though he was merely Jesus' stepfather, as it were, is important for legal genealogical considerations.

So why does Luke tell us that Joseph is of Eli while Matthew tells us that Jacob begot Joseph? Obviously Joseph didn't have two different fathers. I think Matthew is giving us the physical descendants from Jacob to Joseph. In Luke's Gospel, Joseph is not called "the son of Eli" but "of Eli." In other words, Joseph is "of Eli" in the sense that he was Eli's son-in-law. Noticeable by its absence in Luke's genealogy is any reference to King Jeconiah, who is mentioned twice in Matthew's list. Jeconiah came under the curse of God such that his seed would never be on the throne of David. This means that if Luke had traced Jesus' genealogy through Joseph, Jesus couldn't have been king, but since Jeconiah does not appear in Luke's list, it is likely that Luke's list traces the line through Mary.

Significant about the genealogies is the reference to four women. Although not the norm, including women in such lists was not unheard of in Jewish genealogies. The four women mentioned are all non-Jews. Perhaps the most significant one is Ruth the Moabite, who was the grandmother of David. We see here the promise to Abraham, that through his seed all the nations of the world would be blessed, including Gentiles like Rahab and Ruth.

In Martin Luther's study of the genealogies, he sees Jesus as the Son of David who restores the kingdom to Israel, but as the Son of Abraham He brings the kingdom of God to the whole world. All of that is pointed to by what appears, in the beginning, to be nothing but a list of names.

2

THE BIRTH OF JESUS

Matthew 1:18–25

Now the birth of Jesus Christ was as follows: After His mother Mary was betrothed to Joseph, before they came together, she was found with child of the Holy Spirit. Then Joseph her husband, being a just man, and not wanting to make her a public example, was minded to put her away secretly. But while he thought about these things, behold, an angel of the Lord appeared to him in a dream, saying, "Joseph, son of David, do not be afraid to take to you Mary your wife, for that which is conceived in her is of the Holy Spirit. And she will bring forth a Son, and you shall call His name Jesus, for He will save His people from their sins." So all this was done that it might be fulfilled which was spoken by the Lord through the prophet, saying, "Behold, the virgin shall be with child, and bear a Son, and they shall call His name Immanuel," which is translated, "God with us." Then Joseph, being aroused from sleep, did as the angel of the Lord commanded him and took to him his wife, and did not know her till she had brought forth her firstborn Son. And he called His name Jesus.

When we celebrate the birth of Jesus at Christmastime, our attention is most often given to Luke's account, because it gives us so much information. It tells us of the annunciation of the angel Gabriel to the peasant girl Mary. It includes the story of the shepherds as well as the infancy hymns that are sung by Zacharias and by others during that time. Matthew's version is much briefer.

We notice at the outset that Matthew gives his account from the viewpoint of Joseph, whereas Luke tells his account from the viewpoint of Mary. Luke assures us that what he wrote in his Gospel was well researched from eyewitnesses, and tradition affirms that Luke got much of his information from Mary herself. Of course, when Matthew wrote his Gospel he had no opportunity to interview Joseph.

Now the birth of Jesus Christ was as follows (v. 18). This opening assertion is rich in content, as brief as it is. The word used here for the birth of Jesus is *gennēsis*. Our word *genesis* comes from the Greek *ginomai*, which means "to be, to become, or happen." Matthew is asserting that this is how Jesus came to be, which, as we noted in the last chapter, places the birth of Jesus within the framework of history rather than mythology.

The Betrothal of Mary and Joseph

After his mother Mary was betrothed to Joseph, before they came together, she was found with child of the Holy Spirit (v. 18). This takes place after betrothal and prior to marriage. In our society, a betrothal is considered to be an engagement between two people who intend to become married at a certain time, yet there are countless occasions in which engagements are broken and the marriage never comes to pass. Among the Jews in Jesus' day, however, a betrothal was far more serious. It was an unbreakable pledge customarily undertaken one year before the wedding, and it carried almost the weight of marriage itself; it was so close that it required virtually a writ of divorce to end it.

Following betrothal the bride remained under the roof of her parents. She would not move into the home of her husband until after the actual marriage. Therefore, it was serious when a betrothed woman was discovered to be with child; the implications of such a pregnancy were enormous in Jewish society and could, indeed, result in the execution of the woman who violated her betrothal by becoming pregnant. Yet we are told here in Matthew that before Mary came together with Joseph, "she was found with child of the Holy Spirit." The father of this child in Mary's womb was not some illicit lover, nor was it Joseph: the paternity was accomplished through the supernatural activity of the Holy Spirit. In the Apostles' Creed we recite, "Jesus Christ . . . was conceived by the Holy Spirit, born of the virgin Mary . . ." Those two miraculous aspects—His conception and His birth—were integral to the faith of the Christian church of the early centuries. Jesus' conception was extraordinary, not natural but supernatural, accomplished by the divine work of the Spirit, and as a result a baby born to a virgin.

Perhaps no assertion of biblical Christianity fell under greater attack by nineteenth-century liberalism than the account of the virgin birth. For some reason more attention was given to that than to the resurrection. Because the story is so blatantly supernatural, it became a stumbling block to those who tried to reduce the essence of the Christian faith to all that can be accomplished through natural humanity.

When Mary's pregnancy was discovered, Joseph, being a just man—one who was also kind and gave detailed attention to the observance of the law of God, **not wanting to make her a public example, was minded to put her away secretly** (v. 19). He was not willing to call down the wrath of the courts upon his betrothed, and he decided to deal with it from a spirit of compassion. After he thought it over deeply and carefully, he decided to divorce her or put her away in a private manner, so as to save his betrothed from total public humiliation.

While he thought about these things, behold, an angel of the Lord appeared to him in a dream, saying, "Joseph, son of David" (v. 20). The New Testament makes so much out of the fact that Jesus is the Son of David that it's almost amazing to find Joseph being given that same title, but this is also important for the lineage of Jesus. For Jesus to be a Son of David in Jewish categories, legally His father also had to be a son of David. That is why the angel gives this honorific title to Joseph when he addresses him, saying, **"Do not be afraid to take to you Mary your wife, for that which is conceived in her is of the Holy Spirit"** (v. 20). This is the second time in this brief narrative that the conception of Christ in the womb of Mary is attributed to the work of the Holy Spirit.

In Luke's version, when the angel Gabriel told Mary that she had conceived the child and would bring forth a baby, she was stunned and said, "How can this be since I know not a man?" (Luke 1:34). The angel replied, "With God nothing will be impossible" (v. 37).

Then Gabriel explained to Mary how the birth would take place. The Holy Spirit would overshadow her so that the child would be born as a result of this supernatural work. Luke uses the same language that is used at the dawn of creation: "In the beginning God created the heavens and the earth, and the earth was without form and void, and darkness was upon the face of the deep" (Gen. 1:1–2), and then we are told that the Holy Spirit came and hovered over the waters, and God said, "Let there be light" (v. 3). In the act of creation, the Spirit is moving on the face of the deep, and out of the nothingness of that darkness God, through the power of His Spirit, brings forth the whole of creation.

From the biblical perspective, the genesis of life in the first place was through the power of the Spirit of life, of the Spirit of God. Gabriel was declaring to Mary that same power by which the universe was made; that same power that brought life out of the darkness originally is the power that will overshadow her womb and produce a son. God doesn't need a human father to bring this to pass.

The Authority to Name

"She will bring forth a Son, and you shall call His name Jesus, for He will save His people from their sins" (v. 21). It was the privilege of Jewish parents to name their children. The very first enterprise given to humanity in the garden was the scientific task of taxonomy, that is, the task of naming the animals, and in that task of naming, the superior names the subordinate. God gave to Adam and Eve the responsibility and authority to name everything in the animal kingdom. Yet throughout the Old Testament, when a child was born into specific historical and redemptive purposes, God took away the privilege from the parent and named the child Himself, indicating that the child belonged to Him.

That is what happened with Zacharias in the birth of John the Baptist. God told Zacharias what to name his son (Luke 1:13). The same thing happens here in Matthew. The Lord is saying to Joseph, "You are not going to choose a name for this boy. You will name Him what I tell you to name Him, because ultimately He is my Son, and you shall call his name Jesus." The etymology behind that name is "Jehovah saves." Name Him Jesus "for He will save His people from their sins."

The idea of salvation in the Bible in general means some kind of rescue from a threat of destruction or calamity, and the highest, ultimate sense of salvation is rescue from the worst of all possible calamities. The worst calamity that could ever befall human beings is to fall under the judgment of God for their sin. That is the calamity that awaits every person who does not rush to Christ for salvation. However, the baby is called "Jesus" because He is a savior, and He will save His people from the consequences of their sins.

The Virgin Birth

So all this was done that it might be fulfilled which was spoken by the Lord through the prophet saying, "Behold, the virgin shall be with child, and bear a Son, and they shall call His name Immanuel," which is translated, "God with us" (vv. 22–23). This verse, in which Matthew is quoting Isaiah, was sharply attacked by the critics of the nineteenth century. In the Jewish language there are two words that can be used to describe a virgin. The most precise and technical word is not the one that Isaiah chose. Rather, Isaiah chose the other word, which can be translated "young woman" or, more appropriately, "maiden," which presumes virginity but doesn't necessitate it. The critics point to that and say that Isaiah wasn't speaking of a virgin but saying only that a young woman, a maiden, would conceive. Therefore, the critics say, the Bible does not teach a virgin birth. That's what we call the exegesis of despair, because if you just give a cursory look at the context of this text, there is no doubt that Matthew is teaching that Jesus was born from the womb of a woman who had never been with a man—a virgin.

Isaiah said, "Behold, the virgin shall conceive and bear a Son, and shall call His name Immanuel" (Isa. 7:14), but here in Matthew the angel says they will call His name "Jesus." Those names are not the same, and they do not mean the same thing. Isaiah does not tell us why they will call Him "Immanuel." The term *Immanuel* describes what Christ does. It describes the event of incarnation. He will be called Immanuel because He will be the incarnate presence of God with us, but His proper Jewish name will be Jesus, because "He will save his people from their sins."

Then Joseph, being aroused from sleep, did as the angel of the Lord commanded him and took to him his wife, and did not know her till she brought forth her firstborn Son. And he called His name JESUS (vv. 24–25). This reflects not only the obedience and submission of Joseph to what the angel had directed him to do but also that Joseph fully embraces Jesus as his son and fulfills the legal requirements of the genealogy that we examined in the last chapter. Joseph did this even though the child's name was not selected by him but by the angel. In the ultimate sense, Jesus was named by God, who is His ultimate Father. In the proximate sense, Jesus was named by Joseph, who was given the unspeakable privilege of being the Lord Jesus Christ's earthly father.

3

VISIT OF THE MAGI

Matthew 2:1–12

Now after Jesus was born in Bethlehem of Judea in the days of Herod the king, behold, wise men from the East came to Jerusalem, saying, "Where is He who has been born King of the Jews? For we have seen His star in the East and have come to worship Him." When Herod the king heard this, he was troubled, and all Jerusalem with him. And when he had gathered all the chief priests and scribes of the people together, he inquired of them where the Christ was to be born. So they said to him, "In Bethlehem of Judea, for thus it is written by the prophet:

> 'But you, Bethlehem, in the land of Judah,
> Are not the least among the rulers of Judah;
> For out of you shall come a Ruler
> Who will shepherd My people Israel.'"

Then Herod, when he had secretly called the wise men, determined from them what time the star appeared. And he sent them to Bethlehem and said, "Go and search carefully for the young Child, and when you have found Him, bring back word to me, that I may come and worship Him also." When they heard the king, they departed; and behold, the star which they had seen in the East went before them, till it came and stood over where the young Child was. When they saw the star, they rejoiced with exceedingly great joy. And when they had come into the house, they saw the young Child with Mary His mother, and fell down and worshiped Him. And when they had opened their treasures, they presented gifts to Him: gold, frankincense, and myrrh. Then, being divinely warned in a dream that they should not return to Herod, they departed for their own country another way.

We Three Kings from Orient Are" has been sung throughout church history, but the only historical accuracy in the hymn is that those who came to Jesus came from the East, or the Orient. Nothing in Scripture teaches us that they were kings or that there were exactly three of them. Those assumptions are drawn chiefly from the fact that there were three gifts brought to Jesus, and the particular gifts presented indicated great wealth of the sort that was usually found at that time only among royalty. The majority of the hymn is based on speculation and assumption, and unbridled speculation has led many to ruin. When we speculate, we must underscore that we are making hypothetical inferences.

The people who came to visit Jesus bringing their lavish treasures are identified by Matthew as *magi*, from which we get the English word *magic*. The title was usually reserved for those who consulted the stars to learn the future, a common practice in ancient times. In a sense, they were identified as magicians, not necessarily of black arts but as those who were counselors of sorts, perhaps to kings.

They came **after Jesus was born in Bethlehem of Judea in the days of Herod the king** (v. 1). We know that Herod died in 4 BC, and historians estimate that Jesus was born in either 6 or 7 BC. We assume that this visitation from the magi came sometime after the birth of Jesus. Most artwork depicts the magi and the shepherds gathered around the Christ child in a stable, but the biblical text tells us that when the magi came, Mary and Joseph and the Baby were in a house.

The journey from the East would have taken some time, so the magi arrived perhaps as much as a year or two after Jesus had been born. The reason for assuming as much as two years is that Herod ordered the slaying of all male children under the age of two years old (v. 16).

The Star

The wise men did not come directly to Bethlehem but to Jerusalem, and they came with a question on their lips: **"Where is He who has been born King of the Jews? For we have seen His star in the East and have come to worship Him"** (v. 2). Perhaps no text has been subjected to more speculation than the description of the star that led these men from the East. Some scholars have indicated that it was likely a comet's tail that gave guidance to the people in their sojourn. Johannes Kepler, for example, argued that there was an unusual conjunction of the two planets in the constellation Pisces in 7 BC that would have given off an extreme luster. Still others say that these men, perhaps being astrologers, had seen in their astrological charts the appearance of certain stars that heralded the birth of a great king. The other possibility is that the star that led these men to Jerusalem and then to Bethlehem was a specific creation by God for this particular event, something like the shekinah glory cloud that led the people of Israel in their wilderness wandering.

If I had to choose from among these options, I would choose the latter. I think it would be very difficult to follow the tail of a comet, or even an inordinately bright conjunction of two planets, to Jerusalem and then from Jerusalem to Bethlehem. I suspect that this is another account of a miraculous work of God to guide the men to the proper place.

We do not know how they knew that they were looking for the King of the Jews; Matthew doesn't give us that information. But he does say that they had seen His star in the East and had come to worship Him, that is, to give obeisance to Him. The implication here is that the men were coming not merely to give homage to a monarch but to worship before deity.

Herod's Dilemma

When Herod the king heard this, he was troubled, and all Jerusalem with him (v. 3). Herod was troubled because the birth of a foretold king would pose a clear and present threat to his position. Of course, had he known the time of his own death, he would not have had to worry about a child's coming of age and eventually replacing him. Not only was Herod troubled, but all Jerusalem with him. We would think that the city of Jerusalem would have been filled with excitement rather than troubled at the news that the King of the Jews had been born. Perhaps the arrival of an entourage (whether of three or three hundred) bearing gifts simply created a great stir in the city.

When Herod **had gathered all the chief priests and scribes of the people together, he inquired of them where the Christ was to be born** (v. 4). They answered Herod according to their knowledge of the Old Testament, saying, **"In Bethlehem of Judea, for thus it is written by the prophet: 'But you, Bethlehem, in the land of Judah, are not the least among the rulers of Judah; for out of you shall come a Ruler who will shepherd My people Israel'"** (vv. 5–6). They reported to Herod that the prophet Micah had predicted the exact town in which the Messiah would be born, namely, Bethlehem. We see in the prophecy of Micah the unusual linkage between king and shepherd, and we see again the link to David in the Old Testament, who was the great shepherd king. So Jesus comes not only as a King for His people but also, as He described Himself, as a good shepherd who came to tend and care for His sheep (John 10:11).

Then Herod, when he had secretly called the wise men, determined from them what time the star appeared. And he sent them to Bethlehem and said, "Go and search carefully for the young Child, and when you have found

Him, bring back word to me, that I may come and worship him also" (vv. 7–8). Such treachery—how evil is the heart of man. Herod said he wanted to come and worship the Child King, but all the while he really wanted to kill Him.

The Child Worshiped

When they heard the king, they departed; and behold, the star which they had seen in the East went before them, till it came and stood over where the young Child was. When they saw the star, they rejoiced with exceedingly great joy. And when they had come into the house, they saw the young Child with Mary His mother, and fell down and worshiped Him (vv. 9–11). Their journey from the East was long and dangerous. Most likely they traveled from ancient Persia, which is now Iran, or from the part of Babylonia that may now be Iraq. In any case, the travel involved was significant. When the guiding star brought them to Mary and Joseph and the Child, they were filled with joy, and they went in to worship Him. We must wonder what was going on in the mind of Mary and Joseph when the entourage came bearing treasures and falling on their knees to worship their Son.

And when they had opened their treasures, they presented gifts to Him: gold, frankincense, and myrrh (v. 11). Biblical scholars see a certain symbolism contained in the particular gifts that were offered. The first gift was gold, which was the only fitting gift to give a king in the ancient world. Gold was the metal of royalty, and the fact that gold was lavishly spread at the feet of Jesus' parents, and Jesus Himself, is another indication that the men were paying homage to Him as a king.

The reason behind the gift of frankincense is more difficult to pinpoint. In the ancient world incense was primarily used by priests in worship. Central to Jewish worship in the tabernacle and then in the temple was the altar of incense, which was tended by the priests. It symbolized the sweet aroma and fragrance of the prayers of God's people to Him. Matthew in his Gospel makes much of Jesus' being both a king and a priest.

The third gift, myrrh, is the strangest of the three. The chief use of myrrh among ancient people was for anointing the dead at the time of their burial. When Jesus died and was laid in the tomb, women came early in the morning with precious spices in order to anoint His body, and myrrh is what they would have used for that occasion.

Many speculate that, taken together, there was one gift for a king, one for a priest, and one to signify death. This should not surprise us in light of the announcement made to Mary and Joseph when they took the Child to the temple where they were told, "Behold, this Child is destined for the fall and rising of many in Israel, and for a sign which will be spoken against (yes, a sword will pierce through your own soul also), that the thoughts of many hearts may be revealed" (Luke 2:34–35).

Investing in God's Kingdom

I was told about a sermon that Billy Graham preached in 1957 about tithing. In his sermon he referenced Paul's command, "Let him who stole steal no longer" (Eph. 4:28). We can make a similar application from this text in Matthew's Gospel. If you are not a tither, you are robbing God. The magi brought lavish gifts to Christ because they believed He was worthy of their sacrifice and honor.

It is difficult to separate people from their money. I have been a tither throughout my Christian life. I have tithed even when it was difficult to do so, and I have never regretted a single cent of it. I tithe my gross pay, and I pay God before I pay the government. Additionally, I have for many years practiced the principle of delayed gratification and sought to invest as much money as I tithe, which all together takes 20 percent right off the top. In the providence of God, I have been blessed with some fruitful investments, but I have also made some bad ones. When you make an investment, you do not know how it will turn out, because, as the financial experts say, even in the middle of a bull market, there is a bear loose in the woods seeking whom he may devour. The greatest investment one can make is in the kingdom of God, and there are no bear markets in heaven. Every investment that we make in the kingdom of God returns thirtyfold, sixtyfold, or a hundredfold.

I do not encourage people to tithe in hope of becoming rich, nor do I encourage people to tithe simply because it is their duty. I encourage people to tithe for the joy of it. Tithing is joyous because the Lord loves a cheerful giver. When we pinch our money and are reluctant to give it, God is not pleased. Consider the magi. They traveled a great distance and poured out their wealth to honor Jesus. I have been told that if you really want to know how deep your spiritual life is, look at your checkbook, because your checkbook reveals more objectively than anything else the place of your heart. The magi gave not knowing about the cross or the resurrection. We know what Jesus did, and the application, while painful, is clear: give of your best to the Master, and do not ever rob God.

4

THE SLAUGHTER OF THE INNOCENTS

Matthew 2:13–23

Now when they had departed, behold, an angel of the Lord appeared to Joseph in a dream, saying, "Arise, take the young Child and His mother, flee to Egypt, and stay there until I bring you word; for Herod will seek the young Child to destroy Him." When he arose, he took the young Child and His mother by night and departed for Egypt, and was there until the death of Herod, that it might be fulfilled which was spoken by the Lord through the prophet, saying, "Out of Egypt I called My Son." Then Herod, when he saw that he was deceived by the wise men, was exceedingly angry; and he sent forth and put to death all the male children who were in Bethlehem and in all its districts, from two years old and under, according to the time which he had determined from the wise men. Then was fulfilled what was spoken by Jeremiah the prophet, saying:

> "A voice was heard in Ramah,
> Lamentation, weeping, and great mourning,
> Rachel weeping for her children,
> Refusing to be comforted,
> Because they are no more."

Now when Herod was dead, behold, an angel of the Lord appeared in a dream to Joseph in Egypt, saying, "Arise, take the young Child and His mother, and go to the land of Israel, for those who sought the young Child's life are dead." Then he arose, took the young Child and His mother, and came into the land of Israel. But when he heard that Archelaus was reigning over Judea instead of his father Herod, he was afraid to go there. And being warned by God in a dream, he turned aside into the region of Galilee. And he came and dwelt in a city called Nazareth, that it might be fulfilled which was spoken by the prophets, "He shall be called a Nazarene."

Now when they had departed, behold, an angel of the Lord appeared to Joseph in a dream, saying, "Arise, take the young Child and His mother, flee to Egypt" (v. 13). The magi, after they had presented their gifts to the Christ Child and were warned not to return to Herod, left the region. Immediately afterward, we read that an angel appeared to Joseph in a dream.

In Luke's history of the birth and infancy of Jesus we see repeated visitations of the archangel Gabriel, who comes in person and speaks audibly to Zacharias and Mary, whereas in Matthew's version, the angelic visitation typically takes place in a dream. The two accounts are not incompatible by any means; what we see is that the early days of Jesus (and, indeed, His whole life) were bathed in the supernatural and with narratives of angels.

Protected

Because of the many references to angels in the New Testament, modern skeptics continue to discount the events as having any historical reality. They have sought to reconstruct a Christian faith and a New Testament content without any references to angels. That is dangerous business, because in the New Testament there are far more references to angels than to sin. Additionally, the word *angelos*, which means "angel" or "messenger," occurs in the New Testament with greater frequency than the word *agapē*, which means "love." It is striking to note that in terms of numerical frequency the New Testament says more about angels than it says about love. We cannot have a biblical portrait of Christ apart from the reality of the angelic beings that attended His life. It is the angelic visitation in the midnight dream that warns Joseph to flee into Egypt and later instructs him to return to Israel.

Later on, Satan tempts Jesus to throw Himself down from the pinnacle of the temple to prove the biblical passage, that His angels would be given charge over Him, a temptation to which Jesus responded with the Word of God (Matt. 4:5–7). The reality is that at every point in Jesus' life, He was under the protection of the angelic host. Even at the time of the cross to which He voluntarily submitted, He declared that if He so desired He could call down legions of angels from heaven to fight on His behalf (Matt. 26:53). Surely there was a heavenly host concealed from human vision observing the cross, and they were ready at any second to move in at the bidding of Christ. This is part of biblical truth—that God has appointed from the foundations of the earth that His army, the heavenly host, would observe and protect the life of this Baby. We see Herod's attempt to do away with the Baby, but we are told in these verses what was going on behind the scenes. In the providence and sovereignty of God, the Baby was in no danger, and Herod was impotent to carry out his schemes.

The angel tells Joseph to take the young Child and His mother and flee to Egypt. The angel places emphasis on the Child here rather than on the mother. At this time in Jewish history, Egypt was a classic place of refuge for Jews fleeing from the oppressive reign of the Romans, particularly under King Herod. At the time that Joseph and Mary and the Christ Child went down into Egypt, there were one million residents in the city of Alexandria alone. If we consider the land of Egypt as a whole, there were surely far more than a million Jews. That means that when Joseph fled from the wrath of Herod, he went to a place of safety where he was not surrounded by aliens but by his own people living there in exile.

Herod's Mission

"Herod will seek the young Child to destroy Him" (v. 13). Those who serve in the military undertake "search and destroy" missions. Such a mission is not simply a matter of being prepared for a defensive struggle in the event of an attack. In these missions the military takes the initiative to go out and find its enemies in order to destroy them. In this case Herod is on a search-and-destroy mission, and he brings all of his resources to carry it out. He is not searching for enemy combatants or military units. He is searching for a baby under two years of age, and his purpose is to destroy that Child.

Extrabiblical history gives us much information about Herod, but it says nothing about the episode that we call the "slaughter of the innocents." Because secular history does not mention it, some have speculated that the account was a figment of Matthew's imagination; however, if we look at the scope of this particular mission and indeed at the scope of Herod's life, we see that this particular mission would not have warranted any kind of mention. Our best guess as to how many such boys were in the Bethlehem region at that time is twelve to fifteen, and given Herod's history of cruelty, his massacre of twelve to fifteen little boys would hardly warrant a mention against the broader scope of his escapades.

In 40 BC Mark Antony, part of the Second Triumvirate in Rome, together with Octavian, who later became Caesar Augustus, jointly appointed a ruler over the Jewish people, who himself was not Jewish but had been a ruthless chieftain known for his strength and cruelty. Antony and Octavian then appointed Herod to be king over the Jews. This is the man who engendered the slaughter of the innocents, probably thirty-five years after he began his reign.

King Herod had magnificent administrative powers, which he used to appease the Jews, who were hostile toward him because he was not a Jew. He undertook the building of the new temple, which exceeded the temple of Solomon in its grandeur and became known as one of the wonders of the ancient world. The size of the blocks used in the building of the temple was monumental, and extraordinary engineering skill was employed to construct that edifice. Additionally, Herod built his winter palace on the high peak of Masada. The palace had, among other niceties, a working sauna, which was a marvel in itself. Herod enjoyed a widespread reputation for his administrative abilities and his building projects.

His reputation as a builder, however, was far exceeded by his reputation for cruelty. He had ten wives, two of whom he murdered. One of the two was supposedly his favorite wife. He murdered in cold blood three of his own children as well as several other family members. He was so ruthless that in his last months, when he knew that his death was imminent, he issued a decree that on the day of his death principal men of the entire Jewish nation were to be killed.[1] He did it so that there would be widespread mourning. As it turned out, his henchmen did not carry out his decree, but that he ordered it is a matter of historical record. All this gives us a clue as to the character of the man who sought to kill Jesus.

Upon Herod's death his kingdom was divided in fourths or *tetrarchia* and given to his sons. The son who was given the region of Jerusalem was Archelaus, who is mentioned here in the text (v. 22). He was no better than his father, although he was far less able to manage, and shortly after becoming a tetrarch, he was removed by Rome.

When he arose, he took the young Child and His mother by night and departed for Egypt, and was there until the death of Herod, that it might be fulfilled which was spoken by the Lord through the prophet, saying, "Out of Egypt I called My Son" (vv. 14–15). It was Hosea who had uttered these words originally, and when he spoke prophetically about God's calling His Son out of Egypt, he was referring to the exodus, when God acted to bring His people out of slavery and into freedom. However, Matthew tells us that this prophecy did not meet its fullest completion in the exodus but, rather, in this return of Jesus from Egypt to Israel.

This is significant because, in the Old Testament, the whole nation of Israel was called metaphorically the "son of God," but now that title "Son of God" is

[1] Josephus, *Antiquities* 17.173.

reduced to a single person. The text teaches its fullest fulfillment when the only begotten Son is called out of Egypt. This also adds credibility to the fact that the Old Testament uses types and shadows that indicate a deeper fulfillment in later times. In one sense we see that Jesus' life was a recapitulation of the history of Israel. He is the tabernacle. He is the Passover. We see repeatedly that points of interest and significance in the Old Testament find their striking fulfillment in the person and work of Jesus. We must be careful, however, not to seek a shadow or type behind every bush in the Old Testament, as some are wont to do.

Then Herod, when he saw that he was deceived by the wise men, was exceedingly angry; and he sent forth and put to death all the male children who were in Bethlehem and in all its districts, from two years old and under, according to the time which he had determined from the wise men (v. 16). The Greek indicates that Herod's anger was filled with passion. This was no mild displeasure. Herod was enraged when he found out that the magi went their way without coming back to give their report.

Then was fulfilled what was spoken of by Jeremiah the prophet, saying, "A voice was heard in Ramah, lamentation, weeping, and great mourning, Rachel weeping for her children, refusing to be comforted, because they are no more" (vv. 17–18). When Jeremiah spoke of the weeping and lament of Rachel, it was Rachel's weeping for her children when they were sent into exile. Of course, Rachel was long since dead when that took place, but the people of Israel were seen as the children of Rachel, the favorite wife of Jacob.

I cannot read this text without thinking of a more recent application of it in the literary history of the United States. My favorite novel is Herman Melville's *Moby Dick*, which is a theologically symbolic piece of literature. Throughout the book multiple allusions are made to biblical characters and events; even the infamous captain of the *Pequod* is named after Ahab, a wicked king of Israel. While Ahab was engaged in a monomaniacal pursuit of the albino whale, he came upon a ship in distress. The rules of the sea in that day required the approaching ship to assist the befallen ship. So when the captain of the distressed ship saw the *Pequod* approaching, he called to Ahab and implored him to help find a member of his crew who had fallen overboard. Ahab was so obsessed with his desire that he broke all maritime conventions and shut his ears to the pleas of the troubled captain. He was too busy with his mission, so he passed on. The name of the ship was the *Rachel*, and Melville cited the Old Testament reference of Rachel's grieving for her lost children (Genesis 30). The story shows us how the Bible has made its way into the literature of the Western world.

Safe in God's Care

Now when Herod was dead, behold, an angel of the Lord appeared in a dream to Joseph in Egypt, saying, "Arise, take the young Child and His mother, and go to the land of Israel, for those who sought the young Child's life are dead" (vv. 19–20). We then read that Joseph followed the instructions and returned not to Jerusalem or Judea or Bethlehem but to Nazareth in Galilee, the region that is a focal point later in the public ministry of Jesus.

What this story indicates is that God's Son was in the hands of the Father from His conception, to His birth, through His infancy, through His temptation in the wilderness, through His public ministry, and through His betrayal, death, resurrection, and ascension. We have forgotten the power of divine providence.

I have been rebuked for worrying. In fact, I am known as a worrywart, which is inconsistent with my theology. We all tend to get anxious when we cannot foresee the outcome of future events. Indeed, God may take us to the valley of the shadow of death. He may bring us into a place of tribulation. But one thing we can know for certain as Christians is that God will never abandon us and that His providential care will be on our life. He knows exactly how many hairs are on our head, and if His eye is on the sparrow, how much more is His eye on you and on me?

When we think of the extraordinary care that God the Father took to preserve the life of His Son, assigning an angelic host to be over Him, remember that the same God and angelic host are assigned to take care of everyone who puts their trust in Christ, because we too are now by grace the children of God.

5

JOHN THE BAPTIST

Matthew 3:1–12

In those days John the Baptist came preaching in the wilderness of Judea, and saying, "Repent, for the kingdom of heaven is at hand!" For this is he who was spoken of by the prophet Isaiah, saying:

> "The voice of one crying in the wilderness:
> 'Prepare the way of the LORD;
> Make His paths straight.'"

Now John himself was clothed in camel's hair, with a leather belt around his waist; and his food was locusts and wild honey. Then Jerusalem, all Judea, and all the region around the Jordan went out to him and were baptized by him in the Jordan, confessing their sins. But when he saw many of the Pharisees and Sadducees coming to his baptism, he said to them, "Brood of vipers! Who warned you to flee from the wrath to come? Therefore bear fruits worthy of repentance, and do not think to say to yourselves, 'We have Abraham as our father.' For I say to you that God is able to raise up children to Abraham from these stones. And even now the ax is laid to the root of the trees. Therefore every tree which does not bear good fruit is cut down and thrown into the fire. I indeed baptize you with water unto repentance, but He who is coming after me is mightier than I, whose sandals I am not worthy to carry. He will baptize you with the Holy Spirit and fire. His winnowing fan is in His hand. He will thoroughly clean out His threshing floor and gather His wheat into the barn; but He will burn up the chaff with unquenchable fire."

After two thousand years of redemptive history, recorded for us in the prophecies of the Old Testament, the voice of God became silent, and there was not a single word from God in prophetic utterance for a period of four hundred years. The last prophecy in the Old Testament is found in the book of Malachi: "Behold, I will send you Elijah the prophet before the coming of the great and dreadful day of the LORD, and he will turn the hearts of the fathers to the children and the hearts of the children to their fathers, lest I come and strike the earth with a curse" (Mal. 4:5–6). Here at the end of the Old Testament God is saying that instead of bringing a curse upon the world, He is going to bring back the voice of Elijah the prophet. Four hundred years later that prophecy was fulfilled, according to Jesus, in the person of John the Baptist. Our Lord declared that John came in the spirit and power of Elijah (Luke 1:17).

John's Message

Turning to Matthew's account we read: **In those days John the Baptist came preaching in the wilderness of Judea** (v. 1). The fact is that the one anointed by God to restore the voice of prophecy to the land did so with the vocation of preaching. This reminds us that it is through preaching that God has chosen to save the world. God traditionally met with His prophets in the desert or wilderness, places removed from the frenetic activity of the city, where God could whisper in a still small voice to those whom He anointed to be agents of revelation. Just like the Old Testament prophets, this new prophet comes out of the wilderness, and his message is simple: **"Repent! For the kingdom of heaven is at hand!"** (v. 2).

The other Gospels record John as saying, "Repent! For the kingdom of God is at hand." Some have seen the difference between the language of Matthew and that of the other Gospel writers as indicating that there are two different kingdoms under God's reign—a heavenly kingdom and an earthly one. That is wrong, however. We must remember that Matthew is a Jew writing for Jews using the customary literary form of circumlocution. The Jews, who were loathe to pronounce the name of God, found substitute expressions, so instead of saying "kingdom of God," Matthew says "kingdom of heaven."

John was sent to Israel, and he called upon them to repent and be baptized. His message would have scandalized the Jews, because the only people baptized prior to this time were those converting from paganism to Judaism. These converts, Gentiles, were considered unclean, so they were required to participate in a symbolic washing of their filth so as to become worthy to join the community of Israel. The convert baptized himself, as if he were taking a bath before he could join the community of Israel.

Then out of the desert came John, who resembled Elijah in dress and manner, telling the Jews that they needed to be baptized. His message was clear: the Jews too were unclean. God's own people were not ready for His coming, and they needed to repent. The force of that verb, *repent*, is no mere hat tip to the holiness of God with a mere acknowledgment of one's sin. The call here is to radical conversion—to turn from sin and intoxication with this world and direct one's soul and heart to the things of God. And there is no inclusion for anyone in the kingdom of God who has not done that. That is as true today as it was when John made that announcement by the Jordan. John speaks with a sense of urgency. Something new and radical is about to happen—the breakthrough of God's kingdom is at hand.

John's Role

This is he who was spoken of by the prophet Isaiah saying: "The voice of one crying in the wilderness: 'Prepare the way of the Lord. Make His paths straight'" (v. 3). The language of heraldry is used when the New Testament speaks about Christ's coming, even when it speaks of the rapture. Such fanfare happened in the Middle Ages when a king came into a village. The trumpeters gave a blast of the trumpet indicating that the king was about to appear. That was the role of John the Baptist. John's entire function, the purpose for which he was made and raised up, was to herald the kingdom of God, because the kingdom of God was made manifest by the appearance of the King. Just as trumpeters would blow their trumpets to announce the visitation of the king, so the purpose of John the Baptist was to cry in the wilderness to prepare the pathway of the Lord.

Now John himself was clothed in camel's hair, with a leather belt around his waist; and his food was locusts and wild honey (v. 4). The camel hair that John wore was not the sort we find today in expensive outer garments. It was one of the roughest, most crude, and cheapest forms of outer garment of the ancient world. John was not adorned with suede but with the roughhewn skin of the camel. The honey he ate to survive was not the sort cultivated by beekeepers. It was the wild honey obtained only at the risk of a thousand bee stings.

Then Jerusalem, all Judea, and all the region around the Jordan went out to him and were baptized by him in the Jordan, confessing their sins (vv. 5–6). The Jews referred to common people as *`am hā'āretz*. The Greeks used the expression *hoi polloi*. These were the people of the land in contrast to those titled with nobility. The *`am hā'āretz*, the common folk, heard John gladly and were obedient to his word, whereas the clergy, the professional religious people, were absolutely outraged that this strange man would come out of the wilderness and tell them they were unclean and unready for the coming kingdom. How would we have responded if we had heard John? Would we have gone to the Jordan River for cleansing, or would we have refused to participate in the humbling ritual?

But when he saw many of the Pharisees and Sadducees coming to his baptism, he said to them, "Brood of vipers! Who warned you to flee from the wrath to come?" (v. 7). The Pharisees and Sadducees were not coming to be baptized but merely to examine what John was doing so that they could report it to the authorities in Jerusalem. John knew what was in their minds, which is why he rebuked them sharply. We see here an important part of John's message—impending judgment.

The Greek word translated "judgment" is *krisis*, from which we get the English word *crisis*. John is saying that his baptism is not a meaningless ritual; it is a moment of supreme crisis, because the kingdom of God is at hand. It will be heaven for those who receive it but wrath for those who do not.

"Therefore bear fruits worthy of repentance, and do not think to say to yourselves, 'We have Abraham as our father.' For I say to you that God is able to raise up children to Abraham from these stones" (vv. 8–9). The Pharisees and Sadducees must not think that circumcision or their pedigree as descendants of Abraham will save them. God can make people children of Abraham who were not children of Abraham. God can make people living stones who before were nothing but recalcitrant sinners. I am a child of Abraham, and I once had a heart of stone. I had no more spiritual life in me than the stones along the Jordan River, but God changed my heart of stone to a heart of flesh, which He has done for every person who is in Christ.

"Even now the ax is laid to the root of the trees" (v. 10). Do you see the urgency? The kingdom of God is not going to come in some distant time. The woodsman has penetrated that tree down to its very core, the root, so that one more swing of that ax and the tree will come crashing down. That is how close things are, John is saying.

"Therefore every tree which does not bear good fruit is cut down and thrown into the fire" (v. 10). Our Lord gave this same metaphor: "If anyone does not abide in Me, he is cast out as a branch and is withered; and they gather them and throw them into the fire, and they are burned" (John 15:6). If you profess to be a Christian and do not bring forth the fruit of repentance, you will be like the branches that are cast off and are thrown into the fire. Have you thought about that? We live in a culture where no one is afraid of the judgment of God, but the biblical portrait is of a God who will judge the earth, a God who will call every living creature to account. If we do not bring forth fruits worthy of repentance, we will be cast into the fire, where we belong.

"I indeed baptize you with water unto repentance, but He who is coming after me is mightier than I, whose sandals I am not worthy to carry. He will baptize you with the Holy Spirit and fire" (v. 11). Every Christian is united to Christ in His suffering, humiliation, death, and resurrection, and we have been baptized by His Spirit, and that baptism is a baptism of fire. This fire cleanses us, it purges and purifies us, and it produces what the crucible was designed to produce—the pure gold of sanctification. Think not that you come to a Savior who will keep you out of the fire. He will keep you out of the eternal fire, but in the meantime you stand in the furnace like Shadrach, Meshach, and Abednego.

"His winnowing fan is in His hand, and He will thoroughly clean out His threshing floor, and gather His wheat into the barn; but He will burn up the chaff with unquenchable fire" (v. 12). The fan John mentions here is the winnowing fork that Jewish farmers used to separate the good wheat from the chaff. With the fork farmers tossed the wheat into the air. The chaff was so light that even the slightest current of wind would carry it away, but the good wheat would fall to the floor. That is the metaphor John is using here, and the fork is already in the hands of the farmer. That time of separation, that time of division between the wheat and the chaff, is right now.

Do you see the crisis? The visible church is always made up of both wheat and chaff. At the last day Jesus will separate true church members from false. He will gather His wheat into His Father's house, and the rest will be burned with unquenchable fire.

To which group do you belong? That is the question we all have to answer at some point. Am I part of the wheat or the chaff? Is my destiny my Father's house or my Father's wrath? I pray that we will have nothing to fear from the future judgment of God. But if I assume that about each of us, I would be absolutely foolish. Statistically there have to be those among us who are not in Christ, who have nothing to face in the future except the punishment of God. If that is you, you need to flee to the Savior and to the cross so that He will clean you, and change you, and make you His own.

6

THE BAPTISM OF JESUS

Matthew 3:13–17

Then Jesus came from Galilee to John at the Jordan to be baptized by him. And John tried to prevent Him, saying, "I need to be baptized by You, and are You coming to me?" But Jesus answered and said to him, "Permit it to be so now, for thus it is fitting for us to fulfill all righteousness." Then he allowed Him. When He had been baptized, Jesus came up immediately from the water; and behold, the heavens were opened to Him, and He saw the Spirit of God descending like a dove and alighting upon Him. And suddenly a voice came from heaven, saying, "This is My beloved Son, in whom I am well pleased."

Then Jesus came from Galilee to John at the Jordan to be baptized by him (v. 13). We do not want to miss the significance of the purpose clause in this verse. It tells us that Jesus made the trip from Galilee to where John was baptizing at the Jordan for a specific purpose. Jesus did not come to observe what John was doing, nor did He come to criticize, as the Pharisees and Sadducees had done. Whereas the Sadducees, who represented the priestly class of the Jews, were offended by the ministry of John the Baptist and sought to repudiate it, the great High Priest came to be baptized. It is ironic that the One whom God the Father had appointed to be our great High Priest had a completely different view of the matter from that of the Sadducees.

The Lamb without Blemish

John tried to prevent Him, saying, "I need to be baptized by You, and are You coming to me?" (v. 14). We can fill in the gaps here with what we are told by the account in the Gospel of John. From that we know that when Jesus approached the Jordan, John saw Him and issued the *Agnus Dei*, saying, "Behold! The Lamb of God who takes away the sin of the world!" (John 1:29). John's reference to the Lamb of God pertains to the Old Testament sacrificial system. The lamb that was slain on the Day of Atonement had to be a lamb without blemish. A blemished lamb could not serve as an atonement for sins. John recognizes Jesus as the fulfillment of this practice. The Lamb without blemish, without sin, came to John in order to be baptized by him. John did not understand this and tried to stop it.

Because I preach often on the holiness of God, people often assume that I must be a very holy man. They do not understand that I am preoccupied with the holiness of God because God is radically different from me. I have to keep my eye on the holiness of God all the time, because it reveals to me so clearly my desperate need for the Savior. Do not ever think that ministers preach only on matters that they themselves have mastered. The first audience of every preacher's sermon should be and often is himself. That is what we see here in the text. John recognizes that he has a need to be baptized by Jesus, who has come to meet his need rather than the reverse.

But Jesus answered and said to him, "Permit it to be so now, for thus it is fitting for us to fulfill all righteousness." Then he allowed Him (v. 15). It is as if Jesus does not want to take the time to give John a lengthy, theological explanation. Instead Jesus tells John simply to do what He tells him, because it is necessary. Why did Jesus see it as necessary that He be baptized? Some critics take this as proof that Jesus did not see Himself as sinless.

Fulfilling all righteousness for a Jew meant that every jot and tittle of the law of God had to be fulfilled. God's standard is perfection; we are to be holy even as God is holy. In order that Jesus be the Lamb that takes away the sin of the world, He had to obey every jot and tittle of the law. Commentators raise their objection to this, claiming there is no law in the Old Testament that would require Jesus to be baptized, but these scholars overlook something of vast importance. When John the Baptist came, God was bringing forth a new requirement of His law that goes beyond the requirements He gave through Moses and the prophets in the Old Testament, and that new requirement, imposed upon all of Israel, is to be baptized in preparation for the coming of the kingdom of God.

An acute dimension of Jesus' ministry was His coming as the new Adam. He came as the embodiment and personification of Israel. To fulfill His mission, He had to obey every requirement that God had placed upon Israel and has given to man. Jesus had no sin of which to repent; His entire ministry was vicarious. He was a substitute. He was killed on the cross not for His sins but for the sins of His people. That is what He meant when He said, "It is fitting for us to fulfill all righteousness." Even though He had no need for baptism, Jesus submitted to this rite as part His corporate solidarity with His people. John finally acquiesces and baptizes Jesus.

The Veil Removed

When He had been baptized, Jesus came up immediately from the water; and behold, the heavens were opened to Him, and He saw the Spirit of God descending like a dove and alighting upon Him (v. 16). The obvious import is that the veil that covers the eyes of human beings to the inner chambers of heaven was removed, just as the veil was removed from the eyes of Elisha's servant when he saw that host of angels that had been invisible to him. The same thing happened to Stephen while he was being executed. As the earthly court was killing him, he beheld the inner sanctuary of heaven and saw the Son of Man standing at the right hand of God. There have been those few moments in history when the veil that hides the glory of heaven from human sight has been removed. It happened here as Jesus came out of the water. As Jesus was being initiated into His earthly ministry, He looked up and saw heaven itself.

As the heavens were opened to Him, He saw a dove descending from the sky and lighting on top of His head, indicating the anointing of the Lord for His ministry. It was at His baptism that Jesus was anointed and empowered by the Father for His earthly ministry in fulfillment of the words of Isaiah: "The Spirit of the Lord God is upon Me" (Isa. 61:1).

It is important to notice that in this event all three members of the Trinity are present and involved. The Father speaks to the Son, the Spirit anoints the Son, and the Son is anointed and initiated for ministry. Just as all three members of the Trinity were present in creation, so here in this moment of the initiation of redemption, all three are present.

And suddenly a voice came from heaven, saying, "This is My beloved Son, in whom I am well pleased" (v. 17). This will become important again when we look later at the temptation of Jesus. Jesus heard the voice of God audibly, which is a rare occurrence in the Bible. Only three times in the New Testament is the audible voice of God heard, and on every one of those occasions that voice is testifying to Christ. People claim to have heard the voice of God telling them to do all kinds of things, but God does not speak audibly today, and He did it so rarely in the New Testament that He reserved those audible declarations for occasions such as this.

Jesus heard the voice of the Father: "This is My beloved Son, in whom I am well pleased." In Psalm 2 we are told that the whole world sets itself against the Lord and against His Anointed, saying, "Let us break Their bonds in pieces" (v. 3), but in the final portion of the psalm the psalmist instructs, "Kiss the Son, lest He be angry and you perish in the way" (v. 12). In the beginning of the last section of the book of Isaiah, we find God's announcement: "Behold! My Servant whom I uphold, My Elect One in whom My soul delights!" (Isa. 42:1). Is Christ your beloved? God is filled with affection for His only begotten Son. Do you have affection in your heart for Christ? If there is no affection in your heart for Him, you do not belong to Him. Do you take pleasure in Christ? Are you well pleased with Him? In the value system of God, God's love is poured out on His Son. God's good pleasure is revealed toward His Son. On another one of those occasions when God spoke audibly, He said: "This is My beloved Son. Hear Him!" (Mark 9:7). If you love Christ, you hear Him. If you do not listen to Him, that is the clearest indication that there is no love in your soul for the Son of God.

7

THE TEMPTATION OF JESUS, PART 1

Matthew 4:1–11

Then Jesus was led up by the Spirit into the wilderness to be tempted by the devil. And when He had fasted forty days and forty nights, afterward He was hungry. Now when the tempter came to Him, he said, "If You are the Son of God, command that these stones become bread." But He answered and said, "It is written, 'Man shall not live by bread alone, but by every word that proceeds from the mouth of God.'" Then the devil took Him up into the holy city, set Him on the pinnacle of the temple, and said to Him, "If You are the Son of God, throw Yourself down. For it is written:

> 'He shall give His angels charge over you,'

and,

> 'In their hands they shall bear you up,
> Lest you dash your foot against a stone.'"

Jesus said to him, "It is written again, 'You shall not tempt the LORD your God.'" Again, the devil took Him up on an exceedingly high mountain, and showed Him all the kingdoms of the world and their glory. And he said to Him, "All these things I will give You if You will fall down and worship me." Then Jesus said to him, "Away with you, Satan! For it is written, 'You shall worship the LORD your God, and Him only you shall serve.'" Then the devil left Him, and behold, angels came and ministered to Him.

Jesus was led up by the Spirit into the wilderness to be tempted by the devil (v. 1). The other Gospel accounts agree with this rendering, though one or two words are different. After the Holy Spirit descended upon Jesus at His baptism, we are told immediately that the Spirit of God led Jesus into the wilderness. However, the Spirit did not merely lead Him there but drove Him to that place. The Spirit impelled Jesus to go into the wilderness for the specific purpose of being tempted.

The Scriptures tell us clearly, in James's epistle, that temptations arise from within, from the evil inclinations of our hearts, and we succumb to these temptations as a result of our corrupt spirit (James 1:14–15). James writes, "Let no one say when he is tempted, 'I am tempted by God'; for God cannot be tempted by evil, nor does He Himself tempt anyone" (v. 13). For that reason, we know that here in Matthew God is not tempting Jesus. The word Matthew uses can mean "tempt" or "test." God sent His Son into the wilderness in order that He would be tempted by Satan, and the purpose for the temptation was to test Him.

The Sinlessness of Jesus

In our last lesson we considered that when Jesus submitted to the baptism of John, He did so in part to identify with His people, to demonstrate the corporate solidarity between Jesus and the covenant people of God. Jesus did not need to be baptized as repentance for sin, because He had no sin. Nonbelievers attack the veracity of the virgin birth and the resurrection of Jesus because these two events are so manifestly miraculous. Yet there is something in the Scripture about Jesus that is even more astonishing than His resurrection from the dead, and that is His sinlessness.

The most righteous among us have not made it without sin since we got out of our bed this morning. Not one of us has ever loved the Lord our God with all our heart, mind, and strength. To imagine a human being, no matter how sanctified, living a life of complete righteousness without the smallest moral blemish is almost impossible to conceive. We must remember that one of Jesus' roles was to serve as the new Adam, the second Adam. He was called to do for us what the first Adam failed to achieve. This parallel contrast between the original Adam and the new Adam is set forth frequently in the New Testament to show that by the first Adam's disobedience, the world was plunged into ruin, but by the second Adam's obedience, His followers are redeemed. Both Adams were subjected to a probationary test to see if they would achieve obedience and righteousness. For Christ to redeem us as the second Adam, He had to be put to the test. Like the first Adam, He was placed on probation, and He could not fail His test.

The redemption that Christ accomplished for us was not achieved by His death alone. He not only had to take our punishment for sin, but He also had to achieve righteousness on our behalf. Therefore, His perfect obedience is as necessary to our salvation as His death upon the cross. Here, in this experience in the wilderness, that righteousness and obedience are at stake.

The First Test

The location of the first Adam's test was the garden of Eden, an unspoiled place filled with the luscious fruit that God had given to His creatures, saying to them, "Of every tree of the garden you may freely eat; but of the tree of the knowledge of good and evil you shall not eat" (Gen. 2:16–17). The setting for Adam and Eve's test was a gourmet feast in this pristine garden of Eden. The setting of the test of the second Adam was in the Judean wilderness, which, far from being a lush garden, is one of the most desolate places on earth. Its only inhabitants are spiders, scorpions, and a few varieties of birds. It was a place forbidding and foreboding into which the Spirit drove Jesus to be tempted.

The circumstances of His test were to take place on an empty stomach after a forty-day fast reminiscent of the forty days and nights of the fast of Moses in the Old Testament before God gave him the law. The Serpent came to Adam and Eve when their stomachs were full; he came to the new Adam in the midst of profound hunger. Additionally, Adam and Eve's test was not given in the midst of solitude or loneliness, but in the midst of companionship. They faced their test with mutual support and encouragement, whereas Christ faced the devil alone. Unlike Adam and Eve, Jesus faced the devil at a time when the world was accustomed to sin. You can see the strong contrast between the two tests.

At the same time, there is a point of similarity that we do not want to miss: the same issue was at stake. In the garden of Eden the Serpent came to Adam and Eve with a question: "Has God indeed said, 'You shall not eat of every tree of the garden'?" (Gen. 3:1). Of course God had not said that; God had said they could freely eat. There was only one place in the garden that was off-limits. Eve responded to Satan, saying, "We may eat the fruit of the trees of the garden; but of the fruit of the tree which is in the midst of the garden, God has said, 'You shall not eat it, nor shall you touch it, lest you die.'" Satan then told her, "You will not surely die. For God knows that in the day you eat of it your eyes will be opened, and you will be like God, knowing good and evil" (vv. 2–5). So, seeing that the fruit seemed good, they did eat and plunged the world into ruin.

When the Spirit drove Jesus into the wilderness, Satan also came with a question: **"If You are the Son of God, command that these stones become bread"** (v. 3). The last words echoing in Jesus' ears had come from heaven itself, when God audibly spoke, saying, "This is My beloved Son in whom I am well pleased." The devil's point of attack was the same in both cases—the trustworthiness of the word of God. Adam and Eve did not believe God, but Jesus did.

The question of whether Jesus could have sinned comes up in every generation. Many theologians say it is impossible that Jesus could have sinned, and they base that argument on the eternal decrees of God. Did not God decide that Christ would come to this world and be our Redeemer, and if indeed Christ was ordained to redeem us, then surely, in light of that divine foreordination, it would have been impossible for Him to sin. There is some weight to that argument, because if God ordains from all eternity that something is going to happen, it most certainly will happen.

There is a tiny but important theological distinction between the necessity of the consequence and the necessity of the consequent. From the eternal perspective, there is no possibility that Jesus would have sinned, just as it would have been impossible for Adam and Eve or Judas not to sin. However, in terms of the consequent, God's eternal decrees work in and through the means that He appoints, and the appointed means for the fall of the human race was through the decision of Adam and Eve, which they did without coercion. In like manner, our Lord was obedient through no coercive power of God, and in that sense, considering His human nature, He could have sinned.

Even more important is the Christological issue. Throughout church history theologians have argued that it would have been impossible for Jesus to sin because He is God incarnate, and God cannot sin. However, God incarnate has two natures—a divine nature and a human nature—and though we cannot divide them, we must distinguish between them. During His lifetime Jesus got hungry, He sweated, and He died. Those were manifestations of His human nature, not His divine nature. God does not sweat. Those who think that Jesus' divine nature so overshadowed His human nature so as to make it impossible for Him to sin have slipped into monophysitism, an old and lethal heresy in which divine attributes are imputed to the human nature. Jesus' human nature was a real human nature with all of the limitations that go with it. Jesus had the ability to sin, or He would not have been truly human. Moreover, if Jesus had been incapable of sinning, the temptation in the wilderness would have been nothing but a sham.

8

THE TEMPTATION OF JESUS, PART 2

Matthew 4:1–11

Then Jesus was led up by the Spirit into the wilderness to be tempted by the devil. And when He had fasted forty days and forty nights, afterward He was hungry. Now when the tempter came to Him, he said, "If You are the Son of God, command that these stones become bread." But He answered and said, "It is written, 'Man shall not live by bread alone, but by every word that proceeds from the mouth of God.'" Then the devil took Him up into the holy city, set Him on the pinnacle of the temple, and said to Him, "If You are the Son of God, throw Yourself down. For it is written:

> 'He shall give His angels charge over you,'

and,

> 'In their hands they shall bear you up,
> Lest you dash your foot against a stone.'"

Jesus said to him, "It is written again, 'You shall not tempt the LORD your God.'" Again, the devil took Him up on an exceedingly high mountain, and showed Him all the kingdoms of the world and their glory. And he said to Him, "All these things I will give You if You will fall down and worship me." Then Jesus said to him, "Away with you, Satan! For it is written, 'You shall worship the LORD your God, and Him only you shall serve.'" Then the devil left Him, and behold, angels came and ministered to Him.

And when He had fasted forty days and forty nights, afterward He was hungry. Now when the tempter came to Him, he said, "If You are the Son of God, command that these stones become bread" (vv. 2–3). The One being tempted here is the God-Man, who possesses a perfect divine nature and a perfect human nature. He is, as the Council of Chalcedon declared, *vera homo, vera Deus*, truly man and truly God. The text tells us that after the forty-day fast Jesus suffered from hunger, which manifests the humanity of our Lord. He experienced severe pangs of hunger, as anyone would who went without food for forty days and forty nights.

During this time of vulnerability Satan came to tempt Jesus, not to commit some blatant evil but simply to satisfy a natural inclination and desire for food. Satan comes saying, "If You are the Son of God . . ." Satan is seeking to plant the suggestion that if Jesus were really the Son of God, He shouldn't have to endure such hunger but should use His divine authority to get food from the stones.

Every Word

Jesus responds to Satan, **"It is written, 'Man shall not live by bread alone, but by every word that proceeds from the mouth of God'"** (v. 4). Jesus was not referencing something contained in a book from the library of Alexandria or in the manuscripts of the ancient Greeks or Romans. "It is written" was shorthand that every Jew understood. Jesus was referencing sacred Scripture. Jesus responds to the temptation by citing the Bible.

Jesus does not despise our human need for food. In the Lord's Prayer He instructs us to pray for our daily bread. We need the nutrients that food provides to sustain human life. His point here is that life requires more than physical nutrients. We cannot live by bread alone; we need bread and something else. Notice that Jesus did not say that man needs bread and *also* the word of God. He said "every word." We do not live that way, which distances us immediately from Jesus. We think that the Bible is like a smorgasbord so that we can choose a bit of Matthew and Luke and some of Romans but leave behind Leviticus.

Centuries before, God had led His people to the Promised Land and told them to drive out the Canaanites from that land so that His people would not become defiled by mixing with those of pagan religions. But they did not, and the Old Testament spells out the consequences of what happens to God's people when they fail to listen to every word that proceeds from His mouth. That's why, when the Scriptures sound difficult to our ears, we simply need to increase our attention and understand that it is the Word of God. The Word of God in Judges is no more or no less true than the Word of God in the book of Romans. Jesus' meat and drink was to do the will of the Father. He had a zeal that consumed Him. He understood that God had never uttered a desultory word. There is no such thing as an insignificant statement from the lips of God, and Jesus understood that. John Calvin called the Bible the *vox Dei*, the voice of God, and said that we should receive this word as if hearing it audibly from the lips of God Himself.

When Satan came to destroy Jesus, the defense of the Savior was the Word of God. At that point of the temptation, Satan realized that he had lost. Jesus may have had the authority to turn the stones into bread, but He was committed to fast for the sake of His Father's will. The word that came from His Father was more important to Him than His bread.

Jesus' Use of Scripture

Then the devil took Him up into the holy city, set Him on the pinnacle of the temple, and said to Him, "If You are the Son of God, throw yourself down" (vv. 5–6). Since Jesus had cited the Word of God, Satan decided to do likewise, saying, **"For it is written: 'He shall give His angels charge over you,' and, 'In their hands they shall bear you up, lest you dash your foot against a stone'"** (v. 6). In other words, "Isn't that the word of God, Jesus? Isn't that what the Bible says? Well, let's see if the Bible is true. Jump and see if the angels catch you."

Jesus replied again with the Word of God: **"It is written again, 'You shall not tempt the Lord your God'"** (v. 7). Satan's hermeneutics were wrong. Hermeneutics has to do with the laws that govern the interpretation of Scripture. People say that the Bible is the Word of God but still take that Word and twist it to support what they want to do, and this violates the principles for interpreting Scripture. The first principle of interpretation we call "the analogy of faith," which means that Scripture is its own interpreter; in other words, we are to interpret Scripture with Scripture. God never speaks a lie, and His Word is coherent and unified. God never contradicts Himself. Therefore, what He says in the book of Judges can never contradict what He says in Ephesians. If we set one part of Scripture against another part of Scripture, we violate the most fundamental principle of biblical interpretation, and that is exactly what Satan was doing.

Jesus tells Satan that if He were to jump off the temple to prove that the Scripture is true, He would be violating the very Scripture that forbids Him from doing it. Besides that, Jesus knew who He was. He did not have to jump from some great height to know that the angels had been given charge over Him, nor did He have to worry about dashing His foot against a rock, because He knew that angels were protecting Him.

Again, the devil took him up on an exceedingly high mountain, and

showed Him all the kingdoms of the world and their glory. And he said to Him, "All these things I will give You if You will fall down and worship me" (vv. 8–9). Adolf Hitler said to his henchmen, "We can lie to the people now, but after we have victory no one will remember." He meant that no one would later care about his lies because he would bring glory to Germany, a new kingdom that would encompass Czechoslovakia, the Sudetenland, Poland, the low countries, Belgium, Netherlands, France, England, and then the world. Hitler made a notation in his diary that said, "Today I have made a covenant with Satan for all the kingdoms of the world and for all their glory."

Have you ever considered your personal point of vulnerability if Satan were to come to you with a test? What would he put in front of you: glory, a kingdom, riches, or power? He offered all these things to Jesus in exchange for one thing—worship. The offer that Satan presented to Jesus was not his to give. Satan has no glory to give anyone.

Perhaps you have heard the story of a congressman from Tennessee who, after serving his first term in Washington, was seeking reelection. He returned to his home state of Tennessee to seek support for reelection, and in those efforts he went to the home of a wealthy farmer who had been a key supporter in his first election. The congressman said to the farmer, "I'm running for a second term. Will you support me again?" The farmer shook his head no and said, "No, I'm sorry, Mr. Crockett. I'm not going to support you again." He continued, "Do you remember what happened last year when there was a fire in Washington that displaced people from their home? You voted to give the displaced people the money they needed to build a new house. You didn't take that money from your own pocket, but you voted to take it from mine." In other words, the money distributed by the congressman had not been his to give.

The Father has set before His Son all the kingdoms of the world and promised Him the glory that had been His from the beginning. Jesus did not need to get it from Satan. At stake here was the cost of getting it. The price of His inheritance was Calvary. Satan was offering glory without that necessary suffering and humiliation.

How do you respond to Satan's temptations when you are alone and no one can see what you do? Here is how Jesus responded: **"Away with you, Satan! For it is written, 'You shall worship the Lord your God, and Him only you shall serve'"** (v. 10). Jesus refused to give Satan even the slightest genuflection, because the only One worthy of that is the Father. We are to serve Him and Him alone. We are snared more by that word, *alone*, than by any other word in Scripture, but that is how Jesus silenced the devil.

Then the devil left Him, and behold, angels came and ministered to Him (v.

11). The other Gospel narratives give us a bit more information here, saying that the devil left Him *for a season*. This was not the end of the battle. Satan watched the ministry of Jesus every single day, always looking for a way to trap Him.

The most glorious moment in Jesus' earthly ministry was at the Mount of Transfiguration. Shortly after that Jesus asked His disciples, "Who do men say that I, the Son of Man, am?" and Simon gave the great confession: "You are the Christ, the Son of the living God" (Matt. 16:13, 16). Peter did not say, "*If* you are the Son" but "You are the Son." At that time Jesus looked at Simon and said, "Blessed are you, Simon Bar-Jonah, for flesh and blood has not revealed this to you, but my Father who is in heaven. And I also say to you that you are Peter, and on this rock I will build My church, and the gates of Hades shall not prevail against it" (vv. 17–18). Before hardly any time had passed, Jesus foretold that He would be delivered to His enemies, and in his boldness Peter said, "This shall not happen to You!" to which Jesus replied, "Get behind Me, Satan!" (vv. 22–23). Right before Jesus went to Jerusalem, Satan showed up in the lips of his most trusted disciple.

It is almost always our closest friends and relatives who seek to dissuade us from our duty, if that duty promises suffering.

Jesus' test in the wilderness concludes with exquisite irony. As soon as Satan left, the angels appeared and ministered to Him. They were there all the time. The fast was over. The Bible does not say this, but I believe the angels set before Jesus the most incredible breakfast that had ever been served to any human being. It was a gourmet feast. The angels that were not present there but were up in heaven surely noted what an honor it was for those angels who *were* there to minister to Him, because He is the Son of God in whom God is well pleased.

9

JESUS GOES TO GALILEE

Matthew 4:12–17

Now when Jesus heard that John had been put in prison, He departed to Galilee. And leaving Nazareth, He came and dwelt in Capernaum, which is by the sea, in the regions of Zebulun and Naphtali, that it might be fulfilled which was spoken by Isaiah the prophet, saying:

> "The land of Zebulun and the land of Naphtali,
> By the way of the sea, beyond the Jordan,
> Galilee of the Gentiles:
> The people who sat in darkness have seen a great light,
> And upon those who sat in the region and shadow of death
> Light has dawned."

From that time Jesus began to preach and to say, "Repent, for the kingdom of heaven is at hand."

Immediately after Matthew recounts the testing of Jesus in the Judean wilderness, he transitions to an account of the earthly ministry of our Lord. **Now when Jesus heard that John had been put in prison, He departed to Galilee** (v. 12). We do not know how much time passed after Jesus' baptism and temptation before this news reached Him, but presumably it was a short interlude. Jesus might have gone north rather than south in order to escape the vengeance of the king; however, that king ruled both places. Therefore, I have to think there was another reason that Jesus went to Galilee.

Galilee of the Gentiles

And leaving Nazareth, He came and dwelt in Capernaum, which is by the sea, in the regions of Zebulun and Naphtali (v. 13). We learn that Jesus moved from His place of residence in Nazareth and resided for most of His earthly ministry in Capernaum, which was on the northernmost point of the western edge of the Sea of Galilee. In most of our records, Jesus' earthly ministry is seen taking place in the villages around that area.

Isaiah called Galilee "Galilee of the Gentiles" because there was a heavy population of Gentiles there in the north, and they should not have been there. The book of Judges tells us that God was angry because His people had failed to drive out the pagans from that land. God predicted that, because of this, the pagans with their deities would be a snare to His people, as the whole history of the Old Testament exhibits. Two of the tribes that failed to carry out this divine mandate were Zebulun and Naphtali. Jesus goes to that very region, which by this time was simply called "Galilee of the Gentiles." The region was densely populated. Virtually every village there had at least fifteen thousand inhabitants. It was a center of commerce and trade with other nations. Earlier, before Herod became king, Aristobulus had invaded Galilee and forced the Gentile residents to be circumcised. Their hearts were not circumcised. They still despised the things of the God of Israel and continued in their pagan practices, but here we see that Jesus goes to this pagan region in and around the Sea of Galilee.

Light in the Darkness

God rarely does what we expect Him to do. He has never been bound by the expectations of men. God exercises His mission—His redeeming grace—when and where and how in His sovereignty He pleases. So now Jesus doesn't go to Jerusalem but He goes to the regions of Zebulun and Naphtali. Matthew, as he does throughout his work, is eager to point to fulfillments of Old Testament prophecy, so he writes that Jesus went to the regions of Zebulun and Naphtali **that it might be fulfilled which was spoken by Isaiah the prophet, saying: "The land of Zebulun and the land of Naphtali, by the way of the sea, beyond the Jordan, Galilee of the Gentiles: The people who sat in darkness have seen a great light, and upon those who sat in the region and shadow of death Light has dawned"** (vv. 14–16).

This last portion of the citation from Matthew is recited every year during the Advent season because we see its ultimate fulfillment, the entrance of Christ into the world, as the entrance of the light into the darkness. However, its first reference was not to the whole world; it was to that region of Palestine that was occupied largely by pagans. The appearance of Jesus in Galilee was the appearance of light in the darkness. In Isaiah's metaphor we see the image of darkness and the image of death. It describes the inhabitants as Gentile people sitting in darkness and overshadowed by death.

Most of us are familiar with these words from John's Gospel: "For God so loved the world that He gave His only begotten Son that whoever believes in Him should not perish but have everlasting life. For God did not send His Son into the world to condemn the world but that the world through Him might be saved" (John 3:16–17). That passage is so well-known because it announces the gospel. The love of God for a fallen world is so great that He sent His Son so that anyone who believes on Him won't perish but will live forever. We tend to be much less familiar with what John wrote immediately after: "And this is the condemnation, that . . . men loved darkness rather than light, because their deeds were evil" (v. 19).

The metaphor of light and darkness is used abundantly in the New Testament. It gives a vivid contrast between righteousness and evil and between life and death. The Bible teaches us that by nature we are children of darkness. The darkness that enveloped the Gentiles in Galilee did not stop at the border. That darkness cast a pall over the whole planet, and every one of us is born in that state of darkness. Every one of us is by nature a child of the darkness. Every one of us is by nature a person who prefers darkness to light, because in the light of day our sins are made manifest. One of the things we most fear is exposure.

When the prophecy speaks of those in darkness seeing a great light, it does not mean that everyone embraced the light. Jesus was killed because He was the light of the world and because men prefer the darkness to the light. Otherwise that light would not have been extinguished. At the beginning of his Gospel John wrote, "In the beginning was the Word, and the Word was with God, and the Word was God. He was in the beginning with God. All things were made through Him, and without Him nothing was made that was made. In Him was life, and the life was the light of the men. And the light shines in the darkness, and the darkness did not comprehend it" (John 1:1–5).

Another way to translate that text is "the darkness could not overcome it." Whenever there is a real clash between darkness and light, the outcome is certain. If you sit in a dark room at night, with no lights on and no moon shining through the window, light floods the room the second you flip on the light switch. Darkness is no match for the light. Yet when the Light who is the life of the world came, the darkness did not understand it. John continues:

> There was a man sent from God, whose name was John. This man came for a witness, to bear witness of the Light, that all through him might believe. He was not that Light, but was sent to bear witness of that Light. That was the true light which gives light to every man coming into the world. He was in the world, and the world was made through Him, and the world did not know Him. He came to His own, and His own did not receive Him. (vv. 6–11)

When someone becomes converted to Christ, others say of him, often sarcastically, "He has seen the light." As much of a mockery as this tends to be, it is a statement of profound truth, because by nature our souls are shrouded in darkness, and until the soul embraces Christ, that darkness continues to rule. When the Holy Spirit removes the scales from someone's eyes and changes the disposition of his heart, then that light of Christ bursts into the soul so that it cannot be contained.

If you have been converted, you know exactly what I mean; if you have not been converted, you have no idea what I am saying. If you could use an instrument to peer into your soul, what would you see? Would you see a soul that was still sitting in darkness? Or would that instrument explode with light? Galilee was not the only place where people sat in darkness and under the shadow of death. That shadow covered the entire world, and Jesus' appearing was a life-or-death matter.

I have estimated that at Christmastime there must be in metropolitan Orlando a billion lights adorning the yards and the stores of our neighborhoods, but upon further consideration I think that is a gross underestimation. There are more likely several billions of those little lights. I wonder if those who string them understand what they represent. This next Christmas season, every time you pass a house festooned with such lights, stop and remember that those lights signify the entrance of the Light into the world. Then ask yourself whether you rejoice in that light or if you are one of those who cannot wait until the end of December so that all those will go away and you can return to the darkness. The last place we want to be is in the darkness, but the Scriptures indicate that if we reject this One who came into the darkness, our destiny will be the outer darkness where the light of God's grace will never shine.

This was a critical moment for the people of Galilee. The light was in their midst. If they wanted to stay blinded to it, they would stay that way forever, fulfilling the warning of the prophet Amos, who said, "Is not the day of the Lord darkness, and not light? Is it not very dark, with no brightness in it?" (Amos 5:20). There is no worse fate than to be consigned to utter darkness for all eternity, and how foolish that would be when the light is right here.

10

JESUS' DISCIPLES AND MINISTRIES

Matthew 4:18–25

And Jesus, walking by the Sea of Galilee, saw two brothers, Simon called Peter, and Andrew his brother, casting a net into the sea; for they were fishermen. Then He said to them, "Follow Me, and I will make you fishers of men." They immediately left their nets and followed Him. Going on from there, He saw two other brothers, James the son of Zebedee, and John his brother, in the boat with Zebedee their father, mending their nets. He called them, and immediately they left the boat and their father, and followed Him. And Jesus went about all Galilee, teaching in their synagogues, preaching the gospel of the kingdom, and healing all kinds of sickness and all kinds of disease among the people. Then His fame went throughout all Syria; and they brought to Him all sick people who were afflicted with various diseases and torments, and those who were demon-possessed, epileptics, and paralytics; and He healed them. Great multitudes followed Him—from Galilee, and from Decapolis, Jerusalem, Judea, and beyond the Jordan.

Matthew does not give us the record of Jesus' call of all twelve disciples, but of four, who are identified here as two sets of brothers: Peter and Andrew, and James and John. It is important to note at the outset that the biblical terms *disciple* and *apostle* are not interchangeable. A disciple was, in the first instance, a student. The Greek word for *disciple* means "one who is a learner." An *apostle* refers to someone commissioned by an authority figure to speak for him in such a way that the words of the commissioned one carry the weight of the authority himself. The terms get confused because those whom Christ made apostles were first disciples. He did not commission them to the office of apostle until they had been trained as His students.

Jesus was a peripatetic rabbi, which means that He moved around as He taught. He did not have a particular school building in which He held classes. His disciples literally walked behind Him, listening to His lectures, and they committed these lectures to memory. What we see here is Jesus recruiting students for His rabbinic school.

Ready to Follow

Jesus, walking by the Sea of Galilee, saw two brothers, Simon called Peter, and Andrew his brother, casting a net into the sea; for they were fishermen (v. 18). We might think that this is the first time that Simon Peter and his brother Andrew had ever met Jesus and perhaps had not even heard of Him, but from John's Gospel we know that was not the case. Andrew had been a disciple of John the Baptist. John's Gospel mentions only Andrew specifically and leaves the other disciple unnamed, but scholars believe it was John, since he characteristically did not refer to himself by name in his Gospel. As they had listened to John the Baptist's message about Christ, they left John to follow Jesus. We are told in John's Gospel that Andrew went to his brother Simon and told him, "We have found the Messiah" (John 1:41), and presumably the other disciple, John, gave the same message to his brother.

Here Jesus comes to these brothers, two of whom had been present when John the Baptist announced His identity as the Messiah, and two who obviously had heard about Jesus from their brothers. Almost every time we see Andrew in the New Testament, he is bringing someone to Jesus. Andrew is not mentioned nearly as much as Peter, who emerges in the pages of the New Testament as the leader of the Twelve and as the one called "the rock" by Jesus.

These four men are called into discipleship from different careers, and they make different levels of impact on the kingdom. James was the first of the disciples to be martyred for the cause of the kingdom. Of the four who are mentioned in this text, three were killed for their allegiance to Jesus. Simon Peter was crucified upside down. Andrew was crucified on an X-shaped cross after saying that he could not preach the cross without welcoming the opportunity to be put to death on one. The one who lived the longest was John, who presumably was the only one not martyred. He lived to write the Gospel of John, the Epistles of John, and the book of Revelation while he was in exile on the island of Patmos. God uses people in different ways for different times.

My wife, Vesta, and I were involved in the 1993 Amtrak train crash in Alabama, where many people perished. We were unable to answer the media when they asked us why our lives had been spared while others had not. When my close friend and ministry comrade James Boice died in 2000, I wondered why God would take him out of the battle when we needed him so desperately. I had always assumed that I would die before Jim, because he kept his body in excellent shape whereas I neglected mine. All our lives are in the hands of the Father, and He takes us home when He pleases. We can trust God's sovereign control not only over our life but also over our death, as we see in the lives of these four men.

Then He said to them, "Follow Me, and I will make you fishers of men" (v. 19). They were already disciples, but they were being called to full-time discipleship. They had made a commitment to Jesus, but they had not yet given their lives over to His leadership.

Early in my Christian life one of my favorite hymns became "Where He Leads Me I Will Follow":

> I can hear my Savior calling,
> I can hear my Savior calling,
> I can hear my Savior calling,
> "Take Thy cross and follow follow me."

It took hold of my heart and became a prayer: "Lord, wherever you want me to go, I will go." That is a great old hymn, because it expresses what it means to be a Christian. A Christian is someone who follows Jesus.

Thirteen times in Matthew's Gospel we hear Jesus saying to people, "Follow Me." Although the disciples were called to follow Jesus literally, in the sense of tagging along behind Him, the call meant so much more than that. It meant placing themselves in submission under His authority and living in obedience to Him as their Master. It meant being like yoked oxen who labor in His service. Even though we are not part of the original Twelve, every obligation that Jesus imposed on His disciples then is imposed upon us now. If you would be a disciple of Jesus, if you would follow Him, you must submit to His authority. You must regard Him as the Master of your life, must be willing to follow Him wherever He leads you, and must be willing to trust Him with your life.

They immediately left their nets and followed Him (v. 20). Elsewhere Jesus said, "No one, having put his hand to the plow, and looking back, is fit for the kingdom of God" (Luke 9:62), and to the one who said, "Lord, let me first go and bury my father," Jesus said, "Let the dead bury their own dead" (vv. 59–60). In those days, people did not play at being Christians. They were willing to leave everything to follow Him because they had found the pearl of great price. It wasn't a sacrifice to leave their businesses and move into a different vocation, because what they had found was so much more wonderful. They dropped their nets and immediately followed after Him.

An Imperial Summons

Going on from there, He saw two other brothers, James the son of Zebedee, and John his brother, in the boat with Zebedee their father, mending their nets. He called them, and immediately they left the boat and their father, and followed Him (vv. 21–22). Obviously their enterprise was their father's fishing business, and presumably one that was quite lucrative. They were not fishing at this time; they were seated and mending their nets.

When Vesta and I lived on the North Shore of Boston, we would drive up to Gloucester and have lunch on the wharf. Gloucester is famous for its great fishing fleet, which is made up mostly of Greek fishermen. These men go out into the sea and labor for hours, yet when they return and empty their nets, the work is not over. Vesta and I would sit on the wharf and look out at these grizzled veterans of the sea as they sat meticulously sewing their nets. That task is as important to their enterprise as is actually going out to sea, because if a net has a hole in it, it is worthless. A diligent fisherman not only learns to fish, but he pays close attention to the equipment that he uses. Just so, if you want to be a fisher of men, you must constantly mend your nets. You must constantly fortify yourself by feeding on the Word of God so that you have something of which to use when you're fishing for people.

The great Baptist preacher Charles Spurgeon, in looking at this text, saw some dimensions of this call to discipleship that we sometimes overlook. He said that the call that came from Jesus was an imperial summons. The call of Jesus is not like getting a ticket from the local police department, which sometimes gets tossed aside. It is a summons that comes from the King, and such a summons cannot be ignored. Andrew, Peter, James, and John had known who Jesus was before He came to them, so there was no hesitation when the King called them to leave their earthly security. They understood His authority to make that demand on their lives.

Charles Spurgeon also observed that this imperial summons was appropriate for people to obey. As the King of kings, Jesus not only had the authority, but He had the right to call these people to leave what they were doing and follow Him and give Him their lives. There is nothing inappropriate about Jesus making that kind of claim on your life. It is, however, inappropriate to ignore the call of Jesus. Can you imagine anything more inappropriate than saying no to a summons from Jesus? Ignoring it isn't just foolish; it is sinful. That is why I am uncomfortable when someone is "invited" to come to Christ. When Paul declared the gospel to the Athenians on Mars Hill, he said, "Truly, these times of ignorance God overlooked, but now commands all men everywhere to repent" (Acts 17:30). The problem with issuing an "invitation" is that it implies that you have the option to decline. You may send in your regrets and say, "I'm sorry; I can't come." God never invites people to come to Christ; He commands it.

Finally, Spurgeon said that this call was not only imperial and appropriate but also effectual. Every one of us ought to know what the *doctrine of effectual calling* means. It refers to a special kind of call that comes from God as distinguished from an external call. Many hear the gospel message, yet it has no impact on them. They have received only an outward, external call. An effectual call is something God does on the soul of a human being. When God calls you outwardly, you might not respond, but when the Holy Spirit calls you inwardly, He changes the disposition of your heart so that you are made willing and eager to come to Him. God's effectual call works a life-changing effect in the hearts of those who hear it.

Not all of the men who were called to be disciples of Jesus in the New Testament received the effectual call. Judas certainly did not. Even though for His own purposes God had called him, Jesus said that Judas was a devil from the beginning and that he had been appointed as the one through whose hands Jesus would be delivered to death. The others received the effectual call. When Christ called them, His call not only reached their ears but pierced their souls and penetrated their hearts so that when they left their nets they were changed.

You may have heard the external call, but have you heard the inward call? Has the call of Jesus done its work in your soul? I hope you will not put your head on your pillow tonight until you are sure in your spirit that you have heard the call of Christ to follow Him inwardly in your soul.

11

THE BEATITUDES, PART 1

Matthew 5:1–4

> And seeing the multitudes, He went up on a mountain, and when He was seated His disciples came to Him. Then He opened His mouth and taught them, saying: Blessed are the poor in spirit, for theirs is the kingdom of heaven. Blessed are those who mourn, for they shall be comforted.

We begin now a study of the Sermon on the Mount, and there are many dimensions to this sermon that have been fraught with controversy. The first is the question of where this sermon was actually preached. The mountain is not identified. Luke's version has Jesus teaching His disciples on a plain, "a level place" (Luke 6:17). Critics use this to say that the Bible is contradictory; however teachers teach important matters on more than one occasion and in more than one place, so we should not be disturbed that the biblical record has Jesus preaching on a mountain in one Gospel and on a plain in another.

Three Errors

Of greater importance is the matter of interpreting the Sermon on the Mount. There are three serious errors that are widely held in the church with regard to understanding the sermon. The first error teaches that all the ethical mandates found in the sermon have no bearing on us today. Rather, this sermon is seen as being about the ethics of the kingdom of God, and since the kingdom of God has not yet come, the sermon is irrelevant to us now. That is a serious distortion, which is based on an equally serious misunderstanding of the concept of the kingdom of God in the New Testament.

Jesus ascended to heaven to assume the role of King of kings, so even though the final consummation of His kingdom is in the future, to think that the kingdom is something completely future misses one of the central thrusts of the New Testament. I believe that the content of the Sermon on the Mount is very much relevant to us today, as it is to Christians in every generation. In fact, the virtues spelled out here in the sermon are spelled out in the teachings of the Apostles.

The second error is to see that the Sermon on the Mount is merely a new declaration of law by which an impossible ethic is set before us so as to reveal the necessity of the gospel. That is indeed one of the things that the law does—expose our desperate need for the gospel—but I think that again misunderstands the basic essence of the sermon.

Perhaps the worst distortion was brought to bear in nineteenth-century liberalism. It holds that the Sermon on the Mount is about the social gospel and that the ethic of Jesus is not about personal redemption but about teaching the church ethical behavior so that the mission of the church is to be an agency of mere humanitarianism. That, of course, scuttles not only the relevance of the Sermon on the Mount but the entire New Testament.

If you look closely at the content of the Sermon on the Mount, in it Jesus sets forth our response to Him as the ultimate test by which we and all men will be judged eternally. Therefore, let us be careful not to get caught in the trap of those erroneous views. The sermon is the Word of God for us today and for Christians in every age.

Blessed

The beginning of the Sermon on the Mount is filled with a list of beatitudes. They are called "beatitudes" because, in the Latin version of the New Testament, the Latin word *beati*, which is translated "blessed," means simply a pronouncement of blessedness upon those who are included in the categories. We see this formula, "Blessed are . . . ," used repeatedly by Jesus in the beatitudes and in the Sermon on the Mount. Some modern translations have instead "Happy are . . . ," which is a poor choice because it fails to include the intensely spiritual depth, which is lacking in the English word *happy*. To be sure, happiness is an element of blessedness but by no means an exhaustive one.

The prophets of the Old Testament and Jesus, who is a prophet in the New

Testament, use a particular literary form of address. When Old Testament prophets made an announcement, it would be "the word of the Lord," because God had put His words in the prophets' mouth. The prophets would announce doom and prosperity, or what we call "oracles of woe" and "oracles of weal." These oracles were divine pronouncements, like those the Greeks believed they received from the oracle of Delphi. The Hebrew prophets used the oracle to announce the word of God. The oracle of doom was introduced by the word *woe*. Jesus used that same literary form when He warned the Pharisees of their impending judgment: "Woe to you, scribes and Pharisees, hypocrites!" (Matt. 23:13). He then went on to castigate them for their sinfulness. In the book of Revelation, when the great time of judgment comes, an angel flies over saying, "Woe, woe, woe . . . !" (Rev. 8:13). When God announces woe, there is no worse calamity one can imagine. The beatitudes, on the other hand, are oracles of weal, not woe, and the literary form that the prophets used to describe this divine favoring of individuals was the word *blessed*.

That word occurs all through sacred Scripture. The book of Psalms begins with a beatitude: "Blessed is the man who walks not in the counsel of the ungodly, nor stands in the path of sinners, nor sits in the seat of the scornful; but his delight is in the law of the Lord, and in His law he meditates day and night" (Ps. 1:1–2). The consequence of blessedness is not something he merits or earns; it flows from his devotion to the Word of God.

When Gabriel came to Mary and announced that she would be the mother of the Son of God, he said, "Rejoice, highly favored one, the Lord is with you" (Luke 1:28). When the pregnant Mary visited Elizabeth, the child in Elizabeth's womb, who would be John the Baptist, jumped for joy at the approach of Jesus, and Elizabeth said to Mary, "Blessed are you among women" (Luke 1:42). An integral part of the Roman Catholic rosary is, "Hail Mary, full of grace, blessed art thou among women, and blessed is the fruit of thy womb, Jesus." "Hail Mary," or *Ave Maria*, is a simple greeting, and it is the greeting of Gabriel to Mary that pronounces to her that she is blessed among women. Although Protestants do not embrace the theology that attends the veneration of Mary in the Roman Catholic Church, we certainly agree that the most singularly blessed woman in history was the mother of Jesus. The New Testament was right when Elizabeth said to her, "Blessed are you." To be "blessed among women" means to experience a singular benefit from the grace of God, and all who receive the visitation of the Holy Spirit experience that state of blessedness.

The classic Hebrew benediction, which is set forth in a certain poetic form called *parallelism*, gives us a classic description of biblical blessedness. It comes in three verses, and each verse repeats the assertion of the first verse with different words. This benediction is a beatitude:

> The LORD bless you and keep you;
> The LORD make His face shine upon you,
> And be gracious to you;
> The LORD lift up His countenance upon you,
> And give you peace. (Num. 6:24–26)

The supreme blessing that we are promised in the New Testament is that in heaven we will see God face-to-face. We call that the "beatific vision," the vision that will flood our soul with the highest degree of blessedness imaginable. All of that is why I am not satisfied with the word *happy* as a way to translate Jesus' pronouncements in the Sermon on the Mount. To be blessed of God is to receive spiritual benefit from Him that lasts forever, and this is what Jesus is pronouncing upon the various groups that He mentions here in the sermon.

And seeing the multitudes, He went up on a mountain, and when He was seated His disciples came to Him. Then He opened His mouth and taught them (vv. 1–2). As we noted earlier, rabbis in that time did not stand when they preached or taught. They sat down, and then the disciples would sit on the ground, literally at the feet of their master. Matthew is describing here a session given by the rabbi as he assembles his disciples and prepares to teach them. It seems unnecessary to add that He opened His mouth to teach them, but in fact this was a way of signaling that a teacher, rabbi, or prophet was about to declare a word from God.

The Poor

"Blessed are the poor in spirit, for theirs is the kingdom of heaven" (v. 3). Matthew qualifies this first beatitude, whereas Luke does not have a qualifier. He simply says, "Blessed are you poor" (Luke 6:20). Some have drawn from this the idea that the kingdom of God belongs essentially to poor people, so all one has to do to enter the kingdom of God is to be poor in the material sense. There arose in the Middle Ages something called "poverty mysticism" in which poverty was elevated to a level of virtue that gave merit to those who were in such a state. That idea ignores the broader teaching of the Bible concerning the poor.

The Old Testament distinguishes among four different types of poor people. The first are those who are poor as a result of their sloth. They are poor because they are too lazy to sow their seed or to be engaged in meaningful and productive industry, and this group of the poor comes sharply under the judgment of God. This indicates that biblically there is no inherent virtue in poverty.

The second group includes those who are poor as a result of calamity through no fault of their own. They are not poor because they are lazy but because a farmer experienced a drought or a storm that destroyed his crops, or a person had a serious accident that left him in such a crippled fashion that he was unable to engage in productive labor. There is no judgment upon that group of the poor; rather, there is a mandate to make sure that this class of poor is helped by God's people.

The third group is made up of those who are poor as a result of the exploitation of the rich and powerful, which, in biblical terms, was hardly ever the wealthy business people but the rulers who drained their people of all of their wealth. We see an example of this with Ahab, who confiscated unjustly Naboth's vineyard.

The fourth category are those who are poor for righteousness' sake, that is, those who willingly choose a vocation that leaves them destitute. Those in this category are concerned about things other than what the market produces. To them is promised the kindness of God, who notices their personal sacrifice.

It is important that we understand from a biblical perspective that not all poverty arises from laziness. At the same time, not all poverty is virtuous. There is no inherent merit in poverty, and there is no inherent sin in the fact of someone's being poor. The same distinction can be made concerning the wealthy. Those who make their wealth through illegitimate means come under the judgment of God, but, at the same time, the Scriptures recognize that one can be wealthy and virtuous.

Therefore, those whom Jesus addresses here are not necessarily living in poverty, although it may include some in that state. Specifically in view here is a poverty of spirit, but not in the sense that they lack what it takes to exercise courage or industry. Matthew is also not speaking of those who are mean-spirited. To be poor in spirit in biblical terms means that someone has a poverty of arrogance. Such people are the polar opposite of the scribes and Pharisees, who boasted of their riches in virtue, their personal righteousness. Such people do not enter the kingdom of God.

The myth persists even in our culture that people can get to heaven by their good works, by the righteousness that they achieve by their particular virtues. If we trust in our own righteousness to get us into the kingdom of God, we will miss the kingdom of God altogether. To enter the kingdom of God, we must understand that, in light of the perfection of God, our virtue is bankrupt. We have no merit to offer God except for that earned for us by our Savior. Jesus spells out here a necessary condition for entering into His kingdom. We have to be broken of our pride. The psalmist writes, "A broken and contrite heart—these, O God, You will not despise" (Ps. 51:17), and just before this he writes, "For You do not desire sacrifice, or else I would give it; . . . The sacrifices of God are a broken spirit" (vv. 16–19).

A friend of mine had come out of the Roman Catholic Church and become a believer. She was excited about her newfound faith and felt free from her previous church atmosphere of constant scolding. She said, "When I found that I was justified by faith and not by works, I felt that everything was all said and done, until I read your book *The Holiness of God*. I was upset by your book because in it you reiterate that I am a sinner. I didn't want to hear it, but as I began to think about the character of God, I got the message that there is no righteousness in me apart from Christ." Her experience was one of coming to poverty of spirit.

We must not think that the poor in spirit get in the kingdom by that means and others get in by some other way—by being a peacemaker or being hungry or thirsty, as we see in the other beatitudes. Everyone has to be poor in spirit to receive the supreme blessing of the kingdom of God.

12

THE BEATITUDES, PART 2

Matthew 5:4–9

Blessed are those who mourn, for they shall be comforted.
Blessed are the meek, for they shall inherit the earth.
Blessed are those who hunger and thirst for righteousness,
for they shall be filled.
Blessed are the merciful, for they shall obtain mercy.
Blessed are the pure in heart, for they shall see God.
Blessed are the peacemakers, for they shall be called sons of God.

Blessed are those who mourn, for they shall be comforted" (v. 4). Most commentators see this as a particular type of mourning, one so specific that it does not include a broader understanding of mourning. The first beatitude qualifies the poor as the poor *in spirit*, so scholars assume that Jesus is talking about those who mourn over their sin in broken contrition. I think that element is present, and we will look at that briefly in a moment, but the application is broader than simply sorrow for sin.

Mourning

Those who mourn but remain alienated from God will never receive the comfort that is promised here. The promise of comfort for those who mourn is not universal. Nevertheless, mourning was something that sounded a discordant note in the lives of the Jewish people in the Old Testament. Theirs was often a difficult lot as they suffered oppression from many nations, and poverty and disease abounded. Mourning was such an integral part of their lives that the Scriptures make this observation: "The heart of the wise is in the house of mourning, but the heart of fools is in the house of mirth" (Eccles. 7:4). Herman Melville once observed, "Until we understand that one grief outweighs a thousand joys, we will never understand what Christianity is trying to make us."[1] Our Lord was known as a man of sorrows, and He was acquainted with grief. There is a mourning beyond the mourning of sin that is part of the believer's life even to this day.

When Joseph and Mary brought Jesus to the temple for the dedication of the infant and Simeon saw the Babe, he said, "Lord, now You are letting Your servant depart in peace, according to Your word; for my eyes have seen Your salvation" (Luke 2:29–30). That was a marvelous moment in redemptive history. Just prior to this recounting, we read that Simeon was a just and devout man who had been waiting for the Consolation of Israel (v. 25). If you look at that verse in your Bible, you will see that "Consolation" is capitalized. The term was a Jewish title for the coming Messiah, because they were looking to the Messiah as their redeemer and as their consolation.

The New Testament speaks frequently of the ministry of the Holy Spirit, who brings that consolation and dries the tears of God's people. When we lose a loved one, we mourn, but we mourn knowing that mourning will turn to joy and comfort on the day of resurrection. Therefore, if we wish to qualify this beatitude, we have to do so by saying, "Blessed are the godly who mourn, for they shall be comforted," with respect to every pain that they experience in this world.

The experience of comfort on a human level is a Christ-less experience. I have boyhood memories of getting hurt while playing in the street and suffering insults. When so wounded I would come home crying. My mother, busy working in the kitchen, would take the edge of her apron and wipe away my tears. I think of that every time I read the promise in the book of Revelation, that in heaven the Lord will wipe away all of our tears once and for all (Rev. 21:4). As comforting as it was to feel the edge of my mother's apron on my cheek, I would later cry again; but when the comfort that is promised here in Matthew is fully accomplished, it will be an everlasting comfort that will be the end of all tears.

There is also the element of mourning over our sin. In theology we make an important distinction between two types of repentance. One type is called "attrition," which may be defined as repentance that is motivated from a fear of punishment. It is the kind of repentance your children express when their hands are caught in the cookie jar and they say, "Please don't punish me. I won't

[1] Herman Melville, *Redburn: His First Voyage* (Garden City, NY: Doubleday, 1957).

do it again." That is different from authentic repentance, which is defined by what we call "contrition." Real repentance over sin is generated by a profound sorrow from the soul in which we are heartily sorry for our sins. When Christ sees the righteous person who is broken by the conviction of the Holy Spirit, who reveals to us our sins so that our pillows are wet with our weeping, then we know what true contrition is from which God promises His comfort. Those who acknowledge their sins in a glib manner reflect the kind of repentance that Esau had, which was not real. A truly godly person mourns not only the loss of his loved ones or his health but also his sin before God.

Therefore, when our Lord said, "Blessed are those who mourn," the blessing is not in the mourning; it is in the comfort. The comfort God's people can expect, in part now but in full at the final day, is that spoken by the prophet: "'Comfort, yes, comfort My people!' says your God. 'Speak comfort to Jerusalem, and cry out to her, that her warfare is ended, that her iniquity is pardoned; for she has received from the LORD's hand double for all her sins'" (Isa. 40:1–2).

The Meek

The next of the beatitudes is this: **"Blessed are the meek, for they shall inherit the earth"** (v. 5). There is often great misunderstanding about what is in view here. We have a tendency to think of meekness as a synonym for weakness. We think of the meek as personified by Caspar Milquetoast. Meekness seems to describe someone who lacks a backbone, who has a vacancy of courage in his heart, but that is not at all what is meant by the biblical concept of meekness. It is a quality frequently manifested by exceedingly strong people who do not use their strength or power to crush others or to lay them low.

The preeminent model of meekness in Old Testament times was Moses, yet from another perspective we know that he was one of the most powerful men in human history. He used his strength and the power God gave to him with gentleness. There was one in the New Testament far stronger than Moses, even our Lord Himself, and yet it was said of Jesus that a bruised reed He would not break (Isa. 42:3). We observe how Jesus dealt with the Pharisees and the scribes. He responded to strength with strength, but when He encountered people who were lowly, broken by their sin, Jesus ministered to them with gentleness. Our Lord Himself was a paragon of meekness. No one has ever really mistaken Jesus for someone weak or spineless.

The promise given to those who are meek is that they will inherit the earth. When someone dies and a will is read, the heirs of the deceased discover the contents of the estate that has been left to them. The heirs are excited to find out that the family home or the family farm will pass into their hands. However, in terms of the vastness of this earth, such parcels are small. The inheritance in the beatitude is the whole earth.

We are told that we are heirs of God, joint heirs with Christ. All things in this world have been given to Jesus, and the redemption He brings is not simply for the sins of people but for a fallen planet. At the present time the whole creation groans together waiting for the redemption of the sons of God, but at the consummation of His kingdom the Lord will usher in a new heaven and a new earth, and that earth will be owned by the meek.

Do you see the pattern here? It is not that some Christians are called to be poor in spirit while others are called to mourn and others are called to be meek. All these attributes or qualities are to be made manifest in every Christian's life. We are all called to be poor in spirit rather than self-righteous. We are all called to mourn over our fallenness, and we are all called to manifest meekness, because to us has been given the earth to inherit, the comfort that we will be given, and the possession of the kingdom of God.

Real Righteousness

"Blessed are those who hunger and thirst for righteousness, for they shall be filled" (v. 6). Commentators say that what Jesus had in mind here are those believers who passionately search for the imputation of the righteousness of Christ by which we receive our standing before God. We do not have enough righteousness of our own to get us into heaven, they say. Only those who are clothed with the righteousness of Christ will ever enter into His kingdom. Certainly that is true, but I doubt that is what Jesus had in mind here, because even though we are justified by faith and not by our works, we are justified unto works. We have been elected by God and received His grace unto righteousness. Even though our righteousness will never justify us, the fruit of our justification is growth in real righteousness. As Martin Luther said, we were dead in our sins, but God raised us from the dead, and He declared us well while we were still in sin. That is what justification by faith means. Not only did He give us that declaration, but He gave us the medicine by which we actually do become conformed to the image of Jesus, and every Christian is called to grow up into maturity and righteousness.

Elsewhere in this Gospel we are going to see this quest for righteousness, but we have an allergy to it because we tend to link righteousness with self-righteousness, that which the Pharisees displayed, rather than with real righteousness. Real righteousness is, simply, doing what is right. That should be a concern for us, and not just a passing concern. The images used here are those of hunger and thirst. This message was given to people who, for the most part, lived in the desert, who knew what it meant to have such a parched palate that their thirst was so consuming that just one cup of cold water would dramatically improve their condition. They also knew what it meant to endure starvation, to go hungry for long periods of time. For someone who is in that state of hunger, like one who crosses the desert and runs out of water and prays every second for the appearance of an oasis, the pursuit of that oasis is the only thing that keeps him going. The intensity of that sort of thirst and hunger is what Jesus says should mark our lives.

As a young man Jonathan Edwards wrote down resolutions for the virtues that he sought to achieve in his life, and by the grace of God he became a model of righteousness. At almost the same time there was another man in colonial America who also sought after righteousness without the aid of God. His name was Benjamin Franklin. Franklin made a list of the virtues that he wanted to manifest. Each day he would examine himself as to whether he had accomplished a particular righteousness during the preceding twenty-four hours. He confessed that, after noting for a number of consecutive days his success with humility, he was becoming proud of his humility. Even the unregenerate understand at certain points their failure to achieve real righteousness.

That would be a wonderful thing to have on our tombstone, that we were righteous. We ought not to despise righteousness as something that belongs only to the self-righteous; rather, we should love righteousness enough to pursue it intensely as those who hunger and thirst, because God promises that if we hunger for righteousness, we will not be sent away empty. We will receive the bread of life that will feed us for eternity. If we thirst for righteousness, the Son of righteousness will come with living water that will well up in our souls to eternal life. We will be filled. We will be satisfied from these pursuits.

13

THE BEATITUDES, PART 3

Matthew 5:7–9

Blessed are the merciful, for they shall obtain mercy.
Blessed are the pure in heart, for they shall see God.
Blessed are the peacemakers, for they shall be called sons of God.

B**lessed are the merciful, for they shall obtain mercy"** (v. 7). This beatitude contains a glorious promise, but there is also something a bit frightening about it. The promise for divine blessing in this case is reserved for the merciful. As we have seen throughout our study of these beatitudes, Jesus is not singling out different groups of people and giving particular rewards to those who manifest particular virtues. Each of us should embrace and manifest all the virtues contained in the beatitudes.

A Spirit of Mercy

The character of the Christian manifests a spirit of mercy. That is not always manifested among Christians, to our great shame. We cannot draw a single breath except by the mercy of God. We are to manifest a spirit of mercy because we ourselves live by it every day and inherit eternal life strictly on the basis of mercy rather than justice. This theme is echoed even in the Lord's Prayer, which we will examine in more detail later: "Forgive us our debts, as we forgive our debtors" (Matt. 6:12). The frightening aspect of the beatitude is that if God's forgiveness toward me in any way reflects my spirit of forgiveness toward others, I am in serious trouble. Since the granting of forgiveness is in some nature a granting of mercy, we who live by mercy should be willing to be merciful to others.

This concept is so important in Jesus' teaching that we find it later on in Matthew's Gospel in the parable of the unforgiving servant. A servant was unable to repay a debt he owed, so, when he begged for mercy, his master forgave him. Later, however, the servant refused to forgive a fellow servant who was indebted to him, so the master who had forgiven the first servant's debt withdrew his mercy and turned that servant over to the jailers. Jesus concludes the parable with these words: "So My heavenly Father also will do to you if each of you, from his heart, does not forgive his brother his trespasses" (Matt. 18:35).

The warning should ring in our ears. If we refuse to extend mercy to those who ask it of us, how can we possibly expect to receive mercy from the hand of God? That is the downside of this blessing. If we stated it in negative terms, the oracle would be one of doom: "Cursed are you who are unmerciful, for you will not receive the mercy of God." Jesus frames this in a positive way, of course, promising the Father's blessing on those who are merciful, because if they are, they in turn will receive mercy.

We have already received such mercy from the hand of God that if He were never merciful another time as long as we live, we would have nothing to complain about. The good news is that the mercy we have already received is not the end of the mercy that we shall receive. It shall go on into eternity.

Purity and Clear Vision

"Blessed are the pure in heart, for they shall see God" (v. 8). We have noticed throughout our study of the beatitudes thus far a pattern of consistency between that which is received as the blessing of Christ and the reward that is a consequence of it. Here we see that the promise of the beatific vision is given to the pure in heart. One of the most difficult things about being a Christian is that we serve an invisible God.

"Out of sight, out of mind," we say, yet God is always out of sight for His people. We never see Him. From the time of the expulsion of Adam and Eve from the garden of Eden, the vision of God has been prohibited, and we are told that the soul who sees Him will die. Even Moses, who had seen wonderful aspects of God that no other man had ever seen, was denied a glimpse of God's face. God told him, You cannot see My face; for no man shall see Me, and live.' And the Lord said, 'Here is a place by Me, and you shall stand on the rock. So it shall be, while My glory passes by, that I will put you in the cleft of the rock, and will cover you with My hand while I pass by. Then I will take away My hand, and you shall see My back; but My face shall not be seen'" (Ex. 33:20–23). Even Moses was denied the supreme blessing of seeing the face of God.

Why is it that we cannot see God's being? Some would say that this is basically an ontological problem, that is, that God is a spirit. He has no mass, no form to behold, and we as creatures do not have the strength of vision to see the invisible being of God. However, the reason provided for us in Scripture is not a problem with our optic nerves. Our inability to see God is not a deficiency in our eyes but a deficiency in our hearts. God will not allow Himself to be seen by those who are impure.

This is not just a particular issue of impurity that may be in our hands or on our lips; it is an impurity in the very core of our being. If there is one impurity there, the direct vision of God is denied us. In Scripture we see manifold occasions in which God manifests Himself through what we call a "theophany," a visible appearance of the invisible God such as that in the burning bush in the Midianite wilderness that Moses beheld, the manifestation of God's glory in the shekinah cloud. At the incarnation the glory of God shone around the fields of Bethlehem, and the shepherds were desperately afraid. That glory was only an outward manifestation of the inner being of God; it was not the very essence of God Himself. If men tremble before theophanies, we can only imagine how terrifying it would be to see God as He is.

This particular promise is expanded in the New Testament and gives Christians hope of what we call the "beatific vision." We call this vision "beatific" because it is this sight more than any other that will flood the human soul with utter blessedness. "Behold what manner of love the Father has bestowed on us, that we should be called children of God!" (1 John 3:1). John expresses a sense of apostolic astonishment that we would ever be considered God's children. People have questions about heaven, but most of them cannot be answered because they concern things that God has not revealed. John addresses our inability to understand heaven: "It has not yet been revealed what we shall be, but we know that when He is revealed, we shall be like Him, for we shall see Him as He is" (v. 2). This is the promise to every Christian—that we will see Him as He is. The Latin is *eum sicuti est*, which means we shall see Him "as He is." This will be no mere outward perception; we will be able to penetrate to the very reality of the being of God Himself. Edwards comments in great detail about this experience of seeing not just outward appearances but the very essence of something. Such seeing includes an immediate and direct apprehension, one not dependent on physical sensations, and that's what we can expect in heaven when we see God as He is.

John continues, "Everyone who has this hope in Him purifies himself, just as He is pure" (v. 3). One reason we cannot now see God as He is, is that we are not pure in heart, but once we become pure in heart, our eyes will be opened to this immediate knowledge of God Himself. In other words, when we go to heaven and receive the end of our sanctification whereby every remnant of sin is removed from us, then we will be equipped to see the Lord face-to-face, as He is. Others say that our purity of heart will come as a result of our vision of God in His purity. We cannot look into the face of God without that experience cleansing our soul perfectly. I think the answer is the former rather than the latter, but these things may happen simultaneously, and there may be an interconnection between the vision and our glorification. But however the order occurs, the promise remains firm. We have a promise that the God whom we have worshiped without seeing is the One whom we will behold face-to-face.

Peacemakers

"Blessed are the peacemakers, for they shall be called sons of God" (v. 9). I think this is one of the toughest beatitudes to understand. The blessing is not pronounced on peacekeepers but upon peacemakers, those who work to bring peace out of conflict. Some people can sense conflict and alienation and work to help bring about reconciliation. In that sense, all of us are called to be peacemakers. However, there is more to being a peacemaker in the biblical sense.

I was involved many years ago in a group that had been convened to solve a church dispute, which included the minister, the elders, and the congregation. After seeking to know the grievances from all sides, the chairman of our group determined that we needed to find a way to pacify everyone on all sides of the dispute. I objected to that. Our task was to administer justice, not to satisfy every party in the dispute. Our task was not to work out a compromise of the flesh and cry "'Peace, Peace!' when there is no peace" (Jer. 6:14). We can mistakenly think that peace is more important than truth and righteousness.

When ministers are ordained, they are called to maintain the peace, unity, and purity of the church. If someone comes along teaching rank heresy, a minister must oppose it. The minister will be chastised for disturbing the peace and unity of the church, but to sacrifice purity for the sake of the peace is nothing but carnal peace. It is a false peace.

The peacemakers that Jesus has in view here in Matthew are those who bring true peace to bear without compromising integrity or truth or justice. Peace that comes at the cost of justice has brought the church to ruin many times in church history. At the same time, we are not to be contentious. Our task is to be agents of reconciliation and bring peace to bear as representatives of the Prince of Peace, even though doing so can be complicated and difficult. God grant that we may be known as merciful people, that we may seek purity of heart, and that we will be agents of peace.

14

THE BEATITUDES, PART 4

Matthew 5:10–12

Blessed are those who are persecuted for righteousness' sake, for theirs is the kingdom of heaven. Blessed are you when they revile and persecute you, and say all kinds of evil against you falsely for My sake. Rejoice and be exceedingly glad, for great is your reward in heaven, for so they persecuted the prophets who were before you.

These last two beatitudes in the Sermon on the Mount have a common theme with respect to persecution. These two have been considered as perhaps the most unexpected of the beatitudes because those who endure such persecution do not usually consider such experiences as occasions for blessedness.

Persecuted for Righteousness

Blessed are those who are persecuted for righteousness' sake, for theirs is the kingdom of heaven" (v. 10). Notice that this beatitude does not say that persecution for just anything is blessed. People all over the world experience persecution of all kinds, but not always for the sake of righteousness. Peter writes, "It is better, if it is the will of God, to suffer for doing good than for doing evil" (1 Pet. 3:17). In other words, it is one thing to suffer because we have done evil, but it is quite another thing to suffer for doing what is right. In that regard we are merely seeking to be imitators of Jesus, who suffered perhaps more hostility, loathing, and persecution than any individual in the history of the world, and yet every ounce of His suffering was altogether for the sake of righteousness.

Righteous behavior provokes persecution because the unrighteous in this world cannot stand to behold righteousness. Those who hated Jesus most fiercely were the Pharisees because they had a public pretense of righteousness that was not real. Their sin chiefly involved hypocrisy, because while they pretended righteousness they were in fact unrighteous, and they, in their pretense of righteousness, crucified the Son of glory. Nothing exposes the counterfeit faster than the authentic. When true righteousness appeared in the person of Jesus, the false righteousness of the Pharisees was exposed for what it was, and they hated it.

I once had a student with a 4.0 grade point average, which in those days was the highest there could be. She was brilliant, and her grade point average broke the curve. As she broke the curve I noticed that the rest of the students did not applaud her. In fact, they did not like it and tended to scorn her. In the second semester of her senior year I gave her an examination that she failed. I told her I thought that she had failed the test deliberately, and she began to cry. She admitted that she had done just that because none of the men wanted to date her; they all thought she was too smart. She made a pretense of failure in order to be accepted. This woman in her way had suffered for doing what was right.

The same thing happens when Christians refrain from participating in worldly activities. Even if you say nothing outright against the activities, those who participate in them will look at you askance and call you "holier than thou." That kind of persecution is hardly the same as that experienced worldwide for the sake of Christ. People lose their jobs and their lives if they so much as publicly declare their allegiance to Jesus. There are different levels of persecution, yet no Christian can go through life without receiving some form of it. Jesus goes into greater detail in the next beatitude.

Reviled for Christ's Sake

"Blessed are you when they revile and persecute you, and say all kinds of evil against you falsely for My sake" (v. 11). Our Lord has in view here the type of persecution that includes slander. People so persecuted are reviled and falsely accused, and their reputations become tarnished. Again, we are not promised blessing just because people speak evil against us; the blessing is promised when these things happen for Jesus' sake.

For the sake of Jesus, have you ever been slandered or falsely accused? If you have experienced that, you know how painful it can be. Our reputations are precious to us, and it is difficult to be accused of things that we have not done or of saying things that we have not said. How can that be an occasion for blessedness? Jesus tells us: **"Rejoice and be exceedingly glad, for great is your reward in heaven"** (v. 12).

As a student I was once selected by the seminary to give a sermon in chapel on a special occasion. It was an annual event at which the entire presbytery convened. There were ministers present from about two hundred churches, along with the student body of the seminary and the faculty. It was a great honor to be selected to deliver the sermon. I chose to preach on the doctrine of sin, and in the sermon I explained what I had been taught at seminary about sin—that sin is an existential failure to achieve authentic existence. I'd been taught that sin in the final analysis is simply a matter of finitude, a necessary component of creatureliness, and a psychological malady. Then I told the audience that while I agree that we struggle in all these ways, not one of them comes close to the biblical understanding of the nature of sin. According to Scripture, sin is a violation of the holiness of God. Sin is a transgression of His law, and such transgression cannot be minimized by explaining it away in psychological categories of neurosis or in existential categories of inauthenticity or by reducing it simply to finitude.

When the sermon was finished, I stepped down from the pulpit, and a rush of students came toward me. The students, most of them liberal thinkers, came to me moved and excited about the sermon. I was amazed. I thought they would want to tar and feather me. However, not everyone was happy. As I made my way to the back of the chapel, the dean of the seminary approached me, and he was irate. In fact, his face was contorted with rage. He began to yell at me in front of the crowd, and he physically pushed me up against the back of the wall and said, "You have distorted every truth of Protestantism in that sermon this morning." I was devastated, and I walked out of the chapel and wondered if I had really made such distortions.

I went to see my mentor, John Gerstner. When I told him what had happened, he grinned and said, "You should be exceedingly glad." I told him that I did not feel exceedingly glad, and he replied, "Every Calvinist from John Calvin to B.B. Warfield is rejoicing in heaven this morning for what they heard out of that pulpit. You are blessed because you have just been reviled for Christ's sake." I certainly did not feel blessed, but in a small way, I was able to experience the wrath of men for the sake of the truth of God.

Rewards

The concept of rewards is something with which we often struggle. We put so much emphasis on justification by faith rather than by works that we sometimes despise the works we might be able to achieve. How can we reconcile the truth that Christ is our only merit with our receiving great reward in heaven? There are at least twenty-five texts in the New Testament that teach that rewards in heaven will be distributed by Christ according to our works. We get to heaven by faith alone, but the reward we experience once we are there is based upon the works that we do in this world. Therefore, those who are justified are called to live fruitful, godly lives that produce good works, and those works will receive a heavenly reward.

Augustine said that when God rewards us for our works, even those works are so tainted by sin that they are at best splendid vices. The best work we do will not deserve a reward in heaven. Nevertheless, even though we do not deserve it, we will receive it. When God distributes rewards in heaven, He will be crowning His own gifts, which means that God is the one who has gifted you to do the work you do. It is only by grace that you are able to do it.

The reward promised is a future one, although if we look at the last clause of this beatitude, we see that there is a present reward: **"for so they persecuted the prophets who were before you"** (v. 12). If you have been slandered in this world for the sake of Christ, for righteousness' sake, you will indeed receive a great reward when you get to heaven, but even now you will be numbered among the prophets of the Old Testament. Even now, in God's sight, you are included in the select company of those who have gone before and tasted the same slander. If you have experienced this, you are in the company of Isaiah, Jeremiah, and all the prophets before you. That is splendid company in which to be numbered. The reward is not future only but comes to us even now, if we understand the blessed way in which our Lord looks at us. He sees us. He observes us. He encourages us.

15

SERMON ON THE MOUNT

Matthew 5:13–16

You are the salt of the earth; but if the salt loses its flavor, how shall it be seasoned? It is then good for nothing but to be thrown out and trampled underfoot by men. You are the light of the world. A city that is set on a hill cannot be hidden. Nor do they light a lamp and put it under a basket, but on a lampstand, and it gives light to all who are in the house. Let your light so shine before men, that they may see your good works and glorify your Father in heaven.

There is a subtle shift here in the Sermon on the Mount. The beginning of the sermon was Jesus' list of beatitudes in which He pronounced His benediction or blessing upon those who experience certain things. Here Jesus moves away from pronouncing His benediction to announcing responsibilities.

He addresses these words to the disciples: **"You are the salt of the earth"** (v. 13). When we wish to compliment someone, we might say, "He is the salt of the earth." Jesus, however, did not utter these words in that vein. Jesus uses this esteemed title for a different reason. He is explaining who and what His disciples are and, being what they are, defining what they are to do. So when we look at this metaphor of salt, we want to consider the primary function of salt in the ancient world. Salt was used to give zest or tang to food, just as it is today. More importantly, salt was used as a preservative. People in the ancient world did not have refrigerators, so if they wanted to keep their food from spoiling, they had to cover it with salt. Salt was used also to provoke a sense of thirst.

Salt's Zest

Our Lord uses this metaphor for His disciples, and by extension for us, to show that they are to be people who add zest to the world. We are to be the tang that makes life more delicious. Christians are not called to withdraw from the world. We are not salt merely *of* the earth, but we are salt *for* the earth, that we may add this tasteful zest to life itself. Some Christians are perceived as sourpusses. They seem to be dour and do not add joy or zest to life. Of all people, Christians should be the most filled with love for life, and we should have a contagious sense of the joy of living.

A few decades ago Rebecca Manley Pippert wrote a bestselling book, *Out of the Saltshaker*.[1] I found the title somewhat provocative because it captures the idea that salt within a saltshaker cannot add any zest to anything. Salt must come out of the saltshaker. Jesus is saying that we are supposed to be salt that comes out of the shaker. For salt to be worthwhile, it must be used.

The tagline of the Morton Salt company is "When it rains it pours." The saying is memorable not only for the claim it makes for its product but also for the falseness of the claim. We know what happens when we attempt to get salt from a saltshaker in the midst of great humidity. Even Morton salt will not come out by mere shaking.

Salt's Function

More so than the idea of zest is Jesus' principal point, which has to do with salt's function as a preservative. One task of the church is to help keep the world from self-destruction. Historic Christianity is often criticized for bringing warfare and great pain to the world. Indeed, zealous Christians have brought division, but the criticisms leveled are a serious distortion of the historical record. If we consider the history of Western civilization, we see that by the time Christ came, the golden age of Greece had turned to rust, and the culture of Athens had degenerated into barbarianism. That empire gave way to Rome, and Rome ended in the same depth of pagan corruption.

It has been said that the intellectual history of the Western world was saved by the intellectual contributions of the apostle Paul, in particular, and of Christianity, in general. It has also been said that the advent of Christianity is what saved Western culture from pure barbarianism. If we look over the influence of the Christian church, particularly in the West from the first century to the present day, we will see that the Christian church more than any other institution has been responsible for the inauguration of higher education. The university system was the brainchild of the Christian church. It was the Christian church that brought in the arts—music, painting, and literature. Many of the world's greatest

[1] Rebecca Manley Pippert, *Out of the Saltshaker and into the World: Evangelism as a Way of Life* (Downers Grove, IL: InterVarsity, 1979).

artists have been Christians, and the same is true in the realm of music, with Christians such as Bach, Mendelssohn, Handel, and Vivaldi. Additionally, the Christian church began the hospital movement in the West. It was the Christian church, following the mandate of Jesus to care for orphans, that ushered in orphanages. Although the New Testament was written at a time when slavery was still in vogue, John Murray once made the observation that all the seeds for the abolition of slavery were sown in the pages of the New Testament. So, in a very real sense, the church of Christ has been the preservative that God has used to keep Western civilization from imploding from internal corruption.

Some historians say we are living in the post-Christian era. Others have described our culture as neo-pagan. Others have gone further and described it as neo-barbarian. It seems to me that only barbarians would slaughter their unborn children at the rate of one-and-a-half million per year. A nation that tolerates that kind of corruption cannot last. The church is trying to be salt to help preserve our culture while the culture is doing everything in its power to remove the influence of the church from the mainstream of American life. At present, we still have some protection from persecution. We are free to meet for public worship, but our freedom is limited by those who say that Christians will be tolerated only if they keep out of the public square. The minute we take the message of Christ into the culture, we run into the resistance of the pagan culture.

When the settlers came to this country and were met by Native Americans, a war broke out. The Indians were subdued. They were allowed to live in America but only under restrictions, and they were relegated to reservations, which isolated them from the mainstream of cultural life. I fear that is similar to the lot of the Christian church in our day: we are allowed to exist as long as we stay on our reservation. If we were salt like the disciples were salt, if we ventured as boldly into the public square as Paul did in the early church, we would experience jail and beatings and persecutions. We have been taught to keep the salt in the saltshaker, where it will do no harm.

Despite the resistance of a decaying culture, that same culture is kept from self-destruction by the influence of Christ and His people. We are called not to wring our hands and groan about how bad things are becoming; we are called to preserve what is worth preserving in the world around us.

Salt's Provocation

Finally, salt provokes thirst. We are to provoke thirst in those who watch us, that they might be thirsty to drink of the waters from which we have drunk. Jesus said, **"If the salt loses it flavor, how shall it be seasoned?"** (v. 13). That is a rhetorical question, of course. Some critics might point out that sodium chloride, what we call "salt," does not lose its saltiness, so why would Jesus speak about salt in this way? Jesus was speaking to the experience of people in first-century Palestine, and their primary source of salt was the Dead Sea. The salt from the Dead Sea was mixed with other minerals, many of which would contaminate the purity of the salt and leach the saltiness out of the content. Jesus is telling His people that they are the salt of the earth, and they must not allow the saltiness to be leached away. It must not be destroyed by contaminating minerals. If we are not the salt of the earth, it is probably because we have allowed the world to contaminate us.

Some polls have shown that the rates of divorce and abortion among Christians are the same as that of non-Christians. These pollsters try to show that there is no discernable difference between the behavior of born-again Christians and pagans. Those statistics may be true of those who merely claim to be Christians, but the difference between a real Christian and an unconverted person is profound, not simply in what they believe but in how they live. If your life is no different from the lives of your secular friends, then you ought to reassess whether you are truly a Christian or whether whatever Christianity you thought you had has leached out and is worthy only to be trampled underfoot by men.

Reflected Light

"You are the light of the world" (v. 14). That seems strange, because Jesus said that He is the light of the world (John 8:12). It is Jesus who came into the darkness, and the darkness could not overcome Him. Here Jesus takes that title, "light of the world," and transfers it to His disciples. Of course, the light that Christ brings to the world originates in Himself, whereas the light that we have is borrowed. Our light is a reflection of His light. But if we have His light in us, that light cannot be hidden. It will be made manifest.

My best friend in college and in seminary was a young man who had been born and raised in the mission fields of Sudan and Ethiopia. His father was a pioneer missionary for fifty years among primitive tribes, for many of which he was the first white man they had ever seen. One day my friend showed me a photograph of a group of natives from an animus tribe to which he had ministered. "There are twelve natives in this picture who are Christians. See if you can identify them," he said. There was nothing distinctive about those in the picture. They all looked and dressed the same way. Nevertheless, choosing the twelve was an easy task—they were the ones who were radiant. The joy and life of Christ was written plainly on their countenance. Having come out of utter darkness, they reflected the light of Christ.

Just as salt preserves against decay, so light brings truth to bear and rescues people out of darkness. During the Middle Ages the darkness of this world had cast a huge shadow over the church itself and all but eclipsed the gospel. When the gospel was recovered, light burst on the scene. Christ came into a world that was completely engulfed by darkness, and He said to His people, **"A city that is set on a hill cannot be hidden. Nor do they light a lamp and put it under a basket, but on a lampstand, and it gives light to all who are in the house"** (vv. 14–15). No one in the ancient world would have been so foolish as to take his lantern or candle and put a bushel basket over it, because a candle covered by a basket has no value. It might start a fire, but it certainly would not give light. Candles were put onto a stand so that the house would be well-lit. We are to let our light shine that way rather than conceal it.

"Let your light so shine before men, that they may see your good works and glorify your Father in heaven" (v. 16). In this same sermon Jesus is sharply critical of the Pharisees, who paraded their piety for all to see, prayed on the street rather than in their closets, and did not anoint their heads when they fasted but displayed their self-denial. Jesus is sharply critical of the hypocrisy of appearing pious, but the light He puts in His people is designed to be seen by all. When His light shines through, people see your contribution to a dying world. They will see your mercy to the widow, to the orphan, to the imprisoned, to the sick, and to the dying, not so that you will receive the applause of men but so that God may be glorified.

The reason for our Christian lives is to glorify God. What is man's chief end? Man's chief end is to glorify God and to enjoy Him forever. Johann Sebastian Bach understood that, which is why he wrote, at the end of each of his compositions, "Soli Deo Gloria." He offered his musical works as praise to the glory of God. Likewise, whatever we do, whatever we achieve, is to be done for His glory to manifest His light. We are supposed to be the salt of the earth and the light of the world.

16

CHRIST AND THE LAW

Matthew 5:17–20

Do not think that I came to destroy the Law or the Prophets. I did not come to destroy but to fulfill. For assuredly, I say to you, till heaven and earth pass away, one jot or one tittle will by no means pass from the law till all is fulfilled. Whoever therefore breaks one of the least of these commandments, and teaches men so, shall be called least in the kingdom of heaven; but whoever does and teaches them, he shall be called great in the kingdom of heaven. For I say to you, that unless your righteousness exceeds the righteousness of the scribes and Pharisees, you will by no means enter the kingdom of heaven.

In the Sermon on the Mount we find the most in-depth exposition of the law of God of any in the New Testament. Here Jesus begins to set forth His understanding of the law over against the understanding of the scribes and the Pharisees. As we examine this, we will see how the best Jewish scholars were profoundly wrong in how they understood the Law and the Prophets. The scribes and Pharisees were highly educated and deeply dedicated to understanding and keeping the law. This serves as a warning for us. The Bible is clear enough for any Christian to understand its basic meaning; nevertheless, the Word of God in every generation becomes distorted and misunderstood. These distortions happen not because there is something wrong with the clarity of the Word of God but because there is something wrong with us. We come to the Bible with our minds clouded by sin. We must resist the temptation to read into the Bible something that is not there or to try to use the Bible, as Luther said, as a wax nose that we can twist to support our own biases and prejudices. Here our Lord undertakes an important warning about how we are to understand the law of God.

Law and Gospel

We are living in an age of unprecedented antinomianism. *Antinomianism* means literally "anti-law-ism." It is the belief that the Old Testament law has no claim on the New Testament Christian because it has been supplanted by the greatness of the gospel.

Several years ago I was invited to give a conference in New York on the subject of the holiness of God. Following the first service of that event, the conference committee asked me to join them in prayer. I went to the home of one of the committee members with almost twenty others, and we gathered for prayer. Someone turned off the lights, and then they all got down on their knees and began to pray to their dead relatives, calling upon them to appear. When I questioned what was occurring, they explained that they were "in the Spirit," so I said, "Do you realize that what you're doing would have gotten you the death penalty in the Old Testament, that God said that sort of thing is so offensive to Him that He would punish the whole nation if it were permitted?"

They replied, "We know that, but that's the Old Testament. We are free from that now."

I countered, "What do you think has taken place in the history of redemption that would make something that was formerly so repugnant to God now pleasing in His sight?" Their wrong beliefs were the essence of antinomianism.

One of the chief criticisms of dispensationalism historically has been its tendency toward antinomianism. I once gave a critique of dispensationalism and afterward received a letter from a well-educated dispensationalist. He was upset that I had misled people by connecting dispensationalism with antinomianism. He told me that dispensationalists believe in the commandments of Jesus in the New Testament even though they reject the application of the Old Testament law to their lives today. I wrote him back and told him I could find no better a definition of antinomianism than the one he had described in his letter to me.

We struggle with the relationship between law and gospel. We know that one of the functions of the law of God is to expose our sin and show us our need for Christ, but then we think that after we come to Christ, the law no longer has any bearing upon us. We sing, "Free from the Law, O blessed condition, I can sin all I want and still have remission," and forget that when Paul speaks of our being saved by grace, he says, "Shall we continue in sin that grace may abound? Certainly not!" (Rom. 6:1–2).

Beyond the law's function of exposing our sin and driving us to the cross, it also reveals to us what is pleasing to God. The psalmist wrote, "Oh, how I love Your law!" (Ps. 119:97). If we love God, we must love His law. Our Lord said, "If you love Me, keep My commandments" (John 14:15). With all these controversies in our world today, we need to pay heed to what Jesus says.

The Law Fulfilled

He begins with a warning: **"Do not think that I came to destroy the Law or the Prophets. I did not come to destroy but to fulfill"** (v. 17). There is something here in the Greek that just cannot be carried over into the English. The Greek word for "law" is *nomos*, from which we get *antinomianism*. However, the word Jesus uses at the beginning of verse 17 is a portion of the verb *nomizō*, which means "to think or to suppose." It has a stronger significance than the simple translation "Do not think." Once when looking for a parking spot, I came across a sign that said, "Don't even think about parking here." It got the message across, and it conveys the force of what Jesus is saying here: "Do not let this kind of thinking ever enter your mind. Do not think that I have come to destroy the Law." The verb there, *kataluō*, comes from the root word *lyō*, which means "to loose, to loosen, to destroy." It was the word used in Greek culture when a building was demolished. Jesus was saying, "Do not think for a minute that I have come to demolish the law."

Jesus says a great deal in the two sentences of verse 17. He reminds us that He has come. Elsewhere He tells us from whence He has come. The one who at the end of His life ascended into heaven is the one who first descended from heaven. Jesus also says here that one of the reasons He came was to fulfill the law of God. Certainly Jesus fulfills the function of the law by obeying it at every point. He also fulfills the teaching of the prophets by embodying all of the future predictions that they made. We know that both the law and the prophets point to the coming of Jesus, and when He came, that revelatory significance found its fulfillment. Many say, "Jesus didn't come to demolish but to fulfill, so since it has been fulfilled, it has been demolished." That is wrong, because the context makes clear that when Jesus speaks of fulfilling the law, not only does He fulfill it in every dimension in His perfect obedience, but He fulfills it without destroying it, as we will see in His exposition of the commandments.

"The Law and the Prophets" in verse 17 incorporates the whole of the Old Testament. In the law, the Pentateuch or the Torah, the Pharisees were able to find 613 specific laws, which they sought to explain and follow. In all probability, the full measure of those 613 laws was never kept by a single Pharisee, but in the fullness of their requirements they were kept perfectly by Jesus.

"For assuredly, I say to you, till heaven and earth pass away, one jot or one tittle will by no means pass from the law till all is fulfilled" (v. 18). Often in the New Testament we find Jesus saying, "Truly I say to you . . ." In some cases we read, "Truly, truly I say to you . . ." The translation comes from the Hebrew word for "truth," which in Aramaic is rendered by the term *amēn*. When the people of God say "amen" after the preacher preaches or after a prayer is made, they are saying, "That is true," or, "So let it be." Jesus, however, begins His pronouncements with the word "amen." In doing so He is saying, "This truth that I am about to say to you is absolutely certain." He introduces this segment of the sermon with that heavy language.

In recent times there has been a new attempt to undermine the full inerrancy of sacred Scripture. Some seminary professors have proposed a view called "limited inerrancy" in which only part of the Bible is inspired by God. The classic view of inspiration is plenary verbal inspiration, which holds that not only are the general concepts of the Bible inspired by God, but every word. On many occasions Jesus settled a controversy by an appeal to a single word. Jesus did not teach just verbal inspiration; He taught jot-and-tittle inspiration, down to the smallest letter. Here He says that the whole of creation may be removed, but not one jot or tittle of the law shall be removed till everything is fulfilled.

The Whole Law

Now Jesus comes to His conclusion: **"Whoever therefore breaks one of the least of these commandments, and teaches men so, shall be called least in the kingdom of heaven; but whoever does and teaches them, he shall be called great in the kingdom of heaven"** (v. 19). If you break or dismiss the slightest point of the law or teach others to do so, you will be least in God's kingdom.

One time recently, I turned into a driveway without using my turn signal. My wife, who was seated next to me, pointed out that I had broken the law. I argued that this is a trivial issue, but she replied, rightly so, that it is not. How quick we are to dismiss what we think are the little things. Our Lord said that if we cannot be faithful in the little things, he cannot entrust to us the big things (Luke 16:11). Conversely, Jesus said whoever does the commandments shall be called great in the kingdom of heaven.

The opposite error to antinomianism is legalism. People who think they can get to heaven by obeying the law have deceived themselves. They become preoccupied with the law, which is what the Pharisees did. However, the corrective to that is not to dismiss the law. Jesus makes a weighty and frightening statement: **"For I say to you, that unless your righteousness exceeds the righteousness of the**

scribes and Pharisees, you will by no means enter the kingdom of heaven" (v. 20). It may seem that since the Pharisees were so corrupt that exceeding their righteousness would be easy. However, Jesus said to them, "Woe to you, scribes and Pharisees, hypocrites! For you pay tithe of mint and anise and cumin, and have neglected the weightier matters of the law" (Matt. 23:23). If the Pharisees found an extra piece of mint on the floor, they tithed a portion of it. If they found a coin on the street, they made sure to add a fraction of its worth to the collection plate.

Do you tithe? "Woe to you, scribes and Pharisees, hypocrites! For you travel land and sea to make one proselyte, and when he is won, you make him twice as much a son of hell as yourselves" (Matt. 23:15). Would you go over land and sea for one convert? "You search the Scriptures, for in them you think you have eternal life" (John 5:39). The Pharisees and the scribes were diligent students of sacred Scripture. The Pharisees did all this, and yet they missed the kingdom.

Jesus is saying that we have to do all these things the Pharisees did and more. How can this be, since we possess the righteousness of Christ, which is imputed to us? Without that we would perish, and maybe that is all Jesus is saying here. You have to achieve a higher righteousness than even the scribes and the Pharisees, or you will not get into heaven. However, I do not think that is what Jesus meant. Rather, He is saying that those who receive His righteousness must go beyond the scribes and the Pharisees. The Pharisees were so scrupulous about keeping the letter of the law that they missed the spirit. The antinomian way is to attempt to keep the spirit of the law and not bother with the letter. And what do we do? Well, what God really cares about is the spirit of the law, not the letter of the law. What God wants is people who keep the spirit and the letter of the law.

Many say we are not obligated to follow the Old Testament ceremonies, and in one sense that is true. However, even though we do not practice the ceremonies of Old Testament law, the principles of the ceremonies are still central to the worship of Christians. Some do not want to be bothered with the Old Testament, but the Old Testament is the autobiography of God. It is God's revelation of who He is, what He plans, and what He commands from His people. We learn from the Old Testament what pleases God. That is why we must never throw away the Old Testament as if it were of no importance today.

17

JESUS' VIEW OF MURDER

Matthew 5:21–26

You have heard that it was said to those of old, "You shall not murder, and whoever murders will be in danger of the judgment." But I say to you that whoever is angry with his brother without a cause shall be in danger of the judgment. And whoever says to his brother, "Raca!" shall be in danger of the council. But whoever says, "You fool!" shall be in danger of hell fire. Therefore if you bring your gift to the altar, and there remember that your brother has something against you, leave your gift there before the altar, and go your way. First be reconciled to your brother, and then come and offer your gift. Agree with your adversary quickly, while you are on the way with him, lest your adversary deliver you to the judge, the judge hand you over to the officer, and you be thrown into prison. Assuredly, I say to you, you will by no means get out of there till you have paid the last penny.

Here we find the beginning of Jesus' exposition of particular laws found in the Ten Commandments. There is considerable misunderstanding concerning this teaching. Many believe that Jesus is contradicting Old Testament law. However, as we considered in the last chapter, Jesus has just said that He did not come to destroy the law but to fulfill it, and therefore He is warning us against this particular misunderstanding. He is not critiquing the law of God; rather, He is critiquing a misinterpretation of the law that had arisen through the scribes and the Pharisees.

"You have heard that it was said to those of old, 'You shall not murder, and whoever murders will be in danger of the judgment.' But I say to you that whoever is angry with his brother without a cause shall be in danger of the judgment" (vv. 21–22). Every Jew would have understood the formula, "You have heard that it was said." In using it Jesus was referencing the *halakha*, the oral tradition of the rabbis that was passed down from generation to generation, and it is this superficial understanding of God's law that Jesus is criticizing. In this section Jesus contrasts the wrong understanding with the right one: "You have heard that is was said to those of old. . . . But I say to you . . ." We are going to see the difference between how the rabbis incorrectly understood the law and how Jesus corrects those misunderstandings.

Sanctity of Life

The rabbis assumed that one kept the commandment to not kill by refraining from committing murder in the first degree, but Jesus shows that this commandment is far more profound than the external act of murder. Jesus indicates that the law was given by Moses in an elliptical fashion, which means that not everything inherent in the commandment was set forth in words. Whenever you see three or four dots in the middle of a sentence or a paragraph, the dots indicate that material has been deliberately left out. Those dots are called "ellipses." When it comes to the ellipses in the law, it means that whatever the law specifically forbids, it also forbids the broader nexus of the context of that law. So when God says we should not murder, that means, by extension, that we should not do anything that damages our neighbor's life. Murder begins with unjustifiable anger and hatred, and it includes insults, slander, and estrangement from people. That is why Jesus said that no one escapes the weight of the law merely by refraining from actual murder.

By extension, in order to keep the commandment, one must do no harm of any kind. The other aspect of the ellipses is this: whatever the law prohibits, it, at the same time, enjoins its opposite, and whatever the law enjoins, it prohibits its opposite. Therefore, Jesus is saying here that not only is human life so important that we ought never to murder, but also we are to work to promote the safety, welfare, and sanctity of life.

Larry King once said, "Until the Christian community speaks out against capital punishment, I'm not going to take seriously their protest against abortion." King failed to understand that the same principle governs both of those issues. Both the case against abortion and the case for capital punishment are based upon the biblical principle of the sanctity of life. God instituted capital punishment because the life of a human being is sacred. If someone willfully, maliciously, and with malice aforethought kills someone, the killer has slaughtered a creature who bears the image of God.

Jesus is saying that the law against murder prohibits actual murder but also potential murder. In other words, what is prohibited is not only the actual killing of a human being but those things that represent potential destruction of a human being. In the case of abortion, some say, there is no destruction of actual human life but only of potential human life. I believe it is the actual destruction of an actual life. At the very minimum a growing embryo is moving from potentiality to actuality, and to destroy it is to destroy a potential life. If Jesus says you can go to hell for the potential destruction of an actual life, it is much more serious to be involved in the actual destruction of a potential life.

Several years ago I read an essay by a scholar who was skeptical about the ethical teaching of Jesus. The scholar could not understand how hating or slandering one's brother could be as bad as murdering him, or how lusting could be as wrong as adultery. The point he missed is that Jesus does not say it is just as bad to be angry with your brother as to kill him. Jesus never collapsed the difference in degree of heinousness of various sins. His point is that just because you have not gone all the way to murder does not mean that you are free from the full-orbed responsibility of the law.

Fool!

"Whoever says to his brother, 'Raca!' shall be in danger of the council. But whoever says, 'You fool!' shall be in danger of hell fire" (v. 22). We do not know definitively what "Raca" means, but the majority of commentators indicate that it connotes calling someone "stupid." There is a difference between being foolish and being stupid. Stupidity has to do with a lack of intellectual capabilities, so to call someone stupid is insulting, however much deserved. Yet Jesus says that this is not just a matter of saying, "Raca!" Even calling someone a fool is spiritually dangerous.

Denoting someone as stupid is an intellectual judgment, but in Hebrew categories labeling someone as a fool is a moral judgment. In the Old Testament, foolishness is set in contrast to wisdom, and there we are told that the beginning of wisdom is the fear of the Lord (Prov. 1:7; 9:10). The necessary condition for obtaining wisdom is an attitude of reverence and awe before God. The psalmist wrote, "The fool has said in his heart, 'There is no God'" (Ps. 14:1). Paul expands on that when he talks about human beings' rejection of God's plain self-revelation: "Although they knew God, they did not glorify Him as God, nor were thankful, but became futile in their thoughts, and their foolish hearts were darkened" (Rom. 1:21).

A fool in biblical categories may have a high IQ. He might be a brilliant scholar, but he is a skeptic with respect to God. He remains rebellious, cynical to the sweetness and excellency of God, who has revealed Himself so plainly. Someone who cannot stand the thought of God rejects Him, not for lack of evidence but because of hardness of heart. Unbelief is a sin, not a mistake. It is willful, and we need to guard our hearts against it.

Murderers Saved

"Therefore if you bring your gift to the altar, and there remember that your brother has something against you, leave your gift there before the altar, and go your way. First be reconciled to your brother, and then come and offer your gift. Agree with your adversary quickly, while you are on the way with him, lest your adversary deliver you to the judge, the judge hand you over to the officer, and you be thrown into prison" (vv. 23–25). If you are estranged from your brother due to unjustifiable anger, or slander, or whatever has brought about disharmony, before you go to church and drop your offering in the offering plate, go and be reconciled to your brother. This is about establishing a love relationship with your brother and sister and neighbor. We need to get these things settled before we are required to go before the law court of God, when it will be too late. We do not love our neighbor as ourselves; we have not kept all the implications of even this one commandment since we got out of bed this morning. We all harbor anger to a degree that is unjustifiable. We are guilty of slander toward our neighbor and our brother. In a word, we have failed to love our neighbor to the degree that we do everything we can to adorn his life.

Were it not for the murder of Christ, we would go to that place from which we would never be released, but our Lord was murdered for us because we are murderers. We have committed murder in our hearts. We have committed murder against Him, but in that murder comes our salvation.

18

JESUS' VIEW OF ADULTERY

Matthew 5:27–30

You have heard that it was said to those of old, "You shall not commit adultery." But I say to you that whoever looks at a woman to lust for her has already committed adultery with her in his heart. If your right eye causes you to sin, pluck it out and cast it from you; for it is more profitable for you that one of your members perish, than for your whole body to be cast into hell. And if your right hand causes you to sin, cut it off and cast it from you; for it is more profitable for you that one of your members perish, than for your whole body to be cast into hell.

Jesus noted a contrast between the tradition of the rabbis and His own understanding of the law about murder, and we see His same elliptical approach here in the command against adultery. The prohibition against adultery includes within it every aspect that is part of the broader complex of this particular sin. Again Jesus starts out by contrasting the views of tradition with His own: **"You have heard that it was said to those of old, 'You shall not commit adultery'"** (v. 27).

Before we look specifically at what Jesus says, we should note the authority by which He says it. Elsewhere our Lord declares, "All authority has been given to Me in heaven and on earth" (Matt. 28:18), and, "I have not spoken on My own authority; but the Father who sent Me gave Me a command, what I should say and what I should speak" (John 12:49). Therefore, the pronouncement that Jesus makes here in Matthew 5 is nothing less than the pronouncement of God Himself.

A Promiscuous Age

We are living in an age in which God's opinion is considered merely that—a solitary opinion easily cancelled out by a majority report that contradicts His opinion. Our culture has undergone a moral revolution, which originated with the sexual revolution of the 1960s. Many factors were involved in that particular cultural revolution. Gael Greene, in her book *Sex and the College Girl*, stated that she had discovered a radical shift in the mores or the behavioral pattern of the coeds. Her findings indicated a change in conscience among college girls. In the 1950s, Green noted, if a single girl was known to be active sexually, it destroyed her reputation, but when the sexual revolution of the 1960s came along, everything reversed so that a woman feared that her reputation would be destroyed as a result of not being sexually active. Virginity had become the great shame of the unmarried young woman.

When I taught 1 Corinthians to college students, I reminded them of the rationale their parents had given them about sexual ethics: they were to be chaste in order to avoid venereal disease or unwanted pregnancy or cultural shame. But in a short time all that changed. Modern medicine can effectively treat sexually transmitted diseases, and there are a variety of birth control methods to prevent unwanted pregnancy, and, if those fail, abortion is readily available. Additionally, the fear of cultural shame is no longer a factor. So, I asked them, what is left to keep them from engaging in premarital sex? The only thing is that it is an offense against the holiness of God, and that God, who has the eternal authority to command our obedience, prohibits this behavior. That discussion was like a lightning bolt hitting the classroom. My student counseling load multiplied significantly afterward.

Like no other time in the history of Western culture, people today are bombarded with erotic stimuli. Where can we go and not be exposed to sexually suggestive, erotic literature and images? Certainly not to Hollywood movies, television, modern novels, or the Internet. The church today must deal with the pervasive problem of addiction to pornography. The problem is prevalent not just in the secular culture but also in the church. Paul taught that biological urges are strong and intense. The natural passions with which we have been created can be so intense that it feels like we are set aflame. If the sexual urge was burning in the first century, how much more have the incendiary influences of our culture intensified it?

As a pastor, I have to skate carefully between two things. On the one hand, it is my duty to make clear to everyone in my flock what God commands with respect to premarital and extramarital sexual relationships. At the same time, I have to be acutely conscious of people's frailty and the difficulty of the battle for chastity—a battle, it seems, that more Christians are losing than winning. We must hold to the biblical standard while at the same time administering the mercy of God to fallen people.

One student, a senior who was engaged to be married, came to talk to me. She told me she was overwhelmed with guilt because she had been sexually involved with her fiancé before their marriage. She had spoken to the college chaplain about it, but he told her that her guilt sprang from trying to live by an outdated, puritanical ethic. She would be free from guilt, he said, if she would accept that her sexual activity was simply an expression of mature adulthood. Despite what the chaplain told her, she still felt guilty, which is why she had come to me. I told her, "It is possible, as the chaplain indicated, to have a false sense of guilt. However, the reason that you feel guilty is that you are guilty." The solution for guilt is not to deny it or rationalize it. The only solution for real guilt is real forgiveness, and the necessary condition for real forgiveness is real repentance. This young woman needed to repent and seek the forgiveness of God.

Radical Commitment

"But I say to you that whoever looks at a woman to lust for her has already committed adultery with her in his heart" (v. 28). Jesus is not saying that it is just as evil to lust as it is to actually commit adultery, but He is saying that even if you have refrained from actual adultery, you haven't necessarily fulfilled the full dimension of God's law.

This is where Jesus gets radical: **"If your right eye causes you to sin, pluck it out and cast it from you; for it is more profitable for you that one of your members perish, than for your whole body to be cast into hell"** (v. 29). Jesus focuses here on the offending eye, because He understands how adultery begins. It usually begins with a glance, a look. King David, a man after God's own heart, just happened to be walking outside on his roof when he looked over and saw the nude Bathsheba on an adjacent roof. From that look came lust, and from lust came adultery. The visual aspect of erotic stimulation must not be minimized.

Every marketer in America understands that sex sells, which is why seductive women are used as props to sell everything from automobiles to Eskimo Pies. That is why there is so much focus on erotic images on television and in the movies, and nowhere is this more prevalent than on the Internet. Jesus says we have a problem here—a radical problem that requires a radical solution: "If your right eye causes you to sin, pluck it out." There are few, however, who are so committed to chastity that they inflict themselves with blindness to ensure it. Jesus is speaking hyperbolically here. He is not saying that if we have a lustful look, it is time for eye surgery. Rather, He is saying that preserving chastity is so important that we must do whatever it takes to accomplish it.

Odysseus, traveling in his ship on the way home from Troy, had himself lashed to the ship's mast to avoid the temptation of the sirens' song. He knew how easily he could veer off course and sail his ship into ruin. Sometimes that sort of radical action is necessary.

If you are addicted to pornography, find a way to keep it off your computer, but if you cannot, throw the computer in the garbage. Do not think that you cannot live in the twenty-first century without a computer. Sometimes the benefits of technology can offer as much peril as blessing. Jesus is saying that we must do a self-evaluation and consider which is more important: our soul or our computer? Our sanctity or our erotica? We cannot have both. Today we have become jaded. Our consciences have been seared. We have experienced what Jeremiah said to the people of Israel: "Were they ashamed when they had committed abomination? No! They were not at all ashamed; nor did they know how to blush" (Jer. 6:15; 8:12).

Luther, who was every bit a man, admitted that he struggled with lust, but he dealt with it, saying, "I cannot help it if birds fly around my head, but I can keep them from nesting in my hair." Just so, Jesus says we are to take every opportunity to keep our chastity before and after marriage. **"If your right hand causes you to sin, cut it off and cast it from you; for it is more profitable for you that one of your members perish, than for your whole body to be cast into hell"** (v. 30). Better to go through life maimed than to have your soul delivered into hell. One theologian said it is better to limp into heaven than to leap into hell. One of the greatest enticements to sexual sin is that everyone else is doing it. Another is the cultural acceptability of such sin. It takes moral courage to march against the tide, but Jesus is the one who calls us to this, and He never rescinded that call.

In the second century the apologist Justin Martyr defended Christianity before the emperor Antoninus Pius, and in his apology he said, "If you want to see visible proof of the truth of Christianity, observe our chastity." He pointed to the Christian ethic of chastity as proof of the power of the gospel. No apologist today could ask critics of Christianity to examine our sexual behavior as proof of the gospel.

If the Word of God reveals that you have been in sin, get it cleansed. Young women, if you are not married, yet you are no longer a virgin, you can become a virgin again in the sight of God, because when He forgives us our sins He makes us clean.

19

OATHS AND VOWS

Matthew 5:33–37

Again you have heard that it was said to those of old, "You shall not swear falsely, but shall perform your oaths to the Lord." But I say to you, do not swear at all; neither by heaven, for it is God's throne; nor by the earth, for it is His footstool; nor by Jerusalem, for it is the city of the great King. Nor shall you swear by your head, because you cannot make one hair white or black. But let your "Yes" be "Yes," and your "No," "No." For whatever is more than these is from the evil one.

In many English translations of the biblical text, the translators have helped us by dividing the portions of Scripture into various sections and giving each of those sections a subhead. It is important to realize that those subheadings are not part of the original text. The subhead supplied for this passage in the New King James translation is "Jesus Forbids Oaths." However, that subhead misunderstands what Jesus taught in this section.

Godly Oaths

The whole of the Christian faith is rooted and grounded in the biblical principle of covenant, and the covenants could not take place without an essential element—a sworn oath. The late Old Testament scholar Meredith Kline and George Mendenhall from the University of Michigan analyzed the structure of ancient covenants from various nations, and they saw that in all those covenants, oaths were sworn. The oaths were sworn not only by the covenant's subordinate parties but also by the superordinate parties. Our faith rests upon the fact that the Lord God omnipotent, in entering into a covenant with His people, swore an oath to seal that covenant. As the author of Hebrews tells us, "because He could swear by no one greater, He swore by Himself" (Heb. 6:13). He put His character on the line to underscore the trustworthiness of the promises He made to His people.

Throughout the New Testament we see that oaths are sworn by godly leaders. Paul the apostle, for example, when he writes to the Romans and declares his heart's passionate desire for the redemption of Israel, swears an oath to make sure that people understand the sincerity of his affirmation. Our Lord Jesus Himself, when He was placed on trial toward the end of His life, testified before the authorities under oath. So however we understand this text, it must be understood in light not only of its immediate context but also of the entire context of sacred Scripture. We cannot take a simple statement that Jesus makes and come to an understanding of it without considering everything else He teaches on the subject.

On another occasion Jesus said, "If two of you agree on earth concerning anything that they ask, it will be done for them by My Father in heaven" (Matt. 18:19). This does not mean that because we would like to see war end or a cure for cancer that we can simply agree about it, ask God to do it, and it will be done. That is a wrong understanding of what Jesus said. We must understand this in light of everything else He taught about true and effective prayer, which He restricts to what is in keeping with the will of the Father. So, in like manner, when Jesus says we are not to swear oaths, we have to understand that in light of everything else He teaches as well as everything else the Scriptures teach about oaths.

Jesus is setting His teaching here in contrast to the rabbinic traditions. The rabbis had written volumes about the various types of oaths and vows that Jewish people could recite, some of which were binding and obligatory and others that were not. This collection of oaths and vows among the Jewish people degenerated into a type of legal casuistry so that the spirit of taking vows and oaths had been obscured. Jesus is trying to correct the misunderstandings that were prevalent among His people in the first century.

In our last two studies we examined Jesus' exposition of the law against murder and adultery. We would think that He would continue through the rest of the Ten Commandments and give His understanding of the other eight, but He does not do that. Why didn't Jesus talk about coveting or about keeping the Sabbath? The reason is, His exposition of the law here was not exhaustive but illustrative.

He was teaching us with those two examples—murder and adultery—the deeper implications of the law. We should apply that depth dimension to our keeping of all God's laws.

The Sanctity of Oaths

There are at least five places in the Old Testament that teach about the sanctity of oaths and vows. We find it in Leviticus, Numbers, and Deuteronomy—three of the five books of the Torah. We find it in the Psalms, and we find it in the teaching of the prophet Zechariah, where the emphasis is on not taking false vows. When we swear an oath or make a vow, God is a witness to it and expects us to keep it. However, the Bible tells us that we are all liars. Each of us at one time or another breaks his or her word. We do not always keep our promises.

Several years ago *Family Life* magazine did an article on the Sproul family. The magazine sent reporters to our home who interviewed not only Vesta and me but also our children, whom they took aside to ask provocative questions. One of the reporters asked my daughter, "Has your daddy ever let you down?"

My daughter said that, yes, I had let her down. Her birthday coincided with a conference I attended each year, so I was not home to celebrate with her. My daughter told the reporter, "Every year he promises me that he will be home, but he doesn't keep his promise."

I thought, *What is so important about speaking at a conference that would allow me to break a promise to my daughter?* When I saw her answer in print, I felt terrible. It is true that our children sometimes twist our words. If our child asks, "Can we go to Disneyworld this week?" and we say, "We'll see," when the weekend comes and we decide we cannot do it, our child complains, "You promised!" We did not promise. However, there are times when we do promise something, thereby creating an expectation. When the promise goes unfulfilled, the result is disappointment, hurt, anger, or alienation.

A simple yes or a simple no is not enough of an answer in certain circumstances. To be married in most churches requires the taking of vows. We know that if in the backseat of a car a man makes a promise to a woman, that is not the same as making it in front of witnesses—parents, relatives, friends, the state, and the church, but most importantly in front of God Himself. When I perform the marriage of two people, I remind them that even if they or their friends and family do not take their vows seriously, God takes them seriously. The warning comes to us in the Word of God: "Better not to vow than to vow and not pay" (Eccles. 5:5).

Israel trivialized vows and oaths. Vows were dragged out and used in all kinds of circumstances for which they should not have been required. This happened because they realized that, given our humanity, a verbal commitment is not always binding. I was once wooed to a teaching position at a particular school. The school's president promised many advantages if I agreed to take the post, so I moved there with my family. Not all of the promises came to fruition, however, and I felt disillusioned. When I tried to discuss with him the broken promises, he asked, "Did you get those promises in writing?" I said, "No, sir, but I trusted you."

In one sense, Jesus is saying that because of our integrity it shouldn't be necessary for Christians to make vows. Christian people should never have to swear an oath, even if the state requires it. We still do it lest we commit perjury when we are in a courtroom, but we should be known as people whose word can be relied upon.

James gives many admonitions concerning godly living, and He concludes: "But above all, my brethren, do not swear, either by heaven or by earth or with any other oath. But let your 'Yes' be 'Yes,' and your 'No,' 'No,' lest you fall into judgment" (James 5:12). When the brother of Jesus says, "Above all," we should take note. If you say you are going to do something, do it. If you do not want to do it, then say you are not willing to commit yourself to it. We are much too loose about our commitments today.

The Bigger Picture

In this passage of the Sermon on the Mount, there are at least two commandments in broader view here. Jesus says, **"Do not swear at all: neither by heaven, for it is God's throne; nor by the earth, for it is His footstool; nor by Jerusalem, for it is the city of the great King. Nor shall you swear by your head, because you cannot make one hair white or black"** (vv. 34–36). In the Old Testament oaths were to be taken in the name of God. The Pharisees worked this so that, for lesser pledges, they would not swear by the name of God; rather, they would swear by the temple, the earth, the city of Jerusalem, and all things holy.

As children we learned how to give sacred vows: "Cross my heart, hope to die, stick a needle in my eye." If we wanted to elevate it to the next level, we would say something like, "I swear on my mother's grave." We did not realize that a statement like that violates at least two of the Ten Commandments. The second commandment prohibits idolatry, and the third prohibits a vain use of the name of God. If I swear by my mother's grave, I am saying that if I do not keep my promise, let my mother's grave be a witness against me. However, there is nothing about the grave or my mother in it that can see what I do. Even if my deceased mother could see what I do with respect to my promises, she would be utterly powerless to enforce the integrity of my promises. When we swear by heaven, our mother's grave, or anything else, we are attributing to created things the power and authority that belong only to God. To attribute to my mother's grave omnipotence and omniscience is to make of my mother's grave an idol, which does dishonor to God.

There is a place for the taking of vows and oaths, but Jesus is making the point that apart from very special circumstances, if you are a Christian you should be known for your word. Your word should not require even a handshake. Whatever you promise to do, do it. We are not required to make promises, and we should be aware of that. If someone asks us to make a promise, we can say we will try our best to help, but we cannot promise it, because with a promise comes the burden of the responsibility to keep it, even when it is not expedient to do so. So let us be people of the Word, who, because of God's Word and His faithfulness to it, can reflect that kind of integrity so that people can trust what we say.

20

LOVING OUR ENEMIES

Matthew 5:38–48

You have heard that it was said, "An eye for an eye and a tooth for a tooth." But I tell you not to resist an evil person. But whoever slaps you on your right cheek, turn the other to him also. If anyone wants to sue you and take away your tunic, let him have your cloak also. And whoever compels you to go one mile, go with him two. Give to him who asks you, and from him who wants to borrow from you do not turn away. You have heard that it was said, "You shall love your neighbor and hate your enemy." But I say to you, love your enemies, bless those who curse you, do good to those who hate you, and pray for those who spitefully use you and persecute you, that you may be sons of your Father in heaven; for He makes His sun rise on the evil and on the good, and sends rain on the just and on the unjust. For if you love those who love you, what reward have you? Do not even the tax collectors do the same? And if you greet your brethren only, what do you do more than others? Do not even the tax collectors do so? Therefore you shall be perfect, just as your Father in heaven is perfect.

Of all Jesus' teachings in the Sermon on the Mount, the one in the passage before us is the most challenging. Once again Jesus announces a contrast between His teaching and what the people were accustomed to learning from the oral tradition of the rabbis. Here He focuses on the principle called the *lex talionis*, or the "law of the talon" or "claw," which is found to some degree in the Old Testament but is also found widely among ancient Semitic people going all the way back, for example, to the Code of Hammurabi.

Vengeance Belongs to God

You have heard that it was said, 'You shall love your neighbor and hate your enemy'" (v. 43). I have heard critics complain that the Old Testament system of justice was harsh and cruel. They point to the law of an eye for an eye and a tooth for a tooth as an example of such cruelty. Yet I cannot imagine a more just system than to have a punishment fit the severity of the crime. If one were to put out the eye of another, taking out both eyes of the offender would be unjust; in such a case the penalty would be more severe than the crime.

However, Jesus here is not establishing a new system of justice for government or for those who are in positions of authority; He is speaking specifically to the arena of personal ethics, how we are to behave as Christians. Most important in this teaching is Jesus' speaking against individual pursuits of vengeance and retaliation.

"But I tell you not to resist an evil person. But whoever slaps you on your right cheek, turn the other to him also" (v. 39). In other words, we are not to retaliate, slap for slap. As Christians we are called to turn the other cheek. I find it strange that Jesus would speak of slapping someone on the right cheek, since most people are right-handed. How would we go about slapping someone on the right cheek if he is standing in front of us?

Someone posed that enigma to me back when I conducted a Bible study for the Pittsburgh Steelers. There were twenty-eight team members who professed faith and came to the study. The study met in the home of Terry Bradshaw at the time. I was trying to explain the difficulty of this text, and I asked the defensive end L.C. Greenwood if he would volunteer to help me illustrate it. He stood up, towering over me. I got up on a folding chair so that I could look L.C. in the eye, and, after promising not to hurt him, I reached around his neck and tried to hit him on the right check. I could barely get there; I could only tap him. I was trying to illustrate that in view here is hitting someone on the right cheek with the back of your hand, which was the ancient gesture of insult.

Jesus is talking here about insult and slander. If someone slanders you, make yourself vulnerable to be slandered again. If someone insults you, do not respond by insulting him in return; make yourself vulnerable to being insulted again. This has great application to us in the twenty-first century, an age when the Internet provides a medium for any manner of insult or slander with impunity. Theologians of note are attacked all the time. I know of a website that was dedicated to attacking me, not theologically but personally. When that happened I offered no response.

We are told not to seek revenge or retaliation for the injuries we suffer at others' hands. Paul wrote, "Beloved, do not avenge yourselves, but rather give place to wrath; for it is written, 'Vengeance is Mine, I will repay,' says the Lord" (Rom. 12:19). Vengeance is not yours or mine; it is God's. Jesus Himself said, "Shall God not avenge His own elect who cry out day and night to Him, though He bears long with them?" (Luke 18:7). We are to leave vindication in the hands of the One who, unlike us, is perfect in His vindication. We do not want to get even; we want to get one up. God knows that, which is why He instructs His people to let Him handle vindication.

If anyone wants to sue you and take away your tunic, let him have your cloak also. And whoever compels you to go one mile, go with him two (vv. 40–41). According to Roman law, the authorities had the right to compel someone to transport goods up to the length of one mile without compensation. It was under that law that Simon of Cyrene was compelled to carry the crossbeam of the instrument of Jesus' execution. Jesus says here that if someone is afflicted with this unjust oppression, go even an extra mile. Is this not what Jesus Himself did? "He was oppressed and He was afflicted, yet He opened not His mouth; He was led as a lamb to the slaughter, and as a sheep before its shearers is silent, so He opened not His mouth" (Isa. 53:7).

Charity

Give to him who asks you, and from him who wants to borrow from you do not turn away (v. 42). Jesus is putting forth a spirit of charity, a spirit of being willing to help those in need and those who ask you for support. This does not mean, of course, that we are not to be discerning in its application. If we were to give to everyone who asks us for absolutely anything, we would be completely depleted at the end of a week. What Jesus is instructing is the willingness to give and to help.

In the early Christian writing called the *Didache,* or *Teaching of the Twelve Apostles*, there is this aphorism: "Let your donation sweat in your hand." The principle enjoined there is to be wise in your giving. We are not to give to just anything; rather, we must make sure that we give to worthwhile causes. Such qualifications come from the overall teaching of Scripture about almsgiving.

Love for Enemies

Then we get to the crux of the matter: **"You have heard that it was said, 'You shall love your neighbor and hate your enemy.' But I say to you, love your enemies"** (vv. 43–44). According to Jesus, we must love those who slap and slander us. Jesus was not speaking of warm, fuzzy feelings of affection. "Love" here is a verb. Therefore, Jesus is not advocating feelings of love toward our enemies but doing the loving thing. We are to deal with our enemies by doing the loving thing for them. Jesus does not leave that in the abstract. He gives a list of examples to illustrate His point: **"Bless those who curse you, do good to those who hate you, and pray for those who spitefully use you and persecute you, that you may be sons of your Father in heaven; for He makes His sun rise on the evil and on the good, and sends rain on the just and on the unjust"** (vv. 44–45). That goes against everything in our natural makeup. However, Jesus wants us to imitate our Father in heaven, who has treated the wicked with love.

People claim that God loves all men unconditionally, but the Bible is clear about how it defines the love of God for people. We can distinguish among three types of divine love. The first is God's *benevolent* love, His good will. God has a good disposition to all of His creatures even in their fallenness. Added to God's benevolent love is His *beneficent* love whereby God not only has a good will toward His creatures but does good things for them, as Jesus illustrates here. God is beneficent toward wicked people in letting them bask in the sun. He lets His sunlight fall upon the evil and the good. He lets the rain fall for the just and the unjust, so that the unjust farmer receives the benefit of God's kindness of rain for his crops. People curse God and use His name in vain every day. They blaspheme Him. Yet whereas we curse Him, He blesses us. Whereas we do evil, He does good. God does not engage in retaliation against those who stand against Him. Every wicked person enjoys the love of God at least in terms of the first two kinds of love—benevolent love and beneficent love.

The third kind of love, the love of *complacency*, refers to the unique delight and affection God has especially for His only begotten Son. It is His Son that the Father calls His "beloved." The Father has a special love for Christ that He does not have for everyone else in creation, but that special love of complacency is not limited to Jesus. It is extended to all who are in Christ Jesus. None of us deserves God's love of complacency, but every Christian enjoys love from God that the wicked do not enjoy.

God's Standard

"For if you love those who love you, what reward have you? Do not even the tax collectors do the same? And if you greet your brethren only, what do you do more than others? Do not even the tax collectors do so? Therefore you shall be perfect, just as your Father in heaven is perfect" (vv. 46–48). Many argue, "Jesus doesn't really mean that we're called to be perfect, because He understood that no one's perfect. Everyone falls short of the glory of God, so He must have meant something else." But He meant what He said—we are called to be perfect, just as in the Old Testament God said to His people, "Be holy; for I am holy" (Lev. 11:44).

We cannot be holy the way God is holy, nor can we reach perfection before we get to heaven. Jesus knows that, and He knows that this ethic is a difficult one. He also knows that we adjust our personal standards to our level of performance. Every last one of us has done this. Instead of elevating our performance, we reduce the standard. Jesus is explaining that God's standard does not change, and God's standard is perfection.

When people tell me they do not need Jesus, I ask, "Are you perfect?" Most people admit that they are not. "To err is human," they say, to which I respond, "If you are not perfect, you need Jesus in order to survive the judgment of God." The only place to get perfection is in Christ, who kept the standard perfectly.

That is what the gospel is about, and that is why the law drives us to the gospel every time. When I read Jesus' words, I hear the law. I hear what I am required to do, which causes me to pray, "Lord, I cannot do these things. Help me!" He gives me One who did do those things, and He cloaks me in the righteousness of Christ, which is what grace is. Grace is not that God abolishes or compromises the standard. Grace is what He gives us as a gift. He has given us a Savior who is not only adequate but also perfect. That is the amazing thing about grace.

21

PRIVATE PIETY

Matthew 6:1–4

Take heed that you do not do your charitable deeds before men, to be seen by them. Otherwise you have no reward from your Father in heaven. Therefore, when you do a charitable deed, do not sound a trumpet before you as the hypocrites do in the synagogues and in the streets, that they may have glory from men. Assuredly, I say to you, they have their reward. But when you do a charitable deed, do not let your left hand know what your right hand is doing, that your charitable deed may be in secret; and your Father who sees in secret will Himself reward you openly.

We have come to a portion of the Sermon on the Mount that includes a warning with respect to the practice of piety in three areas: (1) charitable giving or almsgiving; (2) fasting; and (3) prayer. In this study we will restrict our focus to the first of those, the giving of alms.

Godly Giving

"Take heed that you do not do your charitable deeds before men, to be seen by them. Otherwise you have no reward from your Father in heaven" (v. 1). At first blush it would seem that what Jesus is speaking about here is on a collision course with what He taught earlier in the sermon about Christians letting their light shine before men so that their good works may be seen by a watching world and give honor to God. Here Jesus talks about a certain spiritual practice that is not to be done before the watching world but in private. Earlier, Jesus described good deeds and manifestations of righteousness that are to be done in full view of the world, such as showing mercy and speaking the truth, so that observers will notice a certain integrity of character. Here, however, Jesus is not talking about righteousness with respect to doing good deeds but about the practice of personal piety. Such things, Jesus says, are not to be done before men.

"Therefore, when you do a charitable deed, do not sound a trumpet before you as the hypocrites do in the synagogues and in the streets, that they may have glory from men" (v. 2). The most common charitable deed done by the Jew in antiquity was to give alms to the poor, and he could do that in more than one way. He could make a donation at the synagogue that then would be passed on to the poor, or, if he saw a beggar in the street, he could give alms directly. In that case, obviously, the one who received the alms would see his benefactor. In such cases, the giving could not be done in secret. However, Jesus is talking about the spirit behind our giving. We are not to give in order to receive applause and glory from men. In other words, we are not to parade our piety in front of a watching world, because, He tells us, that is exactly what the hypocrites of His day were doing. The primary emphasis here is that giving is to be done for the glory of God. Jesus is teaching us that our charitable giving is an act of worship.

Two of the sons of Adam and Eve brought sacrifices to the altar. Abel brought an animal sacrifice, and Cain brought a cereal sacrifice or one of produce. We are told that God loved the one and despised the other (Gen. 4:4–5). Many say that the reason God received Abel's offering and not Cain's was that Abel's was a blood sacrifice. In a sense, Abel's offering did foreshadow the ultimate blood sacrifice that would be made for us by Jesus, but to think that is why God accepted Abel's sacrifice is wrong. God's prescriptions made it abundantly clear that grain offerings were perfectly acceptable to Him; acceptable offerings were not restricted simply to blood offerings. A herdsmen was expected to take an animal from his herd and offer it as a sacrifice, and a farmer was to take from his produce and offer that to the glory of God.

We learn in the New Testament why Abel's offering was acceptable to God: "By faith Abel offered to God a more excellent sacrifice than Cain" (Heb. 11:4). Old Testament worship was communicated through the making of sacrifices, and these were to be sacrifices of praise, not sacrifices to inflate the ego of the giver or to make his offering appear noble. A sacrifice not given from the heart was not offered in faith. Whatever reward God might give for the sacrifice would be withheld if the offering had not come from the heart. Sacrifices offered for self-serving reasons were hypocritical. Just as the author of Hebrews makes a distinction between sacrifices made in faith and those that are not, so Jesus here makes a distinction between a gift that is given genuinely from a gift that is given hypocritically.

Hypocrisy

The term *hypokritēs* that occupies much of Jesus' attention throughout the Gospel of Matthew, particularly as He chastens the Pharisees, comes from the ancient theater. A *hypocrite* was a play actor in the theater. When actors take on a role, they pretend to be someone they are not. The whole idea of acting and pretense was borrowed from the theater and later became a pejorative term to describe someone who merely goes through the motions and plays a role.

Maybe you have noticed that when Academy Award-winning actors give unscripted television interviews, they stumble over their words. They are unable to make an intelligible sentence without the crutch of a script—lines that someone else has written for them to utter. They memorize those scripts so well that they can assume the identity of the character they are playing while acting onscreen. That is good in the theater, but if we in the church seek to portray an aura of greater piety than we actually possess, it is ghastly.

One of the ten most frequent objections that people give to becoming a Christian is that the church is full of hypocrites. D. James Kennedy used to answer, "That's all right. There is always room for one more." He added, "If you ever find a perfect church, don't join it. You'll ruin it." His premise was that the church is filled with sinners. In fact, it is the only organization I know of that requires an acknowledgment of sin to belong. If people outside the church see us sin, they really should not be surprised. What those outside fail to see is that a Christian is only a hypocrite if he says that he does not sin. Hypocrisy is pretending to be something you are not or trying to get people to believe that you are not doing a certain thing that in fact you are doing.

Nevertheless, the sin of hypocrisy does indeed exist in the church. Sometimes the blame for it lies with the preacher. Preachers constantly exhort and admonish people to grow their faith to a higher level of obedience. So much pressure is put on Christians to grow spiritually that sometimes they fear being rejected if others realize they are not quite as righteous as they ought to be.

No two people in the Christian community started their Christian life at the same place, and no two people in the church are at exactly the same place in their spiritual pilgrimage and growth into conformity to the righteousness of Christ. That is why the Bible enjoins us to have a love that covers a multitude of sins. We are not to be spiritual policemen, judging everyone and looking down our noses at those in the congregation. "There but for the grace of God go I," says an old adage. Winston Churchill once played on that adage when he mentioned someone who manifested arrogance, saying, "There but for the grace of God goes God." May it be that no one can say that about us.

I am a Calvinist, which means that the doctrine of *sola gratia* is in my bones and blood. I know that only through the grace of God could I ever enter into His kingdom. I hope we all understand the primacy of grace in the Christian life. Grace is not a license to continue in sin and take advantage of God's grace. "Should we continue in sin that grace may abound?" Paul asks, and then he answers, "Certainly not!" (Rom 6:1–2). At the same time, we have to guard against adding hypocrisy to whatever weaknesses and sins still plague us.

That is why Jesus urges us here to be sure that we do not make our contributions in order to be seen by men. Surely there are times when it is impossible to conceal a contribution. **"But when you do a charitable deed, do not let your left hand know what your right hand is doing, that your charitable deed may be in secret; and your Father who sees in secret will Himself reward you openly"** (vv. 3–4).

When Paul was put under a microscope and criticized by some of his fellow Jews, he became fed up with it and responded:

> Seeing that many boast according to the flesh, I also will boast. For you put up with fools gladly, since you yourselves are wise! For you put up with it if one brings you into bondage, if one devours you, if one takes from you, if one exalts himself, if one strikes you on the face. To our shame I say that we were too weak for that! But in whatever anyone is bold—I speak foolishly—I am bold also. Are they Hebrews? So am I. Are they Israelites? So am I. Are they the seed of Abraham? So am I. Are they ministers of Christ?—I speak as a fool—I am more. (2 Cor. 11:18–23)

The spirit of Paul's response, which he gave when he reached the end of his patience, was that if the people wanted to level charges against him, he would outwork them, outlove them, and outgive them. He was answering the fool according to his folly. Do you want to talk about giving? Each of us ought to embrace the principle of the sacrifice of praise.

The head of a large ministry once told me that every time the organization asked people to give, letters of protest came back. He said that when someone complains about a request for giving, he goes immediately to his donor record. "Ninety-nine times out of a hundred," he said, "the person complaining about the request to give is someone who doesn't give." We do not like to be told to give if we are not giving; however, when we are giving from the heart, such requests do not bother us because we know it is what God expects from His people—to do that which is pleasing to God, not to man.

Rewarded

"Assuredly, I say to you, they have their reward" (v. 5). The reward for the hypocrite is not much. Those who boast about their giving, those who parade their almsgiving, those who put their name up in lights so that the whole world can see their sacrifice, have received their reward. Yet it is not from God. They receive the reward they are looking for—the praise of men—which is worthless from the viewpoint of eternity. They are like Cain, who brought his gift not from faith, not to manifest the glory of God and serve Him, but for his own glorification. It was more important to Cain to be known as a giver than actually to give. If you give, and you are the only one who knows it, you are not the only one who knows it. God knows it, too. That is all that matters.

Your Father, who sees in secret, will reward you openly. He will do it Himself, directly. He is not going to delegate that to someone else. If you give in secret, your reward is open. If we give openly, we are not to expect public acclamation. The most marvelous thing about charitable giving is that it is impossible to outgive the Lord.

22

SINCERE PRAYER

Matthew 6:5–9

And when you pray, you shall not be like the hypocrites. For they love to pray standing in the synagogues and on the corners of the streets, that they may be seen by men. Assuredly, I say to you, they have their reward. But you, when you pray, go into your room, and when you have shut your door, pray to your Father who is in the secret place; and your Father who sees in secret will reward you openly. And when you pray, do not use vain repetitions as the heathen do. For they think that they will be heard for their many words. Therefore, do not be like them. For your Father knows the things you have need of before you ask Him. In this manner, therefore, pray:

> Our Father in heaven,
> Hallowed be Your name.

There are few areas of our spiritual life in which we need more instruction and encouragement than godly prayer. In this brief passage Jesus tells us how not to pray, and then He gives us some words that teach us how indeed we ought to pray. Jesus has just talked about giving gifts in secret in order to honor God rather than giving them openly to receive the praise of men. Here He carries this motif further, explaining that we are not to make an ostentatious display of our piety before the eyes of the world.

When I attended seminary, the institution at which I was studying was in the process of merging with another seminary. The blended seminary had lofty goals of academic excellence, and we students were required to write term papers exceeding two hundred pages. Our reading lists were so large that we could but read only the first line of each paragraph of a particular book in order to meet the requirements. In a sociology of religion class, we were required to write a twenty-page paper analyzing the image of the minister in contemporary culture. We were asked to leaf through magazines and newspaper comic strips to see how ministers were portrayed. We students considered that assignment as hardly worthy of our time, yet when I did the study I made a discovery that has stayed with me ever since. Ministers are caricatured as pious, wimpy sourpusses with pursed lips. That image has expanded so that it now includes all Christians in general. I fear that the caricature has come from the posture that Jesus teaches us we should never adopt, a posture that makes us appear holier than everyone around us and paints us with a facade of hypocrisy.

Private Piety

As we saw earlier, hypocrisy has a devastating impact on the life of the church and on the representation of Christianity to a dying world. For that reason, our Lord warns us here not to parade our piety before the world. **"And when you pray, you shall not be like the hypocrites. For they love to pray standing in the synagogues and on the corners of the streets, that they may be seen by men"** (v. 5).

The solution is not to stop praying. Rather, **"when you pray, go into your room, and when you have shut your door, pray to your Father who is in the secret place; and your Father who sees in secret will reward you openly. And when you pray, do not use vain repetitions as the heathen do. For they think that they will be heard for their many words"** (vv. 6–7). Pagans have historically been those who recite mantras, and people today repeat nonsensical syllables in order to achieve a mystical transcendence. Prayers are used as magical incantations to try to change the environment or one's circumstances. This is the approach of the New Age movement, which believes that one can make things happen by applying mind over matter.

"In this manner, therefore, pray . . ." (v. 9). Jesus did not instruct that we are to use these very words. Rather, He has given us in the Lord's Prayer an outline or model that suggests to us the types of things that we should include in our prayers. It certainly is not wrong to pray or to sing the Lord's Prayer; it has a rich history in the church. Whenever we hear or recite it, we are being reminded of the priorities that Jesus sets before us to pray about. However, praying the Lord's Prayer can become as mindless and vain as the magical incantations and mantras that pagans use. So when we pray the Lord's Prayer, we need to pray it thoughtfully, giving attention to the content of the prayer. Therefore, I want to consider the elements found in the Lord's Prayer so that we can see why Jesus includes them as He does in teaching us how to pray.

God's Omniscience

"Therefore do not be like them. For your Father knows the things you have need of before you ask Him" (v. 8). The psalmist said, "For there is not a word on my tongue, but behold, O Lord, You know it altogether. . . . Where can I go from Your Spirit? Or where can I flee from Your presence? If I ascend into heaven, You are there; if I make my bed in hell, behold, You are there" (Ps. 139:4, 7–8). Jesus is simply seconding that affirmation when He says that the Lord knows what you need before you ask Him and knows what you are going to say before you say it. I am asked frequently whether I think prayer changes God's mind, but how could prayer ever change the mind of God? We cannot give Him information that He lacked before we informed Him. We cannot correct His counsel, showing that what He has determined to do is wrong. God does not have a Plan B that He puts in motion at our request.

"If that is the case," people say, "why should we pray?" We pray because it changes us. We pray also because God uses our prayer as the means to bring about the ends that He has decreed from all eternity. God commands us to pray and to do so earnestly, but we do not pray to instruct Him or give Him our counsel.

Approach to God

There are two things we must always remember when we pray. The first thing we have to remember is to whom we are speaking. We must remember who God is. He is not a cosmic bellhop on call to give us everything on our wish list. The second thing we have to remember is who we are. So often the prayers of God's people are irreverent. They lack a sense of adoration and awe. We sometimes speak to God as if He were our pal; however, if God were to appear before us, such familiarity would vanish from our soul and we would be on our face groveling in the dust before His majesty. That should be our posture when we come before Him. We have been invited to come before Him boldly but never arrogantly.

Years ago there was a barber named Peter who made his living cutting hair and shaving faces. One day as he was cutting the hair of a customer, he looked up and saw a man come in the door whom he recognized immediately as an outlaw, one with a large bounty on his life. When the outlaw got into the barber's chair, the barber put the apron on him and then, taking out the sharpest knife he had, applied soap to the man's chin and neck and pressed the razor to his jugular vein. Just a little more pressure and the reward would be his. However, the barber had no intention of even nicking his client in the neck, because the barber had profound respect for his customer. The outlaw was Martin Luther, and the barber saw Martin Luther not as an outlaw but as his mentor. One day when the barber was shaving Martin Luther, he said to him, "Dr. Luther, can you teach me how to pray?" Luther said, "Of course, Master Peter. I'd be happy to do that." When the shave was finished, Martin Luther went back to his cell and wrote a book just for his barber titled *A Simple Way to Pray.*

Everyone should read that book. It is the best book I have ever read on prayer. Luther's simple suggestion was to pray the Ten Commandments, the Apostles' Creed, and the Lord's Prayer. He did not mean that we should get down on our knees and recite the law, the creed, and the Lord's Prayer. Luther meant that if we really want to learn how to pray, we must focus on the things that God reveals in His law, in the creed, and in the Lord's Prayer. Luther would pray, "You, Lord, are the one who brought your people out of the land of bondage. You are a God who is so offended by idolatry in every form that you have told us not to allow any other gods before you. May we never tolerate in our hearts the very presence of an idol that would tarnish the glory that belongs to You." Luther would take the Apostles' Creed and pray, "Oh, Lord, I am so grateful that I can call you 'Father' and that you are not the Father impotent or the Father abusive, but you are the Father almighty. There is no power or force in this universe that can resist the power of your word. It is by your word, God, that the heavens and the earth were made, by which you said, 'Let there be light,' and the lights came. My soul is overcome when I consider the work of your hands, the sun and the moon and all that you have ordained, and I am forced to ask the question, What is man that you are mindful of him? Or the son of man that you visit him?"

That is what Luther meant by praying the Lord's Prayer. Rather than praying, "Our Father who is in heaven, hallowed be Your name," he would say, "Oh, God, I have not regarded your name as holy, because I have not regarded you as holy. I live in the midst of a people that think nothing of using your name in an irreverent manner. God, I know that your kingdom and your will won't be done on this earth as it is in heaven until or unless we begin to exalt the majesty of your name."

The first thing that Jesus instructed His disciples to pray was that the name of His Father would be considered holy and sacred, that it might never be blasphemed, that the name would never be taken in vain or used as an occasion for cursing. Do you realize that nothing reveals the state of your soul more clearly than the words that come out of your mouth? I know that Christians are capable of all kinds of sin, but I cannot understand how a regenerate person could use the name of Jesus in a blasphemous way. How can we worship someone whom we routinely blaspheme? I do not see how it is possible.

What does your mouth tell you about the state of your soul? Jesus put that at the top of the list. "If you want to pray for something," he is saying, "pray that my Father, who sent me to redeem you, might be regarded as holy and that you would have the same reverence and adoration for Him and for His name as the angels in heaven who surround His throne daily, singing, 'Holy, holy, holy is the Lord of hosts. The whole earth is filled with his glory.'"

We want to learn how to pray and get beyond not only the childlike but also the childish methodology of praying, "Dear God, please bless Mommy and Daddy and Sarah and Jane and Uncle Sam and Aunt Gertrude," to where we focus our pleas on the work of the kingdom and for the sake of the kingdom.

23

OUR FATHER'S HOUSE

Matthew 6:9

In this manner, therefore, pray:

> Our Father in heaven,
> Hallowed be Your name.

"Our Father in heaven." I have often wondered why Jesus taught His disciples to acknowledge in prayer the place of God's abode. Heaven, not earth, is the primary residence of our God. He dwells and inhabits eternity, and there is no house on this planet that can contain His presence. We understand that He is in very nature infinite, ubiquitous, and omnipresent, and He cannot be contained in any one locality. Yet Jesus said that when we come before Him in prayer, we ought to think of Him as being in heaven.

When the first Russian cosmonaut, Yuri Gagarin, returned from his flight into space, he made a cynical observation. Looking as hard as he might while he was out in space, he saw no evidence of the presence of God. He did not realize that one need not go into outer space to see the manifold evidence of the existence of his Creator, as the whole earth is filled with His glory.

Where God Dwells

We have a tendency to think of heaven in somewhat geographical terms. The word used in the New Testament Greek for "heaven" is the same word that is used for the sky, so we are accustomed to think of heaven as being somewhere above us, up in the sky, beyond outer space, where even the Hubble telescope cannot with its precise lens capture the residence of God. However, we ought not to think of heaven so much in geographical terms and certainly not in terms of altitude. Rather, we should think of it more in the way the Bible communicates it. To that end, a couple of analogies might aid us.

In the early 1940s a man named Guido Gallerdini came from his native Italy, took up residence in my hometown, and opened a barbershop. Guido was the first barber to cut my hair, and I had great affection for him. He spoke little English, but he loved to sing opera while he was working. His barbershop had mirrors on one side, which I faced while sitting in the barber chair, and behind me was another set of mirrors. The mirrors reflected my image both to me and to the mirrors on the other side so that there seemed to be an infinite number of images reflected in the glass until they simply reached a vanishing point. When I saw the vanishing point in the mirror I wondered whether the images end there or whether they continued on beyond what I could perceive. The idea of mirrored images caused me to ponder.

In mirrors we see the reality of something three dimensional as if it were reconstructed before our eyes in two dimensions. That is what happens when we see a reflection. Such reflections tell us that there are at least three dimensions, and in three dimensions we live and move and have our being. However, I do not believe that this is the end of reality. There is, as we say, more to reality than meets the eye. I believe the boundary between earth and heaven, between nature and super-nature, is not geographical but dimensional, and therefore heaven is not up there; it is right here. It is not in our three-dimensional reality, but it is near us all the same, and there is a veil that covers this reality right beside us. Heaven breaks through into the third dimension by the reality of God's presence. We do not need a stepladder or an airplane or an elevator to get closer to heaven. It is right here in the next dimension.

Our constituent nature is made up of body and soul. There is a physical aspect to our lives, but there is also a nonphysical aspect. One of the oldest philosophical conundrums is trying to discern the relationship between our mind and our body, in other words, that between our physical activity and our thoughts. The extent of our thoughts cannot be measured. Thought belongs to the realm of the nonphysical, yet our lives are driven by them every moment. There are some who argue that even our thoughts are purely physical responses, but if that were the case, why argue anything? If that were true, none of us could help what we think.

Men such as René Descartes, Baruch Spinoza, and Gottfried Leibniz worked for years trying to figure out how a thought could produce an action. No one can figure out how a thought interacts with a physical action and a physical action interacts with a thought. We live every day in that tension of dimension, because thought belongs to one dimension and the body belongs to another.

Plato, Augustine, and Edwards all understood that the more we probe the things of God with our mind and the deeper our thinking about Him becomes, the closer we approach the fullness of His reality. That is why God gave us His Word, and the Word is meant to be intelligible and understood by the mind.

Sacred Holiness

"Hallowed be Your name." All of sacred Scripture makes clear that God is altogether holy. The most important thing Jesus says we ought to pray for is that the name of His Father will be regarded as holy. We live in a culture that profanes His name. When we profane the name of God, we reveal our deep lack of respect and reverence for the God whose name it is.

When we went about the task of building St. Andrew's Chapel, we tried to build an appropriate place where God and His people can meet. We call it the "house of God," but that word "house" has more than a function. It also communicates something about its intent. When God told the Israelites to build Him a tent, a tabernacle—a house—He had in mind a place where He would meet with His people and reveal His glory:

> Then the cloud covered the tabernacle of meeting, and the glory of the Lord filled the tabernacle. And Moses was not able to enter the tabernacle of meeting, because the cloud rested above it, and the glory of the Lord filled the tabernacle. Whenever the cloud was taken up from above the tabernacle, the children of Israel would go onward in all their journeys. But if the cloud was not taken up, then they did not journey till the day that it was taken up. For the cloud of the Lord was above the tabernacle by day, and fire was over it by night, in the sight of all the house of Israel, throughout all their journeys. (Ex. 40:34–38)

For fifteen chapters in Exodus and more in Leviticus, exquisite instructions were given by God Himself for how that building was to be constructed. There was more ink given to the construction of the tabernacle than was used in the entire book of Romans, Paul's magnum opus of theology. God was so explicit for two reasons: for glory and for beauty. He did not give so much detail for the purpose of creature comforts. He wanted the tabernacle built for His glory and honor and for the beauty of His holiness.

We are far from that today. When we do not honor God with our lips, we turn His name into something ugly and profane. God is the fountainhead of not only all that is good and true but also all that is beautiful. We built St. Andrew's not to bring God from heaven to earth but to reflect His glory and the beauty of His holiness. I still am breathless when I come into our church building. There is something special about it—the arches, the vaulted ceiling—everything points to that other dimension, which we can address only in symbols.

Along the bottom of the St. Andrew's weekly bulletin are these words: "We cross the threshold of the secular to the sacred, from the common to the uncommon, from the profane to the holy." We hope that those who enter sense that they are crossing a threshold and leaving behind the dimension of the commonplace. We hope that as they enter our building, they leave the secular and step across a boundary into the sacred.

When the tabernacle was built, it was divided into three stages—the outer court, the holy place, and then the *sanctum sanctorum*, the Holy of Holies, where was enshrined the throne of God. God was the architect; He designed the place where He would meet with His people. It was the intersection at which His people could come near to Him and get a taste of heaven.

That is what we want every time we come together for worship, a taste of heaven.

24

HALLOWED BE YOUR NAME

Matthew 6:9–10

In this manner, therefore, pray:

> Our Father in heaven,
> Hallowed be Your name.
> Your kingdom come.
> Your will be done
> On earth as it is in heaven.

There are many today who say with assurance that the universe in which we live came into being out of nothing. That statement is not based on scientific fact. If you have an upset stomach and go to the doctor, the doctor is going to ask you questions and do an examination to try to find out the reason for your ailment. He considers all the possibilities before coming up with a diagnosis. When we consider the possibilities of anything, we first must eliminate the impossibilities. Once we have done that, we can examine the possibilities to see which one has the most evidence.

If we ask why are we here and why the world is here, we can eliminate the possibility that anything can ever come from nothing. The most fundamental principle of science is *ex nihilo nihil fit*, which means out of nothing, nothing comes. It is impossible for something to come out of nothing. Even God cannot bring Himself out of nothing. Therefore, anything or anyone in existence today has come from something that has always existed. If there ever was a time in which there was nothing—no God, no matter, no energy—then nothing could be in existence now. The fact that there is something now proves indisputably that there has always been something.

The naturalists say that such reasoning is philosophical or theological and not scientific. However, formal proof always trumps material proof. If you want me to prove that I use glasses, I can show them to you. You can then see them and are thereby given material proof. Conversely, formal proof is rational proof; it is logical and mathematical: 2 + 2 = 4. So which is a higher form of proof? Formal proof always trumps material proof. Logic always beats physical evidence. When the logic of a question is clear—in this case, that nothing can come from nothing—all the so-called mountain of evidence produced against that is always trumped by the formal principle.

Of First Importance

I mention all that because there is a certain logic in the Lord's Prayer. There is an interconnectedness to all the elements that Jesus taught us to pray in this prayer. The first petition is **"Hallowed be Your name"** (v. 9). When Jesus' disciples asked about how they should pray, Jesus tells them first to pray that the name of God would be regarded as holy, because God is holy. This means that God is other and different from anything that we experience or find in the material universe. That God, the Creator, differs from all creatures, and God differs from all creatures in that He is uncreated and eternal. Each of us has been created; we have a measurable age. We are not eternal; we are temporal. The Creator is separated from the creature by that high, transcendent element of God's own being. He is so majestic that He is worthy of the adoration of every creature.

Jesus is saying that, at the beginning of your prayer, you must distinguish the One to whom you are praying. The two things we must always remember when we pray are who God is and who we are. Doing so sets the structure and atmosphere of our conversation. So, Jesus says, when you pray, the first thing to do is identify the One to whom you are praying. The form of address that Jesus taught in this prayer is this: **"Our Father in heaven"** (v. 9).

With the rise of European continental liberalism in the nineteenth century, the effort, particularly in Germany, was to reduce Christianity and all world religions to a primary core. Along with this came the effort to reduce the essence of Christianity to its core. People such as Adolf von Harnack said that the essential message of Christianity is the universal fatherhood of God and the universal brotherhood of man. That concept is utterly alien to biblical Christianity, because the Bible does not teach the universal fatherhood of God. The Bible teaches that God is the universal Creator. It also teaches the universal neighborhood of man, that we are all neighbors and have been made by the same Creator. The language of family, however, has a narrow and special meaning in the Scripture.

Our Father

The German New Testament scholar Joachim Jeremias wrote a book several years ago in which he made the startling assertion that at no time in Jewish history and in no extant Jewish literature until the tenth century in Italy do we find a Jew addressing God as Father. The notable exception, he said, is found in Jesus' prayers in the New Testament. In all His prayers except one, Jesus addressed God directly as Father, and whenever He did it, His contemporaries picked up stones to kill Him, accusing Him of blasphemy. The point I am trying to make is that we use the opening statement of this prayer so routinely that we completely miss its radical significance. In biblical categories God has one Son, His only begotten Son. Therefore, the only person in history who ever had a legitimate right to call God "Father" was Jesus. Yet Jesus, when He tells His disciples how to pray, instructs them to address God as "our Father."

How can we legitimately address God as our Father when, by nature, we are the children of Satan? According to Scripture, we are children of wrath, and God is not our Father. We can call upon Him as our Father only because He has adopted us. The Scriptures tell us that it is only by the Holy Spirit, who has linked us to Christ and brought about our adoption into the family of God, that we can now say, "Abba, Father." Every time we pray the Lord's Prayer, we ought to be reminded that we are praying as God's adopted children and that our elder brother Jesus is the only natural child of God.

There is another sense in which the Old Testament speaks about the son of God. Metaphorically, Israel the nation was referred to as God's son. Earlier in Matthew's Gospel we read that Joseph was warned in a dream to flee from the wrath of King Herod. We are told, "When he arose, he took the young Child and His mother by night and departed for Egypt, and was there until the death of Herod, that it might be fulfilled which was spoken by the Lord through the prophet, saying, 'Out of Egypt I called My Son'" (Matt. 2:14–15). This refers to the exodus, when Israel, as God's child, was put into bondage in Egypt until God delivered them.

The Lord's Supper, which is rooted in the Old Testament Passover, was instituted by Jesus in His celebration of the Passover on the night before He was killed. During the Passover, the angel of death came at the bidding of God to bring the worst of all plagues against Pharaoh and Egypt. He came to slay the firstborn son in every Egyptian household, including Pharaoh's. God was saying to the most powerful ruler of the planet, "Pharaoh, since you will not respect my son, I am going to kill yours." The kings of this world have no respect for the son of God—His metaphorical son, Israel, or His perfect Son, Christ, or His adopted sons and daughters, us.

God's Will Be Done

"Your kingdom come. Your will be done on earth as it is in heaven" (v. 10). We live in a secular world in which people are doing everything in their power to erase any idea whatsoever that the world in which we live comes from the hand of God the Father Almighty, Maker of heaven and earth. If they can get rid of creation, they can get rid of God, and if they can get rid of God, they can get rid of law. If they can eliminate the Creator, they have no need for a redeemer, and there is nothing sacred left. Before God's kingdom can come and His will be done on earth as it is in heaven, the name of God has to be hallowed. There is no blasphemy in heaven. There is nothing profane in heaven. No one in heaven—seraphim, cherubim, or the spirits of men departed to the assembly on high—ever does anything but the will of God, and there it is done joyously, happily, and for His glory.

Jesus is telling His disciples that His Father, who dwells in heaven, sent Him to earth. The world is blinded to Him and to heaven, but our inheritance is in heaven. We cannot be a Christian while at the same time assuming that this world is all there is, because the radical proclamation of Jesus is that He comes from the presence of our Father, who is in heaven. Although He abides in heaven, He does not absent Himself from the earth.

25

THY KINGDOM COME

Matthew 6:9b–11

> Our Father in heaven,
> Hallowed be Your name.
> Your kingdom come.
> Your will be done
> On earth as it is in heaven.
> Give us this day our daily bread.

I had been a Christian for only a few months when I was invited to a Christmas party hosted by my pastor and his wife at their home. The minister did not believe in the miracles of Jesus or in the resurrection of Christ and was somewhat annoyed at my newfound zeal for biblical Christianity. At the party he called me aside and asked me, "R.C., what is the kingdom of God?" I did not know how to answer him. How would you answer that question? The easy answer is that any king's kingdom extends to the limits of his realm. Since we understand that God is the creator of all things and that He reigns omnipotent over all, the extent of His realm must be the whole world. So the easy answer is that the kingdom of God is wherever He reigns, and since He reigns everywhere, the kingdom of God is everywhere.

However, I think my pastor was getting at something else, and certainly the New Testament gets at something else when we see that John the Baptist begins his ministry with an announcement capped with urgency: "Repent, for the kingdom of heaven is at hand!" (Matt. 3:2). Jesus began His earthly ministry with the same pronouncement, saying, "Repent, for the kingdom of heaven is at hand" (Matt. 4:17). If the kingdom of God is simply all the universe over which God reigns, why would they have announced that the kingdom of heaven or of God was near or about to come to pass? Obviously John the Baptist and Jesus meant something more than what we would think of in these general terms. In fact, if there is any one motif that ties together the Old and New Testaments, it is the kingdom of God.

God's Kingdom Come

At the heart of that theme is God's messianic kingdom, a kingdom that will be ruled by God's Messiah, whom He has appointed to be not only the Redeemer of His people but also their King. So when John comes on the scene and speaks of the radical nearness of this breakthrough of the kingdom, he is speaking of the kingdom of the Messiah.

As Jesus was about to depart from this earth and stood on the mount of ascension, His disciples asked Him, "Lord, will You at this time restore the kingdom to Israel?" (Acts 1:6). I imagine that even in His resurrected state He might have been somewhat frustrated by their question, but He gave them a patient, gentle answer: "It is not for you to know times or seasons which the Father has put in His own authority. But you shall receive power when the Holy Spirit has come upon you; and you shall be witnesses to Me in Jerusalem, and in all Judea and Samaria, and to the end of the earth" (vv. 7–8).

During His trial before Pilate, Jesus was asked whether there was truth to what people were saying, that Jesus was a king. Jesus replied, "My kingdom is not of this world. If My kingdom were of this world, My servants would fight, so that I should not be delivered to the Jews; but now My kingdom is not from here" (John 18:36). The Old Testament was calling attention not to a kingdom that would simply appear in people's hearts but to a kingdom that would break through into this world under the rule of God's anointed Messiah. During His earthly ministry Jesus said, "If I cast out demons with the finger of God, surely the kingdom of God has come upon you" (Luke 11:20). On another occasion He said, "The kingdom of God has come near to you" (Luke 10:9, 11). The kingdom of God was in their midst because the King of the kingdom was in their midst.

Jesus inaugurated God's kingdom when He came. He did not consummate it, but He started it, and He promised a time when that kingdom would reach a penultimate climax, when He ascended into heaven and sat enthroned at God's right hand. He did not ascend just to be our High Priest. He went up for

His coronation as the King of kings and the Lord of lords. His kingship is not something delayed for the future. Christ is King right this minute. He is in the seat of the highest cosmic authority. All authority on heaven and on earth has been given to God's anointed Son.

"Your kingdom come" (v. 10). Several years ago I accepted an invitation to do a series of lectures in Eastern Europe. The third leg of the trip was in Romania, and as we prepared to go there from Budapest, we were warned that the border guards in Romania were hostile to Americans. We boarded a train and rode throughout Hungary until we reached the border of Romania. There were four of us traveling together. At one stop two guards got on the train. They could not speak English, but they indicated rudely that they wanted to see our passports and our luggage. Suddenly another burly officer boarded the train who did speak some broken English. He looked over and noticed that one of my traveling companions had a paper bag on her lap, and the guard opened the bag and pulled out a Bible. The guard began leafing through the Bible. He finally stopped and looked at our group, and he said, "You are not Americans." He pointed to the Bible text he had open, which said, "We are citizens of the commonwealth of heaven." The guard was a Christian, and he turned to his subordinate and told him to not harass us. With much relief I realized that this guard understood something about the kingdom of God—our first place of citizenship is in the kingdom of God.

Many years ago an evangelist named John Guest came from England to Philadelphia. He recounted to me that he spent his first few days in America going to antiques stores in the Germantown section of the city, particularly those that focused on Revolutionary War memorabilia. He came across a placard that dated back to the eighteenth century and contained the phrase "We serve no sovereign here." He shared with me the dilemma this posed: "How can I preach the gospel of the kingdom of God to people who will not have a sovereign to rule over them?"

I experienced a crisis on this same point when I was a student pastor at a small Hungarian refugee church in Western Pennsylvania in a steel mill town. Someone donated to the church an American flag, and I put the flag across the chancel from the Christian flag. The next week one of the elders, a war veteran, told me that any time a flag is displayed alongside the American flag, it must be placed in a subordinate position to the American flag. I thought, *How can the Christian flag be subordinate to any national flag?* The kingdom of God trumps every earthly kingdom. I did not want to break the American law, so I solved the dilemma by removing the flags. I love America, and I honor its traditions, but I am a Christian first and an American second. I owe allegiance to the American flag, but I owe a higher allegiance to Christ, because He is my King.

As I mentioned before, there is a certain logic that runs like a ribbon through the Lord's Prayer. Each of the petitions is connected to the others. The first petition that Jesus taught us to pray is "Hallowed be Your name." We pray that the name of God will be regarded as holy, because until or unless the name of God is regarded as holy, His kingdom will not and cannot come to this world.

The Lord says elsewhere that a day will come when the kingdom will be consummated and that every knee of every tribe and people will bow before Jesus (Rom. 14:11), but if you read that text closely, you will see that some who bow will get on their knees in joyful adoration and love, but others will be forced to their knees because they will not have Him as their King. There are multitudes today who will not submit to His kingdom, but God tells us that on the last day every knee will bow, some willingly and others reluctantly. They will have no choice but to bow, because God is going to break their knees with a rod of iron and make sure that everyone pays homage to His Son.

John Calvin said it is the task of the church to make the invisible kingdom visible, but how do we bear witness to the reality of a kingdom that already exists? We live in such a way as to bear witness to the reality of the kingship of Christ, at work, within our family, in our school, and with our checkbook, because God in Christ is King over every one of these spheres of our life. The only way the kingdom of God is going to be manifest in this world before Christ comes is if we manifest it in our lives.

God's Will

Immediately after that, Jesus says that we should pray, **"Your will be done on earth as it is in heaven"** (v. 10). If you look at the New Testament and examine the concept of the will of God, you will see that the words translated as the English word *will* are multiple and have a variety of meanings. There are six or seven different meanings pertaining to the will of God in the Bible. But the two most numerous and most basic are what we find here.

The first one refers to what we call the "sovereign, efficacious will of God," the will of God that comes to pass according to His decree. When God created the heaven and the earth, He did not ask permission. When God said, "Let there be light" there wasn't any debate; the lights came on. That is a manifestation of the sovereign will of God. Whatsoever God wills must necessarily come to pass. That is the sovereign will not only by which the worlds were made but also by which God redeemed our soul. It is the will whereby He sovereignly bestowed

His grace upon us and brought us to Himself. Sometimes that is called God's hidden will, as distinguished from His revealed will.

When people ask me how they can know the will of God for their life, they are usually speaking about His hidden will. I try to be gentle with my answer. We cannot know the hidden will of God, because it is none of our business. That is precisely why it is the hidden will of God. We need to spend far less time worrying about the hidden will of God and more time focused on the revealed will of God. The Scriptures say, "This is the will of God, your sanctification" (1 Thess. 4:3). Therefore, whatever job you have, whatever town you live in, whom you marry, and the names you give to your children are all of secondary importance to the primary will of God for your life, which is your sanctification.

That immediately ties this concept of the will of God to the second most important meaning of it in Scripture, and that is His prescriptive will, which is revealed in His precepts and commandments. When Jesus instructed us to pray, "Your will be done on earth even as it is in heaven," He was not talking about the sovereign will of God, because we do not need to pray for that. It is done on earth as it is done in heaven. Obviously Jesus was talking about the prescriptive will of God, which is to be obeyed here as it is every second by everyone in heaven. This is simply a reflection of what Jesus said elsewhere: "If you love Me, keep My commandments" (John 14:15).

We would be dreadfully hypocritical if we were to pray that God's name be hallowed, that His kingdom come, and that His will be done on earth as it is in heaven if we are really thinking, "But not in my life." Every time we pray the Lord's Prayer we are asking that God will work in us to obey His will on earth as it is obeyed in heaven. We are not supposed to wait until Jesus comes back to be working on the manifestation of His kingdom and His will.

26

DAILY BREAD

Matthew 6:11

Give us this day our daily bread.

Christians commonly use the acrostic ACTS to guide their prayers. The letters represent the four elements of our prayer: adoration, confession, thanksgiving, and supplication. We tend, however, to start with "S." We cannot wait to get into the presence of God with our wish list and supplications. I like that acrostic because it puts the elements of prayer into balance.

The beginning of our prayer should be adoration, which is how the Lord's Prayer begins: "Hallowed be Your name." As we grow in the discipline and delight of prayer, more of our time is spent in that first element, adoration. The psalms, inspired examples of godly prayer, are heavily weighted on the side of adoration. Additionally, we should confess our sins in all our prayers—the "C" of the acrostic—remembering who we are when we come into God's presence. The Apostle Paul tells us that we should always pray with thanksgiving (1 Thess. 5:18). Those are important elements to every prayer, and then we come to the end of the acrostic, which is "S" for supplication. Here we ask God to meet our needs.

The hymn "Breathe on Me, Breath of God" contains a line that I do not like: "Teach us the patience of unanswered prayer." There is no such thing as unanswered prayer. God answers all our prayers, but when He says no, we assume that He either has not heard or has not answered. No is an answer, and we need to be ready to hear it, even as our Lord was willing to hear that answer in His agony in Gethsemane.

Supplication

The pattern of the Lord's Prayer begins with the form of address and moves through the petitions so that the focus of the prayer in its initial stages is on God's glory and on God's kingdom. Our prayers must be kingdom focused, yet at this point in the Lord's Prayer, there is a shift where now we ask God to do something for us: **"Give us this day our daily bread."**

There is a lot contained in that simple request. It does not say, "Sell us this day our daily bread," nor is there any attempt to bribe God. We are asking for God to give us a gift. We should ask God to give us our daily bread, which reveals to us our constant dependence on the gifts of God. Every good and perfect gift we receive comes ultimately from His hand (James 1:17). He is a giving God. He is a God of providence. This is a request of His providence. "In your sovereign providence, Oh God, as you relate to us, as you care for us, please provide us with our necessities for life in this world." Our necessities are basically summarized in this concept of daily bread.

After God promised Abraham that he would be the father of a great nation and that his descendants would be as the grains of sand on the seashore and as the stars in the sky, many years elapsed until finally Sarah brought forth a son whose name was Isaac. There was no happier set of parents in all of history than those two were the day that that promise was fulfilled. Later, however, God came to Abraham and said, "Take now your son, your only son Isaac, whom you love, and go to the land of Moriah, and offer him there as a burnt offering on one of the mountains of which I shall tell you" (Gen. 22:2). In other words, "I gave you this gift, and now I want you to give it back." As father and son made a three-day journey in the middle of this heart-wrenching episode, Isaac looked at the wood for the fire that the beast of burden was carrying, but he was puzzled and turned to his father and said, "Where is the lamb for a burnt offering?" (v. 7). Abraham replied, "My son, God will provide for Himself the lamb for a burnt offering" (v. 8).

Daily Bread

That is the first time in the Bible that the idea of divine providence is mentioned. Providence is about God's provision, and an integral element of that provision is not only what we need for salvation but also food to eat, water to drink, clothes to wear, and shelter for our bodies. In God's providence He makes the crops grow; He gives us what we need for daily life, and that gift of providence is all summed up in the element of bread.

It is important to note that there is a synergistic relationship between divine providence and our labor. God commands and demands that we be productive in our labor. With respect to the provision of our daily needs, the Apostle Paul tells us that he who fails to provide for his own household is worse than an unbeliever (1 Tim. 5:8). So on one hand we have to trust in the benevolent providence of God to help us receive our daily bread, and on the other hand we are to be industrious, doing all that we can to provide for our families. We call the wage earner of a household the "breadwinner." Even in American slang the word *bread* is a synonym for money. There is a link between providing for the welfare of our families and the rudimentary basis of that provision being found in bread, which has been called historically the staff of life.

We are to ask God to give us our daily bread. There is some debate about the exact import of the word "daily" here. Presumably, if the prayer is made in the morning, we are praying for bread for that day, and if we pray at night, we are asking for bread for tomorrow. There are basically three reasons for the emphasis on "daily" bread. One reason is that we need to be on our knees acknowledging our dependence upon the good providence of God to sustain us day to day. The second reason comes from the fact that the majority of wage earners at that time were paid on a daily basis. They would get a small sum every day for their wages, and they had to make it count every day.

When we lived in Holland in a village where hardly anyone spoke English, Sherrie, our daughter, was about three years old. The first Dutch word she learned was *snopje*, which means "a little piece of candy." A knock would come on the door every morning as the baker arrived, and Sherry's job was to answer the door. She would look at the baker and say in Dutch, "Good morning, Mr. Baker—a half a loaf of sliced bread, please." That is the first basic sentence she learned to speak, and she mastered that phrase because she said it every day. The reason we had bread delivered every day was that it was virtually inedible after one day. There were no preservatives used, and the nutrients had not been emptied from it.

However, this petition speaks far beyond the need for simple bread. It is a request that God will give us what we need to eat. Maybe there are times when people have to subsist on bread and water; such is the case for prisoners of war and for people in the midst of famine.

I remember the poignant story recounted by a nurse who worked in an orphanage after the Korean War. Some children who had experienced severe hunger before coming to live at the orphanage were unable to fall asleep at night. Their inability to sleep came from the fear that they might again find themselves destitute. The nurse came up with an idea: every night when she tucked the children into bed she gave each one a piece of bread. This served to remove the children's anxiety, and each night they went to sleep clutching that bread and knowing that tomorrow they would not starve.

I doubt that any of us have experienced real hunger. We have food and water in abundance in our country while literally millions of people around the world, particularly in Africa, go to bed each night wondering if they are going to die of hunger or thirst. It is God who provides these necessities, so we ought to pray not only for our daily bread but for daily bread for others. We should pray that they will have water fit to drink not only for themselves but for their livestock. Even today there are many people who suffer malnutrition and death because their animals are undernourished. That's the world we live in, the world that Christ came into. It is our Father's world, and He has invited us to go to Him and ask for our daily bread and water.

27

FORGIVE US OUR DEBTS

Matthew 6:12

And forgive us our debts,
as we forgive our debtors.

We have already considered the prayer acrostic ACTS, in which "C" stands for confession. The confession of sin ought to be a regular part of both our private and corporate prayers. Here our Lord is teaching that the prayer of confession and the request for forgiveness are an integral part of the model prayer, so He says in this petition that we are to say to God, **"Forgive us our debts, as we forgive our debtors"** (v. 12).

Another rendering of this petition is, "Forgive us our trespasses as we forgive those who trespass against us." Either one is correct. Both accurately communicate the sense of the text here in Matthew and also how it is framed in Luke's Gospel. Luke uses the word "sins" and Matthew uses the word "debts." As we consider the nature of the sin for which we need to be forgiven, we will consider three different dimensions or aspects of sin. The New Testament describes sin in three primary ways: (1) as a debt; (2) as a crime or transgression against the law of God; and (3) as an act of enmity or hostility that estranges us from our Creator. When we ask for forgiveness, we are asking it for all three of these elements of sin.

Sin Is Debt

First, then, sin is a debt. Debts are obligations that we owe to another. We usually think of debt in monetary terms, but there are pecuniary debts, which are monetary, and moral debts. Picture a young boy who walks into an ice cream parlor and orders an ice cream cone with two scoops. When the server hands the cone to the child, she says, "That will be two dollars." The boy's lips begin to quiver, and he looks helplessly to the waitress and says, "My mommy gave me only one dollar." What would you do if you were a witness? You would do what anyone would do. You would reach in your pocket, hand the server a dollar, and say, "Let me satisfy the young boy's debt." The money you supply is legal tender. The server has to accept that in payment, and the little boy can now enjoy his ice cream cone.

Suppose we look at the scenario a bit differently. The boy places his order, and as soon as the server hands him the cone, he runs out of the store without paying. Unfortunately for him, he runs right into the arms of a policeman on his beat while the employee is screaming, "Stop, thief!" So the policeman brings the boy by the scruff of his neck back into the store and asks the employee what has happened. She explains that the boy has stolen the ice cream cone. You witness all this, so you reach into your pocket and say, "Wait a minute, officer. Please don't put this boy in jail. Don't press charges against him. I'll pay the two dollars." This time the employee does not have to accept your money because the debt is moral, not simply monetary.

I typically use this illustration to deepen our understanding of what took place on the cross, when the Son paid our debt that the Father was not required to accept but did in mercy and grace. The Bible uses a metaphor of debt to describe us as sinners who cannot possibly pay our debts. We are debtors who simply cannot pay.

If someone claimed that I owed him $10,000 and threatened me with jail unless I could come up with the money, I think I could find a way to raise the money to keep myself out of jail. But if someone claimed that I owed him $4 billion, there is no way I could pay him. That is a poor analogy, because our obligation to God is far greater than that. He has commanded us to be holy even as He is holy; He commands us to be perfect even as He is perfect. We have fallen so short of His standard that it is virtually impossible for us to pay our debt. We hear it said that everyone is entitled to one mistake, but the only thing we are entitled to is everlasting punishment in hell. By virtue of our sin we hold the title to our own just punishment. God never said we are entitled to one mistake, and even if we were, how long ago did we make it? We have sinned against God and His perfect holiness multiple times since we got out of bed this morning, and when we sin against God, we add to our accounts before Him one more bit of wrath.

The Apostle Paul describes impenitent people as those who are treasuring up wrath against the day of wrath. Every day that you linger in this life without falling on your knees and asking God to forgive you of your debts, you increase that treasury of wrath. Jesus loved people enough to warn them and to teach them to beg God for forgiveness. We are debtors who cannot pay our debts, and when that debt is called in, it will be the most severe crisis that you can imagine if you must pay it yourself. We have witnessed in recent years the calamity of multiple foreclosures on mortgages because people cannot pay their debts, but that is nothing to be compared with the debt that we owe to God. That is why Jesus said that when we pray, we are to ask the Father to forgive our debts.

Sin Is Crime

Sin is also a crime. The Westminster Catechism asks, "What is sin?" and the answer given is, "Sin is any want of conformity to or transgression of the law of God." Imagine if someone were to be arrested for first-degree murder. A video camera captured his bloody act, and there are witnesses who will testify that he boasted days earlier of his intent to murder. The evidence is brought before the court and indicates overwhelmingly the guilt of the accused, but the defendant pleads not guilty and asks to function as his own lawyer. He tells the judge, "I cannot be guilty, because I do not feel guilty." That is not a legitimate defense. The question of guilt is not one of feeling. It is not subjective but objective. It is a question of whether someone has, in fact, broken the law. If he has broken the law, he has transgressed the law and is therefore guilty.

Jeremiah criticized the people of Israel for becoming so hard of heart that they had acquired the forehead of a harlot (Jer. 3:3). Jeremiah was saying to the people of Israel that they had seared their consciences to the point that they could sin with no pangs of guilt. It bears repeating that God will not judge us by our feelings. He will judge us by His law, and His judgment will be perfect and completely just. The one thing we never want to have to face is the just judgment of God.

The only hope we have is His grace and mercy. The whole of Christianity is about forgiveness. A Christian person is a forgiven person. As someone put it, "I have no righteousness in myself, so when I proclaim the gospel, I am just one beggar telling other beggars where they can find food." That is our state. As people who have violated God, we have committed treason against Him. In every sin we commit, no matter how small, we assert our authority and will over His and defy His power by our own. That is the folly of sin.

Sin Is Hostility

Sin is also an act of hostility. It is an act of estrangement whereby we are left in a serious need for reconciliation. The Bible is all about reconciliation. The one necessary condition that must exist before reconciliation can happen is estrangement. People who are not estranged have no need for reconciliation. We are by nature the enemies of God. In our natural state we are, as Scripture tells us, at war with God Himself. Man in his natural state does not believe he is hostile to God, but the Bible tells us that man prior to regeneration hates God.

In Jonathan Edwards's sermon "Man Naturally God's Enemies," he explored why man in his natural state is hostile toward God, and he identified a few aspects of God's nature that provoke hostility within us. First and foremost is that God is holy and we are not, and unholy people do not appreciate a standard that reveals their unrighteousness. If God were not so holy and we were not so sinful, perhaps we could get along, but there is that irreparable breach between fallen humanity and the eternal holiness of God that can be healed only by the mediating work of the Savior and the forgiveness He offers.

The second reason we hate God by nature, Edwards said, is that God is omniscient, and since that is the case, there is nowhere we can hide from Him. We can hide from the gaze of humans in our private sin, but there is nowhere we can hide from God. David said:

> Where can I flee from Your spirit?
> Or where can I flee from Your presence?
> If I ascend into heaven, You are there;
> If I make my bed in hell, behold, You are there. (Ps. 139:7–8)

When I was a boy, my mother worked at the office with my father, so I had a lot of free, unsupervised time. My mother would tell me, "I can't watch you today, but God is watching you." After growing up, going to college and seminary, and learning some theology, I realized that the simple way in which my mother had talked about God was exactly right. Nothing escapes His notice. Jesus said that every idle word we speak will be brought into judgment (Matt. 12:36). I can imagine standing before the bar of God's justice while He brings out a recording of my life so that I have to listen to every offensive thing I said during my life. I do not want that to happen. I want my sin to be covered long before I get to that point.

The third thing Edwards said we hate about God is His omnipotence. If He were impotent, we would have nothing to worry about, but He is all-powerful.

There is no force in heaven and on earth that can subdue His strength. As the psalmist declares:

> The kings of the earth set themselves,
> And the rulers take counsel together,
> Against the LORD and against His Anointed, saying,
> "Let us break Their bonds in pieces
> And cast away Their cords from us."
>
> He who sits in the heavens shall laugh.
> The Lord shall hold them in derision.
> Then He shall speak to them in His wrath,
> And distress them in His deep displeasure:
> "Yet I have set My King
> On My holy hill of Zion." . . .
>
> Now therefore, be wise, O kings;
> Be instructed, you judges of the earth.
> Serve the LORD with fear,
> And rejoice with trembling.
> Kiss the Son, lest He be angry,
> And you perish in the way. (Ps. 2:2–6, 10–12)

Jeremiah cried out to God, "You induced me, and I was persuaded; You are stronger than I, and have prevailed" (Jer. 20:7). If God overwhelms us, nothing could be more tautological than to say that we have been overwhelmed. Nothing we do can defeat the power of God.

Edwards gave those three and then one more. The fourth thing about God that we hate is His immutability. God is unchanging. Why would we be hostile toward God's immutability? Edwards anticipated our mystification and explained that since God is immutable, not only has He been absolutely holy from everlasting to everlasting, but there is no hope that He will ever stop being holy. Sometimes we root for righteous people to fail so that we will not be embarrassed by their excellence. God's holiness is an immutable holiness. We cannot hope that at some day in the future, God's omniscience will fail Him.

When we talk about being forgiven, we say that God not only forgives our sin but also forgets it. We are tempted to think of this as some sort of memory lapse on God's part so that once He has forgiven us, He cannot recall that we had ever sinned. That is not what God's forgetting is about. God still knows every sin that we have ever committed and that He has forgiven. He will always have that knowledge because that knowledge is immutable. When the Bible speaks of His forgetting our sins, it means that He remembers them against us no more. He is fully aware of our transgressions, but He does not remind us. He does not call them to mind or hold them against us. That is the essence of forgiveness, and we need to imitate that in this world. When we offer someone forgiveness, we are making a commitment never to bring up the wrong again. If he does the same sin to us again, we still cannot hold it against him. To forgive is to erase the slate. Our culture today, however, has a cheap understanding of forgiveness.

Finally, there is no hope that God will ever lose any of His power. His right arm will not be weakened. He will be in eternity as omnipotent then as He is today. All of this teaches us that God is a formidable opponent. When we are hostile toward Him and estranged, we are in a battle we cannot possibly win. The only way the battle can end is by our unconditional surrender, which is what we are doing when we get on our knees and say, "Forgive us our debts." That is an act of giving up and saying, "God, I cannot fight you. I do not want to be estranged from you but restored. I want to be able to love you, not hate you, and I want you to love me in spite of my hostility toward you."

Forgive Us Our Debts

With respect to this petition we are told to ask God to "forgive us our debts, as we forgive our debtors." The best commentators tell us at this point that if we were to take this literally, we would be finished, because if God forgave us in exact proportion to how we forgive others, we would perish. Thank God that this is an aspiration rather than a condition. Jesus is teaching us to aspire to reflect the kindness of God and to be ready to forgive anyone who has sinned against us or offended us when he repents.

There is a lot to learn in this petition; we have only scratched the surface of what sin is about and what forgiveness means. There is no greater experience than to get up off your knees knowing that in God's sight you are clean and that He has forgiven every sin you have ever committed. That grace—that forgiveness—is something we all need, and we need it desperately.

28

LEAD US NOT INTO TEMPTATION

Matthew 6:13a

And do not lead us into temptation,
but deliver us from the evil one.

The petition in verse 12 of the Lord's Prayer, "Forgive us our debts, as we forgive our debtors," concerns our past sins. Here in verse 13 the accent of the prayer turns to our vulnerability to sins beyond today and into tomorrow. The structure of this verse follows a typical Hebrew literary strategy called "parallelism," in which two statements are linked together so that the second statement illumines the significance of the first.

The first statement reads, **"Do not lead us into temptation."** That very idea should jar our sensibilities to some degree, because nothing would be further from the character of God than that He would entice us to sin. James teaches, "Let no one say when he is tempted, 'I am tempted by God'; for God cannot be tempted by evil, nor does He Himself tempt anyone" (James 1:13). He goes on to explain that enticement and temptation to sin arise from within, from our own evil inclinations and desires. External temptations can come to us from fellow sinners or from Satan himself, who is known frequently in the Bible as "the tempter." The way to understand this petition in the Lord's Prayer is through an alternate rendering: "Lead us not into the place of testing." Jesus is teaching us to pray that the Father will never ever put us in a place where we will have to undergo a severe test of our faith or obedience.

The second clause of verse 13 reads, **"but deliver us from the evil one."** Some translations render "Deliver us from evil"; however, the context and grammar of this passage lean heavily in the direction of the former translation. We are not merely to pray that we will not be delivered into evil in general but that we will be protected from the wiles of Satan. We are to pray that we will not be exposed to the onslaught of his attacks against us, to the ways in which he tries to entice us to sin or destroy our confidence in our Savior by accusing us of our failures and imperfections. In view in this portion of the Lord's Prayer is being kept from a place of testing.

The Place of Testing

In Genesis 1 and 2 we read of the creation of the universe and how our first parents, Adam and Eve, enjoyed the pristine purity of the garden of Eden. However, when we get to Genesis 3 there is a sense of foreboding as something dark and sinister is introduced into redemptive history with the seemingly innocuous words, "The serpent was more cunning than any beast of the field" (Gen. 3:1). What follows in that narrative is the attempt by the Serpent to persuade Adam and Eve to follow him rather than their Creator, and he comes simply with a question about God's authority: "Has God indeed said?" (v. 1). This is followed immediately by a frontal assault: "You will not surely die. For God knows that in the day you eat of it your eyes will be opened, and you will be like God, knowing good and evil" (vv. 4–5).

From a theological perspective we see this encounter as integral to the outcome of Adam's probation. There was a tree from which he was not allowed to eat, but he failed the test. He succumbed to the subtle wiles of the Evil One and plunged the entire race into ruin and brought death into the world. That was a monumental test, a supremely important trial; and the one God had created in His own image failed it miserably.

Job, although a member of the fallen race of Adam, nevertheless distinguished himself by his extraordinary righteousness and obedience. In the opening scene of the book of Job, God rebuts the accusation of Satan with a question: "Have you considered My servant Job, that there is none like him on the earth, a blameless and upright man, one who fears God and shuns evil?" (Job 1:8).

The response of Satan is one of sneering contempt. "Does Job fear God for nothing? Have You not made a hedge around him, around his household, and around all that he has on every side? You have blessed the work of his hands, and his possessions have increased in the land. But now, stretch out Your hand and touch all that he has, and he will surely curse You to Your face!" (vv. 9–11).

God replies, "Behold, all that he has is in your power; only do not lay a hand on his person" (v. 12).

If any man in the history of the world was subjected to every dreadful attack that Satan could make, it was Job. He lost his livestock, his family, and his reputation. His friends deserted him. His body became covered with sores so that he sat in misery on a dung hill cursing the day he was born. In the midst of his hellish suffering, his wife, who was feeling the horror that her husband was enduring, became an instrument of the Serpent when she said, "Curse God and die!" (2:9).

Job could hardly speak, but during his ordeal he said, "Though He slay me, yet will I trust Him" (13:15). That is what it means to be a servant of God. He also said, "I know that my Redeemer lives, and He shall stand at last on the earth" (19:25). Job passed the test, and God honored and blessed him and restored the things he had lost.

Our father Abraham, believing against all things that were seen, hung tenaciously to God's promise that Abraham would be a father of a great nation and that he would have a son from his wife. He waited, and his wife laughed in scorn, yet in their old age God fulfilled His promise and the child of promise was born. To Abraham and Sarah's household came unmeasured jubilation. They exulted in the lad until that dreadful day when God put Abraham to the test: "Take now your son, your only son Isaac, whom you love, and go to the land of Moriah, and offer him there as a burnt offering on one of the mountains of which I shall tell you" (Gen. 22:2).

Can you imagine a test more terrifying than the one God gave to Abraham? He rose up early in the morning and saddled his beasts of burden and took his son and the wood that he himself had hewn on a journey to Mount Moriah. He tied Isaac with ropes, put the wood on the altar, and raised his knife. At the last possible second, we read:

> The Angel of the Lord called to him from heaven and said, "Abraham, Abraham!" So he said, "Here I am." And He said, "Do not lay your hand on the lad, or do anything to him; for now I know that you fear God, since you have not withheld your son, your only son, from Me." Then Abraham lifted his eyes and looked, and there behind him was a ram caught in a thicket by its horns. So Abraham went and took the ram, and offered it up for a burnt offering instead of his son. And Abraham called the name of the place, The-Lord-Will-Provide; as it is said to this day, "In the Mount of the Lord it shall be provided." (vv. 11–14)

He had provided a substitute to be slain in the place of Abraham's son. Tradition indicates that this was the spot where, two thousand years later, God offered His only Son, the Son whom He loved, Jesus. The mountain was by then no longer called Moriah but Calvary, and this time there was no ram caught in the thicket.

The worst test ever endured by a human being was the one given to Jesus, when immediately after His anointing as the Messiah of Israel, the Spirit of God drove Him into the Judean wilderness to be tempted by the devil for forty days. We looked at that trial in an earlier study, yet we still have no idea all that was endured by our Lord. Whereas the first Adam fell to a simple seductive suggestion, the last Adam endured everything that hell could throw at Him in His isolated, lonely forty-day trial. We are told by Luke that after Jesus had passed the test, Satan "departed from Him until an opportune time" (Luke 4:13). Satan kept coming back to tempt Him, to try to make Him fall.

Church history is replete with further examples of Christians being put to the test. We think sometimes because people make fun of us for being Christians that we are tested, yet none of us has been tested like Adam, Abraham, Job, or our Lord. Hugh Latimer and Nicholas Ridley were burned at the stake for teaching justification by faith alone, and when they were tied together at that stake, Latimer said, "Be of good comfort, Mr. Ridley, and play the man; we shall this day light such a candle by God's grace in England, as I trust never shall be put out." John Huss burned for his faith. Polycarp, the bishop of Smyrna, was taken into the stadium in his late eighties and told by the proconsul, "Renounce Jesus and the atheists and your life will be spared." (The emperor considered Christians to be atheists because they did not believe in the deity of the emperor himself.) Polycarp said, "Eighty and six years has Christ been faithful to me and I would betray Him now?" He looked to the stands of the stadium and to the box that held the proconsul and said, "Away with the atheists." He was martyred a few moments later.

I ask myself what I would do if faced with a similar test. I do not know, and I do not want to have to find out. Every time I pray the Lord's Prayer, I am asking that I will not be placed in such a situation. This petition is for divine protection from all the forces of evil that surround us, and we should be praying it not only for ourselves but also for each other, so if the test comes we will stand.

29

THINE IS THE KINGDOM

Matthew 6:13b

For Yours is the kingdom and the power and the glory forever. Amen.

My normal procedure in sermon preparation is to study the text, then carefully look at it in Greek and Latin, and then consult four or five commentaries to see what insights I might gain from others who have studied it. In preparing for this study, I examined no less than ten commentaries, and I was astonished to discover that not a single one included more than two sentences about this conclusion to the Lord's Prayer.

There are two reasons for the lack of space given to it in the commentaries. The first concerns a textual problem. Many of the ancient manuscripts include this doxological ending to the prayer, but some other ancient manuscripts do not, among them the Codex Vaticanus, which is one of the most important of these ancient texts. As a result, there is widespread opinion among scholars that the ending was not in the original prayer but was added soon afterwards because it was customary among the Jews to conclude their prayers with a doxology. Even among the scholars who are persuaded that this was in the original prayer, little or no attention is given to it. They tend to treat it as a sort of postscript, a line not all that important, particularly in light of the major petitions that precede it. I am bothered by that because this is one of the most important portions of the Lord's Prayer, if not *the* most important. There are four or five things to notice as we incline our hearts to these words.

Reverence

First, it is likely that the vast majority of us learned to recite "Thine is the kingdom" rather than "Yours is the kingdom." On the one hand, there is no difference at all, because the word *thine* means the same thing as the word *yours*. On the other hand, there is all the difference in the world. Our study of Matthew is based on the New King James Version of the Bible, which is distinguished from the old King James Version. The principal difference between the two is that the New King James Version as well as other more recent translations change all the Elizabethan personal pronouns because they are seen as impediments to our reading of the text. People just do not speak that way anymore, so, in order to make the Bible more accessible, translators have modernized the personal pronouns. In my study of languages, I have noticed that almost every language in the Western world makes a clear distinction between the informal and the formal personal pronouns. When I went to school in a foreign culture I had to learn the difference. If I had addressed my professor with the informal usage of "you," I expect I would have been expelled on the spot because the formal use of the pronoun is built into the language to communicate respect.

Similarly, worship is to be marked by a spirit of reverence and adoration. We are to come, as it were, on bended knee, paying homage to our God. Well-meaning translators change the divine pronouns to make God seem less distant and more approachable, but, as the cliché says, familiarity breeds contempt. There is a thin line here, because the Bible encourages us to come boldly into the presence of God. We are even told to address Him as "Abba, Father." At the same time, we are never to be casual in the presence of God.

I like the ancient personal pronouns because they remind me, particularly when I use them in prayer, to whom I am speaking. I am in the presence of the Holy One. I am in the presence of the transcendent majesty of God, who deserves every ounce of respect I can possibly give Him and then some. For that reason, I prefer to say, "*Thine* is the kingdom."

Ruler of All

The other aspect of the word *thine* that is so vitally important is its possessive dimension. The Lord's Prayer ends with an acknowledgment of what is owned by God alone. The first thing we see in this conclusion is that the kingdom belongs to Him—"Thine is the kingdom." It is not our kingdom; it is His.

While reading the newspaper recently, I came across a ten-question quiz designed to test readers' knowledge of the Revolutionary War and the founding of the United States. One question in the quiz bothered me: "What kind of government did we establish—an oligarchy, an aristocracy, an indirect democracy, or a direct democracy?" The correct answer was not provided as an option: none of the above. The United States of America was not founded as a democracy, either direct or indirect. It was founded as a republic. There is a huge difference between the two. Another question asked which thinkers influenced the framers of our Constitution and the Declaration of Independence, and among the choices was the British empiricist John Locke, who along with others contributed the social contract theory of government. In our country the rulers rule on the basis of the consent of the governed. It is a social contract. It is a government of the people, by the people, and for the people. Not so the kingdom of God. The kingdom of God is not of the people, by the people, or for the people; it is God's kingdom. God does not rule by consent of the governed. God rules by His sovereign authority. His reign extends over us whether or not we vote for Him.

God's Power

Martyn Lloyd-Jones was one of the greatest preachers of the twentieth century. While in the heyday of his preaching ministry in London, there were three world-famous preachers in that city. A visitor in London visited the church where each man preached, and afterward he said that the first man preached the love of God, the second one preached Jesus, and the third, Lloyd-Jones, preached God. That is what preaching ought to be. Martyn Lloyd-Jones said that no matter how eloquent or persuasive a preacher, without the accompanying power of God the Holy Spirit his sermons are impotent. That is why the Old Testament priests were called to weep between the porch and the altar and to pray between the study and the pulpit, because unless the Spirit takes this Word to his heart, he is completely helpless.

I hear people say that they have gone to a particular church and got nothing out of it. I want to reply, "So what! It is not about you." How can anyone sit under the Word of God and get nothing out of it? How could we even hear the Word read and get nothing out of it? If we get nothing out of it, that ought to spark an alarm in our brain that maybe we are unconverted. A converted person feasts upon the Word of God, no matter how poorly it is communicated.

The Greek word for "power" in verse 13 is *dynamis*. The Holy Spirit is frequently called the power of God, the *Dunamis*. From that word we get the English word *dynamite*. When you hear the Word, and the Spirit takes it to you, it explodes in your soul. Every Christian knows that to be true. It is never the preacher's power or the power of those listening in the pews. The greatest weakness in the church today is that it no longer believes that Scripture is where God invests His power. Everyone is looking for power in a program or a methodology—everywhere but where God has placed it, in His Word. The power of the Word of God is His power and His alone.

God's Glory

If we were to recite only the concluding verse of the Lord's Prayer every day, our life would be changed. If we come to the realization that it is His kingdom, His power, and His glory, then we get what Jesus is teaching in this prayer. *Sola gratia*—our salvation is by the grace of God alone, and to God alone is the glory.

At the bottom of every one of his compositions Johann Sebastian Bach wrote the initials *SDG* to remind himself and anyone who played his composition that to God alone is the glory. He did not write simply *DG*, "to God the glory"; it was always *SDG*, "to God alone the glory." That is what we are to say at the end of our prayer. "God, it is your kingdom. You own it and rule over it. It is your power, without which we are helpless, and we have no glory in us. We know that you will never share your glory with men." We also sing the *Gloria Patri*: "Glory be to the Father and to the Son and to the Holy Ghost," ascribing glory to the Godhead, because that is where the glory belongs.

The original temptation in Eden was to usurp the glory of God. The Serpent told Adam and Eve that they would not die but would become like God and participate in deity. That temptation is there every day that we want to achieve glory. Yes, we should strive for significance and to make our lives count, but the glory belongs to God alone.

God's kingdom and His power and His glory are forever. They are not temporary but go into eternity.

30

TREASURE IN HEAVEN

Matthew 6:19–24

Do not lay up for yourselves treasures on earth, where moth and rust destroy and where thieves break in and steal; but lay up for yourselves treasures in heaven, where neither moth nor rust destroys and where thieves do not break in and steal. For where your treasure is, there your heart will be also. The lamp of the body is the eye. If therefore your eye is good, your whole body will be full of light. But if your eye is bad, your whole body will be full of darkness. If therefore the light that is in you is darkness, how great is that darkness! No one can serve two masters; for either he will hate the one and love the other, or else he will be loyal to the one and despise the other. You cannot serve God and mammon.

Through a strange set of circumstances, I was able to come into the possession of the 1543 Latin edition of John Calvin's *Institutes of the Christian Religion*. There are only seven known copies of this treasure. When I actually held the book in my hands and looked at the pages, two pressing problems came to mind. First, I wondered how we could insure the book, knowing, of course, that no amount of money could replace it if it were to be destroyed. The second problem concerned where to store the book so bugs would not get into the binding and eat away the glue. It happened to come during the same week that I was preparing to preach the text before us now: **"Do not lay up for yourselves treasures on earth, where moth and rust destroy and where thieves break in and steal; but lay up for yourselves treasures in**

heaven, where neither moth nor rust destroys and where thieves do not break in and steal" (vv. 19–20). Some translations read, "Where moth and vermin destroy," because in the ancient world people kept their valuables hidden under the dirt floors of their houses. The houses themselves were basically made of mud bricks, and there were various types of vermin that could gnaw their way through to the valuables that were stored in the home and destroy them. Clothing was also easily destroyed. A distinguishing sign of the Jewish upper class was the fine and stylish clothes they wore. They did not keep their clothes in protected cedar chests or closets, so their finery was exposed to the destruction wrought by moths. So Jesus borrows from the everyday problems people experience with their most cherished possessions.

Our Treasure

Have you ever had an important possession stolen from you? I have, and I remember the accompanying sense of personal violation. A thief takes what someone else worked to achieve and acquire. That is why Paul writes, "Let him who stole steal no longer" (Eph. 4:28). We live in a world in which anything we own can be lost or stolen from us, yet here in Matthew, Jesus turns the values of the world upside down. Life is not about the treasures that we amass but about the treasures we have in heaven.

However, the Bible does teach us that we are to be diligent in providing for our family: "If anyone does not provide for his own, and especially for those of his household, he has denied the faith and is worse than an unbeliever" (1 Tim. 5:8). Additionally, the Bible does not teach that those who are wealthy must therefore be evil. Jesus is talking about our hearts and what ignites our passion. His concern is our deepest level of concern and commitment.

In Paul's epistle to the Romans, he warned about another kind of treasuring: "In accordance with your hardness and your impenitent heart you are treasuring up for yourself wrath in the day of wrath and revelation of the righteous judgment of God" (Rom. 2:5). The apostle was saying that every offense we have committed against God will be on the docket when we are brought before His tribunal. Paul warns us against making new deposits into the wrath being built up against us. Therefore, we are either storing up treasure or storing up wrath. What are you storing up? Are you storing up treasure in heaven, or are you storing up wrath?

When I taught elementary economics at the Geneva School in Orlando, I told my students about the principle of delayed gratification, the importance of investing rather than consuming their earnings. There is a principle that I call the "eighth joyful mystery," which is the law of compounded interest. We must always consider where we are investing. I believe that the best investment we can make is in the kingdom of God, and that is because there are no moths in heaven, nor is there a single thief. That is what Jesus is saying here.

How do we store up treasures in heaven? Some commentators believe that Jesus was referring to good works, which may strike you as somewhat offensive—we know that justification is by faith alone and not by works. Justification is indeed by faith alone, but our reward in heaven will be according to our works. There are at least twenty-five places in the New Testament that show that the distribution of heavenly rewards will be based upon our good works. Our good works are never good enough to get us to heaven or to merit reward; these rewards are of grace. This is what Augustine called God's crowning His own gifts. At the same time, we are called repeatedly in Scripture to bring forth the fruits of righteousness and obedience. When we are obedient to Christ, we are treasuring up treasures in heaven. There is nothing more valuable than our obedience, and the value of it is eternal. The market in heaven is never a bear market. There are no recessions. The glory of the kingdom of God is from everlasting to everlasting.

"For where your treasure is, there your heart will be also" (v. 21). We must ask ourselves on a regular basis where our treasure is and likewise where our heart is. Where is that point of ultimate concern that grips our life? That is the diagnostic question Jesus is asking. He is saying to us, "Where is your heart? Where is your ultimate commitment? Is it to prestige or success or wealth, or is to my kingdom?" He is asking whether He holds our heart. Our treasure lies in what we cherish.

I love the traditional marriage vows because they go beyond the pledging of love and honor and include the promise to cherish. If we would just keep that promise, we would never wound each other the way we do; people never intentionally damage what they cherish. To cherish something is to assign a high value to it, to esteem it greatly. When we get married, that is what we promise—to value our spouse above any other person in this world.

Light and Darkness

Jesus continues, **"The lamp of the body is the eye. If therefore your eye is good, your whole body will be full of light. But if your eye is bad, your whole body will be full of darkness. If therefore the light that is in you is darkness, how great is that darkness!"** (vv. 22–23). Our eyes are what opens the vista of the world to us. To be consigned to blindness, therefore, is to be consigned to darkness. Some time ago I heard a report of a man who had lost his eyesight and had been blind for thirty-one years. He did not see his wife all that time, and he had never seen his children. After undergoing a corneal transplant, he was able to see his wife and, for the first time, his children. We can imagine what he had experienced only by closing our eyes so that no light gets in.

Jesus is asking the same question with this metaphor as He asked through the metaphor of treasure: what is in our souls? If our souls are filled with darkness, how great is that darkness! This metaphor of light and darkness is found throughout the New Testament. When a person comes to Christ, he "sees the light." In the past he did not see anything special about Jesus or about the gospel. If the light of Christ has not come into your eye, then your soul is in darkness, and Jesus says, "How great is that darkness!" It's the most dreadful darkness that anyone can endure.

Jesus concludes this section by saying, **"No one can serve two masters; for either he will hate the one and love the other, or else he will be loyal to the one and despise the other. You cannot serve God and mammon"** (v. 24). Jesus is not saying that wealthy people cannot be God's children. Jesus knew of the wealth of Abraham and Job, and He knew that He would be buried in the tomb of a wealthy man. Yet neither Abraham nor Job was a slave of riches. Job, when he lost everything, said, "Though He slay me, yet will I trust Him" (Job 13:15). You are a slave to that which you serve, and if your life is consumed by the acquisition of mammon, then you are a slave, and if you are a slave of mammon, you cannot be a servant of God. The two are absolutely incompatible.

We all need a wakeup call, because it is easy to get caught up with the pursuit of everything but the kingdom of God. Yet even in this world, we have had a glimpse of that heavenly treasure. Every Christian possesses a pearl of great price, which pearl is far more valuable than the 1543 edition of *The Institutes of the Christian Religion*. Would you trade your soul for that? Your house maybe, but not your soul. Let us seek treasure. Let us seek the kingdom of heaven with passion.

31

DO NOT BE ANXIOUS

Matthew 6:25–34

Therefore I say to you, do not worry about your life, what you will eat or what you will drink; nor about your body, what you will put on. Is not life more than food and the body more than clothing? Look at the birds of the air, for they neither sow nor reap nor gather into barns; yet your heavenly Father feeds them. Are you not of more value than they? Which of you by worrying can add one cubit to his stature? So why do you worry about clothing? Consider the lilies of the field, how they grow: they neither toil nor spin; and yet I say to you that even Solomon in all his glory was not arrayed like one of these. Now if God so clothes the grass of the field, which today is, and tomorrow is thrown into the oven, will He not much more clothe you, O you of little faith? Therefore do not worry, saying, "What shall we eat?" or "What shall we drink?" or "What shall we wear?" For after all these things the Gentiles seek. For your heavenly Father knows that you need all these things. But seek first the kingdom of God and His righteousness, and all these things shall be added to you. Therefore do not worry about tomorrow, for tomorrow will worry about its own things. Sufficient for the day is its own trouble.

When I was a young man, I watched my father die an inch at a time. He had four serious strokes, which completely incapacitated him. He sat in a chair for the last three years of his life unable to work or to derive any income whatsoever. I can still hear him saying to me, in a thick voice because of the paralysis from the strokes, "Take no thought for tomorrow, what you should eat, what you should drink, what you should put on." He lived and died by that text, yet I hated it with every fiber of my being. Even today, as a Christian, I have trouble with this text because it is as if Jesus is speaking direct to me, saying, "You say that you believe in the providence of God, and if you believe that, why are you such a worrywart?"

The Futility of Worry

Obviously Jesus here is teaching His people the doctrine of providence. When we speak theologically of the providence of God, we speak of that means by which God governs the entire universe, the means by which in His sovereignty He leaves no maverick molecule running loose outside of His sovereign authority. The word *providence* comes from the root word *pronoeō*, which meant originally "to see in advance" or "to see beforehand." However, *providence* actually refers to much more than God's knowledge of the future; it refers to God's provision for the future, His perfect plan that cannot fail and which includes everyone of us and everything about us, even the hairs on our head. "This is our Father's world," as the hymn goes, and there is no one I would rather have governing this world than Almighty God Himself, who does all things well.

Jesus knew that, and He knew it far more profoundly than we do. Jesus understood the practical implications of the sovereignty of God and of God's divine providence. He has just warned us that we cannot serve two masters and that we ought not to be heaping up treasures on earth but rather looking to heaven and to the kingdom of God, which is why He begins this section with a conclusion: **"Therefore I say to you, do not worry about your life, what you will eat or what you will drink; nor about your body, what you will put on. Is not life more than food and the body more than clothing?"** (v. 25).

One of the things Jesus stresses in this admonition about worry is its futility. All the worry in the world cannot possibly change anything. All we do when we worry is get ourselves upset, and the only changes wrought by our worry are negative changes to our own health. Jesus says it is silly to worry, because worry is futile.

Jesus goes on to tell us that worry is a matter of lacking faith and that worry is not only futile but in a certain sense also foolish. Despite His words, we still worry about things. Sometimes it seems that we just cannot help it. However, worry is one of our greatest incentives to prayer, because prayer is the greatest antidote to worry. When I worry, I am driven immediately to my knees, although I recall Vesta asking me, "Shouldn't we go to our knees before we worry rather than having worry as the catalyst to drive us to more earnest prayer?"

A Lesson from Wildlife

Jesus asks some rhetorical questions: **"Is not life more than food and the body more than clothing?"** (v. 25). Obviously life is more than food, and the body is much more than clothing. Worrying about the results of a medical test is not the same as worrying about the sale price of our next clothing purchase; we all realize that our human bodies are more important than the things we use to cover them.

Then Jesus tells us to look at nature: **"Look at the birds of the air, for they neither sow nor reap nor gather into barns; yet your heavenly Father feeds them"** (v. 26). There are several things in Jesus' analogy that we ought not miss. We have never seen a bird plowing a field and planting seeds in furrows, then fertilizing that field and weeding it during the growing process so that when food emerges from the earth, the bird can come and take it to a barn that it has constructed for a rainy day. What we have seen is man plowing the ground and sowing the seed, and then the birds coming down and eating the seeds that man has provided for them. Birds are not like people; they do not have to pay attention to growing seasons. As a rule, God just takes care of their needs without their sowing and reaping and storing. Yet, Jesus says, "Your heavenly Father feeds them."

Critics say of this text that apparently Jesus was not knowledgeable about natural disasters that afflict the earth and kill birds by the thousands. Birds perish during famines or when there is an oil leak on the sea. For these reasons critics deny the rightness of Jesus' words about birds. However, Jesus was using a common, everyday phenomenon to illustrate a point. He was not giving the doctrine of the providential concern for wildlife. Luther says that Jesus was directing us to nature to allow the birds to be our teachers. John Stott, who was an avid birdwatcher in England, said that this is not Jesus' doctrine of ornithology. Rather, it is His doctrine of orni-theology. We have a lesson to learn from the normal operations of nature. Jesus was simply saying that when we see birds pulling worms out of the ground and seeds from our garden, we know they are not starving to death.

The other point I want us to notice is that Jesus says it is our heavenly Father who feeds the birds. We used to have a birdfeeder near our driveway, and each day I would pile birdseed on top of the feeder and then try to keep the squirrels away from it. We could look out the window and watch the various species of birds come to that feeder. I fed the birds, but they were not my birds, nor was I their father. My heavenly Father was feeding those birds through my hand in that particular instance. I was able to participate in the providence of God by taking care of those creatures, but we must understand that it is our Father who is taking care of the animals, the birds, and the fish.

Then Jesus asks what is clearly another rhetorical question: **"Are you not of more value than they?"** (v. 26). When asking a first-century Palestinian a question as obvious as that, there would have been no dispute. "Of course," they would say. "Yes, we as human beings are more valuable than the birds of the air." Even the pagans in that environment understood that human life was more valuable than turtle eggs. Today, however, we live in such an upside-down culture that the eggs of turtles are deemed more valuable than the embryos of human beings. That is why, perhaps, some who read this text today would not know what Jesus was talking about. God does not say that we are to value human life and despise animals. To the contrary, He tells us to value the creatures He has put here; but we are to value human life even more. There is a calculus of value assigned to nature by God.

God's Providence

Jesus again points out the futility and foolishness of our anxiety: **"Which of you by worrying can add one cubit to his stature?"** (v. 27). The primary inference of this text is probably not with reference to height but to the span of our lives. We worry more about death than about any other reality we face. All our fear responses are inherently related to our fear of death. Jesus is saying that our lives are in the hands of His Father, and, because of that, our anxiety cannot add to the duration of our lives. Our days have been appointed by God. He appointed the day of our birth, and so has He appointed the day of our departure from this world. The problem is that He has not given us that information; we do not know the day of our death, so we worry about it, even though our worry does not change anything.

"So why do you worry about clothing? Consider the lilies of the field, how they grow: they neither toil nor spin; and yet I say to you that even Solomon in all his glory was not arrayed like one of these" (vv. 28–29). As magnificent as the clothing worn by the king may have been, it was not nearly as beautiful as the nuanced shades of color found in wildflowers along the pathway. Jesus did not think that wildflowers evolve; He believed that the regal clothing of the wildflowers is exactly the result of the appointed providence of God. It is our Father who adorns the flowers with the beauty they display.

Jesus comes to His conclusion: **"Now if God so clothes the grass of the field, which today is, and tomorrow is thrown into the oven, will he not much more clothe you, O you of little faith?"** (v. 30). Jesus points out God's "how much more" and concludes, **"Therefore do not worry"** (v. 31). In other words, since Jesus says there is no need to worry, we have no need to worry. That's the end of the matter.

"For after all these things the Gentiles seek. For your heavenly Father knows that you need all these things" (v. 32). Our Father knows what we need before we ask Him. That does not mean, of course, that we are not supposed to ask Him. In fact, He not only encourages us to ask Him but also commands it. We do not inform Him of our needs; He already knows them. He asks us to come to Him so that we can put our hearts at rest, knowing that we have spoken to the Father about our concerns. God says in essence, "I know what you need, but come and tell me what it is." It's for our benefit, not for His.

The Antidote to Worry

"But seek first the kingdom of God and His righteousness, and all these things shall be added to you" (v. 33). Jesus gives the alternative to worrying about our lives in what is perhaps the climactic verse of this discourse. It may be the most important verse in the entire Sermon on the Mount. Jesus does not tell us to forget about our concerns but rather to focus our concern and thoughts on His Father's kingdom. All the things that are added to us will be the consequence of our focusing our desires on His kingdom.

I once offended a family member by making a decision he thought was fiscally irresponsible: I decided to sell all my possessions and go to school. He asked me how I intended to provide for my family, and I quoted to him, "I have been young, and now am old; yet I have not seen the righteous forsaken, nor his descendants begging bread" (Ps. 37:25). That is a truism, but it is not a universal absolute. Righteous people do starve from time to time. The principle that David set forth in the psalm was the same as Jesus is saying here. If you seek first the kingdom of God, the rest of what you need will be added to you. You do not need to worry about it.

The force of that mandate is found in the word *first*. It comes from the Greek word *prōtos*, which here does not indicate the first in a series chronologically. In other words, Jesus is not saying that we are to seek the kingdom first and clothes second and a house third, and so on. Rather, He is talking about priority. Jesus is saying that the most important thing we can do is to seek His Father's kingdom and His righteousness. Set your heart on that, and everything else will take care of itself. The number-one priority of the Christian is seeking after the kingdom of God.

I find myself irritated when unbelievers are described as "seekers." No unbeliever seeks after God. There are millions of unbelievers seeking the benefits that only God can give them, but all the while they are fleeing from God. Worship services should be tailored to believers, not to unbelievers, because seeking the kingdom of God does not start until one has found it through conversion. In our natural condition, as the apostle says, there is none who seeks after God (Rom. 3:11). That is why Jonathan Edwards said that the seeking of the kingdom of God is the main business of the Christian. We do not stop seeking the kingdom the day we are converted; we start seeking it. From the day of our conversion onward, our whole life is to be defined as a quest for the kingdom of God and for His righteousness. That is the priority.

Finally Jesus says, **"Therefore do not worry about tomorrow, for tomorrow will worry about its own things. Sufficient for the day is its own trouble"** (v. 34). I do worry about tomorrow, and I repent of that. However, I never worry about yesterday, because it is gone. I worry about the consequences for tomorrow of what happened yesterday, but I do not worry about yesterday. Jesus says that we have enough on our plate today without worrying about tomorrow. Jesus is not saying that we do not need to study for an upcoming exam, or prepare a sermon, or budget to buy groceries. We are not to be reckless when it comes to seeking provision for the normal things of life. We are to make preparation but not with anxious hearts.

32

JUDGE NOT

Matthew 7:1–6

Judge not, that you be not judged. For with what judgment you judge, you will be judged; and with the measure you use, it will be measured back to you. And why do you look at the speck in your brother's eye, but do not consider the plank in your own eye? Or how can you say to your brother, "Let me remove the speck from your eye"; and look, a plank is in your own eye? Hypocrite! First remove the plank from your own eye, and then you will see clearly to remove the speck from your brother's eye. Do not give what is holy to the dogs; nor cast your pearls before swine, lest they trample them under their feet, and turn and tear you in pieces.

Almost everyone, Christian or not, knows these words are in the Bible: **"Judge not, that you be not judged"** (v. 1). Because we live in a culture that claims everyone has a right to do what he or she wants to do, this verse gets quoted whenever the church makes a pronouncement against some form of sinful behavior.

Years ago a parishioner brought her troubled son to see me. The young man had been taking drugs and practicing a licentious lifestyle. His anger was immediately apparent to me, and I asked him who he was mad at. "I'm mad at my mother," he said.

"What is it your mother does that makes you so mad?" I asked.

"Well, she's religious, and she tries to stuff religion down my throat all the time."

I asked him, "What is your life's ethic?"

He said, "I believe people have a right to do their own thing."

"Well," I said, "if that's the case, why are you angry with your mother? What if your mother's thing is to shove religion down people's throats?"

At that point he began to laugh. I said, "If you came to me as a Christian and explained that you've been having a hard time with your mother because she is critical, judgmental, and harsh, then I'd be willing to make an appointment with your mother on your behalf, but by your ethic you have no complaint to make."

Judging Rightly

That story of the troubled boy illustrates the inconsistency of the relativistic ethic of our world today, and it also illustrates that this well-known Scripture passage, Matthew 7:1, is one of the least understood passages. First, the warning that Jesus gives, "Judge not, that you be not judged," is directed to relations between Christians. Second, in view here with respect to the concept of judging is not the judgment of discernment. We are called in the light of God's law to evaluate human behavior and determine or discern whether it is good or evil, but what is in view here is not that kind of judgment. Rather, it is the judgment of condemnation. The word used in the text is borrowed from the legal vocabulary of the day, and it has to do with the gavel of the judge coming down when he issues a sentence of punishment. That is the judgment of condemnation. So, we could interpret Jesus' words as "Condemn not, that you be not condemned."

John in his Gospel gives the account of the woman caught in adultery. The Pharisees let the offending man go, but they dragged the woman in shame and humiliation to Jesus. The Pharisees were not looking for sound judgment; they were using the opportunity to trap Jesus. They asked Him, "Now Moses, in the law, commanded us that such should be stoned. But what do You say?" (John 8:5). Under Roman occupation the Jews were forbidden from exercising capital punishment, but, according to the Law of Moses, stoning was the penalty for adultery. Therefore, Jesus was on the horns of a dilemma. Many miss the point that Jesus did choose between Moses and Caesar, and He chose Moses. Jesus knelt down and with His finger began writing in the dust. The Bible doesn't tell us what He wrote; my guess is that He began to list the sins of the woman's accusers. Then He stood up and said, "He who is without sin among you, let him throw a stone at her first" (v. 7). One by one the woman's accusers walked away, leaving Jesus alone with her.

At that point, Jesus asked her a question: "Woman, where are those accusers of yours? Has no one condemned you?" She said, "No one, Lord," and Jesus replied, "Neither do I condemn you; go and sin no more" (vv. 10–11). Jesus was the only sinless one present and therefore the only who had the right to stone her. However, instead of exercising justice He granted mercy and kindness, and He did it without repudiating the law against adultery. Jesus had the judgment of discernment. He recognized the woman's sin, yet He gave her forgiveness.

One thing that defines the life of the Christian is forgiveness. Of all people in this world, we are the ones who have the least right to be judgmental, harsh, or critical. Those with a critical spirit are always picking at something. They are not happy unless they are unhappy and criticizing something or someone.

Jesus is not advocating here in Matthew a Pollyannaish view of the world. While there are people who cannot look at anything without finding some fault in it, there are also those who look at the world through rose-colored glasses. Jesus is speaking out against having a harsh judgment of people. He is not asking that His people be naïve; He is asking for the judgment of charity. As Christians, we are those who are quick to charity and slow to condemnation.

A pastor I knew years ago claimed that there is no resurrection from the dead and that those who believe in the resurrection are fools. When I verbalized my distress at his claim, someone said to me, "That dear soul doesn't really believe that. He's just trying to get you to think." She just could not bring herself to believe poorly about this man, and that is what we ought to be—charitable to a fault. The judgment of charity means that we interpret other people's actions, particularly actions toward us, in the best of all possible lights.

Judging Wrongly

The judgment of condemnation does just the opposite. It interprets people's actions and motives in the worst of all possible lights. Jesus calls attention to our tendency to give the judgment of charity to ourselves but not to others. We interpret our failures and sins in the best of all possibly lights. In fact, we often do not call our sin "sin." We refer instead to our "mistakes" and "bad decisions." We must never judge the motives of another because we cannot possibly know what motivates another unless we are told. It is safest to avoid even attempting to read someone's motives. We can look at what was done and evaluate whether the action was good or bad, but only God knows the heart of what motivated that particular behavior.

Jesus' point is that nothing will tear up the church faster than those who make harsh judgments about others. He is speaking here about brothers and sisters in Christ: **"Why do you look at the speck in your brother's eye, but do not consider the plank in your own eye? Or how can you say to your brother,**

'Let me remove the speck from your eye'; and look, a plank is in your own eye? Hypocrite! First remove the plank from your own eye, and then you will see clearly to remove the speck from your brother's eye" (vv. 3–5). Jesus uses hyperbole to teach a point. The two objects He uses for radical contrast were found in the carpenter's shop in that day. Carpenters were builders of houses, and great strength was required to carry the large wooden beams used to construct the houses' ceiling. The word translated as "plank" referred to one of those very large logs or beams. In contrast to that beam is a speck of sawdust. Jesus' point is that someone whose eye is covered by a thick plank cannot see others clearly. He is saying that although each of us is guilty of major sins and failures, we so easily call attention to a tiny blemish in the life of someone else.

One reason we direct attention to the speck in someone's eye is to distract attention away from the plank in our own eye. When we have planks in our eyes, we consider them specks. When we see specks in others' eyes, we view them as planks. That is how sin destroys human relationships and community, and that is why Jesus is warning us to be careful. If we adopt a judgmental spirit toward others, what goes around is going to come around, and we will be judged.

Judging with Discernment

Jesus does make a distinction in His teaching, and throughout the New Testament, between what we call gross or heinous sins and what we call peccadilloes, our little sins. We are called to have the kind of love that covers a multitude of sins. To cover up a major sin is serious, but if we are not considering a heinous sin that affects the entire church or community, we are to cover each other with that love. If I see a speck in my brother's eye, I must cover it in my soul with love. If my brother sees a speck in my eye, he must do the same. We must not destroy the body of Christ over sawdust, which is Jesus' point here.

The rest of this passage contains irony, because in order to fulfill it, we must be able to execute judgment—not the judgment of condemnation but the judgment of discernment. Our Lord has just said, "Judge not, that you be not judged," and then He concludes this discourse by saying, **"Do not give what is holy to the dogs; nor cast your pearls before swine, lest they trample them under their feet, and turn and tear you in pieces"** (v. 6). In order to obey this dictum, in the first instance we have to be able to discern between what is holy and what is not.

Dogs in Israel were not gentle, fuzzy, household pets. They were despised scavengers. They were held in the same regard as pigs in a pigsty. Jesus is pointing out that people had the good sense not to take holy things and give them to dogs. Who are these dogs? They are people who make it their business to hate the kingdom of God. Jesus is not advising us to hate such people. When He sent out His disciples on their mission, He said, "Whatever city or town you enter, inquire who in it is worthy, and stay there till you go out. And when you go into a household, greet it. If the household is worthy, let your peace come upon it. But if it is not worthy, let your peace return to you. And whoever will not receive you nor hear your words, when you depart from that house or city, shake off the dust from your feet" (Matt. 10:11–14). While it is right to care about people who are hostile to the kingdom, we must not spend all our time giving them holy things.

Paul went to Mars Hill, to the cultural center of Athens, and engaged in a dispute with the philosophers. When he was finished, some embraced what he said, some mocked him, and others wanted to hear more. For those who responded, Paul had all the time in the world; for those who wanted to hear more, he would talk to them and answer every question he could; but for those who abjectly refused to hear the gospel, he did not spend any more time with them. He left them to God. Perhaps they would really hear the truth at another time from someone else.

In Matthew 7 Jesus is issuing a warning. He has given us the pearl of great price, and we are not to take that valuable gem and throw it to the pigs. The pig in his slop has no appreciation for the value of the pearl. In fact, the pig would think that an acorn has more value than the pearl.

Again, Jesus is not saying that we are to adopt a hard-hearted attitude to the unbeliever. He just wants us to be discerning in our proclamation of the gospel. We are to discern the mind while not judging harshly with the heart. That is what we're called to do, and it is a very weighty call indeed.

33

ASK AND RECEIVE

Matthew 7:7–12

Ask, and it will be given to you; seek, and you will find; knock, and it will be opened to you. For everyone who asks receives, and he who seeks finds, and to him who knocks it will be opened. Or what man is there among you who, if his son asks for bread, will give him a stone? Or if he asks for a fish, will he give him a serpent? If you then, being evil, know how to give good gifts to your children, how much more will your Father who is in heaven give good things to those who ask Him! Therefore, whatever you want men to do to you, do also to them, for this is the Law and the Prophets.

When we look at a Scripture text, it is imperative that we consider the context in which it is found. That is especially true when Jesus frames His teaching in the form of aphorisms, which are terse sayings. These brief little sayings communicate truisms from His lips, but they must never be taken as a magical formula for prayer. The context in which Jesus speaks here about asking, seeking, and knocking is in the broader context of the Sermon on the Mount in which He has focused heavy attention on the matter of prayer.

Two of the most important means of grace by which we grow spiritually are hearing the Word of God and praying. The disciples themselves, who were devoted to studying the Word of Christ every day, recognized the close connection between His uncanny power and His singular prayer life. We recall that earlier the disciples came to Jesus and asked to be taught something crucial. They did not ask to be taught how to cast out demons, how to walk on water, or how to turn water into wine. Their request was this: "Lord, teach us to pray" (Luke 11:1).

That passion to learn how to pray did not end with the death of the last apostle. Christians in every generation are commonly frustrated by the impoverished strength of their prayer life. We all know that prayer is vital to our spiritual lives, and sometimes we simply see it as a duty that must be performed or a discipline that must be carried out rather than as an unspeakable privilege and joy and opportunity we have been given by the Father.

What Prayer Is Not

In the immediate context, Jesus has just addressed the problem of worry and anxiety, telling His disciples not to worry about food and drink and clothing. Jesus reminded them that their heavenly Father knows that they need all these things, and then He reduced the spiritual quest to its most important priority: "Seek first the kingdom of God and His righteousness, and all these things shall be added to you" (Matt. 6:33). It is in this context that Jesus adds His teaching about prayer. The three things He conjoins here are these: asking, seeking, and knocking. We have a tendency to think that these refer to three different aspects of the Christian life—seeking some goal to be reached, or knocking at the gates of heaven in order to enter—but all three are really about the overall matter of prayer.

This does not give us a room-service menu that we can call in to a cosmic bellhop and ask him to provide whatever we might want. I make that warning because we are living in a culture that has been enormously influenced by New Age thinking. Even people who are not self-consciously New Age in their outlook nevertheless have often been influenced by New Age ideas. New Agers practice a type of magic, the very kind of magic about which the people of Israel were so clearly warned by God in the Old Testament. The basic point of New Age thinking is that one can, by concentration and internal effort, change his or her environment. It is mind over matter, which is simply a form of magic. This notion has crept into the church so that people think, *If I just use the right formula in prayer and ask exactly in the right manner, believing, I can make anything happen.*

Jesus said, "If two of you agree on earth concerning what they ask, it will be done for them by My Father in heaven" (Matt. 18:19). However, this does not mean that because we agree that war should end tomorrow, if we simply pray that way, warfare will end tomorrow. If we are going to understand what Jesus meant, we have to understand the whole of Jesus' teaching on prayer, and not isolate individual aphoristic statements and turn them into magic formulae.

Ask, Seek, Knock

Having given that warning on how not to interpret Jesus' words, let's see what Jesus says here in Matthew 7: He says, **"Ask, and it will be given to you; seek, and you will find; knock, and it will be opened to you. For everyone who asks receives, and he who seeks finds, and to him who knocks it will be opened"** (vv. 7–8). To fully understand what Jesus is saying, we have to realize that when we ask, we must ask aright. We must not ask for selfish reasons. We must not ask in an attitude that blasphemes the Holy Spirit. We must ask according to what God endorses in His Holy Word. He could have expanded that little aphorism to give a thousand qualifications, but He did not do that, because He is giving us a general truth. It is important that we understand, without all of the technical qualifications, that Jesus wants us to realize that our Father is a God who loves to give to those who ask. As James wrote, "You do not have because you do not ask" (James 4:2).

Jesus has just told this crowd that our Father knows what we need before we ask Him (Matt. 6:32). So why now does He add this invitation for taking our requests before God? We do not improve God's knowledge by our prayers. Our prayers benefit us. Distorted Calvinists believe that since God ordains all things, we need not bother to pray at all, but that is an offense to the biblical teaching. We are told in James's epistle that "the effective, fervent prayer of a righteous man avails much" (James 5:16).

Jesus does qualify His teaching: "Seek, and you will find." I think He is talking about seeking in the context of asking. Scripture uniformly addresses our need to learn to ask aright. How can we know that our prayers are legitimate and not just selfish grasps for personal gain? In order to know how to pray correctly, we have to search the Scriptures. We do not know what to pray for, nor do we know how to pray.

So what do we do? We search the Word of God. Seeking is not something that unbelievers do; seeking is the business of believers, and in this case we are called to search the Scriptures. Paul wrote that "the Spirit searches all things, yes, the deep things of God. For what man knows the things of a man except the spirit of the man which is in him? Even so no one knows the things of God except the Spirit of God" (1 Cor. 2:10–11). The Holy Spirit does not search for His benefit. The Holy Spirit is God. The Holy Spirit knows the mind of God perfectly. Rather, the Spirit searches the Word of God for us. This is His work of illumination in which He shines light on the text. Have you ever read a text of Scripture, a text that you've read maybe ten times or fifty times or a hundred times and all of a sudden it jumps out at you in a fresh new way? This is the work of the Spirit, who has worked with the Word to pierce your heart. That is the Holy Spirit searching the Word, and as the Spirit searches the Word of God, so we are called to search the Word of God. Those who have the most powerful prayer life are those who have mastered the Word of God.

How to Ask

When we ask God for something, the two things we must always keep in mind are who God is and who we are. Our requests can never be demands. Jesus is not establishing for us an entitlement mentality. When we ask, we are to search the Scriptures, and when we ask God, we do not ask Him rudely. When we come into the presence of God, we knock at the door; that is, we come to God politely. We come with a gentle wrap, but if that does not open the door, we do not assume that God is absent. We learn elsewhere from Jesus that when we knock and God does not answer, we keep on knocking.

In the parable of the unjust judge (Luke 18:1–8), Jesus tells of a widow who persistently sought for a hearing before the judge, but the judge had no regard for men or for justice and did not want to be bothered by this poor widow. Finally, her persistence annoyed him so much that he listened to her case. Jesus' application was that if an unjust judge who has no regard for God or for man would listen to a widow solely to make her go away, how much more will our heavenly Father, who is just and does care, hear our prayers? Jesus taught this parable "that men always ought to pray and not lose heart" (Luke 18:1). I have seen some spectacular answers to prayer, and the most spectacular answers have come after I have prayed with the utmost fervency and persistence. I have seen a correlation between effective prayer that involves seeking and knocking, not just asking.

We are encouraged to do this, Jesus said, because God is not like a human being. Jesus draws an analogy from our natural state when He says, **"What man is there among you who, if his son asks for bread, will give him a stone? Or if he asks for a fish, will he give him a serpent?"** (vv. 9–10). If your little boy is hungry and comes to you asking not for steak or lobster but simply a piece of bread, you would not hand him a stone and say, "Chew on this and be quiet." Surely there are parents like that in this world, but I have never seen anyone that heartless. Jesus says that since even in this natural world of fallen human beings, we give our children bread and fish rather than stones and serpents, **"how much more will your Father who is in heaven give good things to those who ask Him!"** (v. 11).

The Golden Rule

Finally, in what seems like a postscript, Jesus says, **"Therefore, whatever you want men to do to you, do also to them, for this is the Law and the Prophets"** (v. 12). This is also the Golden Rule: "Just as you want men to do to you, you also do to them likewise" (Luke 6:31). Jesus did not invent the Golden Rule. That principle of reciprocity was found in antiquity, in the Old Testament, and also even among other nations.

On one occasion a cynical Gentile came to Rabbi Shammai and said, "Rabbi, converse with me on the condition that you teach me the whole Torah while I stand on one foot." Shammai pushed him aside. So the Gentile went to Rabbi Hillel, who conversed with him, saying, "What is hateful to you, do not do to your neighbor. That is the whole Torah; the rest is commentary." Hillel there stated the Golden Rule in negative terms.

Some say that the essence of Christianity is "Do unto others what you would have them do unto you," but they leave out personal salvation and the cross. The reason we need the cross is that we turn the Golden Rule into rust. The reason we need redemption is that we have not treated our neighbor as we would have our neighbor treat us. We need salvation because we have violated each other and because we have violated God. However, if we want a simple summary of how God wants His redeemed to live, it is this summary: "Do unto others as you would have them do unto you." We cannot control what others say about us or do to us, but we can control what we say about them and do to them. We should be thinking about doing *for* them rather than doing *to* them.

34

THE NARROW WAY

Matthew 7:13–20

Enter by the narrow gate; for wide is the gate and broad is the way that leads to destruction, and there are many who go in by it. Because narrow is the gate and difficult is the way which leads to life, and there are few who find it. Beware of false prophets, who come to you in sheep's clothing, but inwardly they are ravenous wolves. You will know them by their fruits. Do men gather grapes from thornbushes or figs from thistles? Even so, every good tree bears good fruit, but a bad tree bears bad fruit. A good tree cannot bear bad fruit, nor can a bad tree bear good fruit. Every tree that does not bear good fruit is cut down and thrown into the fire. Therefore by their fruits you will know them.

I once had an English professor who never missed an opportunity to attack the Christian faith in her classroom. She knew that I was a Christian, and on one occasion she called on me in class and asked, "Mr. Sproul, do you believe that Jesus is the only way to God?" I still remember my discomfort at that moment. I knew that if I answered truthfully, the teacher's wrath would come down me, but I also knew that if I fudged my answer, I would be denying my Lord. So, I said, "Yes, I believe that Jesus is the only way to God." Just as I had anticipated, she became apoplectic and said, "Young man, that is the most arrogant thing I've ever heard a student say." I could feel not only her hostility but the hostility of my classmates, who regarded me as a narrow-minded bigot because I believed that Jesus was the only way to God.

When the class was dismissed, I approached the teacher and said to her: "I know you don't believe that Jesus is the Son of God, but I do. I want you to understand that if I were to believe that Jesus is the only way to God simply because He is *my* way, that would be, without a doubt, the most arrogant thing a man could say. But I believe that Jesus is the only way to God because Jesus taught that He is the only way to God, and therefore I cannot believe there are other ways without betraying Him. Not only did *He* say it, but the New Testament elsewhere declares that 'there is no other name under heaven given among men by which we must be saved' (Acts 4:12) and 'there is one God and one Mediator between God and men, the Man Christ Jesus' (1 Tim. 2:5)." So, I was able to share my faith with that professor who was hostile to the idea that there is only one way to God.

Those who hate the idea that Jesus is the only way to God often champion the belief that there are many ways. This view is exemplified by the mountain analogy, which appeared in the nineteenth century. According to this analogy, God is on top of a mountain, as it were, and there are many paths that go up this mountain. Some go by circuitous routes and others more directly, but in the end, all the paths lead to the top, where God is. The idea arose that God would be not just if He allowed only one way of salvation. In recent decades, this idea has been exaggerated exponentially, so that now, in a culture that embraces relativism and its twin, pluralism, it seems that nothing is more offensive and more politically incorrect than the notion that there is only one way to God.

Two Gates, Two Paths

I say all this by way of preface because we have come to a saying in the Sermon on the Mount that is highly offensive to those who embrace relativism and pluralism. Most people consider this to be a benign sermon, one that is basically concerned with how we are to get along with one another. But Jesus gives this mandate: **"Enter by the narrow gate; for wide is the gate and broad is the way that leads to destruction, and there are many who go in by it. Because narrow is the gate and difficult is the way which leads to life, and there are few who find it"** (vv. 13–14).

Followers of Christ were first called "Christians" in Antioch during the first century. The term was applied derisively. Before that, Christians called themselves, and were called by others, "people of the Way" (cf. Acts 9:2), because Jesus repeatedly used the metaphor of the road for the Christian life. For example:

> Most assuredly, I say to you, I am the door of the sheep. All who ever came before Me are thieves and robbers. (John 10:7–8a)

> I am the door. If anyone enters by Me, he will be saved, and will go in and out and find pasture. (John 10:9)

> I am the way, the truth, and the life. No one comes to the Father except through Me. (John 14:6)

So, the idea of exclusivity, of Himself as the only way to God, was a major teaching of Jesus. Thus, it is really not surprising that He touched on the same theme in the Sermon on the Mount.

In this teaching, Jesus painted a stark contrast. He said there is a narrow gate and a broad gate. In addition, the narrow gate leads to life, but the wide gate leads to destruction. In saying that the wide gate leads to destruction, Jesus was speaking gently, using *destruction* as a synonym for *hell.* The problem is that it is difficult to get through the narrow gate, and it leads to a difficult path, so very few people choose it. By contrast, it is easy to get through the wide gate, and it opens onto a massively broad highway, so it is packed with people. So, many are on the road that leads to destruction.

Most people assume that we are justified in God's sight by works. They believe that all they need to do to get to heaven is to live a good life. If their good deeds outweigh their bad deeds, they will make it into heaven. Yet there is an even more insidious and pervasive doctrine of justification—justification by death. Some time ago, a famous comedian died, and one commentator, extolling the comedian's virtues, said, "Heaven is a much funnier place today." I don't know whether the comedian was a Christian, and I doubt the commentator knew either. He just assumed that since the comedian had died, he had gone to heaven. Doesn't everyone go to heaven when they die? Well, not according to Jesus. He taught that most people do not go to heaven; those numbered among the redeemed are few.

Some are quick to say that perhaps these words of Jesus were relevant only to first-century Palestine. They note that there had been much corruption and many people had fallen away from Orthodox Judaism, leaving only a remnant—the few who embraced Jesus at that time. Perhaps that is the case. However, those who embraced Him had far more firsthand evidence of His identity than we do, and if that evidence produced only a small contingent of followers, I cannot imagine that, in the Western world today, regenerate people are in the majority. It is exciting to hear of revival happening in places such as South Korea, China, Africa, Latin America, and the Middle East. Multitudes are coming to Christ, and perhaps in some nations the redeemed are in the majority. However, in America, I fear that the vast majority is on the broad way, the path to destruction.

Prophets and Charlatans

Jesus then identified one of the problems that make the narrow way difficult—false prophets. He said, **"Beware of false prophets, who come to you in sheep's clothing, but inwardly they are ravenous wolves"** (v. 15).

In the period of the Old Testament, the greatest threat to the survival of Israel was not the military power of the Philistines, the Amalekites, or the Assyrians. Always the greatest threat to the well-being of the people of God was the false prophets among them. This was a major issue during the time when God sent the prophet Jeremiah to call his people to repentance. It seemed that every time Jeremiah opened his mouth and told the Israelites what God was going to do if they did not change their ways, a hundred false prophets would step forward to contradict him. Jeremiah clearly told the Israelites that God was going to destroy the temple (7:14; 9:11) and send them into exile in Babylon for seventy years (chap. 25), but the false prophets said: "No, God is not like that. God is a God of love. Nothing will ever happen to the temple. He wouldn't allow the children of Abraham to be taken captive in a foreign land. Don't listen to this Jeremiah, for we have peace" (see 6:14; 8:11; 14:13).

Eventually, Jeremiah got sick of it. He went to God and said:

> I am in derision daily;
> Everyone mocks me.
> For when I spoke, I cried out;
> I shouted, "Violence and plunder!"
> Because the word of the LORD was made to me
> A reproach and a derision daily.
> Then I said, "I will not make mention of Him,
> Nor speak anymore in His name."
> But His word was in my heart like a burning fire
> Shut up in my bones;
> I was weary of holding it back,
> And I could not. (20:7b–9)

Do you see what he was saying? He was complaining that his unpopular message of impending judgment meant that he was constantly under attack by the false prophets, and therefore he had to endure the reproach of the people. So he decided to quit, to speak no more in God's name. However, he could not do it. He said, "His word was in my heart like a burning fire shut up in my bones; I was weary of holding it back, and I could not." He could not stop preaching the message God had given him.

Eventually, God comforted Jeremiah by promising to deal with the false prophets. He said: "Their way shall be to them like slippery ways; in the darkness they shall be driven on and fall in them; for I will bring disaster on them, the year of their punishment" (23:12).

False Prophets in Disguise

The false prophets of Jeremiah's time propagated their false teachings openly, but Jesus warned of a more insidious type of false teacher—one who wears a mask. These false prophets do not look like false prophets. In fact, they seem kind and gentle. They look like lambs. In reality, however, they are ravenous wolves disguised as lambs. They whisper into the ears of people, trying to send them through the wide gate.

How can such false teachers be spotted? Jesus gave an identifying mark: **"You will know them by their fruits"** (v. 16a). In other words, they can be identified by what they produce, by the consequences they bring to the life of the church. Nineteenth-century liberalism was perhaps the biggest wolf the church has ever faced. Though few could see it at the time, the fruit of those liberals is now evident. The great cathedrals of Europe today are, for the most part, mausoleums. The preaching of nineteenth-century liberalism left the church empty. It produced nothing of value, no fruit. This is always the outcome of false teaching in the church.

Building on the theme of fruitfulness, Jesus asked a rhetorical question with an obvious answer: **"Do men gather grapes from thornbushes or figs from thistles?"** (v. 16b). In places such as the Napa Valley of California, well-cultivated vineyards stretch for miles across the hills. On those vines grow marvelous clusters of grapes. But nowhere can grapes be seen growing on thornbushes or thistles. The grapes infallibly indicate which plants are grapevines. If there are grapes, the plant on which they are growing is assuredly not a thornbush or a thistle.

Jesus continued: **"Even so, every good tree bears good fruit, but a bad tree bears bad fruit. A good tree cannot bear bad fruit, nor can a bad tree bear good fruit"** (vv. 17–18). The farmer looks for trees that are productive, trees that bear fruit, not trees that produce corrupt fruit. He is able to tell the good trees from the bad trees by the fruit they bear, for the quality of the tree determines the quality of the fruit. This isn't even complicated agronomy. If the tree is corrupt, its fruit will be corrupt. Of course, the farmer has no use for such a tree. Therefore, **"Every tree that does not bear good fruit is cut down and thrown into the fire"** (v. 19).

Jesus summarized His teaching by saying, **"Therefore by their fruits you will know them"** (v. 20). We have to open our ears to the teaching of Jesus and close our ears to the teaching of the culture, which has everything upside down. If we want to live, we need to stay off the broad way. We need to look for the door through which men must enter. Every other door leads to destruction. We must pursue the narrow way, for only that way leads to life—no matter what men may say.

35

"LORD, LORD"

Matthew 7:21–23

> Not everyone who says to Me, "Lord, Lord," shall enter the kingdom of heaven, but he who does the will of My Father in heaven. Many will say to Me in that day, "Lord, Lord, have we not prophesied in Your name, cast out demons in Your name, and done many wonders in Your name?" And then I will declare to them, "I never knew you; depart from Me, you who practice lawlessness!"

In the previous few verses of Matthew's Gospel, Jesus issued sober warnings to His hearers about the road they chose to follow, because the way to destruction is broad and the gate that leads to it is wide, and many go that route, but the way to life is difficult and the gate is narrow, so that few find it. He then warned them to be on guard against wolves who dress in sheep's clothing in order to come in and corrupt the congregation. These warnings seem to be rising toward a crescendo of sorts, and that crescendo appears to arrive in the passage before us now. I consider these to be the most terrifying words that ever came from the mouth of Jesus.

Jesus' warning seems straightforward: **"Not everyone who says to Me, 'Lord, Lord,' shall enter the kingdom of heaven. . . . Many will say to Me in that day, 'Lord, Lord, have we not prophesied in Your name, cast out demons in Your name, and done many wonders in Your name?'"** (vv. 21–22). Yet, this statement employs an unusual Hebrew literary structure that is found in the

Bible only about fifteen times. It is a rare type of expression that was used among the Jews to show emphasis. When Jesus or anyone from a Hebrew background wanted to give emphasis to something they said, they would simply repeat it. For instance, Jesus would often preface His teaching by saying not just, "*Truly*, I say to you," but, "*Truly, truly,* I say to you" (see John 1:51; 3:3; 5:24; 13:38, ESV), adding emphasis by repetition.

Similarly, there are times in Scripture when names are repeated, and we need to take note of these occurrences, for they are expressions of deep and profound personal affection. When one person greets another by the repetition of his or her name, it shows that they have not just a casual acquaintance but a very deep bond. It is worth taking the time to make a brief reconnaissance of the Bible in order to look at examples of this phenomenon so that we will not miss the import of what Jesus said here in the Sermon on the Mount.

"Abraham, Abraham!"

One of the most poignant and dramatic occurrences of this literary device anywhere in the Old Testament appears in Genesis 22. Abraham and his wife Sarah had waited many years for God to fulfill His promise of offspring. At long last, Isaac was born, but then God asked Abraham to do the unthinkable. He said, "Take now your son, your only son Isaac, whom you love, and go to the land of Moriah, and offer him there as a burnt offering on one of the mountains of which I shall tell you" (v. 2). Abraham rose early in the morning, gathered wood for the offering, saddled his donkeys, and began that horrible trek to Mount Moriah with Isaac. On the way, Isaac looked at his father and said, "Look, the fire and the wood, but where is the lamb for a burnt offering?" (v. 7b). Abraham replied, "God will provide for Himself the lamb" (v. 8). Finally, they came to Mount Moriah, and Abraham built an altar, put the firewood around it, bound Isaac, and laid him on the altar. Then Abraham drew a knife and lifted it high. Just as he was about to plunge the blade into the bosom of his son, at the last possible second, God spoke to him. He said: "Abraham, Abraham! . . . Do not lay your hand on the lad, or do anything to him; for now I know that you fear God, since you have not withheld your son, your only son, from Me" (vv. 11–12). Isaac was spared. Jehovah provided a substitute for Isaac (v. 13), just as He would provide a greater substitute two thousand years later, when He would give His Son, His only Son, the Son whom He loved, Jesus.

Later in the patriarchal history, Isaac had a son named Jacob, who in turn had sons of his own. One of them, Joseph, was killed, according to the report of his brothers. In a time of famine, Jacob sent his sons to Egypt to buy food from the storehouses there. In Egypt, they met their long-lost brother, Joseph, who was actually alive and prime minister of Egypt. Joseph told his brothers to go back and bring their father to Egypt. So, they came back to Jacob with the joyous news that Joseph was still alive and that he wanted them to move to Egypt, where there would be ample provisions, all the food that they would ever need. At that, Jacob hesitated. He thought: "I'm too old for this. I don't want to leave this land that God has promised to my family." As he hesitated, God appeared to him at night and said: "Jacob, Jacob! . . . Do not fear to go down to Egypt, for I will make of you a great nation there. I will go down with you to Egypt, and I will surely bring you up again" (Gen. 46:2–4). So, Jacob took his possessions and his family, and he moved to the land of Goshen in Egypt, and there they prospered and multiplied.

Years passed. Finally, a Pharaoh came to power who did not know Joseph. All the promises were thrown away. This Pharaoh took the opportunity to enslave this foreign people and make them work for his own economy. He was cruel, not giving them even straw to make their bricks. So, the descendants of Jacob—the Israelites—cried, groaned, and prayed, and God heard them.

"Moses, Moses!"

In the meantime, one of the Israelite children had been set adrift on the Nile to be spared from the wrath of the Pharaoh, but he had been found and adopted unknowingly into Pharaoh's own household, where he was raised as a prince of Egypt. One day, when he had grown to manhood, he saw an Egyptian mistreating a Hebrew slave. He became so angry he rose up and struck the Egyptian, killing him. This prince, whose name was Moses, hid the body of the slain Egyptian. However, someone had witnessed the killing, so Moses had to leave the palace of Pharaoh and flee for his life. He went to the outer wilderness of the Midianite desert. There, he labored for decades in obscurity and loneliness as a shepherd. One day, as he was tending his flocks, he noticed something strange. He saw a bush that was burning but was not consumed. So, Moses drew near to that phenomenon, and as he approached he heard a voice coming out of that bush, calling to him: "Moses, Moses! . . . Take your sandals off your feet, for the place where you stand is holy ground" (Ex. 3:4–5).

Then God identified Himself to Moses, saying: "I AM WHO I AM. . . . This is My name forever" (vv. 14, 15). Then He sent Moses back to Egypt to tell Pharaoh to let the Israelites go from their slavery. Eventually, by means of great miracles, God forced Pharaoh to free the Israelites, and Moses led them out of Egypt in the most important redemptive event in the whole Old Testament, the exodus.

After many years of wandering, the Israelites conquered the Promised Land of Canaan under Joshua. They became secure and the tribes were established.

They were ruled by men and women of unique charismatic gifts who were called judges. This period lasted about four hundred years. At the end of that time, a man named Eli became judge. He was also a priest, and his sons were priests with him, but they profaned the worship of the people, and Eli did nothing about it.

In the meantime, a barren woman named Hannah had prayed for a child, and God had given her a son, whose name was Samuel. Hannah had promised that if God gave her a son, she would dedicate him to the service of God for all of his days. Therefore, she entrusted Samuel to Eli's care, and Samuel was under his tutelage. One night, Samuel heard a voice say, "Samuel." He went to Eli, thinking the old man had called him. Eli, however, assured Samuel that he had not called him, then sent him back to bed. Three times the voice called, and three times Samuel went to Eli, but Eli told him he had not called. Finally, Eli realized God must be calling the boy, so he told Samuel that if he heard the voice again, he should say, "Speak, Lord, for Your servant hears" (1 Sam. 3:9). Samuel went back to bed, and again God called him, but this time He called the young boy by saying, "Samuel! Samuel!" (v. 10). God proceeded to tell Samuel of the awful judgment He was about to bring on the house of Eli and his sons.

In time, Samuel became the judge of Israel and a prophet of God. He anointed the first king of Israel, Saul, and the second, David, who ushered in the golden age of Israel. However, in his later years, David had to suffer the ignominy of an uprising against the crown led by his own son Absalom. At one point, David had to flee in disgrace from his palace. Finally, a key battle took place between David's men and Absalom's, and the followers of Absalom were defeated and Absalom was killed. When David heard the news, he did not rejoice that the rebellion was over. He cried in agony: "O my son Absalom—my son, my son Absalom—if only I had died in your place! O Absalom my son, my son" (2 Sam. 18:33). Even Absalom's treachery could not quench David's love and affection for him.

Later, the era of the great prophets was introduced by Elijah. As Elijah came to the end of his days, God sent him on a journey to the place where he would be taken up to heaven. He told his protégé, Elisha, not to come, but Elisha begged to accompany him, and Elijah relented and let him come along on the journey. After they had traveled far, suddenly, without warning, a chariot and horses of fire appeared, and Elijah was translated into heaven before Elisha's eyes. When Elisha saw it, he cried out: "My father, my father, the chariot of Israel and its horsemen" (2 Kings 2:12). With that, Elisha's beloved mentor was gone, and he was left to carry on the prophetic ministry.

"Martha, Martha"

Now fast-forward to the New Testament. During the ministry of Jesus, on one occasion He came to Bethany, and He stayed at the home of Lazarus and his sisters, Mary and Martha. Mary sat at Jesus' feet and asked him every question she could think to ask, but Martha was consigned to the kitchen. She was preparing the meal, taking care of the dishes, and working away while her sister basked in the glory of the Christ. Finally, Martha had enough of it and complained to Jesus. He, in turn, rebuked her, but with wonderful tenderness: "Martha, Martha, you are worried and troubled about many things. But one thing is needed, and Mary has chosen that good part, which will not be taken away from her" (Luke 10:41–42).

Soon thereafter, Jesus came to the holy city, Jerusalem. As He approached the city, He was aware of its corruption and sin. He began to lament, saying: "O Jerusalem, Jerusalem, the one who kills the prophets and stones those who are sent to her! How often I wanted to gather your children together, as a hen gathers her brood under her wings, but you were not willing!" (Luke 13:34). Even in rebuking Jerusalem for its corruption, Jesus still expressed His undying affection for the city of God.

On the night Jesus was betrayed, when He was in the upper room with His disciples and celebrating the Passover, Jesus announced to the group that one of them would betray Him (referring, of course, to Judas). One by one they asked Him, "Lord, is it I?" (Matt. 26:22). Finally, Judas said, "Rabbi, is it I?" and Jesus replied, "You have said it" (v. 25). But Jesus was not finished; He still needed to tell the disciples that one of them would deny Him publicly. He looked at him and said: "Simon, Simon! Indeed, Satan has asked for you, that he may sift you as wheat. But I have prayed for you, that your faith should not fail; and when you have returned to Me, strengthen your brethren" (Luke 22:31–32). Even when He announced Peter's eminent denial, He addressed him in terms of personal affection.

Perhaps the most radical example of this took place the very next day, when our Lord was on the cross, under the curse of God, receiving the unmitigated wrath of His Father. In that hell, He cried out, saying, "My God, My God, why have You forsaken Me?" (Matt. 27:46). Even in His forsakenness, crying from the midst of His torment, He addressed His Father in terms of personal affection.

Let me mention one more example. Saul was the scourge of the early church. He was so committed to eradicating the Christian faith that he went from house to house, dragging people away, putting them in prison, and having them executed. He even asked for papers of authority so that he could continue this persecution in Syria. But as he was traveling along the desert road to Damascus, he was blinded by a light that was brighter than the noonday sun. He fell to the ground, and then he heard a voice from heaven speaking to him: "Saul, Saul, why are you persecuting Me?" (Acts 9:4). Saul was dumbfounded. He asked, "Who are You, Lord?" The voice said, "I am Jesus, whom you are persecuting. It is hard for you to kick against the goads" (v. 5). Even when Saul was raging against the church, Jesus called to him in deep personal affection.

Spurious Terms of Endearment

I have labored this history so that we can feel the import of the warning Jesus gave near the end of the Sermon on the Mount. Listen again to what He said: "Not everyone who says to Me, 'Lord, Lord,' shall enter the kingdom of heaven. . . . Many will say to Me in that day, 'Lord, Lord, have we not prophesied in Your name, cast out demons in Your name, and done many wonders in Your name?'" These are stunning words. Jesus was saying that not everyone who addressed Him in terms of deep affection would be saved. Some of them, He said, would come to Him on the day of judgment and, still addressing Him in terms of intimate affection, would remind Him of all they had done for Him. In modern terms, they would say: "Dearest Lord, didn't we preach for You? Didn't we share our testimonies for You? Didn't we teach Sunday school for You? Didn't we go to the mission field for You? Didn't we give tithes for You?" These people would honestly believe they were in intimate relationships with Jesus and that they had served Him faithfully.

But Jesus said they would be deceived. He said, **"And then I will declare to them, 'I never knew you; depart from Me, you who practice lawlessness!'"** (v. 23).

Can you imagine that? Can you imagine people coming to the judgment seat of Christ, calling upon Him as a close friend, appealing to Him to accept their devotion and service, only to hear Jesus say, in essence: "It's not a question of whether you know Me; the question is whether I know you"? I do not believe there could be anything more terrible than to stand before Jesus and hear Him say: "I don't know who you are. You do not belong here. Please leave. I don't know you now; I never knew you."

Do you see now why I say these are the most terrifying words Jesus ever uttered? Anyone can say, "Lord, Lord," but many who do so are only honoring Him with their lips. Many make false professions of faith and deceive themselves into thinking that they belong to Jesus, but they have never repented, never put their trust in Christ, and never embraced Him with their hearts. Only those whose hearts have been changed by God the Holy Spirit can say, "Lord, Lord," and mean it.

On the other hand, can you imagine any greater joy than to stand before Christ at the end of the age and to hear Him speak your name and say, "Come, you blessed of My Father, inherit the kingdom prepared for you from the foundation of the world" (Matt. 25:34)? There are no more comforting words than those. Therefore, I exhort you, make sure that you know that He knows you.

36

A FIRM FOUNDATION

Matthew 7:24–29

"Therefore, whoever hears these sayings of Mine, and does them, I will liken him to a wise man who built his house on the rock: and the rain descended, the floods came, and the winds blew and beat on that house; and it did not fall, for it was founded on the rock. But everyone who hears these sayings of Mine, and does not do them, will be like a foolish man who built his house on the sand: and the rains descended, the floods came, and the winds blew and beat on that house; and it fell. And great was its fall." And so it was, when Jesus had ended these sayings, that the people were astonished at His teaching, for He taught them as one having authority, and not as the scribes.

In the early 1970s, I was preaching and teaching in a church in Cincinnati, Ohio. Every year the church had a special event that was called a preaching mission, which was a kind of evangelistic outreach. An outstanding preacher from out of town was invited to lead the mission. One year, we invited a famous preacher from California, and he stayed in our home during that time. After the mission, I drove him to the airport, and he departed on his flight for California. But while his plane was en route, Southern California was hit by a major earthquake, and the epicenter was near the city of Glendale, where this man ministered. When he got home, he was relieved to find that none of the people in his congregation were injured. Furthermore, the church's magnificent sanctuary did not have so much as a broken window. Everything seemed to be intact. But in the weeks that followed, as engineers examined the various structures in the city to see whether they were still safe after the earthquake, it was found that the foundation of the sanctuary had shifted. Therefore, the city condemned the building as unsafe.

Jesus brought the Sermon on the Mount to its conclusion by asking His hearers to think about sound and unsound foundations. Specifically, He presented the example of two houses, one that was able to withstand the catastrophic forces of nature and another that could not. It all came down to the foundations. One house was built on a sound foundation, but the other was built on an unsound foundation. The decisions that were made as to where to lay those foundations determined the eventual fate of those houses.

Hearing and Doing

Jesus said: **"Therefore, whoever hears these sayings of Mine, and does them, I will liken him to a wise man who built his house on the rock: and the rain descended, the floods came, and the winds blew and beat on that house; and it did not fall, for it was founded on the rock. But everyone who hears these sayings of Mine, and does not do them, will be like a foolish man who built his house on the sand: and the rain descended, the floods came, and the winds blew and beat on that house; and it fell. And great was its fall"** (vv. 24–27).

Recently, I was in Phoenix, Arizona, a city that has risen out of the sands of the desert. In that city, there are many concrete canals. For most of the year, these canals are empty of water. But on those rare occasions when the rains come, the water that falls is directed into these canals, which become raging torrents. Big signs warn people not to drive in these canals because they can be unsafe when the rains come. The city of Phoenix has an ordinance saying that if a person gets caught in one of these canals during a flood, he has to pay the cost of his rescue, plus a fine. However, people are so foolish that they ignore these warnings and drive in the canals anyway. So, it isn't unusual to see a report on CNN about the rescue of someone who has driven into one of the canals and gotten into trouble when the rains came unexpectedly.

In some dry places in the world, there are natural features much like the canals in Phoenix. In the southwestern regions of the United States, there are arroyos, which are creekbeds that remain dry until the rainy season comes. Likewise, in the Middle East, including Israel, there are wadis, which are much like arroyos. Wadis are so common, many places are named for them. The wadis in Israel are dry except for twice a year, when the rains come. They call them the former rains, which come in the spring, and the latter rains, which come in the fall.

When those rains come, the same thing that happens in the Phoenix canals happens there. The water runs off the desert and fills the wadis to overflowing, and anything that gets in the way of the torrents ripping through the wadis faces immediate destruction.

Jesus was certainly aware of these climactic conditions of His native land. Furthermore, as a carpenter, Jesus was familiar with the process of building a house. One of the most important parts of that process was selecting a good site on which to build and then laying a solid foundation. The location and the foundation were critical because of the rains. If a house did not have a sure foundation, it was likely to be washed away when the torrents came and rushed across the landscape, destroying everything in their path. So Jesus concluded His sermon with a very down-to-earth illustration that communicated a profound truth—the difference between a wise man and a fool. That difference had to do with foundations.

When we read through the New Testament and see the teaching of Jesus and the Apostles about the church, we see that they describe the church by many metaphors. It is called the people of God. It is called a body. It is called a family. It is called the bride of Christ. Yet one of the key metaphors for the church is a building. Believers are called "living stones" that make up a "spiritual house" (1 Pet. 2:5). The church is also called God's temple (1 Cor. 3:16) and the household of God (Eph. 2:19).

As part of this building metaphor, the New Testament identifies the foundation of the church. If I were to take a poll among Christians as to what or who is the foundation of the church, I am quite certain that most would answer, "Christ." We sing, "The church's one foundation is Jesus Christ her Lord."[1] However, this may be a case of our hymnody informing our theology more than the New Testament does. According to the New Testament, Jesus is *not* the foundation of the church. Jesus is the cornerstone, but the foundation is the prophets of the Old Testament and the apostles of the New Testament (Eph. 2:20).

Elsewhere, the Bible indicates that the Apostles are the primary element of the foundation. When the Apostle John was given his glorious vision of the New Jerusalem—an image of the glorified church—descending from heaven, he seemed hard-pressed to describe how glorious it was. The city was so extraordinary, it had not one but twelve foundations, and those foundations, John says, bore the names of the twelve Apostles (Rev. 21:14).

Rejecting the Foundation

Why is it so important for us to understand that the Apostles are the foundation of the church? The Apostles were those men Jesus commissioned and to whom

[1] From the hymn "The Church's One Foundation" by Samuel J. Stone, 1896.

He gave His authority. The believers in the early church devoted themselves to the study of the Apostles' doctrine (Acts 2:42). Eventually, the writings of the Apostles were collected in the New Testament. However, in the past two hundred years, there has been an unbridled assault, a kind of vandalism, against the trustworthiness, the sufficiency, and, above all, the authority of the New Testament. In attacking the Bible, the skeptics have attacked the authority of the Apostles. That is an assault on the very foundation of the church. Sadly, we have seen church after church, denomination after denomination, repudiate the God-given foundation. That means they have constructed their houses on sand. Those churches and denominations will not stand in times of trouble for the simple reason that they cannot stand. When the church moves away from her apostolic foundation, she inevitably falls.

The attack on the foundation of the church did not start in the eighteenth century during the Enlightenment, during the nineteenth century with European liberalism, or during the twentieth century with neo-liberalism. It started much earlier. In the second century, the assault came from the Gnostic heretics. The word *Gnostic* comes from the Greek word for knowledge, *gnōsis*. The Gnostics claimed to have secret knowledge, insights that were superior to the teaching of the Apostles. They wanted to keep Jesus in the church but get rid of the Apostles. We hear this same kind of thing from radical feminists, who say they love Jesus but cannot stand the Apostle Paul. They do not like what Paul and the other Apostles teach about the role of women in the home and in the church. They forget that we know nothing about what Jesus said or taught except through the Apostles.

In the second century, God raised up a great apologist whose name was Irenaeus, who wrote to combat the Gnostic heretics. Irenaeus went back to the New Testament and reminded the people of how Jesus had to defend Himself against the Pharisees of His own time, showing them that their positions were inconsistent. The Pharisees said they loved Abraham, but Jesus said, "Your father Abraham rejoiced to see My day, and he saw it and was glad" (John 8:56). The Pharisees said they loved Moses, but Jesus said, "If you believed Moses, you would believe Me; for he wrote about Me" (John 5:46). The Pharisees claimed to love God the Father, but Jesus said, "He who rejects Me rejects Him who sent Me" (Luke 10:16b) and "He who does not honor the Son does not honor the Father who sent Him" (John 5:23). The Pharisees could not reject Jesus without rejecting Abraham, Moses, and even God the Father.

Do you see it? Jesus was refuting the religions of the world that say they believe in God but reject His only begotten Son. If someone has the Father, he has the Son. If he has the Son, he has the Father. He cannot have one without the other.

When Jesus commissioned His Apostles and sent them out, He bestowed His authority on them. Just as the Father sent the Son, so the Son sent the Apostles. He told them, "He who hears you hears Me; he who rejects you rejects Me" (Luke 10:16a). It was Christ who established the Apostles as the foundation of His church. If a person rejects the apostolic writings, He rejects the authority of Christ. If he rejects the authority of Christ, he rejects God Himself.

Therefore, the wise thing to do is to believe and act on Jesus' words. Those who do, find that their lives are built on a solid foundation. Those who do not, eventually find that their lives are built on no foundation at all, and one drop of rain can sweep them away.

Matthew tells us, **And so it was, when Jesus had ended these sayings, that the people were astonished at His teaching, for He taught them as one having authority, and not as the scribes** (vv. 28–29). When Jesus opened His mouth and preached, He did not speak as one who had opinions. He spoke as one having authority. The Greek word translated as "authority" here is *exousia*. It also can be translated as "power." It literally means "out of being" or "out of substance." Whenever Jesus spoke, His words were substantive. They were not trivial. They were binding on the consciences of all who heard. We cannot come into the church if we will not submit our lives to the authority of Jesus, because the Father has bestowed upon Him all authority in heaven and on earth (Matt. 28:18).

37

THE CLEANSING OF THE LEPER

Matthew 8:1–4

> When He had come down from the mountain, great multitudes followed Him. And behold, a leper came and worshiped Him, saying, "Lord, if You are willing, You can make me clean." Then Jesus put out His hand and touched him, saying, "I am willing; be cleansed." Immediately his leprosy was cleansed. And Jesus said to him, "See that you tell no one; but go your way, show yourself to the priest, and offer the gift that Moses commanded, as a testimony to them."

I have talked to many people who have set out to read the Bible. Very often, they relate experiences such as this: "I started well. I read through the whole book of Genesis, and it was somewhat familiar to me and interesting reading, like a novel. Then I moved on to the book of Exodus, and it was like a Cecil B. DeMille spectacle, and that also kept my interest. But when I got to Leviticus and all of those details about the requirements for worship and the laws that are recorded there, they were so unfamiliar and boring that I lost my interest."

Maybe that's been your experience. Maybe you were stopped in your efforts to read through the Bible when you encountered passages like this:

> And the Lord spoke to Moses and Aaron, saying: "When a man has on the skin of his body a swelling, a scab, or a bright spot, and it becomes on the skin of his body like a leprous sore, then he shall be brought to Aaron the priest or to one

> of his sons the priests. The priest shall examine the sore on the skin of the body; and if the hair on the sore has turned white, and the sore appears to be deeper than the skin of his body, it is a leprous sore. Then the priest shall examine him, and pronounce him unclean. But if the bright spot is white on the skin of the body, and does not appear to be deeper than the skin, and its hair has not turned white, then the priest shall isolate the one who has the sore seven days. And the priest shall examine him on the seventh day; and indeed if the sore appears to be as it was, and the sore has not spread on the skin, then the priest shall isolate him another seven days. Then the priest shall examine him again on the seventh day; and indeed if the sore has faded, and the sore has not spread on the skin, then the priest shall pronounce him clean; it is only a scab, and he shall wash his clothes and be clean. But if the scab should at all spread over the skin, after he has been seen by the priest for his cleansing, he shall be seen by the priest again." (Lev. 13:1–7)

This goes on for three chapters. I admit, it is difficult for us to get excited about this kind of biblical material because it seems so alien to our experience. I doubt anyone reading this book, upon waking up in the morning and finding a rash on his or her body, has wondered whether it might be leprous.

On the other hand, if you or a loved one have ever had a biopsy done for one reason or another, and then had to wait for the results, you know the anxiety that can provoke in your heart. A few years ago, my son was diagnosed with Hodgkin's lymphoma. It was caught in the early stages, but he still went through the full sequence of treatments of chemotherapy. However, the doctors did not go with radiation because they pronounced him completely free of cancer. More recently, he called and said that he had discovered a new lump, and they had to do a biopsy on that. But he was not the least bit concerned. He said: "Dad, I trust the Lord in these things. I'm not worried about it." I thought, "Well, good for you, but I'm worried." I was a nervous wreck for three weeks waiting for the outcome of that biopsy. By the grace of God it was completely clean. The feeling of relief you have when you get a good report on a biopsy is wonderful.

For an ancient Israelite, waking up with a strange mark on his skin and having to go through all of the prescribed examinations by the priest was an exercise in terror, because the worst disease that he could ever contract was leprosy. In fact, it was the only disease in Israel that involved not only a medical judgment but also an ecclesiastical one. There was no cure for leprosy and no medicine that could even alleviate the symptoms, so the classic treatment for leprosy in Israel at that time was quarantine. Once the scab had been determined to be leprous, the person was removed from his family, from his village, and from all interaction with other human beings, except other lepers. The leper was pronounced to be unclean, which meant he was no longer able to participate in the religious community of the Israelites. To get that diagnosis was a dreadful thing indeed.

A Leper with Faith

That brings me to Matthew 8. In this chapter, Matthew presents accounts of several miracles Jesus performed. The first of these involved the healing of a leper, which, at that time in history, was as astounding as raising someone from the dead.

Matthew writes, **When He had come down from the mountain, great multitudes followed Him** (v. 1). The Sermon on the Mount only increased Jesus' following; He was basically mobbed when He continued His ministry. Matthew then notes, **And behold, a leper came and worshiped Him, saying, "Lord, if You are willing, You can make me clean"** (v. 2). The word that is translated "worshiped" here is not clear in the Greek. It could simply mean that the man showed obeisance to Jesus, such as one might show to a king or to some other person who is worthy of great respect.

In any case, the leper bowed before Jesus and said, "Lord, if You are willing, You can make me clean." What an amazing statement of faith this was. This leper clearly had heard of Jesus. I do not know how he could have received any kind of news from the grapevine, given how isolated lepers were from the mainstream of life. Yet, somehow the word that had gone through the whole land about this remarkable healer had found its way to the lepers, and this man was convinced. So, he bowed before Jesus and confessed, "I don't know whether You will, but I know that You are able to make me clean."

When I'm on my knees before God about whatever matter is concerning me, I know beyond a shadow of a doubt that He can handle anything I bring before Him. But I also know enough about the sovereignty of God to understand that quite often when I ask God to do things, He hears me but He answers no. In other words, He is not always willing to do what I ask Him to do. When we hear that answer from God, we have to be able to carry on in our Christian lives, saying, "God, if that is not what pleases You, if it is not Your will, that's OK; Your will be done, not mine." That is what Jesus taught us to pray (Matt. 6:10) and that is what He Himself did when He wrestled with the Father in the garden of Gethsemane, saying, "Not as I will, but as You will" (Matt. 26:39). The leper seems to have understood this, for he expressed confidence that Jesus *could* heal him, *if* it were His will to do so.

How did Jesus respond? The first thing He did was astonishing: **Then Jesus put out His hand and touched him** (v. 3a). He put His hand upon the loathsome body of a leper. This violated all the principles of the society of His day. Then He said, **"I am willing; be cleansed." Immediately his leprosy was cleansed** (v. 3b). Jesus made this miserable creature whole. This man who could do nothing to cleanse himself was made clean by the touch of Jesus. Jesus did for this man what no one else in the world could do for him.

Matthew then writes, **And Jesus said to him, "See that you tell no one"** (v. 4a). Jesus did not want everyone flocking to Him for healing and missing the point of His ministry. Instead, He told the man, **"but go your way, show yourself to the priest, and offer the gift that Moses commanded, as a testimony to them"** (v. 4b). He instructed the man to do what the law of God in Leviticus required. He needed to go back to the priest and let the priest examine him. The priest could then declare that he was clean and allow him to go back to his village and his family.

What did Jesus mean by saying, "offer the gift that Moses commanded, as a testimony to them"? The law of God in the Old Testament required lepers who were cured to make a sacrifice. They had to bring a gift. However, these were poor people. What kind of productivity, what kind of enterprise or commerce could a leper have in antiquity? In fact, because the poverty of lepers was often so severe, the law of God made special provisions. If a leper who was cured was particularly poor, he was allowed to give a lesser sacrificial gift than what was required of the general population.

A Reaction of Gratitude

So, in this story we see wonderful demonstrations of Jesus' compassion (in touching a leper and being willing to heal him) and His power (to heal the man of a deadly disease). But there is another application here we dare not miss.

If you are regenerate by the power of the Holy Spirit, if you are a converted person, you have been cleansed from something far more deadly than leprosy. You have been made clean from all of your sins. When, by the Spirit's call, you came to Christ and humbly asked for His deliverance from the guilt and shame of your sin, He said, "I am willing; be cleansed." So, you now can stand before God cleansed of sin and clothed in the perfect righteousness of Christ. But if Jesus commanded the leper to make a gift in response to His healing, what should be our response?

When Jesus saved us, He bought us at a great price (1 Cor. 6:20; 7:23). We do not own ourselves. In fact, we do not own anything. He owns us and all we have. But He has given us the pearl of great price (Matt. 13:46). In return, He asks us for a simple affirmation of gratitude: "Bring all the tithes into the storehouse" (Mal. 3:10a). He asks us to give a tenth of all our increase. Yes, this can be hard to do, but He expects it. It is not a cliché that the Lord loves a cheerful giver. He loves it when a person comes with his gifts and says: "Here, Lord, is my gift. I can't wait to give it. I am delighted to have the opportunity to give it to You, because I give You only what You have given me."

I cannot imagine the leper saying to Jesus: "Thank you for making me whole. I'm happy to go and show myself to the priest, and I want the priest to give me that certificate that I can take home to my family and my village and say: 'Here I am. I'm cured. I don't have to cry, "Unclean! Unclean!" when I see you coming.' But please don't ask me for a gift. You really don't expect me to make a sacrifice after what You have done for me, do You?" I can only imagine the leper was delighted to give his gift, for he must have been grateful beyond all words. Therefore, we who have been cleansed of far worse than leprosy should be willing to give the gift our gracious healer requires.

38

THE CENTURION'S SERVANT AND PETER'S MOTHER-IN-LAW

Matthew 8:5–15

Now when Jesus had entered Capernaum, a centurion came to Him, pleading with Him, saying, "Lord, my servant is lying at home paralyzed, dreadfully tormented." And Jesus said to him, "I will come and heal him." The centurion answered and said, "Lord, I am not worthy that You should come under my roof. But only speak a word, and my servant will be healed. For I also am a man under authority, having soldiers under me. And I say to this one, 'Go,' and he goes; and to another, 'Come,' and he comes; and to my servant, 'Do this,' and he does it." When Jesus heard it, He marveled, and said to those who followed, "Assuredly, I say to you, I have not found such great faith, not even in Israel! And I say to you that many will come from east and west, and sit down with Abraham, Isaac, and Jacob in the kingdom of heaven. But the sons of the kingdom will be cast out into outer darkness. There will be weeping and gnashing of teeth." Then Jesus said to the centurion, "Go your way; and as you have believed, so let it be done for you." And his servant was healed that same hour. Now when Jesus had come into Peter's house, He saw his wife's mother lying sick with a fever. So He touched her hand, and the fever left her. And she arose and served them.

In his Gospel, Matthew often arranges his material topically rather than chronologically. We see this in the sections immediately following the Sermon on the Mount, where he gathers together a series of miracle stories.

We looked at the first of these miracles, the healing of a leper, in the previous chapter, and we will examine two more in this chapter. The first of these two healings, that of the centurion's servant, is very important for us because it speaks volumes to me about what it means to be a Christian. As we will see, there is an element of application here that touches the very heart of Christianity.

Matthew begins, **Now when Jesus had entered Capernaum, a centurion came to Him, pleading with Him** (v. 5). Capernaum, the city where Jesus lived and made His headquarters during his Galilean ministry, was one of many towns and villages along the northwest shore of the Sea of Galilee. It had a bustling fishing industry, as well as numerous merchants, artisans, and scribes. Although it was not a strong Roman outpost, there were some soldiers stationed there. A centurion was one who had command of a hundred soldiers. It is very possible that, as small as the garrison at Capernaum was. the man who came to Jesus in this story was the top Roman officer in the city. But he came in abject humility, not asking Jesus for help but begging for it.

What was the centurion's request? Matthew tells us that he said, **"Lord, my servant is lying at home paralyzed, dreadfully tormented"** (v. 6). The centurion did not explain why the servant was paralyzed. It could have been the result of an injury, a stroke, or some other malady. Sadly, in that day, when someone suffered paralysis, it was considered to be a permanent condition. But not only was the servant paralyzed, he was "dreadfully tormented." Here we are even more in the dark; it is unclear whether the servant was tormented by pain or some other factor.

When we looked at Jesus' healing of the leper in the previous chapter, we saw that the leper said, "If You are willing, You can make me clean." There was no question in the leper's mind about Jesus' ability or power to cure leprosy; his only question had to do with Jesus' willingness. Jesus assured him, "I am willing," and cleansed him. The willingness of Jesus to enter into the torment of those around Him was made manifest once again in His ready response to the centurion's plea for his servant: **"I will come and heal him"** (v. 7).

The Faith of a Gentile

Now, I would expect the centurion to have been delighted by Jesus' answer and to have said: "Great, let's go. Let's hurry. Let's not waste a moment, because as we speak my servant is in agony." But that is not what he said. Instead, **the centurion answered and said, "Lord, I am not worthy that You should come under my roof. But only speak a word, and my servant will be healed"** (v. 8). The centurion replied: "No, Jesus, You don't need to come with me. In fact, it wouldn't be appropriate for You to come to my home. I am not worthy to have You in my home."

As we have already seen in Jesus' willingness to touch a leper, societal conventions meant nothing to Him when it came to redeeming people who were suffering. Jesus had no hesitation about going to the home of a Roman centurion. Yet, the centurion was hesitant about Jesus' coming under his roof. Perhaps this centurion was aware that the Jewish rules and regulations barred Jews from entering the private residences of Gentiles, because the Gentiles were considered to be ceremonially unclean. Perhaps he knew that the Jews hated the Romans as much as any conquered people hate their conquerors. In any case, he was reluctant for Jesus to go so far as to come to his house.

The centurion continued, **"For I also am a man under authority, having soldiers under me. And I say to this one, 'Go,' and he goes; and to another, 'Come,' and he comes; and to my servant, 'Do this,' and he does it"** (v. 9). The centurion was saying that he was thoroughly familiar with authority, being one who was under the authority of superior officers and one who exercised authority over soldiers. However, I think there is a subtle hint here of recognition that Jesus spoke under authority, the authority of God. He communicated the authority of God whenever He spoke, as we saw in Matthew 7:29. Furthermore, the centurion clearly recognized that Jesus had authority to heal. So, he simply acknowledged Jesus' authority and ability to heal the servant with a word from a distance.

Matthew then writes, **When Jesus heard it, He marveled** (v. 10a). This is one of only two times in all of the New Testament that the Greek verb *thaumazō* is used with respect to Jesus. It means "to wonder at" or "to marvel." This word is used frequently in accounts of Jesus' miracles, but there it describes the reaction of those who witnessed His signs. Their normal response was astonishment or amazement. Here, however, Jesus is astonished. That which astonished Him was the faith of this Gentile. He **said to those who followed, "Assuredly, I say to you, I have not found such great faith, not even in Israel!"** (v. 10b).

But Jesus did not stop there; He went on to remark about the larger implications of the presence of such faith in a Gentile rather than an Israelite: **"And I say to you that many will come from east and west, and sit down with Abraham, Isaac, and Jacob in the kingdom of heaven. But the sons of the kingdom will be cast out into outer darkness. There will be weeping and gnashing of teeth"** (vv. 11–12). This is incredible. Jesus said people from all over the earth would be part of the kingdom of heaven, while many Israelites would be cast out, to their everlasting grief. Jesus was prophesying the opening of the kingdom of God to the Gentiles, which began to happen in the early church, as recorded in the book of Acts.

The Promise of God

A friend of mine who lives in the western United States wrote to me recently and told me that he was planning a surprise fiftieth birthday party for his wife. He was going to have a "Scripture party." I had never heard of a Scripture party, but he explained it in the letter. During the party, all the guests would quote their favorite Bible verses and say why those verses meant so much to them. My friend knew that Vesta and I would not be able to attend the party because we live so far away, so he asked us to record our favorite verses on video to be played at the party. We thought that was a wonderful idea, so we recorded a short video clip in which I shared my favorite verse and told why I like it, and then I recorded one for Vesta, because she could not talk about her favorite verse without tearing up.

Now, my favorite verse of Scripture is Genesis 15:17: "And it came to pass, when the sun went down and it was dark, that behold, there appeared a smoking oven and a burning torch that passed between those pieces." Sometimes at conferences people ask me to sign books or even their Bibles, and sometimes they ask me to add my "life verse." I'm not sure what a life verse is, but at some point I began writing down Genesis 15:17. Almost invariably, when I write that verse with my signature, the person will come back ten or fifteen minutes later to ask, "Did you mean to write this verse?" When I assure the person that I did, he will ask, "That's your favorite verse?" When I say yes, he will always ask why, so I have to explain.

Genesis 15 recounts the occasion when God renewed His promise to give Abraham the land of Canaan, and Abraham said to God, 'How shall I know that I will inherit it?" (v. 8). God condescended to Abraham's weakness, which was really unbelief. He commanded Abraham to get a heifer, a goat, a ram, a turtledove, and a pigeon, then to cut them in pieces, and to arrange the pieces in two rows, forming a path. After Abraham obeyed, God made him fall into a deep sleep, and during that sleep, "a smoking oven and a burning torch . . . passed between those pieces."

The book of Hebrews unwraps this strange event for us: "For when God made a promise to Abraham, because He could swear by no one greater, He swore by Himself, saying, 'Surely blessing I will bless you, and multiplying I will multiply you'" (6:13–14). The author of Hebrews understood that this was a theophany, that God was manifesting Himself in the smoking oven and the burning torch, and that He was forging a covenant with Abraham and symbolically saying to him: "If I do not keep My word, may I be torn asunder, just as you have cut these animals in two. I am swearing by Myself, by My holy character." That was how God reassured Abraham. And God's reassurance to Abraham reassures me. It reminds me that God cannot break His word.

Vesta's favorite verses are 1 John 3:1–2: "Behold what manner of love the Father has bestowed on us, that we should be called children of God! Therefore the world does not know us, because it did not know Him. Beloved, now we are children of God; and it has not yet been revealed what we shall be, but we know that when He is revealed, we shall be like Him, for we shall see Him as He is." This passage reminds us that someday we will have the beatific vision. We will see God face-to-face, and the light of His countenance will flood us with glory.

Experience versus Scripture

Back in the early 1960s, the charismatic movement began to make inroads in Lutheran circles, Episcopalian circles, and even Presbyterian circles. The first year I taught college, it seemed to me that all the students in my theology class had been turned on to the Pentecostal faith. They were speaking in tongues, having exotic experiences, and asking me all kinds of questions that I couldn't answer. These students became very interested in and excited about the power of God, and they started to live by believing in this power. For instance, if they were in a car that ran out of gas, they would lay hands on the gas tank, believing that God would cause the car to operate without gasoline. I became swept up in their enthusiasm, but as I went through this stage, I kept being disappointed by unfulfilled expectations. Thankfully, God helped me see that I could not live my Christian life by my feelings and experiences. I realized I needed the Word of God, for that is where I find my stability, my confidence, my ability to persevere, and my hope. Whether this experience or that experience is of the Holy Spirit, I never know for sure. But I know this—the Bible is God's Word.

In my life, I have had some ineffable experiences of being overwhelmed and enveloped by the presence of God. Those experiences were so profound, so acute, that I was content to die on the spot. I said: "This is enough. I don't need anything else." I'm sure that many of you reading this book know what I'm talking about, having had similar experiences of the sweetness of the presence of Jesus. There is nothing like it. But in fifty years of being a Christian, those experiences have been very rare, and they cannot be conjured up. There is no formula to create a sovereign manifestation of the presence of God.

However, I can always rely on God's Word. I do not have to have a mystical experience in order to hear the Word. It is available to me every day. All I have to do is open the book, and when I open the book, I behold the Word of God. Every time I'm tempted to pursue the ecstasies of experience, I think back to the time of Jesus' great temptation and testing in the wilderness, when Satan unleashed all of the horrors of hell against Him. But Jesus responded to the devil by saying, "Man shall not live by bread alone, but by every word that proceeds from the mouth of God" (Matt. 4:4). We will enjoy God's immediate presence for eternity, but for now, we are to live by His Word.

That's the lesson of the centurion. He was saying to Jesus: "You don't have to come. Just say the word and my servant will be healed. I know the power of Your word. I know that the universe is here because You spoke it into being. You said, 'Let there be light,' and there was light. I believe all authority in heaven and on earth is given to You."

Jesus marveled at the faith of this Roman. Then He said, "**Go your way; and as you have believed, so let it be done for you." And his servant was healed that same hour** (v. 13). Jesus never touched the paralyzed man like He touched the leper. He simply commanded His healing, and it happened.

This is what the Christian faith is all about: "Speak, LORD, for Your servant hears" (1 Sam. 3:9). The Word of God has the power to change our lives. We can depend on it and live by it.

Matthew tells us: **Now when Jesus had come into Peter's house, He saw his wife's mother lying sick with a fever. So He touched her hand, and the fever left her. And she arose and served them** (vv. 14–15). Jesus parted from the centurion and went to Peter's house, but there He found Peter's mother-in-law sick in bed. Jesus healed her also, and as a measure of how thorough was her healing, she got out of her bed and served Jesus and those with Him. The Greek word that is used here is *diakoneō*, from which we get the word *deacon*. This is appropriate, for the only legitimate response to the healing power of Jesus is to serve Him.

39

THE HEALER WHO WAS TO COME

Matthew 8:16–17

When evening had come, they brought to Him many who were demon- possessed. And He cast out the spirits with a word, and healed all who were sick, that it might be fulfilled which was spoken by Isaiah the prophet, saying: "He Himself took our infirmities and bore our sicknesses."

Since concluding his account of the Sermon on the Mount, Matthew has set before us a series of episodes that show Jesus engaged in healing the sick, the broken, and the dying. We saw the healing of the leper (8:1–4), the healing of the centurion's paralyzed servant (vv. 5–13), and the healing of Peter's mother-in-law of a fever (vv. 14–15). The next two verses of Matthew's Gospel basically summarize the healing aspect of Jesus' ministry.

Matthew writes, **When evening had come, they brought to him many who were demon-possessed. And He cast out the spirits with a word, and healed all who were sick** (v. 16). After three accounts of specific healings, Matthew tells us about a session of multiple healings, showing us the power of Christ in casting out evil spirits and delivering people from sickness.

Then Matthew tells us why He did this. Certainly Jesus was moved by compassion for the pain of the people to whom He ministered. We read again and again in the Gospels that Jesus was deeply moved by the suffering that He observed among the people (Matt. 14:14; 20:34; Mark 1:41; 6:34; Luke 7:13).

Out of His profound sense of compassion, He ministered to their needs. But there was more.

As we have seen, Matthew often takes pains to show how the ministry of Jesus fulfilled Old Testament prophecies, and he does so again in this passage. Matthew says Jesus healed the people **that it might be fulfilled which was spoken by Isaiah the prophet, saying: "He Himself took our infirmities and bore our sicknesses"** (v. 17).

In the Greek, this verse includes a literary device called a purpose clause, so this passage tells us why Jesus ultimately did these things. He consciously wanted to fulfill a very special Old Testament prophecy, a prophecy regarding the Suffering Servant of God.

In Isaiah 53, the prophet wrote:

> Who has believed our report?
> And to whom has the arm of the LORD been revealed?
> For He shall grow up before Him as a tender plant,
> And as a root out of dry ground.
> He has no form or comeliness;
> And when we see Him,
> There is no beauty that we should desire Him.
> He is despised and rejected by men,
> A Man of sorrows and acquainted with grief.
> And we hid, as it were, our faces from Him;
> He was despised, and we did not esteem Him.
>
> Surely He has borne our griefs
> And carried our sorrows;
> Yet we esteemed Him stricken,
> Smitten by God, and afflicted.
> But He was wounded for our transgressions,
> He was bruised for our iniquities;
> The chastisement for our peace was upon Him,
> And by His stripes we are healed.
> All we like sheep have gone astray;
> We have turned, every one, to his own way;
> And the LORD has laid on Him the iniquity of us all.
>
> He was oppressed and He was afflicted,
> Yet He opened not His mouth;

> He was led as a lamb to the slaughter,
> And as a sheep before its shearers is silent,
> So He opened not His mouth. . . .
> For He was cut off from the land of the living;
> For the transgressions of My people He was stricken. . . .
>
> Yet it pleased the Lord to bruise Him;
> He has put Him to grief. . . .
> By His knowledge My righteous Servant shall justify many,
> For He shall bear their iniquities.
> Therefore I will divide Him a portion with the great,
> And He shall divide the spoil with the strong,
> Because He poured out His soul unto death,
> And He was numbered with the transgressors,
> And He bore the sin of many,
> And made intercession for the transgressors.

If there was any text in the Old Testament that the New Testament church seized upon to explain the ministry of Jesus, it was this one. It is not difficult to understand why—Isaiah 53 focuses on the reality that God laid the sins of His people on His sacrificial Lamb. When we think of the atoning death of Jesus, we almost exclusively fix our vision on Jesus' redeeming us from sin and rescuing us from the wrath of God that is to come at the last judgment. But in a way, that's a simplistic understanding of the ministry of Jesus.

Saved from Sin and Its Consequences

Jesus did not save us only from the wrath of God that is due to sin, but from all of the consequences of sin. Of course, the ultimate consequence is the judgment of God. But we live in a fallen world, a broken world, a corrupt world, a sick world, a dying world. It is a world that is called "the vale of tears," because in the fallen state in which we live, the joy of life is constantly marred by pain, illness, suffering, and death. If your church lists items for prayer in the worship bulletin, you no doubt see the names of brothers and sisters who are suffering or bereaved each week. All of this sickness, pain, and death, according to the Bible, is in the world because of sin.

Of course, we must be careful not to jump to the conclusion that there is a direct correlation between someone's sin and suffering. We cannot conclude that anyone who suffers from a disease or grief of some sort has committed a particular transgression. Job's friends made this mistake when they told Job that he must have sinned or else he would not be suffering so acutely. Likewise, Jesus' disciples came to Him and asked, "Rabbi, who sinned, this man or his parents, that he was born blind?" (John 9:2). Jesus replied, "Neither this man nor his parents sinned, but that the works of God should be revealed in him" (v. 3). Jesus did not mean to say that the man and his parents never sinned, but that none of their sins was the cause of the man's blindness. Rather, he was born blind so that Jesus might be glorified in his healing. So, we may not always know the reason we or others suffer.

What we do know is that all suffering is ultimately related to sin. If there were no sin in the world, there would be no disease, no suffering, and no death.

Paul taught that "just as through one man sin entered the world, and death through sin, . . . thus death spread to all men, because all sinned" (Rom. 5:12). When the human race fell with Adam, not only sin came into the world but also death, and the whole creation was brought into a state of suffering and pain. That is why Paul says "the whole creation groans and labors" (Rom. 8:22), waiting for the redemption of the children of God, for the final consummation of the triumph of Jesus.

A Day of No More Tears

The book of Revelation gives us a lovely picture of what life will be like when the world is made new. We read:

> Now I saw a new heaven and a new earth, for the first heaven and the first earth had passed away. Also there was no more sea. Then I, John, saw the holy city, New Jerusalem, coming down out of heaven from God, prepared as a bride adorned for her husband. And I heard a loud voice from heaven saying, "Behold, the tabernacle of God is with men, and He will dwell with them, and they shall be His people. God Himself will be with them and be their God. And God will wipe away every tear from their eyes; there shall be no more death, nor sorrow, nor crying. There shall be no more pain, for the former things have passed away." (21:1–4)

When the final work of divine redemption has been accomplished and all things have been made new, God will tabernacle in the midst of His people in the new heaven and new earth. When that day comes, "God will wipe away every tear from their eyes."

When I was a little boy, while I was outside playing, I would often suffer some minor hurt—a skinned elbow or a stubbed toe—and I would start to cry. Whenever I began to cry, I made a beeline to my house, because what I wanted more than anything else was my mother. Even today, when I hear a child start to cry and say, "I want my mommy," I remember that feeling. I wanted my mother, too. So I would go to her. I usually found her in the kitchen, and she usually had an apron on. As she held me, she would lean over, take the edge of her apron, and wipe away my tears. I still remember that. One of the most tender experiences a human being can know is that of having his tears wiped away. My mother would say, "Chase that gremlin away, and let me see a smile on your face." Having been comforted, I would smile, and then I would go back outside and play some more.

Of course, sooner or later I would get hurt again. Sooner or later I would seek out my mother once more, and she would wipe away my tears yet again. But God says the day is coming when He will wipe away our tears, and when God wipes away our tears, that's the end of it. In the new heaven and the new earth, there will be no more need for tears of sorrow, for there will be no more death, no more disease, and no more pain.

This sounds too good to be true. Nevertheless it is true, because Jesus fulfilled Isaiah's prophecy about the Suffering Servant of Yahweh, the Servant that God would send into the world for the explicit purpose of suffering in place of His people.

When we look at the cross, we see that God the Father placed the sin of all of His people on His Son. God imputed your sin and my sin to His Servant. While He was hanging on the cross, Jesus was under God's curse for all our cosmic treason. But that's not all. Not only was our sin laid on Jesus, so were all of our illnesses. God put cancer on Him. He put heart disease on Him. He put diabetes on Him. He put leprosy on Him. He put every disease that has been painful to the human race on Jesus. "He has borne our griefs and carried our sorrows." It was not just our sin that was removed, but all the consequences of our sin.

You might well ask, "If that's true, why do people still get sick and die?" It is for the same reason we still sin. The work of redemption is not yet complete. But when God finishes that great work, sin will be no more, and therefore all the consequences of sin will vanish with it. The time is coming: no more disease, no more sorrow, no more pain, no more death, and no more tears.

40

THE COST OF DISCIPLESHIP

Matthew 8:18–22

And when Jesus saw great multitudes about Him, He gave a command to depart to the other side. Then a certain scribe came and said to Him, "Teacher, I will follow You wherever You go." And Jesus said to him, "Foxes have holes and birds of the air have nests, but the Son of Man has nowhere to lay His head." Then another of His disciples said to Him, "Lord, let me first go and bury my father." But Jesus said to him, "Follow Me, and let the dead bury their own dead."

During Jesus' ministry, the scribes and the Pharisees, almost to a man, were extremely hostile toward Him and resisted Him at every turn. That is why this passage from Matthew's Gospel is so extraordinary. Here we read of a scribe, of all people, who approached Jesus in a spirit of profound enthusiasm and willingness to be His disciple.

Matthew tells us, **when Jesus saw great multitudes about Him, He gave a command to depart to the other side** (v. 18). Perhaps Jesus wished to cross the Sea of Galilee in an effort to find a quiet place that would offer a respite for Himself and His disciples after a busy season of ministry. As they were about to set out, **a certain scribe came and said to Him, "Teacher, I will follow You wherever You go"** (v. 19).

This is an amazing affirmation and statement of dedication. When we read the pages of Scripture carefully, we occasionally find similar declarations of commitment. However, we often find that these grandiose professions of allegiance faded into nothing when tribulation came. The Apostle Paul warned, "Therefore let him who thinks he stands take heed lest he fall" (1 Cor. 10:12).

Think for a moment of Peter in the upper room, celebrating the Lord's Supper with Jesus and the other disciples. Jesus looked at him and said: "Simon, Simon! Indeed, Satan has asked for you, that he may sift you as wheat. But I have prayed for you, that your faith should not fail; and when you have returned to Me, strengthen your brethren" (Luke 22:31–32). How did Simon Peter respond when Jesus looked him in the eye and said Satan wanted him? Simon said, "Lord, I am ready to go with You, both to prison and to death" (v. 33). Statements of allegiance do not get much stronger than that. But Jesus only said, "I tell you, Peter, the rooster shall not crow this day before you will deny three times that you know Me" (v. 34). The rest, as we say, is history.

Likewise, in Paul's last letter, his second epistle to Timothy, he spoke of Demas. We have to believe that Paul never would have taken Demas with him had Demas not expressed a strong commitment to Paul's apostolic enterprise. He worked side by side with Paul. But when Paul was left alone in prison, he told Timothy, "Demas has forsaken me, having loved this present world, and has departed for Thessalonica" (2 Tim. 4:10).

Responding to the Call

At the time of my conversion, I was part of a group of Christians who gathered often to study the Bible and sing hymns together around the piano, and it was then that I learned some of the old gospel hymns that I have never forgotten. One of them was "Where He Leads Me I Will Follow." I sang that hymn every week with gusto and commitment. But in the years of my ministry, there have been many times when Jesus went one way and I went another. I certainly meant the words when I sang them: "I can hear my Savior calling, take thy cross and follow, follow Me. . . . Where He leads me I will follow, I'll go with Him, with Him all the way." But I was like Augustine, who prayed in his youth, "Lord, give me chastity and continence, but not yet." Sadly, I think this hesitation when it comes to following Jesus is characteristic of many of us.

Another of those old gospel hymns is "Softy and Tenderly Jesus Is Calling." I love that hymn, or at least part of it. There is a portion of that hymn that I do not like. It is the verse that says, "Why should we tarry when Jesus is pleading, pleading for you and for me?" We get the image of Jesus calling sinners to come to Him in faith, but He does not just call them, He pleads with them. Jesus Christ will never beg anyone to come to Him. He commands everyone to come to Him. The only pleading He does is when He intercedes with the Father for

His people. In truth, no one ever comes to Jesus apart from His intercession on his or her behalf.

Reformed theology is very careful to distinguish between the outward call and the inward call. The outward call is what people heard when Jesus spoke to the multitudes and said, “Come unto Me.” He called people to Himself. He still issues that call today as the gospel is proclaimed. But the only people who come to Jesus and stay with Him are the ones who are called not just outwardly but also inwardly by God the Holy Spirit. The prevailing theology in the Western world today is that Jesus invites people to come. They choose Him, they put their trust in Him, and as a direct result of their faith they are born again. But that is not the view of Paul, of Augustine, and of countless other giants of the faith. The Bible teaches that the heart has to be changed by the inward call of God the Holy Spirit, which then produces faith. After that, a person is able to come to Christ. It is crucial for us to understand the difference between a profession of faith and the possession of it. There are multitudes of people in the world who say they believe in Jesus. Maybe they went forward at an evangelistic meeting, wrote their names on cards, or said the sinner’s prayer. They may have performed any number of actions that are equated with professions of faith, but their hearts remained unregenerate. These are the people Jesus warned at the end of the Sermon on the Mount when He said, “Not everyone who says to Me, ‘Lord, Lord,’ shall enter the kingdom of heaven” (Matt. 7:21a). It is vital that we know we have heard the inward call of Christ, because only those who have heard that call will persevere unto the end.

So, this scribe came to Jesus with a lot of confident bluster. How did Jesus respond? He gave the scribe a stern warning: **And Jesus said to him, “Foxes have holes and birds of the air have nests, but the Son of Man has nowhere to lay His head”** (v. 20). It is as if Jesus looked at him and said: “I appreciate your words, but are you sure you understand what you’re signing up for? Have you counted the cost of being a disciple?”

In the late 1930s, with World War II looming, German pastor Dietrich Bonhoeffer wrote a little book titled *The Cost of Discipleship*. In it, he wrote about the widespread appearance in the European church at that time of what he called cheap grace—the idea that grace does not require a willingness to follow Jesus even into prison and to death. Bonhoeffer protested publicly against the evils committed by Adolf Hitler. He even went so far as to participate in a plot to assassinate Hitler. In the end, Bonhoeffer was executed by Hitler, paying the ultimate cost of discipleship. Jesus wants followers who will go with Him to the end, and Bonhoeffer was one who did.

The Son of Man

Jesus said, "The Son of Man has nowhere to lay His head." This is the first time in Matthew's Gospel that we see Jesus using the title "Son of Man" for Himself. Of all the titles that the New Testament uses for Jesus, Son of Man ranks third on the list in terms of numerical frequency. The title that is used most often for Jesus in the New Testament is "Christ." This is not Jesus' last name. It is one of His titles. It means "Messiah" or "Anointed One." The second most frequently used title for Jesus in the New Testament is "Lord." However, Jesus' favorite self-designation, far and away, is Son of Man. This was Jesus' favorite way to define who He is.

Why did He use it? The common misunderstanding is that Jesus called Himself the Son of Man rather than the Son of God out of a spirit of humility, not trying to be too grandiose in His self-description. This misunderstanding grows out of the declaration of the Counsel of Chalcedon that Jesus is truly God and truly man, one person with two natures, a divine nature and a human nature. Knowing this to be true, we assume that the title Son of God refers to His divine nature and the title Son of Man refers to His human nature. But that is not the case.

Yes, the title of Son of Man indicates Jesus' identification with us. But the overarching emphasis of this title is His deity, not His humanity. We know this because Jesus borrowed the title from Daniel 7, where Daniel relates a powerful vision of heaven. We read:

> "I watched until thrones were put in place,
> And the Ancient of Days was seated." (v. 9a)

Daniel saw the judgment seat of God. The throne was prepared and the Ancient of Days, who is God the Father, took His seat on the throne. He is described in magnificent terms:

> "His garment was white as snow,
> And the hair of His head was like pure wool.
> His throne was a fiery flame,
> Its wheels a burning fire;
> A fiery stream issued
> And came forth from before Him.
> A thousand thousands ministered to Him;
> Ten thousand times ten thousand stood before Him.
> The court was seated,
> And the books were opened." (vv. 9b–10)

Then another actor steps onto the stage:

> "I was watching in the night visions,
> And behold, One like the Son of Man,
> Coming with the clouds of heaven!
> He came to the Ancient of Days,
> And they brought Him near before Him.
> Then to Him was given dominion and glory and a kingdom,
> That all peoples, nations, and languages should serve Him.
> His dominion is an everlasting dominion,
> Which shall not pass away,
> And His kingdom the one
> Which shall not be destroyed." (vv. 13–14)

This is a prophecy of the return of Jesus to heaven following His earthly ministry. He is carried into the heavenly palace with Shekinah clouds of glory to receive dominion and honor forever and ever. It is the Son of Man who is exalted in this manner. Thus, this is clearly not a title of humility.

There were times throughout His ministry when Jesus used this title as part of startling statements about Himself. On one occasion, He got into a dispute with the Pharisees about the Sabbath. Jesus declared, "The Son of Man is also Lord of the Sabbath" (Luke 6:5). How did the Jews understand that statement? They knew who had created the Sabbath and issued regulations about it. It was God, of course. Thus, even though Jesus called Himself the Son of Man, He claimed to be God. That was not an exercise in humility.

On another occasion, He told a paralytic, "Son, your sins are forgiven you" (Mark 2:5b). The Jews were shocked. They said: "Why does this Man speak blasphemies like this? Who can forgive sins but God alone?" (v. 7). When Jesus perceived their thinking, He said: "'But that you may know that the Son of Man has power on earth to forgive sins'—He said to the paralytic, 'I say to you, arise, take up your bed, and go to your house'" (vv. 10–11). Jesus' use of the title Son of Man as part of an assertion of His right and power to forgive sins was not an example of humility.

When you're reading your Bible, every time you see the title Son of Man, it is good to stop and ask, "How does Jesus' use of this title in this text reveal who He is?" Let's apply that question to Jesus' reply to the scribe. He said, "The Son of Man has nowhere to lay His head." It is as if He was reminding the scribe of His humiliation. He, God in the flesh, had nowhere to lay His head. He had all the riches of heaven, but He laid it all aside to come in the flesh and live without even a pillow on which to sleep. The message for the scribe is not difficult to see—he should expect humiliation, too. Following Jesus has a cost.

Burying the Dead

Matthew then writes: **Then another of His disciples said to Him, "Lord, let me first go and bury my father." But Jesus said to him, "Follow Me, and let the dead bury their own dead"** (vv. 21–22). This disciple professed himself ready to enlist in the cause, but he had some pressing matters to take care of before he could give his full attention to Jesus. Specifically, he said he had to bury his father. In the Jewish culture of that day, when the father in the house died, it was the supreme responsibility of the eldest son to see to it that the father had a proper burial. According to Jewish law at that time, in order to carry out this responsibility, the eldest son was excused from all other duties. Even his religious responsibilities were set aside until he buried his father.

But Jesus did not allow for that cultural expectation. "Follow Me," He said, "and let the dead bury their own dead." If ever Jesus sounded as if He lacked compassion, it was here. Of course, we know that was not true; Jesus was filled with compassion for the people to whom He ministered. Jesus was simply reminding this man that the call of God on his life was absolute and immediate. There was no earthly excuse that would permit him to avoid the call. Jesus was saying: "If you are not the one who buries your father, don't worry. He will be buried. There are masses of people out there who are dead in sins. Let them take care of these earthly matters. I want you and I want you now. Follow Me."

When I was a small boy, I enjoyed playing in my sandbox in the back yard. I would play with my little cars—and they were cast-iron cars, if you want to know how old I am. I would really get involved in it. After a time, my mother would stick her head out of the window and say, "Son, come in for dinner." I would say, "Coming, Mother," but I still had a little more to do with my cars. So, a few minutes later, there would come a second call. My mother would say, "Young man, you get in this house immediately." When she said "immediately," it seemed to have about eight syllables. I knew then that I was in big trouble. I knew that when she told me to do something immediately, I needed to get moving. So I can relate to an urgent call.

The urgent call I got at that time was from someone whose authority was not absolute. Her authority was not sovereign. Her authority was not divine. But when Jesus calls us, it is an absolute call, a sovereign call, a divine call. Such a call demands an immediate response.

41

THE CALMING OF THE SEA

Matthew 8:23–27

Now when He got into a boat, His disciples followed Him. And suddenly a great tempest arose on the sea, so that the boat was covered with the waves. But He was asleep. Then His disciples came to Him and awoke Him, saying, "Lord, save us! We are perishing!" But He said to them, "Why are you fearful, O you of little faith?" Then He arose and rebuked the winds and the sea, and there was a great calm. So the men marveled, saying, "Who can this be, that even the winds and the sea obey Him?"

In my ministry through the years, I have taught not only theology but apologetics and philosophy. In fact, when I first began teaching at the seminary level in the 1960s, I was assigned to teach a senior course on atheism. In that course, I required the students to study the writings of the major atheists of recent centuries, men such as Karl Marx, Ludwig Feuerbach, Friedrich Nietzsche, Jean-Paul Sartre, and Sigmund Freud. One of the things my students and I noticed in that course was that a particular theme repeatedly surfaced in the thinking of these philosophers, particularly those who labored in the nineteenth century: they wanted to know why religion was so pervasive in the world.

There was a reason for that interest among the philosophers. In the eighteenth century, Western civilization experienced what the historians have called the Enlightenment, the *Aufklärung*, which began in Germany and spread to

France and to England. One of the central themes of the Enlightenment was the declaration that the God hypothesis was no longer necessary to explain the origin of the world or of human life. Science, it was said, had revealed how these things had come to be, apart from God. Of course, the scientific discovery that was hailed as the death knell for the God hypothesis was spontaneous generation. This was the belief that things could and did come into existence out of nothing. So, the ancient axiom *Ex nihilo nihil fit*, "Out of nothing, nothing comes," was set aside by this new theory that was said to explain the origin of all things.

Let me note in passing that in recent years, this idea has been disputed. A few years ago, I read an essay by a Nobel Prize-winning physicist, who said that we no longer can believe in spontaneous generation. He said things cannot come from nothing spontaneously. He said we have to amend the paradigm and substitute gradual spontaneous generation. I could not believe that what I was reading was written by such a distinguished scientist. He simply said it is very difficult to get something out of nothing, so we have to be patient. It only happens gradually.

In any case, the idea of spontaneous generation was accepted by so many people in the eighteenth century that many thinkers came to the conclusion that it was unnecessary to disprove the existence of God, because science had already done it. What was left for the nineteenth-century philosophers was not so much to battle against the existence of God but to explain why, if there is no God, mankind is virtually universally religious. Nearly everywhere we go, we find people engaged in religion. But if there is no God who generates the idea of religion, where does the idea come from?

That was the question that the atheists of the nineteenth century labored to solve, and almost all of them came to the same conclusion. They said that which provokes a belief in God among human beings is a fear of the forces of nature that threaten to destroy us. The idea was that human beings, living in a universe that is not conducive to human life, need some kind of a crutch to help them cope with the misery that nature sets before them. In fact, the universe was seen as not so much hostile toward humanity as indifferent, which was even worse. The philosophers said the universe simply did not care about our fate. At any moment, floods, fires, earthquakes, disease, and a host of other forces of nature might wipe human beings off the face of the earth.

Freud theorized that religion began when human beings sought to impose personality on impersonal forces of nature. He said one of the threats to our well-being is other people, but people have devised various ways to live safely in the presence of enemies. They might flatter them, bribe them, or seek to appease them in some other way. Following that line of thinking, Freud said, humans beings tried to devise a way to negotiate with cancer and to deal with the hostile forces of floods, fires, earthquakes, and such. In the end, they invented animism, that is, the idea of imputing personality to the impersonal forces of nature. They theorized that there was a god in the flood, a god in the fire, a god in the earthquake, and a god in the disease. If there were gods indwelling all of these forces, people could pray to them, make sacrifices to them, and otherwise seek to appease them, hoping to nullify their antagonism. In short, Freud said religion was invented because of the fear of seemingly impersonal forces of nature.

Terror in the Storm

Matthew's account of Jesus' calming of the storm gives us an example of the terror that can come upon men because of these forces. Matthew begins by noting, **Now when He got into a boat, His disciples followed Him** (v. 23). As we saw in verse 18, Jesus had given orders that they should sail to the other side of the Sea of Galilee, but He was briefly detained by a pair of would-be disciples (vv. 19–22). At last, they got under way.

A few years ago, archaeologists in Israel discovered a sunken fishing vessel dating to Jesus' day, so they now have a good idea of the kind of boats that fishermen on the Sea of Galilee used routinely. In all probability, this was the kind of vessel in which Jesus and His disciples were sailing that day. The boat was about twenty-six-and-a-half feet long and seven-and-a-half feet wide. It was not a tiny craft, but neither was it exceedingly large.

Then Matthew writes: **And suddenly a great tempest arose on the sea, so that the boat was covered with the waves. But He was asleep** (v. 24). The Sea of Galilee is surrounded by mountains, and winds sometimes come off the Mediterranean and down through the valleys, suddenly turning the calm waters of the lake into a frothing, turbulent tempest. That is what happened on this occasion. The sea became so rough that "the boat was covered with the waves."

Somehow, Jesus was able to sleep through this tempest, but the disciples were wide awake—and terrified. At least some of these disciples were seasoned fishermen who spent every day on the Sea of Galilee. They were very familiar with the lake and its weather. Nevertheless, they were as terrified by the fury of this storm as the landsmen among them. Matthew tells us: **Then His disciples came to Him and awoke Him, saying, "Lord, save us! We are perishing!"** (v. 25). Just as Freud said, the fear of the forces of nature took hold of these men. So they went to Jesus, shook Him awake, and cried out, "Lord, do something or we are going to die."

The disciples certainly did a good and wise thing when they cried out to Jesus for rescue from the storm. I wish that everyone in the world would do that. Everyone needs to come to Christ and say: "Jesus, save me! If You don't save me,

I'm going to perish!" There is nothing more certain than that truth. If Christ does not save me, I will certainly perish. If He does not save you, you will certainly perish. There is no other Savior whom God has given us apart from Jesus.

Jesus was obviously tired enough to go to sleep in the boat. When the disciples woke Him, it seems He was a bit annoyed to have His rest interrupted by a group of men who were hysterical in their fear. Matthew writes: **But He said to them, "Why are you fearful, O you of little faith?"** (v. 26a). He would soon rebuke the winds and the sea, but first He rebuked the disciples. He asked them: "Are you going to let a little storm like this terrify you? Where is your faith?"

None of the Gospel writers record any answer from the disciples to this question, but I imagine Peter saying: "Jesus, what do you think we are? Look at these waves. They're going to bury us. Why shouldn't we be afraid? What are we supposed to have faith in? You're a fantastic teacher, and what You do with the demons and with people who have leprosy is amazing. But this is different. This is a terrible storm that's going to take us to the bottom of the lake."

A New Source of Fear

In any case, Matthew goes on: **Then He arose . . .** (v. 26b). It is not advisable to stand up in a boat in stormy conditions. Nevertheless, Jesus stood, and then, instead of talking to the disciples, He started talking to the wind and the waves. He **rebuked the winds and the sea, and there was a great calm** (v. 26c). Mark tells us that He gave a command: "Peace! Be still!" and "the wind ceased" (4:39). As soon as Jesus gave His command, the wind stopped. There was not the slightest zephyr in the air. The sea became like glass.

With the wind calmed, the sea peaceful, and the threat of nature removed, we might expect the disciples to cheer their Lord and say: "Thank you, Jesus. This is your best miracle yet. We love what You have done." But that was not their reaction. Matthew writes, **So the men marveled, saying, "Who can this be, that even the winds and the sea obey Him?"** (v. 27). Mark, however, puts it somewhat differently: "And they feared exceedingly" (4:41a). Even though the threat of nature was removed suddenly and completely, there was a palpable increase in the fear of those men.

What was the source of this intense new fear? It was Jesus Himself. He had saved them from the storm, and as a result, they were more frightened of Him than they had been of the storm. Do you see the import of that? This is the point that Freud missed altogether. Yes, human beings are afraid of floods, fires, earthquakes, and disease, but in the heart of every creature made in the image of God, there is a terror far greater than all of these things combined, because there is a threat far greater than any force of nature can present. It is the threat of falling into the hands of the living God.

As we see over and over again in Scripture, that aspect of God that strikes terror into the human heart is His holiness. He is holy and we are not. Above all else, unholy creatures fear the presence of the holy God. So, I think Freud and his fellow atheists had it all wrong. Human beings did not invent religion as a crutch to help them cope with the impersonal forces of nature. As Paul tells us in Romans 1, they invented religion so that they might avoid the one true God.

Matthew tells us that the disciples "marveled" over what Jesus had done. They asked themselves, "Who can this be, that even the winds and the sea obey Him?" They were beginning to see that it was the one true God who had called them to follow Him.

In a Class by Himself

As human beings, we have a host of defensive mechanisms. One of these strategies is to pigeonhole everyone we meet. We make instantaneous judgments. Is this person a threat or is he peaceful? If the person is smiling, we tend to assign him to the friendly category. If he is scowling, we put him into a different category and try to keep our distance as we pass. We categorize everyone. But when the disciples went searching through their mental files, they could not come up with a category for Jesus. A person who can command the wind and the sea is in a class by himself.

Only one man who has lived had the ability to command nature. Why? The Bible tells us that "of Him and through Him and to Him are all things" (Rom. 11:36). The second person of the Trinity created that lake. The second person of the Trinity created the wind. He is the Lord of the wind and the sea, so He could say to His work of creation, "Do what I tell you to do," and receive instantaneous obedience.

It is ironic that the wind and the sea were far more obedient to Jesus than the men who were in the boat with Him. God says, "The ox knows its owner and the donkey its master's crib; but Israel does not know, My people do not consider" (Isa. 1:3). People do not know the voice of their Master.

Human beings are afflicted by all kinds of phobias. Some people suffer from the fear of water (aquaphobia), open spaces (agoraphobia), or small, cramped spaces (claustrophobia). One of the main fears that besets us is xenophobia, which is the fear of strangers, of aliens, of people who are different from us, whose culture we do not understand. We cannot begin to count how many wars and conflicts have been provoked by this fear.

That day on the Sea of Galilee, the disciples encountered a stranger like no other—God in the flesh. In one sense, they were right to be afraid. That day, for just a moment, the shroud that covered and concealed the full deity of Christ was drawn aside as He exercised His authority over the wind and the sea. It bothers me to hear people talk in a cavalier fashion about their relationship with Jesus, as if Jesus were their buddy. If Jesus were to appear to you or me right now, we would be on our faces. Yes, He loves us, redeems us, and comforts us, but He is the Lord God omnipotent. In His presence, we know the fear of the Lord.

42

BEFORE THE TIME

Matthew 8:28–34

When He had come to the other side, to the country of the Gergesenes, there met Him two demon-possessed men, coming out of the tombs, exceedingly fierce, so that no one could pass that way. And suddenly they cried out, saying, "What have we to do with You, Jesus, You Son of God? Have You come here to torment us before the time?" Now a good way off from them there was a herd of many swine feeding. So the demons begged Him, saying, "If You cast us out, permit us to go away into the herd of swine." And He said to them, "Go." So when they had come out, they went into the herd of swine. And suddenly the whole herd of swine ran violently down the steep place into the sea, and perished in the water. Then those who kept them fled; and they went away into the city and told everything, including what had happened to the demon-possessed men. And behold, the whole city came out to meet Jesus. And when they saw Him, they begged Him to depart from their region.

In 1521, Martin Luther was summoned to appear before the Imperial Diet at Worms, which had been convened by the Holy Roman Emperor Charles V. In summoning Luther to this imperial trial, in which the greatest authorities of the state and the church were assembled to examine Luther's writings for heresy, Charles granted him a safe-conduct passage, guaranteeing that no harm would befall him if he would come to the meeting. When Luther received the summons, all of his friends and his colleagues at Wittenberg cautioned him strongly not to go. They told him he should not trust the emperor, that the safe conduct was simply a charade, and that Worms was filled with devils. Luther, however, declared, "I shall go to Worms, though there were as many devils there as tiles on the roofs."[1]

If you were summoned to a dangerous meeting today, I doubt you would think in terms of the number of demons that might be present to harm you there. We almost never think about the devil or demons unless we are watching the latest Hollywood blockbuster about exorcisms or supernatural beings. The concept of evil spiritual beings has all but disappeared from the consciousness of the Christian community.

Why is this? I think the chief reason is that the church has been thoroughly secularized. The term *secular* in and of itself is perfectly harmless, but when you add the suffix *-ism* to it, you have a worldview that is on a collision course with Christianity. Secularism declares that the only thing that exists is this present time in this present world. There is no transcendent realm. There is no place of eternity. You live, you die, and that's the end. Secularism is an extension of naturalism, which argues that there is nothing besides the natural, which means there is no realm of the supernatural.

Christians say they believe in God, who is supremely supernatural, but we live, practically speaking, as if there were no God. We live as if there were no such beings as angels, the devil, and his legion of cohorts that are called demons. Yet, when we look at the biblical worldview, we see that the Scriptures declare that this universe is inhabited not only by animals and by human beings but also by created spiritual beings called angels, some of which are good and some of which are evil.

It may surprise you to know that the word *angel* occurs in the New Testament more often than the word *love* and the word *sin*. But we tend to read the New Testament with a comb, and every time we see a reference to the supernatural, to angels or demons, we sort of brush it aside, just as all good secularists do.

Luther did not do that. He believed very much in the reality of Satan. He said that Satan had launched an unbridled attack against him when he stood for the gospel in the sixteenth century.

A Need for Armor

In his belief in the supernatural, Luther stood with the Apostle Paul, who says in his letter to the Ephesians, "Take up the whole armor of God" (6:13a). Why does the Apostle admonish us to be garbed in the entire armor of God? He does not leave us in the dark as to his intent. His admonition to believers to take up the armor of God is part of a larger passage that reads: "For we do not wrestle

[1] Philip Schaff, *History of the Christian Church, Volume 7: The German Reformation*, 2nd rev. ed. (Peabody, MA: Hendrickson, 1996), 298.

against flesh and blood, but against principalities, against powers, against the rulers of the darkness of this age, against spiritual hosts of wickedness in the heavenly places. Therefore take up the whole armor of God, that you may be able to withstand in the evil day, and having done all, to stand" (vv. 12–13). We need the armor of God because we are in a war against the forces of evil in the supernatural realm.

Do you believe what Paul says here? Do you agree that there are powers and principalities beyond the institutions of this world? Do you believe that there are powers of darkness that have an enormous impact on individuals, on societies, and on nations?

In the middle of the twentieth century, the eminent Swiss theologian Oscar Cullmann wrote a trilogy of books in which he discussed the virtual neglect of the supernatural realm in studies today. He also made the interesting observation that not only can individuals come under demonic influence, as Scripture indicates, but so can whole nations. That is, entire nations can be subjected to the authority and power of the supernatural principalities of darkness and wickedness.

When I went to the Netherlands for doctoral work in the 1960s, it had been twenty years since the end of World War II. I never could walk past one of the bookstores in Amsterdam without going in to see what was on display—that's still true—but I always found it interesting that it seemed 70 to 80 percent of the titles in the stores were about the war. Of course, they had suffered for years under Nazi occupation, so it really was not surprising that so much of their postwar literature was reflections on the war.

One title in particular caught my eye. Its English title was *Hitler: The Scourge of Europe*. It was a study of the life of Adolf Hitler based on many of the documents that were recovered at the end of the war. One page in that book grasped my attention. It was a reproduction of an early entry in Hitler's diary. In that entry, Hitler had written, "This evening I have made a covenant with Satan." He was not speaking hyperbolically. His closest henchmen were profoundly engaged in devil worship. The swastika was intentionally a distortion of the Christian symbol of the cross, and the Third Reich was designed to supplant the kingdom of God. Of course, demonic involvement with governments did not begin with Hitler, nor did it end with him.

Terrified of Torment

Demonic activity was prevalent during Jesus' ministry, and Matthew records a particularly striking encounter in chapter 8 of his Gospel. As we have seen, Jesus and His disciples had set off to cross the sea of Galilee (v. 18), and during the crossing, Jesus calmed a storm in response to the pleas of the disciples

(vv. 23–27). Matthew then writes: **When He had come to the other side, to the country of the Gergesenes, there met Him two demon-possessed men, coming out of the tombs, exceedingly fierce, so that no one could pass that way** (v. 28).

Mark (5:1–20) and Luke (8:26–39) both give us longer accounts of this incident. However, Mark and Luke both write that there was one demon-possessed man, whereas Matthew speaks of two. Of course, that provides plenty of fodder for critics of the Bible, who say that Scripture obviously contradicts itself. Actually, there is no contradiction at all. If there were two men there, there was surely one. If one writer only mentions one and another mentions two, there is a discrepancy, but there is no contradiction.

When Jesus encountered these demon-possessed men, they were coming out of the tombs. Possibly they were finding shelter in vacant tombs or in the antechambers of the tombs. The demons that possessed them had made them extremely fierce. In fact, they were so crazed by this occupation of their souls by evil that the people who lived in that region had been forced to stop using the path that went past the tombs. These men were a danger to anyone who came near them. But Jesus was not afraid to land His boat there.

When these men saw Jesus, **suddenly they cried out, saying, "What have we to do with You, Jesus, You Son of God?"** (v. 29a). It is interesting that the first creatures to recognize the true identity of Jesus that was hidden behind the veil of His humanity were these fallen angels. They instantly recognized Him as God's Son. And because they knew who He was, they knew they had nothing in common with Him. Their realm was totally alien to everything He represented.

Then the demons asked a curious question: **"Have You come here to torment us before the time?"** (v. 29b). The demons that were possessing these men understood the Word of God. They knew their destiny was to be thrown into the outer darkness, where there is only weeping and gnashing of teeth (Matt. 25:30). They knew they would be justly subjected to the torment of God in hell forever (Matt. 25:41). Have you ever thought about God as One who torments? These demons had, because they knew the just judgment of God on their wickedness would be eternal torment.

But there was something the demons did not understand. They could not grasp why they found themselves in the presence of the Son of God that day. They asked, "Have You come here to torment us *before the time?*" (emphasis added). Now, the Greek word that is translated as "time" here is *kairos* rather than *chronos*. Both of these words can be translated as "time," but they have significantly different meanings. *Chronos* describes the ordinary moment-by-moment passage of time as it is measured by a clock. Kairos refers to a special moment that takes place in time and defines the meaning and the significance of that time. We lack a corresponding set of terms in English that capture the nuances of difference between *chronos* and *kairos*. The closest words we have are *historical* and *historic*. Every event that takes place anywhere at any time is historical. But a historic event is of such importance that you put a circle around it. That is why December 7, 1941, was "a date which will live in infamy," as President Franklin D. Roosevelt described it.

The demons understood that from all eternity God has appointed a day when He will judge the world, a day when He will send all of the demons to the torment of hell. That is exactly what Paul told the philosophers in Athens: "Times of ignorance God overlooked, but now commands all men everywhere to repent, because He has appointed a day on which He will judge the world in righteousness by the Man whom He has ordained. He has given assurance of this to all by raising Him from the dead" (Acts 17:30–31).

Do you believe that there really will be a judgment day? It is on God's calendar. He has established it and will not erase it. He will judge the whole world—me, you, everyone—by the one He has appointed to be the Judge, even Jesus. That is bad news for the unbeliever, but it is very good news for the believer, because Jesus is also our defense attorney. When believers go to the final judgment, we will have the Judge as our advocate.

However, few people today believe there will be a judgment day. The vast majority of the people of the United States of America certainly do not expect a judgment day. How could any person live the way most Americans live and still believe in a judgment day? After all, we kill roughly a million and a half unborn children every year. We raise up armies to engage in a war against terror because terrorists killed about three thousand of us, but we wage no war against the terror of the womb because we do not fear God's judgment. We simply do not believe we will be held accountable. The United States is a barbarian country.

Jesus' Value System

It was almost as if the demons thought they could negotiate with Jesus, as if they could demand their rights. They said to Him, in essence: "It's not time yet. You're early. You can't torment us. Go away and leave us alone."

Of course, such arguments were futile, and the demons knew it, so they began looking for a compromise. Matthew tells us: **Now a good way off from them there was a herd of many swine feeding. So the demons begged Him, saying, "If You cast us out, permit us to go away into the herd of swine"** (vv. 30–31). We would think that Jesus would not do anything the demons suggested. But even though He had been given all authority on heaven and earth, including the power to cast out Satan by the finger of God in order to announce and demonstrate the breakthrough of the kingdom of God, it was true that the time for the final judgment was not yet. So, **He said to them, "Go"** (v. 32a). He drove the demons out of the men, and they invaded the pigs.

To our modern eyes, this seems politically incorrect. We can find ourselves wondering why Jesus had so little consideration for the pigs as to allow the demons to enter them. Simply put, Jesus had a value system. He believed that animals were made for man, not man for animals. He did not see whales as more important than unborn babies. The reason is that Jesus was sane, not locked in the insanity that is caused by sin. Jesus wanted to redeem two suffering men, and if it cost the herd of pigs to do it, He did not see that as too high a cost.

Matthew then writes: **So when they had come out, they went into the herd of swine. And suddenly the whole herd of swine ran violently down the steep place into the sea, and perished in the water** (v. 32b). The demons went into the pigs, and the pigs seem to have become as crazed as the two men had been. The pigs rushed down a hillside, plunged into the Sea of Galilee, and drowned.

This strange story has an even stranger conclusion. Matthew writes: **Then those who kept them fled; and they went away into the city and told everything, including what had happened to the demon-possessed men. And behold, the whole city came out to meet Jesus. And when they saw Him, they begged Him to depart from their region** (vv. 33–34). The pig herders ran to town to tell what they had witnessed. They were not so devastated by the loss of the pigs that they neglected to tell what had happened to the two demon-possessed men. As a result, "the whole city," everyone who lived there, came out to the area of the tombs to see Jesus. But when they saw Him, as well as the two redeemed men and all the carcasses of the pigs at the base of the cliff, what did they do? They begged Jesus to go away.

I honestly do not know why they asked Him to leave. It may have been that they were angry over what had just happened to their economy. There were "many swine" in the herd; in fact, Mark puts the number of pigs at two thousand (5:13). However, I think it is more likely that the people recognized in Jesus the same thing the demons saw there, and they wanted no part of Him. When Jesus manifested His holy character, people got nervous. They saw that the Jesus of reality was not "gentle Jesus, meek and mild," which is the popular modern idea of Him. Rather, He was the Holy One of Israel. Confronted by that reality, they wanted Him to go away.

What about you? Do you push Him away? Or do you welcome Him? Only when we know that we have been clothed by His righteousness can we be comfortable in His presence. Until we are so clothed, we will tremble before Him—just as the demons did (James 2:19).

43

JESUS FORGIVES SIN

Matthew 9:1–8

So He got into a boat, crossed over, and came to His own city. Then behold, they brought to Him a paralytic lying on a bed. When Jesus saw their faith, He said to the paralytic, "Son, be of good cheer; your sins are forgiven you." And at once some of the scribes said within themselves, "This Man blasphemes!" But Jesus, knowing their thoughts, said, "Why do you think evil in your hearts? For which is easier, to say, 'Your sins are forgiven you,' or to say, 'Arise and walk'? But that you may know that the Son of Man has power on earth to forgive sins"—then He said to the paralytic, "Arise, take up your bed, and go to your house." And he arose and departed to his house. Now when the multitudes saw it, they marveled and glorified God, who had given such power to men.

Following His healing of the two demon-possessed men (8:28–34), Jesus heeded the pleas of the people in the country of the Gergesenes and left their region (Mark 5:1). Matthew writes, **He got into a boat, crossed over, and came to His own city** (v. 1). Jesus had left Capernaum (8:18) to cross the Sea of Galilee, but when He was rejected by the people, He sailed back across the sea to "His own city." We might think that Matthew is speaking here of Nazareth, the village in which Jesus grew up. However, he is actually referring to Capernaum, for that seaside city had become Jesus' headquarters by this stage of His ministry. So, after a brief trip across the lake, Jesus returned to the same place He had left.

I have mentioned that Matthew is often more brief than Mark and Luke when the three Gospels contain parallel accounts, and that is true of his account of Jesus' healing of a paralytic, which Matthew records here in chapter 9 of his book. In Matthew's account, the story opens simply: **Then behold, they brought to Him a paralytic lying on a bed** (v. 2a). However, we read in Mark (2:1–12) and Luke (5:17–26) that when the men who brought the paralytic to Jesus arrived, they found Him sitting in a house and preaching to a crowd that was so large they could not get to the door. But these men (four of them, according to Mark) were not to be denied; they carried their stricken friend up to the roof, where they began pulling up the tiles and the ceiling material. Eventually, they opened a hole through which they lowered their friend on his bed to Jesus.

Can you imagine what the people in the room with Jesus must have thought when the ceiling began to be pulled apart above their heads? Perhaps they moved aside to avoid falling dust and debris. Eventually, they could see daylight coming through the rapidly widening hole. Then they beheld a stretcher being lowered into the room. We can only imagine that Jesus stopped His sermon and watched what was happening along with the rest.

Now, I do not know precisely why Matthew chose not to record this part of the story. Ultimately, of course, the reason was that the Holy Spirit did not inspire him to write it down. We can thank God that He has given us multiple records of the events of Jesus' life so that we can study His ministry through various lenses, as it were.

An Unexpected Forgiveness

Matthew then continues, **When Jesus saw their faith . . .** (v. 2b). Here Matthew obviously alludes to the extreme exertions of the men who had brought their paralyzed friend to Jesus. He could see that they strongly believed that if they could simply get the paralytic to Him, his broken body would be healed.

When Jesus saw this faith, He spoke to the paralyzed man, but He did not say, "Be healed." Rather, **He said to the paralytic, "Son, be of good cheer; your sins are forgiven you"** (v. 2c).

First, note the very warm term of endearment with which Jesus addressed the man: "Son." If Jesus were to address you as "Son" or "Daughter," you would sense immediately the affection that was being expressed by that form of address. Second, however, note the words Jesus said to the man: "be of good cheer; your sins are forgiven you." I think we can confidently say that this man and his friends had not come to Jesus expecting forgiveness of sins. They had come simply hoping that his paralysis might be healed. But Jesus made this unexpected comment about forgiveness of sins.

Many of you no doubt know of Joni Eareckson Tada, who has been a quadriplegic for several decades. She is confined to a motorized wheelchair. However, she paints by holding the brush in her mouth, she composes music, she writes books and speaks at conferences, and she has a glorious testimony and an international ministry. She says that she knows that when she gets to heaven she will be whole, and she cannot wait for that moment. In the meantime, she is trusting in the love of God to sustain her during this earthly time of travail. She has said that she would rather be in her wheelchair knowing that she is forgiven in Christ than to be whole without His forgiveness.

Jesus, of course, has the power to heal Joni's paralysis in an instant. He had that same power to heal the paralytic who was brought to Him. However, instead of addressing the man's debilitating physical condition, Jesus addressed his spiritual condition by saying to the man, "Son, be of good cheer; your sins are forgiven you."

It is tempting to conclude, based on this statement, that the paralytic was suffering this dreadful affliction as a direct result of some sin he had committed. But the text gives absolutely no reason to make that inference. When people came to Jesus, it did not matter whether they came on stretchers or walked in under their own power, whether they were blind, deaf, crippled, or completely healthy—all of them came into His presence carrying a burden of guilt. To have that burden removed was far more important ultimately than to receive physical healing of their bodies. If Jesus had done nothing else for this man that day than to say, "Son, be of good cheer; your sins are forgiven you," he would have had no reason to do anything other than go to his house rejoicing.

Have you had the experience of having your sins forgiven? It is a wonderful thing. My daughter became a Christian at the age of seven or eight in response to an altar call. I was a bit skeptical about that, because I thought she was too young to understand what it was all about. I was afraid she might be missing the real significance of the gospel. So, I asked her, "Why did you go forward?" She said: "Daddy, I couldn't help it. I had to go. And now I feel as clean as a newborn baby." I got her point. When she said that she felt clean, fresh, and newly born, I saw that she understood what had just happened to her. She had experienced the grace of forgiveness.

Forgiveness is wonderful precisely because the burden of guilt is so horrible. Many years ago, a friend of mine who was not a Christian asked me to leave the ministry and come to work for him in his psychiatric practice. I was shocked because I know nothing about psychiatry, so I asked him why he wanted to hire me. He said: "You may not know anything about psychiatry, but you know something about guilt and forgiveness. Ninety-eight percent of the people who come to me don't need a psychiatrist. They need a priest. You cannot believe how many people are walking around this world with unresolved guilt that's eating them up."

The great Reformer Martin Luther understood this, and that was why, after he left the Roman Catholic Church, he kept the confessional. He understood how important it is in the life of the people of God to hear someone say, "Your sins are forgiven." In reality, the Protestants never had an issue with confession. It was the Roman Catholic sacrament of penance, in which people were sent out to do works of satisfaction by which they supposedly could get some kind of merit before God, that the Reformers opposed. They fully acknowledged that people need to repent of their sins and confess them, and then receive the assurance of forgiveness.

Do you have that? Do you know that your sins have been forgiven by Jesus?

An Unjustified Accusation

As soon as Jesus said to that man, "Son, be of good cheer; your sins are forgiven you," his sins were forgiven. But the scribes, the Jewish theologians, who were sitting there listening to Jesus were outraged. Matthew writes, **And at once some of the scribes said within themselves, "This Man blasphemes!"** (v. 3). According to the Jewish teachers of that time, blasphemy was any violation of the majesty of God. Any action or word that marred or sullied the magnificence and holiness of God was regarded as blasphemy. I believe that no sin is committed more often or more casually in Western culture today than the sin of blasphemy. We hardly blink when the majesty of God is insulted. But to the Jews, it was a major matter.

What exactly did Jesus do that the scribes regarded as blasphemy? Here again, the other Gospels help us understand the root of their concern. Luke tells us that they said, "Who is this who speaks blasphemies? Who can forgive sins but God alone?" (5:21b). They felt that by arrogating to Himself a prerogative that belongs only to God—the right and power to forgive sins—Jesus was making Himself out to be God, and thereby reducing God.

The church, of course, agrees with the scribes that only God can forgive sins. Think again about the Roman Catholic tradition of the confessional. Every moment of every day, somewhere in the world, someone is in a confessional booth, confessing his or her sins to a priest. Typically, after he has heard the confession, the priest gives absolution, saying, "*Te absolvo*," or, "I forgive you." Many today believe that Roman Catholic priests are sinning by pronouncing absolution, taking to themselves a privilege that belongs only to God. But to its credit, the Roman Catholic Church has always understood and taught that in the sacrament of penitence, when the priest grants absolution, that absolution does not rest in any inherent intrinsic authority to forgive sins that rests with the priest. The pronouncement of forgiveness is carried out by a delegated authority, and the only One who has inherent authority to forgive sins is God.

In much the same way, the scribes assumed Jesus was taking to Himself a privilege that belonged only to God. In truth, they were right. This is one of the clearest claims to deity that Jesus ever made. Being God in the flesh, He had every right to pronounce the paralytic's sins forgiven. However, the scribes could not see past His flesh, so they concluded He was only a man making a presumptuous claim to deity.

Matthew records Jesus' response: **But Jesus, knowing their thoughts, said, "Why do you think evil in your hearts? For which is easier, to say, 'Your sins are forgiven you,' or to say, 'Arise and walk'?"** (vv. 4–5). Jesus, being God, knew what the scribes were thinking, and He pronounced their thoughts "evil." They were accusing Him of blasphemy, by which they were committing blasphemy. He then asked a curious question: "Which is easier, to say, 'Your sins are forgiven you,' or to say, 'Arise and walk'?" Jesus did not give the answer to that question. In one sense, both statements are easy to make. Anyone can say, "Your sins are forgiven you," and anyone can say, "Arise and walk." However, if I say to a person, "Your sins are forgiven you," there will be absolutely no visible evidence that what I have pronounced has taken place. No one will be able to call me a liar, because they will not know from what they see whether the person's sins are forgiven. However, if I say to a person, "Arise and walk," there will be an instantaneous validation or refutation of my power. If the person to whom I say this stays on his stretcher, everyone will know immediately that I'm claiming powers I do not have. So, in one sense, it is much easier to say, "Your sins are forgiven you."

However, there were times when others were anointed by the power of the Holy Spirit to work physical healings. Both Peter (Acts 3:1–7) and Paul (Acts 14:8–10) were used by God to heal lame or crippled individuals. But Peter and Paul would have preferred to die than to pronounce someone's sins forgiven on the basis of their own authority. So, on the other hand, it is harder to say, "Your sins are forgiven you," because everything is on the line with that statement.

A Powerful Demonstration

How did Jesus respond? He said: **"But that you may know that the Son of Man has power on earth to forgive sins"—then He said to the paralytic, "Arise, take up your bed, and go to your house." And he arose and departed to his house** (vv. 6–7). Jesus healed the man to show that He had power to forgive.

I am not sure why the English translators opted for the word *power* here. Is the forgiveness of sins a question of power? The Greek word that is used here is more frequently translated as *authority* than as *power*. But when we look at the word in its nuances, we find that the authority that is in view here is a powerful authority, or the power that is in view here is an authoritative power. So, either word is acceptable in the English.

Jesus' message to the scribes was this: "I am going to command this man to rise up and walk, not simply that he might be healed and be of good cheer, but to teach you something about Me." He was about to give them a demonstration of His divine power in healing to show that He also had the divine power and authority to forgive. He did this for the benefit of the scribes and the other bystanders that day in Capernaum, and He did it for us, too. He did it so that we, reading this account two thousand years later, might know that He can and does forgive sins.

When I was a college student, I was struggling with sin in my life. I went to my minister and said, "I've prayed about this again and again, but I just can't get any peace." He made me open my Bible to 1 John 1:9, which says, "If we confess our sins, He is faithful and just to forgive us our sins and to cleanse us from all unrighteousness." I said, "Yes, I have confessed my sins, but I don't have any peace." He had me read the same verse again. I became more and more exasperated as I kept trying to explain that I had confessed my sins but I didn't feel forgiven. Finally, after I had read the verse about five times, he finally said: "You're depending on your feeling of forgiveness rather than the fact of forgiveness. If God says He will forgive you if you confess your sin, and you confess your sin, you can take it to the bank. You're forgiven."

Forgiveness does not depend on our feelings. Forgiveness depends on the authority of God to forgive sins. Jesus wanted everyone to know that He has that authority. So, if your sins are unforgiven, why are you waiting? There is One who has the authority to forgive them, for He took your sin, assumed your guilt, and paid for it all. He has the power and authority to forgive you. Why do you hesitate? What holds you back from the good cheer that the Son of Man has for you?

The actual healing of this paralytic seems almost like a footnote in this story. We must not forget that when Jesus commanded him to rise, "he arose and departed to his house." For the first time since he was afflicted with paralysis, this man got up from his bed, and no one had to carry him home.

Finally, Matthew notes, **Now when the multitudes saw it, they marveled and glorified God, who had given such power to men** (v. 8). As was proper, what Jesus did resulted in praise to God. How we ought to praise Him for the healing of our souls that He has wrought.

44

THE CALL OF MATTHEW

Matthew 9:9–13

As Jesus passed on from there, He saw a man named Matthew sitting at the tax office. And He said to him, "Follow Me." So he arose and followed Him. Now it happened, as Jesus sat at the table in the house, that behold, many tax collectors and sinners came and sat down with Him and His disciples. And when the Pharisees saw it, they said to His disciples, "Why does your Teacher eat with tax collectors and sinners?" When Jesus heard that, He said to them, "Those who are well have no need of a physician, but those who are sick. But go and learn what this means: 'I desire mercy and not sacrifice.' For I did not come to call the righteous, but sinners, to repentance."

In the Scriptures, it is not unusual to find the biblical writers giving accounts of how God called them to service. Several of the Old Testament prophets report on their calls, and Paul asserted his call as an Apostle in several of his letters. Here in Matthew 9, uniquely among the four Gospel writers, Matthew recounts his direct and immediate call by Jesus.

As in many other events that Matthew records, this calling is also reported by Mark and Luke, though both of those writers give Matthew's name as Levi. Of course, it was not uncommon for men in the Jewish world of that time to have more than one name—Gospel examples include Peter (also known as Simon) and Thomas (also known as Didymus)—and there is no doubt that all three Gospel accounts refer to the same man.

Matthew's account is simple and straightforward: **As Jesus passed on from there, He saw a man named Matthew sitting at the tax office. And He said to him, "Follow Me." So he arose and followed Him** (v. 9). Matthew was at the tax office because he was by profession a tax collector. The Jews were called to give their tithe to God, which was 10 percent of their gross income every year. But beyond the tithe, they had to pay taxes to the civil government, and Matthew was one who helped to collect these taxes.

In our day, those who are involved in the collection of taxes are not very popular with those who labor under the burden of paying those taxes. This was even more true in ancient Israel. At this time in their history, the Jews were under Roman occupation. However, whereas Judea was under a Roman governor, Galilee was governed by Herod Antipas, a puppet king appointed by the Romans, so taxes in the north were paid to his administration. Among other taxes, Herod imposed a heavy tax on goods that were imported, and that tax was especially burdensome in Capernaum, which was not only a crossroads for the commercial routes on land but the chief place where goods that were brought across the Sea of Galilee were unloaded. Matthew had his tax office on the shore of the Sea of Galilee, and there he collected these custom taxes, which ran anywhere from 2 percent to 12.5 percent.

The tax collectors received their compensation by taking a share of the taxes they were able to collect. From an economic perspective, the tax collectors had a very enviable economic position, and many of them were quite wealthy. Matthew probably was a wealthy man, and the text even hints at this when it tells us that after he was called by Jesus, he celebrated by throwing a party at his house.

A Life-Changing Call

In any case, Matthew was performing his vocation at the tax office, just as he did on any other day, when Jesus passed by. Jesus saw him and said to him, "Follow Me." With that, Matthew got up and followed Jesus. It was a moment that changed Matthew's life forever. Jesus had a habit of doing that then, and He has a habit of doing it now. When Jesus calls someone not only outwardly but inwardly, that person's life is never the same.

It seems likely that Matthew already knew who Jesus was. He may not have known Him personally, but he could not have been unfamiliar with Him, because by now Jesus had achieved something of local celebrity status for the mighty works He had done in Capernaum.

Jesus' command to Matthew, "Follow Me," had a literal sense to it. Jesus was a rabbi, a teacher, but He did not have a school where He gave lectures. Rather, Jesus was to the Jews what Aristotle was to the Greeks—a peripatetic philosopher, one who taught while walking around. Jesus constantly moved about, and as He walked, His disciples, who were His students, followed closely behind Him and listened to His teaching, trying to memorize what He said. One of the reasons why Jesus spoke in parables and in aphorisms was because those kinds of statements could be easily committed to memory. So, to be a disciple in the band of a peripatetic rabbi was literally to follow him around from place to place. Thus, when Jesus told Matthew to follow Him, He was saying: "I want you to be My student. I want you to come after Me, and I'm going to teach you, train you, and prepare you for a spiritual mission. In order to do that, Matthew, you have to leave your current occupation. You have to forsake all of the revenue that goes with being a tax collector, and come and join My band of disciples."

When Jesus called Peter and his brother Andrew, along with James and his brother John, they were fishermen. They knew that if things did not work out in their new vocation and they had a falling-out with Jesus, they could go back to the Sea of Galilee and resume their trade in the fishing industry. Matthew had no such safety net. Once he left his job as a tax collector, there were fifty men waiting in the wings to apply for that position. So, Matthew understood that when Jesus said, "Follow Me," he had to leave his security. He had to lay everything aside and give His life to Jesus. That was what Jesus was asking him to do.

Remarkably, he was willing to do it. Jesus' call was so compelling, "he arose and followed Him." He put down the ledger, put aside the coins, got up from his chair, closed up shop as a tax collector, and followed Jesus to his death.

I imagine that on that day, the last thing Matthew thought about was that at some point in his life he would pick up a pen and write an account of the ministry of Jesus. I'm certain that he never thought that he would write something that would still be studied two thousand years later. And yet, in the providence of God, that is what Matthew was called to do.

With Tax Collectors and Sinners

Matthew then tells us: **Now it happened, as Jesus sat at the table in the house, that behold, many tax collectors and sinners came and sat down with Him and His disciples** (v. 10). The tax collectors were among the most despised people in the community. They were regarded as collaborators with the enemy. Even though they had wealth, their social status was at the bottom of the barrel. They were so despised they were not permitted to participate in the synagogue. They were regarded as so disreputable they were not permitted to give testimony in the law courts of that day. So, the phrase "tax collectors and sinners" became an epithet for the dregs of society.

The Jews understood in a certain way that everyone was a sinner. But when they called someone a sinner, they were talking about someone whose life was characterized by such immorality that to come in contact with him was to experience spiritual and ceremonial defilement. That is why the Pharisees, who tried to keep themselves holy, did everything in their power to disassociate themselves from tax collectors. They thought that their salvation would come from segregation. They sought to keep themselves clean by avoiding any contact with the dregs of human society.

Many years go, I talked to a young Episcopalian priest who was serving a parish in Clairton, Pennsylvania, where I went to high school. Clairton was a mill town, and at that time the mills were suffering from tremendous levels of unemployment. The priest asked me, "How can I grow my church?" He explained that he was pastoring a mission church with only about twenty-five members. I told him that it takes time to build a church, especially when it starts out with just a handful of people, so he would have to be patient. I went on to tell him: "It's not going to help you in this environment to just put a sign in front of your church. If you want to have a ministry in this town, you're going to have to go where the pain is. If I were starting a church in Clairton, I would spend time every day of the week in the union hall and the bars, because that's where the pain is found in this town. If you want to build a church in Clairton, you have to be willing to get your hands dirty." He gulped when I told him that.

Frankly, I do not know whether he took my advice. As far as I know, that church is still a mission church, if it's there at all. But I was trying to convince him to build his church the way Jesus built His church. He went out to the highways and byways to seek and to save those who were lost, and He associated with people whom none of the religious leaders of the day would be caught talking to. He went where the pain was, to touch the lepers, to free those who were possessed by demons, to comfort those who were downcast. That was His mission, and that was how He built His church.

A Merciful Physician

When Jesus willingly associated with the dregs of society, the Pharisees took note. Matthew writes, **And when the Pharisees saw it, they said to His disciples, "Why does your Teacher eat with tax collectors and sinners?"** (v. 11). In antiquity, sharing a table was an expression of deep intimacy. Matthew expressed his feelings for Jesus and many other despised people by inviting them to a meal in his home, and Jesus showed His love and acceptance for them by participating. But the Pharisees were offended that Jesus would associate with such people, and they asked His disciples why He did it.

When Jesus heard that the Pharisees were asking this question, He confronted them: **When Jesus heard that, He said to them, "Those who are well have no need of a physician, but those who are sick. But go and learn what this means: 'I desire mercy and not sacrifice.' For I did not come to call the righteous, but sinners, to repentance"** (vv. 12–13).

This is a multiple-pronged explanation. First, Jesus gave His reason in obvious terms: the sick need a doctor, not the healthy. The implication is that He was a doctor of some sort, and those He was associating with needed His ministrations. They were sick and needy. Unfortunately, no one can be a doctor unless he is willing to get his hands dirty, because disease and the treatment of it is a dirty business. Jesus declared Himself willing to get His hands dirty to save some filthy sinners.

Then He quoted from the book of Hosea, which is all about mercy, to show that His behavior should be the norm for all of God's people. In Hosea 6:6, God declares, "I desire mercy and not sacrifice, and the knowledge of God more than burnt offerings." By quoting this verse, Jesus was saying, in essence: "I'm on a mission of mercy. I didn't come to bring judgment on the world. My Father is a God of justice, and He will visit justice upon this world in His time. But My Father always tempers His justice with mercy. You should not think that you satisfy the desires of My Father if you merely go to the synagogue, pay your tithes, and give your sacrifices. I want my people to be people of mercy." Christ has not commanded us to shake our fingers at every sinner and every outcast of our society. He has called us to a ministry of mercy. That is what He did, and that is what He wants us to do.

Finally He said, "I did not come to call the righteous, but sinners, to repentance." Given that He came to draw some to repentance, it is plainly obvious that He had to minister among sinners, for the righteous have no need of repentance. Of course, He could have ministered among sinners equally well by associating with Jewish high society, but the difference was that those people did not know they needed to repent, whereas the tax collectors and other despised people knew they needed a Savior.

In effect, Jesus told the Pharisees: "You don't like the people gathered around Me? These are the people I came to redeem. These are the people I came to call to repentance. I'm not involved with sinners because I want to be amid sin. I'm here because I care about them, because they're lost and they're dying, and I've come to be their Savior."

45

THE PRESENCE OF THE BRIDEGROOM

Matthew 9:14–17

Then the disciples of John came to Him, saying, "Why do we and the Pharisees fast often, but Your disciples do not fast?" And Jesus said to them, "Can the friends of the bridegroom mourn as long as the bridegroom is with them? But the days will come when the bridegroom will be taken away from them, and then they will fast. No one puts a piece of unshrunk cloth on an old garment; for the patch pulls away from the garment, and the tear is made worse. Nor do they put new wine into old wineskins, or else the wineskins break, the wine is spilled, and the wineskins are ruined. But they put new wine into new wineskins, and both are preserved."

It was hardly surprising that Jesus came under criticism from the Pharisees for His practice of eating with "tax collectors and sinners" (Matt. 9:10–11). However, in the next incident that Matthew records, Jesus received criticism from a very surprising source—the disciples of John the Baptist.

Like Jesus, John had gathered disciples around him and was mentoring them in his rigorous form of piety. By this time, John was probably already in prison, but his disciples were observing Jesus, because John had pointed Him out as the Lamb of God who would carry away their sins (John 1:29). However, as John's disciples watched Jesus and His disciples, they became offended, for they saw that neither Jesus nor His disciples engaged in the religious practice of fasting.

So, Matthew writes, **the disciples of John came to Him, saying, "Why do we and the Pharisees fast often, but Your disciples do not fast?"** (v. 14). These men wanted to know why Jesus did not prescribe this discipline for His disciples.

In the Old Testament, God commanded His people to fast only on the Day of Atonement and on some special occasions. However, by the time Jesus appeared, the Pharisees had started a religious tradition of fasting twice each week, and it seems that John was following that tradition at least to some extent, so that he and his disciples fasted more than most Jews. Like the Pharisees, they were caught up in the rituals of religion, the externals of piety. Thus, it is not surprising that John's disciples took offense at the way Jesus mentored His own followers. These disciples were sacrificing their own appetites regularly, but Jesus and His disciples not only were not fasting; they were eating and drinking.

A Time to Feast and a Time to Fast

Matthew tells us that Jesus was willing to answer John's disciples. He began by saying, **"Can the friends of the bridegroom mourn as long as the bridegroom is with them?"** (v. 15a). This metaphorical answer was heavily informed by Jewish history. Often, throughout the Old Testament, we see fasting associated with mourning (2 Sam. 1:12; 1 Kings 21:27; Neh. 1:4; Est. 4:3). At the opposite end of the emotional spectrum was a wedding feast, which was a time of joy and celebration—manifestly *not* a time to fast. Obviously, in this metaphor, Jesus cast Himself as the bridegroom, which was appropriate, for God called Israel His bride (Isa. 62:5), and He sent His Son to be the bridegroom. So, Jesus told John's disciples that the bridegroom was present, which meant it was not a time to fast but a time to rejoice. Jesus was telling John's disciples that if they truly understood what was going on, they would not think it was a time for denial or mourning.

Jesus went on to say, **"But the days will come when the bridegroom will be taken away from them, and then they will fast"** (v. 15b). Jesus soon would begin to warn His disciples that He was going to suffer and die, but here He hinted at it. There would come a time, He said, when the bridegroom would be taken away, and that would be an appropriate time for mourning and fasting.

Then, borrowing some illustrations from the common life of the day, Jesus sought to give the disciples of John a fuller understanding of what was going on. According to Matthew, Jesus said, **"No one puts a piece of unshrunk cloth on an old garment; for the patch pulls away from the garment, and the tear is made worse"** (v. 16). Jesus asked the men to consider what would happen if an old garment were patched with a piece of new cloth. When the repaired garment was washed, the new cloth would shrink for the first time, tearing away from the already shrunken fabric of the garment. Thus, the rip in the garment would be even worse. However, Jesus acknowledged that no one would do such a thing. The problem was known and was avoided.

Then He said: **"Nor do they put new wine into old wineskins, or else the wineskins break, the wine is spilled, and the wineskins are ruined. But they put new wine into new wineskins, and both are preserved"** (v. 17). When wine was made and first began to ferment, it was put into wineskins made from animal skins, often goat skins, which had a certain elasticity. As the fermenting continued, the new wineskin could expand to accommodate the gases that were escaping in the process. But an old wineskin had already been stretched to its capacity, so if new wine were put in it, it would not have sufficient elasticity to withstand the fermentation process and would burst. Both the wine and the wineskin would be ruined. But again, Jesus acknowledged that no one would do such a thing. The problem was known, and because new wine was valuable, no one put it in old wineskins.

My best friend in college and seminary was the son of a missionary, and he grew up deep in the wilds of Ethiopia, five hundred miles from Addis Ababa. In the village where they ministered, his father was the first white man the people had ever seen. From time to time, they had to go to Addis Ababa for medical supplies. They had a jeep, but there was no road; they had to travel across rugged terrain, and the trip usually took five to seven days. When they made the trip, they took food, gasoline, two or three extra tires, and a tire repair kit with patches, because the trip was exceedingly rough on the jeep's tires.

On one occasion, my friend set out to make the trip, but he had not gone very far before he had his first flat tire. He changed the tire, patched the flat tire, and set off again. After another twenty miles, he had another flat tire. This happened with such regularity that he used up all the patches in the repair kit. He kept driving on the flat tires, but soon they were reduced to shreds. He knew that if he tried to finish the trip on the bare rims of the jeep, he would destroy the rims, and then he probably would not be able to come back. He solved this dilemma by shooting an antelope and skinning it, then cutting the hide into long strips that he sewed around the rims, stuffing them with grass. He fixed all four tires in this way and finished his journey to Addis Ababa. He came to the realization that patching the problem was not going to work. He needed new tires. He needed a whole new kind of tire, a tire that could not be punctured because it was not inflated with air. He had to be innovative and creative to do something completely new to accomplish his mission.

A Time of Fundamental Change

What was Jesus saying with these colorful replies to John's disciples? What was His point? He was telling John's disciples that a new age and a new covenant had come. He had come to bring radical change, so radical that it was no longer possible to continue with the old ways.

In recent years, politics in the United States have been dominated by calls for change. When I hear that kind of political language, I want to raise my hand and say, "What kind of change?" In and of itself, change is not necessarily good. When someone comes down with a fatal disease, change comes into his life, but it is not a good change. Change can be for the better or for the worse.

Of course, I believe the United States needs fundamental change. Years ago, I had the opportunity to have dinner with a senator who was the chairman of the Senate Appropriations Committee. I asked him about problems facing the nation. I said, "Senator, don't you think we ought to do such and such?" He replied, "Oh, absolutely, we need to do that, but not this year." When I asked why, he said, "Because it's an election year." I raised another issue I regarded as vitally important, and he said, "Oh, that's desperately needed in our country, and we're going to do that, R.C., but we can't do it this year because it's an election year." This went on for about ten questions. It was as if I was listening to a broken record. Every time I asked him about a problem that the nation faced, he agreed that it needed to be addressed but added that it would have to wait. I finally asked him, "Is there anyone up here on Capitol Hill in any party who's thinking about the next generation instead of the next election?" I fear for the United States unless we have fundamental changes at the heart of how we do things in this country.

Jesus told the disciples of John that fundamental change had happened. He was subtly telling them that the Messiah for whom the Jews had been praying for thousands of years had come at last. It was not a time to be worrying about fasting or feasting.

Sometimes during the week I will bump into a member of my congregation, and I'll say, "Hey, where were you last Sunday? I missed you." Someone once said to me, "There are so many people at Saint Andrew's, you couldn't know I wasn't in church on Sunday." I said, "Yes, I can." Some people in my congregation are there every Sunday morning. If they are not there, I know they are either out of town or ill. I know that if they are in town and healthy, they will be in church on Sunday morning.

But there are other people I see maybe once a month. I even have one friend who comes to church only once each year—on Christmas Eve. I go to see him often because he helps me with some physical problems, and he always tells me to come back the next week. I say to him: "What's wrong with this picture? I have to come see you every week, but you only come to see me once a year." We share a laugh about that, but for my part, the laughter is tinged with sadness. I'm glad people come to church sometimes rather than not at all, but I ask myself why they bother. What motivates a person to go to church once a month or, as in the case of my friend, once a year? It's like putting a new patch on an old garment. It's patchwork Christianity. The person figures, "I'll check in with God this week; maybe I'll get something out of it."

That is not what Christianity is about. We are called to put on Christ (Rom. 13:14). Our God wants us body and soul. He does not call us to dabble in religion. He commands us to commit ourselves to Him from the depths of our souls. Christianity is not a part-time thing. There really is a sense in which it is all or nothing at all. But even the disciples of John the Baptist did not get it. They did not understand.

An Anglican bishop in Australia once had a young curate. One morning, when the curate arrived at the diocesan offices, it was obvious he had not shaved. The bishop was a bit taken aback, so he asked the curate, "Why didn't you shave this morning?" The curate said, "Every morning I get up and wait for the Spirit to lead me, and if the Spirit leads me to shave, I shave, and if He doesn't lead me to shave, I don't shave." The bishop said: "Let me give you some advice that will reduce the stress that you have to go through every morning as you're waiting for the guidance of the Holy Spirit. This will save you some effort and the Holy Spirit some effort. From now on, as a matter of principle, I want you to decide every morning when you get up that you're going to shave."

Wasn't that a novel idea? The bishop was helping the curate to see that he could not practice patchwork cleanliness. It was a question of discipline and habit. Church attendance is like that. It needs to be a habit. We need to hear the Word of God. We need the means of grace. We need the fellowship of other Christians. And, of course, this kind of discipline needs to mark every aspect of our Christians lives.

Have you put on the whole Christ? Have you committed yourself to Him body and soul? That is what I am talking about here. God is not interested in adding more religion to your life. He has sent you a Savior who is Christ the Lord, and He wants you to embrace the whole Christ with your whole being. Nothing else will do.

46

TWO DAUGHTERS HEALED

Matthew 9:18–26

While He spoke these things to them, behold, a ruler came and worshiped Him, saying, "My daughter has just died, but come and lay Your hand on her and she will live." So Jesus arose and followed him, and so did His disciples. And suddenly, a woman who had a flow of blood for twelve years came from behind and touched the hem of His garment. For she said to herself, "If only I may touch His garment, I shall be made well." But Jesus turned around, and when He saw her He said, "Be of good cheer, daughter; your faith has made you well." And the woman was made well from that hour. When Jesus came into the ruler's house, and saw the flute players and the noisy crowd wailing, He said to them, "Make room, for the girl is not dead, but sleeping." And they ridiculed Him. But when the crowd was put outside, He went in and took her by the hand, and the girl arose. And the report of this went out into all that land.

Desperation makes people do unexpected things. We see the truth of that statement twice in this passage.

Matthew begins by writing, **While He spoke these things to them, behold, a ruler came and worshiped Him, saying, "My daughter has just died, but come and lay Your hand on her and she will live"** (v. 18). Jesus had barely finished responding to the disciples of John the Baptist (9:15–17) when a man approached Jesus and asked for His aid on behalf of his daughter. As usual, Matthew's account of this incident is more condensed than those in

Mark (5:22–43) and Luke (8:41–56). Whereas Matthew says only that the man was a "ruler," the other accounts tell us that he was a ruler of a synagogue. That meant he was not a rabbi, but he was in charge of the upkeep of the building and had oversight of the services and the selection of readings from the Scriptures. In short, this man, whose name was Jairus, was of extremely high station in the Jewish community. He was one of those who had been most resistant and hostile toward Jesus. Normally, a man in his position would not have humbled himself to seek aid from Jesus, but he did, for he was desperate.

It is clear, however, that this man was not merely desperate; he was transformed. Notice what he did: he "worshiped" Jesus. Then notice what he said: "My daughter has just died, but . . . lay Your hand on her and she will live." This man recognized that Jesus was more than a prophet, more than a good teacher, more than a wise rabbi. Well before Peter confessed Jesus as the Son of God (16:16), this man had seen the truth. He knew that Jesus was God in the flesh, and that He had the power not only to heal the living but to raise the dead. We are not told how he came to this realization, but his actions and words leave no doubt that he was a changed man.

The Healing of the First Daughter

Matthew tells us that Jesus heeded Jairus's plea: **Jesus arose and followed him, and so did His disciples** (v. 19). But before He reached Jairus's home, Jesus was interrupted by a second desperate person: **And suddenly, a woman who had a flow of blood for twelve years came from behind and touched the hem of His garment. For she said to herself, "If only I may touch His garment, I shall be made well"** (vv. 20–21).

This lady is one of my favorite characters in the New Testament. I love her because she was not filled with a sense of entitlement, such as is rampant in Western culture today, where everyone seems to believe the world owes him or her something. This woman did not try to schedule a meeting with Jesus. She did not even go up and interrupt him to ask for His help. She wanted nothing more than to touch the hem of his garment. She had faith that if she could do that, she would be healed.

She had suffered from a hemorrhage for twelve years. It was not a life-threatening condition, but it was difficult because it rendered her ceremonially unclean. That meant that for twelve years she had been prevented from being actively involved in the religious life of the community. Furthermore, Mark and Luke tell us this woman had spent all her money on physicians, trying to find medical help, but her condition had only grown worse. She, too, was desperate.

Again, Matthew's account is quite abbreviated. Mark writes that when she touched Jesus' robe, "Immediately the fountain of her blood was dried up, and she felt in her body that she was healed of the affliction. And Jesus, immediately knowing in Himself that power had gone out of Him, turned around in the crowd and said, 'Who touched My clothes?' But His disciples said to Him, 'You see the multitude thronging You, and You say, "Who touched Me?"' And He looked around to see her who had done this thing" (5:29–32).

If ever there was an incident when the disciples became annoyed with Jesus, it was this one. They were going along to Jairus's home, and "a great multitude" (Mark 5:24) was following to see what Jesus would do. They were jostling Jesus as they moved. But when the woman touched His robe, He knew something had happened. Hers was more than a casual touch. So, He stopped and asked who had touched Him. The disciples thought His question was silly, but He explained, "Somebody touched Me, for I perceived power going out from Me" (Luke 8:46). Jesus was not a magician who performed tricks. His was the power of God, and when that healing power emanated from His person, He was aware of it.

Even though Jesus was on His way to Jairus's home to raise his daughter from death, He was not so preoccupied with that mission that He did not have time for this poor woman. We can learn something from this incident: Jesus is never too busy for us. He does not have managers and assistants to keep people from contacting Him. He knows the number of hairs on our heads (Matt. 10:30), which means He has a complete and comprehensive knowledge of every creature in this world. He knows all the worries that weigh us down. He knows every pain we experience before we tell Him about them. Yes, He is governing, upholding and sustaining the vast universe in all its complexity from moment to moment, but He still knows us, cares about us, and listens to our prayers. Who am I that I should have the ear of God Almighty? Who am I that He should have a moment's concern about my well-being? David said, "When I consider Your heavens, the work of Your fingers, the moon and the stars, which You have ordained, what is man that You are mindful of him, and the son of man that You visit him?" (Ps. 8:3–4). That care is what we see in this story, when Jesus stopped to minister to this hurting woman. Her need was minor compared to the need of Jairus and his daughter. But it mattered to her, and so it mattered to Jesus.

Matthew writes, **But Jesus turned around, and when He saw her He said, "Be of good cheer, daughter; your faith has made you well." And the woman was made well from that hour** (v. 22). The other Synoptic Gospels tell us that the woman came forward in response to His question, and that she trembled and fell at His feet, perhaps expecting a rebuke (Mark 5:33). But Jesus received her kindly; notice how He called her "daughter," just as He had referred to the paralytic as "son" (Matt. 9:2). He then pronounced her healed and pronounced His benediction upon her.

The Healing of the Second Daughter

Jesus did not forget Jairus and his daughter. Matthew writes: **When Jesus came into the ruler's house, and saw the flute players and the noisy crowd wailing, He said to them, "Make room, for the girl is not dead, but sleeping." And they ridiculed Him** (vv. 23–24). Upon arriving at Jairus's home, Jesus encountered a crowd of people who had gathered to comfort the ruler's family. The music of flutes and wailing could be heard. It was customary among the Jews of that time that when someone died, the mourning was public, not private. In fact, when there was a death, even the poorest family was expected to hire at least two flute players and one professional wailing woman. This was to guarantee that no one ever grieved alone. It also reminded the people of God that they were called to rejoice with those who rejoiced and to weep with those who wept (Rom. 12:15). Jairus, however, was a man of means, so he had numerous flute players and wailers. Matthew tells us frankly that the scene was "noisy."

When Jesus arrived, He asked the crowd to "make room," that is, to let Him pass through to where the girl's body was lying. He also declared that she was not dead but only sleeping. At that, people began to mock Him. They knew death when they saw it.

Jesus' comment here has provoked all sorts of strange ideas about the nature of death. However, the Bible sometimes uses sleep as a metaphor to describe the peacefulness and tranquility that is apparent in a person who has died. Also, Jesus said the girl was sleeping because her death was not final. He was going to wake her up.

Matthew then tells us: **But when the crowd was put outside, He went in and took her by the hand, and the girl arose** (v. 25). Despite the mockery, Jesus was able to have the crowd moved outside the house, probably at the insistence of Jairus, who had faith that Jesus knew what He was doing. Jesus then went to the girl and took her hand. Mark and Luke both note that He commanded her to arise. When He did, she came back to life.

Luke adds a footnote: "Her parents were astonished" (8:56). Likewise, Mark writes, "They were overcome with great amazement" (5:42). He does not tell us who "they" were, but certainly it must have included the parents, as well as all those who had gathered to mourn. In both Mark's and Luke's accounts, we read that Jesus commanded Jairus and his wife not to tell anyone what had happened.

And yet, Matthew writes, **the report of this went out into all that land** (v. 26). A miracle of this magnitude could not be kept quiet.

Just as Jesus did for Jairus's daughter, so He will do for all who put their faith in Him. He has power not only over storms, over demons, over paralysis, and over hemorrhaging, but over death. He is the one who has the key to death (Rev. 1:18), for He has defeated death. So, the thing that we fear most as human beings has lost its bitter sting. Life had ended for Jairus's daughter—until Jesus touched her. That is the Jesus we worship and serve. He saves us from the consequences of our sin. When He raises us to new life, we live forever.

47

THE COMPASSION OF JESUS

Matthew 9:27–34

When Jesus departed from there, two blind men followed Him, crying out and saying, "Son of David, have mercy on us!" And when He had come into the house, the blind men came to Him. And Jesus said to them, "Do you believe that I am able to do this?" They said to Him, "Yes, Lord." Then He touched their eyes, saying, "According to your faith let it be to you." And their eyes were opened. And Jesus sternly warned them, saying, "See that no one knows it." But when they had departed, they spread the news about Him in all that country. As they went out, behold, they brought to Him a man, mute and demon-possessed. And when the demon was cast out, the mute spoke. And the multitudes marveled, saying, "It was never seen like this in Israel!" But the Pharisees said, "He casts out demons by the ruler of the demons."

Matthew continues to display the healing power of Jesus as chapter 9 of his Gospel unfolds. Here we see the healing of two men who were blind and the release of a man who was mute because of demon possession. Both of these incidents are instructive as to who Jesus was and is.

Jesus had been in the home of the synagogue ruler Jairus, where He raised Jairus's daughter from death. Matthew then tells us, **When Jesus departed from there, two blind men followed Him, crying out and saying, "Son of David, have mercy on us!"** (v. 27). In the previous chapter, we saw how the woman who had a hemorrhage approached Jesus stealthily, seeking only to touch His robe so as not to interrupt His ministry to Jairus. These blind men, however, approached him boldly, even brazenly, crying out for His help. When they heard about Jesus and were told that He had raised Jairus's daughter from her deathbed, they knew He had the ability to make them see. Like Jairus and the woman with the hemorrhage, they were desperate for Jesus' help.

I simply cannot imagine what it would be like to be in the condition these men were in—without sight. Every year at the Ligonier National Conference in Orlando, Florida, we have a special section for those whose hearing is impaired, and the messages are translated to them by people who are fluent in American Sign Language. It is always a treat for me to watch the response of these people who cannot hear as the words of the speakers are communicated to them. However, while I'm glad they can receive the messages that are delivered, I'm always a bit saddened that they cannot hear the glorious music that we enjoy at the conference. Yet, they can at least see what is around them. The blind man, however, sees nothing. He gropes in the darkness. He's always at risk of bumping into someone or something, of tripping and falling, or of getting lost. His life is in jeopardy with every step he takes.

At certain times in the Old Testament, there were outbreaks of miracles, but we do not find even a single instance when sight was restored to someone who was blind. However, the Gospel accounts show that Jesus healed people who were blind with some regularity. On one occasion, John the Baptist, apparently having doubts about whether Jesus really was the Lamb of God, sent his disciples to ask Jesus, "Are You the Coming One, or do we look for another?" (Matt. 11:3). Jesus replied, "Go and tell John the things which you hear and see: The blind see and the lame walk; the lepers are cleansed and the deaf hear; the dead are raised up and the poor have the gospel preached to them" (vv. 4–5). These deeds were signs that were to mark the ministry of the Messiah, as prophesied by Isaiah (29:18; 35:4–6). The first of these signs was the giving of sight to the blind. Clearly it served Matthew's purpose to mention this particular type of healing as a poignant testimony to who Jesus was.

The Son of David

The blind men cried out, "Son of David, have mercy on us." Two important aspects of this cry need to be highlighted. First, notice what they asked of Jesus—mercy. Actually, that is not a good translation. They were not asking for mercy in place of justice. Rather, they wanted Jesus' pity. This verse would be better rendered as, "Son of David, have pity on us" or "Son of David, have compassion on our pitiable condition." Second, notice what they called Jesus. In the accounts of the healings in Matthew 8 and 9, Jesus is addressed in various ways, such as "Lord" (8:2, 6) and "Son of God" (8:29), and He calls Himself "Son of Man" (9:6). But this is the first time in the Gospel of Matthew when He is called "Son of David." This title is far more than a simple recognition that Jesus was a descendant of David. It is pregnant with significance.

David was the greatest king in Israel's history. Under his leadership, the nation enjoyed its golden age. As a warrior, he conquered Israel's enemies and extended its boundaries. He was a sterling administrator. He was a great musician and the poet laureate of the people, penning the majority of the psalms in our Bibles. But more than all that, God had promised that from the line of David would come a King whose reign would never end (Isa. 9:7).

However, David's kingdom *did* end. The golden age turned to bronze under the reign of David's son Solomon, and then after Solomon the kingdom turned to rust when it was divided in two. The record of the kings of Israel and Judah is a history of a rogue's gallery of Old Testament life and culture until both kingdoms were conquered.

But God said through the prophet Amos, "I will raise up the tabernacle of David, which has fallen down, and repair its damages; I will raise up its ruins, and rebuild it as in the days of old" (9:11). This was a promise that the throne of David would be established once again, and one like David would restore the kingdom of God. Of course, many centuries before Amos prophesied, Jacob had said, "The scepter shall not depart from Judah" (Gen. 49:10a). The scepter, of course, is the symbol of a king. Jacob also said, "Judah is a lion's whelp" (v. 9a). So, the people of God looked for the coming of "the lion of Judah," who would restore the kingdom of David and reign forever.

The relationship between David and Jesus was unique. On the one hand, the New Testament declares that Jesus was the Son of David. But he was also David's Lord. Psalm 110 begins this way: "The Lord said to my Lord, 'Sit at My right hand, till I make Your enemies Your footstool'" (v. 1). So, David, the author of this psalm, is writing about a conversation that he overheard, as it were. It was God talking to someone else. In the Hebrew, David says, "Yahweh said to my Adonai." The word *Adonai* means "Lord," so Yahweh was speaking to the one David acknowledged as his sovereign. This was a conversation that took place within the Godhead, in which God the Father said to God the Son, "Sit at My right hand," which is the position of supreme authority. The Christian church has held from the very beginning that it is Jesus who sits on the right hand of God. This is why, in the Apostles' Creed, we confess that Jesus "ascended into heaven and sitteth on the right hand of God the Father almighty."

It seems as if every time we have an election, people in the church get caught up in the political hype and begin to speak and behave as if our whole future depends on who is elected president of the United States. In those times, I try to emphasize that Jesus is the One who occupies the highest political office in the universe right now. Jesus is the King of the kings and the Lord of the lords. Every earthly ruler should be submissive to Him, because He is the Son of David, and He has inherited the throne of David that will last forever. So, Jesus is both the Son of David and the Lord of David.

Did the blind men understand all of this? I do not know. However, "Son of David" was a messianic title, so the blind men were at least thinking of Him as the Savior. It is significant that Jesus did not tell them not to address Him as such.

A Metaphorical Sign

Matthew then writes: **And when He had come into the house, the blind men came to Him. And Jesus said to them, "Do you believe that I am able to do this?" They said to Him, "Yes, Lord"** (v. 28). Jesus asked whether they truly believed He had the ability to heal their eyes, as opposed to simply hoping for the best. They replied, "Yes, Lord." They may have been saying, "Yes, sir," but in the context of this account, this has to be the imperial usage of the term *Lord*. I believe they understood that if Jesus was the Son of David, He was the Lord, and if He was the Lord, He could give them their sight.

Matthew tells us: **Then He touched their eyes, saying, "According to your faith let it be to you." And their eyes were opened** (vv. 29–30a). We are never told how long these men had been blind. Possibly the first time in their lives when they saw daylight was this moment when Jesus touched their eyes. Can you imagine what it would have been like to have the face of Jesus as the first thing you ever saw? That may be what happened to these men.

There is a metaphorical application to this passage. Every one of us was born blind with respect to the things of God. By nature we cannot see the spiritual realm of God. There are scales on our eyes. We can see well enough in terms of our biological vision, but we cannot see beyond the plane of this world. If we talk to people about Christ, they say, "I just don't see that." They say that because they do not see it, and they do not see it because they cannot see it. It is not because there is something wrong with their optic nerves. It is because there is something wrong with their souls. The sin of our hearts blinds us to the things of God. Until God opens the eyes of our hearts, we cannot see them. If you perceive the things of God today, if you see the sweetness of Jesus, if you see the excellency of God, that is not a natural vision that you have accomplished on your own. That is a gift of God. It is evidence that God has touched you, just as Jesus touched these blind men. But if you do not see it, you need to cry out: "Lord God, pity me! Let me see the sweetness of Christ."

Notice how this incident concludes: **And Jesus sternly warned them, saying, "See that no one knows it." But when they had departed, they spread the news about Him in all that country** (vv. 30b–31). Jesus had taken them inside the house, removing them from the crowds, before He healed them. Still, He knew they would be prone to tell others what had happened to them. But Jesus did not want that, so He told them not to speak about it. This is the so-called "messianic secret," Jesus' oft-expressed desire that people not spread the word about what He did for them.

Why did He do this? The most likely reason is that there was a gross misunderstanding throughout the Jewish culture of what the Messiah was to be. Jesus knew that the people were looking for someone who would deliver them from the power of Rome. But He had His own timetable for communicating His identity. He did not want to excite the masses to improper expectations. It is also possible that He was exhausted from all the healings He had been performing, so He did not want the men whose sight He had restored to spread the word that healing was available for one and all with any ache or pain. Matthew does not tell us precisely why Jesus gave this command, but he does tell us that these men did not do as Jesus asked. As soon as they got away from Him, they told *everyone* in that region what Jesus had done for them. They simply could not keep quiet.

A Note of Foreboding

Matthew then gives us a short account of yet another healing: **As they went out, behold, they brought to Him a man, mute and demon-possessed. And when the demon was cast out, the mute spoke. And the multitudes marveled, saying, "It was never seen like this in Israel!"** (vv. 32–33). Here again, Jesus cast a demon out of a man. In this case, the demon was preventing the man from speaking, but he recovered that ability when the demon was gone. Just as the blind men regained the use of their eyes by Jesus' power, this man regained the use of his tongue and vocal cords. But unlike the healing of the blind men, this miracle seems to have been done outside, with the result that the crowds saw it and marveled at it. They declared, correctly, that they were seeing things that had never before been witnessed in Israel.

The first two chapters of the Bible trace the various stages of creation. At every stage, God steps back from His creation and evaluates it, repeatedly judging it to be good (Gen. 1:4, 10, 12, 18, 21, 25, 31). But Genesis 3 begins with an ominous note: "Now the serpent was more cunning than any beast of the field which the Lord God had made" (v. 1). These words introduce a jarring note of discord into the account of creation.

There is a similar note of discord and foreboding in Matthew 9. As the people are marveling over Jesus' healing of the demon-possessed mute man, Matthew tells us, **But the Pharisees said, "He casts out demons by the ruler of the demons"** (v. 34). This issue would come up again and would prompt Jesus to deliver an extremely important discourse about the unpardonable sin, blasphemy against the Holy Spirit. How could it have been possible for anyone to think that the power behind the compassion of Christ was the power of evil? There was no evil in Him. But all of the evil of this world and hell was marshaled against Him.

Throughout the ministry of Jesus, there was no neutrality. People were either with Him or against Him. That is as true today as it was then. Where do you stand? If you say, "Well, I'm looking into these things, but I haven't come to a conclusion," I have to tell you that you are in opposition to the Lord's Anointed. There is no neutrality. You are with Him or against Him.

48

THE FIELDS READY TO HARVEST

Matthew 9:35–38

Then Jesus went about all the cities and villages, teaching in their synagogues, preaching the gospel of the kingdom, and healing every sickness and every disease among the people. But when He saw the multitudes, He was moved with compassion for them, because they were weary and scattered, like sheep having no shepherd. Then He said to His disciples, "The harvest truly is plentiful, but the laborers are few. Therefore pray the Lord of the harvest to send out laborers into His harvest."

With these verses, Matthew wraps up a series of episodes that highlight the remarkable healing ministry of Jesus. In doing so, he calls our attention back to the primary focus of Jesus' earthly ministry. Though Jesus spent much time healing the ailments of the people, His priority was to preach and to teach, to proclaim the breakthrough of the kingdom of God. Those activities come to the fore as Matthew's account moves forward. Also in this passage, we find a specific prayer that the Lord instructed His disciples to pray, one that we need to continue to include in our petitions to God the Father.

Matthew writes: **Then Jesus went about all the cities and villages, teaching in their synagogues, preaching the gospel of the kingdom, and healing every sickness and every disease among the people. But when He saw the multitudes, He was moved with compassion for them, because they were weary and scattered, like sheep having no shepherd** (vv. 35–36). Three activities are mentioned here—teaching, preaching, and healing. All of these activities were motivated by Jesus' compassion for the people. He saw them as sheep that had no shepherd.

One of the sharp contrasts in Matthew's presentation of the ministry of Jesus is that between His compassion for the people and the attitude of the Pharisees, who held the masses in contempt. They wanted nothing to do with ordinary Jews. They wanted to keep their distance from the people, lest they become defiled by contact with them. They had no compassion, yet the Pharisees should have been the shepherds the people so desperately needed.

Matthew continues: **Then He said to His disciples, "The harvest truly is plentiful, but the laborers are few. Therefore pray the Lord of the harvest to send out laborers into His harvest"** (vv. 37–38). It is interesting how the metaphor of harvest differs in the Old and New Testaments. In the Old Testament, metaphorical references to reaping almost always carry negative implications. They have to do with God coming to judge the wicked at the final judgment. But there is a totally different accent in this teaching of Jesus. When He used the metaphor of the harvest, He was talking about the gathering of God's people into His kingdom. The Pharisees considered the people to be nothing more than chaff that should be burned, but Jesus saw them as wheat that the Father had grown for His kingdom. Furthermore, they were ready. The fields were ripe. God had prepared His harvest, a people to be brought into His storehouse.

However, though the harvest was plentiful, the laborers were few. Following Jesus' metaphor, we understand that one person could not go out into a huge field with multiple acres of grain and singlehandedly bring in the harvest. Many laborers were needed. Basically, Jesus was saying: "I am going to every town, every village, and every synagogue, and I'm preaching, teaching, and healing everywhere I go, but you must pray that God will call other workers to join Me in this enterprise." It is not by accident that we find this text immediately before He called the Twelve and gave them their commission to participate in the harvest.

The message is simple: the kingdom of God needs men and women who will help to bring in the harvest. Preachers, teachers, missionaries, and ordinary believers—all of us are called to participate in the harvest in one way or another. We cannot simply appoint ministers to do this job; they need a galvanized and equipped laity to assist them.

Lord of the Harvest

Notice to whom believers are to direct their prayers for laborers: "the Lord of the harvest." Who is the Lord of the harvest? It is certainly not the preacher, the teacher, or the missionary. As much as the preacher preaches, as much as teacher teaches, as much as the missionary carries out his mission, all of that work is utterly in vain unless God brings in the harvest. I am acutely conscious, every time I step into the pulpit, that no matter what I say, my words are without power and force unless God the Holy Spirit uses them to penetrate the souls of my hearers. There are no programs, no techniques, and no skills that can do the job unless God Himself brings the harvest.

In his first epistle to the Corinthians, the Apostle Paul addresses a division that arose in the congregation between followers of Paul, followers of Apollos, followers of Peter, and followers of Christ. Paul has to rebuke the members of the Corinthian church for their factionalism:

> And I, brethren, could not speak to you as to spiritual people but as to carnal, as to babes in Christ. I fed you with milk and not with solid food; for until now you were not able to receive it, and even now you are still not able; for you are still carnal. For where there are envy, strife, and divisions among you, are you not carnal and behaving like mere men? For when one says, "I am of Paul," and another, "I am of Apollos," are you not carnal? Who then is Paul, and who is Apollos, but ministers through whom you believed, as the Lord gave to each one? I planted, Apollos watered, but God gave the increase. So then neither he who plants is anything, nor he who waters, but God who gives the increase. (3:1–7)

Could the Apostle be any plainer here? When souls are brought into the kingdom of God, God and God alone gets the credit. All of the knowledge and skill of the Apostle Paul, along with all of the eloquence of Apollos (who was perhaps the most eloquent speaker in the early church), could not produce a single convert. They did what they could. One planted. Another watered the seed. But the fruit came through all the planting and watering because God brought the increase.

We see this theme expressed in Psalm 127. It begins with these words: "Unless the Lord builds the house, they labor in vain who build it" (v. 1a). When the congregation I serve, Saint Andrew's, was building a new sanctuary a few years ago, I enjoyed going by the construction site to see what was happening. At the height of the work, nearly a hundred men were working there every day. I could see the labor they were putting into the project. But as I watched the sanctuary going up, I remembered this psalm, and I knew that the workers' labor, plus all of the sacrifice, giving, and praying by the congregation, was an exercise in futility unless God made it happen. And, of course, this is true as well not just for single church buildings but for the church itself. Christ is building His church

(Matt. 16:18), and no matter how much believers do, the church will not grow and advance if Christ does not build it.

The psalmist goes on to say, "unless the LORD guards the city, the watchman stays awake in vain" (v. 1b). Does this mean that a watchman who keeps his eyes open and diligently does his job is engaged in a futile exercise? Should the watchman just sleep through the night? No, that is not the point. The watchman is called to exercise all the vigilance he can muster. Yet, he has to realize that the safety of the city ultimately is not in his hands but in the hands of God.

The Relationship of Faith and Rebirth

Many people think that Reformed theology can be reduced to the so-called five points of Calvinism. However, Reformed theology is far more than the five points. Just as there are systems of doctrine that define Lutheranism, Episcopalianism, and Roman Catholicism, there is a distinct doctrinal system that defines the Reformed faith. But if there is one tenet of Reformed theology that distinguishes it from every other theology on the face of the earth, it is this—the relationship in the order of salvation between faith and rebirth. That is the great divide. This is where many people who say they love Reformed teaching get off the bus.

Here is the difference: Virtually every theology out there teaches that in order to be reborn of the Spirit of God, a person has to have faith. As a consequence of his trust in Christ, God the Holy Spirit causes a new birth in his soul and he comes to a new spiritual life. In contrast, Reformed theology teaches that while a person must have faith and must make a choice to believe on Christ, none of that happens until God the Holy Spirit changes the disposition of his heart. The cardinal point of Reformed theology is this: rebirth or regeneration comes *before* faith.

The idea that lies behind this point of doctrine is the principle that it is God who gives the increase. I may make a choice to trust Christ, but I cannot do that unless God has first quickened my heart. And at the same time, all whom God quickens come to faith and are included in the kingdom of God.

Jesus explained this point to a man named Nicodemus, who was a Pharisee. Nicodemus came to Jesus at night and complimented Him, saying, "Rabbi, we know that You are a teacher come from God; for no one can do these signs that You do unless God is with him" (John 3:2). In the midst of all this flattery, Jesus stopped Nicodemus in his tracks by saying, "Most assuredly, I say to you, unless one is born again, he cannot see the kingdom of God" (v. 3). Nicodemus was dumbfounded. He asked: "How can a man be born when he is old? Can he enter a second time into his mother's womb and be born?" (v. 4). So Jesus elaborated: "Most assuredly, I say to you, unless one is born of water and the Spirit, he cannot enter the kingdom of God. That which is born of the flesh is flesh, and that which is born of the Spirit is spirit" (vv. 5–6).

Do you know what you were when you were born? Flesh. You were not half flesh and half spirit. You were not even 99 percent flesh and 1 percent spirit. You were 100 percent flesh. Jesus had to explain to His contemporaries: "It is the Spirit who gives life; the flesh profits nothing" (John 6:63a). But millions of Christians believe that while God does 99 percent of the work in salvation, the decisive vote is cast by the sinner who is still in the flesh. He still can do something. He still can say yes to the invitation of the gospel. He still can accept the offer of God's grace. But Jesus is saying the sinner cannot do that unless God the Holy Spirit first quickens his soul.

Anyone who is a Christian has had that experience. All believers once were dead in their sins, and it was while they were dead in that state, walking according to the course of this world, that God quickened them to spiritual life. The moment He gave them that spiritual life, each of them said, "Yes, I believe." Maybe others had planted seeds in their lives. Perhaps others had watered those seeds. Still, they were hanging on the stalk in the field until God came. That's the fundamental point of Reformed theology. It is about who is sovereign and who is not. The sovereignty of God in all things—even salvation—defines Reformed theology.

Of course, every Christian who is asked, "Do you believe in the sovereignty of God?" says yes. But if we begin to get specific, the yes often turns to no in short order. We might ask, "Is God sovereign over nature?" Yes. "Does God sovereignly have the right to give commandments?" Yes. "Does God sovereignly bestow His saving grace on some but not on others?" No. These believers need a more biblical understanding as to who is the Lord of the harvest.

The fact that only God can save a soul should not discourage us but greatly encourage us. If I were to focus on my own weakness and impotency to change people's lives, I would give up the Christian ministry. But I know that God has promised that His Word will not return to Him void (Isa. 55:11). I know that God has promised to assign God the Holy Spirit to accompany the faithful and accurate preaching of His Word, so that it does not come to nothing. This is the only reason I can hope in the efficacy of preaching. My only hope is in God. What better place could my hope be? What greater power could we lean on than the power of God?

Jesus said, "Pray the Lord of the harvest to send out laborers." We need to pray that there will be more preachers, more teachers, and more missionaries, and that they may go out knowing that the efficacy of their labor depends not on them but on God.

Stonewall Jackson, the Confederate general during the Civil War, would tell his troops, "Duty is ours; consequences are God's." Oh, how we need to understand that. We need to know we are not the lords of the harvest. We are the workers; He is the Lord.

49

THE COMMISSIONING OF THE APOSTLES

Matthew 10:1–4

And when He had called His twelve disciples to Him, He gave them power over unclean spirits, to cast them out, and to heal all kinds of sickness and all kinds of disease. Now the names of the twelve apostles are these: first, Simon, who is called Peter, and Andrew his brother; James the son of Zebedee, and John his brother; Philip and Bartholomew; Thomas and Matthew the tax collector; James the son of Alphaeus, and Lebbaeus, whose surname was Thaddaeus; Simon the Cananite, and Judas Iscariot, who also betrayed Him.

When we encounter a list of names in Scripture, such as this list of the twelve Apostles, we find it hard to get excited about the revelatory possibilities. However, Jesus' commissioning of these men to be His Apostles was one of the most significant events of His earthly ministry, so we do well to study it and apply it to our lives.

Immediately after exhorting His followers to pray that God the Father would send out laborers to bring in the harvest (God's people), Jesus Himself took action to send laborers into the fields. Matthew writes, **And when He had called His twelve disciples to Him, He gave them power over unclean spirits, to cast them out, and to heal all kinds of sickness and all kinds of disease** (v. 1). We have seen that a disciple was, first and foremost, a student. He was one who was enrolled in a rabbinical school. Jesus had quite a few students in His rabbinical school, many more than twelve, but among the entire student body, there were twelve who had a certain significance. It was these twelve whom Jesus called to Himself, whereupon He commissioned them for an extremely important task and changed their status from that of disciple to that of Apostle.

There is a huge difference between a disciple and an Apostle. By definition, an apostle is one who is sent by someone in authority, who delegates his authority to the sent one. As a result, the one who is commissioned and sent bears the same authority as the sender, and his orders must be obeyed as if they came from the sender himself.

The first apostle of the New Testament—indeed, the supreme Apostle of the Christian church—is Christ Himself, because our Lord was sent by the Father into the world. Jesus said, "I have not spoken on My own authority; but the Father who sent Me gave Me a command, what I should say and what I should speak" (John 12:49). He also said, "All authority has been given to Me in heaven and on earth" (Matt. 28:18).

We deal with problems of authority every day. Often, when a parent tells a child to do something, the child does not want to comply; instead, he wants to do what he wants to do. If the parent says, "You *must*" or "You *will*," the child is apt to plant his feet and ask, "Why should I?" Sometimes the parent is patient enough to spell out the reasons why the child must do as he is told. At other times, the parent simply pulls rank and says, "You will do it because I said so."

This kind of thing happens not only in the family but in the workplace, where we have hierarchical structures of authority. It happens in the schools, where administrators have authority over students and teachers. It happens in the military, where the first two words a recruit is taught to say are "Yes, sir." There are countless other examples of situations in which someone gives directives that must be obeyed. However, we have to understand that no one in any position of authority in this world, whether it's the president of the United States, the foreman on the job, the principal in the high school, or a drill sergeant in the Marine Corps, possesses inherent authority. No authority that we encounter in this world is rooted and grounded in the person who holds that authority. All authority in this world is delegated, because the only One who possesses inherent, intrinsic, absolute authority is God Himself.

It is not by accident that the word *authority* contains the word *author*. God is the author of all that is. It is He who made us and not we ourselves (Ps. 100:3). By virtue of His position as the Creator and the Sovereign over all things, God inherently has the authority to command from His creatures whatsoever He pleases. God alone, in the final analysis, has the authority to bind our consciences. All other authority derives from Him.

Power or Authority?

As noted above, the first major delegation of authority in the New Testament was from the Father to the Son. Jesus could say, essentially, "The Father says it and that settles it." There used to be a popular bumper sticker that read: "God said it. I believe it. That settles it." Whenever I saw one of those stickers, I felt the urge to get a big marker and black out the middle clause. A matter is settled as soon as God speaks. It does not depend on my acceptance of it or belief in it. Whatever the Lord God says is law. That authority was delegated to the Son.

But when Jesus called His disciples to Himself, He created another level of authority by delegating His God-given authority to them. According to the New King James translation, He gave them "power over unclean spirits, to cast them out, and to heal all manner of sickness and all manner of disease." However, other biblical translations say He gave them not "power" but "authority." The reason for this variation is that the Greek word that is used here is *exousia*, which, as we saw previously, can be translated as "power" or "authority." We saw this word used in Matthew 7:28–29, where, following the Sermon on the Mount, we are told, "the people were astonished at His teaching, for He taught them as one having *authority*, and not as the scribes" (emphasis added). Likewise, we encountered it in Matthew 9:6, where Matthew tells us that Jesus said, "'But that you may know that the Son of Man has *power* on earth to forgive sins'—then He said to the paralytic, 'Arise, take up your bed and go to your house'" (emphasis added). So, we have seen *exousia* translated both ways, and both are legitimate, for the word refers to that which has both power and authority.

I wonder, however, why the New King James translators chose to use the English word *power* here in Matthew 10:1. I believe it must have had to do with the context. Jesus gives the Apostles power over demons and diseases. Casting out demons or healing diseases requires a power men do not inherently possess. It is supernatural power. Jesus bestowed it on the Twelve so they would be able to do these powerful works.

Still, I prefer the word *authority*, for two reasons. First, the power Jesus gave the Twelve over unclean spirits was the authority to require them to leave the hosts they were tormenting. They could drive out demons because they had the authority. Second, while this text tells us that Jesus delegated authority over demons and over disease to the Apostles, that was by no means the full extent of the authority He gave to them, nor, in my judgment, was it the most important authority He gave to them. I believe the most important authority He bestowed on His Apostles was the authority of His Word.

The Authority of the Word

At Saint Andrew's, the church I serve, we place a picture of a Celtic cross on the cover of the worship bulletin each Sunday. This cross is adorned by several Latin phrases, which are the "solas" of the Protestant Reformation, and prominent among them is *Sola Scriptura*, or "Scripture alone." Historians tell us there were two main causes of the Reformation. First, there was the so-called "material cause," the chief matter in the dispute, which was how a person can be justified before a holy God. The Protestant position in the debate between the Reformers and the Roman Catholic Church over justification by faith alone was captured in the phrase *Sola fide*, which means, "By faith alone." But in all the debates, lurking in the background was what the scholars call the "formal cause" of the Reformation, which was the question of authority. When Martin Luther challenged the church, the response was, in essence: "Who do you think you are? You're speaking against the pope and church councils." Luther replied: "That's not the issue. The question is, Am I speaking against the Word of God?" When he was summoned to the Diet of Worms and was called upon to recant his views, he replied: "Unless I am convicted by Scripture and plain reason—I do not accept the authority of popes and councils, for they have contradicted each other—my conscience is captive to the Word of God. I cannot and I will not recant anything, for to go against conscience is neither right nor safe. God help me. Amen."[1]

Luther was faced with the same issue that Eve faced in the garden of Eden, when the Serpent came to her and said, "Has God indeed said . . . ?" (Gen. 3:1). Luther said: "I respect the pope. I respect the church councils. I respect the theologians of the church. I take them very, very seriously. But not one of them individually or all of them together can bind the conscience. Only the Word of God can do that." He was calling attention to the authority of the Bible.

The authority of the Bible rests on apostolic authority. In the early centuries of the church, the great theologian Irenaeus had to defend the apostolic writings from heretics. They basically claimed to respect God and have great admiration for Jesus, but they said they could not stomach Paul, Peter, or John. In reply, Irenaeus made a very simple argument. He noted that when Jesus debated with the Pharisees, they essentially said: "We believe in Moses. It's you we have trouble with." Jesus said, "If you believed Moses, you would believe Me; for he wrote about Me" (John 5:46). He was setting forth a principle: "He who rejects Me rejects Him who sent Me" (Luke 10:16). Jesus was claiming to be the Father's apostle, and if His claim was true, to reject His authority was to reject the authority of God. But Irenaeus went on to say that anyone who rejected the Apostles was

[1] Roland H. Bainton, *Here I Stand: A Life of Martin Luther* (Nashville: Abigdon Press, 1950), 144.

rejecting Christ, for He had delegated His authority to the Apostles. Therefore, anyone who rejected the Apostles ultimately rejected the Father.

I think Irenaeus was absolutely right, and I think Luther was absolutely right in the sixteenth century. If we reject the Bible, we reject apostolic authority. If we reject apostolic authority, we reject the authority of Christ. If we reject the authority of Christ, we reject the authority of God. Therefore, if we reject the Bible, we reject the authority of God.

Apostles Known and Unknown

Matthew then writes: **Now the names of the twelve apostles are these: first, Simon, who is called Peter, and Andrew his brother; James the son of Zebedee, and John his brother; Philip and Bartholomew; Thomas and Matthew the tax collector; James the son of Alphaeus, and Lebbaeus, whose surname was Thaddaeus; Simon the Cananite, and Judas Iscariot, who also betrayed Him** (vv. 2–4).

We know a great deal about roughly half of these men because they appear frequently in the record of the New Testament, but the other half are virtual unknowns. They appear in lists here and there, but we know next to nothing about them because their activities as Apostles in the early church remain mostly obscure. Yet, I think the words of Winston Churchill, which he uttered in response to the heroism of the Royal Air Force pilots who protected their nation in the Battle of Britain in the desperate early days of World War II, apply very well to all of the Apostles: "Never . . . was so much owed by so many to so few." These few whom Jesus entrusted with His mission and to whom He gave His authority turned the world upside down (Acts 17:6).

50

THE SENDING OF THE TWELVE

Matthew 10:5–15

These twelve Jesus sent out and commanded them, saying: "Do not go into the way of the Gentiles, and do not enter a city of the Samaritans. But go rather to the lost sheep of the house of Israel. And as you go, preach, saying, 'The kingdom of heaven is at hand.' Heal the sick, cleanse the lepers, raise the dead, cast out demons. Freely you have received, freely give. Provide neither gold nor silver nor copper in your money belts, nor bag for your journey, nor two tunics, nor sandals, nor staffs; for a worker is worthy of his food. Now whatever city or town you enter, inquire who in it is worthy, and stay there till you go out. And when you go into a household, greet it. If the household is worthy, let your peace come upon it. But if it is not worthy, let your peace return to you. And whoever will not receive you nor hear your words, when you depart from that house or city, shake off the dust from your feet. Assuredly, I say to you, it will be more tolerable for the land of Sodom and Gomorrah in the day of judgment than for that city!"

There are certain passages throughout the Scriptures that sometimes are called "hard sayings," statements that are difficult for us to hear and that, at times, even sound a bit harsh. This passage contains one of those hard sayings.

After Jesus appointed twelve of His disciples to serve as Apostles, He sent them out on a trial mission, but not before giving them detailed instructions. First, He told them where they were not to go. Matthew writes: **These twelve**

Jesus sent out and commanded them, saying: "Do not go into the way of the Gentiles, and do not enter a city of the Samaritans. But go rather to the lost sheep of the house of Israel" (vv. 5–6). When Jesus spoke these words, He and the Apostles were in Galilee, the northern part of Israel. He told them not to go north, east, or south, because there were only Gentile lands to the north and east, while to the south was the country of the Samaritans (the Mediterranean Sea was to the west). Jesus was saying, "I want you to focus your missionary activity in Galilee, because I am sending you to seek the lost sheep of the house of Israel." In other words, the first apostolic mission was to the Jews. We see this priority echoed in the Apostle Paul's letter to the Romans, when he writes, "For I am not ashamed of the gospel of Christ, for it is the power of God to salvation for everyone who believes, for the Jew first and also for the Greek" (1:16).

So, the Jews had the priority of receiving the kingdom of God. Why was that? Why did Jesus restrict the missionary enterprise initially to Israel? He did not say, so to answer that question involves some measure of speculation.

Martin Luther made some serious and at times vehement attacks against the Jews in Germany in his later years. He castigated the Jewish bankers for their usurious interest rates that were crippling the people of the land, but he also spoke sharply against the Jews because of their hostility to the gospel. Luther is remembered for these stances, and some have gone so far as to blame the Holocaust on him because of his strong criticisms of Jews. But earlier Luther wrote a magnificent treatise on the Jews in which he reminded the Christian church that the Gentiles are wild olive branches (Rom. 11:17–24) that have been grafted into the tree, and that biblically salvation is of the Jews. It was Israel that God called to Himself to be a blessing to all of the people of the world. So, there is absolutely no foundation in biblical truth for anti-Semitism. Our Lord Himself was a Jew, and it was a priority for Him to reach His own people. We are also told, "He came to His own, and His own did not receive Him" (John 1:11). That's generally true, but the vast majority of the early converts to Christianity were Jewish people who had waited for the coming of the Messiah. So, Jesus sent the Apostles "to the lost sheep of the house of Israel, [to tell them] 'The kingdom of heaven is at hand.'"

Does that message sound familiar? It was the message of John the Baptist when he began his earthly ministry (Matt. 3:2). Also, it was the message Jesus preached when He inaugurated His earthly ministry (Matt. 4:17). He was telling His Apostles, "I want you to go and preach to My people the same message that I have been preaching. Tell them that the time is at hand, that the supreme crisis of history is upon them—the breakthrough of the kingdom of God. Tell them that the One whom the Father has anointed as King is in their midst." As they went out with this message, they were to **"Heal the sick, cleanse the lepers, raise the dead, cast out demons"** (v. 8a), for these signs would authenticate their authority.

Jesus added, **"Freely you have received, freely give"** (v. 8b). He reminded the Apostles that they had received the kingdom, salvation through Him, as a gift. They did not buy it or earn it. Therefore, they needed to offer it as a gift.

What was true of the Apostles at that time in redemptive history is equally true of us today. If you are a Christian, if you have received the greatest benefit that a human being can receive, you need to remember always that you did not earn it. You did not merit it. You did not buy it. Rather, it was a gift given to you by the grace of God freely. Therefore, you need to extend the kingdom to others freely.

Trusting God for Provision

Then Jesus turned to more practical instructions: **"Provide neither gold nor silver nor copper in your money belts, nor bag for your journey, nor two tunics, nor sandals, nor staffs; for a worker is worthy of his food"** (vv. 9–10). He did not want the Apostles to be weighed down with the burden of finances. Furthermore, He did not want them to have to lug extra clothing or food along on their journey. He wanted them to travel light, trusting that God's people would provide the provisions, clothing, and shelter they would need.

The principle of the people of God providing for the ministers of God is deeply rooted in biblical truth, both in the Old and New Testaments. One of the greatest shames of the American church is that the clergy remain among the lowest-paid professional groups. This shows that Americans attach a very low value to the work of ministers. It was no accident that God instituted the tithe in the Old Testament to make sure that those who were entrusted with the sacred things of the nation would have adequate provisions. God knew that if He left the care of His priests and ministers up to the dynamics of the market, they would starve to death, because people do not value what they do. I think this is part of the reason why hundreds of clergy leave the ministry every year in the United States.

Let me exhort you, if you are a church elder or deacon, to make it your business to see that your minister is well provided for according to the Word of God. It is never your duty to ensure someone else's sacrifice. I have heard Christians say things in discussions about ministerial compensation that nearly made my hair stand on end. I once heard someone say, "We can't pay the minister that much because then he'll be making more money than I do." On another occasion, I heard it said, "We want to keep our minister humble." Protestantism has never bought into the kind of mysticism that grew up in the Middle Ages, which perceived great spiritual virtue in poverty. All of these comments are intended to cover up the fact that only about 4 percent of the people in the congregation are paying their tithes, making it almost impossible for pastors to buy the books they need to study in order to preach and teach the Word of God. We should be moving heaven and earth to make sure that ministers are well compensated.

Jesus went on: **"Now whatever city or town you enter, inquire who in it is worthy, and stay there till you go out. And when you go into a household, greet it. If the household is worthy, let your peace come upon it. But if it is not worthy, let your peace return to you"** (vv. 11–13). With these guidelines, Jesus was simply reiterating principles for hospitality that are set forth in the Word of God. He said that if the Apostles found a household to house, feed, and support them in a given town, they should let their peace—that is, a benediction—be upon that house. If they put their benediction on a house, they would be putting Jesus' benediction on it. However, if a house proved unworthy, if it did not support them adequately, they should withhold Jesus' benediction.

Finally, Jesus said: **"And whoever will not receive you nor hear your words, when you depart from that house or city, shake off the dust from your feet"** (v. 14). From the Jews' perspective, Gentiles were ceremonially unclean, and that uncleanness extended to the homes and lands of Gentiles. If a Jew had to travel through Gentile territory or through Samaria, upon arriving back in Israel, it was customary for him to shake his clothes and feet to rid them of the dust from the ground of the unclean places. This was a symbolic gesture of repudiation of everything that was unclean. Jesus told the Apostles to use it if they were not welcomed or believed in a town or a house.

Rewards and Punishments

At last we come to the hard saying I mentioned earlier. Jesus said, **"Assuredly, I say to you, it will be more tolerable for the land of Sodom and Gomorrah in the day of judgment than for that city!"** (v. 15). Was Jesus just speaking hyperbolically here to make a point? I do not think so. What, then, does this statement mean?

The Old Testament represents the towns of Sodom and Gomorrah as the nadir of corruption and of human sin. They were the most wicked cities in all of biblical history, and they met with the unbridled judgment of God. So, Jesus used them to make a comparison. He told the Apostles that if they went to a town to preach the message of the kingdom of God, and the people of that town did not receive them, they should shake the dust of that town off their feet because it would be more tolerable for Sodom and Gomorrah in the day of judgment than for that town. I believe this statement from Jesus is clear and should be taken literally.

We need to learn two things from this passage. First, contrary to many people's assumptions, on the day of judgment there will be degrees and gradations of reward and punishment. In heaven, some will receive great rewards and others will receive smaller rewards. In hell, some will receive great punishments while others will receive lesser punishments. The popular idea is that everyone in heaven gets the same reward and everyone in hell receives the same punishment. However, there are at least twenty-five passages in the New Testament that tell us that there will be levels of rewards in heaven and levels of punishment in hell. To be sure, between heaven and hell there is an unbridgeable chasm (Luke 16:26), and the person who has the lowest position in heaven is almost infinitely better off than the person in the highest level of hell. To get into heaven is the greatest blessing we can hope to receive. But while we get into heaven by faith alone in Christ alone, God in His grace has decided that our place in heaven is determined by our works, by our level of obedience. So, the difference in rewards in heaven will still be gracious.

By contrast, punishments in hell will be strictly meted out according to justice. If a person murders another person in this life, he will receive the just punishment for that in hell. If he murders five, his judgment will be five times as bad. One of my professors in seminary once said that a sinner in hell would do anything to make the number of his sins during his lifetime one less so that his punishment might be that much smaller.

The sad truth is that most Christians have a practical disbelief in hell. I know that is true because if we really believed in hell our zeal for mission would be a thousand times stronger. We engage in all kinds of sophistry, arguing that God does not send people to hell but that they send themselves there by their own evil deeds. The Bible disagrees. It teaches that no one sends himself to hell. It is God who sends people to hell. He created hell for judgment. I cannot think of anything in this world more terrifying than going to hell.

Once, as I was walking down a hallway, I passed a mirror on the wall, and I stopped and stared at my reflection. As I did so, a horrifying question came to my mind. I asked myself: "What if I have deceived myself all these years? What if I'm not regenerate? What if my profession of faith is false? What if my destiny is eternity in hell?" I was terrified. The only thing I could do at that time was to flee to the cross again and to cling to Christ, saying: "Lord, it's Your righteousness alone that can bring me safely into Your kingdom. Nothing in my hands I bring. There's nothing I can do to earn my way into heaven. If You were to exercise Your justice on me, You would send me to hell forever. I know that." As I reminded myself of the grace of God, my assurance of salvation was restored.

There is a second lesson we need to learn from this passage. Jesus said it would be more tolerable for Sodom and Gomorrah than for a town that did not receive the Apostles for a simple reason: the people of that town rejected the gospel, and in rejecting the message of the kingdom of God, they rejected Jesus.

Many people today believe the gospel is an invitation they can accept or reject as they please. But God does not invite people to come to Christ; rather, He commands them to come (Acts 17:30). If anyone refuses that command, he has done the unthinkable. Most people will admit they are not perfect, but they do not have a clue as to the gravity of sin. Above all, they fail to see that the most serious sin a person can commit in this world is to reject Jesus.

Someone always seems to object by saying: "Unless I'm elect, unless the Holy Spirit gives me grace, I cannot come to Jesus. Since I don't want Him, I must not be elect. Therefore, it's not my fault. It's God's fault." No, God does not owe anyone grace, and He will judge everyone justly. Those who refuse to submit to His appointed King deserve a punishment more severe than that meted out to Sodom and Gomorrah.

That's hard. But I believe with all my heart, mind, and soul that it is the truth. It is a truth we desperately need to hear and receive.

51

PERSECUTIONS

Matthew 10:16–23

Behold, I send you out as sheep in the midst of wolves. Therefore be wise as serpents and harmless as doves. But beware of men, for they will deliver you up to councils and scourge you in their synagogues. You will be brought before governors and kings for My sake, as a testimony to them and to the Gentiles. But when they deliver you up, do not worry about how or what you should speak. For it will be given to you in that hour what you should speak; for it is not you who speak, but the Spirit of your Father who speaks in you. Now brother will deliver up brother to death, and a father his child; and children will rise up against parents and cause them to be put to death. And you will be hated by all for My name's sake. But he who endures to the end will be saved. When they persecute you in this city, flee to another. For assuredly, I say to you, you will not have gone through the cities of Israel before the Son of Man comes.

After giving His Apostles some practical instructions for their trial mission, Jesus implicitly acknowledged that some towns and households would not receive them. In such cases, He said, they should shake the dust off their feet upon their departure. However, as Jesus continued, He warned the Apostles that they would face far worse than the rejection of their message; they would have to deal with outright persecution.

According to Matthew's record, Jesus said, **"Behold, I send you out as sheep in the midst of wolves"** (v. 16a). The most important point to note from this verse is who initiated the missionary enterprise. It was not the Apostles' idea to go out to the villages and cities of Israel. Rather, Jesus was the One who sent them: "I send you."

As the Sender, Jesus was honest with His sent ones—they were like sheep in the midst of wolves. He was not saying the Apostles were sheep in the sense of being stupid. Rather, the point of the metaphor is that He was sending them into an environment that was altogether hostile. They were like sheep venturing among a band of ravenous wolves, who could not wait to attack them. In human terms, the Apostles did not stand a chance.

How does this apply to believers in the Western world in the twenty-first century? There are pockets of hostility against Christianity, and there seems to be a growing disenchantment among public officials toward any influence of the Christian faith in the public square. For the most part, however, Christianity is tolerated in the community, and we usually do not feel as if we are lambs about to be devoured by fierce wolves. We may be mocked a little bit, but no one is threatening to send us to the Colosseum to fight with the gladiators, to throw us to the lions, or to put us to use as human torches to light the emperor's gardens. That's not where we are. And sometimes I wonder why we do not see that kind of persecution happening. Why is the preaching of the gospel in our day in the West not nearly as dangerous as it was for these apostles on their initial apostolic mission?

In his book *Christless Christianity*, Michael Horton demonstrates how the gospel has been diluted and radically altered by the popular preachers of our day. The message of the gospel has become a message of therapy. If we are not well-adjusted, God can help us have successful lives. If we will just exercise our wills and follow a few basic steps, we will be wealthy, healthy, and happy.

In his book, Horton discusses one of the men who preaches this kind of message: Joel Osteen, who is perhaps the most popular preacher in the United States today. In a television interview, Osteen was asked whether he uses the word *sinners*. He replied: "I don't use it. I never thought about it, but I probably don't. But most people already know what they're doing wrong. When I get them to church I want to tell them that you can change."[1] It is no wonder his church is filled to the rafters. What is more popular than a Christianity without sin? Later, Osteen was asked whether Jews, Muslims, and other non-Christians are wrong in their beliefs. He said: "I don't know if I believe they're wrong. I believe here's what the Bible teaches and from the Christian faith this is what I believe. But I just think that only God will judge a person's heart."[2] Even the interviewer, who was not a Christian, sensed that something did not sound right about this message, which lacked any concept of sin and judgment.

[1] Michael Horton, *Christless Christianity: The Alternative Gospel of the American Church* (Grand Rapids: Baker, 2008), 75–76.

[2] Ibid., 74

If God is not holy, wrathful toward sin, and concerned about justice, Christianity is completely meaningless and unnecessary. If God is not holy, why should we be concerned about sin? Why should we be concerned about facing Him at the end of our lives? If God is not wrathful and is only one big bundle of celestial love, who needs grace or mercy?

The gospel is not good news to people today because they are not looking for good news. They are looking for good advice. As Horton points out in his book, most of the advice they want—how to have peace with their children, how to get along in their marriages, and how to be successful in their business relationships—they can get from the barber or the hair stylist without reading a page of the New Testament.

But if God is holy, if He has wrath, and if He is concerned about righteousness and justice (and He is), we need the cross. The best news we could ever hear is that Christ has come to satisfy the demands of the righteousness and justice of God, that Christ has taken on Himself the fullness of the wrath of God directed against our sin, and that He has clothed us with His own righteousness, which alone will meet the demands of a holy God. God is holy, which means we are not holy. That means we need a Savior. We need the cross.

The problem is that this message is repugnant to wolves. No sinner wants to hear about his sin. He does not want to hear about a holy God. But Jesus gave that message to His Apostles and sent them out among the wolves to preach it—but not before warning them that they would be despised because of it.

Wise and Harmless

Jesus continued, **"Therefore be wise as serpents and harmless as doves"** (v. 16b). This was His advice to His sheep when they were among the wolves. Well, the church today is often completely harmless, which is why we enjoy peace and security. But what did Jesus mean with this cryptic statement?

First, the Apostles were to be "wise as serpents." In Genesis 3, after the story of creation, we are told, "Now the serpent was more cunning than any beast of the field which the Lord God had made" (v. 1a). The serpent was subtle and shrewd, laying his snares and traps to seduce the people of God, so this particular animal became a metaphor for cunning shrewdness. That is the attribute Jesus wanted to see in His Apostles—shrewdness, but without the malice of the serpent. He basically said: "I don't want you to be stupid like sheep. I want you to be sensible. I want you to be alert to what is going on around you. I want you to be as sharp as serpents." But at the same time, they were to be "harmless as doves." They were not to have any poison under their tongues. They were not to have any destructive hatred in their hearts. They were to be as gentle, kind, and harmless as doves, which are symbols of peace. This is a striking contrast—as sharp as a snake but as gentle as a dove.

Next Jesus said: **"But beware of men, for they will deliver you up to councils and scourge you in their synagogues. You will be brought before governors and kings for My sake, as a testimony to them and to the Gentiles"** (vv. 17–18). Of course, the wolves Jesus has been talking about are actually men, and it was men of whom He wanted the Apostles to be wary. In their hostility to the message of the gospel, Jesus warned, men would drag the Apostles before councils, scourge them, and force them to stand trial before governors and kings.

Nearly everything Jesus mentions here happened to Him. He was taken before the Jewish council, the Sanhedrin. He was scourged. He was taken to the Roman governor of Judea, Pontius Pilate. It is interesting that Jesus here seemed to be looking ahead, far beyond the Apostles' initial mission to the house of Israel, for He spoke of their offering a testimony to the Gentiles. When that phase of their mission occurred, as recorded in the book of Acts, all these things happened to them, as well.

The prospect of standing before kings must have been daunting for the Apostles, many of whom were simple men. But Jesus counseled them to have no fear. He said: **"But when they deliver you up, do not worry about how or what you should speak. For it will be given to you in that hour what you should speak; for it is not you who speak, but the Spirit of your Father who speaks in you"** (vv. 19–20).

In my family room at home, I have a painting by Richard Serrin that depicts the Apostle Paul before King Agrippa (Acts 25–26). It happened near the end of Paul's life, just before he was taken to Rome. Paul openly told the story of his dramatic conversion on the Damascus road. Luke writes:

> Now as he thus made his defense, Festus said with a loud voice, "Paul, you are beside yourself! Much learning is driving you mad!" But he said, "I am not mad, most noble Festus, but speak the words of truth and reason. For the king, before whom I also speak freely, knows these things; for I am convinced that none of these things escapes his attention, since this thing was not done in a corner. King Agrippa, do you believe the prophets? I know that you do believe." Then Agrippa said to Paul, "You almost persuade me to become a Christian." And Paul said, "I would to God that not only you, but also all who hear me today, might become both almost and altogether such as I am, except for these chains." (26:24–29)

I very much doubt that Paul expected the Roman governor to question his sanity, but he responded with eloquent words that clearly stirred the heart of

King Agrippa. That is the scene Serrin captures in his painting—Paul standing before Agrippa, in shackles, reaching out and pleading for the king to believe. It is an extraordinary scene, but it is not the only such scene in the book of Acts. The Apostles were dragged before the authorities, beaten with rods, stoned and imprisoned, and hauled before governors and kings, where the Spirit anointed them and gave them words to say in the midst of persecution.

We do not have the supervision of the Holy Spirit to be agents of revelation as the Apostles were. However, there are times even today when believers who are faced with crises for the sake of the gospel are given the words they need to say in those circumstances.

Betrayal and Hatred

Jesus continued: **"Now brother will deliver up brother to death, and a father his child; and children will rise up against parents and cause them to be put to death"** (v. 21). Jesus said that the hatred against the gospel would sever family ties. Several years ago, I read a history of the oppression that the people of Hungary suffered after World War II, when they were basically imprisoned by their Russian occupiers. At that time, the Hungarians were forbidden to worship Christ. They were not allowed to read their Bibles or pray. When the children went to school, they were questioned as to whether their parents prayed with them or read the Bible to them. If the children said they did, the secret police came to that home in the night and took the parents away. Some children who were older intentionally turned their parents in. Some parents turned their children in. This was one of the reasons for the catastrophic uprising in 1956, when the unarmed people overthrew the Communist government. Sadly, the Soviet Union invaded and reimposed Communism after only a few days. I was in Budapest right after the fall of the Soviet Union and saw the scars on the buildings. But the scars on the buildings could not compare to the scars on the people.

I wonder whether anyone would turn in a disciple of American churches under similar circumstances. Would a government hostile to Christianity have any problem with someone who tells people to be all they can be or to have a positive spirit? I doubt it, because that's not Christianity.

Jesus had still more warnings for His Apostles: **"And you will be hated by all for My name's sake. But he who endures to the end will be saved"** (v. 22). The persecution would not come from just a few or from the government. The Apostles would be hated by all. Under such circumstances, their ministry would not be easy. But Jesus gave them a promise: If they endured to the end, they would be saved.

The New Testament Epistles are filled with words of encouragement to believers to persevere in the midst of persecution. Not everyone did so. In his last letter, as he is waiting for his execution in Rome, Paul appeals to Timothy to come to him soon because he has basically been left alone. In this context he mentions Demas, saying, "Demas has forsaken me, having loved this present world" (2 Tim. 4:10). Now Demas is known forever as the man who abandoned the Apostle Paul for the love of this world. I hope that is not my legacy. I hope I will be one who endures to the end. Of course, I know that will happen only by God's preserving grace.

Finally Jesus said: **"When they persecute you in this city, flee to another. For assuredly, I say to you, you will not have gone through the cities of Israel before the Son of Man comes"** (v. 23). Jesus expectation was that when the Apostles encountered persecution, they would simply move on to another place, but would not abandon the mission. Then He gave them a strange promise that has provoked much confusion. It seems that Jesus was saying that the Apostles would not finish taking the gospel to every town and city in Israel until He returned. That seems to imply a swift return on His part. No one expected a two thousand-year (and counting) hiatus from the time of this statement until the return of Jesus. This is one of the timeframe references that is so problematic with respect to the coming of Jesus. I will not deal with it here but will give it full consideration when we reach Matthew 24, where Jesus has much more to say on this subject.

No one loves persecution. However, as Christians we must be prepared to suffer persecution and endure it—so long as we keep the cross in our Christianity. If we take the cross away from the Christian faith, we will save ourselves from difficulties—but we will be unfaithful to the message our Lord has entrusted to us. This we dare not do.

52

THE FEAR OF GOD

Matthew 10:24–33

A disciple is not above his teacher, nor a servant above his master. It is enough for a disciple that he will be like his teacher, and a servant like his master. If they have called the master of the house Beelzebub, how much more will they call those of his household! Therefore do not fear them. For there is nothing covered that will not be revealed, and hidden that will not be known. Whatever I tell you in the dark, speak in the light; and what you hear in the ear, preach on the housetops. And do not fear those who kill the body but cannot kill the soul. But rather fear Him who is able to destroy both soul and body in hell. Are not two sparrows sold for a copper coin? And not one of them falls to the ground apart from your Father's will. But the very hairs of your head are all numbered. Do not fear therefore; you are of more value than many sparrows. Therefore whoever confesses Me before men, him I will also confess before My Father who is in heaven. But whoever denies Me before men, him I will also deny before My Father who is in heaven.

Very few people have ever heard of Albertus Magnus or, as he is sometimes known, Albert the Great. But his place in church history is very important because he was the teacher of Thomas Aquinas in the thirteenth century. When Aquinas first went to Paris and came under Magnus's mentorship, Aquinas was often mocked and teased by his classmates because he was somewhat awkward and slow of movement. They called him the Dumb Ox of Aquino. But when Magnus heard that, he rebuked the other students and declared that Aquinas someday would astonish the whole world with his learning. In later centuries, of course, Aquinas came to be known as the Doctor Angelicus ("Angelic Doctor") among the scholars of the Roman Catholic Church. It was not Magnus but Aquinas who was decorated with that sobriquet, for Aquinas was arguably the most profound theologian in the history of the church. Clearly he outshone his teacher.

Yet, according to Matthew, Jesus taught, **"A disciple is not above his teacher, nor a servant above his master"** (v. 24). How could He say this when we have such a clear example of a student outshining his mentor, and many other examples that could be cited? Jesus was not saying that no student can exceed the accomplishments of his teacher as he matures and grows in his learning. Rather, He was saying that while someone is a student, while he is in that subordinate relationship to his teacher, there is a hierarchy that means the student does not have authority over his teacher. The authority rests with the teacher.

I lived through the tumultuous decade of the 1960s. I was a college professor of philosophy at the time when the SDS (Students for a Democratic Society) was trying to revolutionize higher education, and every campus was exposed to sit-ins and protests in the president's office, with students demanding the right to determine their own curriculum. At the institution where I was teaching, some freshmen declared that they could tell the faculty what courses they needed to take in order to qualify to be philosophy majors. I asked them what they knew about philosophy, and their answers manifestly demonstrated their entire ignorance of the subject. Yet they were demanding the right to form their own curriculum. That is how upside down the world was at that time. The students thought they were above the teachers. But Jesus said that attitude was silly. The student does not teach the teacher; the teacher teaches the student. What could be simpler than that?

Why did Jesus take time to teach this rather obvious lesson? We must remember the context in which He gave this teaching. He was about to send the Twelve out on a trial mission, and as we have seen, He warned them they would be brought before councils, scourged in the synagogues, and forced to testify before governors and kings. They would be persecuted for spreading the gospel. He was saying to them: "I am your Teacher and you are My disciples. You see how the Pharisees hate Me. I'm sending you out in the midst of these wolves. Do not think that you will escape the same kind of hatred. If they hate Me, they will hate you. A disciple is not above his teacher."

Has anyone ever hated you because you are a Christian? Has anyone ever been hostile to you because of your faith in Christ? Everyone experiences animosity from other people at one time or another, but have you ever experienced animosity because you are a disciple of Christ? If you have not, you should ask yourself why. Ask yourself: "Am I distancing myself from my Master? Am I a secret service Christian?" Jesus was telling His disciples that there is a fundamental animosity toward Him among fallen human beings, and that animosity extends to His followers.

The Bible teaches us that in our inherent humanity we have a natural hatred for God. Of course, if I were to stop an average non-Christian on the street and ask him, "Why do you hate God?" he would reply indignantly: "I don't hate God. What gives you the idea that I hate God?" I might say, "God gives me the idea that you hate God," and I could cite Romans 8:7 ("the carnal mind is enmity against God") or John 3:20 ("everyone practicing evil hates the light and does not come to the light"). If we have any love for God in our hearts today, it did not come to us naturally. Because of that built-in hostility to God and His Son, we, too, will experience that enmity from unbelievers.

Humiliation and Exaltation

Most Christians are baptized, either as infants or soon after they make a profession of faith. Baptism is a symbol of some sort, but what does it symbolize? Among other things, baptism symbolizes cleansing from our sin—that is why we use water in baptism. But baptism signifies much more. It is a sign of God's promise to give all of the benefits of the work of Jesus Christ to all who believe. Of course, He does not give those benefits automatically with the sign. That is why a person can be baptized before he believes or after he believes, just as in the Old Testament a person was circumcised before he believed or after he believed, depending on his circumstances.

Furthermore, baptism is a sign of our identification with Jesus' death and resurrection, that is, with His humiliation and His exaltation. Jesus promised His disciples that all who are His would participate fully in the glory that the Father was to bestow on Him. Paul writes, "The Spirit Himself bears witness with our spirit that we are children of God, and if children, then heirs—heirs of God and joint heirs with Christ" (Rom. 8:16–17a). Isn't that incredible? We are joint heirs with Christ, which means we will take part in His exaltation. We have no claim to the exaltation of Christ in and of ourselves. We have no merit by which we deserve to participate in His glory. But by His grace, we will experience that glory.

At the same time, however, we are called to participate in Jesus' humiliation, and the New Testament says that if we refuse to participate in His humiliation, we will never participate in His exaltation. Immediately after affirming that we are joint heirs with Christ, Paul adds a qualification: "if indeed we suffer with Him, that we may also be glorified together" (Rom. 8:17b). Peter writes, "Rejoice to the extent that you partake of Christ's sufferings, that when His glory is revealed, you may also be glad with exceeding joy" (1 Pet. 4:13). Jesus reserves His glory for those believers who embrace His humiliation.

We all want to participate in His glory, but we do not want to participate in His humiliation, in His rejection, in His suffering. It is natural even for regenerate people to try to distance themselves from their Savior at the point of humiliation. At times, it can be embarrassing to be a Christian. But Jesus said that a disciple is not above his teacher or a servant above his master. It is not that students are inferior to teachers or that slaves are inferior to their masters. More than anyone, Jesus understood that a person's status in a given society is not what determines his or her value or dignity as a human being. Disciples must be prepared to go through what their master goes through. As Jesus put it, **"It is enough for a disciple that he will be like his teacher, and a servant like his master"** (v. 25a).

Then Jesus said, **"If they have called the master of the house Beelzebub, how much more will they call those of his household!"** (v. 25b). Who is Beelzebub? There is some question about the etymology of that term. Many believe that the title Beelzebub was drawn from some titles that were used in ancient pagan religion for gods and goddesses. One form of this word has been translated "Lord of the flies," which William Golding borrowed as the title for his famous novel. Another rendition is "Lord of the dung heap." The Jews borrowed these kinds of terms and applied them to Satan as insults. So, Beelzebub was a reference to Satan.

We know that Jesus is clearly the "master of the house" in this verse, and He is saying that if He, the long-awaited Messiah, the second person of the Trinity, is called Satan, the disciples should expect even worse. That means Christians can expect to be known in the community as people who belong to the lord of the dunghill. That's how much dignity we should expect to be accorded if we are faithful to Christ. That is a daunting prospect. No one likes to be disliked to such a degree.

A Promise of Vindication

Jesus did not leave the Apostles without comfort. He said: **"Therefore do not fear them"** (v. 26a). But then He added, **"For there is nothing covered that will not be revealed, and hidden that will not be known"** (v. 26b), and that seems to be another worrisome thought.

There is a story about a prankster who lived in a small town. He sent identical letters to twenty prominent businessmen and leaders in the community. The letters simply said: "All is known. Flee at once." All twenty of those men left town by the next day. The point of the story is that everyone has skeletons in his closet, things he would rather other people did not know about. We do our very best to cover up the seamier sides of our lives, so it is terrifying to think that everything that is concealed will be made known.

The Scriptures indicate that all of our secrets will be laid bare before God at the last judgment (Eccl. 12:14; Rom. 2:16; Matt. 12:36–37), but that is not what Jesus was talking about here. Rather, He was talking about the full disclosure of the plans, plots, and conspiracies of those who hate Christ and His people. He was saying that all of the secret plans of the Pharisees would be exposed. All of the false accusations against the people of God would be seen as false. As Jesus said in His parable of the persistent widow, "Shall God not avenge His own elect who cry out day and night to Him, though He bears long with them?" (Luke 18:7).

As a young man, Jonathan Edwards took over the pastorate of the church in Northampton, Massachusetts, from his grandfather, Solomon Stoddard, and there he was used by God to help spark the Great Awakening of the eighteenth century. He was the pastor there for many years, but in the end, he was removed from office and publicly humiliated. It happened because there was a man in Northampton who hated the gospel and therefore hated Edwards. He began to spread awful rumors about Edwards. There was no truth in any of it, but Edwards refused to deny the rumors. When the leaders of the community pressed him to defend himself, he replied that God had promised to vindicate His people. He believed that if he tried to vindicate himself, that would be all the vindication he would get, but if he suffered in silence and waited for God, he would be vindicated fully and finally.

I am not sure that the course Edwards chose is the wisest course for every situation. But ten years later, the lying man was brought to repentance and publically confessed to everyone in the town that out of jealousy and enmity toward Edwards he had made up all of these false stories. God vindicates His people.

Jesus was saying to His Apostles that they should not be afraid of people who said evil things against them. Nothing covered would not be revealed, nothing hidden would not be made known. The falsity behind the things said against the Apostles would be revealed, for God would vindicate them.

The Right One to Fear

Jesus continued, saying, **"Whatever I tell you in the dark, speak in the light; and what you hear in the ear, preach on the housetops. And do not fear those who kill the body but cannot kill the soul. But rather fear Him who**

is able to destroy both soul and body in hell" (vv. 27–28). Jesus' message here was simple: fear the right thing. It was natural for the Apostles to fear the Pharisees and others who were hostile toward Jesus and toward them. But those were not the ones they ought to fear. The worst thing those people could do was to kill the Apostles' bodies. But they could not touch the Apostles' souls.

Aleksandr Solzhenitsyn, one of the great dissidents of the Soviet Union, spent years in the Soviet gulags. After he was finally released, he was asked how he had been able to endure the torment and the torture in his captivity. He said that he knew he was defenseless against the torture of his body, but he kept reminding himself that the Soviets had no instrument of pain that was strong enough to pierce his mind and his soul. Therefore, he focused on the well-being of his soul, not his body. This is an object lesson for all Christians facing persecution.

Jesus said we should fear the one "who is able to destroy both soul and body in hell." Was He speaking of the devil? No, the devil cannot touch a Christian's soul. The only One who can throw a human being into hell, body and soul, is God. Clearly, we should have a fear, a healthy reverence, for God's power. However, for the most part today, there is little fear of God in the Western world. There is no godly sense of awe and reverence before our Maker. Yet, "The fear of the Lord is the beginning of wisdom" (Ps. 111:10a). We need a healthy fear of God, not men.

Then Jesus said: **"Are not two sparrows sold for a copper coin? And not one of them falls to the ground apart from your Father's will. But the very hairs of your head are all numbered. Do not fear therefore; you are of more value than many sparrows"** (vv. 29–31). After saying that the Apostles should fear God, Jesus said they should not fear Him. Why? God superintends the life and death of the sparrow, which has almost no value in human terms. That same omniscient, omnipotent God knows the number of hairs on every person's head. A human being is much more valuable than a sparrow. Jesus was saying that since God valued the Apostles so highly as to bring them into His own family, even though He had the power to cast them into hell, they did not need to be afraid of Him. If our lives are hidden in Christ, we have no need to fear the sovereign God.

He then declared: **"Therefore whoever confesses Me before men, him I will also confess before My Father who is in heaven"** (v. 32). This is glorious news. Imagine that you are in heaven. The books are open, the trial is set to begin, and you are standing there in fear. Everything you have ever done in secret is about to be made manifest. Your record will surely condemn you. Then, suddenly, Jesus comes and says: "Father, this one is mine." Can you imagine Christ confessing you before the Father? That is what He promised to do for all who confess Him before men. But there is a down side: **"But whoever denies Me before men, him I will also deny before My Father who is in heaven"** (v. 33). Those who are too embarrassed and ashamed of Christ to acknowledge Him before men will find that He will be ashamed of them before the Father.

What an encouragement for the Apostles. Jesus had told them that the world would hate them, persecute them, and even kill them. But they could endure it all knowing that He would confess them before the Father. We, too, have this promise, and there is no deeper comfort.

53

JESUS AND DIVISION

Matthew 10:34–42

Do not think that I came to bring peace on earth. I did not come to bring peace but a sword. For I have come to "set a man against his father, a daughter against her mother, and a daughter-in-law against her mother- in-law"; and "a man's enemies will be those of his own household." He who loves father or mother more than Me is not worthy of Me. And he who loves son or daughter more than Me is not worthy of Me. And he who does not take his cross and follow after Me is not worthy of Me. He who finds his life will lose it, and he who loses his life for My sake will find it. He who receives you receives Me, and he who receives Me receives Him who sent Me. He who receives a prophet in the name of a prophet shall receive a prophet's reward. And he who receives a righteous man in the name of a righteous man shall receive a righteous man's reward. And whoever gives one of these little ones only a cup of cold water in the name of a disciple, assuredly, I say to you, he shall by no means lose his reward.

It is vitally important for us to understand the mission of Jesus in this world. But rather than study the Gospels and try to determine that mission on our own, we need only to listen to Jesus, for He stated His purpose to His disciples on several occasions. For instance, He said, "I have come that they may have life, and that they may have it more abundantly" (John 10:10). Elsewhere, He said, "The Son of Man has come to seek and to save that which was lost" (Luke 19:10). When He was on trial for His life before Pontius Pilate, Jesus said, "For this cause I was born, and for this cause I have come into the world, that I should bear witness to the truth" (John 18:37). These different statements Jesus made regarding the purpose of His mission are not mutually exclusive. He sometimes emphasized one facet and sometimes another, but they are all aspects of the mission the Father gave Him.

Interestingly, in the passage we are considering in this chapter, Jesus named one thing He did *not* come to do. As He continued preparing His apostles for their trial mission, He told them: **"Do not think that I came to bring peace on earth. I did not come to bring peace but a sword"** (v. 34). This, like the statement we examined in chapter 50 of this book, is a hard saying.

As we seek to understand this statement, we should ask ourselves first why it seems strange to us that Jesus denied that He had come to bring peace on earth. In other words, why would we expect Him to bring peace? Perhaps one reason was that which happened on the plains of Bethlehem on the night of His birth. After an angel announced Jesus' birth to the shepherds, an angelic choir appeared and sang, "Glory to God in the highest, and on earth peace, goodwill toward men!" (Luke 2:14). Likewise, in the upper room on the night when He was betrayed, Jesus said, "Peace I leave with you, My peace I give to you" (John 14:27a). Finally, He is called the Prince of Peace, having been so named by the prophet Isaiah hundreds of years before He was born (Isa. 9:6). Knowing these things, it is natural for us to assume that one of the key aspects of His mission in this world was to bring peace. But He said that was not so, that He came not to bring peace but a sword.

Notice that when Jesus gave His various explanations of His mission, He repeatedly said, "I have come," or "the Son of Man has come." He did not say, "For this reason was I *born*," "For this reason was I *trained*," or "For this reason was I *called*." The fact that He said "I have come" is significant because it shows He came *to* this world *from* somewhere else. He explained this truth elsewhere when He said, "No one has ascended to heaven but He who came down from heaven, that is, the Son of Man who is in heaven" (John 3:13). The fact that He came from heaven shows who He is. This is the Son of Man, the eternal Logos, the Word of God, the second person of the Trinity.

In biblical categories, "the sword" is the symbol of conflict and warfare. It is significant that the universal symbol of Christianity is the cross, a symbol of suffering and death. By contrast, the universal symbol of Islam is the scimitar, a sword. Nothing could seem to be further from the mission of Jesus than the idea of Him brandishing a sword. Yet He said He came to bring a sword. I believe He was speaking metaphorically here, but we still must determine in what sense He brought conflict.

Dividing Families

Recall how Jesus stated His mission for Pilate: "I have come . . . that I should bear witness to the truth." Jesus spoke often about the truth. He said He Himself was "the way, the truth, and the life" (John 14:6a). Obviously Jesus Himself was a cause of division among the Jews, and the truth that He taught was divisive as well. He brought truth that provoked conflict, truth that provoked separation and division, even severing familial bonds.

Jesus showed how divisive His truth is when He said, **"For I have come to 'set a man against his father, a daughter against her mother, and a daughter-in-law against her mother-in-law'; and 'a man's enemies will be those of his own household'"** (vv. 35–36). Jesus here quoted Micah 7:6, which speaks of divisions among family members in a time of turmoil. He was telling His Apostles to expect the same kind of disruptions in response to their message.

Jesus Himself experienced this division; His brothers did not believe in Him for quite some time (John 7:3–5). Many of you reading this book could attest to similar strains and conflicts in your families over your profession of faith in Christ. I, too, have experienced it firsthand.

I became a Christian during my freshman year in college. I had grown up in the church, although it was a rather liberal church where I was taught that the miracles of Jesus did not really happen and that Jesus did not rise from the grave. Still, I was there every Sunday because my parents made me go, and it was the center of the social life of the community. When I came home from college full of excitement about becoming a Christian, I assumed my mother would be pleased to know that her son was a born-again believer. However, when I told her about my newfound faith, she was furious. Why? She took my confession of faith in Christ as a complete rejection of everything that she, my father, and their church had taught me. She said: "What do you mean you became a Christian? You've always been a Christian. You grew up a Christian. We're all Christians in our household. What do you mean that you've just now become a Christian?" She was quite angry with me.

Of course, many believers experience much worse familial conflict when they come to faith. If a Muslim becomes a Christian, he is expelled from the family. Sometimes Jewish families hold funerals for family members who embrace Christianity. Those who are raised in the Roman Catholic Church and leave it to embrace evangelical Christianity often encounter severe family opposition. Believers have a unity of faith in Christ because we share one Lord, one faith, and one baptism, but the same truth that unites believers separates them from those who are outside the faith.

Denying the Differences

Those who embrace pluralism or relativism are motivated by a desire to get rid of this kind of conflict at all costs. They want to end all disunity over religion. So, we are taught that everyone actually believes the same thing. It does not matter which road a person takes because they all go to God. It does not matter whether one is a Jew, a Muslim, a Hindu, a Buddhist, a Christian, or something else, as long as he is sincere. How silly! If we spend five minutes looking at the basic theses of the great world religions, we cannot help but see that they are in irreconcilable conflict. No one can be an Orthodox Jew and believe that Jesus was the Messiah. No one can be an orthodox Christian and believe He was not the Messiah. Manifestly, Jesus could not have been the Messiah and not the Messiah at the same time in the same way. Conflict is inevitable, no matter how strenuously we try to mend the divisions.

Years ago, I had a discussion with a college student who was very solicitous and somewhat patronizing toward my Christian convictions. He said: "Now, let me see. You believe that there's a God." I said yes. "And this faith that you have is meaningful to your life?" Yes. "You pray to God?" Yes. "You sing hymns to God?" Yes. "You go to church and worship God?" I told him I did all of those things. At that point, the student said: "Well, for you, God exists. But I don't find God at all meaningful. I don't go to church, I don't sing hymns, I don't pray prayers, and I don't devote myself to any kind of deity. So, for me, God does not exist."

I told him: "You don't understand what I'm talking about here. I'm not talking about a God for me or a God for you. I'm talking about a being who exists apart from me and apart from you. I'm talking about a being who is not conjured up by my commitment to him, by my prayers, by my songs, and by my devotions. This being actually exists, and all of your unbelief, your disinterest, and your hostility toward Him does not have the power to annihilate Him."

I know that there is such a thing as an either/or fallacy or the fallacy of the false dilemma. I might say that something is red and you might say it is orange, but we can both be wrong because our perceptions might be incorrect. But there are certain issues that are true either/or situations, and this student and I were discussing one of them. Either God exists or He does not. There is no third alternative. But pluralists and relativists want to find an alternative where there is no alternative.

Francis Schaeffer once lamented that the church in the twentieth century lost the concept of antithesis. What did he mean? He was simply saying that for every truth there is a corresponding falsehood that is the antithesis of and a denial of that truth. But the church seemed to forget this in the twentieth century as the calls for unity grew louder. Each individual had his own faith.

In the 1970s and 1980s, I was involved in the International Council on Biblical Inerrancy. We had a summit meeting in Chicago, where two hundred scholars from around the world assembled to draft a statement about the nature of sacred Scripture. The drafting committee asked me to write the first draft of our affirmations, but I strongly believed it was not sufficient to simply write what we affirmed. Instead, we also needed to write what we denied. In a culture that is committed to pluralism and relativism, it is not enough to affirm what one believes. A person also has to be willing to deny the antithesis. So we spelled out about twenty affirmations and denials. We not only affirmed what we believed, we denied what we did not believe. When a person does that, he draws a line in the sand, and when he does that, he inevitably encounters the metaphorical sword Jesus warned His disciples to expect.

Of course, there are people who want to fight over every tiny detail. They have no understanding of the difference between major points and minor issues. That is sinful; "love will cover a multitude of sins" (1 Peter 4:8, citing Prov. 10:12). We are not called to cry "Heresy!" over every little point of difference in the church. However, there are some truths that are so foundational that to deny them is to deny Christ.

Final Warnings

Jesus went on to warn His Apostles that familial divisions must not cause them to waver in their commitment to Him: **"He who loves father or mother more than Me is not worthy of Me. And he who loves son or daughter more than Me is not worthy of Me"** (v. 37). Jesus' followers must love Him more than they love their own mothers and fathers, their own sons and daughters. We must be willing to sacrifice these relationships for Him. Furthermore, we must be willing to sacrifice our own lives: **"And he who does not take his cross and follow after Me is not worthy of Me. He who finds his life will lose it, and he who loses his life for My sake will find it"** (vv. 38–39). We must be ready to do as Martin Luther exhorted believers to do: "Let goods and kindred go. this mortal life also."[1] Only by doing so will we find true life in Christ.

Jesus concluded His warnings to His Apostles with these words: **"He who receives you receives Me, and he who receives Me receives Him who sent Me. He who receives a prophet in the name of a prophet shall receive a prophet's reward. And he who receives a righteous man in the name of a righteous man shall receive a righteous man's reward. And whoever gives one of these little ones only a cup of cold water in the name of a disciple, assuredly, I say to you, he shall by no means lose his reward"** (vv. 40–42). Again we are reminded that the Apostles were vested with Jesus' own authority,

[1] From the hymn "A Mighty Fortress Is Our God" by Martin Luther, 1529.

such that those who received them and believed their message were receiving Christ Himself. But Jesus cautioned the Apostles not to let their authority go to their heads, but to remember to serve even the "little ones," even the seemingly insignificant believers.

54

JOHN THE BAPTIST'S INQUIRY

Matthew 11:1–11

Now it came to pass, when Jesus finished commanding His twelve disciples, that He departed from there to teach and to preach in their cities. And when John had heard in prison about the works of Christ, he sent two of his disciples and said to Him, "Are You the Coming One, or do we look for another?" Jesus answered and said to them, "Go and tell John the things which you hear and see: The blind see and the lame walk; the lepers are cleansed and the deaf hear; the dead are raised up and the poor have the gospel preached to them. And blessed is he who is not offended because of Me." As they departed, Jesus began to say to the multitudes concerning John: "What did you go out into the wilderness to see? A reed shaken by the wind? But what did you go out to see? A man clothed in soft garments? Indeed, those who wear soft clothing are in kings' houses. But what did you go out to see? A prophet? Yes, I say to you, and more than a prophet. For this is he of whom it is written:

> 'Behold, I send My messenger
> before Your face,
> Who will prepare Your way
> before You.'

Assuredly, I say to you, among those born of women there has not risen one greater than John the Baptist; but he who is least in the kingdom of heaven is greater than he."

I find this passage somewhat interesting and at the same time somewhat difficult. In it, Matthew tells us of an inquiry that came to Jesus from John the Baptist, an inquiry that raises all kinds of questions.

Matthew writes: **Now it came to pass, when Jesus finished commanding His twelve disciples, that He departed from there to teach and to preach in their cities. And when John had heard in prison about the works of Christ, he sent two of his disciples and said to Him, "Are You the Coming One, or do we look for another?"** (vv. 1–3). In the previous five chapters, we have examined Jesus' selection of the Twelve Apostles and His words of instruction and warning prior to sending them on a trial mission. Matthew tells us that He then departed to teach and preach, and presumably the Twelve went in other directions doing the same (see Mark 6:12; Luke 9:6). It was during this time, when Jesus was without His closest followers, that John the Baptist sent two of his own disciples to ask Jesus a question. We are told that John "had heard in prison about the works of Christ." Matthew does not explain whether these were the works Jesus did in this specific time or those He had been performing throughout His ministry. Notice, however, that Matthew did not say "the works of *Jesus*." Rather, he spoke of "the works of *Christ*," that is, the Messiah. Matthew had no doubt as to who Jesus was. However, John did. He wanted to know, "Are You the Coming One, or do we look for another?"

Do you feel the pathos in that question? John was languishing in prison, and he seems to have developed some doubts that Jesus actually was the Messiah. It was not always so. When Jesus came to the Jordan River to be baptized, John saw Him coming and cried out confidently: "Behold! The Lamb of God who takes away the sin of the world!" (John 1:29b). John understood that he was God's appointed herald of the Messiah, and he did not hesitate to single out Jesus as that Messiah. This suggests to us that John had a God-given understanding of the identity of Jesus and of the significance of His mission.

However, we see throughout biblical history that when God gave His message to the prophets, the prophets did not always have a complete comprehension of the message that they had been commissioned to deliver. This lack of understanding seems to have been at work in John's case. He identified Jesus as the Redeemer, but his understanding of the work of Jesus obviously was not complete, because he balked when Jesus presented Himself for baptism. If John had had a complete understanding of Jesus and what He was about, he would have been instantly willing to baptize Jesus, for He would have known that even though Jesus was sinless, He needed to obey the whole law of God. But John did not know this. He could not immediately see how it was appropriate for the sinless Lamb of God to undergo a ritual that involved cleansing.

This lack of understanding surfaced again when John was put in prison. He heard reports that Jesus was preaching, teaching, and healing people, but these activities somehow did not meet his expectations for what the Messiah was to do. Perhaps he thought along the same lines as most of the people of the nation—that the Messiah would be a mighty King who would get rid of the Romans and bring to pass a spiritual kingdom where God would reign, not Caesar. But Jesus was doing nothing of the sort. So, John wondered: "What's going on out there? I thought the Lamb of God was going to bring the kingdom of God that I announced. If this is the kingdom of God, what am I doing here?"

Have you ever felt like that? I think we are all prone to ask, "If God is sovereign, why did he allow this to happen to me?" Once we grasp the truth that God is sovereign, we immediately begin to come up with all kinds of expectations as to what God will do. When He does not behave the way we expect Him to, we become a bit disillusioned. I wonder what Joseph was thinking when he was languishing in prison in Egypt. I have to think that Joseph wondered whether his prayers ever got beyond the ceiling. He had no idea what God would bring to pass in his future—that he would become the prime minister of the land. Likewise, Paul languished in house arrest in Rome. I would not be surprised to learn that he, too, wondered, "Where's God?" This is a typical human weakness.

Because of that, I am not all that distressed about John the Baptist. He was bewildered. He had incorrect expectations. He could not figure out what was happening. But to his great credit, he did the right thing. He went to Jesus with His question. He went straight to the source, sending two of his disciples who had visited him in prison. He sent them to Jesus to ask whether He really was the long-expected Savior.

One of the great tragedies of human history is that the vast majority of the Jewish people at that time thought they had this question answered. They were quite sure Jesus was *not* the One who was to come, and so they were determined to wait for another. John writes, "He came to His own, and His own did not receive Him" (John 1:11). Today, two thousand years later, Jews are still waiting for the Messiah. No one has yet met their expectations. They missed the One who did come.

Fulfilling Messianic Prophecies

How did Jesus respond to John's question? Matthew tells us: **Jesus answered and said to them, "Go and tell John the things which you hear and see: The blind see and the lame walk; the lepers are cleansed and the deaf hear; the dead are raised up and the poor have the gospel preached to them. And blessed is he who is not offended because of Me"** (vv. 4–6). It almost sounds as if Jesus is a bit annoyed with the question and therefore a bit dismissive of it. He seems to have told the disciples of John to go back and tell him about the very kinds of works that were not meeting his expectations. However, I do not really think that is what Jesus was saying. Instead, I believe He was simply telling the two disciples, "Go back and tell John to read his Bible, and then see whether he is still in doubt about who I am."

The fact that Jesus told the two disciples to report to John that Jesus was giving sight to the blind, causing the lame to walk, cleansing the lepers, restoring the hearing of the deaf, raising the dead, and preaching the gospel to the poor is significant. These things were direct fulfillments of Isaiah 35:5–6 and 61:1–2. Jesus specifically cited this latter passage on the occasion of His first sermon, which may have been the shortest sermon He ever gave and possibly the shortest sermon ever preached. Luke tells us:

> He came to Nazareth, where He had been brought up. And as His custom was, He went into the synagogue on the Sabbath day, and stood up to read. And He was handed the book of the prophet Isaiah. And when He had opened the book, He found the place where it was written: "The Spirit of the Lord is upon Me, because He has anointed Me to preach the gospel to the poor; He has sent Me to heal the brokenhearted, to proclaim liberty to the captives and recovery of sight to the blind, to set at liberty those who are oppressed; to proclaim the acceptable year of the Lord." Then He closed the book, and gave it back to the attendant and sat down. And the eyes of all who were in the synagogue were fixed on Him. And He began to say to them, "Today this Scripture is fulfilled in your hearing." (4:16–21)

Isaiah 61:1–2, which Jesus read, gives a portrait of the Anointed One who was to come. When He says, "The Spirit of the Lord is upon Me," He means that the Spirit of the Lord has anointed Him. Thus, this passage is speaking of the Messiah, the Christ. This is the most vivid description of the ministry that God the Father gave to His Anointed One.

When Jesus went to the synagogue that day, this was the passage that had been selected for reading. The Jews loved to hear this reading. Their hearts burned when they heard God's promise that He would send His Anointed One, who would proclaim good news to the poor, give sight to the blind, set the prisoners free, and bring the acceptable year of the Lord. After Jesus read it, He was invited to give the sermon, the exposition of the meaning of the text. He sat down to preach. Every eye was on Him, every ear listening to what He would say. Jesus, however, did not go into a detailed exposition of the text. He did not offer three points and a series of applications. Jesus simply looked at the people and said: "Today this text is fulfilled in your midst. Amen." That was his sermon.

What was He saying? He was telling the people gathered there that Isaiah's beloved description of the Messiah was fulfilled then and there. No one had to look around to see whom Jesus was describing. Everyone understood He could be speaking only of Himself.

John the Baptist did not understand these things. So, Jesus sent a message back to the prison: "Tell John to read Isaiah 35 and 61, because these prophecies will tell John what the mission of the Messiah is to be. Then tell him what you have seen with your eyes and heard with your ears. The blind are seeing, the lame are walking, lepers are clean again, and deaf people hear. People are being raised from the dead and I am preaching the gospel to the poor. The prophecies of Isaiah are being fulfilled. Tell John all this and see if he wants to wait for another."

Jesus then said, "Blessed is he who is not offended because of Me." It was as if Jesus was giving John a mild rebuke, saying, "John, be careful that you don't let your improper expectations cause you to question Me." That is good advice for us today. We need to guard against dissatisfaction with what Jesus accomplished in His work of redemption. He has done everything necessary to save us and to secure for us eternal blessedness, but we often resent His "failure" to meet some other expectation we have of Him. We must remember that He is under no obligation to do anything for us. If He were to take our lives today, we would have no reason to do anything but praise Him forever for what He has done for us. Let us take care not to be "offended" because of Him.

A Prophet Who Was Prophesied

If this was a rebuke of John, it was a mild one, and Jesus immediately showed the crowds that He had the highest regard for John. Matthew writes: **As they departed, Jesus began to say to the multitudes concerning John: "What did you go out into the wilderness to see? A reed shaken by the wind? But what did you go out to see? A man clothed in soft garments? Indeed, those who wear soft clothing are in kings' houses"** (vv. 7–8).

Jesus asked the people why they went out to the Jordan River, presenting themselves to John for baptism. He asked a series of questions. Did they go to see "a reed shaken by the wind," that is, someone who could be blown here and there with every wind of doctrine, a pious little clergyman with no backbone? The obvious answer was no, they had not gone to see such a non-spectacle. Did they go to see "a man clothed in soft garments," that is, a high-class dandy such as might be found in a king's palace? Again, the obvious answer was no. John was none of these things. He was a man who preached an uncompromising message of repentance, a man who "was clothed in camel's hair, with a leather belt around his waist" (Matt. 3:4).

Then Jesus asked a third question: **"But what did you go out to see? A prophet? Yes, I say to you, and more than a prophet"** (v. 9). The people obviously went out to see John because he fitted the biblical portrait of a prophet—he preached fearlessly and he dressed in rough clothing. So, everyone considered John a prophet (Matt. 21:26)—and they were right to do so. Jesus affirmed that John was indeed a prophet of God, sent with a divine message for God's people.

However, Jesus said, John was "more than a prophet." He added: **"For this is he of whom it is written: 'Behold, I send My messenger before Your face, who will prepare Your way before You'"** (v. 10). John was a prophet whose coming had been prophesied, specifically in Malachi 3:1. He was the prophet who was appointed to be the herald of the kingdom of God, the one who would come and introduce the King.

Then Jesus uttered very high praise of John the Baptist. He said: **"Assuredly, I say to you, among those born of women there has not risen one greater than John the Baptist"** (v. 11a). Think about what Jesus was saying. Of all the men who have ever lived—Abraham, Isaac, Jacob, Joseph, David, Isaiah, Jeremiah—not one of them was greater than John the Baptist. In fact, no one *at all* had ever surpassed John's greatness since the world began. What a testimonial this was. I sometimes think that John the Baptist is the most underestimated person in the whole New Testament, if not in the whole Bible, but he certainly was not underestimated in Jesus' opinion.

The Least Is the Greatest

However, we must not miss what Jesus said immediately after giving this high praise of John: **"He who is least in the kingdom of heaven is greater than he"** (v. 11b). I am not sure what Jesus meant here. I do not know who the least person in the kingdom of God is. Jesus did not identify who He had in mind, if indeed He was thinking of a specific individual. In a certain sense, we should all regard ourselves as the least in the kingdom of God (Phil. 2:3). However, according to Jesus, whoever this person is, he or she is greater than John the Baptist. How can that be? Jesus extolled John by saying that no man had been greater than he, but then He said that the least person in the kingdom is even greater than John.

I think the key to unraveling the meaning of this curious statement lies in recognizing the subtlety with which Jesus used the word *great*. In Western culture today, we use this word in a very superficial manner. Mohammad Ali, the former heavyweight boxing champion, used to claim that he was "the greatest," by which he meant that he was the most accomplished person in his field. But in biblical categories, to be great is not simply to excel in one thing or another; rather, it is to be in a position of extraordinary blessedness.

When Noah pronounced his patriarchal blessing on his three sons, he blessed Shem and cursed Canaan (the son of Noah's son Ham). But what about Noah's other son, Japheth? Noah prayed that he would be "enlarged" (Gen. 9:25–27). Noah was not asking that Japheth himself would gain weight or that his family line would expand. Rather, he was praying that Japheth would gain a greater capacity for blessedness.

Because God has ordained that we should live in this particular time, we have a greater capacity for blessedness than John ever had. The same is true for all those who have lived on this side of the cross. It is true that we read about John the Baptist in the New Testament, but he lived and ministered in Old Testament history. The new covenant did not begin until Jesus inaugurated it in the upper room on the night when He was betrayed. So, the least person born since the King was crowned is in a greater situation of blessedness than even John the Baptist enjoyed in his time.

We sometimes think how wonderful it would have been to live when Jesus was ministering during His incarnation. Yes, that would have been wonderful in some ways, but we are in a better state now than the people who were living then, because we are on this side of the cross, this side of the resurrection, and this side of the coming of the King. John was the greatest in the old covenant, but we have a greater blessedness today than John ever dreamed of.

55

THE GREATNESS OF JOHN THE BAPTIST

Matthew 11:12–19

And from the days of John the Baptist until now the kingdom of heaven suffers violence, and the violent take it by force. For all the prophets and the law prophesied until John. And if you are willing to receive it, he is Elijah who is to come. He who has ears to hear, let him hear! But to what shall I liken this generation? It is like children sitting in the marketplaces and calling to their companions, and saying:

> "We played the flute for you,
> And you did not dance;
> We mourned to you,
> And you did not lament."

For John came neither eating nor drinking, and they say, "He has a demon." The Son of Man came eating and drinking, and they say, "Look, a glutton and a winebibber, a friend of tax collectors and sinners!" But wisdom is justified by her children.

The prophet Malachi foretold the coming of one who would go before the Messiah to prepare His way, and Jesus confirmed that John the Baptist was the fulfillment of that prophecy (Matt. 11:10). But in the final section of the final chapter of his book—which is the final book of the Old

Testament—Malachi gave another extraordinary prophecy. It reads: "Behold, I will send you Elijah the prophet before the coming of the great and dreadful day of the LORD. And he will turn the hearts of the fathers to the children, and the hearts of the children to their fathers, lest I come and strike the earth with a curse" (4:5–6). Jesus also had some things to say about John the Baptist in light of this prophecy.

Matthew tells us that Jesus said: "**And from the days of John the Baptist until now the kingdom of heaven suffers violence, and the violent take it by force. For all the prophets and the law prophesied until John**" (vv. 12–13). With these words, Jesus acknowledged that the kingdom of God that John had proclaimed and that He Himself was preaching was already encountering violent opposition. The breakthrough of the kingdom had stirred up wickedness. The demonic realm was aroused. Attacks were happening. After all, John had been violently seized and thrown into prison. John was a prophet, God's channel of revelation, just as "the prophets and the law"—the Old Testament revelation—had been. But as Jesus elsewhere made clear, the religious establishment of Israel had always been intolerant of God's prophets (Matt. 23:37), so their treatment of John was no surprise.

This opposition stemmed at least partly from the fact that at the time of John the Baptist's appearance, prophecy seemed like a thing of the distant past in Israel. Between the delivery of Malachi's final prophecy and the appearance of John the Baptist there were four hundred years. Think about that. At the time of this writing, it has not yet been four hundred years since the Pilgrims arrived in the New World. That is how long the Israelites watched and waited for the fulfillment of this prophecy.

Every Jew in Israel knew something about "the great and dreadful day of the LORD." As Malachi's prophecy suggests, it was to be a day of greatness and also a day of darkness. It was to be a day of redemption and a day of judgment. It would be ushered in by the coming of the Lord's Messiah. The people longed for the Messiah to come and bring the day of the Lord. However, they knew that the Messiah would not come before this prophecy from Malachi was fulfilled. Elijah would come before the Messiah. After Malachi gave this prophecy, whenever the Jews gathered to celebrate the Passover, they left an empty chair at the table in the event that Elijah should come that night and join their celebration. To this day, when the Jewish people celebrate the seder feast, they leave an empty chair for Elijah, because they are convinced he has not come yet. And since they believe Elijah has not come, they believe the Messiah has not come.

So, in those four hundred years between Malachi's prophecy and the coming of John the Baptist, the Jews were watching earnestly for the return of Elijah. But not only did Elijah not appear; the voice of prophecy ceased. No new prophets arrived on the scene in all that time.

Different Perspectives on John

Then, to the whole nation's astonishment, a man appeared out of the desert, the traditional meeting place between God and His prophets. He wore camel skins and a leather belt, and he ate locusts and wild honey (Matt. 3:4). These characteristics were reminiscent of the biblical description of Elijah (2 Kings 1:8). Furthermore, this strange figure began to prophesy. When word began to get around that the voice of prophecy was sounding forth the Word of God in Israel once again, people began to flock to the Jordan River to see this strange man.

But John began to stir up controversy by proclaiming that the people of Israel—not the ceremonially unclean Gentiles—needed to undergo a cleansing ritual because they were not ready for the arrival of the Messiah. The Jews had a ceremony for those outsiders who wanted to join the covenant community of Israel. It was called proselyte baptism. John, however, was baptizing Israelites. The religious authorities in Jerusalem were very disturbed by this, so the Pharisees sent a delegation of priests and Levites to question John and ascertain what he was doing. The Apostle John tells us what happened:

> Now this is the testimony of John, when the Jews sent priests and Levites from Jerusalem to ask him, "Who are you?" He confessed, and did not deny, but confessed, "I am not the Christ." And they asked him, "What then? Are you Elijah?" He said, "I am not." "Are you the Prophet?" And he answered, "No." Then they said to him, "Who are you, that we may give an answer to those who sent us? What do you say about yourself?" He said: "I am 'The voice of one crying in the wilderness: "Make straight the way of the LORD"' as the prophet Isaiah said." (John 1:19–23)

John the Baptist first denied that he was the Messiah. So, they then asked him straight out: "Are you Elijah?" What did John say to that? He said, "No, I am not." He denied that he was Elijah.

According to Matthew, however, Jesus had a different perspective on John the Baptist: **"And if you are willing to receive it, he is Elijah who is to come. He who has ears to hear, let him hear!"** (vv. 14–15). Here Jesus affirmed that John *was* Elijah, but He added a strange preface—"if you are willing to receive it"—and a strange postlude—"He who has ears to hear, let him hear!"—to this announcement. Jesus was saying that John the Baptist *was* Elijah in a sense that no one had expected. He was not Elijah in the literal sense; the Old Testament prophet who was taken away in the chariot of fire had not come back to earth. As the forerunner of the Messiah, he ministered in "the spirit and power of Elijah," as the angel told John's father before his birth (Luke 1:17). John was anointed with the mantle of Elijah. In that sense, the prophecy of Malachi was fulfilled in the mission of John the Baptist. But there were many people who could not bear that, people who lacked the ears to hear it.

I grew up in the church, but the church in my community was a social club. We called it the country club. I learned to dance in that church but I did not learn anything about Jesus there. I hated going to Sunday morning services. If any truth was spoken there, I am sure I did not hear it, because when I heard the gospel for the first time in my life when I was eighteen years old, I did not recognize it. It seemed to me that that was the first time I had ever heard it. If I had been exposed to it before, I did not have ears to really hear it. Some people hear the Word of God and some do not.

When Jesus said, "He who has ears to hear, let him hear!" He was making a distinction. He knew that there were people all around Him who were deaf to everything he said. Perhaps you are deaf to the truth as you read this book. I pray you are not.

Expectations and Preferences

Then, having told the crowd what He thought about John the Baptist, Jesus told them what He thought of the culture, of the people of Israel as a body. Matthew writes that He said: **"But to what shall I liken this generation? It is like children sitting in the marketplaces and calling to their companions, and saying: 'We played the flute for you, and you did not dance; we mourned to you, and you did not lament'"** (vv. 16–17). In a word, Jesus regarded that generation of Jews, and particularly the leaders, as childish.

To make His point, Jesus constructed an elaborate comparison based on a scene from everyday life. The marketplace was not only the place where people bought and sold things; it was where all of the social events took place. It was where funerals were conducted. It was where parties were held. It was also a playground for the children, for whenever people came together for commerce, they brought their children. These youngsters played games together while their parents were doing business, and sometimes their games involved music and singing. But Jesus imagined a scenario in which the children were unhappy and complaining because when they played their merry flutes, no one danced. Conversely, when they sang mournful songs, no one lamented. No one would listen to them and do what they asked, so the children were annoyed and dissatisfied.

What was Jesus saying? He went on to explain: **"For John came neither eating nor drinking, and they say, 'He has a demon.' The Son of Man came eating and drinking, and they say, 'Look, a glutton and a winebibber, a friend of tax collectors and sinners!'"** (vv. 18–19a). John the Baptist came out of the wilderness as an ascetic, a person given to self-denial. The response of the people was to regard him as a lunatic, perhaps even a victim of demonic possession. They knew or should have known that the desert was the traditional meeting place between God and His prophets, and that John's clothing and conduct were reminiscent of Elijah. Clearly he had all the characteristics of a prophet, the first in four hundred years. He was bringing them the Word of God. But instead of receiving him, they slandered him.

By contrast, Jesus was not an ascetic. He ate and drank in the normal fashion. He went to parties and attended dinners. In short, He did the things John the Baptist was criticized for not doing. Still, the people were not satisfied, and Jesus was accused of being overly fond of food and wine. In other words, He was regarded as a glutton and a drunkard. This, too, was slander, for Jesus was never drunk in His life. Plus, it was said that He fellowshiped with all the wrong people—tax collectors and sinners. He could not even please the people by the company He kept.

The problem was that the people's expectations and preferences could not be satisfied. I see this kind of thing sometimes following the Ligonier National Conference. We always ask people to fill out sheets to evaluate the conference and tell us what they liked and did not like. The staff reads every one of them. They take these comments very seriously and try to implement requested changes as they are planning the next conference. But sometimes they will end up with a stack of evaluation forms saying, "There was too much music," and another stack saying, "There was not enough music." How can they possibly fix that kind of disagreement? It cannot be done. It is impossible to completely satisfy every person who comes to a conference. In some way, the conference will fail to live up to their expectations and preferences.

Actions and Consequences

Finally Jesus said: **"But wisdom is justified by her children"** (v. 19b). Jesus was not saying wisdom is set into a right relationship with God by having babies. Rather, He was stating that if someone takes a course of action, the consequences of that action will demonstrate whether it was a prudent course or not. A wise course will yield positive "children," that is, results. So, Jesus was saying that the fruit that would come from His ministry and John's ministry would demonstrate that they were godly men.

This is what James was saying when he wrote, "You see then that a man is justified by works, and not by faith only" (2:24). When people try to refute the doctrine of justification by faith alone, they rush to this verse. That is what the Roman Catholic Church did in the sixteenth century. Rome's scholars pointed to this verse to try to convince the Reformers that the Bible says we are justified by faith *and* works. However, when Paul speaks about justification in Romans, he is talking about how we are made right with God. James is speaking to a different situation. He asks: "What does it profit, my brethren, if someone says he has faith but does not have works? Can faith save him?" (2:14). He spends nearly a whole chapter answering the question with an emphatic no, showing that faith that does not yield works, faith without fruit, is a dead faith. The faith that justifies is a living faith that brings forth the fruit of obedience. That obedience does not save. But if it is not present, that is the clearest proof that faith is no faith at all. When James says a man is justified by works, he means that the man's works demonstrate or vindicate his faith.

Jesus is speaking here about people who always have the wrong response to the Word of God. How do you respond to it? Do you embrace the whole counsel of God? Or do you come to the Bible as if it is a smorgasbord where you pick a little love, a little mercy, and a little grace, but you leave the wrath, the justice, and the holiness on the table? Is your God the Lord omnipotent who reigns, or is He an idol of your own making? Is the Savior you embrace the One who calls you to take up your cross and follow Him, or is He simply Jesus meek and mild, who will not ask anything of you? We need to have ears to hear the Word of God.

56

WOES ON THE CITIES

Matthew 11:20–24

Then He began to rebuke the cities in which most of His mighty works had been done, because they did not repent: "Woe to you, Chorazin! Woe to you, Bethsaida! For if the mighty works which were done in you had been done in Tyre and Sidon, they would have repented long ago in sackcloth and ashes. But I say to you, it will be more tolerable for Tyre and Sidon in the day of judgment than for you. And you, Capernaum, who are exalted to heaven, will be brought down to Hades; for if the mighty works which were done in you had been done in Sodom, it would have remained until this day. But I say to you that it shall be more tolerable for the land of Sodom in the day of judgment than for you."

When I am preaching, I frequently conclude my reading of Scripture with an exhortation: "He who has ears to hear, let him hear." But if there is any one topic in the teaching of Jesus that causes us to plug our ears altogether, it is the subject of judgment. Our hearts are recalcitrant and our necks are stiff, so our ears are deaf to the warnings Jesus gave. But we need to take those teachings very seriously, including the passage we are considering in this chapter.

Matthew tells us that Jesus **began to rebuke the cities in which most of His mighty works had been done, because they did not repent: "Woe to you, Chorazin! Woe to you, Bethsaida! For if the mighty works which were done in you had been done in Tyre and Sidon, they would have repented long ago**

in sackcloth and ashes" (vv. 20–21). The cities of Chorazin and Bethsaida—and later Capernaum—came under criticism from Jesus because the majority of His mighty works—that is, His miracles—happened in their jurisdictions, and yet there was no mass repentance there.

The odd thing about this passage is that while Matthew says that "most" of Jesus' miracles were done in these three cities, two of the three cities are rarely mentioned in the Gospels. Of the three, we find by far the most references to Capernaum because that was where Peter resided and where Jesus made His headquarters for His Galilean ministry. However, the town of Chorazin is never mentioned in the Gospels except here and in a parallel passage (Luke 10:13–16), and Bethsaida is mentioned only a few times.

What do we know about Chorazin and Bethsaida? Both were about the same size as Capernaum. In other words, they were cities of no small significance on the shores of the Sea of Galilee. Chorazin was on the northern coast of the sea, slightly west of the point where the River Jordan empties into the lake and just a few miles from Capernaum. Bethsaida also was on the northern coast, but it was slightly east of the Jordan. Three of the disciples of Jesus came originally from Bethsaida—Peter, his brother Andrew, and Philip (John 1:44).

So, here we have a hint that Jesus did many powerful miracles about which we know nothing at all. As we have seen, Matthew's Gospel contains many wonderful accounts of Jesus' miracles, but his record is by no means exhaustive. His Gospel is a selective journalistic record of the things our Lord did. In fact, all of the other Gospels are equally selective. John acknowledges this when he writes, "And there are also many other things that Jesus did, which if they were written one by one, I suppose that even the world itself could not contain the books that would be written. Amen" (21:25). The Gospel writers simply could not record everything Jesus did.

Jesus' Credentials

Jesus rebuked these three cities because, even though the people who lived in them had seen many miracles, they had not repented. In the church, people often take great interest in the miracles of Jesus, but time and time again people miss the fundamental purpose of these signs. To be sure, one of the things that provoked Jesus to perform miracles was His compassion for people who were in need. But far more important was the fact that the miracles of Jesus were His credentials. They accredited Him as an agent of revelation, as one who had the seal of approval from God the Father. This is the point that Nicodemus seems to have grasped when he said to Jesus, "Rabbi, we know that You are a teacher come from God; for no one can do these signs that You do unless God is with him" (John 3:2). He affirmed that Jesus had been sent from God because He was able to do such mighty works. In that instance, Nicodemus was perfectly sound in his thinking.

This is one of the reasons why I get nervous when people claim to be performing extravagant miracles today. If they are performing actual miracles, then God is accrediting them as agents of revelation. In my mind, many of the people who claim these things do not begin to qualify as agents of revelation; rather, they are false prophets. A true miracle is something only God can do, and God will lend that power to someone only as a credential. So, Jesus was saying He had presented His credentials in these cities. He had performed most of His miracles in Chorazin, Bethsaida, and Capernaum. However, while the people probably got excited about the display of power, they did not repent. They did not recognize that the miracles showed He was a messenger from God who commanded them to repent.

Remember, when John the Baptist came out of the wilderness, he preached, "Repent, for the kingdom of heaven is at hand!" (Matt. 3:2). When Jesus began His public ministry, He proclaimed the same message: "Repent, for the kingdom for heaven is at hand" (Matt. 4:17). His miracles showed that He was a messenger from God, endowed with the authority to command them to repent. Somehow, they failed to see it.

Jesus specifically addressed Chorazin and Bethsaida with oracles of woe. When we looked at the Beatitudes, I noted that prophetic utterances in biblical times were delivered through a literary device called the oracle, which was a divine pronouncement. There were positive oracles, or oracles of blessing, and there were negative oracles, or oracles of doom. The positive oracles, which promised good news, were prefaced by the word *blessed*. We saw examples of oracles of blessing in the Beatitudes, where Jesus said, "Blessed are the poor in spirit . . . Blessed are those who mourn . . . Blessed are the meek . . ." and so on (Matt. 5:3–11). Those were prophetic statements, proclamations of God's blessing on certain people. But the flip side of the oracle of blessing was the oracle of doom, the pronouncement of divine judgment on people. This type of oracle was preceded by the word *woe*.

The prophetic literature of the Old Testament is replete with woes: "Woe to the wicked!" (Isa. 3:11); "Woe to him who builds his house by unrighteousness" (Jer. 22:13); "Woe to the foolish prophets" (Ezek. 13:3); "Woe to you who are at ease in Zion" (Amos 6:1); "Woe to those who devise iniquity" (Mic. 2:1); "Woe to him who covets evil gain" (Hab. 2:9); and "Woe to the worthless shepherd" (Zech. 11:17). But oracles of woe are not just an Old Testament feature. In the book of Revelation, John witnessed an angel crying, "Woe, woe, woe to the inhabitants of the earth" (8:13). And, of course, we have the woes Jesus delivered against the Pharisees and the scribes. As we will see when we study Matthew 23, He pronounced a whole series of woes on these Jewish religious leaders.

Thus, when Jesus said, "Woe to you, Chorazin! Woe to you, Bethsaida!" He was pronouncing the judgment of God on these cities for their failure to repent despite having seen Jesus' miracles. To show how serious that sin was, Jesus made a devastating comparison: "For if the mighty works which were done in you had been done in Tyre and Sidon, they would have repented long ago in sackcloth and ashes."

Tyre and Sidon were two chief Phoenician cities of antiquity that were known for their arrogant hostility toward God and His people. Several of the prophets of Israel prophesied against them, and they eventually were conquered by Alexander the Great. But Jesus asserted that if He had done the same miracles in Tyre and Sidon that He did in Chorazin and Bethsaida, those whole cities would have repented. They would have expressed abject repentance, humbling themselves in sackcloth and ashes, ancient symbols of mourning and sorrow. As wicked as they were, they would have done what the cities of Galilee did not do. Despite the divine revelation in their midst, the people of Chorazin and Bethsaida did not turn from their wicked ways.

The Reality of Judgment

For this reason, Jesus added, **"But I say to you, it will be more tolerable for Tyre and Sidon in the day of judgment than for you"** (v. 22). Here we encounter that subject which so often causes our hearing to shut down—judgment. Jesus said quite plainly that there is going to be a day of judgment. However, very few people take seriously the biblical teaching that a day is coming when God will judge the world—a day when God will judge individuals such as you and me.

One of my favorite hymns is "Rock of Ages, Cleft for Me." The final stanza reads:

> While I draw this fleeting breath,
> When mine eyelids close in death,
> When I soar to worlds unknown,
> See Thee on Thy judgment throne,
> Rock of Ages, cleft for me,
> Let me hide myself in Thee.[1]

When you and I draw our last breaths on this planet, when our eyelids close

[1] From the hymn "Rock of Ages, Cleft for Me" by Augustus M. Toplady, 1776.

for the last time on earth, we will soar to worlds unknown, and the first thing we will see is Christ seated on His throne of judgment. If we ever wanted to sing, "Rock of Ages, cleft for me, let me hide myself in Thee," it will be in that moment. If we are not hidden in Christ, clothed in His righteousness, that day of judgment will be absolute calamity. But so many people in this world are filled with conviction that they have nothing to fear from God. There is no fear of Him in their eyes. Their hearts have calluses, so they disregard the warning of the Son of God. This is what the people of Chorazin and Bethsaida did when Jesus came into their midst and showed He was the spokesman for God, the incarnate Word of God, by the blaze of miracles He performed.

But Jesus did not simply affirm the day of judgment here. Many people assume that at death a person goes to heaven or hell, and that's it. You are either in or out, and there is no difference in blessedness or woe from one person to another. But notice that Jesus said to Chorazin and Bethsaida, "It will be more tolerable for Tyre and Sidon in the day of judgment than for you." Just as we have seen several times in Matthew already, Jesus here indicated that there are degrees of punishment in hell.

I have talked to many men who fell into illicit relationships with women. Usually, the problem began with lust, and the men said to themselves, "Well, I have lusted after her, so I might as well go on." I cannot fathom where this kind of thinking originates. When we come before the judgment seat of God, we will face the bar of perfect justice, and we will be convicted for every single sin we have committed in our lifetimes. It is certainly better to refrain from adultery even if lust has already occurred, for the punishment for two sins will be worse than the punishment for one.

Also, we will be judged according to the light we have received. Every time a sinner hears the Word of God and resists it, his judgment is greater. It is better for him to flee from the church and never come back, because then he will not have the light to make him more and more guilty. Of course, he also will not have the light he needs to go to heaven.

The Apostle Paul writes, "And do you think this, O man, you who judge those practicing such things, and doing the same, that you will escape the judgment of God?" (Rom. 2:3). That is the greatest folly a human being can commit—to think that he will escape the judgment of God. How can he do it? Does he have a getaway car reserved at the pearly gates? Is he going to fool God and keep his sins hidden from Him? There is no way to escape. The judgment of God is absolutely unavoidable.

Paul goes on: "Or do you despise the riches of His goodness, forbearance, and longsuffering, not knowing that the goodness of God leads you to repentance? But in accordance with your hardness and your impenitent heart you are treasuring up for yourself wrath in the day of wrath and revelation of the righteous judgment of God, who 'will render to each one according to his deeds'" (vv. 4–6). People read this passage and say, "Oh, I thought we were justified by faith." We are, but all our deeds will be judged. The person who is impenitent and does not have saving faith will be judged according to his sinful deeds. God will render "eternal life to those who by patient continuance in doing good seek for glory, honor, and immortality; but to those who are self-seeking and do not obey the truth, but obey unrighteousness—indignation and wrath, tribulation and anguish, on every soul of man who does evil" (vv. 7–9a).

We might be tempted to think that because Jesus pronounced woes on Chorazin and Bethsaida, He hated them. On the contrary, He loved them. That was why He told them to wake up. The day of salvation had dawned upon them and their Savior was in their midst. If the wicked people of Tyre and Sidon had seen what the people of Chorazin and Bethsaida had seen, they would have repented in abject humiliation.

More Wicked Than Sodom

Jesus also had a word for Capernaum: **"And you, Capernaum, who are exalted to heaven, will be brought down to Hades; for if the mighty works which were done in you had been done in Sodom, it would have remained until this day. But I say to you that it shall be more tolerable for the land of Sodom in the day of judgment than for you"** (vv. 23–24). The people of Capernaum apparently thought highly of themselves and their city, but Jesus warned that they were in danger of being brought down to Hades, to judgment. Like Chorazin and Bethsaida, they had seen mighty works. He then pointed to Sodom, one of the most wicked cities of the Old Testament, and declared that if the Sodomites had seen the works the people of Capernaum saw, Sodom would still exist, for the people would have repented and the city would not have been destroyed by God's judgment. Therefore, the wicked men of Sodom would receive lighter punishments than the people of Capernaum.

Just imagine standing before the judgment seat of Christ and hearing Him say to you: "I know about your life. You had light. You had the Bible preached to you week in and week out. But you never repented. Therefore, your punishment will be worse than what I poured out upon Sodom." What an awful thing it would be to hear such a condemnation.

Do not fool yourself. Do not think that you can escape the judgment. If you have never gone to the cross as a beggar with nothing in your hand, making no excuses and offering no self-justification, I exhort you not to let another day pass before you get your life settled with God. If you do, you will have joy unspeakable. If you do not, you will endure such tribulation and anguish as you cannot imagine.

57

THE YOKE OF CHRIST

Matthew 11:25–30

At that time Jesus answered and said, "I thank You, Father, Lord of heaven and earth, that You have hidden these things from the wise and prudent and have revealed them to babes. Even so, Father, for so it seemed good in Your sight. All things have been delivered to Me by My Father, and no one knows the Son except the Father. Nor does anyone know the Father except the Son, and the one to whom the Son wills to reveal Him. Come to Me, all you who labor and are heavy laden, and I will give you rest. Take My yoke upon you and learn from Me, for I am gentle and lowly in heart, and you will find rest for your souls. For My yoke is easy and My burden is light."

After Jesus took the cities of Chorazin, Bethsaida, and Capernaum to task for their failure to repent despite seeing so many of the miracles that had authenticated Him as the Father's agent of revelation, He turned to prayer. It was a prayer of thanksgiving for the way in which the Father had revealed Jesus' identity.

Matthew writes: **At that time Jesus answered and said, "I thank You, Father, Lord of heaven and earth, that You have hidden these things from the wise and prudent and have revealed them to babes. Even so, Father, for so it seemed good in Your sight"** (vv. 25–26). The clear meaning of these words is that God is selective in determining to whom He will reveal Himself. He conceals Himself from some individuals but gives His gracious self-revelation to others. God gives a general revelation of Himself to all men by means of the creation. Likewise, as long as a Bible is available in the appropriate languages, anyone can access His special revelation in His Word. But there is a disclosure by which God lifts the veil of sin from a person's eyes and reveals Himself to him or her, and Jesus affirmed here that God does not give that disclosure to everyone.

Jonathan Edwards, the great New England preacher of the eighteenth century, is most famous for his sermon "Sinners in the Hands of an Angry God." But that was not the sermon that catapulted Edwards into national prominence. Rather, it was an earlier sermon titled "A Divine and Supernatural Light." In that magnificent sermon. Edwards set forth the remarkable way in which God from heaven supernaturally enlightens our hearts and souls so as to bring us to see the sweetness and the excellence of Christ. Without that divine and supernatural light, no one would trust Christ. But again, God does not give it to all.

When Jesus spoke of "these things." He was referring to His own identity as the Savior and the breakthrough of the kingdom of God, the truths that the people of Chorazin. Bethsaida, and Capernaum had missed. He said the Father had hidden these things from "the wise and prudent," that is, from those who believed they understood God and His ways through their own wisdom. As we saw in the previous chapter, Jesus said Capernaum was "exalted to heaven" (v. 23), an apparent reference to pride and arrogance. Jesus' words in this prayer may indicate that the Father withheld the revelation of His Son from the people of Capernaum because of that pride.

He went on to thank the Father because He had revealed these things to "babes," that is, to those who were lowly of heart and willing to receive Jesus on faith. It is not difficult to understand who Jesus had in mind here. Look at the disciples. Those whom Jesus called to be His followers were not the elite of the community. They were not the intellectuals and scholars. Rather, they were the lowly—fishermen, tax collectors, and such. There were some exceptions. I believe that the most educated man in all of Palestine in the first century probably was Saul of Tarsus, and Jesus called Him and used Him mightily. But Saul, who became the Apostle Paul, well understood that he had come to Christ only because of God's grace.

Jesus went on to say, "Even so, Father, for so it seemed good in your sight." God decrees and wills only what pleases Him, and the only thing that pleases Him is that which is right. If it seemed good to God to hide these truths from some and reveal them to others, it *was* good, for God does all things well. Jesus gave thanks for this expression of God's sovereignty, and we should do the same.

Knowing the Father and Son

Matthew tells us that Jesus then said: **"All things have been delivered to Me by My Father, and no one knows the Son except the Father. Nor does anyone know the Father except the Son, and the one to whom the Son wills to reveal Him"** (v. 27). At first glance, these statements seem odd, suggesting that the Father and Son know one another but that no one else knows either of them. What are we to make of these words?

In his epistle to the Romans, Paul tells us that God has revealed Himself to all men by His creation (1:20), as I noted above. In their fallen state, men do not want anything to do with God. Nevertheless, the things they see in creation are clear evidences that there is a God; the knowledge of God gets through to everyone, and that is the universal basis for God's judgment on the guilt-laden human race. The fundamental sin of man is not that he does not know God, but that knowing God he refuses to honor Him as God (1:21). That is humanity's natural state. We know that God exists, but we do not honor Him.

As a teenager, I often found it difficult to go to sleep at night. I was acutely conscious of the reality of God. I was not a Christian. I was not even religious. But I knew that God existed. In times of crisis, I would throw up a prayer or two. But I struggled to sleep at night because I knew I was a sinner. I knew there was a serious disconnect between my Maker and me. We all know that.

So, the Bible teaches that we know that God exists. My own experience bears this out. What, then, did Jesus mean when He gave these strange statements?

The word that is translated as "knows" and "know" in this verse is in its intense form. That tells us that Jesus was saying something like this: "No one *really* knows the Son except the Father, and no one *really* knows the Father except the Son." In other words, He was saying that our knowledge of God, even as converted people, is infinitesimal. The knowledge that we gain of the things of God in this world, even if we study intently all of our days, is nothing compared to the depths and the riches of who God is in Himself eternally. To know the Son in His fullness is something only the Father (and the Holy Spirit, of course) can do. Likewise, only the Son (and the Spirit) can know the Father fully.

However, *some* human beings can come to know the Father: those "to whom the Son wills to reveal Him." We saw earlier that the Father conceals Jesus from some and reveals Him to others. Here Jesus said that He does the same for the Father. The Son makes the Father known, but not to all.

As we will see later in the Gospel of Matthew, Jesus explained that He used parables to reveal the truth to some and to hide it from others (13:11–17). Also, we will study Peter's great confession of Christ at Caesarea Philippi: "You are the Christ, the Son of the living God" (16:16). We will see that Jesus pronounced a blessing on Peter for this confession, but not because he had figured out who Jesus was on his own. Rather, "flesh and blood has not revealed this to you, but My Father who is in heaven" (v. 17). God the Father had revealed to Peter that Jesus was the Christ. Thus, if you and I know the Father and the Son, it is not because of anything we have done. It is Their unspeakable mercy and grace that allow us to know Them.

Taking on Jesus' Yoke

After this statement of exclusivity, Jesus issued a general invitation: **"Come to Me, all you who labor and are heavy laden, and I will give you rest"** (v. 28). I think it is clear, based on the context of this passage, what burden Jesus was talking about. He was *not* speaking of the burdens that we deal with in our daily lives: business matters, family squabbles, and other things that create trials for us. Instead, He was referring to the burden of sin.

There is no more crushing burden to the human soul than guilt. When we bear guilt that has not been resolved, guilt that has not been forgiven, it weighs on us and saps our joy. Our steps are heavy because of the weight of this burden. In John Bunyan's magnificent allegory *The Pilgrim's Progress*, when Christian set out from the City of Destruction, he carried an enormous weight on his back that troubled him until he was able to lay it down at the cross. That baggage that was bearing him down was his guilt.

As Jesus looked around at the people, He could see they were weighed down with guilt. In His compassion, He said, "Come to Me." Where else can we go with our guilt? Who else can take it away? Then He promised that those who came to Him would receive "rest." In biblical terms, to enter heaven is to enter permanent rest. The Sabbath day each week is designed not only to give us rest from our earthly labors but a foretaste of the permanent rest that is in store for our souls.

Then Jesus used a very vivid metaphor: **"Take My yoke upon you and learn from Me, for I am gentle and lowly in heart, and you will find rest for your souls. For My yoke is easy and My burden is light"** (vv. 29–30). When I think about the word *yoke*, I see a pair of oxen joined together by a heavy wooden yoke that keeps them moving in unison. The Bible sometimes uses that kind of yoke as a metaphor. For instance, we are told not to be "unequally yoked" with unbelievers in marriage; that would be like putting two completely incompatible oxen together and expecting them to work as a team. Such an attempt is doomed to fail.

However, Jesus was not talking about this kind of yoke. In ancient times, when a person carried a load, he might wear a yoke across his shoulders so he could carry his burden in a balanced fashion. Water was typically carried this way, with a bucket on each end of the yoke. That is the kind of yoke Jesus had in mind, and He promised such a yoke to everyone who came to Him. This yoke would make it easy for them to carry the burdens they could not carry without it.

When we take this yoke, Jesus said, we learn from Him. Of course, the primary thing we learn from Him is Himself; He is both the Teacher and the lesson. Learning from Him means submitting to His authority and becoming His servant, as all disciples did. Paul understood that; his favorite self-designation in his letters is "bondservant of Jesus Christ." He was happy to be a slave of Christ, because the supreme irony is that until we become slaves of Christ, we do not know freedom. Our sin and guilt weigh us down and enslave us, but Jesus frees us from those burdens. He is a gentle and lowly Teacher who has the best interests of His students at heart.

So, Jesus' yoke is easy compared to the yoke of slavery under which we labor as unforgiven sinners. His burden is light compared to the burden of guilt we carry.

Every time I read this passage, I think, "Wait a minute, Jesus, my life became much more complicated when I took on Your yoke." Life seemed simple then. I just did the will of Satan and went with the flow. But I had that awful burden. Jesus calls us to surrender our lives to Him, to dedicate ourselves to Him, to sell ourselves to Him body and soul. Yet, He promises that when we do that we will find the burden light. It is incredible but true.

Have you found the rest for your soul that Jesus was talking about here? If you have, then you know that whatever burden Jesus puts on you is an easy one. Jesus is not a tyrant; although He commands obedience and expects us to give Him our all, He never oppresses His people. It is always a sheer delight to wear His yoke.

58

THE LORD OF THE SABBATH

Matthew 12:1–8

At that time Jesus went through the grainfields on the Sabbath. And His disciples were hungry, and began to pluck heads of grain and to eat. And when the Pharisees saw it, they said to Him, "Look, Your disciples are doing what is not lawful to do on the Sabbath!" But He said to them, "Have you not read what David did when he was hungry, he and those who were with him: how he entered the house of God and ate the showbread which was not lawful for him to eat, nor for those who were with him, but only for the priests? Or have you not read in the law that on the Sabbath the priests in the temple profane the Sabbath, and are blameless? Yet I say to you that in this place there is One greater than the temple. But if you had known what this means, 'I desire mercy and not sacrifice,' you would not have condemned the guiltless. For the Son of Man is Lord even of the Sabbath."

To this point in his Gospel, Matthew has not chronicled any major disputes between Jesus and the Jewish religious leaders. He recorded Jesus' warning to the people that their righteousness must exceed that of the scribes and Pharisees (5:20). He showed examples of the scribes and Pharisees muttering among themselves about things Jesus said and did (9:3, 34). And he mentioned an incident wherein the Pharisees asked Jesus' disciples why He ate with tax collectors and sinners. But now Matthew reports on a major dispute in which the Pharisees accused the disciples—and, by implication, Jesus Himself—of violating the law of God.

Matthew writes: **At that time Jesus went through the grainfields on the Sabbath. And His disciples were hungry, and began to pluck heads of grain and to eat. And when the Pharisees saw it, they said to Him, "Look, Your disciples are doing what is not lawful to do on the Sabbath!"** (vv. 1–2). It was perfectly permissible under Jewish law for travelers walking along near fields of grain to help themselves minimally to some of the crop. In fact, God had commanded His people not to harvest their fields to the very edges but to leave some grain standing for the poor and for sojourners (Lev. 19:9). So, the fact that Jesus' disciples plucked heads of grain out of someone else's field was not regarded as trespassing or theft. The problem, in the eyes of the Pharisees, was that they did it on a Sabbath day.

The Sabbath was extremely important to Jewish piety, and rightly so, for God had commanded observance of the Sabbath in the Ten Commandments (Ex. 20:8–11). The Jews took Sabbath-keeping so seriously that they were willing to suffer death to themselves and to their children rather than violate the Sabbath day. This took place during the assault on Jerusalem by the Roman General Pompey in 63 BC. The Jews refused to fight on the Sabbath as a matter of national honor.

However, despite God's emphasis on the Sabbath, the Old Testament contains very few specific rules and regulations regarding behavior on that day. Because of this, the Jewish religious authorities established all kinds of regulations for the Sabbath. Each rule imposed a new burden and made the observance of the Sabbath more unwieldy. It was these manmade rules that Jesus' disciples violated when they plucked the heads of grain. The Pharisees considered this action a violation of the Sabbath because their laws required the Jews to refrain from all unnecessary work on the Sabbath. The Pharisees believed that plucking a head of grain amounted to reaping, and rubbing the grain to separate the wheat from the chaff amounted to threshing. So, they rebuked Jesus for allowing the disciples to violate the Sabbath.

Two Precedents from the Law

I love the way Jesus responded: **He said to them, "Have you not read what David did when he was hungry, he and those who were with him: how he entered the house of God and ate the showbread which was not lawful for him to eat, nor for those who were with him, but only for the priests? Or have you not read in the law that on the Sabbath the priests in the temple profane the Sabbath, and are blameless?"** (vv. 3–5). Jesus answered His accusers with two precedents drawn from Scripture. It was as if He were saying, "Don't you ever look at the Bible when you are formulating your traditions?"

Jesus first referred to an incident in the life of David, from a time when he was basically an outlaw. Samuel had anointed him to become Israel's second king, but Jonathan had warned David that King Saul was trying to kill him, so David and his men were on the run and were hungry. David went to the city of Nob and asked Ahimelech the priest for food. Ahimelech had no food except the showbread, the special bread that was placed before God in the sanctuary (see Ex. 25:30). This bread was replaced on a regular basis with fresh bread, and the priests had the privilege of eating the bread after its ritual use. David explained the situation to Ahimelech and asked for the bread, and the priest willingly acceded to David's request.

Some commentators argue that Ahimelech allowed David to take the bread because it was within his prerogative to exercise mercy to anyone who was hungry. Others say that he allowed this exception because it was David who requested it, assuming that Ahimelech knew that David was the Lord's anointed king, and he was willing to feed David out of respect for his office.

Regardless of the reason Ahimelech gave the bread to David, the incident allowed Jesus to make a very telling point to the Pharisees. First, it was a priest, one of Israel's religious leaders, who permitted a violation of the sanctuary law. But even more important, Jesus was telling the Pharisees that mercy is more important than ritual. Of course, ritual is not unimportant, but there are occasions when higher necessities need to be addressed. As Jesus put it, **"If you had known what this means, 'I desire mercy and not sacrifice,' you would not have condemned the guiltless"** (v. 7). Just as David was guiltless in an apparent violation of the sanctuary law, the disciples were guiltless of violating the Sabbath. The need for mercy overruled ritual.

Jesus then cited a second precedent: "Or have you not read in the law that on the Sabbath the priests in the temple profane the Sabbath, and are blameless?" Again He asked, "Have you not read . . . the law?" God had commanded His people to work for six days and then rest on the seventh day. But the priests, of course, could not rest on that day. Jesus was telling the Pharisees that the priests were exempt from the Sabbath law. They were not considered Sabbath-breakers when they did their God-ordained duties on that day.

One Greater Than the Temple

Then Jesus made a statement that caused a serious escalation in this confrontation with the Pharisees. By pointing out the examples of David and the priests, He had set the stage to make a point by use of an argument from the lesser to the greater. He said, **"Yet I say to you that in this place there is One greater than the temple"** (v. 6).

To grasp the significance of these words, we need to understand the importance of the temple in the Jewish mind. The temple, like the tabernacle before it, represented the presence of God in the midst of His people. It was the center of the Jews' religious life, the central place of worship and sacrifice. Jesus, however, said there was One "in this place"—clearly He was speaking of Himself—who was greater than the temple. The Pharisees must have been absolutely stunned when He said this.

Yet, they should have known this. Everything in the tabernacle and later in the temple, all of the symbolism that God so meticulously prescribed for these magnificent sanctuaries, pointed beyond itself to the living temple, to the living presence of God in the midst of His people, to His incarnate Son. God was actually dwelling in the temple of Jesus' body (John 2:21), whereas He only lived symbolically in the temple made of wood and stone. Jesus was the one to whom the temple pointed. That is why John wrote that "the Word became flesh and dwelt among us" (1:14a). In the original language, this verse says, "the Word become flesh and *tabernacled* among us." Jesus fulfilled the tabernacle and the temple.

So, Jesus was asserting that He was greater than the temple that the priests so diligently served on the Sabbath. Thus, His disciples had a greater service than those priests. Likewise, by implication, Jesus was asserting that He was greater than David. If it was acceptable for David to eat the showbread from the sanctuary, it was acceptable for Jesus' disciples to eat a few heads of grain on the Sabbath.

Jesus then went back to the Old Testament again to say, "If you had known what this means, 'I desire mercy and not sacrifice,' you would not have condemned the guiltless." This verse contains a quotation from Hosea 6:6, but God was not saying that the sacrificial system needed to be abolished. Rather, He was assigning a hierarchy of values. He was saying: "Yes, I want sacrifices. Yes, it's important to offer the sacrifices as part of your religious obligations. But mercy is much more important than ritual. When there is a conflict between ritual and mercy, always default to mercy." Jesus was subtly showing the Pharisees that they had taken the Sabbath, a gift God gave to His people for their refreshment and joy, and made it a cumbersome burden with all of their detailed restrictions. Because of that, they had condemned the guiltless—His disciples.

The Lord of the Sabbath

Finally, Matthew tells us that Jesus said, **"For the Son of Man is Lord even of the Sabbath"** (v. 8). As we seek to understand this amazing assertion, we need to remember the origin of the Sabbath. Yes, as I noted above, it was one of the Ten Commandments God gave to His people through Moses at Mount Sinai. But that was not the origin of the Sabbath. At Sinai, God was simply telling the

Israelites to remember something that was already in effect: that one day out of seven is consecrated and not to be profaned. The Sabbath day was instituted in creation. God formed the heavens and earth in six days, and on the seventh day He rested (Gen. 2:2–3). As the Creator of the Sabbath, God rightly had absolute authority to say how it should be observed. Therefore, this statement by Jesus was nothing less than another assertion of His deity. He was saying that He had instituted the Sabbath.

So, in this incident, when the Pharisees came to Jesus filled with righteous indignation, He ably defended Himself with an argument that must have shocked the Pharisees to the very core of their beings. First He told them that they had entirely missed the point of the Sabbath. They had turned God's wonderful provision for rest and worship into an instrument of slavery for God's people. Then He claimed the right to make that assertion by declaring Himself to be the Creator of the Sabbath and therefore the Lord of the Sabbath.

Certainly the Pharisees did not miss the point of what Jesus was saying. From this point in Matthew's narrative, we will see an escalation in the frequency and stridency of their confrontations. In fact, in the passage we will study in the next chapter, we will see the beginning of the Pharisees' plots to destroy Him.

59

THE SERVANT OF THE LORD

Matthew 12:9–21

Now when He had departed from there, He went into their synagogue. And behold, there was a man who had a withered hand. And they asked Him, saying, "Is it lawful to heal on the Sabbath?"—that they might accuse Him. Then He said to them, "What man is there among you who has one sheep, and if it falls into a pit on the Sabbath, will not lay hold of it and lift it out? Of how much more value then is a man than a sheep? Therefore it is lawful to do good on the Sabbath." Then He said to the man, "Stretch out your hand." And he stretched it out, and it was restored as whole as the other. Then the Pharisees went out and plotted against Him, how they might destroy Him. But when Jesus knew it, He withdrew from there. And great multitudes followed Him, and He healed them all. Yet He warned them not to make Him known, that it might be fulfilled which was spoken by Isaiah the prophet, saying:

> "Behold! My Servant whom I have chosen,
> My Beloved in whom My soul is well pleased!
> I will put My Spirit upon Him,
> And He will declare justice to the Gentiles.
> He will not quarrel nor cry out,
> Nor will anyone hear His voice in the streets
> A bruised reed He will not break,
> And smoking flax He will not quench,
> Till He sends forth justice to victory;
> And in His name Gentiles will trust."

On every page of the Scriptures, God the Father reveals to us something of Himself, as well as something of the person and work of His Son, the second person of the Trinity, our Lord Jesus Christ. The passage before us in this chapter is especially revealing as to the identity of Jesus.

Following Jesus' first sharp confrontation with the Pharisees, when He made a clear claim to deity by saying He was the Lord of the Sabbath, Jesus **departed from there [and] . . . went into their synagogue. And behold, there was a man who had a withered hand. And they asked Him, saying, "Is it lawful to heal on the Sabbath?"—that they might accuse Him** (vv. 9–10). As was His habit, Jesus went to the synagogue on the Sabbath, but the Pharisees came, too, seemingly still angry over the earlier confrontation. Inside, Jesus encountered a man with a withered hand. Before Jesus could do anything for the man, apparently before the man could even ask Jesus' help, the Pharisees were in His face, asking, "Is it lawful to heal on the Sabbath?"

This question obviously was not asked out of a sincere desire to know Jesus' thoughts on the propriety of healing on the Sabbath. It was more of a sarcastic challenge. Perhaps they guessed His intention and basically asked, "Are you really going to do *this*, too?" They were of the opinion that healing a withered hand was not a matter of life and death, so it would amount to unnecessary work on the Sabbath. However, the question was also asked in malice, with the hope that Jesus would say something theologically unorthodox to justify healing on the Sabbath, giving them ammunition they could use against Him.

Matthew writes: **Then He said to them, "What man is there among you who has one sheep, and if it falls into a pit on the Sabbath, will not lay hold of it and lift it out? Of how much more value then is a man than a sheep? Therefore it is lawful to do good on the Sabbath"** (vv. 11–12). Although the Pharisees' question was not sincere, Jesus took the time to teach them that healing on the Sabbath was indeed legal. To do so, He proposed a hypothetical situation—if one of the Pharisees owned a sheep, and it fell in a pit on a Sabbath day, he would surely take steps to rescue it. Then, once again arguing from the lesser to the greater, He declared that if it was acceptable to rescue a sheep on the Sabbath, it was acceptable to heal a man, for a man is far more valuable than a sheep. The principle is that "it is lawful to do good on the Sabbath."

So, **He said to the man, "Stretch out your hand." And he stretched it out, and it was restored as whole as the other** (v. 13). Jesus healed the man's deformity so that there was no apparent difference between his two hands. He did this in plain view of the Pharisees, who had expected that He might do it. They should have fallen on their knees in repentance and adoration on seeing this miracle. However, Matthew tells us, **the Pharisees went out and plotted**

against Him, how they might destroy Him (v. 14). They were slaves of their manmade traditions, and they could not abide the fact that Jesus did not follow their dictates, thereby undermining their authority. So, they began to plot to kill Him.

Jesus Seeks Anonymity

Matthew then writes, **But when Jesus knew it, He withdrew from there** (v. 15a). Somehow Jesus knew what the Pharisees were plotting. Was this knowledge available to Him through His omniscient divine nature? Did a sympathetic Pharisee tell Him? We do not know. In any case, He left that area. Jesus did not flee from this situation as a coward. He knew He was going to die, but He also knew that His Father had set the agenda for His mission, not the Pharisees. He spoke on occasion about His "time" (see Matt. 26:18; John 7:6), the culmination of His work on earth. That time had been set and could not be altered. Jesus knew He had other work yet to do, so He withdrew to another place. In like manner, we sometimes find ourselves in situations where we have to fight or take flight. Sometimes discretion really is the better part of valor.

Once again, Matthew writes, **great multitudes followed Him, and He healed them all. Yet He warned them not to make Him known** (vv. 15b–16). Jesus took up His preaching and healing ministry again, drawing great crowds. Once again, as we have seen previously, He warned them not to make Him know. Here, however, Matthew offers a hint as to why Jesus so often gave this mysterious command. It was, Matthew says, **that it might be fulfilled which was spoken by Isaiah the prophet** (v. 17).

Once again, Matthew casts the activity of Jesus in the light of Old Testament prophecy, as we have seen him do time and time again in this Gospel. In the Old Testament, there are more than three hundred specific prophecies about the coming Messiah. For example, hundreds of years before Jesus' incarnation, it was prophesied that He would be born in Bethlehem (Mic. 5:2), that He would be called out of Egypt (Hos. 11:1), and that His executioners would gamble for His garments (Ps. 22:18). The odds of one person fulfilling all of these specific prophecies is astronomical. Interestingly however, Matthew here cites a prophecy that stated not what the Messiah would do but what He would not do.

The prophecy is this: **"Behold! My Servant whom I have chosen, My Beloved in whom My soul is well pleased! I will put My Spirit upon Him, and He will declare justice to the Gentiles. He will not quarrel nor cry out, nor will anyone hear His voice in the streets. A bruised reed He will not break, and smoking flax He will not quench, till He sends forth justice to victory; and in His name Gentiles will trust"** (vv. 18–21).

The prophecy starts with a call to attention by God the Father: "Behold! My Servant whom I have chosen." There may be a double meaning in this declaration. Obviously God the Father chose His Servant, whom He appointed and anointed to be the Messiah. But I believe there is a deeper level of election in view here. In the biblical doctrine of election, the supreme elect One is the Son. All else who are elected by the sovereign God are elected in Him. So, any discussion about election must begin with the election of Jesus Christ.

In the prophecy, the Father also declares that the Messiah is "My Beloved in whom My soul is well pleased!" The Gospels testify that the Father spoke audibly from heaven three times during the ministry of Jesus: at His baptism (Matt. 3:17), at His transfiguration (17:5), and when Jesus prayed that the Father would glorify His name (John 12:28). On the first two of these occasions, the Father said, "This is My beloved Son, in whom I am well pleased," a near-verbatim repetition of the words of Isaiah's prophecy.

The Father goes on to say, "I will put My Spirit upon Him." This happened at Jesus' baptism, when the heavens opened and the Spirit came down upon Him as a dove, anointing Him for His earthly mission. Furthermore, "He will declare justice to the Gentiles." Jesus' primary mission was to the Jews, but He did occasionally interact with Gentiles, and in the next generation, He led the apostles to take the gospel beyond the ranks of the circumcised to the Gentile masses.

Bruised Reeds and Smoking Flax

Isaiah's prophecy continues, saying: "He will not quarrel nor cry out, nor will anyone hear His voice in the streets. A bruised reed He will not break, and smoking flax He will not quench, till He sends forth justice to victory." It is important that we give close attention to this section.

Who do you think was the smartest man who ever lived? How about the strongest man? The gentlest man? I would give the same answer for all three questions: Jesus of Nazareth. Jesus must have been the smartest man who ever lived because, being sinless, He never suffered what we call the noetic effects of sin, the effect of sin on the mind. His mind was never clouded or confused. He never made a logical error. His thinking was absolutely impeccable. Also, Jesus was the physically strongest man who ever lived. Can you imagine a physical specimen to match a man whose sinews, tendons, and muscles were never weakened by the ravages of sin on the human body? Jesus was the perfect physical specimen.

In the same way, there would be no contest for the title of gentlest man to ever walk the earth. Years ago, I did a seminar for women on marriage, and I took a poll among all the women who were there. I gave them a list of about fifty characteristics and asked them to identify the two main qualities that would be true of an ideal husband. Overwhelmingly, they wanted a man who was tough and tender. These women told me they wanted husbands who would protect them and honor them. Sadly, that is an extremely rare combination. Lots of men are tough but do not know how to be tender. Likewise, lots of men are tender but cannot stand in defense of their women when they need to do so. However, these qualities were combined perfectly in the person of Jesus, as Isaiah shows in his prophecy.

When Isaiah says, "He will not quarrel nor cry out, nor will anyone hear His voice in the streets," he is talking about argumentation. Disagreements and arguments are a fact of human existence. Often when we find ourselves in contentious circumstances, we grow angry or impatient, and we raise our voices. Jesus debated the Pharisees all the time, and sometimes He was strongly provoked. However, He never let Himself get heated. I cannot imagine that He ever raised His voice, much less that He screamed, shouted, or yelled at His opponents. That was not Jesus' style. Jesus did not have to scream or shout at the Pharisees because He was smarter and stronger. As a result, He did not quarrel or cry out, and no one ever heard Him arguing in the street.

What about Isaiah's strange statement that "A bruised reed He will not break, and smoking flax He will not quench, till He sends forth justice to victory"? What are we to make of this?

In the ancient world, people used reeds to make flutes, pens, and a host of other things. Oftentimes, when someone would gather reeds for one of these uses, as he began to inspect the reeds more closely, he would find some that were bruised and imperfect. In such a case, he would simply snap the reed in two and pick up another one. Reeds cost far less than a dime a dozen. The craftsman would simply keep looking through his reeds till he found one that was suitable. If necessary, he would go get more.

Isaiah cites these reeds as a metaphor for people. He is saying that when the Messiah finds people who are bruised and imperfect, He will not destroy them and discard them. Every person is a bruised reed, and every Christian is a bruised reed that Jesus has not discarded but redeemed. We are not in the kingdom because we are perfect. We are in the kingdom because Jesus is pleased to use bruised reeds.

More than thirty years ago, when Prison Fellowship was just beginning, I was on the board of directors of that ministry to prison inmates. I was meeting with Chuck Colson, and Chuck said, "R.C., we have to have a logo for this ministry, a symbol that everyone will be able to recognize." Almost immediately, I had an idea: a bruised reed. I said: "We're trying to minister to the rejected people of this world. These men and women are bruised people. The ministry of the church is not to destroy them, because Jesus would not break a bruised reed." Chuck's eyes lit up and he said, "That's it!" He got an artist to design a symbol depicting a broken reed, and it has been the logo of Prison Fellowship ever since.

Then Isaiah says of the Messiah, "And smoking flax He will not quench." Again, Isaiah borrows imagery from the ancient world to describe the Messiah. The lamps of the ancient Israelites used wicks made of flax, a fibrous plant. If an Israelite tried to light his lamp with a flawed piece of flax, it would not burn brightly and cleanly. Instead, it would smoke, creating an unpleasant acrid smell. In such a case, the Israelite would pinch the wick and extinguish what burning was going on within the flax. He would then find a new piece of flax so his lamp would burn properly.

But the Messiah will not do that in the case of people, Isaiah declares. Of course, He will see all people as smoking pieces of flax. But He will not discard them. He will use them, imperfect though they are.

An Ongoing Mission

The best news of all, according to Isaiah, is that the Messiah will keep on tending bruised reeds and nurturing smoking flax "till He sends forth justice to victory." Jesus will continue to seek and save the lost until the curtain comes down on history and God makes all things right. Furthermore, this mission of the Messiah will go beyond the house of Israel: "in His name Gentiles will trust." He will find bruised reeds and smoking flax among all nations, tribes, and tongues.

This is a wonderful picture of our Savior, painted for us by God's prophet hundreds of years before Jesus was born. It reminds us that Jesus found us bruised but did not break us. He found us smoldering but did not extinguish us. Despite all of our bruises, our brokenness, our impurities, and our imperfections, He chose to set His love upon us and make us His own people.

Jesus told the people He healed not to speak about Him so that He might be able to minister according to the pattern described by Isaiah. There was a very real danger that His growing fame would cause a frenzy of excitement among the people, which might lead to a popular movement to make Him a military ruler, opposing the Romans. Indeed, John tells us that on one occasion "Jesus perceived that they were about to come and take Him by force to make Him king, [so] He departed again to the mountain by Himself alone" (6:15). The people, having been poorly taught, did not know what to expect from the Messiah, but Jesus was determined to carry out His ministry according to the biblical model. He wanted to keep Himself free to minister to the bruised and broken with His unparalleled gentleness.

60

WAR BETWEEN THE KINGDOMS

Matthew 12:22–30

Then one was brought to Him who was demon-possessed, blind and mute; and He healed him, so that the blind and mute man both spoke and saw. And all the multitudes were amazed and said, "Could this be the Son of David?" Now when the Pharisees heard it they said, "This fellow does not cast out demons except by Beelzebub, the ruler of the demons." But Jesus knew their thoughts, and said to them: "Every kingdom divided against itself is brought to desolation, and every city or house divided against itself will not stand. If Satan casts out Satan, he is divided against himself. How then will his kingdom stand? And if I cast out demons by Beelzebub, by whom do your sons cast them out? Therefore they shall be your judges. But if I cast out demons by the Spirit of God, surely the kingdom of God has come upon you. Or how can one enter a strong man's house and plunder his goods, unless he first binds the strong man? And then he will plunder his house. He who is not with Me is against Me, and he who does not gather with Me scatters abroad."

In both of the two previous chapters, we examined passages from Matthew 12 in which Jesus had confrontations with the Pharisees. In the passage we are studying in this chapter, Matthew's narrative initially seems to move away from these skirmishes. It begins with a miracle, the healing of one of the most afflicted men Jesus ever helped. However, Matthew says little about the miracle itself. Rather, he records the Pharisees' response to it and the teaching that Jesus gave on that occasion. So, the confrontations continue.

Matthew tells us, **Then one was brought to Him who was demon-possessed, blind and mute; and He healed him, so that the blind and mute man both spoke and saw** (v. 22). This man was without his sense of sight and his ability to talk, and he also was a victim of demon possession. Matthew does not explicitly say that the demon was the cause of the man's blindness and muteness. However, we saw an earlier incident in which a man who was mute and demon-possessed was brought to Jesus, and when Jesus expelled the demon, the man was able to speak (9:32–33), so it seems reasonable to assume that there was a connection between the presence of the demon and the man's physical affliction.

Jesus, Matthew says, "healed" the man. Usually Matthew does not refer to incidents when Jesus delivered people from demon possession as "healings"; rather, he prefers to say that the demon was cast out (see 8:16). In this case, however, Jesus' healing power and redeeming power worked together to resolve this man's multiple afflictions. As a result, the man was made completely whole. This is typical of the work of Jesus; He never touches just part of a person but deals with the whole person.

This glorious deliverance provoked unusual wonder and reflection in the crowds who saw it: **And all the multitudes were amazed and said, "Could this be the Son of David?"** (v. 23). The way this verse is structured in the original language tells us this was not a cynical question. The people were beginning to sense the truth. They were wondering, "Could we be in the presence of the Messiah?" The Old Testament had foretold that the Messiah would come in the line of David and would restore David's kingdom. In fact, it was Matthew's stated goal to show that Jesus *was* the Son of David (1:1). On this occasion at least, those in the crowd who were familiar with the messianic prophecies were moved to wonder whether those prophecies were coming true before their eyes.

A House Divided?

The Pharisees' reaction to the people's speculation was dismissive and harsh: **Now when the Pharisees heard it they said, "This fellow does not cast out demons except by Beelzebub, the ruler of the demons"** (v. 24). Whereas the people were wondering whether Jesus might be the long-awaited "Son of David," the Pharisees called Him "this fellow," which was not a term of endearment. They were certainly not ready to acknowledge Him as the Son of David; in their eyes, He was just another self-proclaimed teacher and healer.

Notice, however, that with regard to Jesus' miracles, the Pharisees were not like modern liberal theologians, who try to rewrite history and explain how His miracles were really not miracles at all. The Pharisees raised no challenge to the reality of His miraculous healing of the man who was demon-possessed, blind, and mute. The facts spoke for themselves, and the Pharisees acknowledged that Jesus had performed a real miracle. But while modern liberal scholars tend to be nice to Jesus, often describing Him as the greatest moral teacher who ever lived (even while they deny His works), the Pharisees were anything but nice. They recognized Jesus' power, but they attributed it to the wrong source. They said He was casting out demons by the ruler of the demons, Beelzebub, which, as we have seen, was a name for Satan. So, they attributed Jesus' power over demons to Satan.

We have already seen the Pharisees espousing this theory. They expressed it after the earlier incident when Jesus healed a man who was demon-possessed and mute (9:34). Also, Jesus hinted that He knew they were equating Him with Beelzebub when He gave His instructions to His Apostles prior to their trial mission (10:25). When this scurrilous accusation came up again after the healing of the man who was demon-possessed, blind, and mute, Jesus chose to address it.

Matthew writes: **But Jesus knew their thoughts, and said to them: "Every kingdom divided against itself is brought to desolation, and every city or house divided against itself will not stand"** (v. 25). Again, as we saw in the previous chapter (Matt. 12:15), Jesus knew something that apparently was concealed from Him, in this case, the thoughts of the Pharisees. We can only imagine their astonishment when Jesus began to address that which they were thinking.

Jesus' first assertion was this: "Every kingdom divided against itself is brought to desolation, and every city or house divided against itself will not stand." We have all heard it said, "United we stand, divided we fall." There is much truth in that adage. It is a common strategy of military leaders to divide their enemies and thereby conquer them. If a general can somehow induce his enemies to squabble among themselves, his battle is 90 percent won.

So, Jesus mentioned this truism by way of saying that the Pharisees were suggesting that Satan's kingdom was internally split—a theory that made no sense: **"If Satan casts out Satan, he is divided against himself. How then will his kingdom stand?"** (v. 26). Do you see what Jesus was saying? If Satan's kingdom were as divided against itself as they seemed to imagine it to be, it was dead. Yet, everyone knew that Satan was alive and well on planet Earth.

A Very Real Enemy

We cannot read this text and ignore the reality of Satan. Yet the idea of the devil seems very antiquated in our time. So many sophisticated people refuse to believe in Satan because they think the church teaches as fact a view of the devil that originated as a caricature in the Middle Ages—a funny little fellow with horns wearing a red suit and carrying a pitchfork. It is true that this image originated in the church, but not because the church thought Satan looked like that. The medieval church believed very much in the devil and understood his power to disguise himself as an angel of light (2 Cor. 11:14). If the church had authorized portraits of Satan that reflected the actual view of him, they might have depicted a suave and attractive figure. Instead, he was given a ridiculous appearance. They knew that the devil's principle sin was pride, and they tried to take advantage of that and keep him away by mocking him and making him look ludicrous. But no one ever believed he was really like that. He is not a ludicrous figure but a powerful spiritual being with great malice toward God and His people.

Satan has two ways of getting to God's people. The cleverest way is to convince us that he does not exist. If he can do that, we will not be on guard against his attacks. No one resists something he does not believe in. If the devil cannot get us that way, he will try to cause us to become so preoccupied with him that we will exalt him to the same level as God, giving him equal power with God. When that happens, we begin to see demons behind every bush.

I was in seminary when President Kennedy was shot. On that day and in the following days, we listened to every news broadcast that came our way as the authorities tried to sort out the crisis. I remember that the news commentators used distinctive words to describe the egregious nature of the assassination, words such as *devilish, satanic, demonic, diabolical,* and *inhuman*. I kept wondering why they wanted to bring the devil into discussion about the causes of it all. There is more than enough sin in the heart of human beings to account for the assassination of the president without having to say the devil was behind it. We are all capable of such things, and Satan takes advantage of that capability in us.

Several years ago, a pulpit nominating committee contacted me to ask for my advice on interviewing prospective ministers for their church. They had heard stories of ministerial candidates who sounded good and said all the right things, but when they were hired it was found that they did not believe much of what the Bible teaches. So, the members of this committee wanted to know what questions they needed to ask to find the man's true beliefs. I recommended that their first question should be, "What is your view of angels?" You can learn a lot about a man's theology by how he answers that question. Today it seems hardly anyone believes in angels, but the New Testament says more about angels then it does about love or about sin. So, if we choose to disregard the New Testament teachings on angels, we might as well disregard its teachings on love and sin. And, in fact, many popular preachers do just that. They toss all teaching about angels in the garbage can, including the teaching about the chief fallen angel, Satan, and his minions.

Notice that Jesus used the language of kingdoms. He spoke here about the kingdom of Satan, just as He spoke often about the kingdom of God. This theme comes up again and again in Scripture. Jesus referred repeatedly to Satan as "the ruler of this world" (John 12:31; 14:30; 16:11). Paul speaks of "the prince of the power of the air, the spirit who now works in the sons of disobedience" (Eph. 2:2) and of "the rulers of the darkness of this age" (Eph. 6:12). So, Satan is a ruler, and that means there are two realms with two monarchs. However, the realms are not equal by any means. Satan is no match for God. But there is an intense battle between the two kingdoms, and there is no neutral ground. Everyone is in one kingdom or the other. If you are not in the kingdom of God, there is only one other kingdom you can be in—the kingdom of the evil one.

The Kingdom Has Come

Matthew then writes that Jesus said: **"And if I cast out demons by Beelzebub, by whom do your sons cast them out? Therefore they shall be your judges. But if I cast out demons by the Spirit of God, surely the kingdom of God has come upon you"** (vv. 27–28). Jesus again used a hypothetical situation to make a point. "Let's assume," He said to the Pharisees, "that you are right and I am casting out demons by Beelzebub. By whom, then, do your sons cast them out?" There were some among the Jews who performed exorcisms (see Acts 19:13). Jesus was pointing out that it made no sense to accept that other Jews were casting out demons legitimately but that He was doing it by the power of Satan.

Then He declared, quite logically, "But if I cast out demons by the Spirit of God, surely the kingdom of God has come upon you." This was a stern warning. Jesus had refuted their argument that He was casting out demons by Satan's power. Therefore, He was doing it by God's power. Luke records Jesus' words this way: "But if I cast out demons with the finger of God, surely the kingdom of God has come upon you" (11:20). "The finger of God" was a metaphor for the Holy Spirit. The point is that Jesus' ability to cast out demons "with a word" (Matt. 8:16) was an unprecedented display of divine power and clear evidence that the kingdom of God was present—just as John the Baptist had preached and just as Jesus had preached.

Sometimes the idea is put forth that the kingdom of God has not yet begun. Others say that the kingdom has already come in its fullness and nothing is yet to happen. The New Testament view is that the kingdom of God has been inaugurated, having made its advent with the entrance of Jesus to the world. He was elevated to the right hand of the Father and crowned as King of kings and Lord of lords. But His kingdom has not yet been consummated. We still have a future hope—the return of our Lord Jesus Christ, when all things will be given over to Him. So, if we have this confusion, it is perhaps understandable that the Pharisees could be mistaken about the kingdom. That is why Jesus warned them so sternly. It was as if He were saying: "Wake up. Pay attention. You're missing it. Not only that, you're opposing it. The kingdom is here. The display of My power shows it beyond all doubt."

Jesus then gave another illustration to try to break through the Pharisees' blindness: **"Or how can one enter a strong man's house and plunder his goods, unless he first binds the strong man? And then he will plunder his house"** (v. 29). No one walks into a strong man's home and says, "Excuse me, I'd like to help myself to your wide-screen television set, to your jewelry, and to whatever else looks valuable." No, if someone wants to loot a strong man's home, he first needs to subdue the strong man and restrain him so that he cannot protect his home and his goods. Jesus was saying that the man who was under demonic control, blind, and mute had been under the possession of the strong man, Satan. But Jesus had bound Satan and plundered him.

No Room for Neutrality

Finally, Jesus painted the situation in black and white terms: **"He who is not with Me is against Me, and he who does not gather with Me scatters abroad"** (v. 30). We almost never hear unbelievers say, "I'm against Jesus." Instead, they say, "I don't believe in Jesus" or "I don't feel the need for Jesus." They think they can take Him or leave Him. But Jesus said that is not possible. Anyone who is not actively for Him is truly against Him. Again, there is no neutrality.

We need to see how provocative this kind of talk is. Jesus' ministry lasted only three years. I wonder how long His ministry would last if He were to come again in the flesh in twenty-first-century America. Could anything be more politically incorrect than to say, "If you don't believe in Me, you belong to Satan's kingdom; if you don't follow Me, you are My enemy; if you are not for Me, you are against Me"? Jesus was saying that there is only one way, and He is it. That kind of talk would draw even more angry opposition today than it did in Jesus' own time.

So often today our evangelism is too gentle. In order to be politically correct, we invite people to come to Jesus. We ask them if they would like to receive Jesus and tell them they will be glad if they do, for believing in Him will enrich their lives, give them meaning, and so on. But God does not invite people to come to Jesus. He commands them to come (Acts 17:30). It is every person's duty to submit to the Lord of glory. Those who refuse to come to Christ sin grievously against the Son of God and God Himself. They are in rebellion against the King of kings.

61

THE UNPARDONABLE SIN

Matthew 12:31–32

Therefore I say to you, every sin and blasphemy will be forgiven men, but the blasphemy against the Spirit will not be forgiven men. Anyone who speaks a word against the Son of Man, it will be forgiven him; but whoever speaks against the Holy Spirit, it will not be forgiven him, either in this age or in the age to come.

In the previous chapter, we saw that Jesus sternly warned the Pharisees that they were opposing the kingdom of God. That in itself was a grievous sin. However, in the passage we take up in this chapter, Matthew records that Jesus warned the Pharisees that they were perilously close to committing a far worse sin, a sin so heinous it could not be forgiven. Jesus drew a line at the edge of God's forgiveness. He was telling them that even though God is extremely merciful, profoundly gracious, and overwhelmingly forgiving, there is a limit to His mercy.

According to Matthew, Jesus said, **"Therefore I say to you, every sin and blasphemy will be forgiven men, but the blasphemy against the Spirit will not be forgiven men. Anyone who speaks a word against the Son of Man, it will be forgiven him; but whoever speaks against the Holy Spirit, it will not be forgiven him, either in this age or in the age to come"** (vv. 31–32). Once again we see that strange anomaly, wherein a new section of Matthew's Gospel begins with the word *therefore*. At least the editors who divided the text into chapters and verses did not begin a new chapter at this point, which is sometimes the case and always regrettable, because the word *therefore* links what is about to be said with what has come before it. It indicates that a conclusion is about to be announced.

That conclusion is perhaps the most severe warning Jesus ever gave to the Pharisees. In essence, He was saying to them: "Be very careful. I have put up with your slanders and your false accusations. But now you are close to committing a slander so serious that God will not forgive it."

The obvious question that arises when we study this passage is this: What is the unpardonable sin? This is a very important question. We want to know what this sin is so that we do not commit it.

There are all kinds of theories about the unforgivable sin. For instance, some have said it is murder, because the Bible dictates that those who murder should be executed. However, there are many examples in Scripture of men who committed murder but received the pardon of God, including Moses and David. For this reason, I am convinced that murder is not the unforgivable sin. Perhaps the most common definition of the unforgivable sin is persistent unbelief, to the point of going to one's death without embracing Christ. Of course, repentance is impossible once death has occurred, so I do not think this is what Jesus had in mind.

Jesus said the unforgivable sin has to do with blasphemy. Blasphemy is a sin that is committed with words. It can be done by spoken words or written words. This sin is extremely common. We live in a culture that routinely blasphemes the name of God. People use the names of God and Jesus as curse words. Blasphemy is uttered every day in movies, on television, in books and magazines, on websites and blogs, and so on. Certain words are still censored on the public airwaves, but blasphemy against God is allowed.

God takes this sin very seriously indeed. Remember the third commandment: "You shall not take the name of the LORD your God in vain, for the LORD will not hold him guiltless who takes His name in vain" (Ex. 20:7). Likewise, in the Lord's Prayer, the first petition Jesus taught His disciples to pray was "Hallowed be Your name" (Matt. 6:9). This is an acknowledgment that God's name is so holy that it should be set apart, consecrated. Because of that, we ought never to use God's blessed name in a frivolous manner. We need to guard our tongues.

Jesus did not say that blasphemy in general is not forgivable. If that were the case, very few people would have any hope of heaven. Indeed, Jesus specifically said that some kinds of blasphemy can be forgiven. He said, "Anyone who speaks a word against the Son of man, it will be forgiven him." Remember, He was saying this to the Pharisees, who had just said a very serious word against the Son of Man, slandering the source of His power. Even broader, Jesus said "every sin and blasphemy will be forgiven men." Presumably, then, we can blaspheme the name of the Father or the name of Jesus and be forgiven for that. (Of course, Jesus was not granting permission for such blasphemy.)

Repudiating What Is Revealed

However, Jesus identified one kind of blasphemy that cannot be forgiven: "blasphemy against the Spirit." He said, "whoever speaks against the Holy Spirit, it will not be forgiven him, either in this age or in the age to come." This prohibition sounds exceedingly strange to our modern ears. We might be tempted to think that it would be more serious to blaspheme the Father or the Son, for we discuss them and study their work often, and we tend to think of the Spirit as subordinate to both of them. Why, then, did Jesus make this curious distinction?

If we search the Scriptures, the answer emerges rather clearly. It is the job of God the Holy Spirit to apply the work of redemption of God the Son to us and to illumine our minds to an understanding of the truth of Christ. But if the Holy Spirit reveals Jesus' identity, so that a person comes to know that Jesus is the Son of God, and that person then begins to suggest that Jesus is not the divine Son of God, he has committed the unpardonable sin by repudiating the work of the Spirit in his heart.

Why do I say this? As I begin to explain my reasoning, let me first remind you of one of the petitions Jesus prayed as He hung on the cross. He said, "Father, forgive them, for they do not know what they do" (Luke 23:34). Notice that Jesus did not request an unqualified forgiveness for His executioners. He attached a reason to His request. He said, "Father, let Your forgiveness extend even to My executioners because they hate Me so much they do not know what they are doing." In short, He prayed for the forgiveness of those who were taking His life because they were committing that ghastly sin in ignorance.

In moral theology, the church historically has made a distinction between what is called "invincible ignorance" and "vincible ignorance." The distinction is simple. Invincible ignorance is ignorance that cannot be overcome. A person who has invincible ignorance and commits a sin could not have known better, and that kind of ignorance can serve as an excuse for him. But vincible ignorance can and should be overcome. There are things about which I am ignorant because I have been completely lazy when it comes to applying myself to the study of truth. I should know certain things about God because He has plainly revealed them to me in the pages of the Bible, but I have not taken the time to visit the Scriptures and study them. Therefore, I will not be able to say on the last day,

"O God, if only You had said something about this I wouldn't have done it." God will say to me: "I *did* say something about it. I put it right there in plain words in the Bible."

The Pharisees were guilty of vincible ignorance when it came to Jesus. They had no excuse for missing the appearance of the Son of God. The Scriptures plainly taught about what the Messiah would do, and there was Jesus performing miracle after miracle right in front of their eyes. How could they miss it? They did not want God in their thinking. Their minds were blinded by their bias against Jesus, and so they lost themselves in willful ignorance.

The Apostle Peter spoke about the Pharisees' ignorance on the day of Pentecost when he told the multitude: "You denied the Holy One and the Just, and asked for a murderer to be granted to you, and killed the Prince of life, whom God raised from the dead, of which we are witnesses. . . . Yet now, brethren, I know that you did it in ignorance, as did also your rulers" (Acts 3:14–17). So, Peter declared that the Pharisees and the other religious leaders were ignorant.

However, we must keep in mind what the writer to the Hebrews had to say on this subject:

> For if we sin willfully after we have received the knowledge of the truth, there no longer remains a sacrifice for sins, but a certain fearful expectation of judgment, and fiery indignation which will devour the adversaries. Anyone who has rejected Moses' law dies without mercy on the testimony of two or three witnesses. Of how much worse punishment, do you suppose, will he be thought worthy who has trampled the Son of God underfoot, counted the blood of the covenant by which he was sanctified a common thing, and insulted the Spirit of grace? (Heb. 10:26–29)

The writer here implies that "trampling the Son of God underfoot" and "insulting the Spirit of grace" are sins worthy of severe punishment. But notice that such punishment is earned when these sins are committed "after we have received the knowledge of the truth." In every person's life, there is a time when he or she does not understand who Jesus is, and if the person blasphemes Jesus in that time, it can be forgiven. But if the Spirit of God reveals the truth to that person, and he afterward tramples the Son of God underfoot and insults the Spirit, there is nothing to expect but judgment. This leads me and many others to conclude that the unforgiveable sin is blaspheming against the Holy Spirit by blaspheming against Christ after the Spirit has revealed to a person that Jesus is the Son of God.

A Gracious Warning

So, it is now possible to see why Jesus gave this warning at this particular time. The Pharisees had just suggested that He was casting out demons by the power of Satan. This was certainly blasphemy, but because their statements were directed at Jesus, they were not technically blaspheming the Spirit. Still, as we saw in the previous chapter, Jesus said He cast out demons by "the finger of God" (Luke 11:20), which was a metaphor for the Spirit. Thus, the Pharisees were coming perilously close to slandering the Spirit, and Jesus was most gracious to warn them.

Whenever the topic of the unforgivable sin arises, people naturally want to know whether a Christian can commit it. People write me letters and come to me at conferences to tell me they are afraid they have committed the unpardonable sin and to ask if I can help them understand their condition before God. When I am asked whether a Christian can commit the unforgivable sin, I always answer yes and no. I believe that, left to ourselves, believers have the capability in our hearts to blaspheme against the Holy Spirit. That capacity is not erased from our hearts by conversion. However, I am convinced that God, in His mercy and grace, keeps believers from ever committing this sin. The Apostle Paul tells us that "He who has begun a good work in you will complete it until the day of Jesus Christ" (Phil. 1:6). Part of that good work involves keeping us from committing this terrible sin. If God did not keep us from doing so, we could and we would. But because He does, we do not. Therein lies our comfort—that the weakness of our flesh is trumped by the grace of God.

Blasphemy is a very serious slander against God. All blasphemy is a serious sin. If you are guilty of routinely blaspheming God by using the name of the Father or the Son in a frivolous manner, you need to plead with God for forgiveness. We have Jesus' assurance in this passage that blasphemy against the Father or Son will be forgiven. Furthermore, I strongly believe that God preserves all those who are His from committing the unforgivable sin of blaspheming the Holy Spirit. Therefore, if you are trusting in Jesus for your salvation, trust Him also to preserve you from blaspheming the Holy Spirit.

62

THE TREE AND ITS FRUITS

Matthew 12:33–37

Either make the tree good and its fruit good, or else make the tree bad and its fruit bad; for a tree is known by its fruit. Brood of vipers! How can you, being evil, speak good things? For out of the abundance of the heart the mouth speaks. A good man out of the good treasure of his heart brings forth good things, and an evil man out of the evil treasure brings forth evil things. But I say to you that for every idle word men may speak, they will give account of it in the day of judgment. For by your words you will be justified, and by your words you will be condemned.

A few years ago, to my astonishment, some young people told me that I had been quoted by name in a Hollywood movie. That piqued my interest. I wondered what I had ever said that could have been considered worthy to quote on the silver screen. Well, it turned out that I was quoted in a vampire movie titled *The Addiction*, which took away quite a bit of my excitement. Apparently the movie was about a philosophy student who became a vampire and then tried to make sense of her condition, and the writers of this film had the stars quote various philosophers from history—Friedrich Nietzsche, Søren Kierkegaard, and others. Then, toward the end, one of the characters quoted me, saying, "R.C. Sproul said we're not sinners because we sin, but we sin because we're sinners." When I heard that, I thought, "Well, it's nice that they gave me credit for that insight, but someone could sue me for plagiarism because that idea certainly did not start with me."

When we say that we are not sinners because we sin, but we sin because we are sinners, we are simply saying that we commit particular sins because there is something essentially wrong at the core of our being, that our sinful actions are simply manifestations of a deeper problem. In the context of His discussion of the unpardonable sin and in the broader context of the assault on Jesus' integrity by the Pharisees, who had accused Him of casting out demons by Beelzebub, the lord of the demons, Jesus talked about how the heart dictates our actions.

Matthew tells us that after warning the Pharisees about the unforgivable sin, Jesus said, **"Either make the tree good and its fruit good, or else make the tree bad and its fruit bad; for a tree is known by its fruit"** (v. 33). Jesus was aware, as was everyone in that agricultural society, that if a tree was rotten, the fruit of that tree, if there was any at all, would not be acceptable for human consumption. If a farmer wanted to produce good fruit, he had to fertilize the tree, prune it, and care for it. Only by keeping the tree healthy could he get good fruit. Thus, the quality of a tree could be known by the fruit it produced, even if no signs of rot were visible. Jesus' implication was that the Pharisees were showing their true character by the things they were saying about Him.

He then added: **"Brood of vipers! How can you, being evil, speak good things? For out of the abundance of the heart the mouth speaks"** (v. 34). In Romans 3, as the Apostle Paul describes the character of fallen man, he quotes from a number of Old Testament passages, including Psalm 140:3: "The poison of asps is under their lips" (Rom. 3:13b). Fallen people are full of venomous hatred toward the things of God, and they express that hatred through their words. That is what the Pharisees have been doing to Him, especially in suggesting that He was casting out demons by Beelzebub. But, of course, it only stood to reason that they would behave in such a way—being evil, they were incapable of speaking good things. They could not be expected to speak the truth, to applaud the good. They could speak only according to their nature. They could speak only those things that are consistent with what they are inside—vipers.

Notice that Jesus said, "For out of the abundance of the heart the mouth speaks." We have a tendency to connect the mouth more to the brain than to the heart. We think that our words reflect the thoughts in our minds. But Jesus said that the driving force behind the words that we use is not the intellect but the heart, the very core of our being. There is a lot of discussion about "core values" in the culture wars today. If we trace the etymology of the word *core*, we find that its ultimate meaning is "heart." When Jesus spoke of the heart, He was speaking about the very center of our existence, that place within us where our true nature is to be found. So, words are not as unimportant as we often seem to think they are. Instead, they are some of the very best "fruits" that indicate what we are like on the inside.

James notes that the tongue is "a little member" (3:5), yet it "sets on fire the course of nature" (v. 6). It can cause massive damage. When I was a little boy and someone would tease me or insult me, I would come home crying to my mother. She would dry my tears, and then she would say, "The next time that fellow makes those unkind comments, you tell him, 'Sticks and stones will break my bones, but words will never hurt me.'" Of course, my mother meant well, but it did not take me long to figure out that that little ditty just was not true. If someone would hit me with a stick and break my arm, the doctor would set the bone and put my arm in a cast, and a few weeks later I would be just fine. If someone would hit me with a stone and put a lump on my forehead, my mother would put some ice on it and a few hours later I would be okay. But the pain inflicted by a word had the power to paralyze my mind and my heart for the rest of my life. That's why the psalmist speaks of restraining his mouth with a muzzle (Ps. 39:1). Unbelievers cannot help but spread poison with their tongue, but Christians can and should guard their words.

Good and Evil Treasure

Jesus continued to hammer away at the truth that what is inside of a man determines what comes out of the man by saying, **"A good man out of the good treasure of his heart brings forth good things, and an evil man out of the evil treasure brings forth evil things"** (v. 35). Just as a good tree must produce good fruit, a good man, because he has good treasure in his heart, brings forth good things. Likewise, just as a bad tree must produce bad fruit, an evil man, having evil treasure in his heart, brings forth evil.

There is a very popular idea in the world today that man, even though he is capable of doing bad things, is basically good. This is a lie. We are not basically good. Instead, we are basically evil. In the same passage where Paul tells us that natural men have the poison of asps under their lips, he writes, "There is none righteous, no, not one" (Rom. 3:10). This is why Jesus told the rich young ruler, "No one is good but One, that is, God" (Matt. 19:17b).

One of my seminary professors, Dr. John Gerstner, was invited to preach in a little country church one Sunday morning. When he got there, the elders welcomed him and then said that an infant was to be baptized that morning, so they asked him to perform the baptism, which he agreed to do. They then went on to explain that that particular church had a unique ritual—the presiding pastor would pin a white rose to the clothing of the baby before he or she was baptized. My professor asked the elders to explain the significance of the white rose, and the elders told him it was a symbol of the baby's innocence. He then said: "I see. What, then, is the significance of the water?" That was the end of the white rose tradition in that church. The elders realized that it made no sense to symbolically declare a baby to be innocent just before he underwent a ritual that symbolized cleansing from sin.

In light of Scripture's clear and abundant teaching on man's fallenness and inherent evil, why did Jesus here talk about "good" people? No one is good in and of himself. But those who are born again of the Holy Spirit are born unto righteousness. One of the fruits of the Holy Spirit in the Christian's life is goodness (Gal. 5:22). As the Holy Spirit works to bring us into conformity to the image of Christ, He changes our hearts so that we can bring forth good fruit.

Jesus spoke of "treasure" in the heart. A treasure is something on which we place great value, and we go to great lengths to protect it from robbers and from decay. But Jesus spoke of both good and evil treasure. We always see treasure as something good. How can treasure be evil? Turning to Romans once again, we see Paul giving unbelievers a fearful warning: "In accordance with your hardness and your impenitent heart you are treasuring up for yourself wrath in the day of wrath and revelation of the righteous judgment of God" (2:5). Those who are not trusting in Christ are building up a horde of sin, which makes them subject to a "mother lode" of wrath. If sin is what is concealed in your heart, nothing can come out of your heart except evil.

Basically, Jesus was saying that everyone has a treasure. So, we all need to stop and ask ourselves: "What is my treasure? What do I think about day after day? What are my desires? Do I treasure Christ and the righteousness His Spirit produces in me? Or do I treasure evil, in which case I am treasuring up wrath?" If you have trouble answering these questions, listen to the words that come forth from your mouth.

Idle or Empty Words

Jesus continued: **"But I say to you that for every idle word men may speak, they will give account of it in the day of judgment"** (v. 36). This statement scares me to death for two reasons.

The first reason is Jesus' use of the term *idle word*. He indicated here that every casual, thoughtless word that we speak is going to find its way into the last judgment. However, some commentators take issue with that rendition and say that Jesus was talking about not casual speech but empty speech, saying that every *empty word* will be brought into the judgment. What is an empty word? It is a promise that has no substance. It could include a very serious promise, such as a wedding vow. If you stand before God and a group of witnesses on your wedding day and promise to be faithful, but you do not do what you promise, the emptiness of that promise will be made clear on the day of judgment. But I think every promise will be so judged. There have been all kinds of times in my life when I have told people that I was going to do something on their behalf but did not do it. In those cases, my words were empty. These empty words will be brought before God in the day of judgment, and I will be asked to give an account.

The second reason this verse scares me is because Jesus spoke here about a day of judgment. As I said earlier, if there is anything we try to delete from the teaching of Jesus, it is His relentless warnings about the last judgment. However, it is an inescapable truth that at the end of our lives, each one of us will have to stand before an omniscient, holy God as He evaluates our lives. We do not like to think about that, so we act as if there will be no judgment. We blithely assume that everyone goes to heaven at death. Not so, according to the Scriptures. It greatly behooves us, while we still live, to prepare ourselves for that day.

When I was teaching at the college level, I had a brilliant student who went on to graduate school at Harvard. He was studying the physiology of the brain, which seems to be the last frontier of scientific inquiry. I saw him on one occasion while he was still in graduate school, and he said, "R.C., I think I know how the last judgment is going to work." When I asked him to explain, he said: "The brain is an amazing thing. It's like a gigantic computer that records every thought, every impression, every incident of your life, awake or asleep. It's all there, indelibly etched on the brain. I read in Scripture that at the last judgment every tongue will be silenced and there will be no protests as the whole world is brought before God and shown to be guilty. I think God is going to take each person's brain and push 'play' on the controls so that the brain will pour out all of its memories. We'll stand there listening to ourselves condemn ourselves."

Well, that was an interesting idea. I do not think God needs to tap our memories to know what we have done, said, and thought in our lifetimes. However, I do think my friend was close to the truth in saying that our own words will condemn us.

Justified or Condemned

Finally, Jesus said something very strange: **"For by your words you will be justified, and by your words you will be condemned"** (v. 37). I relentlessly teach and preach the biblical doctrine of justification by faith alone. That means no one is justified by anything he does or says. But here Jesus said we will be justified or condemned by our words. What did He mean?

Was He possibly speaking about our profession of faith in Him? Paul writes: "If you confess with your mouth the Lord Jesus and believe in your heart that God has raised Him from the dead, you will be saved. For with the heart one believes unto righteousness, and with the mouth confession is made unto salvation" (Rom. 10:9–10). It is true that we must profess our faith, but no one is ever justified by a profession of faith. Anyone can say, "I believe in Jesus." As we saw when we studied the Sermon on the Mount, Jesus said, "Not everyone who says to Me, 'Lord, Lord,' shall enter the kingdom of heaven" (Matt. 7:21a). Jesus made it clear that it is possible to say the words without meaning them.

Jesus was not speaking here about the doctrine of justification. He was talking about manifesting what is in the heart. When we face God at the last judgment, He will rehearse the records of our own mouths. If that record contains a constant stream of empty words, those words will condemn us. On the other hand, if the words that came out of the treasure of our hearts reveal our affection for Christ and our love for the things of God, then God will bless us in that day.

63

ASKING FOR A SIGN

Matthew 12:38–42

Then some of the scribes and Pharisees answered, saying, "Teacher, we want to see a sign from You." But He answered and said to them, "An evil and adulterous generation seeks after a sign, and no sign will be given to it except the sign of the prophet Jonah. For as Jonah was three days and three nights in the belly of the great fish, so will the Son of Man be three days and three nights in the heart of the earth. The men of Nineveh will rise up in the judgment with this generation and condemn it, because they repented at the preaching of Jonah; and indeed a greater than Jonah is here. The queen of the South will rise up in the judgment with this generation and condemn it, for she came from the ends of the earth to hear the wisdom of Solomon; and indeed a greater than Solomon is here."

We have focused for several chapters on a series of disputes between Jesus and the Pharisees. It began when the Pharisees questioned why Jesus let His disciples pluck heads of grain on the Sabbath (Matt. 12:2). It continued when Jesus healed a man's withered hand on the Sabbath, angering the Pharisees so greatly they began plotting His death (vv. 9–14). It reached something of a crescendo when the Pharisees theorized that Jesus was casting out demons by the power of Beelzebub, which prompted Jesus to warn them about the unpardonable sin and the importance of a "good" heart as opposed to an evil one (vv. 22–37).

In the passage we are addressing in this chapter, the dispute goes on. Matthew tells us it was ignited anew when the scribes and Pharisees banded together and presented Jesus with an exceedingly ridiculous demand: **Then some of the scribes and Pharisees answered, saying, "Teacher, we want to see a sign from You"** (v. 38).

When the scribes and Pharisees asked for a sign, they were asking Him to do what we usually think of as a miracle. But while our English Bibles do use the word *miracle* from time to time, it is not a word that is found in the original language. There is no single word for miracle in the New Testament. Rather, there are three words that are used to describe various events, and it is possible to extrapolate the concept of a miracle from these three scenarios. The three words are *wonder, power*, and, perhaps most common, *sign*. John especially uses the word *sign* in his Gospel.

A sign points beyond itself to something else. In other words, Jesus' acts of healing, raising people from death, feeding the five thousand, turning of the water into wine, and so on were *sign*ificant. They not only showed the power of Jesus but revealed that He was authorized by God to perform His works. I have already mentioned how Nicodemus, when he came to Jesus by night, said to Him, "Rabbi, we know that You are a teacher come from God; for no one can do these signs that You do unless God is with him" (John 3:2b). There was much that Nicodemus did not understand, but he was right on this matter.

So, why did the scribes and Pharisees ask Him to show them a sign? We might have expected Him to say: "You want to see a sign? Where have you been? I've been giving scores of signs, but you still don't believe in Me. You think I'm a servant of Satan. You want one more?" But I think they were asking to see a bigger sign than Jesus had yet done, something even more significant than healing a leper or giving sight to the blind. Perhaps they were a bit jaded because they had their own traveling healers in the ancient world, men who basically were charlatans and only pretended to heal people. Perhaps they suspected Jesus of the same chicanery, so they asked to see a sign that no other healer could possibly perform.

An Evil and Adulterous Generation

Jesus responding by telling them what kind of person would ask for such a sign: **He answered and said to them, "An evil and adulterous generation seeks after a sign"** (v. 39a). Jesus said the scribes and Pharisees showed they were part of "an evil and adulterous" generation for asking for a sign. That sounds rather severe, but it is a warning we need to hear. After all, we sometimes think how nice it would be if God would give us a sign. We daydream about how easy it would be to be faithful after seeing such a sign. But God does not tend to answer such requests. Why? He is not standing by to perform at our beck and call. He is God and we are His creatures, and it is evil for us to demand that He prove Himself to us.

Besides, if we want a sign from God, all we need to do is open our Bibles. If we want to see the transcendent power of almighty God at work before our very eyes, we should read and listen to the Scriptures. It is God's Word, and there is no force on this planet as powerful as that Word. The critics attack it day in and day out, committing vandalism as they try to neutralize, diminish, or destroy the power of the Word. But it will not go away, because it is filled with the power of God. It has been turning people's lives upside down since it was inspired by the Holy Spirit.

During the inerrancy controversy in the 1980s, I was invited to represent the International Council on Biblical Inerrancy to a seminary faculty that had changed its stand on Scripture. I went alone and debated the entire faculty on the subject of the trustworthiness of Scripture. When the debate was over and I was walking to the parking lot, the dean of the institution walked with me. He said, "You know, I don't understand why this means so much to you." I told him: "If you take away this book, you take away my life. I'll fight what you are trying to do until my last breath, because you are undermining the Word of God instead of proclaiming it, obeying it, and defending it."

Of course, people do not see the Bible for the incredible sign that it is. Books seem so ordinary, even one that is bound in leather and printed with red letters here and there. People want to look up in the sky and see a message from God written there. Of course, even that would not make a difference. James Montgomery Boice used to say: "If God decided to give the whole world a sign about Jesus, He could arrange the stars in the sky in such a way that they would spell out the message, "Jesus is My only begotten Son." But if God did that, people would simply say, 'I wonder what astronomical perturbation caused that chance alignment of the stars?'" He was right. No one would believe a message written in the stars any more than they believe the Bible, because they are part of an evil and adulterous generation. The do not believe because they do not *want* to believe.

The Sign of Jonah

Jesus said, **"No sign will be given to [this generation] except the sign of the prophet Jonah"** (v. 39b). What did He mean? Jonah had been dead for centuries. How could he give a sign? Jesus did not mean that Jonah would give a sign but that God would give a sign *like* that which happened to Jonah. Jesus explained a bit more: **"For as Jonah was three days and three nights in the belly of the great fish, so will the Son of Man be three days and three nights**

in the heart of the earth" (v. 40).

Critics today look at this text and raise an objection, and I can imagine that the Pharisees would have done the same. They say that if Jesus was foretelling His resurrection here, He made a mistake, because He died on Friday afternoon and rose on Sunday morning. That is not three days and three nights. So, the critics say, "See, Sproul, you tell people that this is the Word of God and that it's infallible and inerrant, but here's a glaring error."

To properly understand this text, we need to know something about the common speech of the Hebrews of the first century. When they said "three days and three nights," they meant three calendar days. Jesus spent part of Friday, all of Saturday, and a small part of Sunday in His tomb, but in Hebrew terms, that was reckoned as three full days, or "three days and three nights." Jesus saw no need to change the vocabulary He used to communicate to people in the first century in order to shut the mouths of the obstreperous in the twenty-first century. More important, the book of Jonah says that the prophet was in the belly of the fish for "three days and three nights" (Jonah 1:17), and Jesus said He would be in "the heart of the earth" for the same length of time.

When I was a senior in seminary, I had to do a Hebrew exegesis paper. In the paper, I endeavored to show that most of the book of Jonah belongs to the historical literary genre. Well, I got an A+ on the paper, and my professor called me into his office and said: "This is the first time I've ever heard anyone argue reasonably that most of the book of Jonah is in the genre of historical narrative rather than poetry. This needs to be published." I could not believe what he was saying. There was nothing in that paper that had not been said a thousand times by orthodox scholars for two millennia. I did not say it, but I was thinking, "Where have you been?" Actually, I knew where he had been. He had studied at a liberal college, a liberal seminary, and a liberal graduate school. He had never been exposed to an orthodox interpretation of the book of Jonah. All it took was one paper by a student to convince him of the literary genre of that portion of the Old Testament.

The critical scholars have a field day with Jonah, but they might as well not be reading the text. Here's an example: Jonah 2:5 says: "The waters surrounded me, even to my soul; the deep closed around me; weeds were wrapped around my head." The critical scholars read that and say: "There would not have been seaweed in the belly of the fish. This must be mythology." The only problem is that Jonah was not complaining about seaweed in the belly of the fish. He was complaining about seaweed in the sea. It was the sea, not the fish, that threatened his life. He was drowning. He was sinking in the sea and seaweed was wrapped around his head. At that point, God sent a fish to swallow him and then spit him out three days later on the dry land. The fish was the instrument of Jonah's deliverance, not of his torment. I wonder how some of these scholarly interpretations come about.

Just as Jonah was thrown into the sea so that the sailors on the ship might be saved, Jesus was thrown into the depth of the earth for our redemption. He was silent for three days. Then, on the morning of the third day, God the Father took the earth in His hand and shook it, and brought His Son to life again. That was the sign of all signs, the resurrection of Christ.

Paul dealt with this kind of ignorance when he debated the philosophers in Athens. He saw their monument to an unknown god and said:

> "The One whom you worship without knowing, Him I proclaim to you: God, who made the world and everything in it, since He is Lord of heaven and earth, does not dwell in temples made with hands. Nor is He worshiped with men's hands, as though He needed anything, since He gives to all life, breath, and all things. . . . Therefore, since we are the offspring of God, we ought not to think that the Divine Nature is like gold or silver or stone, something shaped by art and man's devising. Truly, these times of ignorance God overlooked, but now commands all men everywhere to repent, because He has appointed a day on which He will judge the world in righteousness by the Man whom He has ordained. He has given assurance of this to all by raising Him from the dead." (Acts 17:23b–31)

When Paul spoke of "times of ignorance," he was talking to the philosophers of Athens, who were worshiping idols they had made with their own hands. Paul warned them that God had put up with such silliness for centuries, but the days of His forbearance were over, and He was commanding all men to repent. What changed? Why did God put up with something for thousands of years, only to announce one day that He would not put up with it anymore? It was because He had "appointed a day on which He [would] judge the world in righteousness by the Man whom He [had] ordained." Furthermore, He had "given assurance of this to all by raising Him from the dead."

No sign authenticates the person of Christ more completely and powerfully than His resurrection from the dead. We simply will not get anything greater than this sign. If we will not acquiesce to it, we will not benefit from the ministry of Jesus. We will remain in the ranks of the scribes and the Pharisees, the "evil and adulterous generation."

The Testimony of Pagans

Matthew then tells us that Jesus said to the scribes and Pharisees: **"The men of Nineveh will rise up in the judgment with this generation and condemn it, because they repented at the preaching of Jonah; and indeed a greater than Jonah is here. The queen of the South will rise up in the judgment with this generation and condemn it, for she came from the ends of the earth to hear the wisdom of Solomon; and indeed a greater than Solomon is here"** (vv. 41–42). He was telling them that people from the pagan city of Nineveh would testify against them at the judgment before the throne of God because they had had the good sense to repent at the preaching of Jonah. They listened to Jonah, but the scribes and Pharisees would not listen to Jesus, "a greater than Jonah." Likewise, the Queen of Sheba would testify against them at the judgment, because she had made a lengthy and arduous journey to hear the wisdom of Solomon while the scribes and Pharisees demanded that Jesus, "a greater than Solomon," do something for them.

This was not someone in league with Beelzebub. This was the Son of God that the scribes and Pharisees were rejecting, denying, hating, and taunting with demands for a sign. Their hardness of heart is terrible to behold.

64

WHO ARE MY BROTHERS?

Matthew 12:43–50

"When an unclean spirit goes out of a man, he goes through dry places, seeking rest, and finds none. Then he says, 'I will return to my house from which I came.' And when he comes, he finds it empty, swept, and put in order. Then he goes and takes with him seven other spirits more wicked than himself, and they enter and dwell there; and the last state of that man is worse than the first. So shall it also be with this wicked generation." While He was still talking to the multitudes, behold, His mother and brothers stood outside, seeking to speak with Him. Then one said to Him, "Look, Your mother and Your brothers are standing outside, seeking to speak with You." But He answered and said to the one who told Him, "Who is My mother and who are My brothers?" And He stretched out His hand toward His disciples and said, "Here are My mother and My brothers! For whoever does the will of My Father in heaven is My brother and sister and mother."

I am a strong proponent of expository preaching, which involves preaching through whole books of the Bible verse by verse. One of the most valuable aspects of this type of preaching, in my opinion, is that it prevents the preacher from beating the same drum Sunday after Sunday and forces him to expound on the whole counsel of God. The minister who practices expository preaching does not go through the Bible picking and choosing what to preach about each week. Rather, the next text is already chosen for him, and the topic or topics that must be preached are right there; he has to take them as they come.

One of the downsides of expository preaching is that sometimes the minister encounters a text that is difficult to apprehend, and the passage we are examining in this chapter is, for me, one of those texts. I am not at all sure I understand what Jesus was talking about here with respect to a demon who leaves a possessed person, wanders in the desert for a time, and then goes back. I have read what others have said and written about this passage, but I am still not convinced as to its meaning.

The problem is that in this passage we are dealing with the extremely difficult subject of demonology. Neither the Old Testament nor the New Testament gives us any extensive teaching on the nature and behavior of demons. We know that they are real. We know that Jesus had a profoundly important ministry of exorcism during His ministry, and obviously He knew much more about the habits of demons than we do. However, our knowledge in this area remains very sketchy.

Jesus uttered these words as part of a series of disputes with the Pharisees. As we saw several chapters ago, the Pharisees accused Jesus of casting out demons by the power of Beelzebub, that is, Satan, which prompted Jesus to warn them against committing the unforgivable sin of blasphemy against the Holy Spirit. Then, as we saw in the previous chapter, the scribes and Pharisees demanded that Jesus show them "a sign," or a miracle. In response, Jesus told them they were part of "an evil and adulterous generation," and the only sign they would see would be the sign of the prophet Jonah. He reminded them that, at the preaching of Jonah, the pagans of Nineveh repented, but one greater than Jonah was in their midst. So, Jesus was calling the Pharisees to repent, to recognize and acknowledge that the kingdom of God was right there in front of them, and they were in danger of missing it. I suspect that in these words that Jesus uttered about this demon, He was continuing to call the Pharisees to repentance.

A Restless Demon

Matthew tells us that immediately on the heels of his rebuke of the Pharisees for demanding a sign, Jesus said: **"When an unclean spirit goes out of a man, he goes through dry places, seeking rest, and finds none. Then he says, 'I will return to my house from which I came.' And when he comes, he finds it empty, swept, and put in order"** (vv. 43–44). In this scenario that Jesus sketched out, "an unclean spirit," or a demon, goes out of a man, apparently not as a result of exorcism but on its own volition. He said that the demon wanders through "dry places," presumably desert. This scenario fits with an Old Testament association between demons and dry places. There seems to have been a notion that deserts were places that were denied the blessing of God as represented by rainfall (see Isa. 13:19–22; Jer. 17:6; Mal. 1:3).

The demon's purpose in this wandering is to try to find rest, but it fails in that quest. I find it interesting that this demon exhibits a restlessness that is characteristic of fallen men and women. Augustine is famous for his prayer, "You made us for yourself and our hearts find no peace until they rest in you."[1] He was making a profound observation about unconverted human beings. A person may be successful, powerful, attractive, and exceedingly rich, having all of the goods that this world offers, but if he is outside of Christ he is tormented by a sense of emptiness and restlessness in his soul. Most people go through life in this state of restlessness. Obviously, the demons have this sense of restlessness because there is nothing of God in their lives. They are completely alienated from their Creator. How horrible it is to contemplate that unsaved human beings are in the same condition as demons.

Eventually, in Jesus' scenario, the demon decides to return to the man it left, whom the demon regards as "my house." It considers the man it left to be its rightful habitation. But when it comes back, it finds the man "empty, swept, and put in order." This is one of the more difficult parts of this passage. Jesus' words paint a picture of a positive change, yet the man is still susceptible to demonic possession, so I believe he remains not only empty of the demon but empty of the Spirit of God that alone could prevent the demon from returning. Perhaps the man had cleaned up his life in something like a self-reformation. Perhaps he gave up a vice or vices, but there is no salvation in that. A vacuum remains in his soul, and whereas nature abhors a vacuum, this demon likes it.

Many misconceptions about salvation abound, and one is that when we are born again, we are restored to the condition of innocence that Adam and Eve enjoyed before the fall. According to this view, salvation is paradise regained immediately. After all, Jesus paid for our sins, so we must be innocent in the sight of God. But if the only thing that has happened to us is that Jesus has paid for our sins, we will not get into heaven. Jesus' atoning death took care of the negative problem of our sin. However, God requires not only that we be innocent of sin but that we come into His presence with true righteousness. That's why I stress the double transfer that is involved in our salvation—our sins are imputed to Jesus on the cross and His righteousness is transferred to us by faith. Therefore, when I put my trust in Christ, He takes my sin and gives me His righteousness, so that when I stand before God, I stand clothed in the righteousness of Christ.

But even that is not all that happens. When we are converted, the Spirit of God comes to live inside of us. Every believer is indwelt by the Holy Spirit, and where the Spirit of God dwells, no demon can take up residence. I do not believe that demons can possess genuine Christians. They can harass, tempt, and annoy

[1] Augustine, *Confessions* (Harmondsworth, England: Penguin Books: 1961), 21.

Christians, but they cannot possess them. In the Christian life, there is no such thing as a vacuum, because God Himself has come into that life.

However, some people have a false sense of repentance, a repentance of the flesh—self-reformation, if you will. This is what Jesus was warning the Pharisees about. It was as if He were saying to them: "You men are dedicated to the achievement of holiness and righteousness, but you think you can be righteous on your own. If you have a bad habit, you confess it and break it. But you've never come to Me. You are resting on your own righteousness, your own performance. You're like this man who had a demon. The demon left, so he cleaned up his house. But he had no way to keep the demon from returning. That's you. You're empty inside."

Jesus then spelled out the danger of leaving the house empty: **"Then he goes and takes with him seven other spirits more wicked than himself, and they enter and dwell there; and the last state of that man is worse than the first. So shall it also be with this wicked generation"** (v. 45). Jesus did not say why the demon gathers seven other demons more wicked than itself; there is no indication that the demon needs help to move back into the man. In any case, the man ends up far worse off than he was before. Then Jesus added, "So shall it also be with this wicked generation," that is, the Pharisees. The obvious message is that self-reformation was not enough. The Pharisees needed a reformation from above, a conversion, a new birth. So, this was a stern warning, a forceful call to repentance.

We must be very careful about what kind of repentance we manifest. It must not be merely repentance of the flesh. It must come from the heart. But it will come from the heart only if the Holy Spirit has taken up residence there.

Jesus' Mother and Brothers

I want to conclude our consideration of Matthew 12 by looking briefly at an incident that Matthew records at the end of this chapter. It is unrelated to the discussion about evil spirits and to the larger context of Jesus' disputes with the Pharisees, but it is very instructive as to discipleship.

Matthew writes: **While He was still talking to the multitudes, behold, His mother and brothers stood outside, seeking to speak with Him. Then one said to Him, "Look, Your mother and Your brothers are standing outside, seeking to speak with You"** (vv. 46–47). This is Matthew's first mention of Jesus' brothers, who also are mentioned in the other three Gospels and in Acts. The fact that Jesus had brothers and that Mary was obviously their mother has caused no small amount of consternation for our friends in the Roman Catholic Church. They have a doctrine called the perpetual virginity of Mary. They teach that after Jesus was born of the Virgin Mary, she remained a virgin until the day she died. This idea has absolutely no foundation in the Bible; indeed the evidence, including these verses from Matthew, strongly refutes Rome's position.

Protestantism historically has recognized that our Lord's mother was one of the greatest women who ever walked the face of the earth, but we teach that she is not to be an object of worship. Rome, by contrast, has shrines to Mary all over the world, and its priests say Masses dedicated to her. Roman Catholic authorities insist that the church practices veneration of Mary but does not worship her. John Calvin, however, said that the Roman distinction between veneration and worship is a distinction without a difference. If you are in the Roman Catholic Church, I challenge you to read the New Testament and try to find an example of the veneration of Mary as it is practiced by Rome or anything that teaches that it should be practiced. It's not to be found.

Some scholars in the Roman Catholic Church say that these "brothers" of Jesus were really sons of Joseph by a previous marriage. Others argue that the word translated here as "brothers" (*adelphos*) can also refer to cousins, so these were not necessarily Jesus' brothers. I think that's nonsense. It seems very clear that these are the blood relatives of Jesus.

Jesus did not go out to His mother and brothers, nor did He invite them in, or at least not immediately. Matthew tells us: **He answered and said to the one who told Him, "Who is My mother and who are My brothers?" And He stretched out His hand toward His disciples and said, "Here are My mother and My brothers! For whoever does the will of My Father in heaven is My brother and sister and mother"** (vv. 48–50).

At first glance, this response seems to be discourteous and dishonoring of His family. However, I do not think that is the case. Jesus was about His Father's business, and His mother and brothers were trying to interrupt him in the middle of His preaching. Mark tells us that "His own people" concluded that He was "out of His mind" (3:21), and it was soon afterward that His family appeared and asked for Him (v. 31). Perhaps they wanted to take Him home with them, to try to bring Him to His senses.

Jesus seized a valuable teaching moment when this happened. He asked, "Who is My mother and who are My brothers?" With a wave of His hand, He then identified His disciples as His mother and brothers, saying, "For whoever does the will of My Father in heaven is My brother and sister and mother." Two points need to be mentioned here.

First, these statements in no way lessen the importance of family relationships, but they show once again that Jesus regarded love for Him as more important than love for family members. Earlier, we saw that Jesus said: "He who loves father or mother more than Me is not worthy of Me. And he who loves son or daughter more than Me is not worthy of Me" (10:37). He was making a similar point in identifying His disciples as His brothers, sisters, and mother.

Second, these words of Jesus point to the beautiful doctrine of adoption into the family of God. Yes, Jesus was the earthly son of Mary, and He honored her and loved her; He even made provision for John to care for her as He hung on the cross (John 19:26–27). But in a higher sense, Jesus understood that He was the Son of God, and He was declaring here that all of those who put their trust in Him become His brothers and sisters. It is only when someone is truly converted that He has the ability to do the will of God. They do it because they have been adopted by the Father.

65

THE PARABLE OF THE SOWER, PART 1

Matthew 13:1–17

On the same day Jesus went out of the house and sat by the sea. And great multitudes were gathered together to Him, so that He got into a boat and sat; and the whole multitude stood on the shore. Then He spoke many things to them in parables, saying: "Behold, a sower went out to sow. And as he sowed, some seed fell by the wayside; and the birds came and devoured them. Some fell on stony places, where they did not have much earth; and they immediately sprang up because they had no depth of earth. But when the sun was up they were scorched, and because they had no root they withered away. And some fell among thorns, and the thorns sprang up and choked them. But others fell on good ground and yielded a crop: some a hundredfold, some sixty, some thirty. He who has ears to hear, let him hear!" And the disciples came and said to Him, "Why do You speak to them in parables?" He answered and said to them, "Because it has been given to you to know the mysteries of the kingdom of heaven, but to them it has not been given. For whoever has, to him more will be given, and he will have abundance; but whoever does not have, even what he has will be taken away from him. Therefore I speak to them in parables, because seeing they do not see, and hearing they do not hear, nor do they understand. And in them the prophecy of Isaiah is fulfilled, which says:

> 'Hearing you will hear and shall not understand,
> And seeing you will see and not perceive;
> For the hearts of this people have grown dull.

> Their ears are hard of hearing,
> And their eyes they have closed,
> Lest they should see with their eyes and hear with their ears,
> Lest they should understand with their hearts and turn,
> So that I should heal them.'

> But blessed are your eyes for they see, and your ears for they hear; for assuredly, I say to you that many prophets and righteous men desired to see what you see, and did not see it, and to hear what you hear, and did not hear it."

We have been working our way through a series of disputes between Jesus and the Pharisees (recounted by Matthew in chapter 12 of his Gospel), a foreshadowing of the titanic conflict that was to follow. These disputes began in or near a grainfield (12:1–8) and continued in a synagogue (vv. 9–14). The climax occurred after Jesus healed a man who was demon-possessed, blind, and mute, prompting the Pharisees to assert that He was casting out demons by the power of Satan (vv. 22–45). Matthew never specifies where this last dispute occurred, but it appears it was in a house, for here at the opening of chapter 13 he writes, **On the same day Jesus went out of the house and sat by the sea** (v. 1). Jesus, it seems, had been ministering in a house, and when He had finally said all He needed to say to the Pharisees, He strolled down to the beach.

However, Jesus was given no time of solitude there on the shore. Matthew tells us, **And great multitudes were gathered together to Him, so that He got into a boat and sat; and the whole multitude stood on the shore** (v. 2). Crowds of people came to Jesus again, eager to hear His teaching. To accommodate them, He got into a boat and put out a little from the shore, and the people stood on the shore to hear Him. It was customary for the people of God in that time to stand for long periods of time in order to avail themselves of His instruction.

Then Matthew notes, **He spoke many things to them in parables** (v. 3a). What follows is the first parable from Jesus that Matthew records, but several others follow it immediately as Jesus delivers the third great discourse found in this book. Every parable Jesus spoke is important and useful, but the first parable in Matthew's record—the parable of the sower—is perhaps the most important of all, having a certain critical significance.

We have a tendency to think that parables were merely illustrations Jesus employed to help make His points. There is a sense in which that is true, but it is a vast over-simplification of the actual function of parables. The word *parable* is made up of a prefix, *para*, and a root, the verb *ballō*. *Para* means "alongside." A paralegal is someone who comes alongside a lawyer to provide legal help. A parachurch ministry comes alongside the church to aid it in its mission. *Baleo* means "to throw or hurl." So, literally, a parable is something that is thrown alongside of something else. In the case of Jesus, a parable was an illustration or a restatement of a truth that He "threw in" with His teaching.

In this chapter, I want to focus on Matthew 13:10–17, which records Jesus' response to a question from the disciples as to the purpose of parables. With that understanding under our belts, we will then move on to a consideration of the parable of the sower and Jesus' interpretation of it in the next two chapters.

The Doctrine of Election

Matthew tells us, **And the disciples came and said to Him, "Why do You speak to them in parables?"** (v. 10). They were asking Jesus a question about His methodology. Something about this teaching technique caught their attention, but Jesus' purpose in using it was not readily apparent to them. The answer Jesus gave them comes as a shock to many who read it today, and perhaps it was shocking to the disciples, as well.

According to Matthew: **He answered and said to them, "Because it has been given to you to know the mysteries of the kingdom of heaven, but to them it has not been given. For whoever has, to him more will be given, and he will have abundance; but whoever does not have, even what he has will be taken away from him. Therefore I speak to them in parables, because seeing they do not see, and hearing they do not hear, nor do they understand"** (vv. 11–13).

This answer drips with the doctrine of election. There is no way to get around it. Some people believe the doctrine of election is found only in Paul's letter to the Romans or in his letter to the Ephesians, but if you pay close attention to the Scriptures, it appears again and again. Here, it jumps up in full view, for Jesus declared that some people are permitted to understand "the mysteries of the kingdom of heaven," but others are not so permitted. Those who have been given new hearts so that they are able to understand the things of God are then given further instruction, but those who have not received the ability to understand are denied divine truth. These latter people have fully functional eyes and ears, but they cannot understand the underlying meaning in biblical teaching.

At this point, someone might raise an objection, arguing that there is nothing here that points to divine election and that the disciples see and hear merely because they have been with Jesus and have learned much. They have received extensive exposure to His teaching and have begun to grasp who He is. Others, however, have not been His students, so they have not had the benefit of hearing the mysteries of the kingdom of God explained by the King Himself. Perhaps Jesus was using parables so that they could get it, too. If that is your thinking, let me ask you to stay tuned, for there is more to come.

Matthew tells us that Jesus continued, saying: **"And in them the prophecy of Isaiah is fulfilled, which says:**

> **'Hearing you will hear and shall not understand,**
> **And seeing you will see and not perceive;**
> **For the hearts of this people have grown dull.**
> **Their ears are hard of hearing,**
> **And their eyes they have closed,**
> **Lest they should see with their eyes and hear with their ears,**
> **Lest they should understand with their hearts and turn,**
> **So that I should heal them.'"** (vv. 14–15)

Over and over again in this Gospel we have seen Matthew connecting things Jesus did and said with Old Testament prophecies. Here, Matthew does not need to do the connecting, for Jesus did it Himself. He told the disciples that He was using parables because some were elect and some were not—just as it was foretold by the prophet Isaiah.

A Prophet of Judgment

This quotation appears in the sixth chapter of Isaiah's prophecy, which recounts his dramatic vision of God, high and lifted up on His heavenly throne, as the seraphim cried out, "Holy, holy, holy is the Lord of hosts; the whole earth is full of His glory!" (Isa. 6:3). After beholding this splendor, Isaiah cried out: "Woe is me, for I am undone! Because I am a man of unclean lips, and I dwell in the midst of a people of unclean lips; for my eyes have seen the King, the Lord of hosts" (v. 5). He abhorred himself when he gazed upon the holy God.

While he was in this state of misery, overcome by the weight of his guilt and unworthiness, one of the seraphim flew to him with a hot coal taken from the altar with tongs, and he touched it to Isaiah's mouth, saying, "Behold, this has touched your lips; your iniquity is taken away, and your sin purged" (v. 7b). After that, he heard God asking, "Whom shall I send, and who will go for Us?" (v. 8b). Isaiah replied (probably through blistered lips), "Here am I! Send me" (v. 8c). So, Isaiah was commissioned as a prophet that day.

However, the instructions that God gave to Isaiah are very interesting:

> And He said, "Go, and tell this people:

> 'Keep on hearing, but do not understand;
> Keep on seeing, but do not perceive.'
> Make the heart of this people dull,
> And their ears heavy,
> And shut their eyes;
> Lest they see with their eyes,
> And hear with their ears,
> And understand with their heart,
> And return and be healed." (vv. 9–10)

What a mission Isaiah was given. Can you imagine being ordained to the task of telling people, "Look, but don't see; hear, but don't understand"? Can you imagine working to make people's hearts dull, to clog their ears, and to cover their eyes, all so that they would *not* understand? God was sending Isaiah as a prophet of judgment, because God had had enough of people who did not want to hear or see the truth.

The New Testament tells us that we are born with an impulse to exclude God from our thinking. We want nothing to do with Him. Our basic posture is the same as that of Adam and Eve after they sinned. They hid from God. They tried to escape the presence of God. Many today are like that. They may attend church services and sit under the preaching of the Word of God, but they do not care for what they hear and they want no part of God and Christ.

When Isaiah heard these instructions for his ministry, he cried out, "Lord, how long?" (v. 11a). God replied:

> Until the cities are laid waste and without inhabitant,
> The houses are without a man,
> The land is utterly desolate,
> The LORD has removed men far away,
> And the forsaken places are many in the midst of the land.
> But yet a tenth will be in it,
> And will return and be for consuming,
> As a terebinth tree or as an oak,
> Whose stump remains when it is cut down.
> So the holy seed shall be its stump. (vv. 11b–13)

Do you see what God was saying here? He was explaining to Isaiah that He had kept for Himself a remnant, "a tenth," from which He would raise up His people again. But Isaiah's mission was to the rest, to clog their ears and blind their eyes.

The Blessing of the Disciples

Matthew then tells us that Jesus said to the disciples: **"But blessed are your eyes for they see, and your ears for they hear; for assuredly, I say to you that many prophets and righteous men desired to see what you see, and did not see it, and to hear what you hear, and did not hear it"** (vv. 16–17). Here the disciples receive a hint of the blessing that is theirs—they can see and hear God's truth, a truth that many prophets and righteous men earnestly hoped to see and did not. Abraham longed to see these things, but he never saw them. Moses would have given anything to have seen what the disciples were seeing, but he died with that aspiration unfulfilled. What of David? What of Isaiah? What of Jeremiah? What of Amos? What of Hosea? All of those who lived in ages past looked to the future, looked to the promises that God had given to them, but they died in faith without seeing and without hearing. The disciples, however, had seen and heard.

So, in answer to the disciples' question, Jesus explained that He used parables both to reveal and to conceal. To those who had "ears to hear," the parables were words of life. To those whose hearts were hardened and who could not hear so as to understand, the parables were indecipherable stories, impenetrable mysteries. The first of them was the parable of the sower.

66

THE PARABLE OF THE SOWER, PART 2

Matthew 13:1–9, 18–23

On the same day Jesus went out of the house and sat by the sea. And great multitudes were gathered together to Him, so that He got into a boat and sat; and the whole multitude stood on the shore. Then He spoke many things to them in parables, saying: "Behold, a sower went out to sow. And as he sowed, some seed fell by the wayside; and the birds came and devoured them. Some fell on stony places, where they did not have much earth; and they immediately sprang up because they had no depth of earth. But when the sun was up they were scorched, and because they had no root they withered away. And some fell among thorns, and the thorns sprang up and choked them. But others fell on good ground and yielded a crop: some a hundredfold, some sixty, some thirty. He who has ears to hear, let him hear! . . . Therefore hear the parable of the sower: When anyone hears the word of the kingdom, and does not understand it, then the wicked one comes and snatches away what was sown in his heart. This is he who received seed by the wayside. But he who received the seed on stony places, this is he who hears the word and immediately receives it with joy; yet he has no root in himself, but endures only for a while. For when tribulation or persecution arises because of the word, immediately he stumbles. Now he who received seed among the thorns is he who hears the word, and the cares of this world and the deceitfulness of riches choke the word, and he becomes unfruitful. But he who received seed on the good ground is he who hears the word and understands it, who indeed bears fruit and produces: some a hundredfold, some sixty, some thirty."

The parable of the sower is unique in its structure. Normally, parables are interpreted as communicating one basic message, not as allegories with several points to be made. Looking for allegorical interpretations in most of Jesus' parables leads to all kinds of trouble. The temptation is to treat them like wet clay that can be shaped to teach whatever truth is desired. However, the parable of the sower *does* have an allegorical interpretation, as we learn when Matthew gives us Jesus' explanation of its meaning (vv. 18–23).

This parable illustrates four different responses to the preaching of the Word of God, only one of which is ultimately positive. For this reason, the parable of the sower is intensely comforting to me, and I believe it should be comforting to everyone who is called to preach the gospel. This story involves a man who sows seed in a field, and the sower is representative of Christ Himself, while the seed is the gospel of the kingdom of God. However, not all of the seed bears fruit, and that was certainly true in the ministry of Jesus. So, I find comfort in the fact that Jesus, the greatest preacher in the history of the world, whose cogency was without peer, whose eloquence was never marred by the influences of sin, was rejected by the vast majority of those who heard Him preach and teach. Not that this widespread rejection was a good thing in and of itself, but it reminds me that the power of preaching is not in the preacher or in the hearer. It resides in the Spirit of almighty God alone.

In order to demonstrate the various responses to the Word, Jesus crafted an illustration based on an agricultural economy. He began by saying, **"Behold, a sower went out to sow"** (v. 3b). In other words, a farmer set to work to plant seeds. Notice, however, that Jesus said nothing about the farmer preparing his field before scattering his seeds. This was because the method of sowing seed in the ancient world was very different from the methods typically used in the West today. Modern farmers usually plow their fields and prepare the soil meticulously before planting seeds. By contrast, ancient farmers sowed their seeds first, then plowed the seeds into the earth, and that was how it was done in Israel. However, this method was inefficient because the seeds sometimes fell in very inauspicious places.

In His parable, Jesus listed various places where the sower's seeds came to rest. Some fell on pathways people had made by walking through the field, packing the soil down tightly. Others landed in rocky areas, and still others came down in areas where thorns were growing. In modern agriculture, the hard places would have been broken up, the stones removed, and the thorns eradicated before the seeds were cast down, but, as I noted, ancient farmers did their plowing after the seed was on the ground. Of course, as Jesus noted, some of the seeds fell on good ground, and after it was plowed in, they yielded a significant harvest.

Because Jesus' hearers already knew these details about farming in the ancient Near East, they formed the ideal basis for an allegorical parable. As I noted above, this parable is about four kinds of people who display different responses when the Word of God is preached to them. These four types were not unique to Israel in Jesus' time, but can be found in all places and eras. By nature, we are no different from the people who heard Jesus teach this parable, so each of us could be in any of the four groups He identified. My hope is that everyone reading these words is the fourth type of hearer, the one in whom the Word of God takes root and brings forth its fruit in its season.

The Seeds on the Wayside

Let us take a closer look at each of these groups. Jesus said: **"And as he sowed, some seed fell by the wayside; and the birds came and devoured them"** (v. 4). In Jesus' metaphor, these seeds fell on earth that was packed down. Therefore, they remained on the surface of the earth rather than sinking into soil that was soft and loose. That meant they were easily spotted and consumed by birds, so they never had a chance to germinate and grow.

When asked to explain the meaning of this type of soil, Jesus said: **"When anyone hears the word of the kingdom, and does not understand it, then the wicked one comes and snatches away what was sown in his heart. This is he who received seed by the wayside"** (v. 19). He was speaking of individuals with stony hearts, people who will not hear the Word of God. The good news of the gospel bounces off them like seed bounces off a hardened path, and then Satan comes, like the birds of the air, and snatches it away.

Hardness is used frequently in Scripture as a metaphor for man's fallen condition. We are told that we have hearts that are recalcitrant, as if there were stones implanted in our chests (Job 41:24; Ezek. 11:19; 36:26). Obviously, stones are not capable of pumping blood through a living human person, but when this image is used biblically, it is with respect not to biological life but to spiritual life. Our hearts are hard to the things of God.

So, the first group is made up of people who hear the Word of God and immediately dismiss it out of hand. They have no interest in it. In fact, they are hostile to it. We all know people like that. Furthermore, we were like that until God's Spirit softened the hardness of our hearts. Thus, this group is easy to understand theologically.

The Seeds on Stony Places

Jesus continued: **"Some fell on stony places, where they did not have much earth; and they immediately sprang up because they had no depth of earth.**

But when the sun was up they were scorched, and because they had no root they withered away" (vv. 5–6). The picture here is of seeds that fell onto an area that was full of rocks, with a thin layer of soil spread across them. In that shallow soil, the seeds got water, so they sprouted up quickly, giving initial promise of healthy growth and a harvest to follow. But with the rocks below, they could not put down deep roots. Therefore, when the sun rose, the heat caused them to wither away.

Explaining this type of soil, Jesus said: **"But he who received the seed on stony places, this is he who hears the word and immediately receives it with joy; yet he has no root in himself, but endures only for a while. For when tribulation or persecution arises because of the word, immediately he stumbles"** (vv. 20–21). These are people who make professions of faith in Christ in an emotional moment, but soon, when all the implications of what they have done become apparent, including persecution, they quit the faith. They pass off their flirtation with Christianity as a momentary rush of excitement in their lives, then give it no more thought.

The night I was converted to Christ, I was with my college roommate, and he, too, made a profession. Later that night, we both sat down at our desks and wrote to our girlfriends that we had become believers. When I woke up the next morning, I was still filled with joy and gladness for the forgiveness of my sins. My roommate, by contrast, had no concern for it whatsoever. He had an initial response that was positive, but in less than twenty-four hours, his enthusiasm died away. This is why I constantly stress that no one is ever justified by a *profession* of faith. Rather, we are brought into a justified relationship with Christ by the *possession* of faith. We are not saved simply by responding to an altar call, signing a prayer card, or reciting a sinner's prayer in the moment. These kinds of techniques produce all kinds of examples of people who seem to demonstrate a positive response to the gospel, only to fall away in no time at all. A superficial, surface profession of faith is no assurance of the reality of one's faith.

The Seeds among Thorns

Next, Jesus said, **"And some fell among thorns, and the thorns sprang up and choked them"** (v. 7). These seeds took root and actually started to grow. But the thorns that were growing in the same area had a head start, and as they continued to grow, they overshadowed and crowded the sprouting seeds, Eventually, the seeds could no longer grow, and so died. Jesus explained the meaning behind this soil type by saying, **"Now he who received seed among the thorns is he who hears the word, and the cares of this world and the deceitfulness of riches choke the word, and he becomes unfruitful"** (v. 22).

Love for the world and especially riches proves more powerful in these people than love for Christ and the treasures of His kingdom.

Years ago, I taught at the Young Life Institute in Colorado, and I commended the Young Life leaders for establishing what was, in my opinion, the most sophisticated and effective evangelistic outreach program for high school students that I had seen to that time. But I felt I had to give them a warning, too. In Young Life at that time, there was a phenomenon of young people exhibiting a positive response to Christ, then coming into the group and being actively involved for two or three years, only to leave Young Life and the faith after that time. They rejected their original profession of faith.

This is a difficult issue. I firmly believe that once a person is in grace, he or she will always be in grace. The Bible is full of promises that those who are saved cannot lose their salvation. Paul tells us, "He who has begun a good work in you will complete it until the day of Jesus Christ" (Phil. 1:6). Yet, we see individuals, like those Young Life students, who make eager responses to the gospel, become involved in Bible classes, maybe even become the teachers in those Bible classes, become very active in church, and then, after a period of time, simply walk away from all involvement and from God. Did they reject their salvation? I believe the only possible explanation is that they were never really converted. The Apostle John said of some people who had abandoned the faith, "They went out from us, but they were not of us; for if they had been of us, they would have continued with us" (1 John 2:19a). These people gave the outward appearance of being with the apostolic bond, but when the cares of this world came upon them, they left. I think something similar was going on with the Young Life students.

Now, I cannot say why anyone who is not really converted would want to be around the church and around Christians. Perhaps they find some mild pleasure in the fellowship and the intellectual stimulation. Whatever the reason, I warned the Young Life leaders, "Be careful that when people are converted, they are converted to Christ and not just converted to Young Life." It is possible to be converted to a movement and miss the very object of faith.

This truth is illustrated in the life of Jesus Himself. As we saw in the previous chapter, Jesus taught this parable from a boat because such a large crowd gathered on the shore to hear Him. It is possible that many of them followed along with Him as He moved about. They probably were numbered among the multitude that put palm branches in front of Him on Palm Sunday and cried: "Hosanna to the Son of David! 'Blessed is He who comes in the name of the Lord!' Hosanna in the highest!" (Matt. 21:9). But when push came to shove, when crunch time came, they were the same people who cried, "Let Him be crucified!" (27:22b).

One of the serious controversies that arose in the evangelical world in the last quarter of century was the so-called lordship salvation controversy. The central question was this: When a person is saved, must he receive Jesus as Savior *and* Lord, or can he be saved simply by receiving Jesus as Savior? One camp insisted that a person cannot have Jesus as Savior without at the same time bowing the knee before Him as Lord. The other group said this amounted to adding something to the gospel of free grace, and that a person needs to receive Christ only as Savior.

This latter view led to the concept of the carnal Christian, which states that someone may receive Christ as Savior but not give Him the throne of his life. Jesus is in the person's life and heart, so he is truly saved. However, the person gives no evidence of salvation. He does not actively obey Christ, but continues to sin freely. He is a Christian, but he behaves in a carnal manner; hence, he is a carnal Christian.

Of course, all true believers have a carnal element in their souls until they are fully glorified in heaven. When we are converted, the Spirit of God takes residence in us. After that, our lives become a battleground between the flesh and the Spirit, but over time the Spirit gains ground while the flesh retreats. However, no true Christian is entirely carnal, which this doctrine permits.

In each of the first three soil types in the parable of the sower, Jesus was talking about people who, in the final analysis, are unconverted. They are not Christians who are simply struggling with carnality. Rather, they are not Christians at all, for it is impossible to be converted and not bring forth some fruit. In saying this, I am not preaching justification by works. We are justified by faith alone, but not by a faith that is alone. True faith always yields the fruit of obedience to one degree or another. That variation of degrees is a subject that Jesus addressed in the fourth soil type He mentioned in His parable, which will be the subject of the next chapter.

67

THE PARABLE OF THE SOWER, PART 3

Matthew 13:8–9, 18–23

But others fell on good ground and yielded a crop: some a hundredfold, some sixty, some thirty. He who has ears to hear, let him hear! . . . Therefore hear the parable of the sower: When anyone hears the word of the kingdom, and does not understand it, then the wicked one comes and snatches away what was sown in his heart. This is he who received seed by the wayside. But he who received the seed on stony places, this is he who hears the word and immediately receives it with joy; yet he has no root in himself, but endures only for a while. For when tribulation or persecution arises because of the word, immediately he stumbles. Now he who received seed among the thorns is he who hears the word, and the cares of this world and the deceitfulness of riches choke the word, and he becomes unfruitful. But he who received seed on the good ground is he who hears the word and understands it, who indeed bears fruit and produces: some a hundredfold, some sixty, some thirty.

Having examined that portion of Jesus' parable of the sower that focuses on the three types of unfruitful soils in the previous chapter, I now want to consider the fourth soil type, that which yields a harvest to one degree or another. Matthew tells us that Jesus said: **"But [other seeds] fell on good ground and yielded a crop: some a hundredfold, some sixty, some thirty. He who has ears to hear, let him hear!"** (vv. 8–9). Then, giving His explanation of this soil type, He said, **"But he who received seed on the good ground is he who hears the word and understands it, who indeed bears fruit and produces: some a hundredfold, some sixty, some thirty"** (v. 23).

It would be easy to read this parable and assume that the good ground refers to good people. That would lead to the ghastly conclusion that those of us who are believers were saved because we were smart enough or righteous enough to listen to the Word of God and understand it sufficiently so as to respond to it in a positive manner. However, anyone who knows anything about the Word of God should totally reject such an understanding. Jesus was not talking about good people.

Someone might object: "But R.C., you have been saying that the various soil types in Jesus' parable represent various types of people. Doesn't the good soil therefore represent good people?" It is true that Jesus calls this group "good ground," but what made this soil good? We know from Scripture that the Word of God comes to people who are not good, to people who are dead in trespasses and sins (Eph. 2:1). All of us are in this condition by nature. However, some of these people hear the Word of God. Why is that? Why do some who are dead in trespasses and sins hear the Word of God while others who are dead in trespasses and sins reject the Word? Are those who respond simply better people?

Obviously, if a person is in a condition of spiritual death, in order for him to take hold of the Word of God and respond fruitfully to the preaching of the kingdom of God, something must happen to him first. If nothing happens to change his condition, he will remain spiritually dead, with ears that cannot hear and eyes that cannot see.

One day, when I was in seminary, one of my professors wrote three words on the chalkboard. Those three words changed my theology forever. He wrote, *Regeneration precedes faith*. If any assertion distinguishes Reformed theology from every other belief system in the world, it is this one. Even the vast majority of evangelical Christians do not believe this statement. Instead, they reverse the order of the words so that they read, *Faith precedes regeneration*. They believe that a person is born again because of the exercise of faith in the heart of the believer. I believed that for at least five years—until that day in my seminary classroom, when my professor wrote those three words on the chalkboard and explained what he meant.

The Order of Salvation

When I talk about the precedence of regeneration over faith, I am talking about what we call in theology the *ordo salutis*, that is, the order of salvation, the order in which things happen to bring us to a state of salvation. Paul gives a very brief summary of that order when he writes: "For whom He foreknew, He also predestined to be conformed to the image of His Son, that He might be the firstborn among many brethren. Moreover whom He predestined, these He also called; whom He called, these He also justified; and whom He justified, these He also glorified" (Rom. 8:29–30). As you can see, there is an order there, a sequence.

When we talk about the order of these things, we are discussing not so much a temporal order as a logical order. What's the difference? When we say that we are justified by faith, we mean that in the order of salvation, faith comes before justification. How long before? How long must we have saving faith before God justifies us? Five minutes? Five days? Five months? Five years? None of the above. The moment true faith exists in our souls, justification exists in them. But logically, faith comes before justification in the sense that justification depends on faith. Likewise, I do not think there is a temporal delay between regeneration and faith. But if we are discussing which depends on which, the vast majority of Christian people believe faith logically precedes regeneration.

When I became a Christian, I began reading through the New Testament for the first time. Soon I came to John 3, the Apostle's account of how Nicodemus came to Jesus by night and said to Him, "Rabbi, we know that You are a teacher come from God; for no one can do these signs that You do unless God is with him" (v. 2). Jesus told Nicodemus, "Most assuredly, I say to you, unless one is born again, he cannot see the kingdom of God" (v. 3). Nicodemus was confused and asked: "How can a man be born when he is old? Can he enter a second time into his mother's womb and be born?" (v. 4). I thought, "What's wrong with you, Nicodemus?" When I read that text for the first time, my heart leaped for joy. I said to myself: "I know what Jesus is talking about here. I know what it means to be born again. I have experienced it, and my whole life has changed." Even so, if you had asked me what caused my new birth, I would have replied that it was because I had believed in the Word of God and placed my faith in Christ. I would have told you about what I had done.

Then came that day in my seminary class, when I had the opportunity to study John 3 under the tutelage of one of the greatest theologians in America at that time. He showed me that rebirth is the work of God the Holy Spirit alone; it is not a joint venture between the believer and God. Regeneration is an immediately supernatural act by which God changes the disposition of the human heart and quickens that person to spiritual life. Spiritually dead people cannot even assist in this operation. It is something that God alone can do.

So, Jesus was telling Nicodemus that if he did not become born again, he would not see the kingdom of God, much less enter it. The very first step is a divine initiative, a supernatural work of grace. Paul describes that work when he writes, "You He made alive, who were dead in trespasses and sins" (Eph. 2:1).

The point is this: By nature, there is no fertile soil in our hearts. There is nothing in us in which the seeds of the Word of God can germinate and take root. All that we bring to the table is the flesh, and the flesh profits nothing (John 6:63).

Going back to John 3, notice how Jesus continued in His discussion with Nicodemus: "Most assuredly, I say to you, unless one is born of water and the Spirit, he cannot enter the kingdom of God. That which is born of the flesh is flesh, and that which is born of the Spirit is spirit" (vv. 5–6). Jesus was not trying to be redundant when He said, "That which is born of the flesh is flesh." He was showing Nicodemus that that which is born of the flesh is not a mixture of spirit and flesh. It is only flesh—fallen, corrupt human nature with no tinge of goodness in it at all. The Spirit must effect the new birth.

Later, Jesus said, "No one can come to Me unless it has been granted to him by My Father" (6:65b). Jesus explained the human situation with respect to our ability to receive the seeds of the Word and nurture a fruitful crop. When He said that "no one *can*," He was speaking of ability. No person has the power or capacity to come to Christ unless something is done to that person first. The Father must give him the ability to believe. In short, the Father makes the soil good, so that it is receptive to the seeds.

If you have come to Christ, if you have heard His voice and embraced Him as your Savior, you did so not in the flesh, not because you were "good soil" in and of yourself, but because God in His mercy and grace was pleased to change your heart and give you the faith by which you believed. The good soil is the heart that has been regenerated by the Holy Spirit. When the Spirit does this work, the heart hears the Word of God so that it takes root and brings forth fruit.

Sanctification: A Joint Venture

At the end of His explanation of this parable, Jesus hinted about sanctification. It happened when He spoke about the different degrees by which the seed bears fruit in good soil. Everyone who receives the Word of God brings forth some fruit. Anyone who is truly regenerate, who therefore truly has faith, is fruitful. But not everyone who is regenerate brings forth the same fruit. This is why Jesus distinguished three different levels of fruitfulness: "some a hundredfold, some sixty, some thirty" (v. 23b).

Why does this variation occur? Is it God's fault? Is His work of regeneration more extensive in some than others? By no means. The Spirit's work of regeneration is uniform; it does not differ from person to person. It simply moves a person from spiritual death to spiritual life. There are two positions, with nothing in between.

But regeneration is just the first step. The rest of the Christian life, as we grow in grace and sanctification, is a joint venture. God is at work and we are at work with Him. We see this clearly when Paul writes, "Work out your own salvation with fear and trembling; for it is God who works in you both to will and to do for His good pleasure" (Phil. 2:12b–13). In this scenario, it is clear that God is working and we are working. That is because Paul is talking here about sanctification, which is a cooperative process, not regeneration, which is God's work alone.

With that background, it is easy to see why some people are more fruitful than others. Some cooperate with God in their sanctification better than others do. Some are more disciplined than others. Some are more diligent than others. Some work harder at growing in Christ than others. Some seed yields thirty bushels for every bushel planted, but some yields sixty bushels, and some a fantastic one hundred. So it is with believers and their fruit. On the other hand, some believers produce very little fruit at all.

One of the key factors in our degree of fruitfulness is our use of the means of grace. Every time we willfully miss worship on Sunday mornings, we miss out on the grace that God extends to His worshipers, and it costs us in terms of productivity. Every time we squander an opportunity to be nurtured by the grace of God through prayer, through Bible study, through fellowship, or through the sacraments, there are eternal consequences. There will be that much less fruit in our lives.

It should be our desire and delight as believers to be as fruitful as possible. We come together for fellowship, for worship, for instruction in truth and righteousness, to the end that we might be productive and fruitful, pleasing and glorifying our God.

68

THE PARABLE OF THE TARES

Matthew 13:24–30, 36–43

Another parable He put forth to them, saying: "The kingdom of heaven is like a man who sowed good seed in his field; but while men slept, his enemy came and sowed tares among the wheat and went his way. But when the grain had sprouted and produced a crop, then the tares also appeared. So the servants of the owner came and said to him, 'Sir, did you not sow good seed in your field? How then does it have tares?' He said to them, 'An enemy has done this.' The servants said to him, 'Do you want us then to go and gather them up?' But he said, 'No, lest while you gather up the tares you also uproot the wheat with them. Let both grow together until the harvest, and at the time of harvest I will say to the reapers, "First gather together the tares and bind them in bundles to burn them, but gather the wheat into my barn."'" . . . Then Jesus sent the multitude away and went into the house. And His disciples came to Him, saying, "Explain to us the parable of the tares of the field." He answered and said to them: "He who sows the good seed is the Son of Man. The field is the world, the good seeds are the sons of the kingdom, but the tares are the sons of the wicked one. The enemy who sowed them is the devil, the harvest is the end of the age, and the reapers are the angels. Therefore as the tares are gathered and burned in the fire, so it will be at the end of this age. The Son of Man will send out His angels, and they will gather out of His kingdom all things that offend, and those who practice lawlessness, and will cast them into the furnace of fire. There will be wailing and gnashing of teeth. Then the righteous will shine forth as the sun in the kingdom of their Father. He who has ears to hear, let him hear!"

After the parable of the sower, Jesus told another parable that was built around an agricultural metaphor, but with this parable, the parable of the wheat and the tares, Jesus introduced an element that we will see repeated again and again through the remainder of Matthew's Gospel: He began by saying, "The kingdom of heaven is like . . ." From the very beginning of His ministry, Jesus preached about this kingdom (4:17), and it was an important topic in His Sermon on the Mount (5:3, 10, 19, 20; 7:21). With this parable, however, the kingdom becomes the major focus in His parables.

Given this focus on the kingdom, let me remind you, as we noted earlier, that the terms "kingdom of heaven" and "kingdom of God" are synonymous. Matthew, being a Jew, was exceedingly scrupulous about using the name of God, so he chose to refer to the kingdom of heaven. But why this term instead of some other? The kingdom of God is that realm over which God is the sovereign Monarch, but the original locus of that kingdom is heaven. When Jesus came to this planet, He announced the breakthrough of that heavenly kingdom in this world. It was as if Jesus was invading enemy territory, expanding the borders of heaven. Thus, it was appropriate for Him to speak of the arrival of the kingdom of heaven.

Matthew tells us, **Another parable He put forth to them, saying: "The kingdom of heaven is like a man who sowed good seed in his field; but while men slept, his enemy came and sowed tares among the wheat and went his way"** (vv. 24–25). The action that Jesus spoke of here—sowing tares, or weeds, in another farmer's field—was one way in which people in the ancient world sought vengeance against their enemies. In addition to sowing weeds, they sometimes salted the fields—anything to disrupt the harvest. In fact, this kind of activity was such a problem that the Roman government stipulated punishments for those who were caught in this type of act.

Jesus then said, **"But when the grain had sprouted and produced a crop, then the tares also appeared"** (v. 26). Vengeful farmers typically sowed a particular type of weed that had seeds that were almost identical to wheat. In the beginning, all of the sprouting plants looked the same, so the naked eye could not discern the presence of the tares among the wheat. But as the plants matured, the weeds became readily apparent.

The servants brought the bad news to their master: **"So the servants of the owner came and said to him, 'Sir, did you not sow good seed in your field? How then does it have tares?' He said to them, 'An enemy has done this'"** (vv. 27–28a). The servants could not understand what was happening, but the master knew. He knew he had sowed good seed, so the weeds could only be the work of an enemy.

Jesus went on to say: **"The servants said to him, 'Do you want us then to go and gather them up?' But he said, 'No, lest while you gather up the tares you also uproot the wheat with them. Let both grow together until the harvest, and at the time of harvest I will say to the reapers, "First gather together the tares and bind them in bundles to burn them, but gather the wheat into my barn"'"** (vv. 28b–30). The master made no attempt to resolve the problem during the growth of the crop, lest the good plants be damaged. He resolved to separate the plants at harvest time, storing the wheat away but burning the tares.

The World or the Church?

So, what is the point of this parable? Thankfully, we do not have to guess, for as He did with the parable of the sower, Jesus provided an explanation for the parable of the wheat and the tares. Matthew writes: **Then Jesus sent the multitude away and went into the house. And His disciples came to Him, saying, "Explain to us the parable of the tares of the field"** (v. 36). It seems the disciples were still getting used to interpreting parables, so they asked Him for an explanation.

Matthew tells us: **He answered and said to them: "He who sows the good seed is the Son of Man. The field is the world, the good seeds are the sons of the kingdom, but the tares are the sons of the wicked one. The enemy who sowed them is the devil, the harvest is the end of the age, and the reapers are the angels. Therefore as the tares are gathered and burned in the fire, so it will be at the end of this age. The Son of Man will send out His angels, and they will gather out of His kingdom all things that offend, and those who practice lawlessness, and will cast them into the furnace of fire. There will be wailing and gnashing of teeth. Then the righteous will shine forth as the sun in the kingdom of their Father. He who has ears to hear, let him hear!"** (vv. 37–43). What we have here, then, is a picture of the work of Jesus, "the Son of Man"; some brief insight into His conflict with the devil; and some information about the end of the age.

Even though we have this interpretation, there has been an age-old dispute about what this parable actually means. Does it refer to the world in general or is it speaking specifically of the church? When we look at the terms of the parable, we understand why it is difficult to choose between those options. There is no argument that the sower in the parable is Christ Himself. But then we read that "the field is the world," so some commentators say that Jesus was talking about sowing the seed of the kingdom of God, the seed that brings forth the fruit of salvation, even while the devil is sowing his seed to disturb the kingdom of God and stunt its growth.

This is a possible interpretation, but the rest of the parable is strikingly similar to Jesus' teaching about the problem that will always exist in the church in this age. We saw Jesus' dreadful warning in the Sermon on the Mount: "Not everyone who says to Me, 'Lord, Lord,' shall enter the kingdom of heaven" (7:21a). He will say to many who call Him Lord, "I never knew you; depart from Me, you who practice lawlessness!" (v. 23). This warning was given clearly to those who profess faith and are therefore inside the visible church. But though they are inside the church, they are not really in the kingdom.

The problem seems less significant when we realize that in either case, whether the parable refers to the sowing of the seed of the kingdom in the world or the sowing of the seed in the church, the application is essentially the same. The church is the place where the kingdom of God in the world is made manifest. When Jesus left this world and ascended into heaven, the last question the disciples asked Him was this: "Lord, will You at this time restore the kingdom to Israel?" (Acts 1:6b). Jesus told them, "It is not for you to know times or seasons which the Father has put in His own authority" (v. 7). He basically told them that the timing of future events was none of their business. Their primary task as part of the visible church was to bear witness to the presence of the kingdom of God (v. 8).

It is important to note that the devil does not have to plant fresh seed to thwart and obscure the presence of the kingdom of God in the world. The tares are already covering the world. It appears, then, that Jesus must have been saying that Satan strives to undermine the kingdom by planting tares in the church.

In the first year I was a Christian, I learned a rather cynical piece of verse. It went something like this:

> Wherever God erects a house of prayer,
> The devil always builds a chapel there.
> And 'twill be found upon examination,
> The latter has the largest congregation.[1]

These two factors, then—what the Bible says about people in the church who honor the Lord with their lips while their hearts are far from Him, as well as what the parable says about the activity of the devil—tip the balance for me. I believe the parable is speaking primarily with regard to the presence of wheat and tares in the visible church.

[1] Daniel Defoe (1661–1731), *The True-Born Englishman: A Satire.*

The Church: A Mixed Body

The great Augustine argued that the church in the world is always a *corpus permixtum*, which simply means "mixed body." He was saying that the church is a mixture of those who are true believers and those who have made professions of faith but who are not actually regenerate or numbered among the elect. Because of this reality, Augustine also introduced the very important distinction between the visible church and the invisible church. The visible church refers to all of those people whose names appear on the rolls of a given congregation. The invisible church refers to those people who are truly saved.

Many people have the idea that when Augustine put forward the idea of the invisible church, he was speaking of individuals who believe they do not need to be a part of a local church. There are people who maintain that they can worship God on their own. Hence, they are never visible, never seen, inside the walls of a church. It may be possible to be a Christian and have such disdain for the local church, but I am doubtful. All believers are called to be members of congregations, to be involved in the visible body of Christ. Of course, there are extreme examples of people who are part of the invisible church but cannot be in the visible church. An example might be someone who is converted in isolation in a prison camp where no expression of the visible church is permitted. However, Augustine argued that the invisible church exists substantially and primarily within the visible church.

The invisible church is called invisible because the real state of any individual's heart, the condition of his or her soul—regenerate or unregenerate—is beyond the scope of anyone's vision, except God's. We look on the outward appearances, but God looks on the heart (1 Sam. 16:7). He knows those who are His. Thus, Augustine said that the invisible church is made up of God's elect, whom He has gathered to Himself, the Holy Spirit having regenerated them and begun to bring them into conformity to the Son.

If we are in the invisible church, God charges us to make our membership visible. We are told, "By their fruits you will know them" (Matt. 7:20). We can produce fruits that may be indicators that we are indeed in the kingdom of God, but sometimes the fruit that people show is counterfeit. We all know of people whom we thought were dedicated Christians, but in the end they departed the faith and repudiated everything to do with it. As John tells us, "They went out from us, but they were not of us; for if they had been of us, they would have continued with us" (1 John 2:19a). The possibility of deception is always there because we cannot know what is in the soul of another person.

Uprooting the Tares?

If the church is indeed made up of wheat and tares, we immediately come to the question of church discipline. From time to time at St. Andrew's, the congregation I serve, the bulletin includes a notice that a person has been excommunicated from the membership. You may be scratching your head at this point and saying, "I thought only the Roman Catholic Church excommunicated people." Actually, every church is responsible under God to practice both self-discipline and discipline of one another (see Matthew 18). When one-on-one discipline fails, church discipline should be brought to bear, even in Protestant churches and especially in cases involving very public and scandalous sin that is harmful to the sinners, to others, and to the body of Christ.

Of course, church discipline is not to be enacted over every wrongdoing or failure of people in the congregation. The church is made up of sinners, so some sin is to be expected. Also, we are told in the New Testament that "love will cover a multitude of sins" (1 Peter 4:8). We are to practice forbearance and patience with one another, not being contentious and judgmental, trying to bring church discipline to bear at the drop of a hat. We are here to encourage one another, to pray for each other, and to build one another up, not to destroy each other.

The purpose of church discipline is twofold. On the one hand, it is practiced to purify the church from scandal. But even more important, it is undertaken to reclaim brothers and sisters who have fallen into serious sin in a protracted way. Many different transgressions may trigger church discipline, but in reality there is only one sin for which a person can be excommunicated from the body of Christ—impenitence. Whenever a person is brought under church discipline, there are stages in the process, and he or she is given opportunities along the way to repent and be restored to good standing in the church. If the person refuses to repent through all the stages of discipline and multiple admonitions, then and only then is he or she excommunicated. Of course, even excommunication is not final. If the person who has been put out of the body of Christ comes to repentance, he or she can be restored.

We can trace how this process unfolded in the Corinthian church in New Testament times. A scandalous situation arose in which a man was having sexual relations with his father's wife, but the congregation did nothing (1 Cor. 5:2–3). Apparently there was no exhortation, no admonition, and no exercise of discipline. When the Apostle Paul heard about this, he wrote to the Corinthians and essentially ordered them to deal with this matter. So, discipline was brought to bear on the incestuous man. He was turned over to Satan; that is, he was put outside of the visible church. In a word, he was excommunicated (vv. 4–5). After that, the man repented. However, the Corinthians refused to let him come back to the church. Paul had to write another letter. He told them: "First you were too lax; now you're too harsh. The purpose of excommunication has been accomplished. The man has repented. Restore him now to your fellowship" (see 2 Cor. 2:5–11).

That is something of a microcosm of the history of the church. At some times, the church becomes lax and lets any behavior go unchallenged. At other times, the church tries to tighten the reins and goes on a witch hunt. That was why, in Jesus' parable, the owner told the servants not to separate the wheat and tares until harvest time—he did not wish to see the wheat wounded. Only in extreme circumstances do we pluck up the tares. We do not actively seek to root them out, even though we know they are there.

The fact that there are both saved and unsaved people sitting in the pews each Sunday morning creates a dilemma for pastors. They wonder how much of their preaching should be evangelism and how much should be nurture. Some churches issue an evangelistic invitation every Sunday morning. However, the purpose of Sunday morning worship is the assembling together of the saints. It is not a time designed for unbelievers. There are other opportunities and programs for evangelism. With that in mind, I emphasize biblical exposition in my preaching, so that the wheat under my care may grow in sanctification and understanding of the things of God.

However, in light of this parable, I recognize that there are tares in my church each Sunday morning, and they need to hear the gospel. For that reason, from time to time, I aim to include elements of evangelism in my preaching. Lord willing, I hope to both nurture the wheat and see the tares converted.

69

THE MUSTARD SEED AND THE LEAVEN

Matthew 13:31–35

Another parable He put forth to them, saying: "The kingdom of heaven is like a mustard seed, which a man took and sowed in his field, which indeed is the least of all the seeds; but when it is grown it is greater than the herbs and becomes a tree, so that the birds of the air come and nest in its branches." Another parable He spoke to them: "The kingdom of heaven is like leaven, which a woman took and hid in three measures of meal till it was all leavened." All these things Jesus spoke to the multitude in parables; and without a parable He did not speak to them, that it might be fulfilled which was spoken by the prophet, saying:

> "I will open My mouth in parables;
> I will utter things kept secret from the foundation of the world."

We are in the midst of a section of Matthew's Gospel that records a number of Jesus' parables that all begin with the words "The kingdom of heaven is like . . ." I would have expected Jesus to compare the kingdom to grand and glorious things. He might have said, "The kingdom of heaven is like a mighty mountain range in its strength" or "The kingdom of heaven is like the ocean in its width and depth." Instead, He chose to compare it to unexpectedly ordinary things. The two short parables I want to consider in this chapter are both cases in point—Jesus compared the kingdom to mustard seeds and to leaven. At first glance, these seem very odd choices for comparison to the kingdom of God, but with some reflection, we can see the genius behind the comparisons.

Matthew tells us: **Another parable He put forth to them, saying: "The kingdom of heaven is like a mustard seed, which a man took and sowed in his field, which indeed is the least of all the seeds"** (vv. 31–32a). Critics have jumped all over this statement from Jesus in recent years, using it to question the authority and infallibility of the Bible, as well as the reliability of the teaching of Jesus. Here, they say, is an instance where not only Scripture but Jesus Himself committed a grievous error. What is this terrible error? Jesus said the mustard seed is the smallest of all seeds, but we know that there are seeds that are smaller than the mustard seed.

However, before we all throw our Bibles into the garbage over the relative size of a seed, I want to make sure we do not miss the point of what Jesus is saying. We can put seeds into three categories—seeds that are small, seeds that are smaller, and seeds that are smallest. The mustard seed belongs in the third category, in the category of the superlative degree of smallness. It is certainly one of the smallest of all seeds, even if it is not *the* smallest. But Jesus referred to it as the smallest because He was employing the literary device known as hyperbole, the intentional use of exaggeration to make a point. He did this frequently throughout His ministry.

We hear, read, and even use hyperbole all the time with no qualms at all. For instance, when a professional sports team wins a championship and returns home, the team typically is given a victory parade through its home city. On such occasions, the local newspapers are apt to write, "The whole city turned out to welcome the team." No one cancels his subscription to the newspaper when he reads that, thinking the paper is guilty of intentional inaccuracy. Any sentient human being who reads such a report understands that the writer is making a point by saying "the whole city." He does not mean that every last person in the city came to the parade, merely that a large number of the residents attended.

Jesus was telling His listeners that the kingdom He had come to announce and inaugurate was very small at that moment. Jesus and His disciples comprised the entire citizenry. Compared to the other religions and cults in the Roman empire at that time—the gods and goddesses of the pantheon of Rome, the cult of Mithras, the mystery religions that abounded in the Mediterranean region (all of which have vanished from the face of the earth)—the kingdom of heaven appeared insignificant. It was so small, it was nearly invisible. That was His point in comparing the kingdom to a mustard seed.

Small but Growing

However, Jesus added, **"but when it is grown it is greater than the herbs and becomes a tree, so that the birds of the air come and nest in its branches"** (v. 32b). It was as if Jesus was saying: "Yes, the kingdom is minute now. But wait. The mustard seed can barely be seen when it is put it in the earth, but then it begins to grow and expand until it becomes a tree that is large enough for birds to use as a nesting place. So will the kingdom of God be."

In the late 1990s, my wife, Vesta, and I were hosting a Bible study in our home. Fewer than ten people attended regularly. However, one night after the Bible study, some of the people came to me and said, "R.C., why don't we start a church and have you be the minister?" I laughed. I said: "I have a day job. In fact, I have two of them, teaching full-time in seminary and working full-time at Ligonier Ministries. There are only so many full-time jobs that you can have if you're one person. I'm sorry, but that's just not an option." They said, "Well, will you at least pray about it?" That's what you say to a person when you ask him to do something and he says no. I agreed, and the more I prayed and thought about it, the more I realized how empty my life seemed because I was involved only in the teaching ministry of the truth of God and not in preaching the Word on a regular basis to a congregation. So, a week later, when our Bible study met again, they asked me whether I had prayed about it and was willing to do it, and I told them I would if I could be responsible only for the preaching and teaching, allowing others to handle pastoral care so I would have time for my other responsibilities. I also told them: "Let's not call it a church. Instead, let's call it a chapel, because we have to keep it small." So, St. Andrew's Chapel was started with about thirty charter members.

There is a rule in the business world that when people plan what they are going to do, they tend to radically overestimate what they can accomplish in a year but radically underestimate what they can accomplish in five years. I had no idea what would happen with St. Andrew's Chapel five and ten years down the road, but we have since built a sanctuary, outgrown it, and built another. We have more than a thousand members. Never in my wildest dreams did I imagine anything like this. Finally, in 2011, I suggested that we drop the word *chapel* from the name because, despite my intentions, it would not stay small.

The growth of St. Andrew's does not amount to a blip on the timeline of church history. In cosmic terms, its growth is insignificant. Yet, it reflects the truth of what Jesus said. Though it began small, it has grown beyond my wildest imagination. That is what Jesus was telling His disciples—that the kingdom of heaven would become something they could not imagine.

If we consider the condition of the kingdom of God from the perspective of twenty-first-century Western culture, it can seem to be declining rather than growing. In Western Europe, the average attendance at Sunday morning worship services is about 2 percent of the population. The great cathedrals have become, in the words of the skeptics, the mausoleums of a God who is dead. Historians say the United States has entered the post-Christian era, and that Christianity, if it is not dead, is irrelevant. The federal government of the United States has declared independence from God, interpreting separation of church and state to mean the autonomy of the state from God. So, the things of God are banished from the public square, from the schools, from the halls of Congress, and from the courts. The church seems to be forgotten unless there is a national catastrophe along the lines of the 9/11 terrorist attacks; then the churches are revisited for a little while until the panic subsides.

But we cannot get a real picture of the health of Christianity in the twenty-first century by looking at the West. We have to look elsewhere. The kingdom of heaven is experiencing explosive growth in places such as China, Korea, Japan, South America, Eastern Europe, Australia, and many places in Africa. In many of these locations, Christianity has become the dominant influence on the culture—just as it has been in the West for two thousand years.

I was reminded of this a few years ago when I visited the Rijksmuseum in Amsterdam, the Netherlands, one of my favorite museums in the world. It has the largest Rembrandt collection of any museum. Among Rembrandt's paintings, and indeed among all the classical artwork collections of the Rijksmuseum, most of the themes are of a biblical nature. It's the same if you go to the Louvre in Paris—you see wonderful landscapes, still-life paintings, and sculptures, but again, most of the themes are biblical.

Christians have made enormous contributions in art, as well as music and literature. Without the Christian church, there would have been no Bach, no Mozart, no Beethoven, no Handel. Christianity has been the cradle of the classical music that has influenced the Western world. Likewise, if you take away the Geneva Bible, there may have been no Shakespeare, no Pilgrims, no Plymouth Colony, no Mayflower Compact. Would there be a United States of America? Who can say?

What we can say beyond any doubt is that the kingdom of heaven began small but has grown enormously over the past two thousand years. It has expanded to every nation on the face of the earth. And it is growing still.

Hidden but Working

Matthew then writes: **Another parable He spoke to them: "The kingdom of heaven is like leaven, which a woman took and hid in three measures**

of meal till it was all leavened" (v. 33). In this brief parable, Jesus compared the kingdom of heaven to leaven in the context of baking. The Jews typically took a piece of a loaf of bread and put it into a batch of new dough, and that morsel provided enough fermentation to cause the entire lump of dough to rise. Jesus spoke of a woman performing this baking task, but notice the word He used: He said she "hid" the leaven in the dough. So, Jesus was saying that the kingdom of heaven was hidden from the sight of most people for the moment, but it was working nonetheless.

Matthew then steps away from his role as a reporter to become a commentator again, writing: **All these things Jesus spoke to the multitude in parables; and without a parable He did not speak to them, that it might be fulfilled which was spoken by the prophet, saying: "I will open My mouth in parables; I will utter things kept secret from the foundation of the world"** (vv. 34–35). Matthew wants to emphasize just how heavily Jesus relied on the use of parables at this point in His ministry. In Matthew's words, *all* of Jesus' teaching at this phase was by parables. Also, Matthew once again draws a connection to show how Jesus fulfilled prophecy, in this case by His use of parables. He tells us this teaching methodology was a fulfillment of Psalm 78:2.

Do you ever get discouraged because of the secularization of the society around you? Do you sometimes feel as if you are out of step because you are in church on Sunday mornings while your friends and neighbors are on the golf course, at the beach, or sleeping in? They do not know what they are missing. You are in the midst of the kingdom of heaven. Every time believers gather together in the name of Christ for the purpose of public worship, we experience a taste of the kingdom of God. Soon we will experience the full banquet.

70

THREE PARABLES

Matthew 13:44–58

"Again, the kingdom of heaven is like treasure hidden in a field, which a man found and hid; and for joy over it he goes and sells all that he has and buys that field. Again, the kingdom of heaven is like a merchant seeking beautiful pearls, who, when he had found one pearl of great price, went and sold all that he had and bought it. Again, the kingdom of heaven is like a dragnet that was cast into the sea and gathered some of every kind, which, when it was full, they drew to shore; and they sat down and gathered the good into vessels, but threw the bad away. So it will be at the end of the age. The angels will come forth, separate the wicked from among the just, and cast them into the furnace of fire. There will be wailing and gnashing of teeth." Jesus said to them, "Have you understood all these things?" They said to Him, "Yes, Lord." Then He said to them, "Therefore every scribe instructed concerning the kingdom of heaven is like a householder who brings out of his treasure things new and old." Now it came to pass, when Jesus had finished these parables, that He departed from there. When He had come to His own country, He taught them in their synagogue, so that they were astonished and said, "Where did this Man get this wisdom and these mighty works? Is this not the carpenter's son? Is not His mother called Mary? And His brothers James, Joses, Simon, and Judas? And His sisters, are they not all with us? Where then did this Man get all these things?" So they were offended at Him. But Jesus said to them, "A prophet is not without honor except in his own country and in his own house." Now He did not do many mighty works there because of their unbelief.

In January 1980, we were living in the mountains of Western Pennsylvania. A friend of mine who was a real estate broker told me there were some sixty acres of wooded property nearby that were being sold in a dispute over a divorce at what was basically a fire-sale price of $200 per acre. He encouraged me to join him in buying those sixty acres, and I did so. A few weeks later, we put a for-sale sign on the property, asking $400 per acre. Then we waited to see what would happen.

One night, there was a knock at my door, and I opened it to find two strangers in work clothes. It was rather cold outside, so I invited them in. After we exchanged pleasantries, they told me they were inquiring about the property. They explained that they were involved in strip-mining operations and had traced a great seam of coal all the way from West Virginia, through Pittsburgh, and into the mountains where we lived. They told us they were virtually certain that there were two large seams of coal beneath the surface of the property we were trying to sell, They got down on our living-room rug with their tablets and their papers, and they drew an outline of the property showing the seams of coal that they were sure were down there. They wanted my permission to do a test drill on the property to confirm their expectations, and they explained to me that if they were able to discover these seams, my share of the coal would be $2 million. I readily gave them permission to dig their test hole.

A few days later, they called and said they were ready for the test dig, and they invited my friend and me to come out and witness it. We had to trudge through two feet of snow to get to the place where they had set up their drilling rig. The machinery was running and dirt was spewing out of the ground as the drill penetrated deeper and deeper. All of a sudden, in the midst of the soil, a black material came spewing out of the ground in abundance. The operator turned off the drill, jumped down, and picked up a handful of this material. Then he put a piece of it in his mouth and bit it. With that, he started to dance around and cry out, "It's coal, we've found the coal." As you can imagine, I was watching all of this and enjoying my new membership in the millionaires' club.

However, my experience as a millionaire lasted only about fifteen minutes. After the men resumed drilling, the drill soon began spewing out dirt instead of coal. The operator got down and looked things over, then he told me: "I'm sorry, but this coal seam is only an inch thick. The seam we've been tracing must have cropped out down below and didn't come up to this property." He thanked me for my willingness to let him make his test drill; then they packed up their gear and left.

My friend and I shrugged off the experience. A few weeks later, we sold the parcel for $400 per acre. I made a nice profit on the venture, but far short of the $2 million the coal men had mentioned.

About a month later, I happened to drive back by the property. As I drove by, I noticed that the property was covered with giant earthmoving equipment and huge trucks filled with coal. I told my wife, "We've been had." The coal operator had bought the land in order to possess the coal that was hidden beneath the surface.

True Treasure

I tell this story because it was the only parallel in my life to Jesus' parable of the treasure hidden in a field. Matthew tells us that He said: **"Again, the kingdom of heaven is like treasure hidden in a field, which a man found and hid; and for joy over it he goes and sells all that he has and buys that field"** (v. 44). In the ancient world, there were no banks, no safe-deposit boxes, and so on. The normal procedure for hiding and protecting one's valuables was to bury them in some secret place. The law of the land provided that if someone happened to stumble upon buried valuables, he was entitled to that property—unless he was in the employ of the owner of the property. In that situation, the only way he could get his hands on the valuables was to buy the field. That is the scenario Jesus was referencing in this parable. A man found a treasure hidden in a field, so he sold everything he had to gain the funds to purchase the field and thus possess the treasure.

In the previous chapter, we examined two parables that were about growth. Jesus said the kingdom of heaven is like a mustard seed and like leaven. He was saying that the kingdom was small and hidden at the moment, but it was working, and in time it would grow beyond all expectation. However, the theme of the parable of the hidden treasure is value. Jesus said that the kingdom of heaven is a treasure that is worth giving up all one has in order to acquire it. All a man has, all of his property, all the wealth he has accumulated in his whole life is worth nothing by comparison to the value of the kingdom.

He then told another parable that made the same point: "**Again, the kingdom of heaven is like a merchant seeking beautiful pearls, who, when he had found one pearl of great price, went and sold all that he had and bought it"** (vv. 45–46). Here, the subject was a merchant who was in the business of buying and selling pearls. Again, in antiquity, there were no artificial pearls, such as are commonplace in our day, so a pearl was an extremely rare and valuable commodity. We are told that the gates of the New Jerusalem will each be made of a single pearl (Rev. 21:21) because of the extreme value of these particular gems. The merchant in Jesus' parable searched near and far until he found one exquisite pearl that was so lustrous and magnificent it surpassed all other pearls in value. When he found it, he was willing to divest himself of everything else that he owned to possess that one pearl. Again, Jesus' point was that what that man did for a valuable pearl is exactly what a believer should do to gain the kingdom. It is worth far more than all he has.

In the science of economics, there is a theory known as the subjective theory of value. It teaches that value is not inherent but is determined by individuals. In other words, no one can tell another person how valuable a certain thing is, for the two of them will necessarily value the object differently. This is what makes business possible. Any time a merchant prices his shoes more than I value the shoes, I will not buy them. It's that simple. There is no such thing as an objective value for a pair of shoes.

I was reminded of this theory when I was shopping for a car recently. I found a car I liked, I talked to the dealer, and we were about to conclude the sale when we turned our attention to the trade-in value of the car I already owned. I was not happy with the price he offered me. So, he brought out his little book and said, "This is the objective value of your car." I said, "It may be the objective value of my car *to you*, but it is not the objective value of my car *to me*." I went down the street and found another dealer whose objective value of my car was $2,000 more than the first fellow's. You see, value has to do with the degree to which we appreciate and esteem things.

Values Examined

I have noticed an increasing confusion in our culture between the term *ethics* and *values*. Ethics has to do with objective standards as to what is good. But we live in a culture that eschews any objectivity in regard to ethics. We are told that there are no absolutes, no transcendent norms that dictate what is right and wrong. Instead, what is right and wrong is determined by individual preference, that is, by each person's value system. However, ethics and values meet in the mind of God, and our task as Christians throughout the whole course of our sanctification is to adjust our value systems to God's value system. When the Bible tells us to seek the mind of Christ (1 Cor. 2:16), that means that we are to esteem the things that He esteems and abhor the things that He abhors. According to these parables, one of the things He esteems most highly is the kingdom of heaven. It is so valuable from God's perspective that people in their right mind do well to sell everything they have in order to possess it.

In light of this teaching of Jesus, it is clear that we are called to examine our values, to consider that which we esteem most highly. I encourage you to ask yourself these kinds of questions: "What do I value the most in this world? My wife? My husband? My children? My house? My car? My job? My redemption?" Elsewhere, Jesus posed some serious questions about value: "For what profit is it to a man if he gains the whole world, and loses his own soul? Or what will a man give in exchange for his soul?" (Matt. 16:26). The main characters in the parables of the hidden treasure and the pearl of great price were able to gain what they wanted by divesting themselves of all the property they owned at that time. But there is not enough property in this world to pay for a man's soul. What would you give in exchange for your soul? What price would you put on your soul?

Wherever I go, I like to watch people. I like to wonder what they are thinking about. Sometimes when I look at people scurrying about with so much energy and concentration, I think: "Do they know about the kingdom of heaven? Do they care about it? Or are they so caught up in the pressures, responsibilities, and burdens of their lives that they never step back and ask themselves why they are here, why they are even living?" That's the oldest question the philosophers asked: "Why am I here?" But there are millions of people in this world who have no idea about the kingdom of God. It remains as hidden to them as that treasure was before the man discovered it. They have no idea of the valuable thing they are overlooking.

Which Kingdom?

Matthew tells us that Jesus then changed His focus, telling a third parable that was essentially an exhortation and a warning: **"Again, the kingdom of heaven is like a dragnet that was cast into the sea and gathered some of every kind, which, when it was full, they drew to shore; and they sat down and gathered the good into vessels, but threw the bad away. So it will be at the end of the age. The angels will come forth, separate the wicked from among the just, and cast them into the furnace of fire. There will be wailing and gnashing of teeth"** (vv. 47–50).

Jesus was talking about one of the methods employed by fishermen on the Sea of Galilee. Sometimes they would use the dragnet, which was a vertical net that was pulled behind one boat or stretched between two boats, and it would sweep up large quantities of fish. There were twenty varieties of fish in the Sea of Galilee. Some of them were edible and some were not, but the net did not differentiate. It caught everything in its path. So, after the net had been dragged and filled with fish, it was brought to shore, and the fishermen sorted the fish. Some they could take to market, but others were inedible, so they piled the good fish and bad fish in separate piles.

Jesus said the kingdom of heaven is like that. In the visible church, which I discussed in chapter 68, there are both believers and unbelievers—wheat and tares, to use the terms of Jesus' parable (Matt. 13:24–30). But at the last day, the angels of God will separate the saved from the unsaved, the just from the unjust, those who embrace the kingdom that Jesus proclaimed from those who ignore it or reject it. Then, the wicked will be punished.

Again, we see Jesus teaching on one of the most neglected of all the subjects He taught about—the last judgment. He was saying that every human being will be held accountable for his or her actions. At the end of our days, all of us will stand before God, and there will be an examination. That examination will be all about which kingdom we joined. To find that kingdom is to find the most valuable thing we can find in this world. To overlook it is a tragedy beyond words.

Matthew then tells us: **Jesus said to them, "Have you understood all these things?" They said to Him, "Yes, Lord"** (v. 51). Jesus wanted to make sure the disciples were not struggling to grasp His meaning, as they had with the parable of the wheat and tares (see v. 36), and they assured Him they understood. He then told another short parable, not about the kingdom but about those who are instructed about the kingdom: **Then He said to them, "Therefore every scribe instructed concerning the kingdom of heaven is like a householder who brings out of his treasure things new and old"** (v. 52). Jesus was saying here that those who find the treasure of the kingdom are to point others to it, sharing the treasure, as it were.

The Missed Prophet

At the end of this wonderful series of parables, Matthew writes: **Now it came to pass, when Jesus had finished these parables, that He departed from there. When He had come to His own country, He taught them in their synagogue, so that they were astonished and said, "Where did this Man get this wisdom and these mighty works? Is this not the carpenter's son? Is not His mother called Mary? And His brothers James, Joses, Simon, and Judas? And His sisters, are they not all with us? Where then did this Man get all these things?" So they were offended at Him** (vv. 53–57a).

According to Matthew, Jesus went to "His own country." Although He had been ministering from Capernaum on the Sea of Galilee, in this case Matthew seems to be referring to Nazareth, Jesus' true hometown, the place where He grew up. Why did He go there? We know that His mother and brothers had recently tried to speak with Him (12:46); perhaps He went to Nazareth in response to a plea from them. In any case, while He was there, He taught in the synagogue, to the astonishment of those who clearly had known Him in His formative years. It was that longtime knowledge that caused the problem. Knowing Jesus' humble origins and upbringing, the people of Nazareth assumed He had no right to act as a teacher. His apparent exaltation of Himself offended them.

When this happened, **Jesus said to them, "A prophet is not without honor except in his own country and in his own house"** (v. 57b). Of course, the calling and anointing of a prophet by God was a supernatural thing, having nothing to do with human ability. Therefore, it makes perfect sense that those who knew him best, in all his failings and limitations, were most skeptical when he claimed to be speaking for God. Jesus was no exception. By making such a claim, He ranked Himself with the prophets of the Old Testament, a comparison that was more than enough to inspire contempt for Him in Nazareth.

Matthew closes this episode by noting that **He did not do many mighty works there because of their unbelief** (v. 58). This does not mean the people's lack of faith somehow hindered His power. He simply refrained from performing signs because He knew they would be wasted on these people. Sadly, the people of Jesus' hometown missed the treasure, the pearl of great price, when He stood before their very eyes.

71

THE DEATH OF JOHN THE BAPTIST

Matthew 14:1–12

At that time Herod the tetrarch heard the report about Jesus and said to his servants, "This is John the Baptist; he is risen from the dead, and therefore these powers are at work in him." For Herod had laid hold of John and bound him, and put him in prison for the sake of Herodias, his brother Philip's wife. Because John had said to him, "It is not lawful for you to have her." And although he wanted to put him to death, he feared the multitude, because they counted him as a prophet. But when Herod's birthday was celebrated, the daughter of Herodias danced before them and pleased Herod. Therefore he promised with an oath to give her whatever she might ask. So she, having been prompted by her mother, said, "Give me John the Baptist's head here on a platter." And the king was sorry; nevertheless, because of the oaths and because of those who sat with him, he commanded it to be given to her. So he sent and had John beheaded in prison. And his head was brought on a platter and given to the girl, and she brought it to her mother. Then his disciples came and took away the body and buried it, and went and told Jesus.

As we saw in the previous chapter, Jesus said, "A prophet is not without honor except in his own country and in his own house" (Matt. 13:57). This was certainly true of Jesus when He returned to Nazareth, and ultimately with respect to the whole nation of the Jews. It also was true of John the Baptist, that prophet who came before Jesus and restored the voice of prophecy in Israel after four hundred years of silence. Though he was highly honored at one time, Matthew tells us that John ultimately was senselessly executed by a dissolute ruler.

Matthew begins his account by writing, **At that time Herod the tetrarch heard the report about Jesus** (v. 1). Keeping track of the family tree of Herod the Great is extremely difficult. Herod, a client king of the Roman Empire, ruled Judea from 37 BC until his death in 4 BC. When he died, his kingdom was divided into several parts. His son Archelaus became the ethnarch (that is, a ruler over a nation, one rank below a king) of Judea, the territory where Jerusalem was located. Herod's son Antipas, known as Herod Antipas, was called a tetrarch (one rank below an ethnarch). He ruled over an area west of the Sea of Galilee and another to the east of the Jordan, known as Perea. Though he was officially a tetrarch, he assumed to himself the title of king. Another of Herod's sons, Philip, who was the half-brother of Archelaus and Herod Antipas, received a territory north and east of the Sea of Galilee.

The Herod of whom Matthew is speaking in this passage is Herod Antipas. Because he ruled over Galilee, the territory where Jesus carried out so much of His ministry, it was natural that he heard of Jesus and His great miracles. But when Herod Antipas heard of Jesus, he was terrified: **and [Herod Antipas] said to his servants, "This is John the Baptist; he is risen from the dead, and therefore these powers are at work in him"** (v. 2). Immediately, Matthew tips us off that John the Baptist was dead, but Herod Antipas was of the opinion that Jesus was actually John resurrected, and that this resurrection had somehow given John new supernatural powers. Why did Herod Antipas come to this conclusion? We can only guess as to the reasons, but it may have stemmed from a profound sense of superstition and even more from a troubled conscience. As we will see, Herod Antipas was himself the cause of John's death, so perhaps he was fearful that John had come back to life to bring the vengeance of God upon him.

The Voice of a Prophet

After that introduction, Matthew begins filling in the backstory, explaining what had happened to John the Baptist. He writes: **For Herod had laid hold of John and bound him, and put him in prison for the sake of Herodias, his brother Philip's wife. Because John had said to him, "It is not lawful for you to have her"** (vv. 3–4). Herodias was the daughter of Aristobulus, yet another son of Herod the Great. She had married her half-uncle Herod Philip, but then entered an adulterous relationship with her uncle Herod Antipas. Antipas was married to a princess, Phasaelis, the daughter of King Aretas, ruler of Nabatea, which adjoined Herod Antipas's territory of Perea. However, he divorced Phasaelis to marry Herodias, his niece and the wife of his half-brother.

When this happened, two men were extremely upset and exercised about it. The first was King Aretas, who did not like to see his daughter rejected by the tetrarch of Galilee and Perea, Herod Antipas. So, Aretas went to war against Herod Antipas. He defeated Antipas's army and captured some territory along the Jordan River. The other person who was upset about this marriage was the prophet John the Baptist. He publicly admonished and rebuked Herod for breaking the law of God, not only for committing adultery but for entering an unlawful marriage. For this indiscretion, Herod Antipas had John arrested and imprisoned.

When John the Baptist criticized Herod for his immorality, he was standing in an ancient tradition of the prophets. At the head of the office of prophecy in the Old Testament stood Moses, whom God sent to Pharaoh to say, "Let My people go" (Ex. 5:1). Then came Elijah, who pursued King Ahab for his godlessness and for his transgressions (1 Kings 18:18). Isaiah was often in the palaces of the kings, and he brought word to King Hezekiah that Judah would be taken into exile after Hezekiah showed his treasures to envoys from Babylon (2 Kings 20:12–18). Daniel stood before King Nebuchadnezzar of Babylon and warned him of his coming humiliation (Daniel 4). Amos cried out against the sins of King Jeroboam II of Israel (Amos 7:10–11).

From Old Testament Israel to the New Testament church and down through Reformed history in the Western world, the church has taught that it is an institution created by God and given a particular mission to carry out in the name of God—to preach the gospel, to administer the sacraments, to care for the sick and the needy, and so on. But the church has also taught that God created another institution for a different kind of ministry—government, to which He gave the power of the sword (Rom. 13:1–4). It is the responsibility of civil magistrates to promote justice and righteousness in the land. Both church and state are instituted by God, are to serve as ministers of God, and are under the authority of God. The state is to maintain a safe and just culture in which the church can thrive, and the church is to act as the conscience of the state and the culture. In other words, the church sometimes must perform a prophetic role when the state oversteps its bounds.

Sadly, just as Herod Antipas disliked hearing John the Baptist's admonitions, the state in modern times does not like to hear any correction from the church. The psalmist writes:

> Why do the nations rage,
> And the people plot a vain thing?

> The kings of the earth set themselves,
> And the rulers take counsel together,
> Against the LORD and against His Anointed, saying,
> "Let us break Their bonds in pieces
> And cast away Their cords from us." (Ps. 2:1–3)

What do we hear in this psalm? We hear rulers declaring their independence from God. That is the mantra that is chanted constantly in the United States of American when secular authorities insist that there must be a separation of church and state. I believe this is simply a nice way of saying that the state should be separate from God, of declaring independence from God.

This cry of separation of church and state becomes especially shrill when the church begins to cry out against unrighteous laws, such as those that allow for abortion on demand. When that happens, the newspapers are suddenly filled with editorials denouncing the church, and talk shows find plenty of pundits to say: "This is not the church's business. The church shouldn't be involved in legislation. The church is not to be a lobbying group. Christians just need to mind their own business. They can preach the gospel and pray and sing their hymns in private. But they should keep their religion out of the marketplace, out of the schools, out of the courts, and out of government."

On occasion, when I have been interviewed about the fight against abortion on demand, I have been asked, "Are you trying to take over the state?" I say: "No. I do not want the church to be the state. I'm asking the state to be the state. I'm asking the state to do what God has ordained it to do—to promote and protect the sanctity of life and to promote justice and righteousness." I made this same point several years ago when I was invited to give the address at the inaugural breakfast of the governor of the state of Florida. In that address, I said to the governor: "You're here for your inauguration. But I see it as your ordination to minister, because God has established the state to be His minister of justice and righteousness." I reminded the governor that ultimately he was answerable to God Himself.

Notice God's response to the efforts of the kings of earth to throw off His rule: "He who sits in the heavens shall laugh; the LORD shall hold them in derision" (Ps. 2:4). It is one thing to *declare* independence from God; it is another thing to *gain* independence from Him. There is no magistrate in this world who is free from the sovereign government of almighty God. People like to think they can separate the government from God, but God does not allow it. He uses His church to be the voice of prophetic criticism to the government.

Unfortunately, the church does not always exercise prophetic criticism, because it can be dangerous to do so. John the Baptist was imprisoned and ultimately killed because he called the king to repentance. He did not ask Herod to be a priest or a prophet. He only asked him to be a godly tetrarch, to submit to the law of God, as all civil magistrates are called to submit. The same dire fate befalls many Christians today who speak out against injustice and unrighteousness by governments and rulers.

The Death of a Prophet

Matthew continues, **And although he wanted to put him to death, he feared the multitude, because they counted him as a prophet** (v. 5). Herod Antipas wanted to get rid of John, to remove the thorn in his side, but he did not put him to death because he was slightly concerned over how the populace might react to John's execution, for John was widely regarded as a prophet. However, seeing John imprisoned was not enough for Herodias; she wanted him dead.

We are told: **But when Herod's birthday was celebrated, the daughter of Herodias danced before them and pleased Herod. Therefore he promised with an oath to give her whatever she might ask. So she, having been prompted by her mother, said, "Give me John the Baptist's head here on a platter"** (vv. 6–8). Herod Antipas held a birthday party for himself, and many dignitaries were present. In the midst of the party, Antipas called on his stepdaughter to dance before him and his guests. I am sure her dance was more than provocative. The king was pleased, so he promised to reward her with anything she wanted. She, naturally, asked her mother for advice on how she could best capitalize on this tremendous offer, and Herodias saw her opportunity. She told the girl to ask the king to have John the Baptist beheaded and his head brought to her on platter.

Matthew then writes: **And the king was sorry; nevertheless, because of the oaths and because of those who sat with him, he commanded it to be given to her** (v. 9). Herod Antipas suddenly had scruples about keeping the laws of God regarding oaths. He knew there were grave penalties for failure to keep one's promises. Of course, he was probably more motivated by the desire that his guests not see him as backing down from his extravagant promise. His pride was on the line. That was enough to overcome his concerns about the reactions of the people to John's execution. So he gave the command that the girl's request be fulfilled: **So he sent and had John beheaded in prison. And his head was brought on a platter and given to the girl, and she brought it to her mother** (vv. 10–11).

This narrative concludes on both a mournful and hopeful note: **Then his disciples came and took away the body and buried it, and went and told Jesus** (v. 12). John's loyal followers collected his body and gave it a proper burial.

Then they brought word of John's death to Jesus. Why did they go to Him? Were they seeking comfort? We cannot know why they went, but I do not doubt their grief was assuaged by the One their master had identified as "the Lamb of God" (John 1:36). In grief, pain, and loss, there is no better place to go than to Jesus.

72

THE FEEDING OF THE FIVE THOUSAND

Matthew 14:13–21

When Jesus heard it, He departed from there by boat to a deserted place by Himself. But when the multitudes heard it, they followed Him on foot from the cities. And when Jesus went out He saw a great multitude; and He was moved with compassion for them, and healed their sick. When it was evening, His disciples came to Him, saying, "This is a deserted place, and the hour is already late. Send the multitudes away, that they may go into the villages and buy themselves food." But Jesus said to them, "They do not need to go away. You give them something to eat." And they said to Him, "We have here only five loaves and two fish." He said, "Bring them here to Me." Then He commanded the multitudes to sit down on the grass. And He took the five loaves and the two fish, and looking up to heaven, He blessed and broke and gave the loaves to the disciples; and the disciples gave to the multitudes. So they all ate and were filled, and they took up twelve baskets full of the fragments that remained. Now those who had eaten were about five thousand men, besides women and children.

The eighteenth-century movement known as the Enlightenment changed the course of Western civilization forever. It did so by, among other things, spawning a school of philosophy known as naturalism. As the word suggests, naturalism holds that nothing exists beyond what is found in nature. There is no transcendent realm, nothing that is supernatural or beyond nature.

Obviously, this new philosophy presented a crisis for the Christian church, because historical Christianity is tethered to the supernatural. If naturalism is true, then all of the supernaturalism found in sacred Scripture must be discarded—and Christianity along with it. Some indeed abandoned the faith. Others, however, attempted to read the Bible through the lens of naturalism and thus salvage some meaning and significance for the church. This desperate effort to reconstruct Christianity gave birth to nineteenth-century theological liberalism, which originated in Germany and spread throughout the rest of Western Europe, and eventually across the sea to America.

One of the primary concerns of the liberals was to reexamine the miracles of Jesus, those supernatural works He performed. Because they hoped to preserve some vestige of Christianity in the face of naturalism, they did not simply dismiss the miracles. Rather, they treated them as myths that had some basis in reality. However, they believed that basis could not be gleaned just from reading the text of Scripture.

For example, some of the more militant of the nineteenth-century liberals studied the passage we are examining in this chapter, which recounts Jesus' miracle of the feeding of the five thousand, and gave it a natural explanation. They said that the deserted place to which Jesus retreated after learning of the death of John the Baptist was pockmarked with caves. In one of these caves, the disciples had hidden a cache of bread and fish well in advance. When the people became hungry, Jesus stood in front of the hidden entrance of the cave, and the disciples secretly passed bread and fish to Him through the back of His robe, which He then dispersed out of His flowing sleeves, making it appear that He was creating the bread and fish in His hands. This explanation of the miracle, of course, reduced the feeding of the five thousand to unscrupulous fraud.

Others proposed less literal interpretations. When I was growing up in Pittsburgh, the minister of my church once told the youth group that what really happened on this occasion was that some of the people came prepared with food but that others brought none. Those who had brought food for themselves did not want to share with those who had been negligent. So, Jesus called on anyone there who had food and was willing to share it to come forward, and a little boy came up and offered to share his loaves and fishes. This generosity shamed the people who were hoarding their food. Thus, Jesus was able to persuade the "haves" to share with the "have-nots." My minister called this an ethical miracle.

Others have suggested that Jesus was preparing people for the institution of the Lord's Supper and its perpetual celebration by breaking the bread that

He had into tiny bits that He then passed around to the multitude, just as we distribute the elements when we celebrate the Lord's Supper. However, it still seems miraculous that Jesus could have been able to break five loaves into enough bits to give one to each of the five thousand men who were there, plus the women and children, which meant that the crowd probably numbered well over ten thousand people. It would take a lot of bits to satisfy so many people, not to mention filling twelve baskets with leftovers.

When we consider these attempts to reconcile Christianity and naturalism, what we see are people bending over backward so far that they break their necks. So these supposed explanations are nothing other than sheer, unadulterated dishonesty. Going even further, Emil Brunner, the Swiss theologian of the twentieth century, wrote a book titled *Der Mittler* (*The Mediator*), in which he asserted that nineteenth-century liberalism and its successor movements are nothing other than unbelief. I believe Brunner was correct. I have much more respect for the skeptic than for someone who twists and distorts the Word of God to try to make it accommodate an incompatible philosophical system.

Of course, I believe that this account is nothing less than the truth of almighty God, that what Matthew records for us is a faithful account of exactly what happened. In short, I have no doubt that the feeding of the five thousand was a real miracle. It is one of only two miracles that are mentioned in all four of the Gospels, the other being the resurrection of Jesus. Clearly, the Holy Spirit regarded this event as something of great importance for the saints who would live in generations to come.

A Miracle of Compassion

Matthew begins his account by writing: **When Jesus heard it, He departed from there by boat to a deserted place by Himself. But when the multitudes heard it, they followed Him on foot from the cities** (v. 13). Jesus learned of the death of John the Baptist from John's disciples. This news prompted Him to depart by boat to a deserted place somewhere on the shore of the Sea of Galilee, apparently to grieve for His cousin and herald. However, His whereabouts became known, and people from all around the Sea of Galilee came to the place where He was.

If I had been in Jesus' shoes, desiring a little time by myself to mourn the death of John the Baptist, I would have been irritated by the arrival of huge crowds. But Jesus showed no such annoyance: **And when Jesus went out He saw a great multitude; and He was moved with compassion for them, and healed their sick** (v. 14). He saw the needs of these people and had compassion for them, so He healed those among them who were sick. Apparently He kept at it until evening drew near, which caused the disciples some anxiety: **When it was evening, His disciples came to Him, saying, "This is a deserted place, and the hour is already late. Send the multitudes away, that they may go into the villages and buy themselves food"** (v. 15). In a way, the disciples also were being compassionate; they were worried as to how the people would find food if they remained with Jesus in the deserted place too late into the evening. So, they gently suggested that He send them off to buy food in the nearby villages.

Jesus did not heed this suggestion: **But Jesus said to them, "They do not need to go away. You give them something to eat"** (v. 16). I am sure that Jesus surprised His disciples quite frequently by the things He said and did, and I believe this must have been one of those times. On the face of it, His suggestion that they should give the huge multitude food was ridiculous. That was essentially what they told Him: **And they said to Him, "We have here only five loaves and two fish"** (v. 17). John adds the detail that it was Andrew who located this meager amount, which belonged to a boy, but he could not help asking, "What are they among so many?" (6:8–9).

As it turned out, the five loaves and two fish were sufficient in the hands of the Son of God: **He said, "Bring them here to Me." Then He commanded the multitudes to sit down on the grass. And He took the five loaves and the two fish, and looking up to heaven, He blessed and broke and gave the loaves to the disciples; and the disciples gave to the multitudes. So they all ate and were filled, and they took up twelve baskets full of the fragments that remained. Now those who had eaten were about five thousand men, besides women and children** (vv. 18–21). By His mighty power, Jesus multiplied the food so that all of those in this great multitude had enough to satisfy their appetites after a long day with Him.

The Question of Ability

After Jesus was baptized (Matt. 3:13–17) but before He began His public ministry (4:12), the Holy Spirit drove Him into the wilderness to be tested by Satan (4:1–11). For forty days He was without food. Then the enemy came in the midst of His hunger and began to tempt Him by saying, "If You are the Son of God, command that these stones become bread" (v. 3). How did Jesus respond? "It is written, 'Man shall not live by bread alone, but by every word that proceeds from the mouth of God'" (v. 4). He refused to abandon His trust in God to provide for Him. However, the point I want to stress is that Jesus *could* have changed the stones to bread. He had the ability to do it. If He could multiply five loaves and two small fish enough to feed five thousand men, plus women and children, there is no question that He could have transformed some rocks into a meal for Himself.

This question of ability is at the crux of the debate between supernaturalism and naturalism. The naturalist says no human being has the ability or power to multiply loaves and fishes to feed thousands and thousands of people. Naturally speaking, they are right. But what about someone who has supernatural power, power that is above and beyond nature. In fact, without the supernatural (that is, without God), the natural would not and could not exist. Naturalists want to deny this fact above all else, and they tie themselves in philosophical knots to do so.

By contrast, Christianity declares that all of nature is the result of the One who is eternal and self-existent, who has the power of being within Himself, and who alone can bring something out of nothing. Only God has this power. If He had not exercised that power in creating all that now is, I would not be writing this book and you would not be reading it. You can take this to the bank—it is utterly impossible to get something from nothing by natural means. If there ever was a time when there was nothing, there would be nothing now. There would be no people. There would be no churches. There would be no Bibles. There would be no philosophers and scientists. Unless something exists eternally in and of itself, something that has the power to give rise to something else, there would be nothing.

Naturalism is a fool's errand, and the New Testament is on a collision course with that kind of thinking. If you could persuade me of naturalism in its full skepticism, I would sleep in tomorrow morning, because I would have no reason whatsoever to get out of bed. If the naturalist is correct, then Jean-Paul Sartre's assessment is accurate—humanity is a useless passion. That means that all the things we care about, all of our feelings of love, hope, aspiration, honor, and joy are futile and meaningless. If the naturalist is right, there is more meaning in an ant on the ground than in the aspirations of our hearts.

Yet, I constantly encounter naturalists who have both feet firmly planted in midair. They tell us that all we have is nature. However, we still have dignity, significance, and meaning. They have no basis for that assertion if man is nothing more than a biological accident.

I cannot live as a naturalist. I believe that Jesus fed those people that day, because I believe that Jesus is the incarnate Son of God, who made me and has absolute authority over me. That is why I call him Lord.

73

JESUS WALKS ON WATER

Matthew 14:22–36

Immediately Jesus made His disciples get into the boat and go before Him to the other side, while He sent the multitudes away. And when He had sent the multitudes away, He went up on the mountain by Himself to pray. Now when evening came, He was alone there. But the boat was now in the middle of the sea, tossed by the waves, for the wind was contrary. Now in the fourth watch of the night Jesus went to them, walking on the sea. And when the disciples saw Him walking on the sea, they were troubled, saying, "It is a ghost!" And they cried out for fear. But immediately Jesus spoke to them, saying, "Be of good cheer! It is I; do not be afraid." And Peter answered Him and said, "Lord, if it is You, command me to come to You on the water." So He said, "Come." And when Peter had come down out of the boat, he walked on the water to go to Jesus. But when he saw that the wind was boisterous, he was afraid; and beginning to sink he cried out, saying, "Lord, save me!" And immediately Jesus stretched out His hand and caught him, and said to him, "O you of little faith, why did you doubt?" And when they got into the boat, the wind ceased. Then those who were in the boat came and worshiped Him, saying, "Truly You are the Son of God." When they had crossed over, they came to the land of Gennesaret. And when the men of that place recognized him, they sent out into all that surrounding region, brought to Him all who were sick, and begged Him that they might only touch the hem of His garment. And as many as touched it were made perfectly well.

Immediately after feeding the five thousand, Jesus performed another miracle that struck terror into the hearts of His disciples. However, with that terror came an acute sense of reverence, and a new recognition and confession of who Jesus was.

Matthew tells us, **Immediately Jesus made His disciples get into the boat and go before Him to the other side, while He sent the multitudes away** (v. 22). Jesus' disciples had urged Him to dismiss the crowds as evening approached, but Jesus chose to feed them miraculously first. Once they had eaten, He sent the disciples to the other side of the Sea of Galilee and then sent the multitudes to their homes.

Why was Jesus so abrupt in His dismissal of the people? Matthew does not tell us, but John does. He writes: "Then those men, when they had seen the sign that Jesus did, said, 'This is truly the Prophet who is to come into the world.' Therefore when Jesus perceived that they were about to come and take Him by force to make Him king, He departed again to the mountain by Himself alone" (6:14–15). The people were very struck by the power of the miraculous feeding, so they were on the verge of demanding that He become their king. Jesus moved quickly to stop this campaign in its tracks. The political ambitions of this multitude were not in line with His mission, so He firmly and swiftly dismissed them. Perhaps the disciples were being carried along by the delirium of the crowd, and that was why Jesus sent them away, too.

Matthew continues, **And when He had sent the multitudes away, He went up on the mountain by Himself to pray** (v. 23a). This is one of several instances in the life of Jesus when He purposefully went apart by Himself for prayer. No clear reason is given for this season of prayer, though a mission into Gentile lands was in the near future (15:21) and His passion was drawing closer. After He had been there several hours, He and the disciples were separated by a great distance and an expanse of the sea: **Now when evening came, He was alone there. But the boat was now in the middle of the sea, tossed by the waves, for the wind was contrary** (vv. 23b–24). It seems the disciples were headed west, into the prevailing winds, which would indicate that Jesus was somewhere on the eastern shore of the Sea of Galilee.

One summer when I was a college student, I served as a counselor at a boys' camp in Ohio. This camp had a lake that was about a thousand feet long by eight hundred feet wide. It was a small lake, but it was big enough for the boys to have a good time. One afternoon, a violent storm arose. The alarm system sounded across the camp, signaling that all of the children were to assemble at the cafeteria to be counted, so we could be sure that all of them were safe and sound. On that occasion, when the count was made, we were horrified to discover that two campers were not present. I and a couple of other counselors went out and looked all around the camp without success. Finally, I happened to look out on the lake, and at the far end I could see two boys in a canoe. They were trying desperately to get out of the storm, but in order to get back to the area of the cabins, they had to go directly into the wind. Every time they tried to head up the lake, the wind blew the canoe back. They could not make any headway.

I was in charge of the waterfront and the canoes, so I ran down to the lake and jumped into a canoe. I had no trouble getting to the boys because the wind was behind me. But when I got there to assist them, I encountered the same problem they were experiencing—getting back up the lake into the wind was nearly impossible. I'll never forget that. It took us the better part of an hour to get back to safety, with the lightning flashing and the thunder booming. We had to labor as hard as we could just to make that thousand feet or so to safety.

I think of that incident every time I read this story, because the disciples were not young children. They were seasoned veterans of the Sea of Galilee. They were strong men, and there were several of them. Still, although they had been in the boat for hours, they were stuck in the middle of the Sea of Galilee. No matter how hard they pulled on their oars, the wind blew them back.

A Terrifying Surprise

I noted in the previous chapter that Jesus had a propensity for surprising His disciples. He surprised them by suggesting that they themselves should give the huge multitude something to eat. But that surprise was as nothing to what He did to rejoin His disciples en route to the western shore of the sea: **Now in the fourth watch of the night Jesus went to them, walking on the sea. And when the disciples saw Him walking on the sea, they were troubled, saying, "It is a ghost!" And they cried out for fear** (vv. 25–26). The disciples were not only surprised, they were terrified.

Remember, it was evening when the disciples suggested that Jesus send the people away (v. 15). He did not come to them until "the fourth watch," that is, between 3 and 6 a.m., and if we read between the lines of this story, it seems that He came to them closer to dawn than to 3 a.m. So, the disciples must have been very tired after rowing fruitlessly almost all night. That exhaustion probably exacerbated their fear.

Imagine this experience from the disciples' point of view. Their attention was fixed ahead, to the west, as they struggled to move the boat forward. Then, they caught sight of something behind them on the sea. Looking closely, they finally discerned the figure of a man, but he was not swimming or wading; he was *walking* on the surface of the heaving sea. They ran through the categories that reason offered to explain this extraordinary phenomenon, and they quickly came to a conclusion: "It is a ghost!" What else could it be? They understood the basic principles of buoyancy. They knew that human beings could not remain on the surface of the water but always sank into it. But a ghost, a disembodied spirit, would have no problem coasting across the water without sinking. I doubt that it ever crossed their minds that they were seeing Jesus. So, on top of the stress caused by the storm, by their exhaustion, and by the unnatural sight of a human figure walking on water, they believed they were encountering a ghost. It is little wonder they cried out in fear.

Jesus did not leave the disciples in this state of terror: **But immediately Jesus spoke to them, saying, "Be of good cheer! It is I; do not be afraid"** (v. 27). Why did He say "Be of good cheer"? Friedrich Nietzsche was one of the giants of philosophy in the nineteenth century. He was contemptuous of nineteenth-century Europe, for he thought Christianity had made Western culture weak and fearful. He said the world's only hope was the emergence of the *übermensch*, the superman. The *übermensch* would build his house defiantly on the slopes of Vesuvius and sail his ship into uncharted waters, for his major quality would be what Nietzsche called "dialectical courage." That was a fancy way of speaking of absurd, irrational, or illogical courage. With this courage, the *übermensch* would defy the meaninglessness of life. So, Nietzsche's message was basically this: life is meaningless, but be of good cheer anyway.

Jesus did not ask His disciples to defy meaninglessness, to take a blind leap of faith. He said, "Be of good cheer, I have overcome the world" (John 16:33b). As He walked toward the disciples in their boat, they could see that He was no ordinary man. They could see that the supernatural is real. They could see that there is a God. Therefore, life is not meaningless.

Perhaps the best news for the disciples was hearing Jesus' own voice say, "It is I." But this little statement is packed with meaning. One of the fascinating features of the Gospel of John is his record of Jesus' "I am" statements. Jesus repeatedly crafted metaphors for Himself: "I am the way, the truth, and the life" (14:6), "I am the vine, you are the branches" (15:5), "I am the good shepherd" (10:11, 14), "I am the door" (10:9), "I am the bread of life" (6:48), and so on. Each time Jesus said "I am," He used a unique combination of Greek words, *egō eimi*. Both the word *egō* and the word *eimi* mean "I am," so it was as if Jesus were saying, "I am, I am." However, this same combination of words, *egō eimi*, was used in the Septuagint, the Greek translation of the Old Testament, to render the ineffable name of God, "I AM WHO I AM" (Ex. 3:14). Thus, every time Jesus said, "I am," He was equating Himself with God. *Egō eimi* is rarely found outside of John's Gospel, but here it is in Matthew as Jesus said, "It is I." I am sure the disciples noticed this and were comforted by it.

Peter's Brief Walk

Peter, ever impetuous, was still not sure of what he was seeing. So, as Matthew tells us: **Peter answered Him and said, "Lord, if it is You, command me to come to You on the water." So He said, "Come." And when Peter had come down out of the boat, he walked on the water to go to Jesus** (vv. 28–29). Peter had the incredible experience of walking on water, defying the laws of gravity and buoyancy.

This episode is a metaphor for the ministry of the Apostles following Jesus' return to heaven. Peter had no power within himself to walk on water. If he had clambered over the gunwales of the boat before Jesus gave him permission, he surely would have plunged into the sea. But when Jesus empowered him, he was able to walk on the water. Likewise, after they were empowered by the Holy Spirit, the Apostles performed many miracles, but not because they had the power within themselves to do so. It was because Jesus gave them His authority over the things of nature.

Peter's stroll on the sea did not last long: **But when he saw that the wind was boisterous, he was afraid; and beginning to sink he cried out, saying, "Lord, save me!"** (v. 30). Thousands of sermons have been preached on this verse, and the basic application is this: Keep your eyes on Jesus. As long as Peter was directing his vision toward his Master, he walked on water. But then his eyes shifted. His attention was diverted from Jesus. He turned his gaze from super-nature to nature, and when he saw the boisterous wind and the heaving sea, his faith deserted him and he started to sink.

All of us are like Peter. Our faith is firm until adversity shows up. When we see the obstacles that we face and the threats that confront us, our hearts begin to sink, our confidence vanishes, and we have to cry for help. Nature is too much for us. At least Peter had the good sense to make the right call: "Lord, save me!" That is the most important cry any human being can ever make.

I essentially became a Christian with those very words. I knew where my life was going, and I knew I could not get out of the place where I was by myself. So, my conversion was a desperate cry to Christ for help. Some people do not make that cry until after they start sinking, and some do not make it until they sink all the way to the bottom. But there are multitudes that will not make that cry even on the bottom of the sea. We see people who have made shipwreck of their lives and we reach out to try to help them, but they want no help. Peter made a better choice. He knew where he was headed, and he did not wait to hit the bottom before he cried for help.

How did Jesus respond to His disciple's cry? Did He berate Peter for becoming distracted? Did He let Peter get a good dunking to teach him a lesson? No. Matthew writes, **And immediately Jesus stretched out His hand and caught him, and said to him, "O you of little faith, why did you doubt?"** (v. 31). Yes, Jesus chastised Peter for doubting, but only after He "immediately" caught him.

Finally, we read: **And when they got into the boat, the wind ceased. Then those who were in the boat came and worshiped Him, saying, "Truly You are the Son of God"** (vv. 32–33). Jesus and Peter got into the boat, and at that second the wind died away, just as it had died away upon Jesus' command during an earlier crossing of the sea (Matt. 8:23–27). This miracle, combined with seeing Jesus' supernatural mastery of the water, brought the disciples to their knees. They worshiped Him and confessed Him to be the Son of God, an important confession, though not quite as extensive as Peter's great confession that was yet to come (Matt. 16:16).

Matthew 14 closes with a brief mention of events that followed this momentous crossing of the sea: **When they had crossed over, they came to the land of Gennesaret. And when the men of that place recognized him, they sent out into all that surrounding region, brought to Him all who were sick, and begged Him that they might only touch the hem of His garment. And as many as touched it were made perfectly well** (vv. 34–36). They came to Gennesaret, an area on the western side of the Sea of Galilee south of Capernaum. Word quickly got around that Jesus was there, so many brought sick relatives and friends that Jesus might heal them. Like the woman who had a flow of blood (Matt. 9:20–21), as many of the sick as touched the hem of His robe were healed.

I suspect the people who were healed were deeply grateful to Jesus, but I doubt they realized fully who He was. They did not have the benefit of the disciples' experience, of seeing Him demonstrate His sovereignty over nature and hearing Him declare Himself to be *Egō eimi*, "I am." They did not yet recognize Him to be the Son of God. But with each expression of His power, that recognition was growing in the disciples. It is a recognition we all need to make.

74

INNER DEFILEMENT

Matthew 15:1–20

Then the scribes and Pharisees who were from Jerusalem came to Jesus, saying, "Why do Your disciples transgress the tradition of the elders? For they do not wash their hands when they eat bread." He answered and said to them, "Why do you also transgress the commandment of God because of your tradition? For God commanded, saying, 'Honor your father and your mother'; and, 'He who curses father or mother, let him be put to death.' But you say, 'Whoever says to his father or mother, "Whatever profit you might have received from me is a gift to God"—then he need not honor his father or mother.' Thus you have made the commandment of God of no effect by your tradition. Hypocrites! Well did Isaiah prophesy about you, saying:

> 'These people draw near to Me with their mouth,
> And honor Me with their lips,
> But their heart is far from Me.
> And in vain they worship Me,
> Teaching as doctrines the commandments of men.'"

When He had called the multitude to Himself, He said to them, "Hear and understand: Not what goes into the mouth defiles a man; but what comes out of the mouth, this defiles a man." Then His disciples came and said to Him, "Do You know that the Pharisees were offended when they heard this saying?" But He answered and said, "Every plant which My heavenly Father has not planted will be uprooted. Let them alone. They are blind leaders of the blind. And if the blind leads the blind, both will fall into a ditch." Then Peter answered and said to Him, "Explain this parable to us." So Jesus said, "Are you also still without understanding? Do you not yet understand that whatever enters the mouth goes into the stomach and is eliminated? But those things which proceed out of the mouth come from the heart, and they defile a man. For out of the heart proceed evil thoughts, murders, adulteries, fornications, thefts, false witness, blasphemies. These are the things which defile a man, but to eat with unwashed hands does not defile a man."

As we move into Matthew 15, we encounter the last significant episode in Matthew's record of Jesus' ministry in Galilee. He was about to leave Galilee for a brief retreat in the north before proceeding south to Jerusalem. The things Jesus said on this occasion were among His most significant teachings. I can think of a host of ghastly episodes in church history that would have been avoided had the church hearkened to these words. It is important that we listen carefully to our Lord's words here, understand them, and heed them.

Matthew begins by writing: **Then the scribes and Pharisees who were from Jerusalem came to Jesus, saying, "Why do Your disciples transgress the tradition of the elders? For they do not wash their hands when they eat bread"** (vv. 1–2). A delegation of scribes and Pharisees came to Jesus, but it is significant that they were not from the local vicinity. Instead, they had traveled all the way from Jerusalem. Obviously they were an official delegation sent to investigate Jesus, as an earlier delegation had been sent out to examine the ministry of John the Baptist (John 1:19). These men were not content merely to listen to Jesus and then report back to their superiors in Jerusalem; they observed something that raised doubts in their minds about Jesus' orthodoxy, so they asked Him a question. Specifically, they wanted to know why His disciples did not wash their hands before eating bread, for the disciples' failure to do so, they said, constituted a transgression.

What is a transgression? In biblical terms, it is crossing a line, and that line is the law of God. In short, a transgression is a sin. But that which the disciples transgressed here was not a mandate found in the Old Testament. The Old Testament has abundant laws with respect to ritual purity and cleanliness. The priests were required to wash their hands and feet before ministering in the tabernacle (Ex. 30:20–21). But no such requirement was passed on to the general public in connection with eating foods. The rabbis had added to the law of God. The *halakhah*, the oral tradition, was codified in the *mishnah*, the writings of the scribes and the rabbis, and there it was written that it was incumbent upon all Jews, any time they ate anything, to wash their hands first. But Jesus and His disciples paid no attention to this tradition.

The Greek word for tradition, *paradosis*, refers literally to that which is given over from one person to another, from one group to another. *Tradition* is not a bad word in the Bible. For example, the Apostle Paul speaks of the Apostolic tradition that Jesus gave to the church and which the Apostles enshrined in Scripture (1 Cor. 11:2; 2 Thess. 2:15; 3:6). So, the Bible itself is a kind of tradition. However, it is an inspired tradition, a divine tradition.

Every church, every family, and every nation has traditions. For instance, at St. Andrew's, we have several stained-glass windows depicting a man, a lion, an ox, and an eagle. Why do we have these pictures? These windows are a continuation of a tradition that began very early in church history. The creatures depicted in the glass were used to signify the four Gospel writers—Matthew, Mark, Luke, and John, respectively. These symbols can be found in Christian art throughout church history. However, God does not command the church to use them.

Another example—we have corporate worship because God commands it, but He nowhere tells us that our worship must be at 11 a.m. on Sunday morning. That particular time, which is the most popular time for worship in the United States, is a church tradition. There is nothing wrong with worshiping at 11 a.m., but there is no rule that is binding on the conscience.

Scripture and Tradition?

So, traditions are not bad in and of themselves. The problem occurs when traditions supplant or trump the law of God. That is precisely what had happened in rabbinic Judaism; the human traditions devised by the rabbis had taken the place of the law of God in some instances.

One of the mottos of the Reformation was *sola Scriptura*, "Scripture alone." *Sola Scriptura* does not deny the value of traditions that enrich the worship of God's people. It does not negate the importance of human confessions of faith, such as the Heidelberg Catechism, the Westminster Confession of Faith, or the Nicene Creed. But *sola Scriptura* says that there is only one source of special revelation that has the authority to bind the consciences of human beings and to impose absolute obligation. It is the Word of God.

In 1521, Martin Luther was summoned to appear before the Imperial Diet at Worms and there called upon by church and state to recant his teaching, particularly his doctrine of justification by faith alone. Luther declared: "Unless I am convicted by Scripture and plain reason—I do not accept the authority of popes and councils, for they have contradicted each other—my conscience is captive to the Word of God. I cannot and I will not recant anything, for to go against conscience is neither right nor safe. God help me. Amen."[1] In taking that stand, Luther was voicing the doctrine of *sola Scriptura* even before it had a name.

However, the Roman Catholic Church refused to listen to Luther. In the middle of the sixteenth century, at the fourth session of the Council of Trent, the church declared that the special revelation of God's truth is found in Scripture *and* in the tradition of the church, a dual source of ultimate authority that was confirmed as late as 1950 in the papal encyclical *Humani Generis* ("Of the Human Race"). So, this has been a point of contention for centuries. Is the Bible the one absolute source of divine truth, or are the traditions of the church on an equal plain with Scripture? The Reformation said *sola Scriptura*.

The same kind of debate was going on in Israel when the traditions of the rabbis began to occupy an equal place of authority to the Word of God and, in some cases, actually began to swallow up the authority of Scripture, because the leaders of the church preferred *their* traditions to the commandments of God. So, the scribes and Pharisees were questioning Jesus not about a violation of a biblical injunction but of a manmade tradition.

Transgressing God's Law

Jesus replied with an example designed to show the Jewish religious leaders that they, too, were transgressors—not of mere human tradition but of the law of God: **He answered and said to them, "Why do you also transgress the commandment of God because of your tradition? For God commanded, saying, 'Honor your father and your mother'; and, 'He who curses father or mother, let him be put to death.' But you say, 'Whoever says to his father or mother, "Whatever profit you might have received from me is a gift to God"—then he need not honor his father or mother.' Thus you have made the commandment of God of no effect by your tradition"** (vv. 3–6). What was Jesus speaking about here?

The fifth commandment, "Honor your father and your mother" (Ex. 20:12a), imposed a divine obligation on families to take care of their elderly parents. However, people would sometimes attempt to get around this obligation by pledging their estates to the temple. This meant that while they were alive, they could not spend so much as a farthing to take care of their parents, for the money was pledged to go to the temple when they died. By this method of subterfuge and evasion of the responsibility God had given to them, they really kept their money for themselves. Jesus was telling the scribes and Pharisees that their tradition sanctioned such reprehensible behavior and permitted violation of the commandment of God. As He put it, they had "made the command of God of no effect by [their] tradition." He was saying to them: "There is no law

[1] Martin Luther, cited in Roland H. Bainton, *Here I Stand: A Life of Martin Luther* (Nashville: Abingdon Press, 1950), 144.

of God that says My disciples have to wash their hands before they eat a piece of bread, but there is a law of God that tells you what you are to do with regard to your parents. Let's look at obedience to God rather than obedience to men."

One of my earliest appointments as a professor was at a Christian college. The first day Vesta and I arrived on campus before the school term started, there was a campus-wide picnic by the lake. When we arrived, we saw some students sitting on the shore of the lake. They had spread out a blanket and they were playing cards. Vesta and I enjoyed playing bridge, so we walked over to see what the kids were playing. When we got there, I asked what game they were playing, and they told me they were playing Rook. I was surprised because Rook was a game we had played when we were six years old. So, I asked them why they were playing Rook, and they said: "It's the only card game we're allowed to play." When I asked if they ever played bridge, they said, "Oh, no, we would be expelled if we were caught playing bridge." I eventually discovered that the students were not allowed to go to movies or to dance. The college had lists of rules and regulations that defined what a Christian is. It broke my heart, because these young people were being taught a radical distortion of what it means to be Christian. Which is easier—to cultivate the fruit of the Spirit or abstain from movie going? Such traditions trivialize the kingdom of God and create a sense of guilt that has nothing to do with the Christian life.

The scribes and Pharisees did the same thing. They made the traditions of men more important than the commandments of God.

The Source of Defilement

Jesus always called a spade a spade. Matthew tells us that He said: "**Hypocrites! Well did Isaiah prophesy about you, saying: 'These people draw near to Me with their mouth, and honor Me with their lips, but their heart is far from Me. And in vain they worship Me, teaching as doctrines the commandments of men'"** (vv. 7–9). First, He declared that the scribes and Pharisees were guilty of hypocrisy. Then He declared that they were the fulfillment of Isaiah 29:13. In that passage, the prophet described the people of God as giving Him only lip service—praising His name, singing hymns, and praying, but not loving Him from their hearts. They obeyed the external traditions, but internally there was nothing but decay and spiritual death. Furthermore, they taught manmade rules as God's commandments. In essence, Jesus told the scribes and Pharisees that their spirituality was pointless and empty.

Then Matthew adds, **When He had called the multitude to Himself, He said to them, "Hear and understand: Not what goes into the mouth defiles a man; but what comes out of the mouth, this defiles a man"** (vv. 10–11). We can put all kinds of things into our mouths that are harmful to our bodies, but nothing that goes in defiles us before God. It is what comes out—our words, and the filth, blasphemy, and slander they contain—that causes defilement.

Jesus expanded on these thoughts when the disciples sought Him out for clarity: **Then His disciples came and said to Him, "Do You know that the Pharisees were offended when they heard this saying?" But He answered and said, "Every plant which My heavenly Father has not planted will be uprooted. Let them alone. They are blind leaders of the blind. And if the blind leads the blind, both will fall into a ditch"** (vv. 12–14). The disciples wanted Jesus to know that He had offended the Pharisees, but He counseled them not to worry about it. He noted that every plant not planted by the Father would be uprooted, a comment that is reminiscent of His parable of the wheat and tares (see 13:30). Then He gave His famous characterization of the Pharisees as blind leaders of the blind, a situation that would end with both the leaders and the led in a ditch—a complete failure of leadership.

When Peter prompted Him, Jesus said more about the source of defilement: **Then Peter answered and said to Him, "Explain this parable to us." So Jesus said, "Are you also still without understanding? Do you not yet understand that whatever enters the mouth goes into the stomach and is eliminated? But those things which proceed out of the mouth come from the heart, and they defile a man. For out of the heart proceed evil thoughts, murders, adulteries, fornications, thefts, false witness, blasphemies. These are the things which defile a man, but to eat with unwashed hands does not defile a man"** (vv. 15–20).

The problem, Jesus said, is the heart. There, evil thoughts, murders, adulteries, fornications, thefts, false witness, and blasphemy are born, to be expressed as words and actions that are sinful in the sight of God. It is by sin that a man is defiled, that is, brought under the judgment of God. As James said, "When desire has conceived, it gives birth to sin; and sin, when it is full-grown, brings forth death" (James 1:15).

External rules—taste not, touch not, handle not—cannot address the real problem, which is the evil that lies in men's hearts. Only Jesus, working by the power of His Holy Spirit, can change the heart. That change is essential if there is to be real obedience to the commands of God.

75

A GENTILE WOMAN

Matthew 15:21–39

Then Jesus went out from there and departed to the region of Tyre and Sidon. And behold, a woman of Canaan came from that region and cried out to Him, saying, "Have mercy on me, O Lord, Son of David! My daughter is severely demon-possessed." But He answered her not a word. And His disciples came and urged Him, saying, "Send her away, for she cries out after us." But He answered and said, "I was not sent except to the lost sheep of the house of Israel." Then she came and worshiped Him, saying, "Lord, help me!" But He answered and said, "It is not good to take the children's bread and throw it to the little dogs." And she said, "Yes, Lord, yet even the little dogs eat the crumbs which fall from their masters' table." Then Jesus answered and said to her, "O woman, great is your faith! Let it be to you as you desire." And her daughter was healed from that very hour. Jesus departed from there, skirted the Sea of Galilee, and went up on the mountain and sat down there. Then great multitudes came to Him, having with them the lame, blind, mute, maimed, and many others; and they laid them down at Jesus' feet, and He healed them. So the multitude marveled when they saw the mute speaking, the maimed made whole, the lame walking, and the blind seeing; and they glorified the God of Israel. Now Jesus called His disciples to Himself and said, "I have compassion on the multitude, because they have now continued with Me three days and have nothing to eat. And I do not want to send them away hungry, lest they faint on the way." Then His disciples said to Him, "Where could we get enough bread in the wilderness to fill such a great multitude?" Jesus said to them, "How many loaves do you have?" And they said, "Seven, and a few little fish." So He commanded the multitude to sit down on the ground. And

> He took the seven loaves and the fish and gave thanks, broke them and gave them to His disciples; and the disciples gave to the multitude. So they all ate and were filled, and they took up seven large baskets full of the fragments that were left. Now those who ate were four thousand men, besides women and children. And He sent away the multitude, got into the boat, and came to the region of Magdala.

After yet another clash with the Pharisees, this one with a delegation from Jerusalem, as well as a brief discourse on the source of defilement (the heart, not external things), Jesus moved out of the area of Galilee. He went in a most unexpected direction: **Then Jesus went out from there and departed to the region of Tyre and Sidon** (v. 21).

Tyre and Sidon were ancient cities on the Mediterranean coast north and west of Galilee. They had been major cities of Phoenicia, a significant civilization that flourished in Canaan hundreds of years before Christ. By Jesus' time, Phoenicia had long since fallen, and Tyre and Sidon were part of the Roman province of Syria. These cities were cultural centers because they were major seaports, an important inheritance from their Phoenician past. Both cities still exist today and are part of Lebanon.

Why did Jesus venture into this area, which was outside the regions of the Jews and therefore largely Gentile and pagan? Perhaps He simply wanted the anonymity that would give Him a breather from all of the ministry activity that followed Him everywhere He went in Galilee. Perhaps He wanted to escape the imminent danger posed by the Jewish officials. We do not really know why He went there, but we do know this is the only time during His ministry that Jesus left the ancient borders of Israel and went into a pagan land.

If Jesus sought anonymity and a complete break from ministry, He did not find it. Matthew tells us: **And behold, a woman of Canaan came from that region and cried out to Him, saying, "Have mercy on me, O Lord, Son of David! My daughter is severely demon-possessed"** (v. 22). A Canaanite woman, that is, a pagan woman from that region, somehow recognized Jesus. We can only surmise that Jesus' reputation had spread all over that region of the ancient world. It seems likely that His abilities as a healer were especially talked about, for the woman appealed to Him to heal her daughter, just as so many had appealed to Jesus in Galilee. She did not state the symptoms of that particular experience of demonic possession, as sometimes happens in the Gospel accounts, but she indicated that her daughter was *severely* demon-possessed. So, she asked Him to have mercy on the girl.

Nearly everything about this woman's appeal to Jesus is remarkable, beginning with the fact that she addressed Him by saying, "O Lord, Son of David." In this instance, "Lord" may have simply been a title of respect, but she also called Him "Son of David." We saw earlier that this was a highly significant title for Jesus, for it had been prophesied that a king from the line of David would rule forever (Isa. 9:7). Matthew identifies Jesus as "the Son of David" from the beginning of his Gospel (1:1). Two blind men cried out to Jesus in much the same words as the Canaanite woman: "Son of David, have mercy on us!" (9:27). Later, the crowds at His triumphal entry would laud Him as "the Son of David" (21:9). This was a messianic title. We cannot know how this pagan woman came to know and use this title for Jesus, but it is interesting that she was willing to identify Him as the Messiah when so many in Israel were unwilling to do so.

Pressing Appeals for Help

While the woman's initial appeal was remarkable, Jesus' initial response was even more so: **But He answered her not a word** (v. 23a). How absolutely unlike Jesus this non-response was. There was a consistent pattern throughout His earthly ministry—whenever someone looked to Him for help, He stopped in His tracks and dealt with that person's need. His ministry was marked, above all things, by compassion. However, it seems, at least at first glance, that Jesus ignored this Canaanite woman.

Matthew then notes, **And His disciples came and urged Him, saying, "Send her away, for she cries out after us"** (v. 23b). In this plea, were the disciples urging Jesus to hastily heal the woman's daughter so that she would stop crying out and attracting attention? Or were they being as coldhearted as Jesus seemed to be, simply urging Him to dismiss her because they were tired of listening to her cries? I like to think that the disciples were making an implied request for Jesus to minister to the woman.

But Jesus made another odd response, saying it was not His job to help a Canaanite woman: **But He answered and said, "I was not sent except to the lost sheep of the house of Israel"** (v. 24). What should we make of this pronouncement? It was not that Jesus was saying He would not exercise His power except within the confines of Israel. Rather, He was saying: "I am a missionary. I was sent by God to a particular place at a particular time for a particular task. I was sent to the lost sheep of Israel. This woman is not one of those lost sheep. She does not fall within the parameters of My mission." I believe that was what Jesus was saying, but it still seems as if He was becoming more and more insensitive.

How did the woman react to this? Amazingly, Matthew says, **she came and worshiped Him, saying, "Lord, help me!"** (v. 25). Jesus had just said that she was not in the purview of His mission, and yet, she worshiped Him. Then she said the three words that are among the most important words any human being can utter in the presence of Jesus: "Lord, help me!" She recognized Him as God incarnate and appealed to Him for help. She did not want any sort of recognition. She did not care what Jesus said to her or how He seemed to treat her. She was convinced that He was the only hope for her daughter, so she kept pressing Him for help.

I love to talk to Christians and hear their testimonies of how they came to Christ. One pattern that I find is that people frequently come to the end of themselves and only then do they turn to Christ. When they reach the end of their ropes, they do not seek Jesus out to negotiate or debate. They come on their knees, crying out for help. That is what happened to me at my conversion beside my bed in my college dorm room more than fifty years ago. I put my head on the bed and cried out to heaven, "God, help me!" At some point, every one of us has to come to that point. I hear many foolish utterances by unbelievers, but there is none more foolish than the statement, "I don't need Jesus." When I hear a person say that, I want to grab him by his collar and say: "What's the matter with you? Don't you know that there's nothing in this world that you need *more* than Jesus?"

This Canaanite woman knew she needed Jesus, so she came with a simple but urgent plea. Jesus, however, still hesitated. Then He uttered what seems to be His most insensitive statement yet: **But He answered and said, "It is not good to take the children's bread and throw it to the little dogs"** (v. 26). In ancient Israel, one of the worst ways to insult someone was to call him or her a dog. Commentators have pointed out that Jesus spoke here of "the little dogs," which were small dogs that were kept as pets, not feral dogs roaming the streets. Also, the setting He pictured was that of a family meal, with children seated at the table and the small dogs on the floor below. He rightly said that it would not be right for the parents to take the food that was intended for the children and give it instead to the dogs. But no matter how we cut it, Jesus called this woman a dog.

A Proper Understanding of Self

I think this woman is one of the most remarkable people we meet anywhere in Scripture. I am frankly amazed that she did not become angry at this point and accuse Jesus of slandering her. Instead, she answered very humbly: **And she said, "Yes, Lord, yet even the little dogs eat the crumbs which fall from their masters' table"** (v. 27).

We have already seen that this woman knew who Jesus was. She knew that He was the Lord and the Son of David, that is, the Messiah. But equally important, she knew who she was. That is why, when Jesus likened her to a dog, albeit the household pet variety, she did not protest. That was a tacit acknowledgment that she knew she was not one of Jesus' people and He owed her nothing. In short, she did not come with a sense of entitlement.

In the United States today, there is a burgeoning sense of entitlement. We seem to hear it everyday—people making the argument that the society or the government owes them something. We're all susceptible to this mind-set, but we need to resist it with all our beings. The problem with such an entitlement mentality is that it can grow to the point where we believe God Himself owes us something—health, wealth, happiness, and myriad other things.

The tenth commandment says, "You shall not covet your neighbor's house; you shall not covet your neighbor's wife, nor his male servant, nor his female servant, nor his ox, nor his donkey, nor anything that is your neighbor's" (Ex. 20:17). The Heidelberg Catechism, Question 113, asks, "What is God's will for you in the tenth commandment?" The answer says: "That not even the slightest thought or desire contrary to any one of God's commandments should ever arise in my heart. Rather, with all my heart I should always hate sin and take pleasure in whatever is right." When we covet what another person has, we sin against that person. But the sin against the person is not worthy to be compared to the sin against God, because when we covet what belongs to someone else, we are saying to God: "You're not fair. You have given to that person what You should have given to me. I deserve that as much as he does. You have robbed me of what I justly deserve." That is where an entitlement mind-set can take us.

If the United States decided to get rid of the Constitution as we know it and throw away the Bill of Rights in favor of a simplified legal code with only ten laws, what ten rules would you want to see enshrined in this new code? Surely you would want a law that would protect the sanctity of life by outlawing murder. I hope that you would have a law that would protect property rights by outlawing theft, robbery, and burglary. You probably would want to protect the sanctity of marriage, the family, and the home by means of a law prohibiting adultery. Those laws seem rather obvious choices, for they deal with major issues. But would you include a law against envy? God laid down such a law when He created a nation and gave His ten-point summary of the law. The prohibition against covetousness made God's top ten. Maybe God knows something about how destructive envy, jealousy, and a sense of entitlement can be to people.

But there was no sense of entitlement with this Canaanite woman at all. She did not come to Jesus with a chip on her shoulder, demanding His help as her due. She knew she had no right to His help. She acknowledged herself to be a "dog" and said she was only hoping for a few crumbs to fall her way, just as any domestic dog would do.

So, Matthew writes: **Then Jesus answered and said to her, "O woman, great is your faith! Let it be to you as you desire." And her daughter was healed from that very hour** (v. 28). Jesus saw faith in this Canaanite woman. Her eyes had been opened to know Him and believe on Him. For that reason, He granted her petition.

This woman is Exhibit A of what it means to be a Christian. All of us are tempted from time to time to think that God owes us a little more than He has given, and that we deserved what He has given us. That is deadly thinking. The only merit we have before a holy God is demerit. Our only hope to stand before a holy and righteous God is by appealing to His mercy and grace, for it is by His grace alone that anyone enters into His kingdom.

Miracles in Gentile Lands

Matthew goes on to tell us: **Jesus departed from there, skirted the Sea of Galilee, and went up on the mountain and sat down there. Then great multitudes came to Him, having with them the lame, blind, mute, maimed, and many others; and they laid them down at Jesus' feet, and He healed them. So the multitude marveled when they saw the mute speaking, the maimed made whole, the lame walking, and the blind seeing; and they glorified the God of Israel** (vv. 29–31). Leaving the region of Tyre and Sidon, Jesus spent some time in the Gentile areas north of the Sea of Galilee. Multitudes there came to Him for healing, and Jesus granted their requests, causing them to marvel and glorify God.

What follows is a near repetition of the feeding of the five thousand, which we studied in Matthew 14. Here, Matthew writes: **Now Jesus called His disciples to Himself and said, "I have compassion on the multitude, because they have now continued with Me three days and have nothing to eat. And I do not want to send them away hungry, lest they faint on the way"** (v. 32). Jesus was concerned because the people, incredibly, had been with Him for three days, and they either had had nothing to eat in that time or had run out of food. He did not want to send them away hungry.

I would expect that one of the disciples would have jumped in at this point and said, "Lord, why don't You multiply some loaves and fishes the way You did before?" But it was as if they had forgotten that incident: **Then His disciples said to Him, "Where could we get enough bread in the wilderness to fill such a great multitude?"** (v. 33). I am completely unable to explain why they seemingly could not remember such a vivid display of Jesus' power.

Jesus patiently led them through a process much like that of the earlier miracle: **Jesus said to them, "How many loaves do you have?" And they said, "Seven, and a few little fish." So He commanded the multitude to sit down on the ground. And He took the seven loaves and the fish and gave thanks, broke them and gave them to His disciples; and the disciples gave to the multitude. So they all ate and were filled, and they took up seven large baskets full of the fragments that were left. Now those who ate were four thousand men, besides women and children. And He sent away the multitude, got into the boat, and came to the region of Magdala** (vv. 34–39).

Thus, just as Jesus had earlier fed five thousand Jewish men, plus women and children, He fed four thousand Gentile men, plus women and children. Here, then, was a hint of the future expansion of the kingdom of God beyond the borders of Israel to the Gentiles.

76

THE LEAVEN OF THE PHARISEES

Matthew 16:1–12

Then the Pharisees and Sadducees came, and testing Him asked that He would show them a sign from heaven. He answered and said to them, "When it is evening you say, 'It will be fair weather, for the sky is red'; and in the morning, 'It will be foul weather today, for the sky is red and threatening.' Hypocrites! You know how to discern the face of the sky, but you cannot discern the signs of the times. A wicked and adulterous generation seeks after a sign, and no sign shall be given to it except the sign of the prophet Jonah." And He left them and departed. Now when His disciples had come to the other side, they had forgotten to take bread. Then Jesus said to them, "Take heed and beware of the leaven of the Pharisees and the Sadducees." And they reasoned among themselves, saying, "It is because we have taken no bread." But Jesus, being aware of it, said to them, "O you of little faith, why do you reason among yourselves because you have brought no bread? Do you not yet understand, or remember the five loaves of the five thousand and how many baskets you took up? Nor the seven loaves of the four thousand and how many large baskets you took up? How is it you do not understand that I did not speak to you concerning bread? but to beware of the leaven of the Pharisees and Sadducees." Then they understood that He did not tell them to beware of the leaven of bread, but of the doctrine of the Pharisees and Sadducees.

At first glance, the opening verses of Matthew 16 seem to be repeating earlier accounts. In one previous incident, some scribes and Pharisees asked Jesus to show them a sign, but He told them they would see only the sign of the prophet Jonah (12:38–39). In another incident, a delegation of Pharisees from Jerusalem asked why His disciples were transgressing one of the traditions of the Jews (15:1–2). Here in chapter 16, with Jesus apparently back in Jewish lands, it seems that another delegation of Jewish religious leaders arrived with another request for a sign. Yes, this incident is similar in some ways to those that occurred earlier, but it is also unique in some aspects. In fact, there is something significantly different about this event that we could easily miss by working through the passage too quickly.

Matthew begins, **Then the Pharisees and Sadducees came, and testing Him asked that He would show them a sign from heaven** (v. 1). Immediately we see one important difference from the earlier incidents—this delegation is not made up of Pharisees and *scribes* but of Pharisees and *Sadducees*. This is the first confrontation that Matthew records between Jesus and the Sadducees. It is strange that Sadducees came with Pharisees, for these were two distinct parties of the Jews, and they did not get along. For representatives of both parties to come to Jesus in a joint delegation indicates that something had them seriously concerned. Of course, that something was their mutual distrust and hatred of Jesus. So, they teamed up in an unholy alliance to put Jesus to the test.

Their first step was to ask Jesus for a sign from heaven. This was the same kind of thing the Pharisees had asked earlier. They wanted something beyond the miraculous signs that they had seen, the healings, the deliverances from demonic possession, the multiplication of loaves and fishes, because they knew that earlier prophets had also performed healings and other wondrous signs. They asked Jesus for a sign that was unmistakably from heaven, a sign that would settle the question of His identity once and for all. They wanted to see Jesus confirmed by God Himself through a kind of miracle that would transcend anything that they had yet been able to observe. In essence, they were asking Him to show them His divine credentials.

Jesus gave a very interesting answer: **He answered and said to them, "When it is evening you say, 'It will be fair weather, for the sky is red'; and in the morning, 'It will be foul weather today, for the sky is red and threatening'"** (vv. 2–3a). We have a saying: "Red sky at night, sailor's delight; red sky at morning, sailor take warning." This adage reflects the general truism that when the sky is red at sunset, the weather will be fair the next day, but if the sky is red at sunrise, the weather is likely to turn foul very soon. Jesus' answer indicates that this bit of folk wisdom was known in His time, and the Pharisees and Sadducees themselves used it to forecast the weather.

However, in Jesus' opinion, they were better meteorologists than theologians and biblical scholars, for He went on to say: **"Hypocrites! You know how to discern the face of the sky, but you cannot discern the signs of the times"** (v. 3b). It was as if He were asking them, "How can you have missed the unmistakable signs of the breakthrough of the kingdom of God that have been taking place in your midst?" They had heard the teaching of John the Baptist and the teaching of Jesus Himself, and they had seen the mighty signs He had done, all in clear fulfillment of prophecy, but they had not understood or believed what these things indicated.

Longing for a Sign

Then, Matthew tells us, Jesus said: **"A wicked and adulterous generation seeks after a sign, and no sign shall be given to it except the sign of the prophet Jonah." And He left them and departed** (v. 4). Jesus first told the Pharisees and Sadducees that their seeking after a sign showed that they were part of a wicked and adulterous generation, a generation that was not faithful to its God. He was speaking about people whose hearts are hard, so hard they feel God ought to perform a special miracle just for them. However, they already have been given the most stupendous sign of all, the sign of Jonah—just as the prophet was three days in the belly of the fish, so Christ was three days in the earth and then rose again (12:40).

The world today is filled with people just like these Pharisees and Sadducees. They say: "I know what the New Testament says, but I wasn't there, so unless I can see this Jesus with my eyes and touch Him with my hands, I'm not going to give any confidence or consideration to Him." Despite the testimony God has given in His Word to the identity of Jesus, testimony that ought to convict any sentient creature that Jesus is the Son of God, they want more. They want to see Jesus alive and performing miracles.

After Jesus rose again, He appeared to most of the apostles, but Thomas was not there. When he heard the news, Thomas said, "Unless I see in His hands the print of the nails, and put my finger into the print of the nails, and put my hand into His side, I will not believe" (John 20:25). Several days later, Jesus came into the upper room when Thomas was present and said to him: "Reach your finger here, and look at My hands; and reach your hand here, and put it into My side. Do not be unbelieving, but believing" (v. 27). John does not tell us whether Thomas actually touched Jesus' wounds. All he tells us is that Thomas blurted out, "My Lord, and my God!" (v. 28). That prompted Jesus to say: "Thomas, because you have seen Me, you have believed. Blessed are those who have not seen and yet have believed" (v. 29). Not all are given the privilege of seeing Jesus' wounds in order to bolster their belief, but they believe nonetheless.

Remember what Paul told the skeptical philosophers in Athens: "Truly, these times of ignorance God overlooked, but now commands all men everywhere to repent, because He has appointed a day on which He will judge the world in righteousness by the Man whom He has ordained. He has given assurance of this to all by raising Him from the dead" (Acts 17:30–31). People may want more from God, but they are not going to get it. He already has given enough evidence to make every human being culpable to Him by raising Jesus from the dead. Thus, all people everywhere are already under divine obligation to come to Jesus. Coming to Him is not an option. It is a requirement that God Himself has laid upon the world.

Dangerous Leaven

After rebuking the Pharisees and Sadducees, Jesus departed. Matthew adds: **Now when His disciples had come to the other side, they had forgotten to take bread. Then Jesus said to them, "Take heed and beware of the leaven of the Pharisees and the Sadducees"** (vv. 5–6). When Matthew says that Jesus and the disciples went to "the other side," he probably means that they went once again from a Jewish area to a Gentile region. This squares with the fact that upcoming events take place in the neighborhood of Caesarea Philippi and Mount Hermon, a Gentile region north of the Sea of Galilee. Only when they got into these Gentile lands did the disciples realize they had forgotten to bring bread with them. They apparently discussed this aloud, for Jesus unexpectedly gave them a solemn exhortation to beware the leaven of the Pharisees and Sadducees. This is a warning we also need to heed, as I will explain below.

The disciples, as happened so often, were confused by what Jesus said: **And they reasoned among themselves, saying, "It is because we have taken no bread"** (v. 7). They reasoned that they had been discussing bread, whereupon Jesus had told them to watch out for the leaven of the Pharisees and Sadducees, and since leaven was an essential ingredient of bread, they thought perhaps He was advising them about how to bake bread properly or where not to buy bread. But no matter how hard they tried, they could not be sure what He was telling them.

Matthew then writes: **But Jesus, being aware of it, said to them, "O you of little faith, why do you reason among yourselves because you have brought no bread? Do you not yet understand, or remember the five loaves of the five thousand and how many baskets you took up? Nor the seven loaves of**

the four thousand and how many large baskets you took up? How is it you do not understand that I did not speak to you concerning bread?—but to beware of the leaven of the Pharisees and Sadducees" (vv. 8–11). Jesus could always sense their confusion, so He told them His comment had nothing to do with their lack of bread. He pointed out that they should have had enough faith at that point to know that He could provide them with bread if they needed it. He then repeated the warning so that they might hear that He had never used the word *bread* but had spoken of the *leaven* of the Pharisees and Sadducees.

Finally, the disciples saw that Jesus was speaking metaphorically: **Then they understood that He did not tell them to beware of the leaven of bread, but of the doctrine of the Pharisees and Sadducees** (v. 12). He was telling them to watch out for bad doctrine, for it can poison the mind, the heart, and the soul.

In Praise of Doctrine

So often today, *any* doctrine is regarded as bad doctrine. I hear it all the time: "I don't want to learn doctrine. All I need is Jesus. Doctrine divides. Doctrine's not necessary. I only have Jesus as my doctrine." I think that is a dangerous attitude, so when people tell me the only doctrine we need is Jesus, I ask them, "Well, who is Jesus?" If they answer me with so much as one word about Jesus, they are expressing doctrine. The Bible is almost totally about doctrine. Do we dare to tell the author of sacred Scripture that doctrine is not important? Should we tell the apostles who died for their teaching that doctrine is not important? Should we tell Jesus that we do not care about doctrine? That kind of attitude is wicked and silly.

In the sixteenth century, the Dutch humanist, Desiderius Erasmus, wrote a satire titled *The Praise of Folly*, which became one of the classics of Western literature. It was directed against the immorality that had infected the Roman Catholic Church priesthood and even the papacy under the Borgia popes, who were exceedingly corrupt. When Martin Luther read *The Praise of Folly*, he said that Erasmus had attacked the pope in his belly, while he had attacked the pope in his doctrine. He was saying that the Reformation was not about the immorality of the clergy in Rome; it was about the corruption of the true gospel with false doctrine.

Why is doctrine important? It is important because it is not an abstract set of philosophical or theological axioms. Doctrine has as its content the nature and the character of God, Father, Son, and Holy Spirit. How we understand the character of God has a profound impact on how we live the Christian life.

The Pharisees were devoted to obedience to the law of God. They believed that the Jewish Scriptures, the Old Testament, were the Word of God, all of them.

They believed in miracles. They believed in the resurrection of the dead and life after death. They were the conservatives of first-century Israel. Their problem, as is often the problem with conservatives and fundamentalists, was that they were not satisfied with what God had revealed in sacred Scripture. They added their own rules and regulations. By contrast, the Sadducees were the liberals. They said the only part of the Old Testament that was Scripture was the first five books, the Pentateuch. They did not acknowledge the books of the prophets to be the Word of God. They did not believe in miracles. Neither did they believe in the resurrection or life after death. They resembled nineteenth-century liberals in the mainline churches. Jesus told His disciples that both groups had poisonous leaven. They needed to watch out for the conservatives who added to the Bible and for the liberals who subtracted from it. Their duty was to keep their eyes on the Word of God and believe every word of it.

If we are going to know who God is and grow in our Christian lives, we have to study doctrine, because that is the content of the Bible. I know Bible study organizations that tell their people: "We're not going to get into doctrine. All we're going to do is look at the text." Unfortunately, if we want to stay away from doctrine, we cannot look very deeply into the text of Scripture. The best approach is to go to Scripture to *get* our doctrine, for that is what Scripture is, and our doctrine should come from nowhere else.

77

THE GREAT CONFESSION

Matthew 16:13–20

When Jesus came into the region of Caesarea Philippi, He asked His disciples, saying, "Who do men say that I, the Son of Man, am?" So they said, "Some say John the Baptist, some Elijah, and others Jeremiah or one of the prophets." He said to them, "But who do you say that I am?" Simon Peter answered and said, "You are the Christ, the Son of the living God." Jesus answered and said to him, "Blessed are you, Simon Bar-Jonah, for flesh and blood has not revealed this to you, but My Father who is in heaven. And I also say to you that you are Peter, and on this rock I will build My church, and the gates of Hades shall not prevail against it. And I will give you the keys of the kingdom of heaven, and whatever you bind on earth will be bound in heaven, and whatever you loose on earth will be loosed in heaven." Then He commanded His disciples that they should tell no one that He was Jesus the Christ.

We have come to Matthew's account of one of the great moments in the ministry of Jesus, that occasion when Simon Peter gave his great confession of Jesus as "the Christ," the Messiah. Jesus' excitement over this confession is nearly palpable in this passage, and therefore it is something about which we, too, should be excited. The reason, as Jesus Himself explained, is that it is upon this confession of faith that Jesus is building His church.

Matthew begins, **When Jesus came into the region of Caesarea Philippi, He asked His disciples, saying, "Who do men say that I, the Son of Man,**

am?" (v. 13). Caesarea Philippi was a city about twenty-five miles north of the Sea of Galilee. It had been built by one of the sons of Herod the Great, Philip, tetrarch of Iturea, a territory north and east of the sea. He named the city Caesarea in honor of Caesar Augustus, but because there was already a city named Caesarea on the Mediterranean coast, he added his own name to distinguish the two cities. As indicated in Matthew 16:5, Jesus and His disciples were back in Gentile lands again.

However, the place is not as important as what happened there on this occasion. Jesus polled His disciples, saying, "Who do men say that I, the Son of Man, am?" He was calling upon them to tell Him what they were hearing from their loved ones, friends, and others, to give Him the gist of public opinion about Him. I find it interesting that Jesus did not simply ask them, "Who do men say that I am?" In His question to the disciples, He provided the answer the people ought to be giving: "the Son of Man." As we have seen, this was Jesus' favorite designation for Himself, a title borrowed from the book of Daniel, which speaks of a heavenly being who is sent into the world from the Father and then returns to receive a kingdom (Dan. 7:9–14).

The disciples gave Jesus a short list of theories about Him that were current among the people: **So they said, "Some say John the Baptist, some Elijah, and others Jeremiah or one of the prophets"** (v. 14). These answers can cause us to scratch our heads. First, why did anyone think that Jesus was John the Baptist? Remember, without the modern methods of communication that we take for granted, the news of John's death may not have spread to all the people. Besides, few probably knew exactly what John looked like. Thus, when Jesus appeared in Galilee and began preaching and ministering like a prophet, some assumed that they were finally encountering the prophet they had heard about some time earlier. Second, why did some think Jesus was Elijah? As we have seen, the last prophet of the Old Testament, Malachi, had foretold the return of Elijah, saying, "Behold, I will send you Elijah the prophet before the coming of the great and dreadful day of the Lord" (4:5). Jesus was clearly a supernaturally gifted man of God, so it was understandable that some people wondered whether He was the fulfillment of this prophecy. Third, why did some believe He was Jeremiah? The Old Testament said nothing of a promised return of Jeremiah, but there were some Jewish traditions that taught that at the time of the Messiah, Jeremiah would reappear. Jeremiah was seen as standing at the head of a significant series of prophets, so it made sense that Jesus might be Jeremiah. Fourth, why did people think He might be another of the prophets? This seems to have been a default position for those who were not so sure about the other theories.

I find that last idea significant, because even in today's world, people who do not confess the lordship of Christ often give Him high acclaim by saying, "Jesus was a great prophet." The problem with such an accolade is self-evident. If He was a prophet and was not the Son of God, then He was a false prophet, because He taught that He Himself was more than a prophet.

An Enlightened Confession

After hearing these reports from the disciples, Jesus asked them a much more personal question: **He said to them, "But who do you say that I am?"** (v. 15). The word *you* here is plural; Jesus was asking all of the disciples to declare their thinking as to His identity. Peter, however, responded on behalf of them all: **Simon Peter answered and said, "You are the Christ, the Son of the living God"** (v. 16). We see throughout the Gospels that Peter had good days and bad days. In some ways, he was the strongest of the disciples; in other ways, he was the weakest. He actually denied Jesus at the time of His trial (though, to his credit, he was filled with shame and embarrassment when he realized what he had done). I have to say, however, that at least prior to the Day of Pentecost, this was Peter's finest hour. His words in response to Jesus' question have been immortalized in church history: "You are the Christ, the Son of the living God."

You may be wondering what was so startling about this confession. We have seen indications and hints that Jesus' identity as the promised Messiah of Israel was recognized here and there by various people. But the Old Testament teaching about the Messiah was complex, and there was disagreement and confusion as to whether Jesus fulfilled what was written there. As we have seen, John the Baptist went from declaring Jesus to be "the Lamb of God" (John 1:29) to asking Him, "Are You the Coming One, or do we look for another?" (Matt. 11:3). Jesus was not fulfilling John's understanding of the Old Testament.

Many of the Jewish people were focused on the idea that the Messiah would be a King who would deliver them from the oppression of the Romans. The Messiah would indeed deliver His people, but He would deliver them from their sins. He would be not only the King following David but also the Priest who would be the Suffering Servant of Israel, who would offer up for His people the perfect sacrifice once and for all—Himself. Very few understood this priestly role the Messiah would play or the fact that He would suffer. Furthermore, the idea that the Messiah would be divine was something virtually everyone failed to grasp. Given all this confusion, it took some time for the disciples to see the truth, but they finally got it—Jesus was, indeed, the Messiah the Old Testament had foretold.

Peter's confession is glorious, but it is also very important that we pay heed to how Jesus responded: **Jesus answered and said to him, "Blessed are you,**

Simon Bar-Jonah, for flesh and blood has not revealed this to you, but My Father who is in heaven" (v. 17). When Jesus heard Peter's confession, He pronounced him blessed because God the Father had done a wonderful thing for him. God had revealed truth to Peter. Jesus told him that the confession he had just uttered was not the result of ordinary reflection on his observations. It was not the product of ordinary human insight. It was a conclusion he never could have come to on his own. Instead, God had revealed it to him. God had worked supernaturally in Peter's mind to enable him to see that Jesus really was the fulfillment of the Old Testament prophecies about the Messiah who was to come.

You probably have heard of Jonathan Edwards, the magnificent preacher of eighteenth-century New England, and his famous sermon "Sinners in the Hands of an Angry God." But as I mentioned in chapter 57, it was not that sermon that catapulted Edwards to national fame and prominence. Rather, it was his earlier sermon "A Divine and Supernatural Light," in which Edwards expounded the idea that in our fallen humanity we are blind to the truths of God, and unless God the Holy Spirit opens our spiritual eyes, we cannot see the loveliness of Christ. This means that if we think Jesus was "a great man" and "a prophet," we are blind. We have missed the most important truth that can be proclaimed about Him. To see Him in His true dignity and preeminence requires a divine and supernatural work on our souls by God the Holy Spirit. We all need this work. With it, we cannot confess Him as Christ, as Peter did.

I vividly remember the night when the Holy Spirit removed the scales from my eyes and I realized for the first time that Jesus was the Son of God. I know that insight was not a result of my own clever investigations. It was a gift, the sweetest gift I have ever received. Who am I that the Lord would open my eyes? Who are we that we have been visited by such grace as to see Him in His excellence?

As I mentioned, Edwards was known for his sermon "Sinners in the Hands of an Angry God." Largely because of that sermon, he has the reputation of being a dour, mean, and insensitive preacher of hell fire, and damnation, scaring people with vivid images of wrath and judgment. However, scholars who have studied his complete body of work have said that the two words that appear most often in his writings are *sweetness* and *excellence*. Because of the divine and supernatural light of God, Edwards' mind and soul were captured by the sweetness and excellence of Christ.

The Rock and the Keys

Jesus went on to say: **"And I also say to you that you are Peter, and on this rock I will build My church, and the gates of Hades shall not prevail against**

it" (v. 18). There are probably very few verses in all of the New Testament more controversial than this one. This is the text to which the Roman Catholic Church appeals to support its view that the church must be ruled by the successor to Peter, the pope in Rome. Rome maintains that the church is built on one apostle, Peter. Other scholars have argued that the Roman Catholic understanding of Jesus' words completely misses the sense of what He was saying. They insist that Peter was the rock because of his confession, and it is on this confession that the church is built—the conviction that Jesus is the Christ, the Son of the living God. A church that forgets this confession or denies it is no church at all.

In some translations, this verse speaks of "the gates of hell." However, the word *Hades* is the actual Greek word in the text, and *Hades* does not have the same connotation as *hell*. It was the Greek word for the underworld where all people went at death; it made no distinction between those who went into blessedness and those who went into eternal punishment. Jesus was simply saying that not even death, "the last enemy" (1 Cor. 15:26), would be able to overcome His church, His gathered people.

Finally, Jesus said: **"And I will give you the keys of the kingdom of heaven, and whatever you bind on earth will be bound in heaven, and whatever you loose on earth will be loosed in heaven"** (v. 19). This portion of the text is equally controversial. Every attempt to translate this verse runs into difficulty because of the peculiar tense of the verb. A more accurate translation would be, "Whatever you bind on earth will have been bound in heaven, and whatever you loose on earth will have been loosed in heaven." What is in view here is the church's ministry of discipline.

At the time of the Reformation in the sixteenth century, as new churches and communions were emerging, a very important question arose: "What are the marks of an authentic church?" In response, the Reformers identified three essential marks. They said a true church is a place where the gospel is truly preached, the sacraments are properly administered, and discipline is practiced. That third mark is rarely handled correctly. Sometimes churches are harsh and judgmental, punishing members for small infractions. Other churches permit almost anything. But a true church is involved in godly discipline of its members, instructing them in how to grow in their walks with Christ and calling them to repentance when they fall into very serious sin.

When Jesus had finished giving these important teachings, Matthew tells us, **Then He commanded His disciples that they should tell no one that He was Jesus the Christ**. He wanted His disciples to keep His identity secret for a time. Here again we see the "messianic secret," Jesus' frequently expressed desire that people not spread the word about Him too extensively.

I want to close this chapter by asking you an important question: Who do you say Jesus is? The answer to that question is not just a matter of correct theology. Instead, it will determine where you will spend eternity—either in the eternal blessedness of those who know the sweetness and the excellency of Christ, or in the company of the damned, who refuse to submit to the only Son of God.

78

THE SHADOW OF THE CROSS

Matthew 16:21–28

From that time Jesus began to show to His disciples that He must go to Jerusalem, and suffer many things from the elders and chief priests and scribes, and be killed, and be raised the third day. Then Peter took Him aside and began to rebuke Him, saying, "Far be it from You, Lord; this shall not happen to You!" But He turned and said to Peter, "Get behind Me, Satan! You are an offense to Me, for you are not mindful of the things of God, but the things of men." Then Jesus said to His disciples, "If anyone desires to come after Me, let him deny himself, and take up his cross, and follow Me. For whoever desires to save his life will lose it, but whoever loses his life for My sake will find it. For what profit is it to a man if he gains the whole world, and loses his own soul? Or what will a man give in exchange for his soul? For the Son of Man will come in the glory of His Father with His angels, and then He will reward each according to his works. Assuredly, I say to you, there are some standing here who shall not taste death till they see the Son of Man coming in His kingdom."

Matthew has just recorded one of the glorious moments of Jesus' ministry, that occasion when Simon Peter confessed of Jesus, "You are the Christ, the Son of the living God" (v. 16), whereupon Jesus told him, "Blessed are you, Simon Bar-Jonah, for flesh and blood has not revealed this to you, but My Father who is in heaven" (v. 17). It is thrilling for us to see the disciples finally grasp and articulate precisely who Jesus is, and to observe Jesus' obvious excitement and pleasure over Peter's confession.

But immediately on the heels of that wonderful event, Matthew's narrative turns dark and foreboding. He writes: **From that time Jesus began to show to His disciples that He must go to Jerusalem, and suffer many things from the elders and chief priests and scribes, and be killed, and be raised the third day** (v. 21). With His identity clear in the minds of His disciples, Jesus began to enlighten them as to what lay ahead—the suffering and death that awaited Him at the culmination of His ministry as Messiah.

Sometimes English words fail to express the full import of ideas that are in the original biblical languages. In this verse, the English word *must* falls short of the degree of intensity Jesus used in explaining to His disciples that which absolutely *had* to happen. He was not telling them of a necessity that was driven by a human agenda; rather, it was a divine necessity. Therefore, it was nonnegotiable and incapable of being altered. Jesus was saying: "Men, I *must* go to Jerusalem, and in Jerusalem I *must* be delivered into the hands of the Jewish religious authorities, to be judged by the Sanhedrin and to suffer many things. I *must* enter into My grand passion and be killed. But I will be raised on the third day."

I think it is very significant that Jesus chose to talk about these things immediately after Peter's magnificent confession of faith. Even though the disciples recognized Jesus as the Messiah, they still had a very poor understanding of what the Messiah was to do. They did not envision a suffering and dying Messiah. As noted above, Jesus was clearly pleased with Peter's confession, but there was much more for the disciples to learn and understand.

Note the way in which Jesus worded the final portion of this prophecy: "and be raised the third day." Jesus did not say, "I will rise on the third day." Instead, He used the passive voice. He was saying that He would not stay dead, not because He would raise Himself from the grave, but because the Father would raise Him. He would not be abandoned to death. The Father would bring Him back to life.

It seems that the disciples were so stricken by Jesus' prophecy of His death that they did not hear Him foretell His resurrection. This promise of life overcoming death should have brought them such joy as to more than compensate for their sadness over His suffering and death. However, it seems they never took the promise of His resurrection to heart when He mentioned it and were actually surprised when it happened.

Satan's Opportune Time

The next verses, if they were not so tragic, would be almost comical. Matthew tells us: **Then Peter took Him aside and began to rebuke Him, saying, "Far**

be it from You, Lord; this shall not happen to You!" (v. 22). Can you imagine? Peter had just made his great confession of faith, and Jesus had called him "the rock." However, within minutes, the rock began to crumble into dust. Peter, perhaps feeling a bit prideful after giving his confession and receiving Jesus' praise, took it upon himself to *rebuke* the Lord Jesus Christ. To give emphasis to his instruction of Jesus, Peter said, "Far be it from You." Another translation is, "God forbid that this should happen to You." God forbid it? How could Peter presume to know the mind of God so clearly? How could he make such a monstrously arrogant statement that was so completely wrong? God would not forbid the cross for He had ordained the cross. If Jesus did not go to the cross, He would not be able to complete His mission as the Messiah. If Jesus did not go to the cross, there would be no salvation from sin, including the sin of arrogance Peter was committing. Peter was setting himself against God's eternal plan.

Jesus quickly showed Peter the seriousness of his error by rebuking *him*: **But He turned and said to Peter, "Get behind Me, Satan! You are an offense to Me, for you are not mindful of the things of God, but the things of men"** (v. 23). I want to look closely at several points in this sharp rebuke.

First, Jesus said, "Get behind Me." He was saying, in essence: "Get out of My way! Don't stand in front of Me to resist Me!" Jesus was a Man on a mission and did not want to be hindered. It is interesting that when we are called to do a duty that may put us in harm's way or expose us to affliction or suffering, those who are strongest in their urging for us not to do it very often are the people who love us the most. Our loved ones and best friends often counsel us to be careful and to look out for our own skins. That can make it very difficult to be obedient to the call of God on our lives. At this point, Jesus was no different. When He announced that it was His destiny to go to Jerusalem to die, it was His closest friends who wanted to stand in His way. But Jesus refused to hear their entreaties.

Second, Jesus called Peter "Satan." The one Jesus had so recently called "the rock" He now equated with the Evil One. Why did He choose this epithet? I believe we find the answer when we recall Jesus' temptation in the wilderness, when Jesus came under the unrestrained assault of the devil day after day. The main temptation of Satan's attack on Him during that time was to be a Savior without suffering. Satan suggested that Jesus should go the triumphal route. He dared Jesus to turn stones into bread. He tempted Him to throw Himself down from the temple so angels would catch Him. He offered Jesus all the kingdoms of the world without an ounce of pain if He would only bow down and worship the prince of darkness. Satan was willing to give Jesus anything—as long as He did not take the way of suffering that led to the cross. Jesus, however, refused all Satan's offers. Finally, Satan departed from Him "until an opportune time" (Luke 4:13b). That time came when Peter stood up to oppose Jesus' plan to go to Jerusalem, suggesting, just as Satan had in the wilderness, that Jesus should avoid pain and suffering. Peter was opposing Jesus' divine mission just as the devil had. It is little wonder, then, that Jesus called Peter "Satan."

Third, Jesus said Peter was "an offense." The Greek word used here is *skandalon*. Originally, this word referred to a part of a trap to which bait was attached, but in the New Testament it typically carries a broader meaning, referring metaphorically to something that causes a hindrance. Jesus was rebuking Peter for being a hindrance to His mission, for offering Him a tantalizing way out of His deadly mission that would prove to be a trap.

Fourth, Jesus said, "You are not mindful of the things of God, but the things of men." Peter was looking at things from a human perspective, assuming that a living Jesus was better than a suffering and dying Jesus. There is a world of difference between the things of God and the things of men. It is our nature, our habit, to focus our attention on the things of this world and give little thought to the things of God. That ought not to be. Christians, of all people, should know better. Our calling is to bring our thoughts into alignment with God's, to think His thoughts after Him (Rom. 12:1–2).

Deny Self, Following Christ

Next, Matthew tells us, **Jesus said to His disciples, "If anyone desires to come after Me, let him deny himself, and take up his cross, and follow Me"** (v. 24). This is one of the clearest, starkest statements of what the Christian life is about that we find in all of Scripture. To follow Christ is to live in the shadow of the cross. If we want to join Him in His glory, if we want to participate in His exaltation, first we must join Him in His disgrace, shame, and humiliation. We must be willing to die. That is what it means to be a follower of Christ.

When we seek to win converts to Christianity, we often do everything we can to persuade them of all the benefits they will receive if they will give their lives to Jesus. But Jesus talked about the cost of being one of His followers. There was no cheap grace in the evangelism of Jesus.

But that does not mean the Christian life is loss. Ironically, by losing, we experience great gain. Jesus said, **"For whoever desires to save his life will lose it, but whoever loses his life for My sake will find it"** (v. 25). Simply put, Jesus was saying we cannot save ourselves by our own efforts. However, if we surrender all to Him, we gain everything.

Then He borrowed language from the marketplace and said: **"For what**

profit is it to a man if he gains the whole world, and loses his own soul? Or what will a man give in exchange for his soul?" (v. 26). Jesus was speaking of ultimate value, eternal value. Clearly, it is better to choose the way of suffering now if by it we may gain glory for eternity. To choose gain in this life, only to lose one's soul—that is, to suffer eternal condemnation—is a poor bargain indeed.

What do you daydream about? Do you dream about a better job, a nicer home, a fancier car, a larger bank account? What if you could have it all with just one string—your soul? Would that seem to be a good bargain to you? Or would you regard it as a price too dear to pay, even if you could receive the whole world in exchange? Jesus valued the souls of His people so highly He shed His blood to purchase them. He places more value on our souls than we ourselves do. We all need to think very soberly about what we value most and make sure our priorities are in order.

Jesus continued, **"For the Son of Man will come in the glory of His Father with His angels, and then He will reward each according to his works"** (v. 27). Several times in our study of Matthew we have run across this idea of rewards in heaven, and we find the same concept taught elsewhere in the New Testament. As we saw earlier, Jesus here explained that everyone will be rewarded for His works in this life. Clearly, works do not get us to heaven; the New Testament strongly denies that idea in many passages. Only the works of Christ are good enough to get us into heaven, but once we are there, our station in heaven for eternity is determined by our works. So, we are encouraged by Jesus and by the New Testament authors to work for the prize that has been set before us, to "lay up . . . treasures in heaven" (Matt. 6:20) rather than punishments in hell. This is a call to set our minds not on earth but on heaven, not on the natural but on the supernatural. We need to think about where we will be a thousand years from now.

Jesus ended this brief discourse with one of the most enigmatic statements that we have found so far in the Gospel, one that twists the commentators on this book into all kinds of knots. He said, **"Assuredly, I say to you, there are some standing here who shall not taste death till they see the Son of Man coming in His kingdom"** (v. 28). When Jesus said "assuredly," He was emphasizing to His disciples that the statement He was about to utter was completely trustworthy; they could take it to the bank. He then said that some of them would not die until He came "in His kingdom." What did this mean and what was the time frame to which He was referring? Was He referring to the transfiguration that was to happen in just a few days? Was He referring to His ascension? Was He referring to the Holy Spirit coming in power at Pentecost? Was He referring to the destruction of Jerusalem in AD 70? Or was He referring to His final coming in the future? All of these are options scholars have proposed to interpret this verse. I will try to sort through these various interpretations when we reach Matthew 24, which also contains a very controversial time-frame reference.

As we await His final coming, let us not be those that would dare to rebuke the Lord, to be His counselor, to give Him direction. Let us be people who are mindful of the things of God rather than the things of men.

79

THE TRANSFIGURATION

Matthew 17:1–9

Now after six days Jesus took Peter, James, and John his brother, led them up on a high mountain by themselves; and He was transfigured before them. His face shone like the sun, and His clothes became as white as the light. And behold, Moses and Elijah appeared to them, talking with Him. Then Peter answered and said to Jesus, "Lord, it is good for us to be here; if You wish, let us make here three tabernacles: one for You, one for Moses, and one for Elijah." While he was still speaking, behold, a bright cloud overshadowed them; and suddenly a voice came out of the cloud, saying, "This is My beloved Son, in whom I am well pleased. Hear Him!" And when the disciples heard it, they fell on their faces and were greatly afraid. But Jesus came and touched them and said, "Arise, and do not be afraid." When they had lifted up their eyes, they saw no one but Jesus only. Now as they came down from the mountain, Jesus commanded them, saying, "Tell the vision to no one until the Son of Man is risen from the dead."

It is always a joy and a delight for me to work through the Gospel accounts and to read anew the records of those great events that attended Jesus' life and ministry—His birth in Bethlehem, His astonishing miracles, His triumphal entry into Jerusalem, His crucifixion on Golgotha, His resurrection, His ascension to the right hand of God, and so many more. On occasion I have asked myself, if I had lived during Jesus' time, which of these events would I most like to have witnessed? It would be awfully hard not to choose the resurrection.

But of all the events of Jesus' life prior to His death and resurrection, the one I most would have loved to witness was His transfiguration. I think that if I had lived in that time and had seen the transfiguration, I would have been able to sing hymns of praise while the lions were waiting to devour me in the Coliseum. How wonderful it would have been to see Jesus unveiled in His glory.

It is obvious that the three men who were there—Peter, James, and John—never got over it. When John wrote his Gospel, he said, "And the Word became flesh and dwelt among us, and we beheld His glory, the glory as of the only begotten of the Father, full of grace and truth" (1:14). Likewise, Peter wrote, "For we did not follow cunningly devised fables when we made known to you the power and coming of our Lord Jesus Christ, but were eyewitnesses of His majesty" (2 Peter 1:16). Given what these men witnessed on the mountain, it really is not surprising that they went on to turn the world upside down (Acts 17:6).

Matthew tells us, **Now after six days Jesus took Peter, James, and John his brother, led them up on a high mountain by themselves; and He was transfigured before them** (vv. 1–2a). *Transfigured* is a weak word, but perhaps it is the best available English word to translate the Greek word Matthew uses here, which is the passive form of the verb *metamorphoō*. The verb literally means "a change of form." It comes over into the English language as the word *metamorphosis*. We use it to describe the amazing transformation of a caterpillar into a butterfly. But *transfiguration* includes the prefix *trans-*, which means "across." What was crossed in the transfiguration? We might say Jesus crossed the line from the natural to the supernatural, from the human to the divine, as the cloak of humanity that veiled His true glory was removed and His glory became visible.

Notice that Matthew says "He was transfigured before them." In other words, His figure changed right before the disciples' eyes. What did they witness and later report to the Gospel authors for their records?

The Brightness of His Glory

Matthew writes, **His face shone like the sun, and His clothes became as white as the light** (v. 2b). The first thing they noticed was a change to His face; it shone like the sun. When the biblical writers describe something that is intensely bright, the metaphor they usually turn to is the sun. When a solar eclipse occurs, we always see warnings in the media to be very careful when the eclipse is total, for as the moon moves across the face of the sun, the searing brightness of the sun returns with little warning, and it can damage our eyes. When astronomers study the sun, they must gaze at it through media that filter its brightness. That was the kind of intense brightness that suddenly began to emanate from Jesus' face there on the mountain. His visage became refulgent.

When Saul was on the road to Damascus to persecute the Christians there, "suddenly a light shone around him from heaven" (Acts 9:3b). The intensity of this light caused him to fall to the ground and blinded him. It was the splendor of the glorified Jesus that appeared to him on the road to Damascus. It was this glory that the three disciples witnessed on the mountain.

As Moses was communing with God on Mount Sinai, he asked for the ultimate blessing: "Please, show me Your glory" (Ex. 33:18). God replied that no man could look on His face and live, but He said: "Here is a place by Me, and you shall stand on the rock. So it shall be, while My glory passes by, that I will put you in the cleft of the rock, and will cover you with My hand while I pass by. Then I will take away My hand, and you shall see My back; but My face shall not be seen" (vv. 21–23). As He promised, God gave Moses a glimpse of His back (34:6–7). When Moses beheld that sight, he was transfigured. When he came down from Mount Sinai, the people fled from him in terror, for Moses's face was shining, though he did not know it (34:29–30). However, the glory of Moses's face was a mere reflection of the glory of God. Even so, it was enough to terrify the people of Israel.

The glory that Peter, James, and John beheld on the Mount of Transfiguration was not a reflection. It came from inside Him. The source was the being of Christ, whom the author of Hebrews describes as "the brightness of [God's] glory" (1:3). The disciples witnessed the glory of God. Thus, this event was a revelation of the actual nature of Christ, who is God Himself, the second person of the Trinity.

We have another glimpse of the glorified Christ in the book of Revelation. Near the end of the book, John describes the New Jerusalem. One curious feature that he mentions is that "the city had no need of the sun or of the moon to shine in it, for the glory of God illuminated it. The Lamb is its light" (21:23). This city needs no sun or moon because there is a greater light, the glory of God as seen in the Lamb.

Matthew also says, "His clothes became as white as the light." Mark amplifies this description, writing: "His clothes became shining, exceedingly white, like snow, such as no launderer on earth can whiten them" (9:3). Does it ever seem to you that companies that manufacture soap products seem to tout an improvement every year or so? Every commercial, every magazine ad, every product box seems to carry the words "new and improved." It makes you wonder how shoddy those products were just a few years ago. Of course, after a while, it becomes difficult to find new superlatives for soap, so we see the soap companies claiming that their products will make things "whiter than white." When you hear that, you know you are hearing an advertising ploy and not the truth, because there is no such thing as whiter than white. Once white is expressed in its purity, there is no room for improvement.

In the past, when I taught children about the transfiguration, I would ask them a simple question: "What color is a lemon?" They would always answer correctly: yellow. So, I would then ask, "What color is a lemon in the dark?" Some would say it is still yellow, some would say black, and others would make various other guesses. I then would explain that in the dark a lemon has no color at all, because color is not a primary quality of objects; rather, it is a secondary quality. Color is manifest when light is present, but without light, all hues vanish. But the purity of color, the fullness of color, is perfect whiteness. All of the colors of the rainbow are found in pure whiteness.

That was what the disciples witnessed. As Jesus' glory radiated out from His person, His garments shone with pure whiteness. There was no hint of gray, no shadow, no darkness, just pure, unblemished whiteness. The eyes of the disciples had never beheld such whiteness in their lives.

The Law and the Prophets

Matthew then records, **And behold, Moses and Elijah appeared to them, talking with Him** (v. 3). Moses, the mediator of the old covenant, had not been allowed to enter the Promised Land, but he finally stood there on this occasion. As we have seen, God had promised that Elijah would return in conjunction with the coming of the Messiah (Mal. 4:5). It is not difficult to know what they were talking about, since the Old Testament books of the Law and the Prophets all pointed to Christ and His ministry. No doubt they were discussing what was about to happen to Him in Jerusalem, the culmination of God's plan, foretold for so many centuries. In fact, Luke tells us they discussed "His decease which He was about to accomplish at Jerusalem" (9:31b), the trials and death He was shortly to endure. Perhaps Moses and Elijah were reminding Jesus, "This is what you were born for. This is the end of the curse of the law. This is the fulfillment of all the prophecies." In essence, the Law and the Prophets came to Jesus on the mountain to encourage Him in His mission.

Matthew also tells us, **Peter answered and said to Jesus, "Lord, it is good for us to be here; if You wish, let us make here three tabernacles: one for You, one for Moses, and one for Elijah"** (v. 4). Peter expressed his pleasure at being present for this magnificent display of Jesus' glory, and he offered to make three tents so Jesus, Moses, and Elijah could remain there—anything to prolong this "mountaintop experience." Still, it is hard to escape the conclusion that Peter was just babbling, with no clear notion of what He was saying.

In any case, **While he was still speaking, behold, a bright cloud overshadowed them; and suddenly a voice came out of the cloud, saying, "This is My beloved Son, in whom I am well pleased. Hear Him!"** (v. 5). The *shekinah* cloud of God's glory appeared and surrounded them, and a voice spoke from within it, the Father expressing His love and pleasure in the Son. He also spoke an exhortation, clearly aimed at the disciples: "Hear Him!" Not surprisingly, **when the disciples heard it, they fell on their faces and were greatly afraid** (v. 6). This voice was more than they could handle. But in the midst of their terror, **Jesus came and touched them and said, "Arise, and do not be afraid." When they had lifted up their eyes, they saw no one but Jesus only** (vv. 7–8). Once again, Jesus was veiled in His humanity, the *shekinah* cloud had lifted, and Moses and Elijah had departed. The transfiguration was over.

In a brief postscript, Matthew adds: **Now as they came down from the mountain, Jesus commanded them, saying, "Tell the vision to no one until the Son of Man is risen from the dead"** (v. 9). Just as He had commanded many He had healed to tell no one about Him, He instructed the disciples to say nothing about His transfiguration—until after His resurrection. Once again, in an oblique way, Jesus hinted to His disciples that He would die but not stay dead, but they did not seem to catch His meaning.

We tend to think of the transfiguration as a momentary epiphany of the true identity of Jesus. Actually, it was a taste of heaven, where we will live eternally with Jesus, glorified as He is glorified (1 John 3:2). This was not a temporary thing with Jesus, because forever and ever He is the Lord of glory. It is no wonder the disciples were filled with passion for the work of the kingdom after their eyes saw what took place on that mountain. May God give to us the same passion for His kingdom.

80

THE COMING OF ELIJAH

Matthew 17:10–13

And His disciples asked Him, saying, "Why then do the scribes say that Elijah must come first?" Jesus answered and said to them, "Indeed, Elijah is coming first and will restore all things. But I say to you that Elijah has come already, and they did not know him but did to him whatever they wished. Likewise the Son of Man is also about to suffer at their hands." Then the disciples understood that He spoke to them of John the Baptist.

If I had been with Jesus on the Mount of Transfiguration, I believe I could have come up with a thousand questions to ask Him as we descended. However, I am frankly not sure I would have asked a question about the basis for the Jewish scribes' teaching on the return of Elijah, even if I had just seen Elijah talking with Jesus on the mountain. Nevertheless, Matthew tells us Peter, James, and John did indeed ask this question.

Now, I believe the three disciples probably did pepper Him with many questions, for we must never suppose that the conversations between Jesus and His disciples that are recorded for us in the Gospels are the only ones they ever had. John tells us, "And truly Jesus did many other signs in the presence of His disciples, which are not written in this book" (20:30). The Gospel writers were selective, and John helpfully identifies his chief criterion: "These are written that you may believe that Jesus is the Christ, the Son of God, and that believing you may have life in His name" (v. 31). Since Matthew, like John, was guided in his writing by the Holy Spirit, we must approach this text on the assumption that this question about Elijah and Jesus' answer to it are recorded here in this Gospel that our faith in Jesus might be strengthened.

The question was a simple one: **And His disciples asked Him, saying, "Why then do the scribes say that Elijah must come first?"** (v. 10). The scribes were theologians, experts on the Old Testament law. They taught that Elijah had to come before the Messiah. The implication in the disciples' question is that the scribes were contending that since Elijah had not come, the Messiah had not come either. So, any claim Jesus might make to be the Messiah must be regarded as invalid.

As I noted earlier, the prophecy about Elijah's coming is the last prophecy recorded in the Old Testament. We find it at the end of the last chapter of the last book of the Old Testament, the book of Malachi. We read there: "Behold, I will send you Elijah the prophet before the coming of the great and dreadful day of the Lord. And he will turn the hearts of the fathers to the children, and the hearts of the children to their fathers, lest I come and strike the earth with a curse" (Mal. 4:5–6). With this prophecy in mind, the Jewish people had awaited the return of Elijah for four hundred years. Whenever they celebrated the Passover, they kept one chair empty in case Elijah came that night. Jewish people still do this when they celebrate the seder meal. They are still waiting for Elijah.

However, Peter, James, and John were in a different situation. They were convinced that Jesus was the Messiah. As we saw in chapter 77, Peter, speaking on behalf of all the disciples, confessed, "You are the Christ, the Son of the living God" (Matt. 16:16). Furthermore, as we saw in the previous chapter, all three of them had seen Jesus transfigured on the mountain, beholding His divine glory. Now they were wondering why the scribes were so insistent that Elijah had to come before the Messiah. As they saw it, the Messiah had come, but Elijah had not come before Him.

However, Elijah had appeared on the mountain, along with Moses, when Jesus was transformed. As we noted in the previous chapter, Moses and Elijah appeared there with the Messiah. The disciples obviously saw and somehow recognized both Moses and Elijah, for Peter spoke of him by name (Matt. 17:4). So, that extraordinary meeting of Moses, Elijah, and Jesus provoked questions in the minds of the disciples, including one about the basis for the scribes' teaching that Elijah had to come before the Messiah.

The Mistreatment of Elijah

Matthew tells us, **Jesus answered and said to them, "Indeed, Elijah is coming first and will restore all things. But I say to you that Elijah has come already,**

and they did not know him but did to him whatever they wished. Likewise the Son of Man is also about to suffer at their hands." Then the disciples understood that He spoke to them of John the Baptist (vv. 11–13). Jesus essentially said, "The scribes are right." However, He added that "Elijah" had already come, but he was really John the Baptist. What did He mean by this?

We have considered the relationship between Elijah and John the Baptist in previous chapters, so I will briefly recap here what we have discovered. When John appeared out of the wilderness, wearing camel's hair and a leather belt, and eating locusts and wild honey, he provoked comparisons to Elijah (2 Kings 1:8), who spent so much of his time as a fugitive in the desert, even being fed by the ravens on one occasion (1 Kings 17:4–6). So, the Jewish religious authorities from Jerusalem sent a delegation to John and specifically asked, "Are you Elijah?" to which he replied, "I am not" (John 1:21). However, as we saw earlier in Matthew, in the context of commenting on John's greatness, Jesus said, "If you are willing to receive it, he is Elijah who is to come" (11:14). In a certain sense, then, John was the fulfillment of Malachi's prophecy. This link between John and Elijah is explained by the words of the angel Gabriel, when he foretold John's birth to John's father, Zacharias: "He will also go before [the Messiah] in the spirit and power of Elijah" (Luke 1:17a). Thus, Malachi's prophecy was not fulfilled by a second coming of Elijah himself, but by the coming of one who was endowed with the same spirit and power as Elijah, who was John the Baptist. This is why Jesus said, "Elijah has come already, and they did not know him."

Jesus then added, "but [they] did to [John] whatever they wished." John endured persecution, just as Elijah did. Elijah, of course, was persecuted by the idolatrous Queen Jezebel because he courageously struck down the prophets of Baal. That stirring episode in Israel's history is found in 1 Kings 18, where we read that Elijah challenged the prophets of Baal to a contest—he and they would both prepare a bull for sacrifice, lay it on wood, and call upon their deities to send fire. The prophets of Baal went first, and though they prayed, nothing happened. Elijah began to mock them, saying, "Either he is meditating, or he is busy, or he is on a journey, or perhaps he is sleeping and must be awakened" (v. 27). They began to cut themselves with knives, but still nothing happened.

Finally, Elijah built an altar, prepared his bull for sacrifice, and laid it on the wood. He then commanded that water be poured over the sacrifice and the wood, not once but three times. Even so, when Elijah prayed, fire fell from God and consumed the bull, the drenched wood, the stones of the altar, and even the water. The people immediately proclaimed that God was God, and Elijah ordered them to seize and execute all of the prophets of Baal.

When we come to 1 Kings 19, we discover that this incident had serious consequences for Elijah:

> And Ahab told Jezebel all that Elijah had done, also how he had executed all the prophets with the sword. Then Jezebel sent a messenger to Elijah, saying, "So let the gods do to me, and more also, if I do not make your life as the life of one of them by tomorrow about this time." And when he saw that, he arose and ran for his life, and went to Beersheba, which belongs to Judah, and left his servant there. But he himself went a day's journey into the wilderness, and came and sat down under a broom tree. And he prayed that he might die, and said, "It is enough! Now, Lord, take my life, for I am no better than my fathers!" Then as he lay and slept under a broom tree, suddenly an angel touched him, and said to him, "Arise and eat." Then he looked, and there by his head was a cake baked on coals, and a jar of water. So he ate and drank, and lay down again. And the angel of the Lord came back the second time, and touched him, and said, "Arise and eat, because the journey is too great for you." So he arose, and ate and drank; and he went in the strength of that food forty days and forty nights as far as Horeb, the mountain of God. And there he went into a cave, and spent the night in that place; and behold, the word of the Lord came to him, and He said to him, "What are you doing here, Elijah?" So he said, "I have been very zealous for the Lord God of hosts; for the children of Israel have forsaken Your covenant, torn down Your altars, and killed Your prophets with the sword. I alone am left; and they seek to take my life." (vv. 1–10)

This is the classical text that expresses what I call "the Elijah syndrome." This is the condition that afflicts a person who thinks he is the only faithful person, the only one who still serves God amid rampant evil and apostasy. God quickly corrected that incorrect perception in Elijah, saying, "I have reserved seven thousand in Israel, all whose knees have not bowed to Baal, and every mouth that has not kissed him" (v. 18). Nevertheless, it is true that Elijah was relentlessly hunted and pursued by wicked people for much of his ministry.

Like Elijah, John the Baptist was despised and ultimately put to death by a wicked king. He came as the forerunner of the Messiah and ministered in the spirit and power of Elijah, but the authorities still did to him whatever they wished. Herod Antipas imprisoned him and cut off his head during a party.

Why did Elijah suffer so greatly? Why did King Ahab call him, "O troubler of Israel" (1 Kings 18:17), even though he and Jezebel were the true troublers of Israel? It was because he brought the truth of God to a nation in the midst of corruption. As a result of that truth, he was hated, exiled, and pursued. Why was John the Baptist thrown in jail and executed? It was because he spoke truth to power, admonishing the king for his adultery and improper marriage.

The Mistreatment of the Son

Jesus also warned His disciples, "Likewise the Son of Man is also about to suffer at their hands." Just as Elijah was hunted and John the Baptist was put to death, Jesus was going to be mistreated and put to death by the Jewish religious leaders. Like them, His only crime would be speaking the truth.

So many people today are quick to praise Jesus—to a point. They say: "Jesus was a great teacher, a marvelous innovator, a real man of peace. He was centuries ahead of His time. I don't believe He was divine, but He was certainly one of the greatest men who ever lived." When I hear that, I want to ask: Why did virtually no one in Jesus' own time see Him as a great man? Why did so many people hate Him? Why did they kill Him?

Jonathan Edwards once preached a sermon titled "Men Naturally God's Enemies." In that sermon, Edwards developed the New Testament teaching that in our fallen condition, all of us are at enmity with God. No one is born into this world with a neutral mind-set. Our natural disposition is antagonism and antipathy toward the God who made us. We simply do not want God's restraints on our behavior, our thinking, or any aspect of our lives.

I once was invited to address a collegiate atheist club. The club members expected me to give a philosophical defense of the truth claims of Christianity. Instead, I just treated them to a heavy dose of the book of Romans, where Paul declares that God has revealed Himself to every human being with penetrating clarity, but the universal response of fallen men is to suppress that knowledge (1:19). Paul says, "they are without excuse, because, although they knew God, they did not glorify Him as God, nor were thankful" (vv. 20b–21a). The most basic, fundamental, and primeval sin that inhabits the hearts of all humans by nature is the refusal to honor the God whom they know exists.

At the end of my talk to the atheist club, I said to them: "If the apostle Paul is correct, and I believe he is, it seems to me that the problem with the existence of God is not at all an intellectual problem. It's a moral problem. Your problem is not that you don't know that God exists, because you do know that God exists. Your problem is that you hate the God who does exist. You are by nature at enmity with God." As you can imagine, they were not very grateful to hear that summation.

If God were to come down from heaven and put his life at risk before men, He would not survive for five minutes, because fallen human beings want nothing to do with Him. He is not welcome in the marketplace of ideas. A worldview that is theistic, rooted and grounded in the core affirmation of the supreme existence of God and His sovereignty over all things, is wholeheartedly rejected. That is why, more and more in the West, Christians are being told to keep their beliefs on the reservation. They are told, "You're welcome to pray to God, sing to Him, and worship Him, but keep your beliefs in the privacy of your church or your home." As soon as we bring God into the marketplace, the natural hatred of God that Edwards preached about manifests itself, and those who bring Him there are in jeopardy.

Jesus' words were a sobering wake-up call for Peter, James, and John. "Just as John was treated, so the Jews are going to treat Me," He said. "So, in spite of the glory you have just seen on the mountain, this is not a time for a theology of glory. It is a time for a theology of the cross. That is the way My Father has ordained that the restoration of all things should come to pass." Therefore, Jesus set His face as a flint toward Jerusalem (Isa. 50:7).

81

A FAITHLESS GENERATION

Matthew 17:14–21

And when they had come to the multitude, a man came to Him, kneeling down to Him and saying, "Lord, have mercy on my son, for he is an epileptic and suffers severely; for he often falls into the fire and often into the water. So I brought him to Your disciples, but they could not cure him." Then Jesus answered and said, "O faithless and perverse generation, how long shall I be with you? How long shall I bear with you? Bring him here to Me." And Jesus rebuked the demon, and it came out of him; and the child was cured from that very hour. Then the disciples came to Jesus privately and said, "Why could we not cast it out?" So Jesus said to them, "Because of your unbelief; for assuredly, I say to you, if you have faith as a mustard seed, you will say to this mountain, 'Move from here to there,' and it will move; and nothing will be impossible for you. However, this kind does not go out except by prayer and fasting."

Following the glorious experience of the transfiguration, Jesus, along with Peter, James, and John, descended the mountain so that He might take up His journey to Jerusalem and the trials that awaited Him there. It was a descent from glory and transcendence to the normalcy of life and ministry, with Jesus once again having to deal with "a faithless and perverse generation."

As I read this passage, I cannot help but think of a similar descent from a mountaintop experience to an encounter with a distorted, perverse, and twisted generation that was marked by unbelief. We read in the book of Exodus:

> And Moses turned and went down from the mountain, and the two tablets of the Testimony were in his hand. . . . And when Joshua heard the noise of the people as they shouted, he said to Moses, "There is a noise of war in the camp." But he said: "It is not the noise of the shout of victory, nor the noise of the cry of defeat, but the sound of singing I hear." So it was, as soon as he came near the camp, that he saw the [golden] calf and the [people] dancing. So Moses' anger became hot, and he cast the tablets out of his hands and broke them at the foot of the mountain. Then he took the calf which they had made, burned it in the fire, and ground it to powder; and he scattered it on the water and made the children of Israel drink it. (32:15–20)

What Moses saw when he came down from Mount Sinai was probably the most popular worship service ever held. Everyone was in attendance, for this worship service was designed to please the desires of the people rather than the desire of God. The singing was so lustful that it sounded like the outbreak of war from miles away. It was all focused on an image of a calf fashioned from the golden earrings of the people.

The mediator of the old covenant went up the mountain, where he met with God and received the Law, but when he came down from that holy place he saw the nation of Israel totally given to idolatry. Centuries later, our Lord went up the Mount of Transfiguration, where His glory was made manifest, but He came down to a faithless and perverse generation.

An Absence of Faith

Matthew tells us: **And when they had come to the multitude, a man came to Him, kneeling down to Him and saying, "Lord, have mercy on my son, for he is an epileptic and suffers severely; for he often falls into the fire and often into the water"** (vv. 14–15). The term *epileptic* is supplied by the translators based on the symptoms that are mentioned here—the boy had convulsions and often fell into the fire or the water. The text literally says the boy was a lunatic. We think of lunacy as insanity, but in the ancient world people who behaved in a strange and erratic manner were thought to be "moonstruck," and so they were called lunatics from the Latin word *luna*, which means "moon." But while the boy's symptoms indicated that he had an illness, Matthew soon informs us that the real issue was demonic possession.

The father then said, **"So I brought him to Your disciples, but they could not cure him"** (v. 16). Jesus had given the disciples power and authority over demons (Luke 9:1), and they had rejoiced in the power He had given to them (10:17). There is no record that they had had any problems with casting out demons prior to this occasion, but they were stymied in their efforts to help this boy. They probably did everything they knew to do, but all that they tried failed. I can only imagine how the father's frustration with the disciples' inability must have turned to joy when he saw Jesus coming. He ran to Him, knelt, and begged Him to have mercy on the boy.

Matthew gives us Jesus' response: **Then Jesus answered and said, "O faithless and perverse generation, how long shall I be with you? How long shall I bear with you? Bring him here to Me"** (v. 17). If we ever hear an outcry of utter frustration from Jesus, it is here. He described that generation, the people who were alive at that time, as faithless and perverse. Those words, *faithless* and *perverse*, belong together. To be faithless is to lack trust in the truth of God, to not be committed heart and soul to the ways of God. The word that is translated as "perverse" literally means "distorted or twisted." The people's sense of right and wrong was twisted. They embraced vice and ridiculed virtue. Their values were upside down. In short, they were perverse. Does this sound familiar to you? We live in a time when vice is celebrated and righteousness is ridiculed. That is because we live in a time that is marked by the absence of faith.

At this point in His ministry, Jesus had had a bellyful of this perversity. That frustration provoked Him to a lamentation: "How long do I have to put up with this? How long do I have to bear with this generation?" Nevertheless, Jesus commanded the father to bring the boy, and when he did, **Jesus rebuked the demon, and it came out of him; and the child was cured from that very hour** (v. 18).

Jesus' ability to drive out the demon with ease naturally caused the disciples to wonder what they had done wrong. So, they asked Jesus about it: **Then the disciples came to Jesus privately and said, "Why could we not cast it out?" So Jesus said to them, "Because of your unbelief"** (vv. 19–20a). How are we to understand this diagnosis of the reason for their failure? Just days before, Peter, speaking on behalf of all of them, had made a grand and glorious confession of faith: "You are the Christ, the Son of the living God" (Matt. 16:16). They had faith, but it was fragile. It was mixed with doubt. It was diluted with the thinking of this world.

We are called to live lives of faith in a godless society. Every hour of every day we hear viewpoints that are on a collision course with the content of our faith, viewpoints that assault, undermine, and torpedo the precious truths we try to cling to, sometimes by our very fingernails. We believe, but our faith is often overcome by our unbelief. Jesus said this is why the disciples were powerless to defeat the enemy on this occasion, and that is why we often fail to live the faithful lives we aspire to live.

Jesus went on to say, **"For assuredly, I say to you, if you have faith as a mustard seed, you will say to this mountain, 'Move from here to there,' and it will move; and nothing will be impossible for you"** (v. 20b). In the Jewish lore of that day, the idea of moving mountains through faith was part of the metaphorical understanding of the power of trusting God. Jesus said if His disciples had real faith, they could move mountains—and they surely could cast one little demon out of a poor soul.

The Need for Urgent Prayer

Finally, Matthew tells us, Jesus concluded His explanation with a curious statement: **"However, this kind does not go out except by prayer and fasting"** (v. 21). There is some question as to whether this sentence was part of Matthew's original text, for it is not found in all of the early manuscripts. However, this statement is found in Mark's Gospel (9:29), so it seems that it was indeed part of what Jesus said on this occasion. The more pertinent issue for us is what Jesus meant by these words.

I believe Jesus was telling His disciples that when we combine prayer with fasting, the act of refraining from food puts an accent on the significance and the seriousness of that which we are asking from the Father. When we come to God in prayer with fasting, we are coming before Him with a sense of urgency. I believe most believers today do engage in prayer, but I also believe most of our prayer is of a perfunctory character. As children, many of us learned to say: "Dear God, please bless Mommy and Daddy and Uncle Sam and Aunt Gert and all the rest of the family. And watch over me tonight. Amen." For many of us, prayer never progresses much beyond that point. Our petitions are marked by a rote quality lacking in passion.

When we read the pages of the Old Testament, we find a very different style of prayer. Here is just one example:

> And [Jacob] arose that night and took his two wives, his two female servants, and his eleven sons, and crossed over the ford of Jabbok. He took them, sent them over the brook, and sent over what he had. Then Jacob was left alone; and a Man wrestled with him until the breaking of day. Now when He saw that He did not prevail against him, He touched the socket of his hip; and the socket of Jacob's hip was out of joint as He wrestled with him. And He said, "Let Me go, for the day breaks." But he said, "I will not let You go unless You bless me!" So He said to him, "What is your name?" He said, "Jacob." And He said, "Your name shall no longer be called Jacob, but Israel; for you have struggled with God and with men, and have prevailed." Then Jacob asked, saying, "Tell me Your name, I pray." And He said, "Why is it that you ask about My name?" And He blessed him there. (Gen. 32:22–29)

This was a wrestling match to end all wrestling matches, for in wrestling with an angel, Jacob was virtually wrestling with God. But Jacob would not let the angel go. That is the kind of prayer that Jesus was talking about, the kind that we need to conquer the forces of hell. It is prayer with urgency and persistence. It is prayer like the entreaties of the woman who would not give up until the judge heard her case (Luke 18:1–5). It is wrestling all night in prayer if necessary.

I have been a Christian for more than fifty years now, and in that time God has blessed me with a number of incredible, marvelous, overwhelming answers to prayer. I have never had an unanswered prayer, because there is no such thing as an unanswered prayer. Often God's answer is no, but that is an answer. Jesus understood that; when He prayed in the Garden of Gethsemane that the cup of the Father's wrath might pass from Him, the Father said no, so Jesus drank the cup (Matt. 26:39–44). However, God has sometimes answered my requests positively in marvelous ways. I have also seen a strong connection between the most remarkable answers to prayer in my life and the passion and urgency with which I made those prayers. Of course, I care about everything I pray for, but I do not pray for everything with the same passion and urgency.

The author of the New Testament epistle of James was not the Apostle James, the brother of John, but one of the brothers of Jesus (Matt. 13:55). He apparently was not converted until after the resurrection, but he became a leader in the church at Jerusalem (Acts 15:13; Gal. 2:9) and was known as a particularly righteous man. His nickname was "Old Camel Knees" because his knees were heavily callused, like those of a camel, because he spent so much time on his knees in prayer. He knew something about prayer, and he wrote about it in his epistle:

> Is anyone among you suffering? Let him pray. Is anyone cheerful? Let him sing psalms. Is anyone among you sick? Let him call for the elders of the church, and let them pray over him, anointing him with oil in the name of the Lord. And the prayer of faith will save the sick, and the Lord will raise him up. And if he has committed sins, he will be forgiven. Confess your trespasses to one another, and pray for one another, that you may be healed. The effective, fervent prayer of a righteous man avails much. Elijah was a man with a nature like ours, and he prayed earnestly that it would not rain; and it did not rain on the land for three years and six months. And he prayed again, and the heaven gave rain, and the earth produced its fruit. (5:13–18)

Here again, in the example of Elijah, we see an example of earnest prayer.

There is a question I am asked at seminars and conferences all the time: "R.C., does prayer change God's mind?" If ever I can identify with Jesus' frustration with a faithless generation, it is when I hear that question. To ask that question is to answer it. Am I able to change the Almighty's mind? Am I going to give Him information that He lacked before I got on my knees and informed Him of my situation? He knows what I need before I tell Him. Can I correct His counsel by lending my wisdom to His intentions? Prayer does *not* change God's mind. And as soon as I say that, people ask, "Well, then, why pray?" Saying that prayer does not change God's mind does not mean that prayer does nothing. It changes *us*. Also, God uses prayer to bring His secret counsel to pass. He gives us the unspeakable privilege of being part of the means He uses to bring about His saving grace in our lives.

So, should we pray? Yes, and with as much earnestness as we can bring to it, because as James says, "The effective, fervent prayer of a righteous man avails *much*."

If you really want to see the invisible hand of God working in your life, working in times of crisis and emergency, bring urgency to your prayers. Bring fervency to your prayers. Let not your prayers be mere perfunctory statements, but strive to lay hold of God as Jacob did. Wrestle with Him through the evening, through the night. Do not let go until He blesses you. That's the stuff of which true prayer is made. That's the stuff that moves mountains. That's the stuff that avails much.

82

PAYING THE TAX

Matthew 17:22–27

Now while they were staying in Galilee, Jesus said to them, "The Son of Man is about to be betrayed into the hands of men, and they will kill Him, and the third day He will be raised up." And they were exceedingly sorrowful. When they had come to Capernaum, those who received the temple tax came to Peter and said, "Does your Teacher not pay the temple tax?" He said, "Yes." And when he had come into the house, Jesus anticipated him, saying, "What do you think, Simon? From whom do the kings of the earth take customs or taxes, from their sons or from strangers?" Peter said to Him, "From strangers." Jesus said to him, "Then the sons are free. Nevertheless, lest we offend them, go to the sea, cast in a hook, and take the fish that comes up first. And when you have opened its mouth, you will find a piece of money; take that and give it to them for Me and you."

After the transfiguration, Jesus and His disciples moved south, back toward Galilee. Matthew tells us: **Now while they were staying in Galilee, Jesus said to them, "The Son of Man is about to be betrayed into the hands of men, and they will kill Him, and the third day He will be raised up." And they were exceedingly sorrowful** (vv. 22–23). This was the second time Jesus foretold what was to happen to Him in the near future; He had spoken of it just after Peter's great confession (16:21). Again, Jesus told the disciples that He would both die and rise again, but they seem to have focused on His death, with the result that they were "exceedingly sorrowful."

After recording Jesus' prophecy about His suffering, Matthew then recounts an episode that seems much less consequential. I find myself wondering why Matthew decided to preserve a record of this incident; he is the only Gospel writer who did so. I think this incident caught Matthew's attention partly because of his background as a tax collector (9:9). Nevertheless, Matthew's primary interest in writing his Gospel was to tell others about his Master, and this brief passage tells us much about Jesus' identity.

Matthews writes: **When they had come to Capernaum, those who received the temple tax came to Peter and said, "Does your Teacher not pay the temple tax?"** (v. 24). The temple tax had been legislated in the book of Exodus for the maintenance of the tabernacle and later the temple (Ex. 30:11–16). Every male was required to pay the tax, which amounted to half a shekel, at each census. Later, the priests and leaders of the nation began to require it on an annual basis. One of the reasons for the presence of moneychangers in the temple (to Jesus' great annoyance, 21:12–13) was because many of the pilgrims who came to Jerusalem during the Passover needed to pay the temple tax. To do so, they had to exchange their native currency for the local currency, and they had to pay a tariff for the exchange.

It seems that some of those who were responsible for collecting the tax approached Peter to ask whether it was true that Jesus did not pay the tax. Perhaps they had never seen Him pay it, or perhaps they had heard a rumor that He did not pay it. For unspecified reasons, they did not approach Jesus Himself. It is possible that they lacked the authority of the priests and Pharisees, who felt themselves entitled to approach Jesus personally. In any case, they took their question to Peter.

Matthew writes that when the men questioned Peter, **he said, "Yes"** (v. 25a). What did this answer mean? Was Peter saying that Jesus did, in fact, pay the tax? Some scholars interpret his response in that way. Or was he saying that what they had observed or heard was correct, that Jesus did not pay the tax? We cannot be sure, though Jesus' subsequent steps to pay the tax suggest He had not paid it for that year at least. But why would He not have paid it? After all, it was only a half a shekel. Paying the tax would not have been a major financial setback for Him.

We can only speculate as to Jesus' possible reasons for not paying the tax. For one thing, He knew that the whole function of the temple soon would be irrelevant and obsolete, because in just a few days He would offer the perfect sacrifice once for all, and as a result of that sacrifice the veil that separated the Holy Place from the Holy of Holies in the temple would be torn asunder. With that, the whole point of temple worship would be fulfilled. Furthermore, within the life of that generation, not one stone of the temple would be left upon another (Matt. 24:2), for the temple was going to be destroyed in AD 70. So, perhaps Jesus saw no point in investing in a losing proposition, regarding it as wasteful to give to an enterprise that was no longer useful. However, He did not explicitly give a reason for not paying the tax, if He was, in fact, not paying it.

An Adiaphorous Matter

Matthew tells us no more about Peter's exchange with the temple tax collectors, but shifts to a follow-up discussion between Jesus and Peter. He writes: **And when he had come into the house, Jesus anticipated him, saying, "What do you think, Simon? From whom do the kings of the earth take customs or taxes, from their sons or from strangers?" Peter said to Him, "From strangers." Jesus said to him, "Then the sons are free"** (vv. 25b–26).

Peter, who obviously had been detained by the tax collectors' inquiry, joined Jesus and the other disciples in a house. He seems to have been itching to ask Jesus about the discussion, but Jesus already knew what was on His mind. Thus, He raised the issue of taxation in a curious way by asking Peter whether kings taxed their own family members or strangers. Peter gave the natural answer: strangers. Jesus replied that the sons therefore were free. What are we to make of this exchange? Jesus was saying that the King of the temple is God. Jesus, therefore, as the Son of God, the Son of the King, was rightfully exempt from paying the temple tax. With this statement, Jesus was again declaring His identity as the Son of God.

But then Jesus said something that is crucially important: **"Nevertheless, lest we offend them, go to the sea, cast in a hook, and take the fish that comes up first. And when you have opened its mouth, you will find a piece of money; take that and give it to them for Me and you"** (v. 27). Jesus was not required to pay the tax. However, He had submitted to every law that God had imposed upon Israel, and it was important that He submit to this law, too. But there was another principle at play in this episode.

Notice those little words "lest we offend them." By submitting to the tax, Jesus illustrated a principle that the Apostle Paul teaches in Romans and in 1 Corinthians, the principle of dealing with what is called the *adiaphora*, those things that have no inherent moral bearing. Paul writes extensively about the example of meat offered to idols (1 Corinthians 8, 10). His position is that there is nothing inherently wrong with buying and eating meat that has been offered to idols in pagan worship. Paul says that is adiaphorous. But if there are people in your family, your church family, or your circle of friends who believe it to be wrong, it is best to abstain from eating meat rather than make them stumble. So, Jesus chose to acquiesce and to pay the tax, even though the tax had no claim on Him.

Emptying and Submission

Furthermore, this accommodation by Jesus was at the very heart of the incarnation. In the so-called Kenotic Hymn (from the Greek word *kenōsis*, which means "an emptying") in Philippians 2, which some believe was a song that was sung in the early church, Paul writes:

> Let this mind be in you which was also in Christ Jesus, who, being in the form of God, did not consider it robbery to be equal with God, but made Himself of no reputation, taking the form of a bondservant, and coming in the likeness of men. And being found in appearance as a man, He humbled Himself and became obedient to the point of death, even the death of the cross. Therefore God also has highly exalted Him and given Him the name which is above every name, that at the name of Jesus every knee should bow, of those in heaven, and of those on earth, and of those under the earth, and that every tongue should confess that Jesus Christ is Lord, to the glory of God the Father. (vv. 5–11)

It is very important that we understand what Jesus laid aside when He became incarnate. In the nineteenth century, there was a heresy that was known as the kenotic heresy, which held that when Jesus took upon Himself a human nature, He laid aside His divine attributes—His omnipotence, omniscience, immutability, and so on. This is a pernicious heresy, but we can hear it espoused every day on so-called Christian television and in many pulpits throughout the world. God is immutable. God never stops being God. And when God became incarnate, the divine nature did not stop being divine. Jesus laid aside no element of His deity. He took on a human nature that had limits, but the divine nature remained intact.

What, then, did Jesus give up in the incarnation? In the Christmas hymn "Hark! The Herald Angels Sing," one of the stanzas reads, "Mild he lays his glory by, born that man no more may die."[1] The eternal Son of God, the second person of the Trinity, did not lay aside His deity, but He laid aside the glory that attended it and chose humiliation, ignominy, suffering, and death, making Himself of no reputation. He even submitted to the simple temple tax, which was an insult to His glory.

In His High Priestly Prayer in the upper room on the night before His death, Jesus prayed with these words:

[1] From the hymn, "Hark! The Herold Angels Sing" by Charles Wesley, 1739.

> Father, the hour has come. Glorify Your Son, that Your Son also may glorify You, as You have given Him authority over all flesh, that He should give eternal life to as many as You have given Him. And this is eternal life, that they may know You, the only true God, and Jesus Christ whom You have sent. I have glorified You on the earth. I have finished the work which You have given Me to do. And now, O Father, glorify Me together with Yourself, with the glory which I had with You before the world was. (John 17:1b–5)

Do you see it? Jesus was ready to finish the work the Father had given Him to do. But He also wanted to receive back the glory He had laid aside at His incarnation. It was that of which He had emptied Himself, not His deity.

So, Jesus submitted to the tax. But His method of paying the tax showed once again who He was. He told Peter to go to the lake and cast in a line, whereupon he would catch a fish with a shekel in its mouth, enough to pay the tax for the two of them. In this way, He demonstrated His deity and gave a hint of His true glory, which glory has been restored since His ascension to the Father and coronation as King over all things.

83

THE GREATEST IN THE KINGDOM OF HEAVEN

Matthew 18:1–5

At that time the disciples came to Jesus, saying, "Who then is greatest in the kingdom of heaven?" Then Jesus called a little child to Him, set him in the midst of them, and said, "Assuredly, I say to you, unless you are converted and become as little children, you will by no means enter the kingdom of heaven. Therefore whoever humbles himself as this little child is the greatest in the kingdom of heaven. Whoever receives one little child like this in My name receives Me."

Recently, as I was reminiscing about my fifty-plus years of teaching and preaching, I began trying to calculate the number of messages I have given. As near as I could guess, including college and seminary lectures, as well as radio messages, it is somewhere between twenty-five thousand and thirty thousand messages.

Even as I was reflecting on that astonishing number, I could not help thinking that I have preached some really, really bad sermons. I can even pinpoint my very worst sermon. It was the first sermon I ever delivered, which occurred in 1958, when I was a sophomore in college. I wrote the sermon out and memorized it word for word. Then I practiced it like the ancient Greek orator Demosthenes, who spoke with stones in his mouth to overcome a speech impediment. In the end, however, it was not the delivery that was so bad, although it very well may have been bad, too. Instead, as I later understood, it was my handling of the biblical text that made this my worst sermon ever. I completely mutilated and butchered the text from which I preached. Like many young people, I thought that I knew virtually everything, but I had very little biblical and theological understanding.

The text that I so badly mangled in that initial sermon was Matthew 18:1–5, the same text I am considering in this chapter. I hope and pray that I can do a better job of explaining it properly in this instance.

In Matthew 18, we find the fourth of five great discourses contained in this Gospel. It began with a question from the disciples: **At that time the disciples came to Jesus, saying, "Who then is greatest in the kingdom of heaven?"** (v. 1).

Remember the context of this discourse. Just a few days before, Jesus had asked the disciples, "Who do you say that I am?" and Peter had said, "You are the Christ, the Son of the living God" (16:15–16). So, the disciples understood that He was the Messiah who had been prophesied in the Old Testament. Of course, Jesus had subsequently warned them that He was going to Jerusalem to suffer, die, and rise again (16:21; 17:22–23), but the disciples, it seems, still had not grasped the concept of a suffering Savior. Apparently they were still expecting Him to inaugurate the divine kingdom on earth. In thinking about that, perhaps they fell into a discussion of their own places in Jesus' royal administration, wondering who would sit at His right hand. Indeed, Mark and Luke tell us this incident followed a time of dispute among the disciples about which of them ought to be considered the greatest in the kingdom (Mark 9:33–37; Luke 9:46–48). They understood greatness in terms of human abilities. Finally, according to Matthew, they simply asked Jesus to settle the dispute for them.

Jesus did something they did not expect: **Then Jesus called a little child to Him, set him in the midst of them** (v. 2). This child was probably no more than two or three years of age. Jesus called the child to Him and had him stand where all the disciples could see him. Then He said, **"Assuredly, I say to you, unless you are converted and become as little children, you will by no means enter the kingdom of heaven"** (v. 3).

Perhaps I should share with you how I mutilated this text in 1958. I used it to articulate that pernicious idea that invades churches all over the world—that to be a Christian is to have a simple faith. The New Testament, of course, is clear that if we are called of God, if we are believers in Him, we are not to be satisfied with the milk of the gospel but to grow to the fullness of maturity as God's people by consuming the meat God has given to us in His Word. But I told my hearers that day that we do not need to spend copious amounts of time and energy poring over the Scriptures. I told them that we do not need a lot of theology and doctrine. Instead, all we need is Jesus. We need to be simple people with a simple faith. But that is not what Jesus was getting at when He told the disciples they must be converted and become as little children.

The Need for Conversion

What, then, did He mean? As we begin to explore Jesus' meaning, it is crucial that we note His use of the word *unless*. Any time we see this term, we know that it introduces a necessary condition that has to be fulfilled for the desired result to take place. The condition that Jesus said has to be met in order for someone to enter the kingdom of God is conversion.

I would encourage you at this point to ask yourself in all sobriety, "Am I a converted person or an unconverted person?" If you are an unconverted person and you stay in that condition, there is no way, Jesus says, for you to enter the kingdom of God. I hear people say, "I was born a Christian." But the Scriptures tell us that every human being (except Jesus Christ) is born into this world in a state of spiritual death (Eph. 2:1). In that sense, no one is born a Christian. In order to be a Christian, a person must be *reborn*. We have to be born not of the flesh but of the Spirit of God. Unless we are reborn, Jesus told Nicodemus, we will not be able to see the kingdom of God, let alone enter it (John 3:3, 5). Human beings were created to reflect the holiness of God. Instead, we sin against Him from the earliest age.

In Romans 1, the Apostle Paul tells us that God has clearly revealed His eternal power and Godhead to every person in this world by the things He has made (v. 20). However, men universally repress this truth, exchanging the truth for a lie, and worshiping and serving created things rather than the Creator (vv. 21–23). Then he writes:

> Therefore God also gave them up to uncleanness, in the lusts of their hearts, to dishonor their bodies among themselves, who exchanged the truth of God for the lie, and worshiped and served the creature rather than the Creator, who is blessed forever. Amen. For this reason God gave them up to vile passions. For even their women exchanged the natural use for what is against nature. Likewise also the men, leaving the natural use of the woman, burned in their lust for one another, men with men committing what is shameful, and receiving in themselves the penalty of their error which was due. And even as they did not like to retain God in their knowledge, God gave them over to a debased mind, to do those things which are not fitting; being filled with all unrighteousness, sexual immorality, wickedness, covetousness, maliciousness; full of envy, murder, strife, deceit, evil-mindedness; they are whisperers, backbiters, haters of God, violent,

> proud, boasters, inventors of evil things, disobedient to parents, undiscerning, untrustworthy, unloving, unforgiving, unmerciful; who, knowing the righteous judgment of God, that those who practice such things are deserving of death, not only do the same but also approve of those who practice them. (vv. 24–32)

This is a very grim description of the natural condition of human beings who are unconverted, who are dead in sin and trespasses. They reject God's revelation of Himself, for by nature they do not "like to retain God in their knowledge." It is not difficult to see that they need to be converted out of this terrible state.

The Humility of a Child

Jesus also said that conversion must be in the direction of childlikeness. But childlikeness can be understood in different ways. Thankfully, Jesus went on to explain His meaning. He said: **"Therefore whoever humbles himself as this little child is the greatest in the kingdom of heaven. Whoever receives one little child like this in My name receives Me"** (vv. 4–5).

Jesus did not bring a young child into the midst of His disciples to tell them they must be innocent like a child in order to enter the kingdom of God. Jesus knew that young children are not small angels. He knew how self-centered and demanding they can be. Instead, He was telling them to become like children in their humility. A young child does not yet think he knows more than his parents. Rather, he thinks his mother and father know everything. If a mother tells her two-year-old that X, Y, or Z is true, the child believes it. That child has what is called in technical language a *fides implicitum*, an implicit faith. He trusts his mother implicitly. Whatever she says must be true.

This is how we are to relate to God. Of course, true faith in God is not blind faith. It is not taking a leap into the dark and hoping Jesus will catch us. But true faith in God is an implicit faith, because once we are reconciled with Him and know who He is, we know that God is omniscient. His knowledge is perfect. His counsel is perfectly wise. A true believer trusts God implicitly, because he knows that God is altogether trustworthy.

Therefore, the believer wants to learn as much as he can. For this reason, he feeds on God's Word. He is not satisfied with hearing one sermon a week. Psalm 1 says, "Blessed is the man who walks not in the counsel of the ungodly, nor stands in the path of sinners, nor sits in the seat of the scornful; but his delight is in the law of the Lord, and in His law he meditates day and night" (vv. 1–2). We must close our minds to the counsel of the ungodly that assaults us all day every day, and focus instead on the law of God, His Word.

The psalmist goes on to tell us what such a man is like: "He shall be like a tree planted by the rivers of water, that brings forth its fruit in its season, whose leaf also shall not wither; and whatever he does shall prosper" (v. 3). He is not like a small child. Rather, he is like a tree, one that grows beside rivers, which cause it to grow huge, stout, stalwart, and unmovable. Furthermore, he brings forth fruit.

Then the psalmist contrasts this man to the wicked: "The ungodly are not so, but are like the chaff which the wind drives away" (v. 4). In antiquity, farmers would cut their grain and pile it high. Next, the wheat had to be separated from the chaff—stems, seed pods, and so on. To do this, the farmer did not get down on his hands and knees with tweezers and pick out each individual seed. He would beat the pile to separate the wheat from the chaff, then use his winnowing fork to toss piles of the mixed wheat and chaff into the air, letting the breeze carry the chaff away while the wheat fell back into the pile. The psalmist said the ungodly are like the weightless chaff, easily carried away. He meant that they are as gullible as simple children.

Jesus understood that human beings have what I call the primacy of the mind and the primacy of the heart. How can I speak of two primacies? There is a primacy of importance and a primacy of chronology. The primacy of importance for the Christian is the heart. You may be able to get a perfect score on a theology exam even if your heart is far from God. In the final analysis, the primary thing God will look at in judging you is your heart. Is your heart with Him? Does your heart beat for Christ and for His kingdom? However, the primacy of chronology is the mind, because before anything sound can be rooted in the heart, it has to go through the mind. No one can have a godly heart without a godly mind. Scripture says, "As he thinks in his heart, so is he" (Prov. 23:7). The thinking in the heart comes only by first thinking in the mind, by gaining understanding of the Word of God.

Jesus wants us to grow in our thinking, but at the same time He wants us to manifest the sense of dependence, weakness, and humility that the young child has. If you have that kind of humility, you will be great in the kingdom of God. It is not necessarily the one who knows the most theology, the one who wins the most souls, or the bravest martyr who is greatest in the kingdom. It is the one who is most like a child.

84

DEALING WITH TEMPTATION

Matthew 18:6–9

Whoever causes one of these little ones who believe in Me to sin, it would be better for him if a millstone were hung around his neck, and he were drowned in the depth of the sea. Woe to the world because of offenses! For offenses must come, but woe to that man by whom the offense comes! If your hand or foot causes you to sin, cut it off and cast it from you. It is better for you to enter into life lame or maimed, rather than having two hands or two feet, to be cast into the everlasting fire. And if your eye causes you to sin, pluck it out and cast it from you. It is better for you to enter into life with one eye, rather than having two eyes, to be cast into hell fire.

In the passage we are considering in this chapter, Jesus introduced an ominous note of judgment. We will see more such pronouncements, some of them even more dire, as the following chapters of Matthew's Gospel unfold before us. These are hard sayings that are difficult for us to embrace. Yet because they come from the lips of Christ Himself, who is true and righteous in all His sayings, we are bound to receive them as the truth of God.

This passage must be read in the context of the question the disciples brought to Jesus: "Who then is greatest in the kingdom of heaven?" (18:1). As we saw in the previous chapter, when the disciples asked Him this question, Jesus summoned a little child, perhaps no more than two or three years of age, and had him stand in the midst of the disciples. Then He said: "Unless you are converted and become as little children, you will by no means enter the kingdom of heaven" (18:3). He was accenting the way in which little children trust their parents implicitly, and teaching the disciples that they must have that kind of trust in their heavenly Father and the same humility that can be found in little ones. In the passage to which we now turn, Jesus expanded this teaching with severe warnings and even the pronouncement of judgment.

Matthew writes that Jesus said: **"Whoever causes one of these little ones who believe in Me to sin, it would be better for him if a millstone were hung around his neck, and he were drowned in the depth of the sea. Woe to the world because of offenses! For offenses must come, but woe to that man by whom the offense comes!"** (vv. 6–7). It is clear that when Jesus spoke of "these little ones," He was not talking about children in general. Instead, He was speaking of those who have been converted and become like children, that is, new or young believers. We know this because He said "little ones *who believe in Me*." But His teaching was not about these young believers. It was about those who relate to them. Specifically, He gave a warning to anyone who would cause a young believer to sin. He also acknowledged that "offenses," or temptations, will happen in this fallen world, but the one who causes such temptations is deserving of woe, and the world is deserving of woe for its wholehearted devotion to sin.

In the ancient world, grain was processed at a mill, where large, round stones were used to crush the grain and produce flour. At some mills, the grinding stone was small enough that a person could push it around in a circle, but a larger, heavier stone was moved by an ox. It was to such a stone Jesus was referring when He said that anyone who entices young believers to sin is committing such a heinous sin that it would be better if one of these millstones were hung about his neck and he were tossed into the sea, where he would surely drown. In other words, it would be better for such a person to *die* than to continue causing young Christians to sin.

Leading Little Ones into Temptation

The Greek word that is translated as "offenses" is the word from which we get the English word *scandal*. We encountered this word previously, when Jesus said Peter was an offense to Him (16:23). I noted earlier that this Greek word originally had to do with a device that was used in the ancient world to catch wild animals or birds. It was the bait stick that held up a basket, and which could be pulled away when the quarry ventured under the basket. Jesus was applying this imagery to the temptation of young believers, warning those who set traps for them, catch them off their guard, and lead them into sin.

Tourists who go to Europe, particularly Eastern Europe, frequently are warned to keep a close watch on their personal possessions, especially their wallets, because pickpockets often work at will in the public places. The majority of those who practice the trade of the "Artful Dodger" are children who have been forced into it by their parents. When I encountered this in Europe, I felt a sense of sorrow for these children. This kind of thing, in spiritual terms, is what Jesus was addressing here—intentionally leading young and impressionable believers into sinful acts.

When I was ordained to the ministry, I was ordained to the teaching ministry, not to the pulpit or pastoral ministry. My first assignment was as a teacher of philosophy at a Christian college. Later I taught philosophical theology in the seminary. Between that time and the founding of Ligonier Ministries, I spent a couple of years working in a church in Cincinnati, Ohio, where I taught theology. One of my classes was the college group of the church, and the vast majority of the people who were in my class were students at the University of Cincinnati. In that class, I kept getting question after question about the historical reliability of the New Testament documents. So, one day I stopped in the middle of the class and asked why this question kept coming up. One student explained that a professor in their history class at the university never missed an opportunity to ridicule anyone who put his confidence in the biblical documents. He asserted that, from a historical perspective, the biblical books were completely unreliable. Then another student asked me whether I would be willing to debate this professor on the question of the historical reliability of the New Testament documents, so I said I would.

That same week, I received an invitation to appear on a local talk show hosted by Phil Donahue, who had not yet launched his nationally syndicated talk show. He wanted to discuss the credibility of the truth claims of Christianity. However, I said no to that invitation. I had a number of reasons for that choice, but I felt a greater obligation and urgency to confront the professor who was leading my students astray by teaching them that the New Testament was unreliable.

I often hear from distraught parents who have sent their sons and daughters to colleges that they thought were Christian institutions, only to see their children exposed to an avalanche of skeptical criticism about the Christian faith. Parents cannot and should not assume that because a college was once a committed Christian school that it continues to be such. Many schools recruit students on the basis of their past reputation, even though they have abandoned any real commitment to the Christian faith. We have to be extremely careful to monitor the education of our children, lest they be led astray. It is partly because of this danger that my son and his late wife, like many other Christian parents, have homeschooled their children. My son once said to me: "People say we're sheltering our kids. Next they'll accuse us of feeding and clothing them." Just as it is right and proper for parents to feed and clothe their children, it is right and proper for parents to shelter their children from those who would lead them astray. We have a duty as parents to protect our children from the traps that are set for them.

When we looked at the Sermon on the Mount, we studied the Beatitudes (5:3–11). Those expressions of blessedness were couched in the prophetic device known as the oracle, which was a pronouncement from on high. In the Bible, oracles are of two kinds—oracles of weal, which are pronouncements of blessedness, happiness, or prosperity; and oracles of woe, which are pronouncements of judgment and doom. Typically, the word that is used to introduce an announcement of divine judgment is *woe.*

Here in Matthew 18, we see Jesus pronouncing an oracle of woe, a message of judgment, on the whole world: "Woe to the world because of offenses!" The world is filled with offenses, with traps for the saints, with sin. Jesus went on to say that He understood that "offenses must come, but woe to that man by whom the offense comes!" The Bible says that not many should become teachers, for they will incur a stricter judgment (James 3:1). When I think about those college professors who make sport out of trying to destroy the faith of the students who have come into their classrooms, I tremble to think what they will experience on the last day.

Taking Action against Temptation

Jesus then personalized His teaching on offenses: **"If your hand or foot causes you to sin, cut it off and cast it from you. It is better for you to enter into life lame or maimed, rather than having two hands or two feet, to be cast into the everlasting fire. And if your eye causes you to sin, pluck it out and cast it from you. It is better for you to enter into life with one eye, rather than having two eyes, to be cast into hell fire"** (vv. 8–9).

In the early church, some believed Jesus was deadly serious when He gave this startling teaching. There are known instances when, for instance, a pickpocket became a Christian, and, in order to fight the temptation to continue to use his expertise in theft, he cut off his hands. Some saints who suffered from sexual temptation voluntarily underwent castration on the basis of this passage. Today, most scholars agree this is an example of the use of hyperbole, which is intentional exaggeration to make a point. Jesus was stating a comparative value, saying that if something in your life is destroying your soul, you should get rid of it, no matter how much it costs.

In our day, there is an epidemic of addiction to pornography. I do not know how many families and homes I have personally seen destroyed by this problem, which has been enormously exacerbated by the Internet, which allows people to access pornography in the privacy of their homes. If you are struggling with Internet pornography, here is my advice: get rid of your Internet access or the computer itself. I am not kidding. If Jesus were speaking to you in modern terms, He would say that it is far better for you to go through life without Internet access or a computer than to spend eternity in hell. That is what is at stake.

In this teaching, Jesus touched on a subject that comes up again and again in His words that are recorded in Matthew's Gospel—the doctrine of hell. Scarcely one Christian in a hundred really takes Jesus' warnings about hell seriously. We do everything we can to avoid the discussion. We water down His words and reduce hell to symbolism or metaphor. But Jesus taught more about hell than He did about heaven. Most of the New Testament teaching about hell comes from the lips of Jesus. It has been said that if anyone other than Jesus were to tell us the terrible things He taught about hell, no one would believe it at all.

When Jesus spoke about "the everlasting fire" and "hell fire," He was using a metaphor borrowed from His own culture. Mark tells us that Jesus described hell as a place where "their worm does not die, and the fire is not quenched" (9:44). There is a tradition that in Roman times the garbage dump for Jerusalem was in the Valley of Hinnom, just outside the city. Not only garbage but the corpses of criminals and the bodies of animals were deposited there. Why did the worm not die? Worms are parasites that attach themselves to a body of a person or an animal. As soon as they have devoured the flesh of that body, the worms die. But in this garbage dump, there was a constant influx of new corpses, so the worms did not die. Likewise, fires were kept burning constantly in the dump to consume the influx of refuse. This is the awful picture of hell that Jesus painted.

People are often curious as to whether Jesus was using symbolism when He spoke of hell as a place of fire. I usually tell them that it is possible the fire is symbolic. They usually sigh with relief, so I go on to say that Jesus used the most terrifying images and symbols at His disposal for a reason. My guess is that the reality is far worse than any symbol could communicate.

In this passage, Jesus gave a brief foreshadowing of His coming teaching about the last judgment. That judgment is set in the providence of God, and it will never be negotiated. Every one of us will be there. It is better to be there without hands, without eyes, and without computers but with a clean heart than to be there with hands, eyes, and computers along with a record of sin.

85

THE PARABLE OF THE LOST SHEEP

Matthew 18:10–14

Take heed that you do not despise one of these little ones, for I say to you that in heaven their angels always see the face of My Father who is in heaven. For the Son of Man has come to save that which was lost. What do you think? If a man has a hundred sheep, and one of them goes astray, does he not leave the ninety-nine and go to the mountains to seek the one that is straying? And if he should find it, assuredly, I say to you, he rejoices more over that sheep than over the ninety-nine that did not go astray. Even so it is not the will of your Father who is in heaven that one of these little ones should perish.

At the outset of Matthew 18, in response to an inquiry from the disciples as to which of them was the greatest, Jesus stressed the need for those who would be His followers to be converted and become as children (v. 3). Then He talked about the terrible judgment that will come upon those who lead astray His little ones—not children in a physical sense but in a spiritual sense, people who are new to the Christian faith. In the passage we are considering in this chapter, He continues to discuss how these "little ones" should be regarded, uttering one of the more curious statements of His ministry.

Matthew tells us that Jesus said, **"Take heed that you do not despise one of these little ones, for I say to you that in heaven their angels always see the face of My Father who is in heaven"** (v. 10). In this sentence, the Lord Jesus

Christ strongly affirmed the realm of the supernatural. This is important, because Western culture today does everything it can to "demythologize" the teachings of the New Testament and nudge our cultural point of reference to a philosophy of sheer naturalism. Because of this, it seeks to dismiss anything that smacks of the supernatural, of that which is above and beyond the realm of the natural. This is the point of conflict between Christianity and all forms of secularism. From beginning to end, the Christian faith is anchored and rooted in the context of the supernatural. If we take away the supernatural, we eviscerate the faith.

The aspect of this teaching that is most striking is Jesus' mention of angels. The Bible tells us that angels are creatures (Neh. 9:6; Ps. 148:2, 5; Col. 1:16–17). Their primary task is to function as messengers for God; the Greek word *angelos* means "messenger." The Bible calls them "ministering spirits" (Heb. 1:14), which tells us they do not have physical bodies, although they may manifest themselves at times with the appearance of physical bodies. We also learn from this description that angels are responsible to minister to the people of God in times of distress and crisis. I am certain that most Christians have received the benefits of the ministrations of the angels of God, though we are almost always unaware of these occasions.

In His words to His disciples, Jesus pointed to the role of angels in caring for weaker ones, the spiritual infants among His disciples. He warned those who would "despise" or seek to harm them or corrupt them to remember that their angels are in heaven, where they behold the face of God. I cannot read this verse without thinking of Isaiah 6, that marvelous account of Isaiah's vision of the heavenly throne room, where the seraphim were flying around the throne of God, singing, "Holy, holy, holy is the Lord of hosts" (v. 3). What a tremendous vocation angels have—they were created to minister in the immediate presence of God, seeing things none of us have ever seen in this world.

Because of this text and a few others, people have deduced the idea that all Christians have specific guardian angels assigned to them, to watch over them and care for them in times of danger or peril. That may be the case, but I personally do not think these verses give us enough information to come to that conclusion with certainty. I think we could make a somewhat stronger case from this verse that angels in general or at least some of them are tasked with watching over a particular group—little ones who may be in jeopardy.

Of course, we must never forget that other angels are watching us, but not for our good. These are the fallen angels, the demons. It was from the ranks of the angels that Satan and his forces fell. The Apostle Paul warns us that in our spiritual struggles we do not wrestle simply against the flesh; rather, our strife is against powers, rulers of darkness, spiritual wickedness in high places (Eph. 6:12).

A Shepherd Seeking the Lost

Jesus then said, **"For the Son of Man has come to save that which was lost"** (v. 11). This verse is not found in all the early manuscripts, and for this reason it is deleted from some modern translations. However, it agrees fully with other words of Jesus recorded elsewhere (Luke 19:10).

The question is why this statement appears here. It does not seem to relate to Jesus' previous assertion about not despising little ones. At first glance, it seems to fit well with the parable that follows, which has to do with a shepherd looking for a lost sheep, but this parable, at least as Matthew presents it, is not about evangelism but about the shepherding of disciples. This parable is also found in the Gospel of Luke (15:4–7), and Luke's version is about evangelism. There, the lost sheep clearly represents an unbeliever. But here in Matthew, the lost sheep does not represent one who has never come to faith but one who is part of the flock of God and wanders away. This sheep is one who belongs to Him.

As you might expect, the critics jump all over this difference, saying that there is a clear contradiction between the context in which this parable appears in Matthew and in Luke. I find such charges rather amusing. The critics are clearly not preachers or teachers, for any preacher or teacher is apt to use an illustration on more than one occasion and even for different applications. I have any number of illustrations that I have used more than once, and since Jesus spoke and taught so frequently, I think we can safely assume that He did the same.

I believe that when Jesus spoke of His coming to save that which was lost, then followed up with a parable about a shepherd seeking a lost sheep, He was indicating His pastoral concern for His people. It is the natural response of the owner of a flock, when one of his sheep goes missing, to do everything in his power to seek and to save that sheep. Jesus was saying that if His little ones are indeed led astray, He will seek for them and bring them back. None who are truly His will be led away from Him in an ultimate sense. He will keep His own safe in His fold. But as He said earlier, "Woe to that man by whom the offense comes!" (v. 7).

Lost and Found

This parable is simple yet profound. Jesus began with two questions: **"What do you think? If a man has a hundred sheep, and one of them goes astray, does he not leave the ninety-nine and go to the mountains to seek the one that is straying? And if he should find it, assuredly, I say to you, he rejoices more over that sheep than over the ninety-nine that did not go astray"** (vv. 12–13). Sheep absolutely need a shepherd, because they are prone to wander randomly and haphazardly. They easily become lost, and when they do, they are in danger from predators, in danger of falling into streams or ravines, and in danger from the elements. That is the idea Jesus was communicating here.

I once got lost in the mountains in Western Pennsylvania. I was miles from the nearest road. I tried to determine the direction I needed to go by the position of the sun in the sky. When I got thirsty, I looked for water. I had a high-powered rifle with me, and I kept firing it into the air hoping that someone from my party would hear it and come find me. I was lost for hours, and it was one of the scariest experiences of my life. But I *knew* I was lost and I *wanted* to be found.

In either version of this parable, Matthew's or Luke's, I think it is safe to say that the lost sheep does not know it is lost. We all interact every day with people who are lost in sin and do not realize it. I have a friend who always teases me about being a preacher. When I saw him recently, he said, "Praise the Lord!" Then he added, "Come on, R.C., say something religious." So, I looked at him and said: "Okay. You're going to hell." That was not what he was expecting. He almost fell out of his chair. In the next hour, he must have asked me ten times, "Did you say I'm going to hell?" I finally told him: "I don't want you to go to hell, but that's where you're going. You're lost, but you don't know that you're lost."

Likewise, unbelieving men and women do not want to be found by God. One of my pet peeves is churches that design their worship services to be "seeker sensitive." They want their Sunday morning services to be attractive to unbelievers, comfortable times for people who are seeking after God. I cannot understand why they do not see that the Bible says no one seeks after God (Rom. 3:11). Human beings, in their natural, unregenerate state, are fugitives from God. They cannot get as far away from God as they would like to be. The first sin of the human race resulted in a game of hide-and-seek. But it was not a game. Adam and Eve were filled with shame and sought to hide from the presence of God. Men and women have been fugitives from the presence of God ever since. We want nothing to do with God. No one is seeking Him.

Joe Louis was the heavyweight boxing champion from 1937 to 1949. Once, when he was about to face an opponent who was known for his quick feet and dazzling footwork, Louis said, "He can run, but he can't hide." That's how it is with human beings and God. Whether we are lost unbelievers or wandering sheep, we cannot hide from God. David said: "Where can I go from Your Spirit? Or where can I flee from Your presence? If I ascend into heaven, You are there; if I make my bed in hell, behold, You are there. If I take the wings of the morning, and dwell in the uttermost parts of the sea, even there Your hand shall lead me, and Your right hand shall hold me" (Ps. 139:7–10). It is a futile exercise to flee from the presence of God. He is the One who seeks.

God's Will and Salvation

Finally, Jesus said, **"Even so it is not the will of your Father who is in heaven that one of these little ones should perish"** (v. 14). If you struggle against the biblical doctrine of election, the teaching that God sovereignly elects a people and individuals to come to Him, you will be drawn to texts such as this one, which seem to suggest that God does not want anyone to perish, disproving the idea that He coldheartedly elects some and passes over others. If that is your thinking, you need to be careful, because the Bible speaks of the will of God in more than one way.

First, it speaks of God's preceptive will, that will that He states in His commands, in His law. For instance, it is His will that people have no other gods before Him (Ex. 20:3). That is His law. However, that law can be broken. God's preceptive will can and is violated by human beings every time we sin.

Second, there is the decretive will of God, those things He decrees that must come to pass. When the universe was empty and darkness was upon the face of the deep, God willed the creation of light. When He said, "Let there be light" (Gen. 1:3), He was not saying to some cosmic power above and beyond Him, "Please, let the lights come on." The language in the phrase "Let there be light" shows that it is an imperative, a command. When He gave the word, the lights came on. The lights could not refuse to shine, because when God sovereignly wills and commands something to be, it happens every single time.

Third, there is His will of disposition. God takes no pleasure in the death of the wicked (Ezek. 33:11). God does not gain sadistic glee in sending people to hell. Nevertheless, He sends them there because He also wills justice. He is like a judge whose own son appears before him, having been convicted by a jury of his peers. The judge is called upon to set the sentence. If he is a just judge, an honest judge, a judge with integrity, he will send his own son to jail. But he will do it with tears. That's what the Bible is saying when it tells us God does not delight in the death of the wicked. He does not take pleasure in their judgment.

Here in Matthew, Jesus was not talking about the preceptive will of God. He may have been talking about the decretive will, saying that God will not permit any of His elect people to be lost (a point that is made by numerous other passages). The Bible tells us, "He who has begun a good work in you will complete it until the day of Jesus Christ" (Phil. 1:6). So, if you are a regenerate person who has gone on vacation from your spiritual life, if you really are in Christ Jesus and you have wandered away from God, He will not let you stay there. He will bring you back. Jesus also may have been talking about the will of disposition, saying that God does not want any of His sheep to perish.

Jesus identified Himself not only as the Son of Man but as the good shepherd

(John 10:11, 14), who does not merely seek out His lost sheep but lays down His life for them. We are the sheep of His pasture because He bought us at the terrible price of His blood. After paying such a price, He will not let us stray.

86

DISCIPLINE

Matthew 18:15–20

Moreover if your brother sins against you, go and tell him his fault between you and him alone. If he hears you, you have gained your brother. But if he will not hear, take with you one or two more, that "by the mouth of two or three witnesses every word may be established." And if he refuses to hear them, tell it to the church. But if he refuses even to hear the church, let him be to you like a heathen and a tax collector. Assuredly, I say to you, whatever you bind on earth will be bound in heaven, and whatever you loose on earth will be loosed in heaven. Again I say to you that if two of you agree on earth concerning anything that they ask, it will be done for them by My Father in heaven. For where two or three are gathered together in My name, I am there in the midst of them.

The subject of church discipline has been a struggle for believers throughout the history of Christendom, with the pattern of church discipline swinging from one extreme to another. In one era of discipline, there were devices of torture, such as the rack, that were used by the Spanish Inquisition. At other times, the church has fallen into total latitude, allowing any heresy or sinful pattern with no correction, and our own time fits into this category. I think there is some truth to the idea that the church occasionally resorted to torture because its leaders believed that it was better for a person to endure physical pain and thereby be rescued from sin than to suffer an eternity of suffering in hell. Likewise, one of the reasons we have become so lax in our disciplinary patterns is because we do not take hell seriously enough. In any case, Jesus gives His church a clear procedure for discipline here in Matthew 18. We only need to follow it.

Matthew writes that Jesus said: **"Moreover if your brother sins against you, go and tell him his fault between you and him alone. If he hears you, you have gained your brother"** (v. 15). Other translations read, "If your brother offends you . . ." When this happens, I am to go to the one who has sinned against me and tell him privately what he has done. This is step one in resolving problems between believers.

Before we can understand the meaning and application of this directive, we must understand what kind of sin or offense is in view. This text is not a license for Christians to become litigious, filing suits against their brothers over every simple slight or unhappy experience. Elsewhere, the Bible tells us that "love will cover a multitude of sins" (1 Peter 4:8). This means that I do not need to initiate the process of reconciliation every time my brother or sister annoys me, displeases me, or irritates me in some other minor way. Minor offenses are to be covered by grace and charity. If my brother or sister offends me in a minor way, I need to absorb it and not make a big deal out of it. The sins and offenses that Jesus has in view are the more significant ones.

But are not all sins serious? In the medieval era, the Roman Catholic Church made a distinction between venial sins and mortal sins. Venial sins are offenses against God that are not mortal; that is, they do not kill the grace of justification that has been infused into the believer's soul by the sacraments. Mortal sins, however, do kill that grace, requiring the believer to partake of the sacrament of penance in order to be restored to a state of salvation. In making this distinction between very serious sins and lesser sins, Rome was responding to principles that are taught in the New Testament, which occasionally gives lists of sins that are more egregious than others (see Rom. 1:28–31; 1 Cor. 6:9–10; Eph. 5:3–5). John Calvin, in responding to this distinction at the time of the Reformation, offered a very balanced perspective, saying that every sin is mortal in that it deserves death, but no sin is mortal in the sense that it can destroy the grace of justification that we enjoy in Christ.

Initial Considerations

It is also important that we distinguish between an offense given and an offense taken. I wish we all could master this distinction. If I insult you, slander you, or lie to you, I certainly *give* offense to you. However, you may or may not choose to *take* offense against me for such things. Likewise, I may say or do something to you that is not sinful, yet you find it offensive. In that case, I did not *give* offense to you, but you chose to *take* offense. Preachers find themselves in this scenario often. I have the responsibility of preaching the whole counsel of God, so if we come to a text where Jesus is teaching about hell, I have to teach on it. It seems that every time I preach on hell, someone goes out of his or her way to tell me, "I was offended by that." That is an offense taken but not an offense given, because it is not a sin to proclaim the truth of God accurately to the people of God. In fact, I would be sinning against God and offending Christ if I did not preach the whole counsel of God.

Of course, not all confrontations that seem to fit Jesus' model are legitimate. Has anyone ever come to you and said, "I feel I must speak the truth to you in love" (see Eph. 4:15)? I have learned over the years that when a Christian brother or sister comes to me and says this, I need to be on my guard. Of course, this may be the prelude to a legitimate complaint about an offense I have given. If I have sinned against a brother, and he comes to me to make that offense known, it is proper that he should speak truthfully but lovingly to me. But all too often, when someone tells me he must speak the truth to me in love, an offense has been taken even though I have not given one. We need to listen carefully when we are confronted in this way.

Finally, this text does not prohibit us from using intermediaries when it is appropriate to do so. If I suffer a criminal action, even if it is by another church member, I have every right to call the authorities, because that is the responsibility God has given to them. So, clearly Jesus was speaking here of offenses that fall short of criminal actions that require the immediate assistance of the authorities.

When Jesus said, "If your brother sins against you, go and tell him his fault between you and him alone," He was establishing a procedure to prevent His people from gossiping to third parties when offenses occur. We are not to make our complaints known to third parties until we first go to those who have wounded us. That is very hard to do. If someone wounds me in a significant way, the temptation is enormous for me not to go to the person but to go and seek an alliance with someone else who will back me up and agree with me. It is human nature to avoid the confrontation and seek support. But Jesus said we are not to do that. Such behavior is destructive. The way to save a relationship is to go to the person who has given offense to explain the problem.

On some occasions, that is all that is required. If the other person is a Christian and has a sensitive conscience, he may hear the rebuke as it was intended and say: "You're absolutely right. I shouldn't have done that. I apologize. Please, forgive me." If that is the response, you must forgive, and then the matter is closed. As Jesus said, "You have gained your brother." You have restored the relationship between the two of you.

Secondary Steps

However, Jesus knew that in some or perhaps even most cases, this initial step will not solve the problem, because people are loathe to admit they were wrong and to repent. In those cases, Jesus said, **"But if he will not hear, take with you one or two more, that 'by the mouth of two or three witnesses every word may be established'"** (v. 16). The idea is that by going to the one who has sinned against you with one or two others, he will be moved by the wisdom of multiple counselors.

Jesus provided yet another step in case the second fails: **"And if he refuses to hear them, tell it to the church"** (v. 17a). This does not mean making the sin and the refusal to repent public knowledge in the church. Rather, it means taking the matter to the elders, who have the responsibility for administering discipline in such cases. The elders typically take a number of steps. First, they might speak to the other person with biblical counsel. Next, they might administer a rebuke. If he still refuses to repent, they might temporarily ban him from participation in the Lord's Supper, hoping that the loss of access to the Table of the Lord and the grace that is contained in it will soften his heart and show him the seriousness of his sin.

Even these serious steps sometimes fail to bring repentance. Therefore, Jesus said, **"But if he refuses even to hear the church, let him be to you like a heathen and a tax collector"** (v. 17b). Jesus was talking here about excommunication, the removal of a person from the fellowship of the church. In the end, there is only one sin for which a person can be excommunicated—contumacy, which is an obstinate refusal to repent of the sin that involved him in church discipline in the first place. Excommunication is a very serious matter. The person is put out of the church and symbolically delivered into the hands of Satan. For a Christian, that is a horrible thing. Usually when this happens, the person finds another church that is happy to gain a new member and has no interest in honoring the discipline that the first church has administered. Sometimes, however, the horror of excommunication is the final straw that breaks through the hardened heart and brings the sinner to repentance.

Evangelical churches occasionally are too quick to excommunicate members. Most of the time, however, excommunication is a last resort. The church goes through many steps before removing a person from the body of Christ. When the final step is taken, it is with sorrow, but also with the hope that excommunication will lead the person to repentance, in which case he is free to come back and be restored to the church.

We see an example of this process in the Apostle Paul's Corinthian correspondence. Paul heard about a man in the church at Corinth who was living openly in sin, but the leaders of the church were doing nothing about it (1 Cor. 5:2–3). Paul told them they had to bring this man into discipline (vv. 4–5). They did so, with the result that he eventually was removed from the church (2 Cor. 2:6). In the end, excommunication brought the man to repentance, but then the Corinthian church refused to receive him back (v. 7). So, Paul had to write to the church again, asking them to receive their repentant brother (v. 8).

Binding and Loosing

Matthew tells us that Jesus went on to say, **"Assuredly, I say to you, whatever you bind on earth will be bound in heaven, and whatever you loose on earth will be loosed in heaven"** (v. 18). We have seen that, only days before, Jesus had told the disciples, "I will give you the keys of the kingdom of heaven, and whatever you bind on earth will be bound in heaven, and whatever you loose on earth will be loosed in heaven" (16:19). The Roman Catholic Church believes these words were spoken specifically to Peter, so it takes these references to binding and loosing as teaching that the pope, who is regarded as the successor of Peter, holds the keys of the kingdom. Protestants, however, believe that Jesus was granting this power to His apostles, giving them the right to "open" the kingdom to those who share Peter's confession (16:16) and to "lock" it to those who reject Jesus as the Messiah. In other words, by apostolic authority, church elders may admit people to the church and exclude them from it.

Jesus added: **"Again I say to you that if two of you agree on earth concerning anything that they ask, it will be done for them by My Father in heaven. For where two or three are gathered together in My name, I am there in the midst of them"** (vv. 19–20). Both of these verses frequently have been radically misunderstood. First, simply finding two people on earth who agree on something does not guarantee that God will make it happen. If that were the case, we could settle all wars, wipe out cancer, and end poverty in a heartbeat. Remember, Jesus said this in the context of His teaching on church discipline. He basically was restating verse 18, saying that church discipline carried out according to biblical procedures is recognized in heaven.

Second, Christians often comfort themselves that even though their gatherings for worship, Bible study, prayer, or fellowship are small, if there are just two or three of them, Jesus is with them. That is certainly true, but again, the context of this verse is church discipline. Jesus was saying that He is with the leaders of the church to validate their decisions on church discipline, much in the way that Paul said he would be with the Corinthians "in spirit" as they brought discipline against the man who was living in sin (1 Cor. 5:3–5).

On one occasion, I had to go with another minister to confront a married woman who was in the house with her lover. It is terrifying to go into that kind of a situation, to confront people in the midst of their sin. But Jesus said that if two or three are gathered together in His name, He is there. In the difficult situations of church discipline, it is tremendously comforting to know that Jesus is there with us.

In the previous chapter, Jesus told the parable of the lost sheep, showing how He ever works to reclaim His wandering people. One of the ways in which He does that is through church discipline. As unpleasant and terrifying as it can be, we must be diligent to exercise church discipline when it is called for on biblical grounds. Thankfully, we have the assurance that Jesus, the good shepherd, is with us in that troubling process.

87

THE UNFORGIVING SERVANT

Matthew 18:21–35

Then Peter came to Him and said, "Lord, how often shall my brother sin against me, and I forgive him? Up to seven times?" Jesus said to him, "I do not say to you, up to seven times, but up to seventy times seven. Therefore the kingdom of heaven is like a certain king who wanted to settle accounts with his servants. And when he had begun to settle accounts, one was brought to him who owed him ten thousand talents. But as he was not able to pay, his master commanded that he be sold, with his wife and children and all that he had, and that payment be made. The servant therefore fell down before him, saying, 'Master, have patience with me, and I will pay you all.' Then the master of that servant was moved with compassion, released him, and forgave him the debt. But that servant went out and found one of his fellow servants who owed him a hundred denarii; and he laid hands on him and took him by the throat, saying, 'Pay me what you owe!' So his fellow servant fell down at his feet and begged him, saying, 'Have patience with me, and I will pay you all.' And he would not, but went and threw him into prison till he should pay the debt. So when his fellow servants saw what had been done, they were very grieved, and came and told their master all that had been done. Then his master, after he had called him, said to him, 'You wicked servant! I forgave you all that debt because you begged me. Should you not also have had compassion on your fellow servant, just as I had pity on you?' And his master was angry, and delivered him to the torturers until he should pay all that was due to him. So My heavenly Father also will do to you if each of you, from his heart, does not forgive his brother his trespasses."

When we considered Jesus' instructions as to how we are to respond when we are offended in an egregious manner by a brother, I mentioned that the procedure He outlined is not meant to be set in action by every petty irritation or annoyance. The disciplinary process that He spelled out is reserved for serious matters. We are to exercise a love for our brethren that covers a multitude of sins (1 Peter 4:8), especially those that are minor or insignificant.

However, there is a misunderstanding that abounds in the church that Christians are called to unilaterally forgive *every* sin or trespass that we suffer at the hands of other believers and even unbelievers, and that we are to grant this forgiveness automatically without ever engaging in personal confrontation. I believe this misunderstanding arises partly from the example of our Lord Himself, who freely prayed for His enemies who had put Him on the cross, saying, "Father, forgive them, for they do not know what they do" (Luke 23:34). This powerful example teaches us that we certainly have the right at any time to give unilateral forgiveness to those who have sinned against us, but we must not mistake that for a divine requirement. Yes, when others violate us and then repent, we are not to withhold forgiveness. If we refuse to forgive those who injure us and then repent, we risk having God refuse to forgive our own sins (Mark 11:26). However, if we are always and everywhere required to give forgiveness to those who have sinned against us, then Jesus' teaching on church discipline (18:15–20), by which we confront those who offend us and then take them to the church if necessary, was pointless.

After Jesus gave His instructions on church discipline, Peter asked a follow-up question that prompted Jesus to give an explanation of the extent of forgiveness Christians must practice. Matthew tells us: **Then Peter came to Him and said, "Lord, how often shall my brother sin against me, and I forgive him? Up to seven times?"** (v. 21). Peter was asking: "What is the limit of forgiveness? How big is the multitude of sins that love can cover?" In ancient Judaism, the rabbis taught that forgiveness of three offenses was sufficient. By suggesting that he might forgive as many as seven offenses, Peter probably assumed he was being generous.

But Jesus introduced Peter to an entirely different standard of generosity in forgiveness: **Jesus said to him, "I do not say to you, up to seven times, but up to seventy times seven"** (v. 22). This does not mean that Jesus was setting a limit of 490 offenses. Essentially, Jesus was saying there is to be no limit on forgiveness (at least when repentance occurs). Forgiveness is to be a way of life for Christians.

An Unpayable Debt

To reinforce this message, Jesus told the remarkable parable of the unforgiving servant, which is quite frightening in some dimensions. Here we encounter another of Jesus' parables describing the kingdom of heaven, the way the kingdom operates. He began by saying, **"Therefore the kingdom of heaven is like a certain king who wanted to settle accounts with his servants"** (v. 23). Jesus used the word *servants*, but we are not meant to envision a king settling accounts with his slaves. In a kingdom, anyone who is under the dominion of the reigning monarch is considered a servant of the king. Clearly, no slave would have any occasion to compile a debt to a king in the amount of ten thousand talents. Anyone who could find himself so deeply in debt to a sovereign would have to be very high up in the hierarchy of the land, perhaps a duke, an earl, or other nobleman.

In any case, Jesus said that the king decided to settle some or all of his accounts, and **"when he had begun to settle accounts, one was brought to him who owed him ten thousand talents"** (v. 24). At that time in Israel, a denarius was the normal pay for a day's work for a person, and it took six hundred denarii—roughly two years of wages—to make one talent. Biblical scholars have reached for their calculators and tried to figure out how much money ten thousand talents would be in today's economy. For the most part, they have thrown up their hands in despair. The major problem is that the translation "ten thousand talents" does not do justice to the Greek that is used here. It actually says "myriad talents," which is indefinite. So the commentators' estimates of this amount in modern currency range from $1 billion to much higher figures. Simply put, the man owed the king more money that he or anyone else could count.

You may ask how, in a modern kingdom, a duke or an earl could find himself owing so much money to a king. It is true such indebtedness would be very unusual. But this is a parable, and so Jesus was at liberty to arrange the details in ways that did not necessarily reflect real life. In order to make His point, Jesus was saying that the servant owed the king more money than Peter could imagine.

It was a dark day for this servant when the king called him in and demanded that he settle his account: **"But as he was not able to pay, his master commanded that he be sold, with his wife and children and all that he had, and that payment be made"** (v. 25). The king was prepared to send the man and his entire family into indentured servitude, and to confiscate and liquidate all his possessions, to settle the debt he could not pay.

The servant had no recourse other than to appeal for mercy: **"The servant therefore fell down before him, saying, 'Master, have patience with me, and I will pay you all'"** (v. 26). The servant was asking the king to have a great deal of patience. There was no way he could pay back his debt. His best hope was to do some creative accounting, perhaps attempting to borrow from others in order to pay the king. He begged for time to try to come up with the money.

The king was merciful beyond all expectation: **"Then the master of that servant was moved with compassion, released him, and forgave him the debt"** (v. 27). The king did not simply grant the servant's request for an extension of time to try to come up with the money. Instead, the king took an IOU for billions and billions of dollars, ripped it up, and threw it in the fire. He wrote off the debt in total and released his creditor. What an act of mercy and compassion this was.

An Absence of Compassion

The servant must have walked out in a daze. One moment he was facing indentured servitude and the loss of all his possessions. The next he was free and his crushing debt was gone. That is what makes his next action so puzzling. Jesus said: **"But that servant went out and found one of his fellow servants who owed him a hundred denarii; and he laid hands on him and took him by the throat, saying, 'Pay me what you owe!'"** (v. 28). Perhaps there was some sort of history between these two men. Perhaps the newly forgiven servant simply had decided to follow Polonius's advice from Shakespeare's *Hamlet*: "Neither a borrower nor a lender be," and he was now determined to collect from his debtors so as to pay other creditors. In any case, he demanded that this man pay what he owed, one hundred denarii. This was not an inconsiderable sum; it was several months of wages. However, it was a paltry amount compared to that which he himself had just been forgiven. Sadly, his own forgiveness had fostered no compassion in his spirit.

Jesus continued, **"So his fellow servant fell down at his feet and begged him, saying, 'Have patience with me, and I will pay you all'"** (v. 29). It was with nearly these same words that the servant had pleaded with the king (v. 26), leading to his forgiveness. However, he refused to heed the other man's plea: **"And he would not, but went and threw him into prison till he should pay the debt"** (v. 30).

The servant's hardhearted actions did not go unnoticed, Jesus said: **"So when his fellow servants saw what had been done, they were very grieved, and came and told their master all that had been done. Then his master, after he had called him, said to him, 'You wicked servant! I forgave you all that debt because you begged me. Should you not also have had compassion on your fellow servant, just as I had pity on you?' And his master was angry, and delivered him to the torturers until he should pay all that was due to him"** (vv. 31–34). The servants were "grieved" by the man's actions. There is no evidence that the servants had any connection to the other man who was jailed; it seems they were simply upset by the unforgiving spirit of the man who had been forgiven so much. I wonder if others are sometimes upset with me when I exhibit an unforgiving spirit. Such hardheartedness should grieve all of us who love and value mercy and grace.

So, the other servants told the king what had happened, and he summoned the servant and addressed him, quite properly, as "You wicked servant." Basically, he called the man an evil scoundrel. The king then sent the man to be tortured, and he reinstated his debt.

Notice that the king did not throw the servant to the torturers because he failed to pay what he had owed. That which provoked the king to wrath was not how the servant had managed the king's money but how he had managed the king's mercy. He had failed to be a good steward of the king's grace. The only way this servant had continued to enjoy freedom and life was by the grace of the king. But when the king forgave him all that he owed, the servant showed no grace, no mercy for other people. The king was not willing to put up with that.

Jesus ended the parable by saying: **"So My heavenly Father also will do to you if each of you, from his heart, does not forgive his brother his trespasses"** (v. 35). It does not take much thought to apply this story to our redemption. The debt that we owe God is not a pecuniary debt that can be measured in dollars and cents. It is a moral debt. Every sin we commit is deposited in the treasury of wrath that constitutes our debt to God unless we are recipients of the mercy of Christ. On the cross, all of that sin debt was paid by our Savior.

I honestly cannot believe how many people think they can pay the debts they owe to God. They think they can perform ten thousand deeds of righteousness to make up for their ten thousand debts of sin. This is foolishness. The debt is too huge and our so-called good works are actually filthy rags (Isa. 64:6), good for nothing. We absolutely need grace. Since we have received it, we should be the last people to grab our brothers or sisters and demand that they pay their debts to us.

As I said at the beginning of this chapter, we are not required to give unilateral forgiveness, but we must stand ready to forgive every second of the day. As Christians, we should be the most merciful of people.

It has been said that Christians are beggars telling other beggars where to find bread. That saying is somewhat trite, but things tend to become trite when they are repeated frequently, and sometimes things are repeated frequently because they are true. We have nothing before God except His mercy. None of us has even begun to understand the depth of that mercy. We sing "Amazing Grace," but we are not really amazed by it, because we do not like to think of the enormity of the debt that has been canceled by the Father's compassion. We need to think about that debt so that we will grasp that we are forgiven by divine mercy and grace.

We should not be thinking of forgiveness in terms of arbitrary limits, as Peter was. Having been forgiven so greatly, we must be ready to forgive always. If someone offends you and then apologizes, and you withhold your forgiveness, you need to change your ways. If you do not, there is a torture cell waiting for you.

88

MARRIAGE AND DIVORCE

Matthew 19:1–12

Now it came to pass, when Jesus had finished these sayings, that He departed from Galilee and came to the region of Judea beyond the Jordan. And great multitudes followed Him, and He healed them there. The Pharisees also came to Him, testing Him, and saying to Him, "Is it lawful for a man to divorce his wife for just any reason?" And He answered and said to them, "Have you not read that He who made them at the beginning 'made them male and female,' and said, 'For this reason a man shall leave his father and mother and be joined to his wife, and the two shall become one flesh'? So then, they are no longer two but one flesh. Therefore what God has joined together, let not man separate." They said to Him, "Why then did Moses command to give a certificate of divorce, and to put her away?" He said to them, "Moses, because of the hardness of your hearts, permitted you to divorce your wives, but from the beginning it was not so. And I say to you, whoever divorces his wife, except for sexual immorality, and marries another, commits adultery; and whoever marries her who is divorced commits adultery." His disciples said to Him, "If such is the case of the man with his wife, it is better not to marry." But He said to them, "All cannot accept this saying, but only those to whom it has been given: For there are eunuchs who were born thus from their mother's womb, and there are eunuchs who were made eunuchs by men, and there are eunuchs who have made themselves eunuchs for the kingdom of heaven's sake. He who is able to accept it, let him accept it."

The text we are considering in this chapter is certainly not the most inspirational or sensational portion of Matthew's Gospel. However, the words Jesus uttered in this exchange with the Pharisees give us exceedingly important instructions about the sacred institution of marriage and its sanctity as decreed by God, instructions that are particularly relevant for today's Western culture, which virtually despises matrimony.

As we take up this text, it is very important that we come to it to hear what it has to say, not with the intention to shape it to our own prejudices. In other words, we need to be careful to use exegesis, not isogesis. Exegesis is the process of looking at the text and drawing out what it actually says. Isogesis is the practice of reading into the text things that we would like it to say even though it does not. Unfortunately, many churches and scholars have subjected our text in this chapter to what I would call biblical torture, often making it nearly impossible to really hear what Jesus was saying. Our goal is to listen to Him anew.

Jesus and His disciples had completed their Galilean ministry. He had announced to them, after Peter's great confession, that they were going south to Judea and ultimately to Jerusalem, and that is precisely what He was in the process of doing. Matthew writes: **Now it came to pass, when Jesus had finished these sayings, that He departed from Galilee and came to the region of Judea beyond the Jordan. And great multitudes followed Him, and He healed them there** (vv. 1–2). Most likely Jesus was in Perea at this point, a Jewish area east of the Jordan River. Word about His ministry had drifted south from Galilee, and people thronged Him for healing.

Matthew then tells us: **The Pharisees also came to Him, testing Him, and saying to Him, "Is it lawful for a man to divorce his wife for just any reason?"** (v. 3). Matthew wants us to know that these Pharisees were not interested in being instructed by Jesus. The purpose of their question was to test Him and to trap Him, because just as there are many views on marriage and divorce today, the first-century Jewish community was deeply divided over this subject. So the Pharisees knew that no matter how Jesus answered their question about marriage and divorce, He would alienate a lot of people. They were seeking to diminish His popular appeal among those who were rushing to follow Him.

The Pharisees were asking Jesus to comment on a text from Deuteronomy, which reads:

> When a man takes a wife and marries her, and it happens that she finds no favor in his eyes because he has found some uncleanness in her, and he writes her a certificate of divorce, puts it in her hand, and sends her out of his house, when she has departed from his house, and goes and becomes another man's wife, if

> the latter husband detests her and writes her a certificate of divorce, puts it in her hand, and sends her out of his house, or if the latter husband dies who took her as his wife, then her former husband who divorced her must not take her back to be his wife. (24:1–4a)

In this passage, Moses was delivering God's command that if people divorce, get married to someone else, and then divorce again, they cannot go back to the original spouse. That was not permitted by the law of God in the Old Testament. But the rabbis were divided over the reason for the first divorce mentioned here—"some uncleanness" in the wife. This is the only ground for divorce mentioned in the Old Testament, so it was important to understand it clearly. There were two schools of thought, the conservatives and the liberals. The conservatives took the position that the uncleanness was adultery. The liberals believed that it could not be adultery because there already was a stated penalty for that sin, namely, execution (Lev. 20:10). So, the uncleanness had to be something less serious than adultery. The liberals basically concluded that the uncleanness was anything that displeased the husband. This essentially meant that the husband could divorce his wife for any reason.

Command and Permission

Jesus gave a wonderful answer: **And He answered and said to them, "Have you not read that He who made them at the beginning 'made them male and female,' and said, 'For this reason a man shall leave his father and mother and be joined to his wife, and the two shall become one flesh'? So then, they are no longer two but one flesh. Therefore what God has joined together, let not man separate"** (vv. 4–6).

The first part of Jesus' answer took the Pharisees back to the institution of marriage at creation. He reminded them that God created man and woman, God instituted the sacred union of marriage, and God declared that when a man and a woman are joined together, they become one flesh. Therefore, He said, what God has joined together, human beings are not permitted to separate.

Because Jesus based His answer in creation, many people and churches have come to the conclusion that the Bible makes no provisions for divorce whatsoever. I think those who take this position mean well and want to understand what Jesus had in view in the best light, but I think this is one of those cases where the text of Scripture is blatantly twisted to such a degree that it cannot even be recognized. If Jesus had ceased to comment on marriage at that point, it would undoubtedly be true that He taught that there should be no divorce. However, He said more, and we dare not ignore what He said.

The first part of Jesus' answer elicited a response from the Pharisees: **They said to Him, "Why then did Moses command to give a certificate of divorce, and to put her away?"** (v. 7). They challenged His teaching on the basis of their understanding of the Word of God. If divorce is not permitted, they said, why did Moses give a command for how it was to be carried out?

At that point, Jesus had to correct His antagonists: **He said to them, "Moses, because of the hardness of your hearts, permitted you to divorce your wives, but from the beginning it was not so"** (v. 8). Moses did not *command* a husband to put away his wife if she did some unchaste thing; rather, he *permitted* it. There is a huge difference between being commanded to do something and being allowed to do it. Moses, Jesus went on to say, permitted divorce "because of the hardness of your hearts." It was a measure to lessen the harm that could come about in a marriage ravaged by sin, the outgrowth of the hardness of heart produced by the fall. However, "from the beginning it was not so"; divorce was not God's best.

So, Moses gave a provision for divorce. The Old Testament law allowed divorce under certain circumstances. The question, then, was not whether people were allowed to divorce in the Old Testament. The question was about the grounds on which divorce was permitted. Thankfully, Jesus went on to answer that question. He said: **"And I say to you, whoever divorces his wife, except for sexual immorality, and marries another, commits adultery; and whoever marries her who is divorced commits adultery"** (v. 9). Here Jesus gave what has come to be known as the exceptive clause: "except for sexual immorality." It was an exception to God's prohibition of divorce, the only legitimate ground for divorce.

The Greek word translated here as "sexual immorality" is *porneia*. It is the word from which we get our word *pornography*. Scholars differ as to the precise meaning of *porneia* in Jesus' time. Did it mean only adultery or did it include lesser forms of sexual immorality? I personally take the view that "sexual immorality" is broader than pure adultery. For instance, I believe that addiction to pornography violates this passage and is grounds for divorce.

In any case, Jesus was talking about how the union of two people can be violated and fractured by sexual immorality. If this happens, He said, divorce is allowed. However, it does not mean that divorce *must* take place.

Guilt and Forgiveness

It is at this point that this passage is often twisted in the church. I cannot tell you how many women have told me they have been violated by the ruling bodies of churches. What usually happens is that when marital troubles come to the attention of church leaders (almost all of whom are men in conservative churches), they take the man's side. For instance, if a man commits adultery and his wife finds out and asks for a divorce, the church elders will say to her: "You have the right to divorce him. But you're a Christian. Jesus calls you to the higher road." Then the woman feels absolutely guilty if she continues to pursue a divorce, even though the man broke his vows and violated her. He destroyed the trust on which all marriage has to be built, but she is called to walk the higher road. The Lord Himself gave a woman in this situation every right to leave the relationship, and she should be free to choose that option. It is wrong to bind her conscience when Jesus Himself did not.

Sometimes, of course, when a man commits adultery and the wife learns of it, he falls on his knees, cries, and begs for her forgiveness. Does she have to stay married to him? I do not think so. But he has repented, and as we saw in the previous chapter, Jesus wants His people to be forgiving (Matt. 18:35). So, if the husband repents, she has to forgive him. If he commits adultery seventy times seven and repents seventy times seven, she has to forgive him and receive him as a brother in Christ. However, forgiving him does not mean she has to remain married to him. So often the spouse who was violated and chooses to divorce has to wear a stigma the rest of his or her life because he or she was the unforgiving partner. But a man or woman can forgive the spouse who sins against him or her and still choose to divorce.

So, sexual immorality is the one ground for divorce that Jesus mentioned. The Apostle Paul added another, which is the desertion of a nonbelieving spouse (1 Cor. 7:15). However, just as there is debate about what constitutes "sexual immorality," there is debate about "desertion." If one partner leaves the bed of the other and refuses conjugal rights for ten years while still living in the same house, is that desertion? I believe it is. Of course, we have to be careful not to make the definition of "desertion" so broad that we end up in no-fault divorce. But desertion is a legitimate, biblical ground for divorce.

What did Jesus mean when He said, "whoever divorces his wife . . . and marries another, commits adultery; and whoever marries her who is divorced commits adultery"?

He was saying that if a couple gets a divorce not according to the law of God, in the eyes of God they remain married, even though the state may have dissolved the marriage. Someone who divorces unbiblically and remarries, then, has entered an adulterous relationship.

Jesus' teaching led to an interesting exchange with the disciples: **His disciples said to Him, "If such is the case of the man with his wife, it is better not to marry." But He said to them, "All cannot accept this saying, but only those to whom it has been given: For there are eunuchs who were born thus from their mother's womb, and there are eunuchs who were made eunuchs by men,**

and there are eunuchs who have made themselves eunuchs for the kingdom of heaven's sake. He who is able to accept it, let him accept it" (vv. 10–12). The disciples responded with words that seem to express despair over whether marriage is even workable. Jesus did not dispute that it is sometimes better not to marry, but He did gently imply disagreement with their pessimism about marriage itself. Instead, He noted that it can be good not to marry if thereby a person can be of greater service to the kingdom of heaven. Some have a special gift to bypass marriage in order to render this service.

Understanding the principles of marriage and divorce that Jesus laid out here is relatively easy. Applying them to real-life situations often takes the wisdom of Solomon. I do not think I have seen two divorce cases in my ministry that were exactly the same. I have sometimes pondered whether the church should establish a panel of theologians and scholars of Christian ethics that could serve as an appeal board to apply these principles to real situations.

It is important to look carefully at this text and never rush to judgment when we come across complex and difficult cases. Most of all, we need to remember that when we enter into this sacred covenant, we are to be in it for keeps. We ought to be extremely careful not to do the things that would destroy that sacred union.

89

JESUS AND THE CHILDREN

Matthew 19:13–15

Then little children were brought to Him that He might put His hands on them and pray, but the disciples rebuked them. But Jesus said, "Let the little children come to Me, and do not forbid them; for of such is the kingdom of heaven." And He laid His hands on them and departed from there.

We have come to a short passage that recounts an incident that is mentioned in all three of the Synoptic Gospels. It is an interesting event, but I would not normally devote an entire chapter to such a small passage. In this chapter, however, I plan to depart from my verse-by-verse progression through Matthew's Gospel to deal with a subject that touches on the relationship of children to Jesus—namely, infant baptism. This is, of course, a controversial subject, but I believe there is biblical warrant for it. I will not be able to touch on all the aspects of this subject, but will simply highlight some of the arguments for it.

Matthew writes, **Then little children were brought to Him that He might put His hands on them and pray** (v. 13a). As we have seen in Matthew, it was quite common for Jesus to touch people, and people often sought to touch Him or to have Him touch them (8:3, 15; 9:20, 29; 14:36). Usually, those who sought His touch had an ailment, but Matthew does not tell us that these children had any specific need. It seems their parents simply wanted Jesus to touch them and pray over them as a blessing. However, **the disciples rebuked them** (v. 13b). It seems the disciples felt it was a waste of their master's time to touch these healthy children, so they actually rebuked the parents.

Jesus did not want to be so protected. Matthew tells us: **But Jesus said, "Let the little children come to Me, and do not forbid them; for of such is the kingdom of heaven." And He laid His hands on them and departed from there** (vv. 14–15). Mark adds that Jesus was "greatly displeased" that the disciples had rebuked the parents. He directed them to allow the children to come to Him, saying, "of such is the kingdom of heaven." In saying this, He was repeating the point He had made after the disciples argued about which of them was the greatest: "Assuredly, I say to you, unless you are converted and become as little children, you will by no means enter the kingdom of heaven" (18:3). Essentially He was saying that His followers must trust Him with simple, childlike faith, an implicit faith, just as children trust their parents implicitly. With that, He willingly touched the children, then departed to continue His journey to Jerusalem.

Understanding Baptism

Many years ago, I taught theology at the Conwell School at Temple University in Philadelphia. We had students from many denominations; most of them were Episcopalian and Presbyterian, but some were from Baptist churches and other groups. Part of my responsibility was to teach Systematic Theology 3, the senior theology class, in which we covered the doctrines of the church and the sacraments. In the portion of the course devoted to the sacraments, we studied the Lord's Supper first, then baptism, and one of the last things we covered prior to the students' graduation was infant baptism. So, I was charged with teaching them the doctrine of infant baptism in the final weeks of their seminary education, and some of them did not accept that doctrine. This set of circumstances created a moral dilemma for me. I began to ask myself: "What if I persuade them? Many of them already have their ordination dates set. If they suddenly become convinced of infant baptism, that could have a significant impact on their futures and their employment prospects."

In the end, I decided to give my students an assignment that varied according to their positions on infant baptism. My assignment for those who believed in infant baptism was to write a term paper on why they should *not* practice it. In other words, I asked them to defend the believer's baptism position. The assignment for those who were advocates of believer's baptism was to write a term paper on why so many churches historically have practiced infant baptism. I gave these assignments for this reason: Many of us adopt our theology from our love lines—that is, from our parents, from beloved pastors and Sunday school teachers, from the churches we grow up in—without carefully examining the issues involved. I wanted the students who believed in infant baptism to know why and I wanted the students who did not believe in infant baptism to know why. I stressed to them that this debate of all debates within the church requires a certain patience with those who differ from us, because nowhere in the New Testament do we have an explicit command to practice infant baptism or an explicit prohibition of it. With the absence of any explicit teaching in the New Testament on the subject, the case must be determined by an examination of inferences that are drawn from Scripture.

For one of my friends, a well-known Christian leader, the matter is settled by the fact that there are no explicit references in the New Testament to the practice of infant baptism and no explicit commands for it. He says without such references or commands the debate is over, because we should not baptize infants without an explicit example or command. I, on the other hand, believe that the practice of infant baptism can be inferred from the teaching of Scripture. In the remainder of this chapter, I want to provide a quick survey of some of the main reasons and inferences. These are the reasons why a vast majority of churches in church history have practiced infant baptism.

First, there is the relationship of baptism and circumcision as covenantal signs. Baptism, according to the New Testament, is the sign of the new covenant. The sign of the old covenant was circumcision. Both signs signify benefits that are received by faith alone. That is to say, people in the Old Testament were justified in the same way people in the New Testament are justified. Paul labors that point in Romans 3 and 4, using Abraham as his supreme example. In the Old Testament, adult converts to Judaism were required to give a profession of faith before they could receive the sign of circumcision. However, their infant children received the sign of the covenant before they had faith. The classic example is that of Abraham and his son Isaac. Abraham believed God, then received the sign of circumcision. God commanded that he also have his son Isaac circumcised before Isaac had faith.

So, the principle, at least in the Old Testament, was that the sign of faith could be administered before faith was actually present. The question is whether that principle carries over to the New Testament.

Baptism in the New Testament

That leads to my second point, the New Testament teaching on baptism. One passage that sheds some light on this question is found in the Apostle Paul's letter to the Colossians. He writes: "In Him you were also circumcised with the circumcision made without hands, by putting off the body of the sins of the flesh, by the circumcision of Christ, buried with Him in baptism, in which you also were raised with Him through faith in the working of God, who raised Him from the dead" (2:11–12). In this text, Paul does not identify circumcision with baptism, but he does clearly show that there is continuity between them. Also, he makes clear that the circumcision that is made without hands is a spiritual circumcision that is signified by baptism. In his epistle to the Romans, he argues against those among the Pharisees and rabbis who believed that circumcision automatically puts people in a state of salvation (2:25–29). Many people in the history of Christendom have argued that baptism brings a person into a state of salvation through baptismal regeneration. For instance, in the Roman Catholic Church, baptismal regeneration is said to occur for all who receive the sacrament. One of the main reasons why Baptists historically have rejected infant baptism is to do away with this idea. So, Paul's concern over circumcision should be shared by all Christians with regard to baptism—baptism does not save. We are required to receive it, certainly as adults, arguably as infants, but even as adults the sacrament alone does not save us.

Turning to Paul's first letter to the Corinthians, we encounter a statement that is difficult to understand. He says: "And a woman who has a husband who does not believe, if he is willing to live with her, let her not divorce him. For the unbelieving husband is sanctified by the wife, and the unbelieving wife is sanctified by the husband" (7:13–14a). Do you feel the weight of that? As evangelicals, we understand sanctification to be the process that follows justification. First we are justified, and then begins the process of becoming more conformed to the image of Christ, which process goes on throughout our whole Christian lives. But here in 1 Corinthians, Paul is talking about unbelieving people being sanctified. How can that be? He is speaking about a Christian woman who is married to a man who is not a Christian. But, he says, the unbelieving husband is sanctified by the faith of the wife, and the same is true the other way around. Does he mean to imply that there is more than one way to be sanctified and therefore more than one way to be justified? Is he saying that a person can be justified by marriage? Obviously, Paul does not mean that. Many other passages in Scripture rule out that interpretation.

To begin to grasp Paul's meaning, we must remember that the terms *sanctify* and *sanctification* in the Bible refer not only to that process by which the Holy Spirit is molding us into the image of Christ but to the act or state of *being set apart.* In fact, this is the primary meaning of *sanctification* in the Bible. For the Jews, this idea had strong covenantal significance. To be sanctified meant being set apart into a consecrated state. So, Paul was saying that an unbelieving man is set apart, not saved, through the faith of his wife.

But why would that be? Paul answers explicitly: "otherwise your children would be unclean, but now they are holy" (v. 14b). Does this mean "holy" in the sense of being righteous? No. Again, Paul is using covenantal language. In the Old Testament, a person who was circumcised was marked as a member of the house of Israel, a member of the old covenant. Those who were outside the covenant, the Gentiles, were considered unclean. That is, they had no part in this covenant of salvation that God had made with the Israelites. So, Paul says that if just one parent is a Christian, man or woman, husband or wife, the other member of the marriage is holy or set apart, and therefore the children are not unclean but holy. This, then, is an explicit New Testament teaching that children of at least one believer are considered holy and clean. If that is indeed covenantal language—and I cannot see how it can be anything else—it means that the children of one believer are members of the covenant community. And if they are members of the covenant community, why should they not receive the sign of the covenant?

In Israel, for more than two thousand years, when people were brought into a covenantal relationship with God, not only were the adults included in that covenant, but all the children, including the infants, as well. Could it possibly be true that in the New Testament this principle of covenant inclusion, of corporate solidarity, of familial sanctification and consecration was suddenly abandoned and nullified, without a single word being given to that effect? It is virtually unthinkable to me that this principle of covenantal inclusion of infants would be abrogated in silence. So, the major reason why Christians have continued the practice of giving their little children the sign of the covenant is because this is the way it has been from the very beginning of God's covenant with Abraham, the father of all of the faithful (Rom. 4:11).

Our Baptist friends point out that in the book of Acts, those who are baptized are said to believe first. They also note that every example of baptism that we see in the book of Acts is baptism of an adult who first makes a profession of faith; we do not see a single instance of an infant receiving baptism. That is another of the major reasons why Baptists have rejected infant baptism—there is no example of it in Acts and no specific command for it in the New Testament.

However, there is no reason to believe that any of the people whose baptisms are mentioned in Acts were second-generation Christians. They were new converts coming out of the world. They followed the practice that had been in place in Israel for two thousand years: someone converting as an adult first had to give a profession of faith. That is why every church I know that practices infant baptism also practices adult baptism or believer's baptism, and in the case of adults those churches require a profession of faith first. That is the model we have in the book of Acts.

Also, fully one-fourth of the examples of baptism in the book of Acts include "household baptism" (10:44–48; 11:14; 16:15, 31, 34). Not only is the professing believer baptized, so is that person's entire household. Oscar Cullmann, the great New Testament scholar and church historian, said the Greek word *oikos*, which is translated as "household," indicates the presence of children and probably small children. So, we see the principle intact from the Old Testament to the New Testament. Just as circumcision involved households and included infants, so New Testament baptism certainly included the baptism of households, which, in all probability, encompassed infant children. If we could find any evidence that any of the people in the book of Acts were children of Christians at the time of their childhood or youth and yet were not baptized, we would have to question the practice of infant baptism. But we see no such examples.

The New Testament makes very clear that the new covenant is a better covenant than the old covenant (Heb. 7:22; 8:6). A better covenant must be more inclusive, not less inclusive. If we do not allow our infant children to receive the sign of the covenant until they are of age to make a profession of faith, we make the new covenant less inclusive, at least with respect to our children, than was the case for two thousand years in Israel. I think that is an important point to keep in mind when we wrestle with this.

Baptism in Church History

Third, there is the issue of history. I used to remind my students who did not practice infant baptism that the vast majority of Christians in the history of the church have believed in it. I am not going to give you the fallacious argument of *argumentum ad populum*, by which we determine the truth by counting noses. The fact that so many Christians and Christian bodies historically have practiced infant baptism does not make it right. But it puts a burden of proof on those who believe infant baptism is improper to demonstrate why the church was wrong for hundreds of years.

With respect to the historical evidence, the German scholar Joachim Jeremias wrote a tome on the history of baptism in the first four centuries of Christendom. In this book, he indicates that the first question about the legitimacy of infant baptism in the extant literature arose in the middle of the second century, when one of the church fathers objected to it. In his objection, he conceded that infant baptism was the universal practice of the church. This means that in the numerous volumes of Christian literature from the late first century and into the second century, when the church fathers were dealing with all kinds of theological controversies, there was never any controversy over infant baptism.

None of these facts proves that the first-century church universally practiced infant baptism. But they tell us that if infant baptism was a departure from apostolic practice, that departure reached extreme levels of participation by the second century, with virtually the whole church practicing this error of baptizing infants. While it is certainly possible that a deviation from orthodoxy could spread and become universal by the second century, it is not likely, and that argues for the earliest practice of infant baptism. Again, it is possible that all of the literature that contained the debates over this issue has perished and we simply do not have it on record anymore. But the odds that none of that literature should have survived seem very long.

So, I am saying that the overwhelming weight of inferential evidence from the relationship of the old and new covenants, from the New Testament, and from church history, in my judgment, argues strongly that the church not only may but should include the children of believers in the sacrament of baptism.

Given that Jesus welcomed little children into His presence and blessed them, why would we not give them the sign of God's promise? Remember, it is a sign that if that baby exercises faith, he will receive all of the benefits of the new covenant promise, all of the benefits of the person and work of Christ. Those benefits are not received by the act of baptism. They are not received until the child has faith. But by placing the sign upon their child, the parents declare their hope in the future faith of the baby. What makes the sign sacred is not the integrity of the parents or the integrity of the pastor who administers baptism. Rather, it is the integrity of God. Baptism is the sign of God's promise to all who believe and to their children. It is God's promise to our children that if they believe, they will receive all of the benefits that have been achieved for them by Christ.

90

THE RICH YOUNG RULER

Matthew 19:16–22

Now behold, one came and said to Him, "Good Teacher, what good thing shall I do that I may have eternal life?" So He said to him, "Why do you call Me good? No one is good but One, that is, God. But if you want to enter into life, keep the commandments." He said to Him, "Which ones?" Jesus answered, "'You shall not murder,' 'You shall not commit adultery,' 'You shall not steal,' 'You shall not bear false witness,' 'Honor your father and your mother,' and, 'You shall love your neighbor as yourself.'" The young man said to Him, "All these things I have kept from my youth. What do I still lack?" Jesus said to him, "If you want to be perfect, go, sell what you have and give to the poor, and you will have treasure in heaven; and come, follow Me." But when the young man heard that saying, he went away sorrowful, for he had great possessions.

I believe it is significant that this encounter between Jesus and the one who is known as the rich young ruler is recorded in all three of the Synoptic Gospels (Mark 10:17–30; Luke 18:18–30). Even though this man was a real individual of the first century, in a sense we could call him Everyman. The mistakes and errors that he made in his assumptions before Christ are the same that countless millions make everyday.

When we compare Matthew's account of this meeting with those in Mark's and Luke's Gospels, we learn that this man approached Jesus in a state of eagerness if not urgency. He obviously admired Jesus greatly and considered

Him someone whose opinion was important. So, he came to Jesus with a compliment and a question. Matthew writes, **Now behold, one came and said to Him, "Good Teacher, what good thing shall I do that I may have eternal life?"** (v. 16). He called Jesus "Good Teacher" and asked Him what he needed to do to "have eternal life," that is, to enter the kingdom of heaven.

Before dealing with the question, Jesus focused on the compliment. Matthew tells us: **So He said to him, "Why do you call Me good? No one is good but One, that is, God"** (v. 17a). Some critics have looked at this response of Jesus and said that it shows that He did not consider Himself to be God, because He denied His own goodness. But if we read the text carefully, we see that Jesus did not deny His own goodness, and therefore He did not deny His deity. He knew that this young man did not know to whom he was speaking. He did not know the identity of Jesus. It was simply as a courtesy that he said "Good Teacher." He was recognizing that Jesus was a rabbi and a righteous man. But Jesus picked up on his compliment as a way of focusing his attention on his own lack of goodness.

The word *good* is a relative term. Things are good or bad relative to or compared with some standard. I once had a friend who always playfully said, "Compared to what?" when I asked him, "How are you?" I would have to say, "Well, compared to how you were yesterday." I had to give him some standard by which he could answer my simple greeting. When something is deemed to be good or bad, there has to be some norm, some canon of measurement, against which we can determine goodness or badness.

According to the Bible, the standard of goodness is God. The New Testament tells us, "All have sinned and fall short of the glory of God" (Rom. 3:23). We all have failed to measure up to the standard of His glorious righteousness. The Apostle Paul, quoting from a psalm of the Old Testament tells us, "There is none righteous, no, not one. . . . There is none who does good, no, not one" (Rom. 3:10b, 12b).

Of course, we do not really believe we are not good. We believe we do many good deeds, and we are convinced that others do good things, too. Our problem, as Paul elsewhere tells us, is that we judge ourselves by ourselves (Rom. 2:1). But God does not judge us by grading on a curve, comparing us with our neighbors. He knows who is good and who is not according to the standard of His own character. Obviously, no one in the world can be judged to be good when measured against the standard of God's righteousness. Therefore, it is pointless to attempt to determine goodness by the standards of this world.

Keeping the Commandments

Next, Jesus began to deal with the young man's question. He said, **"But if you want to enter into life, keep the commandments"** (v. 17b). The law of God is simply a statement of His holy character, the standard against which we must measure up. But as we have seen, we cannot measure up to this standard. This means we cannot keep God's commands. We have an axiom in our culture, "To err is human," as if error is necessary for us to be human at all. And yet, people cling to the hope that their good deeds will outweigh their bad deeds, so they will go to paradise. But a truly good deed is one that conforms to God's law and is performed out of a heart that is fully in love with Him. Furthermore, every single deed we do must be this kind of deed if we are to make it to heaven by our own works, for conformity to the character of God entails perfect obedience. It should be obvious that it is impossible for anyone to meet that standard.

Jesus had already showed the rich young ruler that he had no understanding of true goodness. In addressing his question, Jesus showed him the standard of goodness—God Himself. The implication was that he must possess within himself a righteousness that perfectly conformed to that standard—or he must somehow acquire a righteousness from outside himself, the righteousness of someone who could meet all of God's requirements.

The righteousness of Christ is at the very heart of our salvation. We are living in a time when even evangelical seminary professors are questioning the idea of the perfect obedience of Christ, His satisfaction of all the demands of God's law, by which He achieved a perfect righteousness that He gives to all who trust in Him. When we say that we are justified by faith apart from the works of the law (Rom. 3:28), we do not mean that faith is a good work that makes up for all our bad works. Saying that we are justified by faith alone is simply shorthand for saying we are justified by Christ alone. The only righteousness by which we will be declared righteous in the eyes of God is the imputed righteousness of Jesus Christ.

In 1936, J. Gresham Machen, one of the founders of Westminster Theological Seminary in Philadelphia, was speaking in the Dakotas during the seminary's Christmas vacation. During that time, he became desperately ill with pneumonia. Soon it was apparent that he was dying. Just before he died on January 1, 1937, he dictated a telegram to his friend and seminary colleague John Murray: "So thankful for the active obedience of Christ. No hope without it." He died in faith, clinging to the righteousness of Christ.

Until we understand that we have no goodness of our own to present before God, we do not understand how desperately we need the gospel. If we think we can merit eternal life without the perfect righteousness of Christ, we do not see our need of Christ.

Uncovering the Idol

Jesus' mention of the commandments sparked a follow-up question from the rich young ruler. Matthew writes: **He said to Him, "Which ones?" Jesus answered, "'You shall not murder,' 'You shall not commit adultery,' 'You shall not steal,' 'You shall not bear false witness,' 'Honor your father and your mother,' and, 'You shall love your neighbor as yourself'"** (vv. 18–19).

I have often wondered why Jesus answered this question by going to the Ten Commandments, and more specifically to what we often call the second table of the law. The first four of the Ten Commandments define our obligations to God, while the other six define our obligations to our neighbors. Why did Jesus start there? Personally, I think Jesus was simply presenting a representative sampling of commandments. Unfortunately, some people look at this answer and say: "See, all we have to do to get into heaven is to avoid the big sins. As long as I don't kill anyone or steal anything, I'll be OK."

Unfortunately, it is clear that the rich young ruler thought along these lines. Matthew tells us: **The young man said to Him, "All these things I have kept from my youth. What do I still lack?"** (v. 20). He was overwhelmed with relief. He told Jesus that he had learned these commandments as a boy and had kept them ever since. But just to be sure, he asked Jesus whether there were any other odds or ends he needed to see to.

Here we see the deep patience of Jesus. Had I been there and heard this young man say, "All these things I have kept from my youth," I would have lost my patience right there. I would have said: "What? You haven't kept these commandments since you got out of your bed this morning." Likewise, Jesus could have said to him, "You must not have been there when I gave the Sermon on the Mount and explained the deeper implications of these commandments. When you become angry with your brother or hate your brother, you violate the commandment against killing. When you have lust in your heart, you violate the prohibition against adultery. When you falsely accuse your brother, not just in a court of law but in the court of public opinion, you bear false witness against him. If you had been there, you wouldn't have the audacity to come to Me and say that you have kept all of these laws since your youth."

Of course, there are people everywhere who really think they keep the law of God. However, as I noted above, for a work to be defined as good biblically, not only must it outwardly conform to the law, it must be internally motivated by love for God. When Jesus was asked which is the greatest commandment, He said, "You shall love the Lord your God with all your heart, with all your soul, and with all your mind" (Matt. 22:37, citing Deut. 6:5). No one has ever loved God perfectly for even one second.

But Jesus did not rebuke the young man for his assumption that he was able to keep the law. Mark tells us that when the young man said this, "Jesus, looking at him, loved him" (10:21). I believe Jesus felt compassion for him, the compassion of a shepherd for a lost, wandering, confused sheep. Therefore, **Jesus said to him, "If you want to be perfect, go, sell what you have and give to the poor, and you will have treasure in heaven; and come, follow Me"** (v. 21).

Commentators agree that with this answer, Jesus was not setting down a law for the whole world, saying that if anyone wants to enter heaven he must get rid of all of his possessions. Instead, He was putting his finger on this man's core problem—he was in love with his money. That love for money was affecting his obedience to all the other commandments. Jesus could have said: "OK, you say you've kept all the commandments. Let's start at number one: 'You shall have no other gods before Me' (Ex. 20:3). Young man, your money is your god. Your wealth is your idol. You cannot love money more than you love God and expect to enter His kingdom." He could have done the same with the other commandments. This young man needed to set aside his idol and follow Jesus so as to gain a treasure that would never rust or fade away.

The man did not get angry. He did not protest to Jesus and say: "That's not fair. I worked hard to get my money, and I've been a good steward of it. I'm not wasteful. I don't live in riotous fashion. So who do You think You are?" No, his response was very different. His heart was broken. He had rushed up to Jesus to find out how to go to heaven. But when Jesus told him what he needed to do, He put His finger on the young man's soul. Matthew tells us, **But when the young man heard that saying, he went away sorrowful, for he had great possessions** (v. 22).

That is one of the saddest commentaries that we read anywhere in sacred Scripture. This man walked away from Jesus because he was not willing to trade his riches for the pearl of great price. He walked away with his money and left his soul and his Savior behind. But as I mentioned above, the rich young ruler is Everyman, and this same transaction occurs every day in this world. Christians have a great calling to show the world that Jesus is a better treasure than any riches this world affords.

91

ALL THINGS ARE POSSIBLE

Matthew 19:23–30

Then Jesus said to His disciples, "Assuredly, I say to you that it is hard for a rich man to enter the kingdom of heaven. And again I say to you, it is easier for a camel to go through the eye of a needle than for a rich man to enter the kingdom of God." When His disciples heard it, they were greatly astonished, saying, "Who then can be saved?" But Jesus looked at them and said to them, "With men this is impossible, but with God all things are possible." Then Peter answered and said to Him, "See, we have left all and followed You. Therefore what shall we have?" So Jesus said to them, "Assuredly I say to you, that in the regeneration, when the Son of Man sits on the throne of His glory, you who have followed Me will also sit on twelve thrones, judging the twelve tribes of Israel. And everyone who has left houses or brothers or sisters or father or mother or wife or children or lands, for My name's sake, shall receive a hundredfold, and inherit eternal life. But many who are first will be last, and the last first."

When we look at the teachings in any text of Scripture, it is important that we search for the context in which they were delivered. In the case of the passage that is before us in this chapter, we recall that the text we examined in the previous chapter concerned the rich young ruler who approached Jesus to ask, "Good Teacher, what good thing shall I do that I may have eternal life?" (19:16). We saw that this young man had a woefully inadequate understanding of what is truly good and a woefully exaggerated view of his own righteousness. Jesus had to strip him of his pretention and then challenge him with regard to his love of money. Our Lord said to him, "If you want to be perfect, go, sell what you have and give to the poor, and you will have treasure in heaven; and come, follow Me" (v. 21). At that point, the man walked away from Jesus because "he had great possessions" (v. 22).

The disciples witnessed this episode, and Jesus immediately put it to good use as a teaching tool. Matthew tells us: **Then Jesus said to His disciples, "Assuredly, I say to you that it is hard for a rich man to enter the kingdom of heaven. And again I say to you, it is easier for a camel to go through the eye of a needle than for a rich man to enter the kingdom of God"** (vv. 23–24). In making these comments, Jesus was not making an ethical pronouncement on the evil of wealth. Rather, He was simply pointing out that people who are endowed with riches have difficulty entering the kingdom of God. The rich young ruler was a prime example of this truth. Wealth can be a god, and as such it must be set aside if one is to follow God. This is no easy step.

Jesus reiterated this point with a metaphor that is strange to our ears: "it is easier for a camel to go through the eye of a needle than for a rich man to enter the kingdom of God." Some commentators have said that in addition to the various gates of Jerusalem, there was a small entrance known as the eye of the needle. It was not normally used by caravan traders, but in a pinch, by forcing a camel to its knees and prodding it forward, a trader could use the opening to enter the city. That's a great story, but there is absolutely no scholarly confirmation that there ever was such a gate by that name in or around Jerusalem. I believe Jesus was simply using hyperbole, an intentional exaggeration to make a point. He chose the largest animal native to the disciples' environs and the smallest opening that came to His mind. He said it was easier for an enormous camel to go through the tiny eye of a needle than for a rich man to enter the kingdom of God.

The Biblical View of Wealth

Of course, we know that a camel cannot possibly fit through the eye of a needle. So, it seems that the irresistible conclusion of Jesus' teaching is that all rich people, in the final analysis, will not make it into the kingdom of God. It is easy to conclude that Jesus was saying that there is something inherently wrong or wicked about the accumulation of wealth. But such an interpretation of Jesus' words would clash with the teaching of the rest of sacred Scripture.

The Bible knows nothing of a worldview that exalts the virtue of poverty or despises the vice of riches. On the contrary, the Old Testament delineates four distinct groups who find themselves in poverty. The largest of these groups is composed of those who are poor because of their sloth and refusal to work. But it is a terrible mistake, one that many people today make, to conclude that people are poor only because they are lazy. Such a view slanders multitudes of people who are poor through no fault of their own. The Bible makes it clear that some are poor because they were victims of great calamities over which they had no control, such as a famine that destroyed their crops. Others are poor because they were exploited by unscrupulous powerful people or rulers. Still others are poor voluntarily for righteousness' sake.

Likewise, there are several groups of wealthy people. First, there are those who are wealthy because they are crooked, unscrupulous, and unmerciful toward other people. Then there are those who are wealthy because they have been industrious and have engaged in good stewardship of their wealth, not squandering it in wasteful consumption. Also, there are those who are wealthy through inheritance. The Old Testament made it obligatory for the Israelites to be productive and to steward what they gained so as to provide for their families. The Apostle Paul was reflecting this ethic when he wrote, "If anyone does not provide for his own, and especially for those of his household, he has denied the faith and is worse than an unbeliever" (1 Tim. 5:8). But not only were they expected to provide for their families; they were to do everything in their power to accumulate an inheritance for their children. As we read through the narratives of the patriarchal period in Genesis, we see that the patriarchs were always careful to provide an inheritance for their children. Throughout the Old Testament, we see the sanctity of the inheritance.

Just imagine that your great-grandfather was exceedingly productive and a good steward of his wealth, so that he died with a surplus, leaving a significant legacy for your grandfather. Imagine that your grandfather built on his inheritance and made it even more valuable, and that he followed in the steps of his father and exercised godly responsibility and stewardship, so that when he died he left an inheritance that was even greater than he received to your father. Then imagine that your father, being diligent and able to avoid catastrophic downturns in the market and so on, was able also to increase the wealth he'd received by wisdom, labor, and industry, so that when he died your great-grandfather's fortune had increased a hundredfold, and you did not have to start at zero. Would it not be wonderful if everyone enjoyed the benefit of the godly labor and stewardship of former generations? Unfortunately, most of us, I believe, have had to start almost at ground zero because we live in a world that is given to wasteful consumption, a world of people who want to spend their grandchildren's inheritance on themselves now.

The Bible has nothing but approval for industry, productivity, and stewardship.

That is why, in part, Jesus' statement was so shocking and astonishing to His disciples. In biblical categories, diligence, hard work, and good stewardship are seen as virtues that usually are attended by the blessing of God. So, if anyone had any right to expect entrance into the kingdom of God, it was those who had been good stewards of the gifts that God had given.

A Blessing and a Curse

But Jesus said that was not so. Why? Jesus was showing His disciples that while wealth is a blessing, it is also a curse, because it can become the very barrier that prevents a person from entering the kingdom of God. There are many problems that come with wealth, three of which bear mentioning.

First, one of the great barriers to entering God's kingdom is to be in possession not so much of wealth but of a sense of self-sufficiency. The more wealthy a person becomes, the less dependent he is on other things. The less dependent he is for his daily concerns in this world, the less dependent he assumes he is in relationship to God. He assumes money can get him out of whatever problems he encounters in this world. But there is no bail from hell. Money can never get a person out of there. So, this kind of false sense of self-sufficiency can rob people of a sense of dependence on the grace of God for everything from eternal life to one's next meal. A false self-sufficiency is a serious barrier to people in their relationship to God.

Second, the acquisition of wealth and the maintenance of it requires an almost total absorption. Wealth forces people to keep their eyes on their businesses, their responsibilities, their purchases, and so on. In other words, being wealthy takes a lot of time and energy. People can become so absorbed with the business of this world that they are not the masters of their wealth, but their wealth is their master. However, Jesus said, "You cannot serve God and mammon" (Matt. 6:24b). In other words, no one can devote himself to the acquisition of wealth and at the same time devote himself to serving God. Every Christian needs to ask himself or herself on a regular basis, "How much of my thinking, how much of my planning, how much of my effort, how much of my concern is about money as distinct from the things of God?"

Third, the acquisition of wealth can become an obsession. What drives the vice of greed? Greed afflicts people when they never seem to have enough. I remember having a conversation many years ago with a friend who mentioned a figure that a friend of his was making each year. We began to dream together, saying, "Wouldn't it be nice if we could make that kind of money?" Well, by the blessing of God, my income has surpassed that figure that once seemed unattainable. Yet I sometimes find myself thinking about what I could do, what

I would not have to worry about, if my income was just a little more. Somehow, in the accumulation of wealth, the goal keeps getting higher and higher. People are never satisfied. I see this every day of my life, and so do you. Wealth becomes a snare, an obsession.

The Bible tells us to be productive, to have an inheritance, and to provide for our families. But above all things we are to seek the kingdom of God (Matt. 6:33). If our pursuit of riches gets in the way of our searching after the kingdom, we are in the same position as the rich young ruler, who walked away from Jesus.

The First and the Last

Matthew tells us, **When His disciples heard it, they were greatly astonished, saying, "Who then can be saved?" But Jesus looked at them and said to them, "With men this is impossible, but with God all things are possible"** (vv. 25–26). The disciples were shocked to hear Jesus say these things and made the obvious conclusion—if it is difficult for a man God has blessed with riches to be saved, it must be nearly impossible for the average person to be saved. But Jesus cautioned them not to leave God out of the equation. Jesus had said it was *difficult* for a rich man to be saved, but not *impossible*, for with God, all things are possible.

The disciples had another question: **Then Peter answered and said to Him, "See, we have left all and followed You. Therefore what shall we have?" So Jesus said to them, "Assuredly I say to you, that in the regeneration, when the Son of Man sits on the throne of His glory, you who have followed Me will also sit on twelve thrones, judging the twelve tribes of Israel. And everyone who has left houses or brothers or sisters or father or mother or wife or children or lands, for My name's sake, shall receive a hundredfold, and inherit eternal life. But many who are first will be last, and the last first"** (vv. 27–30). Peter seems to have been asking how the disciples would be compensated for their voluntary poverty if rich men could enjoy their wealth in the world and then be saved, too. Jesus answered that the disciples would be rewarded in "the regeneration," that is, the new heaven and new earth. He assured them that they would reign with Him and would receive a hundred times what they had given up for His sake. They *would* be rewarded for their sacrifice. They, simple blue-collar men—not the rich of the world—would judge the twelve tribes of Israel.

So it is in the kingdom of heaven: many who are great in the eyes of the world will be "last," while many who are lowly and overlooked in the world will be "first." We must keep "kingdom priorities" in view as we wrestle with issues such as wealth.

92

THE PARABLE OF THE WORKERS

Matthew 20:1–16

For the kingdom of heaven is like a landowner who went out early in the morning to hire laborers for his vineyard. Now when he had agreed with the laborers for a denarius a day, he sent them into his vineyard. And he went out about the third hour and saw others standing idle in the marketplace, and said to them, "You also go into the vineyard, and whatever is right I will give you." So they went. Again he went out about the sixth and the ninth hour, and did likewise. And about the eleventh hour he went out and found others standing idle, and said to them, "Why have you been standing here idle all day?" They said to him, "Because no one hired us." He said to them, "You also go into the vineyard, and whatever is right you will receive." So when evening had come, the owner of the vineyard said to his steward, "Call the laborers and give them their wages, beginning with the last to the first." And when those came who were hired about the eleventh hour, they each received a denarius. But when the first came, they supposed that they would receive more; and they likewise received each a denarius. And when they had received it, they complained against the landowner, saying, "These last men have worked only one hour, and you made them equal to us who have borne the burden and the heat of the day." But he answered one of them and said, "Friend, I am doing you no wrong. Did you not agree with me for a denarius? Take what is yours and go your way. I wish to give to this last man the same as to you. Is it not lawful for me to do what I wish with my own things? Or is your eye evil because I am good?" So the last will be first, and the first last. For many are called, but few chosen.

Following His discussion with His disciples about the difficulties of rich individuals making it into the kingdom of heaven, Jesus told yet another kingdom parable, the parable of the workers in the vineyard. Though this parable is somewhat enigmatic upon an initial reading, it teaches us a profound lesson about the nature of God's grace.

Jesus began by saying, **"For the kingdom of heaven is like a landowner who went out early in the morning to hire laborers for his vineyard"** (v. 1). The time had come for the owner of a vineyard to harvest his grapes. The permanent workers on his farm were not numerous enough to complete the harvest in time, so when harvest time came, as many farmers did in the ancient world and still do today, he went looking for day laborers he could hire. Such laborers customarily came to the marketplace in the hope that they would be chosen to labor that day and would gain the standard pay for a day's work in Israel, which was one denarius. So, Jesus said, **"When he had agreed with the laborers for a denarius a day, he sent them into his vineyard"** (v. 2).

However, it seems that his initial trip to the marketplace happened before all of the available laborers had gathered there, and the owner was not able to secure enough of them to complete the harvest as soon as he hoped. Therefore, Jesus said: **"And he went out about the third hour and saw others standing idle in the marketplace, and said to them, 'You also go into the vineyard, and whatever is right I will give you.' So they went. Again he went out about the sixth and the ninth hour, and did likewise"** (vv. 3–5). The owner kept checking the marketplace throughout the day, and every time he found a few available workers, he sent them off to his vineyard with the promise to pay them "whatever is right."

So zealous was this landowner to complete his harvest, **"About the eleventh hour he went out and found others standing idle, and said to them, 'Why have you been standing here idle all day?' They said to him, 'Because no one hired us.' He said to them, 'You also go into the vineyard, and whatever is right you will receive'"** (vv. 6–7). "The eleventh hour" was about 5 p.m., quite near the end of the workday, but the owner found a few men available even then, men who had not been hired to do any work all that day. So, he sent them to his vineyard with the same promise.

So far, this is a happy story. The economic system of the day seemingly worked to perfection. The labor pool supplied abundant workers and the landowner employed them steadily. His harvest moved forward and the laborers earned their daily bread. A happy ending seemed certain.

But it was not to be. Jesus said: "**So when evening had come, the owner of the vineyard said to his steward, 'Call the laborers and give them their**

wages, beginning with the last to the first.' And when those came who were hired about the eleventh hour, they each received a denarius. But when the first came, they supposed that they would receive more; and they likewise received each a denarius" (vv. 8–10). The owner of the vineyard paid everyone the exact same wage. The people who had worked for an hour received a denarius. Those who had worked for three hours received a denarius. Those who had worked for six hours received a denarius. And those that had been there all day received a denarius.

That seemed unfair to those who had worked the longest: **"And when they had received it, they complained against the landowner, saying, 'These last men have worked only one hour, and you made them equal to us who have borne the burden and the heat of the day'"** (vv. 11–12). The men who had been there all day felt the wages were unfair, for they had borne the brunt of the labor in the heat of the day, while some had worked only a short time in the cool of the afternoon. They believed that if the latecomers received a denarius, they were due more.

So, the owner addressed these grumblers, these malcontents: **"But he answered one of them and said, 'Friend, I am doing you no wrong. Did you not agree with me for a denarius? Take what is yours and go your way. I wish to give to this last man the same as to you. Is it not lawful for me to do what I wish with my own things? Or is your eye evil because I am good?'"** (vv. 13–15). The owner simply pointed out that he had fulfilled his end of the deal they had struck in the early morning. I would guess that he reminded them how happy they had been in the morning to have a day of work ahead of them and the prospect of a denarius at the end of it. They had been satisfied with the deal at that point and had gone to work for the owner of their own volition. But then they saw others get the same wage for less work, and the issue of fairness arose with a vengeance.

A Parable on Sovereign Grace

This parable is not about grapes. It is about grace. It is about the mercy of the living God. It is about the grace of the One who owns the vineyard and who, in His mercy, gives benefits to people who have not earned them. In the parable, those who came later in the day had no possible way of meeting the normal requirements to make a denarius. However, the owner of the vineyard gave them the denarius anyway. The first group received justice. Every group thereafter received mercy and grace. But those who received justice complained that they were victims of injustice and that the owner was not fair.

Furthermore, I believe this parable is about *sovereign* grace, that is, the biblical doctrine of election. We read in the Scriptures that God from all eternity has decreed by His grace alone to save certain people from their sins, not because they deserve it or have earned it, but that His mercy might be made manifest. He chooses to save some and leaves others in their lost condition to receive whatever justice requires.

The Apostle Paul develops this teaching clearly in the eighth and ninth chapters of Romans. He cites the example of Jacob and Esau, of whom God decreed that the older (Esau) would serve the younger (Jacob) before they were born or had done anything good or evil. This was so "that the purpose of God according to election might stand" (9:11).

Having said this, the apostle anticipates a response, the response of protest that every sinner gives to God's electing grace: "That's not fair." Paul asks rhetorically, "Is there unrighteousness with God?" (v. 14). How does he answer? Does he say: "Well, maybe there is a little bit of unrighteousness. Maybe every now and then God does something that is a little bit unfair and unjust, but in the main He's a pretty good God"? You know that is not what Paul says. He answers his own rhetorical question with an emphatic denial: "Certainly not!" Other translations read, "By no means!" "May it never be!" and "God forbid!" What could be more unthinkable than to imagine for a second that there might be a gap in the righteousness of God, as if somehow the perfect righteousness of God could suffer a defect. Paul then reminds his readers what God revealed in the Old Testament through Moses: "I will have mercy on whomever I will have mercy, and I will have compassion on whomever I will have compassion" (v. 15). He concludes, "It is not of him who wills, nor of him who runs, but of God who shows mercy" (v. 16).

At Saint Andrew's, the congregation where I preach, we print the five *"solas"* of the Reformation in the bulletin each week. These great mottos of the Reformers are *sola fide*, justification by faith alone; *sola Scriptura*, the authority of the Scriptures alone; *soli Deo gloria*, to God alone the glory; *solus Christus*, salvation through Christ alone; and *sola gratia*, salvation by grace alone. We have not really understood the gospel until we understand that we are saved by grace alone, not by grace plus merit, not by faith plus works, and not by Christ's righteousness plus our own righteousness. If we do not embrace *sola gratia*, salvation by grace alone, we really do not embrace *sola fide*, justification by faith alone, because the faith by which we are justified is the gracious gift of God (Eph. 2:8), not something that we produce out of our own sinful flesh.

But we have the idea that if God gives His saving grace to one person, in order to be just, He must give the same grace to that person's neighbor. However, if God is required to give His grace to anyone, it is not grace. That is the whole point of this parable. The owner said, "Is it not lawful for me to do what I wish with my own things?" In other words, "I will have mercy on whomever I will have mercy."

Grace and Justice, but No Injustice

In the parable, a large group of the workers received grace. One group received justice. However, no one received injustice. But the workers who labored all day *thought* they received injustice. They thought the owner owed them something.

If we were to try to list everything God owes us, it would be the easiest task we were ever assigned, one we could complete in record time. The truth is, He owes us nothing except His wrath as punishment for all our sins. A much more challenging assignment would be to try to write down all the things we owe God. We would never complete that task. We are much in His debt for our offenses against His righteousness. Yet He still freely gives us good gifts each day, each hour. Everything that we have comes from Him, not because we have earned it but because He mercifully provides it.

If there is any sentiment that has no place in the Christian heart, it is the sentiment that God owes us something. He owes us nothing. The only title we have is to our sin, unless in His mercy He bestows the title of the kingdom of God freely upon us. That is what He has done for everyone who has believed.

So, Jesus capped this parable by saying: "So the last will be first, and the first last. For many are called, but few chosen" (v. 16). First He repeated the point He made at the end of His teaching on rich men: in the kingdom, many who are now last will be first and many who are now first will be last (19:30). Then He declared, "Many are called, but few are chosen." The general call of the gospel goes forth to all nations, tribes, and tongues, but only those who are regenerated by the Spirit respond to it. It is they who were chosen before the foundation of the world. It is they who receive God's unmerited grace.

93

SERVICE

Matthew 20:17–34

Now Jesus, going up to Jerusalem, took the twelve disciples aside on the road and said to them, "Behold, we are going up to Jerusalem, and the Son of Man will be betrayed to the chief priests and to the scribes; and they will condemn Him to death, and deliver Him to the Gentiles to mock and to scourge and to crucify. And the third day He will rise again." Then the mother of Zebedee's sons came to Him with her sons, kneeling down and asking something from Him. And He said to her, "What do you wish?" She said to Him, "Grant that these two sons of mine may sit, one on Your right hand and the other on the left, in Your kingdom." But Jesus answered and said, "You do not know what you ask. Are you able to drink the cup that I am about to drink, and be baptized with the baptism that I am baptized with?" They said to Him, "We are able." So He said to them, "You will indeed drink My cup, and be baptized with the baptism that I am baptized with; but to sit on My right hand and on My left is not Mine to give, but it is for those for whom it is prepared by My Father." And when the ten heard it, they were greatly displeased with the two brothers. But Jesus called them to Himself and said, "You know that the rulers of the Gentiles lord it over them, and those who are great exercise authority over them. Yet it shall not be so among you; but whoever desires to become great among you, let him be your servant. And whoever desires to be first among you, let him be your slave just as the Son of Man did not come to be served, but to serve, and to give His life a ransom for many." Now as they went out of Jericho, a great multitude followed Him. And behold, two blind men sitting by the road, when they heard that Jesus was passing by, cried out, saying, "Have mercy on us, O Lord, Son of David!" Then the multitude warned them that they should be quiet; but they cried out all the more, saying, "Have mercy on us, O Lord, Son of David!" So Jesus stood still and called them, and said, "What do you want Me to do for you?" They said to Him, "Lord, that our eyes may be opened." So Jesus had compassion and touched their eyes. And immediately their eyes received sight, and they followed Him.

As Jesus was making His way toward Jerusalem, indeed, as He was drawing near to the city, He warned His disciples a third time about what was going to happen to Him there (see 16:21; 17:22–23). Matthew writes: **Now Jesus, going up to Jerusalem, took the twelve disciples aside on the road and said to them, "Behold, we are going up to Jerusalem, and the Son of Man will be betrayed to the chief priests and to the scribes; and they will condemn Him to death, and deliver Him to the Gentiles to mock and to scourge and to crucify. And the third day He will rise again"** (vv. 17–19). The main new information in this warning was His impending deliverance from the Jews to the Gentiles, who, He said, would mock Him, scourge Him, and execute Him by crucifixion. Matthew records no reaction from the disciples, but these sad and gruesome new details must have been painful for them to hear.

I do not believe for a second that this warning "just happens" to precede Matthew's account of the incident that follows. Even as Jesus was revealing to His disciples that He was about to perform the ultimate act of servanthood, two of His disciples showed that servanthood was the last thing on their minds. It seems clear that Matthew juxtaposed these incidents to highlight Jesus' servant heart.

Matthew tells us, **Then the mother of Zebedee's sons came to Him with her sons, kneeling down and asking something from Him** (v. 20). Zebedee was the father of two of the men who were part of the inner core of Jesus' disciple band, James and John. Their mother's name is not given here, but many believe her name was Salome (see Mark 15:40: 16:1), and that she was the sister of Mary, the mother of Jesus (see John 19:25), in which case James and John were cousins of Jesus. In any case, she came with her sons in tow and knelt before Jesus, showing respect to Him and acknowledging His authority. Then she made it known that she had a request for Him.

Matthew continues: **And He said to her, "What do you wish?" She said to Him, "Grant that these two sons of mine may sit, one on Your right hand and the other on the left, in Your kingdom"** (v. 21). There is good news and bad news in this request. The good news is that the woman understood and believed that Jesus was about to come into His kingdom. She had confidence in Jesus for the future. In spite of the words of gloom and doom that He had just uttered, she was convinced that the kingdom about which Jesus had preached throughout His earthly ministry was not pie in the sky but a reality that was soon to be made manifest.

The bad news is that she was not concerned first and foremost with Jesus' glory in this kingdom but with the glory of her sons. She wanted one to sit on Jesus' right and one on His left in His kingdom. It is always the case that glory overflows from those who are in positions of power to those who are closest to them, and whenever someone comes to a position of power, be it a king, a president, or a superintendent on the job, people scramble to get close to the seat of power. Thus, it was natural for this woman to assume that those who sat on the right and left of Jesus in His kingship would be in the highest possible seats of power and glory in the entire kingdom, outshined only by the King Himself. So, she said to her sons: "Look boys, I'm going to talk to Jesus. I'm going to talk to the one who will soon be King and make sure that you have the highest positions of power in His kingdom."

A Bitter Cup to Drink

Jesus' response seemed to carry a note of pity: **But Jesus answered and said, "You do not know what you ask. Are you able to drink the cup that I am about to drink, and be baptized with the baptism that I am baptized with?" They said to Him, "We are able"** (v. 22). The word *you* here is plural, so Jesus' words were directed to James and John, not their mother. It was as if He were saying to them: "You have no idea what you're asking. If you knew what you are asking, you would get up off your knees and run for your lives, because whoever sits at My right hand and whoever sits at My left hand will first encounter not glory but infamy, suffering, and humiliation." It was to these He was referring when He asked, "Are you able to drink the cup that I am about to drink?"

A few years ago, I wrote a book for children titled *The Prince's Poison Cup*. It is designed to teach children not about a mythical prince but about the Prince of Peace, who, in order to redeem us, was asked by His Father to drink the most ghastly cup that had ever been served to any mortal in the history of this world. This cup was filled with wrath, suffering, and sorrows. This was the cup from which Jesus was shrinking in horror in the garden of Gethsemane when He prayed, "O My Father, if it is possible, let this cup pass from Me" (Matt. 26:39b). He was asking whether there was any other way to redeem His people. The Father said no. He had to drink that cup. It was His vocation to drink it. In the end, He did.

So, Jesus knew what was coming. He knew what was in the cup He had to drink. He looked at James and John and said, "Can you drink this cup too?"

Some people have said that there is no such thing as a stupid question. I think that is highly debatable. But one thing we know for sure: There are stupid answers to questions. One such answer was given when James and John replied to Jesus' question by saying, "We are able." They had no idea what suffering and humiliation lay ahead.

Matthew then writes: **So He said to them, "You will indeed drink My cup, and be baptized with the baptism that I am baptized with; but to sit on My right hand and on My left is not Mine to give, but it is for those for whom it is prepared by My Father"** (v. 23). Of course, neither of these men, individually or together, had the ability to drink the fullness of the cup that Jesus was about to drink. But Jesus' cup would spill over upon His followers in a smaller measure. He was warning them: "Do you want to follow Me? Do you want to sit in glory on My right or left hand? Then get ready, because you will participate in My suffering first." As the Apostle Paul said, "If we endure, we shall also reign with Him" (2 Tim. 2:12a).

But Jesus went on to say that it was not up to Him to determine who would sit on His right and left in glory; rather, "It is for those for whom it is prepared by My Father." What king does not have the authority to say who will sit on his right and left? Any king has the power to grant positions within his kingdom. But Jesus is the Father's anointed King, and even in His enthronement, He still is subordinate to His Father. Just as the Father has determined from the foundation of the world that His Son will sit as the King in His kingdom, so He has determined who will sit on Jesus' right and left. Jesus was simply telling James and John that it was pointless to ask for such positions, because the Father had already determined who would get them. The decision was not up to Jesus. James and John must submit to the Father, just as Jesus did.

Greatness through Servanthood

Matthew then writes what is perhaps his supreme understatement: **And when the ten heard it, they were greatly displeased with the two brothers** (v. 24). Just imagine how Peter felt when he heard about this. "What? I'm the leader of this group. What do you mean by trying to get on the right hand?" But it was not just Peter; all of them were very displeased. Two of their comrades had just tried an end run to get ahead of them.

Here, then, was another teaching moment for Jesus: **But Jesus called them to Himself and said, "You know that the rulers of the Gentiles lord it over them, and those who are great exercise authority over them. Yet it shall not be so among you; but whoever desires to become great among you, let him be your servant. And whoever desires to be first among you, let him be your**

slave" (vv. 25–27). The rulers of the Gentiles behaved autocratically, "lording it over" their subjects. But that was not to be the model for the disciples. Instead, in the church, the greatest was to be the one with the biggest servant heart. Furthermore, the "first" would be the "slave." Twice in recent passages we have seen Jesus say that in His kingdom, "The last will be first and the first last" (19:30; 20:16). Here He showed that whoever wants to be first must *make himself* a slave to his brethren. The true follower of Christ does not grab for glory; he humbles himself as a servant.

Finally, Jesus said, **"The Son of Man did not come to be served, but to serve, and to give His life a ransom for many"** (v. 28). There are only a few times in the Gospels when Jesus explained why He came into this world. On one occasion, He said, "The Son of Man has come to seek and to save that which was lost" (Luke 19:10). On another occasion, He said, "I have come that they may have life, and that they may have it more abundantly" (John 10:10b). When He was on trial before Pontius Pilate, and Pilate asked Him whether He was a king, He said, "For this cause I have come into the world, that I should bear witness to the truth" (John 18:37b). However, here in Matthew's Gospel, Jesus gave a different explanation for His coming. Why did He descend from heaven and live in the world for thirty-three years? He said, "The Son of Man did not come to be served, but to serve." He was the Servant of the Lord that we read about in Isaiah 53.

Furthermore, He said He came "to give His life a ransom for many." Some scholars say Jesus paid a ransom to the devil to set us free, but that is not the biblical picture. It is true that ransoms were paid in military tribunals in antiquity to secure the release of those who were held captive by the enemy. More frequently, however, ransoms were paid to secure the freedom of those who could not pay their debts and were facing indentured servitude. Jesus paid a ransom to purchase His beloved people out of their bondage to sin. Is it any wonder that the Apostle Paul says, "You were bought at a price" (1 Cor. 6:20)?

This is one of the chief reasons why Jesus came. Now, having been purchased by the Son of Man, we are called to reflect His servanthood. We are not to lord it over anyone, but we are to be slaves to all.

The "Son of David"

Matthew closes this chapter with a short account of a healing: **Now as they went out of Jericho, a great multitude followed Him. And behold, two blind men sitting by the road, when they heard that Jesus was passing by, cried out, saying, "Have mercy on us, O Lord, Son of David!" Then the multitude warned them that they should be quiet; but they cried out all the more,**

saying, "Have mercy on us, O Lord, Son of David!" So Jesus stood still and called them, and said, "What do you want Me to do for you?" They said to Him, "Lord, that our eyes may be opened." So Jesus had compassion and touched their eyes. And immediately their eyes received sight, and they followed Him (vv. 29–34).

This incident is remarkably similar to a healing that is recorded in Matthew 9:27–34, which we studied in chapter 47, so I will not rehearse the details here. It is interesting to note, however, that Jesus was in Jericho at this point. This was not the Old Testament city of Jericho, which Joshua conquered when the Israelites entered the Promised Land, but a different Jericho, located around an oasis about eighteen miles north of Jerusalem. It is clear that Jesus was nearing the end of His journey to Jerusalem.

One other aspect of both of the healings of blind men seems important for what is to follow. In both Matthew 9 and 20, the blind men referred to Jesus as "Son of David," which was a messianic title. We have already seen this title used on several occasions in Matthew (9:27; 12:23; 15:22), and in the next chapter we will see that this title was on the lips of those who welcomed Jesus at His triumphal entry (21:9, 15). Then, in the next chapter, Jesus will ask the Pharisees how it is possible that David, writing in Psalm 110, could speak of his Son as his Lord (22:41–46). These are further clues as to Jesus' true identity.

94

THE TRIUMPHAL ENTRY

Matthew 21:1–11

Now when they drew near Jerusalem, and came to Bethphage, at the Mount of Olives, then Jesus sent two disciples, saying to them, "Go into the village opposite you, and immediately you will find a donkey tied, and a colt with her. Loose them and bring them to Me. And if anyone says anything to you, you shall say, 'The Lord has need of them,' and immediately he will send them." All this was done that it might be fulfilled which was spoken by the prophet, saying:

"Tell the daughter of Zion,
'Behold, your King is coming to you,
Lowly, and sitting on a donkey,
A colt, the foal of a donkey.'"

So the disciples went and did as Jesus commanded them. They brought the donkey and the colt, laid their clothes on them, and set Him on them. And a very great multitude spread their clothes on the road; others cut down branches from the trees and spread them on the road. Then the multitudes who went before and those who followed cried out, saying:

"Hosanna to the Son of David!
'Blessed is He who comes in the name of the LORD!'
Hosanna in the highest!"

And when He had come into Jerusalem, all the city was moved, saying, "Who is this?" So the multitudes said, "This is Jesus, the prophet from Nazareth of Galilee."

It was shortly after the Transfiguration that Jesus set His face "like a flint" (Isa. 50:7) and began to move resolutely southward, toward Jerusalem. We have followed His progress through several chapters of Matthew's Gospel as He moved from a Gentile area north of Galilee down through Capernaum and then into Judea. Finally, in our passage for this chapter, we witness His arrival at Jerusalem, an event that traditionally is known as His triumphal entry. This episode is sometimes obscured by the vastly important events that followed, but it was a watershed not only in the life of Jesus but in the history of the world, one of the great moments of redemptive history.

Matthew tells us, **they drew near Jerusalem, and came to Bethphage, at the Mount of Olives** (v. 1a). It is thought that Bethphage was on the Mount of Olives, just across the Kidron Valley and less than a mile to the east of Jerusalem. It probably was within sight of the city. At that point, **Jesus sent two disciples, saying to them, "Go into the village opposite you, and immediately you will find a donkey tied, and a colt with her. Loose them and bring them to Me"** (vv. 1b–2). Jesus gave specific instructions to two of His disciples, telling them to go into a village, find a donkey and a colt, and bring them to Him, though He did not explain why He needed them. Here again we have a glimpse of Jesus' divine omniscience, by which He knew where the donkey and colt could be found.

Incidentally, Matthew is the only one of the Gospel writers who mentions the colt's mother. Perhaps he wanted to emphasize how young the colt was by telling his readers it was not yet weaned from its mother. Such a young colt would not have been ridden before. Furthermore, keeping the mother with the colt would have helped to keep the colt calm. We can only imagine how skittish the colt would have been, particularly with huge crowds of people shouting and waving palm fronds.

"The Lord Has Need of Them"

Jesus also provided the two disciples with a word of assurance: **"And if anyone says anything to you, you shall say, 'The Lord has need of them,' and immediately he will send them"** (v. 3). Jesus declared that if anyone challenged their right to borrow the animals, they needed only to say that "the Lord" wanted them. It is interesting that Jesus instructed the disciples to use this word to identify Him. It is possible that the owner of the donkeys would have known that "the Lord" meant Jesus, but he also might have taken it to be a reference to God the Father. In that case, He would have understood the disciples to be saying, "God has need of them." In truth, He would not have been wrong in interpreting their words that way, and I actually think Jesus meant the owner to understand "the Lord" as the Father. Jesus understood that it was in the plan of God that He should make His entrance into Jerusalem in this way, so it was by divine appointment that the disciples were fetching the donkeys.

We know it was in the plan of God for Jesus to ride into Jerusalem on a donkey because God had said so. Once again, as he has done so often, Matthew points out how Jesus' actions fulfilled Old Testament prophecy. He writes: **All this was done that it might be fulfilled which was spoken by the prophet, saying: "Tell the daughter of Zion, 'Behold, your King is coming to you, lowly, and sitting on a donkey, a colt, the foal of a donkey'"** (vv. 4–5). Jesus was consciously fulfilling a messianic prophecy, not because He wanted to make a name for Himself by doing what the Old Testament had foretold, but because He was submissive to the Word of God and eager to do what it required the Messiah to do.

Matthew cites the prophecy in these words: "Tell the daughter of Zion, 'Behold, your King is coming to you, lowly, and sitting on a donkey, a colt, the foal of a donkey.'" This is basically a conflation of two texts from the Old Testament, Isaiah 62:11 and Zechariah 9:9. The context of these verses sheds light on what was happening that day on the Mount of Olives.

Chapter 62 of Isaiah begins by saying, "For Zion's sake I will not hold my peace, and for Jerusalem's sake I will not rest, until her righteousness goes forth as brightness, and her salvation as a lamp that burns" (v. 1). God was saying, "I am determined that My righteousness and My salvation will burn like a lamp in the midst of the people." Then, in verse 11, He said, "Say to the daughter of Zion, 'Surely your salvation is coming.'"

Zechariah 9:9 specifically mentions the King's arrival on a donkey: "Rejoice greatly, O daughter of Zion! Shout, O daughter of Jerusalem! Behold, your King is coming to you; He is just and having salvation, lowly and riding on a donkey, a colt, the foal of a donkey." The Israelites understood this to be a prophecy of the Messiah. So, for hundreds of years the people of Israel waited for the arrival of this King. He would not be a warrior who would arrive amid the pomp and ceremony of a conqueror. He would come in humility, on a donkey, bringing salvation.

Jesus knew what was waiting for Him in Jerusalem. He was fully aware of the hostility of the Jewish religious leaders there. He also knew that the people who soon would be clamoring around Him and celebrating Him had a largely misguided understanding of who He was. They wanted a king in a chariot. They wanted a king who would drive out the Roman occupiers. They wanted a king that would set them free in worldly terms, not free from sin. In short, they were not primarily interested in a King who would bring salvation. Thus, it was doubly important in Jesus' eyes to fulfill this prophecy.

In addition to fulfilling a prophecy, by riding a donkey, Jesus was replicating a significant event from the Old Testament. When King David grew old and infirm, his son Adonijah schemed to have himself declared king of Israel. But David had promised Bathsheba that her son Solomon would be king after him. So he had Solomon proclaimed as the heir to the throne, had him ride into Jerusalem on a mule, and had him anointed (1 Kings 1).

"Hosanna in the Highest"

Matthew goes on to say: **So the disciples went and did as Jesus commanded them. They brought the donkey and the colt, laid their clothes on them, and set Him on them** (vv. 6–7). The disciples carried out their assignment and brought the mother donkey and the colt. They then laid their cloaks on them and Jesus mounted. When Matthew says they "set Him on *them*," he is referring to the clothes that were laid on the colt's back, not to the animals; Jesus did not ride both the colt and its mother.

We then read, **And a very great multitude spread their clothes on the road; others cut down branches from the trees and spread them on the road** (v. 8). By laying their cloaks in the road where Jesus would pass, the people symbolized their submission to Him as their Messiah. There was also an Old Testament precedent for this action (2 Kings 9:13). Palm branches were a common Jewish symbol.

Matthew continues: **Then the multitudes who went before and those who followed cried out, saying: "Hosanna to the Son of David! 'Blessed is He who comes in the name of the Lord!' Hosanna in the highest!"** (v. 9). Enormous crowds had turned out to see Jesus make His entrance into Jerusalem. Matthew says there were multitudes before Him and behind Him. Some of these, of course, had followed Him from Galilee, and others had joined the crowd from the nearby villages. In the meantime, word had gotten into Jerusalem, and vast numbers of people had flowed out of the city to meet Jesus on the way.

As Jesus advanced, the crowds cried, "Hosanna." This word meant "Save, now." The people acknowledged that Jesus was bringing salvation, but again, they understood that salvation in terms of deliverance from the Romans. They also cried out, "Hosanna to the Son of David." As we have seen, this was a definite messianic title, an acknowledgment by the people that the Messiah was to come in the line of David, Israel's greatest king. Finally, they cried, "Blessed is He who comes in the name of the LORD!" With these words, the people confessed that Jesus was coming with the authority of God Himself, that He was an emissary or representative of God. They were declaring that Jesus had been sent by God. "This is the One whom God has sent! This is our Messiah! This is our King!"

Matthew gives us a somewhat curious conclusion to this episode: **And when He had come into Jerusalem, all the city was moved, saying, "Who is this?" So the multitudes said, "This is Jesus, the prophet from Nazareth of Galilee"** (vv. 10–11). Jesus' arrival sparked such a tumult that it caught the attention of the whole city. In this case, I do not think Matthew was engaging in hyperbole. Jerusalem was still small enough and Jesus' arrival was significant enough that it could well have been the talk of the whole town. But while many were actively engaged in welcoming Jesus, some were not aware of who He was. They asked: "Who is this?" So, the people told them: "This is Jesus." Sadly, they added, "the prophet from Nazareth of Galilee." Yes, Jesus was a prophet, but He was far more than a prophet. Even though the people had welcomed Jesus in messianic terms, it seems that many of them did not recognize Him as the Son of God.

Luke adds an interesting tidbit to this story. Some of the Pharisees urged Him to rebuke His disciples for their messianic language, but Jesus replied, "I tell you that if these should keep silent, the stones would immediately cry out" (Luke 19:40). He was saying that to silence His disciples and the crowd would have been an exercise in futility, because creation itself, being sick and tired of groaning, was ready to celebrate the arrival of the Savior.

This was a watershed moment. Jesus came to Jerusalem, the ancient capital of God's people, and was openly proclaimed as the Messiah. The stage was then set for the events of the final week of His life, leading to His suffering, crucifixion, death, and resurrection.

95

THE CLEANSING OF THE TEMPLE

Matthew 21:12–17

Then Jesus went into the temple of God and drove out all those who bought and sold in the temple, and overturned the tables of the money changers and the seats of those who sold doves. And He said to them, "It is written, 'My house shall be called a house of prayer,' but you have made it a 'den of thieves.'" Then the blind and the lame came to Him in the temple, and He healed them. But when the chief priests and scribes saw the wonderful things that He did, and the children crying out in the temple and saying, "Hosanna to the Son of David!" they were indignant and said to Him, "Do You hear what these are saying?" And Jesus said to them, "Yes. Have you never read,

> 'Out of the mouth of babes and nursing infants
> You have perfected praise'?"

Then He left them and went out of the city to Bethany, and He lodged there.

It is easy to pass over the familiar story of Jesus' cleansing of the temple without giving it much thought. However, this story is rich in its revelation of Jesus' character, and we therefore do well to consider it thoughtfully.

Matthew tells us that immediately after His triumphal entry, **Jesus went into the temple of God** (v. 12a). It is interesting to me that Matthew chose to refer to the temple as "the temple of God." The original temple in Jerusalem was built by David's son Solomon; hence, it was popularly known as "Solomon's temple." That temple was destroyed by the Babylonians in 586 BC. When the temple was rebuilt after the Babylonian exile, it was often called "Zerubbabel's temple," after one of the men who led the rebuilding effort. That temple stood for more than five hundred years until Herod the Great began to dismantle it in 21 BC in preparation for building a new temple. That temple, which was the one that was standing in Jesus' time, was known as "Herod's temple." However, each of these temples was first and foremost a sanctuary and symbolic dwelling place for God, His house among His people. The temple was established for the honor and the glory of God, for worship, for adoration, for sacrifice, for praise, and for prayer. Matthew was absolutely right to refer to it as he did.

Then Jesus **drove out all those who bought and sold in the temple, and overturned the tables of the money changers and the seats of those who sold doves. And He said to them, "It is written, 'My house shall be called a house of prayer,' but you have made it a 'den of thieves'"** (vv. 12b–13). Jesus entered the temple complex by passing through a massive gate that led into a series of courts. One of the outermost of these courts was the court of the Gentiles. It was there—not in the temple itself or even in its immediate vicinity—that He encountered people exchanging currency and selling animals. What was the reason for this activity?

When Jesus arrived in Jerusalem, the city had just begun the weeklong celebration of the Passover. The Jewish historian Josephus tells us that literally millions of people from all over the Roman world poured into Jerusalem each year to celebrate the annual feast, so that this small city teemed with humanity. The many foreigners in the city needed to exchange their own currency for the authorized coin for paying the half-shekel temple tax (Ex. 30:11–16; cf. Matt. 17:22–27), and the money changers were present to meet this need. Furthermore, some of those who came to Jerusalem desired to make burnt offerings, but in many cases, they chose to purchase animals for sacrifice in Jerusalem rather than go through the laborious process of bringing animals with them on their journeys. Many bought sheep, but those who were poorer could sacrifice doves. This is why Jesus found men selling doves in the court of the Gentiles.

This practice of exchanging currencies and providing animals for the religious ceremonies began with a good purpose in view. It was a service for the pilgrims, particularly for those who were poor, to help them fulfill their obligations. But that which began as a legitimate service for the people had become a means of exploitation, of extortion, and of downright thievery. In order for a pilgrim to exchange his currency for the local currency, he had to pay a 6 percent rate of exchange. Plus, if he did not have the right change, he had to pay another

6 percent to resolve that problem. Then there were the prices for the animals. The cost of a dove inside the temple complex was fifty times higher than it was out on the street. We know that Jesus was displeased about these unfair and exploitative practices because He said that the temple had been turned into a "den of thieves."

A "House of Prayer" Defiled

However, this was not the only reason Jesus was unhappy. He was also upset that the temple's function as "a house of prayer," was being set aside and disturbed. In the Protestant tradition, we tend to think that the basic and perhaps only significant function of the church building is to be a place where we gather to hear the Word of God proclaimed. Certainly that is an extremely important dimension of a church building. But Jesus did not refer to the temple as a "house of preaching." He called it a "house of prayer."

I spoke recently with a friend who is a Roman Catholic. He makes it a practice to visit Roman Catholic churches and spend time in prayer there. He told me he had heard about the beautiful sanctuary we had built at Saint Andrew's, so he decided to visit our church and pray there. However, when he came to Saint Andrew's, he found the sanctuary locked. When he shared this experience, I immediately began to fumble around for an explanation. I mentioned insurance issues, concerns about theft, and so on. I even told him that he was welcome to go to the office and ask for access to the sanctuary, and the staff would unlock the doors and let him in. But even as I said those words, I knew they were hollow. I knew it was not right that the church should be kept locked all day. I decided then and there that I wanted to see our church's doors open for prayer every day, and I really did not care how much it would cost for the insurance. I want to see our people on their way to work, on their way home from work, by themselves or in groups coming into the sanctuary and spending time in prayer, because unless that happens, we just have a pretty building. God's people ought to come to God's house for worship, for edification, and for instruction, but also for prayer.

I am not saying that the only legitimate place to pray is in the church. Obviously we are free to pray at home, in our prayer closets, and wherever we are. But the sanctuaries of our churches need to be known as houses of prayer.

So, when Jesus saw the extortionary practices of the money changes and animal merchants, and when He saw that God's house of prayer was being used for other practices that made prayer next to impossible, He took action. John tells us that He made a whip out of cords (2:15), and with it He literally drove out the merchants. He kicked over the tables of the money changers, scattering their coins across the temple pavement. He knocked over the seats of those who were selling doves, sending birds flying everywhere. It was chaos. In the middle of it all, filled with righteous indignation, was the Son of God.

What does this tell us about Jesus? Among other things, it tells us He was capable not only of feeling but demonstrating anger. But His anger was holy wrath. If ever a man had a right to be angry, it was He, because He was witnessing the desecration of God's house, His Father's house.

In the early chapters of the book of Hebrews, the author compares and contrasts Jesus with the prophets, the angels, and Moses. We read: "Therefore, holy brethren, partakers of the heavenly calling, consider the Apostle and High Priest of our confession, Christ Jesus, who was faithful to Him who appointed Him, as Moses also was faithful in all His house" (3:1–2). Jesus was the supreme Apostle of God, our Great High Priest, appointed by almighty God. He was faithful to the One who appointed Him, just as "Moses also was faithful in all His house." Moses was the mediator of the old covenant and Jesus is the Mediator of the new covenant. Just as Moses was obedient to God in the old covenant, Jesus was faithful to His commission as Mediator of the new covenant. So, initially the author of Hebrews puts Jesus on the same level as Moses.

However, he does not stop there. He goes on to say: "For this One has been counted worthy of more glory than Moses, inasmuch as He who built the house has more honor than the house. For every house is built by someone, but He who built all things is God. And Moses indeed was faithful in all His house as a servant, for a testimony of those things which would be spoken afterward, but Christ as a Son over His own house, whose house we are if we hold fast the confidence and the rejoicing of the hope firm to the end" (vv. 3–6). Do you see the difference? Moses was a servant in the house of God; Jesus is the Father's Son, the One to whom the Father bequeaths ownership of the house. So, in defending His Father's house, Jesus was, in essence, defending His own house.

Praises from the Children

After Jesus cleansed the temple, Matthew writes, the blind and the lame came to Him in the temple, and He healed them (v. 14). Immediately upon arriving in Jerusalem and in the temple, Jesus began to minister to the people, healing people who were blind and lame.

A curious incident then occurred: **But when the chief priests and scribes saw the wonderful things that He did, and the children crying out in the temple and saying, "Hosanna to the Son of David!" they were indignant and said to Him, "Do You hear what these are saying?"** (vv. 15–16a). It seems that as things settled down in the temple, some children at play were repeating the words they had heard adults crying out earlier that day: "Hosanna to the Son of David!" That, combined with the healings Jesus was performing, prompted the Pharisees to take Jesus to task. As we saw in the previous chapter, Luke mentions some Pharisees rebuking Him for the words of the crowd during the triumphal entry itself (Luke 19:39–40), and this seems to have been a similar complaint. The Pharisees felt that Jesus should tell His disciples not to speak of Him in messianic terms.

As He was so wont to do, Jesus replied with the words of Scripture: **And Jesus said to them, "Yes. Have you never read, 'Out of the mouth of babes and nursing infants You have perfected praise'?"** (v. 16b). This was a quotation from Psalm 8:2, which speaks of God ordaining praise for Himself from children. Thus, Jesus not only did not silence those who were speaking of Him as the Messiah; He accepted their praise and justified it from Scripture, saying that it was right for the children to praise Him as God.

Finally, Matthew tells us, **Then He left them and went out of the city to Bethany, and He lodged there** (v. 17). Jesus refused to stay overnight in Jerusalem, probably lodging with His friends Mary, Martha, and Lazarus in Bethany. However, He would be back in the temple each day that week, teaching and sparring with the scribes and Pharisees, as we will see.

96

THE CURSING OF THE FIG TREE

Matthew 21:18–22

Now in the morning, as He returned to the city, He was hungry. And seeing a fig tree by the road, He came to it and found nothing on it but leaves, and said to it, "Let no fruit grow on you ever again." Immediately the fig tree withered away. And when the disciples saw it, they marveled, saying, "How did the fig tree wither away so soon?" So Jesus answered and said to them, "Assuredly, I say to you, if you have faith and do not doubt, you will not only do what was done to the fig tree, but also if you say to this mountain, 'Be removed and be cast into the sea,' it will be done. And whatever things you ask in prayer, believing, you will receive."

The Ligonier Valley Study Center, the forerunner of Ligonier Ministries, was launched in western Pennsylvania in the early 1970s through the generous help of Mrs. Dora Hillman, who donated the fifty-two acres on which the study center was situated. Mrs. Hillman had a profound love for trees. She was constantly planting trees all over the property. On some occasions, she asked me to plant the trees and then told me how to do it properly, because I didn't know. She explained that if you have a $10 tree, you dig a $100 hole, because the hole needs to be ten times bigger than the tree.

Of course, once the trees were planted, they had to be watered. However, some of the trees were planted in places that we could not reach with our hoses. In those cases, we had to depend on Providence to send rain. On one occasion,

I watched one of those beautiful young trees wither and die. When I told Mrs. Hillman about it, she came up to the study center in her Jeep, and she brought along the foreman of her farm to try to redeem this tree. She told him, "I want you to water this tree and make sure that it becomes healthy again." But when he had looked over the tree, he turned to her and said, "It's dead, boss." He was right. There was nothing he could do to bring that tree back to life.

In the passage we are considering in this chapter, we witness the death of another tree, a fig tree. However, this tree died not because of a lack of water but because of a word from Jesus. He cursed it when He found that it was bearing no figs. According to Mark's account of this incident, it was not the season for figs (11:13). Given these facts, Jesus' cursing of the tree can seem arbitrary and capricious. In fact, critics of the New Testament and of Jesus Himself point to this incident to show that Jesus did not always behave in a godly way. Rather, they believe He acted in the manner of a petulant child, who throws a temper tantrum when he does not get his way and takes out his frustration on inanimate objects. Obviously, this view fails to do justice to this text and to Jesus Himself. But what are we to make of this strange incident?

A Deceptive Fig Tree

Matthew writes: **Now in the morning, as He returned to the city, He was hungry. And seeing a fig tree by the road, He came to it and found nothing on it but leaves, and said to it, "Let no fruit grow on you ever again." Immediately the fig tree withered away** (vv. 18–19). Many years ago, when I was a young Christian, I struggled over this passage. Then I had the opportunity in seminary to study under one of the three greatest archaeologists of the twentieth century. The three greatest were William Foxwell Albright, John Bright, and James Kelso. Dr. Kelso, who had worked with Albright and with Bright, was a distinguished professor at the seminary I attended. He was in his eighties by then and taught only one course, "The Geography and Customs of Palestine." It was one of the most brutal courses I had to endure in all of my years of study. We had to memorize the average annual rainfall in the Negev Desert and many similar facts about every region of Palestine. To put it bluntly, it was boring. But every now and then, as Dr. Kelso explained to us the customs, rituals, and practices of the people of ancient Palestine, he would open up the Scriptures to us in ways we had never considered. One of those occasions was when he talked to us about Jesus' cursing of the fig tree.

Dr. Kelso's lecture went on and on about how the production of figs was vitally important to the life and culture of the Jewish people, how the fig season was a time of great rejoicing because of the production of this fruit, and how many varieties of figs were grown in Palestine. He noted that most varieties ripened during a particular season of the year, but some varieties ripened at different seasons. Not surprisingly, when these particular trees brought forth figs outside of the normal fig season, the fruit was particularly satisfying and enjoyable to the people. Because there were these varieties that brought forth fruit in different seasons, the best indication of ripe figs on a tree was not a certain season of the year but an abundance of leaves. When the people noticed a fig tree covered with leaves, they could be certain that figs were there.

That brings me back to Matthew's account. We read there that Jesus was walking back to Jerusalem after spending the night in Bethany, and He was hungry. He happened to see a fig tree beside the road, and He noticed it was covered with leaves, the certain sign of the presence of figs. So, He paused in His journey to pick some figs for His breakfast. However, when He reached the tree, despite the abundance of leaves, He found no figs at all. He responded by doing something that was commonplace in the prophetic tradition of Old Testament Israel. He used that moment to give a dramatic, prophetic object lesson, a parable not in words but in actions. He pronounced judgment on the tree, declaring that it would never again bear fruit. Under the power of that divine curse, the tree withered and died.

Judgment on Hypocrisy

So, Jesus did not curse the fig tree out of petulance. Instead, He did it in order to make a statement about what was going on all around Him in the city of Jerusalem at that time. In other words, this was an object lesson, and its point was simple. It was a picture of God's judgment on hypocrisy.

A hypocrite is a play actor, one who lives his life under the pretense of being something he is not. The biggest hypocrites Jesus had to deal with were the religious leaders of His day, the Pharisees and Sadducees. They were spiritual frauds. In the days ahead, Jesus would denounce their hypocrisy in the strongest terms, as we will see. He would actually pronounce a curse on them by means of the curse language of the Old Testament: "Woe to you!" But before He did that to people, He did it to the fig tree. According to all outward appearances, the fig tree should have been covered with fruit. It had all the external trappings of life, vitality, and fruitfulness. But it was a pretender, a fraud. What it promised on the surface was not the reality. So, Jesus took advantage of this available object lesson, seized the moment, and expressed judgment on the tree for hypocrisy.

Hypocrisy is one of the most insidious sins that infects the church, and we are all exposed to its seduction. Why is that? It is because once we take the name of Christ, once we declare ourselves to be Christians, suddenly the bar is raised.

The watching world rightly expects to see purity, humility, and righteousness in us, but we often display little of it. Of course, there is no such thing as a sinless Christian in this world. All the sinless Christians are gathered together in glory. As long as we are here, we struggle with the ongoing influences of sin in our lives. Naturally, we are embarrassed by that. Since we cannot achieve the level of sanctification that we desire or that is expected from us, we construct our own halos and begin playacting, pretending that we are more righteous than, in fact, we are.

This text, however, does not have to do with falling short of the perfection that is God's standard of righteousness for us. He does not threaten judgment upon us for failing to be as righteous as Christians as we ought to be, for bearing less fruit than we should be bearing. God's judgment is reserved for those who bear no fruit at all. These are those whose Christian testimony is all pretense. Again, I remind you of Jesus' frightening words in the Sermon on the Mount, when He said that many would come to Him at the last day and say, "Lord, Lord, have we not prophesied in Your name, cast out demons in Your name, and done many wonders in Your name?" Jesus said He would tell them, "I never knew you; depart from Me, you who practice lawlessness!" (Matt. 7:22–23). It was these individuals Jesus was condemning, people who gave the impression that they were followers of Christ and who actually believed themselves to be Christians, but who did not know the Lord at all.

A pernicious heresy that was pervasive in evangelical Christianity for a time in recent decades is the doctrine of the carnal Christian. This teaching holds that it is possible to receive Jesus as Savior and yet manifest no fruits of a changed life. Such a person is said to be born again by the Holy Spirit but still carnal in the flesh. Now, we are all carnal in the sense that a tendency toward sin remains in us throughout our lifetimes. But it is foolishness to speak of someone being a born-again Christian in whom no change is wrought and no fruit is manifested. This is a dangerous doctrine, because it gives people a false sense of spiritual safety.

There was a college student who made a profession of faith in Christ. He was living with his girlfriend and involved in the distribution of drugs. His pastor confronted him, saying, "The life that you're living is not consistent with your profession of faith in Christ." The student smiled and said, "It's okay, pastor, I'm a carnal Christian." I believe he was completely deluded about the state of his soul. If a person thinks that he is in a state of grace and in the kingdom of God even though there is no fruit in his life, he is simply deceiving himself.

If I know anything about Jesus, I am sure that when He came to that fig tree and looked it over from top to bottom, if He had found one little fig, there would have been no curse from His lips. He did not curse that tree because it did not have *enough* figs. He cursed it because it had no figs, but it pretended to have something it did not possess at all.

Praying with Faith

Matthew continues, **And when the disciples saw it, they marveled, saying, "How did the fig tree wither away so soon?"** (v. 20). They were astounded. Remember, they had seen Jesus' power over nature in the stilling of the waves of the sea (8:23–27), yet they were amazed that He could cause a tree to wither.

When the disciples expressed their amazement, **Jesus answered and said to them, "Assuredly, I say to you, if you have faith and do not doubt, you will not only do what was done to the fig tree, but also if you say to this mountain, 'Be removed and be cast into the sea,' it will be done. And whatever things you ask in prayer, believing, you will receive"** (vv. 21–22). He was talking about the power of faith that is focused on the nature of God, faith that is so in tune with the mind of Christ that it is a catalyst for unbelievable exploits.

I know of one biblical scholar who argues that the background of this statement was the work Herod the Great had done to build his fortress next to the temple complex. He had moved so much land from one hill to a shallow place that he literally had moved a mountain. That may be so, but I think it is rather beside the point. I know of no saint in the history of the church who ever said to a mountain, "Be removed and be cast into the sea," and it actually happened. I think it is clear that Jesus was speaking metaphorically here. He was saying that people who pray for great things see great things accomplished.

Christ wants His people to be so confident in God's power that they pray for marvelous things to happen, and He promises that when they pray in this way, marvelous things *will* happen. History proves the truth of this statement. Christians have accomplished amazing things throughout the ages: great missionary thrusts, the abolition of slavery, works of mercy such as hospitals and orphanages. Usually there was a person who prayed his or her heart out, asking that, despite all apparent obstacles, the goal would be achieved. Jesus was telling His disciples that He wants His people to pray like that. He wants His people to pray for things and attempt things that other people regard as hopeless causes.

When Jesus said, "Whatever things you ask in prayer, believing, you will receive," He was clearly making a hyperbolic statement. There are people who say that if we believe something can happen, it will happen by the strength of our belief. Prayer is the most powerful force at our disposal, but it is not magic. What Jesus taught about prayer here must be understood in light of everything He taught about prayer. He was not saying that if we ask anything believing in His name, it will happen. But He was encouraging His people to run from indolence, to be bold, to be daring, to attempt those things that few people ever dream of attempting.

97

THE AUTHORITY OF JESUS

Matthew 21:23–32

Now when He came into the temple, the chief priests and the elders of the people confronted Him as He was teaching, and said, "By what authority are You doing these things? And who gave You this authority?" But Jesus answered and said to them, "I also will ask you one thing, which if you tell Me, I likewise will tell you by what authority I do these things: The baptism of John—where was it from? From heaven or from men?" And they reasoned among themselves, saying, "If we say, 'From heaven,' He will say to us, 'Why then did you not believe him?' But if we say, 'From men,' we fear the multitude, for all count John as a prophet." So they answered Jesus and said, "We do not know." And He said to them, "Neither will I tell you by what authority I do these things. But what do you think? A man had two sons, and he came to the first and said, 'Son, go, work today in my vineyard.' He answered and said, 'I will not,' but afterward he regretted it and went. Then he came to the second and said likewise. And he answered and said, 'I go, sir,' but he did not go. Which of the two did the will of his father?" They said to Him, "The first." Jesus said to them, "Assuredly, I say to you that tax collectors and harlots enter the kingdom of God before you. For John came to you in the way of righteousness, and you did not believe him; but tax collectors and harlots believed him; and when you saw it, you did not afterward relent and believe him."

In the previous chapter, we considered Jesus' cursing of the fig tree, which, as we saw, was a prophetic object lesson against hypocrisy and an indication that God's wrath is stored up against this serious sin. Today's passage and those that follow continue to deal with this theme of hypocrisy, specifically the hypocrisy of the leading clergy of Jesus' day. These clergy, of course, were the ones who were chiefly responsible, humanly speaking, for the rejection and execution of Jesus.

Matthew begins by writing: **Now when He came into the temple, the chief priests and the elders of the people confronted Him as He was teaching, and said, "By what authority are You doing these things? And who gave You this authority?"** (v. 23). Jesus entered the temple, perhaps immediately after cursing the fig tree, and began to teach the people. However, the chief priests and the elders interrupted Him. They apparently did not mean to let this rustic prophet from Galilee have free access to the temple precincts. It was only a couple of days earlier at most that they had seen Him turning over the tables of the money changers and expelling those who were trafficking in the sale of birds for sacrifice and exploiting the poor in the process. They could not know what He might do next, what faults in their leadership and lifestyles He might expose. So, as a pretense to shut down or disrupt His teaching ministry, they demanded to see His credentials, to know the source of His authority to teach the people.

All authority in this world—the authority that parents have over their children, that employers have over their employees, that the government has over its citizens, that police officers have over people, that the dogcatcher has over dogs—is delegated. No one has authority inherently or intrinsically; it has to be given by someone else. The only One in all of reality who possesses authority in and of Himself is God. Whatever authority we have is handed down in a line that ultimately goes back to Him. The chief priests and the elders understood that, because they asked Jesus, "Who gave You this authority?"

Jesus could have said: "Some of you are old enough to remember that I was here when I was twelve years old, and that you were astonished by My understanding and My questions. As I explained to My parents then, I had to be about My Father's business [Luke 2:41–50]. It is the same even now. The authority by which I do these things is the authority that comes from the fountain and source of all authority in the universe—God Himself. He gave Me My authority." Of course, that is not what Jesus said. He also could have said, "All authority has been given to Me in heaven and on earth" (Matt. 28:18). Likewise, He might have said, "For I have not spoken on My own authority; but the Father who sent Me gave Me a command, what I should say and what I should speak" (John 12:49). But He saved these comments for other times.

Priests and Elders with a Dilemma

Instead, in a very clever way, He turned the tables on these men who believed that they had all the authority: **But Jesus answered and said to them, "I also will ask you one thing, which if you tell Me, I likewise will tell you by what authority I do these things: The baptism of John—where was it from? From heaven or from men?"** (vv. 24–25a). In other words, Jesus wanted the priests and the elders to tell Him the source of John's authority to baptize—God or men. This question presented the religious authorities with quite a dilemma: **And they reasoned among themselves, saying, "If we say, 'From heaven,' He will say to us, 'Why then did you not believe him?' But if we say, 'From men,' we fear the multitude, for all count John as a prophet"** (vv. 25b–26).

Jesus knew they would not attribute John's baptism and his ministry to God. He was a prophet, and no one could be a true prophet without being called and set apart by the authority of God. So, heaven was behind John the Baptist's ministry. But if the priests and the elders admitted that, the discussion would be over, because Jesus would remind them that John had pointed to Him and said, "Behold! The Lamb of God who takes away the sin of the world!" (John 1:29b). If the priests and the elders attributed John's authority to heaven, they had no basis on which to challenge the authority of Jesus.

But these religious leaders could not attribute John's authority to men, either. Although it is strange to consider, even at this point in time John may have been more famous than Jesus. John was recognized as a prophet by nearly every Jew, the first since the voice of prophecy in Israel had fallen silent four hundred years before. When John the Baptist came on the scene, it was the most exciting moment in four centuries. Thus, if the priests and the elders said that John carried out his ministry on his own authority, they would be saying he was not a real prophet, and if they said that, they would have the whole population on their backs.

Notice that when they went aside and began discussing Jesus' question among themselves, they did not ask one another: "Well, what do you think? Do you think John was sent from God?" Instead, they said to one another: "If we say it was from heaven, He'll ask us why we did not believe him. If we say it was from men, we'll be in trouble with the people." There was no debate among them about the question itself, about which option was the truth, because they did not care about the truth. They were trying to discover the expedient answer, the answer that would not hurt their position in any way.

Finally, they simply gave up: **So they answered Jesus and said, "We do not know"** (v. 27a). They realized that they were facing a lose-lose proposition, and that it would be better for them to simply profess not to know. When they did, **He said to them, "Neither will I tell you by what authority I do these things"** (v. 27b). By showing the priests and elders that He could unmask their hypocrisy, their lack of concern for the truth, with ease, Jesus secured the right to teach in His Father's house. The men who had been demanding His credentials shut their mouths.

Two Sons with Different Responses

Jesus immediately resumed teaching in the temple, starting with the parable of the two sons. It seems this parable was aimed at the same men with whom He had been sparring moments before. Matthew tells us that He said: **But what do you think? A man had two sons, and he came to the first and said, 'Son, go, work today in my vineyard.' He answered and said, 'I will not,' but afterward he regretted it and went. Then he came to the second and said likewise. And he answered and said, 'I go, sir,' but he did not go"** (vv. 28–30). Again, the theme in this parable is hypocrisy. Two sons respond differently to their father's request, one saying he would not go but regretting it and going anyway, the other agreeing to go but failing to do so. The point of the parable is to show that the religious leaders did not respond properly to John the Baptist's ministry.

After setting forth the examples of the two sons, Jesus asked: **"Which of the two did the will of his father?" They said to Him, "The first"** (v. 31a). This was not a trick question. In fact, the priests and elders had no trouble answering. They replied that the first son did the will of the father. He said he was not going to obey his father. He was reluctant to obey his father. He hesitated to obey his father. But in the end, he did obey his father. When push came to shove, he was out there working in the vineyard. By contrast, the second son was very accommodating, agreeing to go to the vineyard, but as soon as his father's back was turned, he went the other way.

When He heard their answer, **Jesus said to them, "Assuredly, I say to you that tax collectors and harlots enter the kingdom of God before you. For John came to you in the way of righteousness, and you did not believe him; but tax collectors and harlots believed him; and when you saw it, you did not afterward relent and believe him"** (vv. 31b–32). What was Jesus saying here?

The chief priests and the elders were like the son who said he would go but did not. When the Father required them to go to the River Jordan and to be baptized, they would not go. That was beneath their dignity. Why should they have to repent? They were not willing to publicly acknowledge themselves as sinners. They were ordained to be the representatives of God, to be His sons working in His kingdom, but they did not obey Him.

However, tax collectors and harlots in Jerusalem went to the river and submitted to the baptism of John in repentance. When they first heard that there was a man who looked and acted like a prophet out at the river, and he was summoning all the people to come there and be cleansed from their sin in repentance because the kingdom of God was coming at any minute, they said no. The tax collector said: "I'm not going out there. I'm too busy. I've got money to make." The harlot said: "Are you kidding? You want me to do something religious? You think I'm going to go out there and confess that I'm a sinner before the whole world and let this man baptize me?" But that night, when the tax collector put his head on the pillow, he said, "I've got to do something about my sin, because my guilt is killing me." The harlot had no illusions about her integrity or purity. She said: "I'm drowning in my sin and in my guilt. Is it possible that someone could make me clean?" So, the tax collector and the harlot went to the river and were baptized. Jesus said that it was they who did the right thing. They submitted to the baptism of John. Therefore, they would go into the kingdom of God before the priests and elders would ever see it.

It is often said that the church is full of hypocrites. No, the church is full of sinners. Only people who claim not to be sinners are hypocrites. I know of no organization other than the church that requires members to publicly declare themselves to be sinners before they can join.

There is one more point about this parable that we must not overlook. No one is ever saved by a profession of faith. Untold millions of people have gone to evangelistic meetings, and when the altar call was issued, they got up out of their chairs and went forward to receive Christ. Or they raised a hand, signed a card, or said the sinner's prayer. Then, the next day, they went right back to wallowing in their sin. No one was ever justified by saying, "I hereby make a decision to follow Jesus." Those who are justified, those who are saved, are the ones who follow Jesus. They do not just say they are going to do it—they do not just profess faith—they actually do it because they actually have faith.

How many times have you made a promise to your spouse, to your children, or to the church that you did not keep? The second son did that. He said: "Well, father, of course I'll go. I'll be in the vineyard first thing in the morning. You can count on it." But when the time came, he did not show up. Are you this kind of person, one who promises but never keeps his word?

The ideal thing, when the Father asks, "Will you go into the vineyard," is to say, "Of course I'll go into the vineyard," and then go. We are God's people, redeemed by His mercy and His grace through the blood of His Son. He calls us as His people to work for Him in His kingdom every day. It is a terrible thing to say that we are going to serve God in His kingdom but never get around to doing it.

98

THE PARABLE OF THE VINEYARD

Matthew 21:33–46

"Hear another parable: There was a certain landowner who planted a vineyard and set a hedge around it, dug a winepress in it and built a tower. And he leased it to vinedressers and went into a far country. Now when vintage-time drew near, he sent his servants to the vinedressers, that they might receive its fruit. And the vinedressers took his servants, beat one, killed one, and stoned another. Again he sent other servants, more than the first, and they did likewise to them. Then last of all he sent his son to them, saying, 'They will respect my son.' But when the vinedressers saw the son, they said among themselves, 'This is the heir. Come, let us kill him and seize his inheritance.' So they took him and cast him out of the vineyard and killed him. Therefore, when the owner of the vineyard comes, what will he do to those vinedressers?" They said to Him, "He will destroy those wicked men miserably, and lease his vineyard to other vinedressers who will render to him the fruits in their seasons." Jesus said to them, "Have you never read in the Scriptures:

> 'The stone which the builders rejected
> Has become the chief cornerstone.
> This was the LORD's doing,
> And it is marvelous in our eyes'?

Therefore I say to you, the kingdom of God will be taken from you and given to a nation bearing the fruits of it. And whoever falls on this stone will be broken; but on Whomever it falls, it will grind him to powder." Now when the chief priests and Pharisees heard His parables, they perceived that He was speaking of them. But when they sought to lay hands on Him, they feared the multitudes, because they took Him for a prophet.

It was common for Jesus to weave agricultural activities into His parables, and the passage we are examining in this chapter features an example of this practice. Like a number of other parables, it features a vineyard. This was a logical image for Him to use, for grapes were a major crop in Palestine. Also, the vineyard was an image for the kingdom of God, for the Old Testament pictured the nation of Israel as God's vineyard. By employing this vivid metaphor, Jesus gave a succinct recapitulation of redemptive history.

Matthew tells us that Jesus, continuing to teach after telling the parable of the two sons and interacting with the chief priests and elders (vv. 23–32), went on to say: **"Hear another parable: There was a certain landowner who planted a vineyard and set a hedge around it, dug a winepress in it and built a tower. And he leased it to vinedressers and went into a far country"** (v. 33). Jesus told of a landowner who went to great pains to develop a productive vineyard. He planted his vines, then planted a protective hedge around the vineyard, dug a winepress that would be used when the grapes ripened, and constructed a tower from which his watchmen could see would-be thieves or marauding animals. Finally, when the vineyard was ready, he leased it to a group of vinedressers, men who were hired to tend the vines, and departed for another country. It is important to note that the New Testament does not look favorably on "hirelings," for they do not have the same care for that which is the owner's as does the owner himself (see John 10:12–13), and this parable only reinforced that idea.

Usually owners of such vineyards were wealthy people, because building a vineyard required a heavy upfront investment that would give no return for several years. It is no different today. In the great grape-producing regions of California, such as the Napa Valley and Sonoma, it is said that a vineyard will produce a small fortune for its owner—so long as he begins with a large fortune. But in ancient Israel, wealthy men were willing to invest in vineyards because the climate was so suitable for grapes and because the economy was so dependent on the production of wine. This landowner, then, was a wealthy man who invested a considerable sum to start his vineyard.

Then Jesus said, **"Now when vintage-time drew near, he sent his servants to the vinedressers, that they might receive its fruit"** (v. 34). The owner was naturally eager to learn how well his vineyard was doing, so when the first wine was ready for consumption, he sent some of his servants to the vinedressers, requesting that they send him samples of the wine they had produced. But here the story took a strange and shocking turn: **"And the vinedressers took his servants, beat one, killed one, and stoned another. Again he sent other servants, more than the first, and they did likewise to them"** (vv. 35–36). The vinedressers not only did not send the requested wine, they mistreated the owner's servants, even killing one. When he got word of this atrocity, the landowner sent another group of servants, more than the first, but they received the same dreadful treatment.

Confronted with this behavior by the renegade vinedressers, the owner decided to send his son: **"Then last of all he sent his son to them, saying, 'They will respect my son.' But when the vinedressers saw the son, they said among themselves, 'This is the heir. Come, let us kill him and seize his inheritance.' So they took him and cast him out of the vineyard and killed him"** (vv. 37–39). The owner believed the vinedressers would respect his son, for the son would come with all the authority of the father behind him. However, the vinedressers treated the son just as they had treated the owner's servants. Somehow they came to the conclusion that by killing the son they would come into full possession of the vineyard. So, they murdered the owner's son in cold blood.

Enmity toward God

We cannot miss the obvious point of the parable. First, the vineyard is God's nation of Israel. We see this clearly in the opening verses of Isaiah 5, where the prophet says, speaking of God:

> Now let me sing to my Well-beloved
> A song of my Beloved regarding His vineyard:
>
> My Well-beloved has a vineyard
> On a very fruitful hill.
> He dug it up and cleared out its stones,
> And planted it with the choicest vine.
> He built a tower in its midst,
> And also made a winepress in it;
> So He expected it to bring forth good grapes,
> But it brought forth wild grapes.
>
> "And now, O inhabitants of Jerusalem and men of Judah,
> Judge, please, between Me and My vineyard.
> What more could have been done to My vineyard
> That I have not done in it?
> Why then, when I expected it to bring forth good grapes,
> Did it bring forth wild grapes? . . .
>
> For the vineyard of the LORD of hosts is the house of Israel." (vv. 1–4, 7a)

God adopted the people of Israel as His people, brought them out of Egypt, and "planted" them in Canaan. He nurtured them, cared for them, and caused them to grow. He expected them to be fruitful, to manifest the fruit of holiness: "You shall be holy, for I the Lord your God am holy" (Lev. 19:2). Israel was to manifest the glory of God to all of the nations of the world. But instead of the good fruit of holiness, the people brought forth wild, spoiled, and rotten grapes as they fell into idolatry and other sins.

Returning to the meaning of the parable, we see, second, that Jesus clearly intended the servants to represent the treatment that was accorded the Old Testament prophets. They were rarely welcomed, their message drew scoffing and disbelief, and they were often badly mistreated. For instance, Queen Jezebel actually massacred prophets (see 1 Kings 18:4) and tried diligently to do the same to Elijah. Jeremiah was beaten and put in stocks (Jer. 20:1–2). Jesus even alluded to the murder of unnamed prophets (Luke 11:47). Finally, the son in the parable is a clear reference to Christ Himself. He was sent by the Father, disrespected by those who should have honored Him, and finally killed.

Rejecting the Son

Lest the religious leaders listening to His parable not get the message, Jesus gave them a quiz. He asked: **"Therefore, when the owner of the vineyard comes, what will he do to those vinedressers?" They said to Him, "He will destroy those wicked men miserably, and lease his vineyard to other vinedressers who will render to him the fruits in their seasons"** (vv. 40–41). In their ignorance, they gave a nearly prophetic answer to Jesus' question—the owner (God) would destroy the vinedressers (the religious leaders) and give the vineyard to others.

Jesus then referred them to the Old Testament, specifically to Psalm 118:22–23: **Jesus said to them, "Have you never read in the Scriptures: 'The stone which the builders rejected has become the chief cornerstone. This was the Lord's doing, and it is marvelous in our eyes'?"** (v. 42). The reference here is to the building industry. A builder would go to the stone pile and select for himself the best stones for use in constructing the finest buildings, tossing the defective stones aside. But the psalmist imagined another builder who came along and noticed one of the stones that the first builder had discarded, and he not only used it in his house but made it the cornerstone. The reference here was to the Son once again. Though He would be rejected and mistreated like the son in the parable, though He would be discarded as defective by those who supposedly knew about such things, He would become the cornerstone, the all-important figure in the Father's plan.

With that, Jesus spoke frankly to the religious authorities: **"Therefore I say to you, the kingdom of God will be taken from you and given to a nation bearing the fruits of it. And whoever falls on this stone will be broken; but on whomever it falls, it will grind him to powder"** (vv. 43–44). Because of their hypocrisy, these priests, elders, and others would lose their privileged task of caring for God's vineyard. Because they were tripping over Jesus (the cornerstone), they would fall and be crushed by Him.

Sometimes we jump to the conclusion that the religious leaders with whom Jesus sparred were very thick-headed. In this case, however, they got the message. Matthew tells us: **Now when the chief priests and Pharisees heard His parables, they perceived that He was speaking of them. But when they sought to lay hands on Him, they feared the multitudes, because they took Him for a prophet** (vv. 45–46). Jesus had made it painfully obvious that He was criticizing them, and they understood Him well. But instead of repenting, they sought to silence Him. They were held back only by fear of the crowds who still were enraptured with Jesus at this point. Nevertheless, they began to plan how they might do away with the Son of the Owner of the vineyard.

99

THE PARABLE OF THE MARRIAGE FEAST

Matthew 22:1–14

And Jesus answered and spoke to them again by parables and said: "The kingdom of heaven is like a certain king who arranged a marriage for his son, and sent out his servants to call those who were invited to the wedding; and they were not willing to come. Again, he sent out other servants, saying, 'Tell those who are invited, "See, I have prepared my dinner; my oxen and fatted cattle are killed, and all things are ready. Come to the wedding."' But they made light of it and went their ways, one to his own farm, another to his business. And the rest seized his servants, treated them spitefully, and killed them. But when the king heard about it, he was furious. And he sent out his armies, destroyed those murderers, and burned up their city. Then he said to his servants, 'The wedding is ready, but those who were invited were not worthy. Therefore go into the highways, and as many as you find, invite to the wedding.' So those servants went out into the highways and gathered together all whom they found, both bad and good. And the wedding hall was filled with guests. But when the king came in to see the guests, he saw a man there who did not have on a wedding garment. So he said to him, 'Friend, how did you come in here without a wedding garment?' And he was speechless. Then the king said to the servants, 'Bind him hand and foot, take him away, and cast him into outer darkness; there will be weeping and gnashing of teeth.' For many are called, but few are chosen."

During the original Holy Week, that week leading up to His betrayal, arrest, trial, crucifixion, and death, Jesus taught extensively in the temple precincts. When Matthew put together his gospel years later and selected material from that crucial week, he chose to include many teachings that Jesus aimed directly at the Jewish religious leaders, as well as some of Jesus' exchanges with them. Much of what Jesus said during this time was designed to confront, challenge, and expose these leaders, and the parable we are examining in this chapter, the parable of the wedding feast, was part of that design.

However, we have seen throughout our study in Matthew that many of Jesus' parables were about the kingdom of heaven. Usually, Jesus would begin one of these parables by saying, "The kingdom of heaven is like . . ." Jesus' entrance into His public ministry was heralded by John the Baptist, who cried to the people, "Repent, for the kingdom of heaven is at hand!" (3:2). Jesus began His preaching with the very same message: "Repent, for the kingdom of heaven is at hand" (4:17). Throughout His teaching ministry, many of His parables focused on this urgent reality of entering the kingdom of God, and the parable of the wedding feast also served this purpose.

Matthew tells us: **And Jesus answered and spoke to them again by parables and said: "The kingdom of heaven is like a certain king who arranged a marriage for his son"** (vv. 1–2). It seems clear that the son for whom the king arranged this great marriage and feast was the crown prince. I cannot imagine a more significant social event in any kingdom than the marriage of the crown prince. The king wants to honor his son on the occasion of his wedding by means of a feast to end all feasts. It is an incredible honor to receive an invitation from the palace to observe the marriage ceremony and to join in the celebration. So, Jesus began this parable by painting a picture of a forthcoming joyous occasion.

But then, Jesus introduced a nearly unbelievable twist to this story: **"and [the king] sent out his servants to call those who were invited to the wedding; and they were not willing to come"** (v. 3). The servants went out to people who had received invitations earlier. It was not that these invitees were incapable of coming or were too busy to come. In other words, it was not that they *could* not come; they simply *would* not come.

We could inject theological ramifications into this development. We know from other passages of Scripture that those who refuse God's invitation to come to the wedding feast designed for His Son really cannot come, for they are dead in their trespasses and sins (Eph. 2:1). The Lord Jesus Himself said on one occasion, "No one can come to Me unless the Father who sent Me draws him" (John 6:44a). So, it would be easy to conclude that it was not really the case that these invitees would not come; rather, they could not come because their hearts needed to be changed so that they would have a desire or disposition to come. That is all true, but it is also true that we cannot do what we will not do. Thus, there is a sense in which these people could not come to the feast precisely because they would not.

I have made the point countless times that every human being in every moment of decision chooses according to his strongest inclination at the moment. That is, no one ever does something that, in the final analysis, he does not want to do. Even if someone points a gun at you and asks for your money, you do not necessarily have to give it to him. You can allow the robber to shoot you and then take your money, gambling that you can survive the gunshot. Or you can hand over your money, gambling that the robber will take the money and run, leaving you unharmed. That is not exactly quintessential free will, but the will is not altogether eliminated in this case. But in any case, the ones who were invited to the king's feast were not willing to come.

In modern evangelicalism, the customary way of doing evangelism is to invite people to place their trust in Christ. However, that concept is virtually foreign to the Scriptures. God does not invite people to come to Christ; He commands them to come. The invitation in Jesus' parable was no different. The invitees were given a royal summons.

Indifference and Hostility

Jesus continued: **"Again, he sent out other servants, saying, 'Tell those who are invited, "See, I have prepared my dinner; my oxen and fatted cattle are killed, and all things are ready. Come to the wedding."' But they made light of it and went their ways, one to his own farm, another to his business"** (vv. 4–5). The king was patient, sending other servants to summon the invitees again. But even though it was their king who was calling them to come, some "made light of it." It was not a matter of concern for them. They just did not care. They were more concerned about their farms and businesses, the ordinary matters of their lives. Others, however, reacted much more negatively: **"And the rest seized his servants, treated them spitefully, and killed them"** (v. 6). They so hated their king that they mistreated and murdered his servants.

If you are a minister of the gospel or you regularly share your faith with others, you know well that many who hear the good news simply shrug it off. They just do not seem to care about what they are hearing. But others get irritated by the message. They show forth the natural human hatred for God and His messengers. His gracious offer of salvation only provokes them to rage.

The king's patience was exhausted by this violence against his servants: **"But when the king heard about it, he was furious. And he sent out his armies,**

destroyed those murderers, and burned up their city" (v. 7). Does God have an army? Yes. The Bible calls Him "the LORD of hosts" (Ps. 24:10; Isa. 1:9; Mal. 1:4). These hosts are armies, heavenly forces, angelic legions that are at His command in every moment.

Jesus continued with His parable, saying: **"Then he said to his servants, 'The wedding is ready, but those who were invited were not worthy. Therefore go into the highways, and as many as you find, invite to the wedding.' So those servants went out into the highways and gathered together all whom they found, both bad and good. And the wedding hall was filled with guests"** (vv. 8–10). The king would not be thwarted. It was his desire that his son should be honored and that every seat be taken at his wedding feast. If the original invitees were not interested in coming or were violently opposed to the king, still the king would find people who would come to the wedding feast.

One of the most remarkable moments in evangelism I ever experienced happened when I was leading a group of laypeople in a church in Cincinnati, Ohio. We used to go out into the community every Tuesday night in teams of three. On one occasion, one of my elders was going to make a presentation of the gospel for the first time. We knocked on the door of an apartment building and the door was opened by a young lady, who was one of two single women who lived there. Her apartment was one of the most weird, scary places I had ever seen. The walls were painted black and strobe lights were scattered around. Nevertheless, the elder who was with me began to go through a gospel presentation with the young lady. However, she interrupted him halfway through and said: "Stop right there, I've heard this a thousand times. I'm just not interested. I don't want to hear it." I was training our people not to be obnoxious and pushy in presenting the gospel, so the elder said quietly: "Well, thank you for listening so far and for inviting us in. And I hope that maybe someday we'll be able to finish this."

At that point, I spoke up. I said to the young lady, "If you've really heard this a thousand times, could it possibly hurt you to hear it one more time?" She said, "Well, no." So, I said, "Will you let me take just five minutes to finish this?" and she agreed. I finished the gospel presentation, but I did not ask her for a commitment. I simply thanked her for her patience with us and bade her farewell. However, six weeks later that young woman showed up in our church's new-member class, and she told all of us who were there that after we walked out of her door that night, she went into her room, dissolved in tears, got down on her knees beside her bed, and gave her life to Christ. She had to hear the gospel a thousand and one times before the Spirit pierced her heart with the Word of God.

This portion of the parable of the wedding feast had much in common with some of Jesus' previous teachings since His triumphal entry. It showed once again that those who had been entrusted with the kingdom—the priests, elders, scribes, and so on—had forfeited their place by rejecting the King, Jesus Himself. Therefore, the kingdom would be taken from them and given to others.

Proper Wedding Attire

Jesus closed this parable with what almost seems to be a footnote, but it is very significant. He said: **"But when the king came in to see the guests, he saw a man there who did not have on a wedding garment. So he said to him, 'Friend, how did you come in here without a wedding garment?' And he was speechless"** (vv. 11–12). Remember, the last group of servants went out to the highway and invited whomever they found there to come to the king's banquet. These people were delighted to come, so they hurriedly prepared themselves. But when the guests were assembled together and the king came into their midst, he encountered one man who had come in without proper attire.

What is the proper clothing to which the parable was pointing? Augustine, the fifth-century bishop of Hippo in North Africa, was convinced that it is righteousness of Christ. If we are not clothed in that righteousness, we will not be welcome at the wedding feast of the Lamb in heaven, because all of our righteousness, the Bible says, is like filthy rags (Isa. 64:6). We can enter the kingdom of heaven only if we are dressed in the righteousness of Jesus, which is imputed to all who believe (Zech. 3:3–4). Other scholars have disagreed with Augustine, saying that there is no direct indication in the parable that the proper attire for the wedding feast pointed to the righteousness of Christ. Well, I read these commentators and I think: "What's wrong with you? What else can it refer to?"

When the king noticed the man in his improper clothes and questioned him about it, what did he say? Did he say: "I'm so sorry, your highness. I was so busy that I had no time to go home and get dressed. I came directly here in response to the invitation from your servants"? Did he say: "What difference does it make how I'm dressed? Why are you so uppity, O king? I don't think I should have to get dressed to the nines in order to be welcome at your party"? No. Jesus said that the man could find nothing to say. Rather, "He was speechless."

This is consistent with what the Bible universally teaches about human responses at the day of judgment, where every human being will be brought to the tribunal of God and the sins of every one of them will be made manifest. We are told in Scripture that every person will be silent before Him (Ps. 76:8–9; Zeph. 1:7; Zech. 2:13). When we stand before an omniscient God who knows everything we have ever done or thought, what excuse can we give Him? Anyone who stands before God at the last judgment will at least have the good sense to keep his or her mouth shut, because there will be nothing to say.

When the man without proper wedding attire said nothing, **the king said to the servants, 'Bind him hand and foot, take him away, and cast him into outer darkness; there will be weeping and gnashing of teeth'"** (v. 13). Without proper attire, he simply could not remain at the feast; his place was in the outer darkness, the place of suffering and torment.

Finally, Jesus said, **"For many are called, but few are chosen"** (v. 14). This verse has caused a great deal of consternation for many people. It drips with the doctrine of election. It says that many receive the outward call of the gospel, but not everyone hears it inwardly. The Apostle Paul speaks of the "effectual call" of the gospel that is given only to the elect: "Whom He predestined, these He also called; whom He called, these He also justified" (Rom. 8:30). Many hear the gospel, and some make a false profession of faith. However, from every nation God not only calls people outwardly, but by the power of His Holy Spirit He calls them inwardly, changing the dispositions of their hearts so that whereas they once were unwilling to come into the presence of the King and His Son, suddenly they are both willing and eager.

None of us can change our hearts like that. Only the Holy Spirit can do it. He makes the unwilling willing. It makes those who do not care to care very much. He does it because God is determined that His Son will be honored. All whom the Father has given to the Son come to the Son with joy.

100

RENDER TO CAESAR

Matthew 22:15–22

Then the Pharisees went and plotted how they might entangle Him in His talk. And they sent to Him their disciples with the Herodians, saying, "Teacher, we know that You are true, and teach the way of God in truth; nor do You care about anyone, for You do not regard the person of men. Tell us, therefore, what do You think? Is it lawful to pay taxes to Caesar, or not?" But Jesus perceived their wickedness, and said, "Why do you test Me, you hypocrites? Show Me the tax money." So they brought Him a denarius. And He said to them, "Whose image and inscription is this?" They said to Him, "Caesar's." And He said to them, "Render therefore to Caesar the things that are Caesar's, and to God the things that are God's." When they had heard these words, they marveled, and left Him and went their way.

From the time of His triumphal entry to Jerusalem, Jesus took on the religious leaders of the Jewish people. He cleansed the temple of the commerce they had allowed to take place there. He sparred with them over the source of His authority (21:23–27). Most of all, He delivered teaching that was directed at them, exposing their hypocrisy. Matthew has told us that "when the chief priests and Pharisees heard his parables, they perceived that He was speaking of them" (v. 45). They could not lay hands on Him because He was popular with the people (v. 46). Therefore, as we see in the passage we are examining in this chapter, they began discussing ways to cause trouble for Him.

Matthew writes, **Then the Pharisees went and plotted how they might entangle Him in His talk** (v. 15). When I read this introductory sentence, I am tempted to laugh, as I find it amusing that these religious leaders, men who obviously were educated beyond their intelligence, tried to come up with a way to trap Jesus. Clearly they did not understand whom they were dealing with. This was the only Man to walk the earth whose brain had not been clouded by the effects of sin. The God-man was the most brilliant genius who ever visited this planet, but these men thought they could trap him. It was their hope to impale Jesus on the horns of a dilemma, to confront Him with a question that would land Him in trouble with someone no matter how He answered it.

It is interesting to me that the Pharisees took the lead in this effort to trap Jesus. Since the triumphal entry, He had interacted with "the chief priests and scribes" (21:15), "the chief priests and the elders" (21:23), and "the chief priests and Pharisees" (21:45). It is possible some of these descriptions were interchangeable, but as we read the Gospels, it seems that the Pharisees usually were the leaders in the opposition to Jesus. That seems to have been the case here.

Matthew goes on: **And they sent to Him their disciples with the Herodians, saying, "Teacher, we know that You are true, and teach the way of God in truth; nor do You care about anyone, for You do not regard the person of men"** (v. 16). Once the Pharisees had their question ready for Jesus, they sent their disciples to Him along with the Herodians, a small party of people who supported the rule of the Herods (and who usually were at odds with the Pharisees). They came to Jesus with lips dripping with praise, heaping flattery upon Him. They called Him "Teacher," even though they had questioned His authority only days before. They said He was true, which was not how they felt about Him at all; they really believed He was false. In a similar vein, they said that He taught the way of God in truth, but, of course, they had challenged His teaching again and again throughout His ministry. They then said, "nor do You care about anyone." They were not saying He had no compassion or affection for people. Instead, they were professing to believe He was not biased or prejudiced in His teaching and treatment of people. Finally, they said He did not "regard the person of men." The Greek used here literally means Jesus was not a "face looker." In other words, He did not spin His words according to the reactions of His audience.

This final bit of flattery touches on one of the banes of preachers. Like all preachers, when I stand in the pulpit, I see every yawn, every hostile look, every smirk. When I see these kinds of responses from the audience, I sometimes think I had better soften my message a little bit so they won't throw tomatoes at me. But Jesus was not like that. He spoke the truth. He never wavered from it, even for a moment.

So, even though the Pharisees did not actually believe what their disciples said about Jesus, it was all true. They wanted to flatter Him, but to do so they had to say things that were true of Him. They should have admired these qualities in Him instead of seeking to destroy Him.

A Question about Taxes

Finally, the Pharisees' disciples and the Herodians got to the point: **"Tell us, therefore, what do You think? Is it lawful to pay taxes to Caesar, or not?"** (v. 17). Basically, they were asking, "Is it right, according to the Mosaic Law, to pay taxes to foreign rulers?" The Bible makes it very clear that it is lawful to pay taxes. The Apostle Paul tells us that we are to render taxes to whom taxes are due (Rom. 13:7). So, it is clearly the will of God that we should pay our taxes. Thus, these men were not really asking whether it is lawful to pay taxes. They were asking, "Is it appropriate?" The Jews of first-century Palestine were one of the most heavily taxed people in the history of the world. When the Romans conquered them, they exacted all kinds of taxes. Of course, the Jews were not happy to pay taxes to the ones who had taken away their freedom. They did not want to support the Roman regime. Plus, they wanted to bring their tithes and offerings to God, and the heavy taxes made it difficult to do that. So, the Roman taxes were deeply resented. We see, then, that the disciples of the Pharisees and the Herodians were asking Jesus, "Is this something that we should do, given that the taxes that are being imposed here are exploitive, confiscatory, oppressive, and unjust?"

So, the trap was set. If Jesus said that the Jews *should* pay taxes to Caesar, the common people would react negatively, for they hated the taxes. But if He replied that the Jews *should not* pay taxes to Caesar, the Pharisees would immediately denounce Him to the Romans as one who was fomenting rebellion against Roman rule.

However, Matthew tells us: **Jesus perceived their wickedness, and said, "Why do you test Me, you hypocrites? Show Me the tax money." So they brought Him a denarius** (vv. 18–19). Jesus saw right through the trap. Of course, in His divine nature, He was omniscient. He also had deep insights into human nature. However, He really did not need to use His divine powers to detect this trap. Since when had the Pharisees genuinely sought out His opinion on any subject? The fact that these disciples of the Pharisees and Herodians came to Him with mouths filled with flattery and a supposedly serious question was enough to tip Him off. So, He rebuked them for their hypocrisy in testing Him.

Of course, seeing the trap and evading it were two different things. Jesus still had to give an answer to what was basically a yes-or-no question. How could He avoid offending the people or the authorities? Since this was the Son of God, He did not have to fumble around for a safe answer. He knew what was right in God's eyes, so He immediately asked someone to show Him the coin that was used to pay the tax, and someone produced a denarius.

Matthew then tells us: **And He said to them, "Whose image and inscription is this?" They said to Him, "Caesar's"** (vv. 20–21a). The denarius was a small silver coin that was minted in Rome. The image on the denarius at that time was that of the Emperor Tiberius, who reigned after Augustus, from AD 14 to 37. Along with his image, an inscription was pressed on the surface of the coin: "Tiberius Caesar, son of the divine Augustus." On the other side was the inscription, "High Priest." The emperor was given this title because he was not only the supreme political ruler of the Roman Empire but the supreme religious leader, as well. He was regarded as a god. The Jews knew well who was depicted on the coin, because they hated the fact that Tiberius was regarded as divine. In their eyes, the fact that the coin bore the image of someone who was declared to be God made the denarius a pagan idol, a violation of the second commandment.

Caesar's status made for great difficulties and trials for the believers of the early church. Every Christian was required to swear a loyalty oath, saying, "Caesar is lord." The penalty for refusal was death. Even so, many, when asked to say, "Caesar is lord," responded instead by saying, "Jesus is Lord," and that affirmation because the first confession of the early church. Those believers said: "Caesar, we'll pray for you. We'll honor you. We'll pay our taxes. We'll be good citizens. But you are not lord. Jesus is Lord. We will not worship you."

Two Divinely Ordained Spheres

When Jesus received their answer to His question, **He said to them, "Render therefore to Caesar the things that are Caesar's, and to God the things that are God's"** (v. 21b). The coin bore the image of Caesar, so it belonged to Caesar. As the ruler who had been raised up by God, he had the right to ask the people under his rule to render to him that which belonged to him. So, Jesus was saying it was the obligation of the Jews, as much as they despised Caesar and his regime, to pay their taxes. At the same time, however, they were to give God those things that were His: the tithe and obedience in all areas. So, whereas the Pharisees set up an either/or question for Jesus, He gave a both/and answer.

This command is for us, too, of course. As we have seen, the entire Bible supports the payment of taxes. We may not like the taxes, but we need to pay them. We are not to defraud the government. And, of course, we always must remember to fulfill our biblical obligations to God. The New Testament sees a distinction between two spheres, the church and the civil magistrate, or the state. The church has been given her task to perform and the state has been given its task to perform. Christians are supposed to support both of those institutions as being ordained of God.

We all know that there are stiff penalties for failure to pay our taxes. If we do not pay, a government auditor is likely to show up. We understand that the obligation to pay our taxes is backed up by the full force of the government. However, the situation is usually different in the church. I know of a few churches that audit the giving of their members, and if they find that some members are not tithing, they discipline them or they publish their findings and embarrass the non-tithers. But most churches do not do that. In most cases, the matter of the tithe is strictly between individual believers and God. It is left to the conscience. However, the tithe is no less important than taxes. Both need to be rendered.

But our obligation to God goes far beyond the tithe. Jesus told the Pharisees and Herodians to render to Caesar the things that are Caesar's, which, in that instance, meant the tax, for it was Caesar's face on the denarius. But whose image is on us? Whose image do we bear? Whose image is stamped on our souls? We are image-bearers of God. We belong to Him. We owe Him not only our tithes but our lives.

At the end of his account of this episode, Matthew writes, **When they had heard these words, they marveled, and left Him and went their way** (v. 22). The disciples of the Pharisees and the Herodians were shocked because they had spent so much time coming up with what seemed to be a very clever question, but Jesus evaded the trap with ease. With their clever plans foiled, they quickly slipped away. Matthew tells us that they "left Him and went *their* way," not God's way. We need to search our hearts and make sure we are going God's way, not just in paying our taxes and our tithes, but in all things.

101

THE RESURRECTION

Matthew 22:23–33

The same day the Sadducees, who say there is no resurrection, came to Him and asked Him, saying: "Teacher, Moses said that if a man dies, having no children, his brother shall marry his wife and raise up offspring for his brother. Now there were with us seven brothers. The first died after he had married, and having no offspring, left his wife to his brother. Likewise the second also, and the third, even to the seventh. Last of all the woman died also. Therefore, in the resurrection, whose wife of the seven will she be? For they all had her." Jesus answered and said to them, "You are mistaken, not knowing the Scriptures nor the power of God. For in the resurrection they neither marry nor are given in marriage, but are like angels of God in heaven. But concerning the resurrection of the dead, have you not read what was spoken to you by God, saying, 'I am the God of Abraham, the God of Isaac, and the God of Jacob'? God is not the God of the dead, but of the living." And when the multitudes heard this, they were astonished at His teaching.

In the previous chapter, we witnessed the party of the Pharisees taking the lead in plotting against Jesus. In the passage that is before us in this chapter, it is the men of a different party, the Sadducees, who attempt to trap Jesus. The Sadducees have been mentioned only a handful of times in Matthew's Gospel to this point, far less frequently than the Pharisees. However, we did see the Sadducees joining with the Pharisees on one occasion in an attempt to trap Jesus (16:1ff), which prompted Jesus to warn the disciples to "beware of the leaven of the Pharisees and the Sadducees" (16:6). As we noted when we studied this passage in chapter 76, the leaven of which Jesus spoke was bad doctrine. Thus, Jesus was warning the disciples to beware of error at both ends of the doctrinal spectrum.

The Pharisees and Sadducees differed on almost everything theologically. The Pharisees accepted all of the books in our Old Testament as Holy Scripture. The Sadducees did not; they restricted their Bible to the Torah, the first five books of the Old Testament. The Pharisees believed in the resurrection of the dead. That is, they believed that there is a heaven and that God will have people with Him there. The Old Testament has scant references to heaven, but there are a few. The Sadducees, however, denied the ideas of the resurrection and heaven, for they believed these teachings were not to be found in the Torah. In a very real sense, the Sadducees were the secularists of their day. They believed that the only sphere in which human life exists is the here and now. When a person dies, the soul perishes with the body. So, their whole focus was on this world, with no view to the world to come. It is no wonder they disliked Jesus, whose public teaching included manifold references to the final judgment, to heaven, and to hell.

The Pharisees hated the Sadducees. The Sadducees hated the Pharisees. But as is often the case in history, those who are enemies suddenly become friends when they have a mutual hatred. In the case of the Pharisees and Sadducees, the object of mutual hatred was Jesus. Therefore, both parties were out to undermine and get rid of Jesus. That is why, after Jesus evaded the trap of the Pharisees and the Herodians, the Sadducees came to Him with a type of argument known as *reductio ad absurdum* ("reduction to the absurd"), which involves taking an opponent's position to its logical conclusion in order to show absurdity.

Matthew tells us: **The same day the Sadducees, who say there is no resurrection, came to Him and asked Him, saying: "Teacher, Moses said that if a man dies, having no children, his brother shall marry his wife and raise up offspring for his brother"** (vv. 23–24). This is an allusion to the law of "levirate marriage," which Moses handed down in Deuteronomy 25:5. It states that if a man died with no children and he had a living brother who was not married, it was the obligation of the brother to take the widow as his wife, so that his dead brother would have offspring. This was a significant law for the Sadducees, who believed that the only sense of life after death a person could experience was through his offspring. So, to die with no children was to be dead and gone forever. Essentially, the only comfort in death was to be found in the legacy of the children one left behind.

We know there were a couple of instances in Jewish history when the levirate principle was followed to the letter, but it seems that over time this procedure passed out of usage among the Jewish people. But the Sadducees, armed with the Word of God, dredged up this principle and used it to pose a question that they believed would perplex Jesus: **"Now there were with us seven brothers. The first died after he had married, and having no offspring, left his wife to his brother. Likewise the second also, and the third, even to the seventh. Last of all the woman died also. Therefore, in the resurrection, whose wife of the seven will she be? For they all had her"** (vv. 25–28). In essence, they were saying, "Look, Jesus, we have practiced leverite marriage to the letter. We did what Moses told us to do. But You say there is going to be a resurrection. If that's so, which of the seven brothers will be married to the woman? How will God sort out all of these marriages?" By posing this absurd scenario, they believed they had cornered Jesus into admitting that the resurrection was nonsense.

Like the Angels of God

I am frequently asked, "Will we be married in heaven?" There are a couple of leading theories on this question. Some say there will be no marriage in heaven at all, that we will not be married there. Others believe we will be married in heaven to all the spouses we had during our lifetimes. That idea is a comfort to the widow and widower who have been remarried. However, I believe Jesus gives a clear answer to this question.

Matthew tells us, **Jesus answered and said to them, "You are mistaken, not knowing the Scriptures nor the power of God"** (v. 29). Jesus began His answer to the Sadducees' question by rebuking them for their faulty understanding of Scripture (they had not grasped the scriptural teaching on the resurrection) and for their lack of knowledge of the power of God to so rule and reign over eternity as to create an existence that would be far more fulfilling and wonderful that the fallen world in which the Sadducees lived. Then He said, **"For in the resurrection they neither marry nor are given in marriage, but are like angels of God in heaven"** (v. 30). This is a key verse, one that is often misunderstood, so we need to think it through carefully.

First, note what Jesus did not say here. He did not say that in heaven we will *become* angels. We are not angels now. Therefore, we will not be angels at any time in the future. Angels are a different order of creation, different beings. However, Jesus said we will be *like* angels in one respect—we will not be married, just as angels are not married.

There is a theory that the phrase "neither marry nor are given in marriage" is a Jewish idiom that refers not to the actual estate of marriage but to the proliferation of divorce. In other words, Jesus was saying that in heaven there will be no divorces. This theory arises from the fact that Jesus said that at the time of His second coming, things on earth would be as they were in the days of Noah (Matt. 24:37). He explained: "For as in the days before the flood, they were eating and drinking, marrying and giving in marriage, until the day that Noah entered the ark" (v. 38). This theory holds that the words "marrying and giving in marriage" indicate that the holy estate of marriage had been undermined by sin and that divorce had become rampant. People were marrying, divorcing, remarrying, and divorcing again. There was no respect for marriage, no long-term commitment. So, according to this theory, in the resurrection, divorce will be unknown and marriage will be sacrosanct.

I believe this theory carries almost no weight. I believe Jesus was simply saying that when the judgment comes from God, life will be moving along as usual. People will be getting married and giving their daughters away in marriage just as they do every day. In other words, people will be thinking they have a future up to the moment when the end of time arrives.

So, I think it is clear that Jesus was saying that heaven will be a different order from what we are accustomed to here. We must not assume that life in heaven will be just like life on this earth. One of the reasons for marriage is the propagation of the species through the bearing of children, which will be completely unnecessary in heaven. Also, another of the reasons for the institution of marriage is that it is not good for a man to be alone (Gen. 2:18). Human beings need intimate relationships in this world, but in heaven God will fulfill that role.

Here's the good news. Even if marriage is no longer an institution in heaven, love will be. I envision it this way. In this fallen world, the closest relationship I have with any other human being is the one I have with my wife. I do not think that the love I have for her or the love she has for me or the closeness that we enjoy will be removed in heaven. Rather, it will get better. I believe that my relationship with Vesta will be superior in heaven to what it is on earth. But the glory is that we will have that kind of communion and that kind of relationship with all of the saints of God. The only bride in heaven will be the church, the bride of Christ. All the people who are a part of the bride of Christ in their glorification will enjoy the communion of saints to such a degree of felicity and blessedness that marriage by contrast will be a very poor substitute or imitation. So, it will not be a question of loss when we get to heaven; it will be a matter of gain.

Jesus was saying to the Sadducees: "Do you really think God cannot handle the problem of a woman who has been married to seven different men? That's no problem for God." Do we believe that? We know what we are supposed to say—God is omnipotent, He can do miracles, He can do wonderful things. But we have not begun to understand the kind of power that is in the self-existent, eternal Being who can form a universe by His word alone. People who doubt that today are just like the Sadducees. They have no concept of the power of God, who is the source of all power there is. We must never limit God in our thinking, for His power is not limited in any way.

The God of the Living

Jesus was not content merely to answer the Sadducees' absurd question. He took a moment to confront them on their denial of the resurrection. He said to them: **"But concerning the resurrection of the dead, have you not read what was spoken to you by God, saying, 'I am the God of Abraham, the God of Isaac, and the God of Jacob'? God is not the God of the dead, but of the living"** (vv. 31–32). It is very significant that when He gave biblical evidence for the resurrection, Jesus did not go to the Historical Books, the Prophets, or the Writings. He went to none of the books of the Old Testament that clearly point to life after death. Neither did He appeal to the resurrections He had already brought to pass in His earthly ministry: Jairus's daughter (9:18–26), the son of the widow of Nain (Luke 7:11–17), or Lazarus (John 11:1–44). Instead, He argued for the resurrection from the Torah. Remember, that was the only section of the Old Testament that the Sadducees recognized as Scripture. And if there was any phrase that the Sadducees knew by heart from the Torah, it was the repeated refrain that God was "the God of Abraham, the God of Isaac, and the God of Jacob." So, there is no doubt that Jesus was arguing for the resurrection on the basis of the authority that the Sadducees recognized.

It is possible that Jesus was merely calling attention to the fact that when God is identified in the Bible, He is always identified with the present tense. We possibly could argue that Jesus was implying that if there is no resurrection from the dead, God would have said He *was* the God of Abraham, Isaac, and Jacob. Thus, by using the present tense, Jesus was declaring that the patriarchs are still alive, and therefore there is a resurrection.

However, it is possible there is more here. God's relationship with Abraham, Isaac, and Jacob was based on an eternal covenant that He made with them. The covenant God made with Abraham was not a covenant that died with the death of Abraham; neither did it die when Isaac and Jacob passed away. The relationship God had entered with the patriarchs was an eternal relationship that was not cancelled by death. That idea has wonderful implications for us, for we are in a better covenant (Heb. 7:22; 12:24). The One who is the firstborn from the dead (Col. 1:18) will be the firstborn of many brethren (Rom. 8:29).

Though we may go through the valley of the shadow of death, the resurrection of Christ is God's guarantee that we will live for eternity.

Matthew writes, **And when the multitudes heard this, they were astonished at His teaching** (v. 33). The people just shook their heads. Jesus had silenced the Pharisees, and now He had done the same to the Sadducees, using their own Scriptures. His teaching was wonderful in their eyes.

102

THE FIRST COMMANDMENT

Matthew 22:34–40

But when the Pharisees heard that He had silenced the Sadducees, they gathered together. Then one of them, a lawyer, asked Him a question, testing Him, and saying, "Teacher, which is the great commandment in the law?" Jesus said to him, "'You shall love the LORD your God with all your heart, with all your soul, and with all your mind.' This is the first and great commandment. And the second is like it: 'You shall love your neighbor as yourself.' On these two commandments hang all the Law and the Prophets."

Jesus' wisdom had proved too much for the Pharisees and the Sadducees in their attempts to trap Him in words, but such was their hatred of Him, Jesus' opponents were not ready to surrender. Nevertheless, there is a definite sense of desperation in Matthew's account of the final question they asked of Him.

Matthew writes, **But when the Pharisees heard that He had silenced the Sadducees, they gathered together** (v. 34). Jesus had easily foiled the Pharisees' carefully laid trap (22:15–22), so they seem to have placed their hopes in the Sadducees. When the Sadducees' effort to entangle Him failed also (vv. 23–33), the Pharisees gathered together to discuss their next step. It is almost possible to hear them saying to one another in frustration, "What are we going to *do*?"

Their chosen course of action, if it can be called that, was to fire another question at Him: **Then one of them, a lawyer, asked Him a question, testing Him, and saying, "Teacher, which is the great commandment in the law?"**

(vv. 35–36). Yet again, Jesus was confronted with a question designed to test or trap Him. This time the question was not posed by a group but by one individual. This man is identified here as a lawyer, which means he was a scribe, an authority on the law of God. The rabbis had catalogued all the laws of the Old Testament and counted them, coming up with a final tally of six hundred and thirteen. They believed that there was a distinction between commandments that were "light" and "weighty," and they spent endless hours discussing which commandments fit into which categories. This lawyer asked Jesus to give His opinion as to which of all the commandments was the most weighty, obviously hoping He would say something that the Pharisees could contradict with their supposedly extensive legal knowledge, perhaps impressing and influencing the people.

Of course, this whole discussion about which commandment was the most important was thoroughly academic and scholarly, having little or nothing to do with faithful obedience to the law. I find it highly ironic that this one who was supposed to be an expert on the law of God was confronting the only person in all of human history who had kept all six hundred and thirteen of God's commandments. By comparison, this expert in the law was thoroughly lawless.

I must say a word at this point about the idea that some commandments are more weighty than others. There is a widely held idea in the Christian world that all of the laws of God hold equal weight. Perhaps one of the reasons for that is the teaching of James, who writes, "Whoever shall keep the whole law, and yet stumble in one point, he is guilty of all" (2:10). However, James does not mean that when we violate one point of the law we thereby violate every particular law. Moreover, there are frequent instances in Scripture where gradations of sin are set forth. God considered certain laws so important that He specified that violations of them deserved the death penalty, but He did not require such grave penalties for other laws. Obviously, therefore, the prohibition against murdering a human being (Ex. 20:13) was of greater import than the prohibition against boiling a goat in its mother's milk (Ex. 23:19). Even Jesus recognized a hierarchy of laws; He said, "Whoever therefore breaks one of *the least* of these commandments . . . shall be called least in the kingdom of heaven" (Matt. 5:19, emphasis added).

Of course, every law that comes from the mouth of God is serious enough to warrant the death penalty if it is violated. The slightest transgression of the slightest law that comes from the mouth of God is an act of cosmic treason, an act of defiance against the Lord God, who rules all things. In our slightest sin we exalt our own preferences over the will of our Maker. That is not only foolish, it is heinous. The fact that not all of the commandments in the Old Testament law carried the death penalty was an expression of God's mercy.

Love for God

How, then, did Jesus respond to the lawyer's question? Matthew tells us: **Jesus said to him, "'You shall love the LORD your God with all your heart, with all your soul, and with all your mind.' This is the first and great commandment"** (vv. 37–38). He referred the lawyer to the *Shema* from Deuteronomy 6, which every pious Jew recited out loud two times a day: "Hear, O Israel: The LORD our God, the LORD is one! You shall love the LORD your God with all your heart, with all your soul, and with all your strength" (vv. 4–5). For unknown reasons, when Jesus cited the *Shema,* He changed the wording slightly, substituting the word *mind* for the word *strength.* I cannot explain this change, but it certainly speaks to our fallen condition as sinful people.

We are called sinners because we sin, but it is more accurate to say we sin because we are sinners. That is, we sin because it is our nature to sin. What is sin? The Westminster Shorter Catechism answers succinctly: "Sin is any want of conformity unto, or transgression of, the law of God" (Q&A 14). I mention that catechetical statement because we have to understand the relationship between sin on the one hand and law on the other. Where there is no law, there is no sin. But where there is law, if the law is violated, there is sin.

Jesus did not go through all six hundred and thirteen commandments and tell the lawyer, "You're guilty of this one, this one, and this one." If He had done so with the lawyer, He would have said "guilty" with regard to each and every commandment. Earlier, we examined Jesus' discussion with the rich young ruler, who came to Jesus thinking that he had kept all of the commandments of God from his youth, but in reality he had not kept a single one of them since he got out of his bed that morning (19:16–22). Likewise, we have not kept a single one of the Ten Commandments since we got out of our beds this morning. We have a terribly low view of what the law of God requires and a frightfully high view of our own performance. If we were to adjust our understanding of both the law and our ability to keep it, we would see that there is an unbridgeable chasm between our performance and the demands of the law of God.

But what about this one commandment, the one Jesus identified as the greatest, the commandment to love God with all our hearts, souls, and minds? How do we do when it comes to keeping this command? I once asked a group of students in a theology class to list the most serious and gross of all human sins, the worst sins human beings can commit. They began to suggest various atrocities such as murder, treason, and adultery. I wrote them all down on the blackboard; then I turned to them and said, "None of the above." Then I told them that if the single most important commandment God ever gave to His people is to love Him with all of our hearts, all of our souls, and all of our minds, it seems to me that the greatest transgression is to fail to love Him with all of our hearts, all of our souls, and all of our minds.

However, we do not feel any particular guilt because we do not love God with all of our hearts, souls, and minds. Why is that? I believe it is because we understand that no one loves God with all of his or her being. I may have some affection for God, but my heart is not given entirely to love for Him. Certainly my soul may have a few positive inclinations toward God, but it is not filled to its capacity with affection for Him. As for my mind, if I loved God with all of my mind, I would have mastered His Word much more thoroughly than I actually have. My mind is usually busy gathering wool about a host of other things. It fixates on ideas that have little or nothing to do with God.

The Fallen Mind

In fact, when Paul describes our fallen condition, he specifically makes the point that we do not want God in our thinking. Because we have rejected the knowledge of God, our minds have become darkened, and this leads to all sorts of wickedness:

> And even as they did not like to retain God in their knowledge, God gave them over to a debased mind, to do those things which are not fitting; being filled with all unrighteousness, sexual immorality, wickedness, covetousness, maliciousness; full of envy, murder, strife, deceit, evil-mindedness; they are whisperers, backbiters, haters of God, violent, proud, boasters, inventors of evil things, disobedient to parents, undiscerning, untrustworthy, unloving, unforgiving, unmerciful; who, knowing the righteous judgment of God, that those who practice such things are deserving of death, not only do the same but also approve of those who practice them. (Rom. 1:28–32)

This is a catalogue of the vices of every fallen human being. One of the results of our fallen condition is that we are "haters of God." We are not merely indifferent. Rather, we have a deeply rooted desire to do our own will rather than God's. He remains the supreme obstacle to our pursuit of pleasure. Therefore, we want to do away with Him, to get rid of Him.

Jesus said the number one commandment is to "love the LORD your God with all of your heart, with all your soul, and with all your mind." I have not kept this commandment for five seconds in my lifetime. I have never loved God with all of my being. No one has. Obviously this is a major problem, because God is not going to grade us on a curve. He is not a relativist; He deals with absolutes. He will judge us all according to these commandments.

Let's look at the other side of it: Why should we love God with all of our hearts, souls, and minds? We have never seen Him or heard His voice. But we know what He is like. He has revealed Himself to each one of us, even His eternal power and deity (Rom. 1:20). What we know of Him is that He is altogether lovely. So, God is not asking us to love the unlovely. He does that, for He loves us in the unloveliness of our sin. He asks us to direct our love to Him because He first loved us (1 John 4:19).

This is an idea that we really need to get our arms around. We are supposed to love God not just for what He does. There is plenty of reason for you and me to love Him with all of our hearts, souls, and minds when we consider what He has done and what He does for us. Jesus said that he who has been forgiven much loves much (Luke 7:47). God has forgiven me of so many things, and that forgiveness should be enough to spark in my heart, soul, and mind a deep affection for Him. But we have not really learned what it means to be Christians until we have an affection for God not simply for what He has done for us but for who He is. As we think about Him in His perfections, in His holiness, in His power, in His knowledge, and so on, those attributes of God should be like matches that set our beings aflame with love for Him.

When we read the Psalms, we understand that every one of them was written by a sinful man such as David. Yet, as we read them, we are eavesdropping on the outpouring of affection from human beings who are intoxicated with love for God. They even express love for His law: "Oh, how I love Your law! It is my meditation all the day. . . . [It] is a lamp to my feet and a light to my path" (Ps. 119:97, 105). The psalmist understood that the law reveals all of God's excellence, wisdom, and righteousness. But the psalmist was really saying, "Oh, how I love Your Word." Are we people who love the Bible? We should be, for in it we hear from Him and He reveals to us who He is. The more we study it and learn it, the more our hearts will be enflamed with affection for Him.

Love for Neighbor

But Jesus did not simply identify the greatest commandment. He pointed to the second greatest, as well: **"And the second is like it: 'You shall love your neighbor as yourself'"** (v. 39). As we have seen, the Bible does not teach the universal brotherhood of all people, but it does teach the universal neighborhood of all. Everyone is my neighbor. Therefore, I am under obligation to love all men. This means I cannot say I love God with all of my heart, soul, and mind if I disregard His commandment to love other people. I can love people and not love God, but I cannot love God and despise my neighbor.

Finally, Jesus said, "**On these two commandments hang all the Law and the**

Prophets" (v. 40). Augustine said it this way: "Love God and do as you please." He meant that love for God is so much at the heart of what the law of God is all about that if we really love God with all of our hearts, souls, and minds, we do not need the rest of the six hundred and thirteen commandments. If we truly love God in this way, we will be so overwhelmed by a desire to please God that we will be able to live in righteousness.

103

DAVID'S SON AND LORD

Matthew 22:41–46

While the Pharisees were gathered together, Jesus asked them, saying, "What do you think about the Christ? Whose Son is He?" They said to Him, "The Son of David." He said to them, "How then does David in the Spirit call Him 'Lord,' saying:

> 'The LORD said to my Lord,
> "Sit at My right hand,
> Till I make Your enemies Your footstool"'?

If David then calls Him 'Lord,' how is He his Son?" And no one was able to answer Him a word, nor from that day on did anyone dare question Him anymore.

In the past few chapters, we have looked at passages in which Jesus was asked questions by His enemies, the Jewish religious leaders. These men believed their carefully crafted questions would entrap or entangle Jesus, forcing Him to give an answer that would get Him in trouble with someone—perhaps the people or perhaps even the Roman authorities. They were stunned to find that Jesus answered their questions with ease, evading the dangerous ground and making them look foolish.

In the passage before us in this chapter, Jesus showed that He not only was adept at answering supposedly tough questions, He was without peer in asking difficult questions of His own. If His answers made them look foolish, His questions removed any doubt.

Jesus asked the Pharisees a question about Psalm 110:1, which is the Old Testament text that is quoted most frequently in the New Testament. It is cited so much because it offers profound insights about the identity of Jesus. It behooves us, then, to give close attention to this passage, that we might extract the gems contained within it.

The Son of David

Matthew tells us: **While the Pharisees were gathered together, Jesus asked them, saying, "What do you think about the Christ? Whose Son is He?" They said to Him, "The Son of David"** (vv. 41–42). We saw in the previous chapter that the Pharisees gathered to take counsel together after Jesus silenced the Sadducees (v. 34). At that point, one of their members, a lawyer, blurted out a question about the law that Jesus handled straightforwardly (vv. 35–40). Then, while the Pharisees were still together in His presence, Jesus asked them for their opinion about the Christ, namely, whose Son He would be, that is, from which family line in Israel would He come.

Christos, or Christ, was the New Testament word for the Old Testament word *Messiah*. So, when Jesus asked the question, "What do you think about the Christ?" He was asking about the Messiah. The whole concept of the Messiah was on everyone's minds in the first century. All of those in positions of authority were concerned about the Old Testament prophecies that promised the future coming of the One whom God had anointed to be the Messiah of Israel.

To ask a question like this to the Pharisees, who were among the most learned people in the land with respect to the Scriptures of the Old Testament and Jewish theology, was like asking someone with a PhD to answer a question that any kindergartener could handle. Everyone in Israel knew the answer to Jesus' question—the Messiah was to come from the lineage of David, the greatest king of Israel, the one who had ushered in the golden age of the nation. Furthermore, God had entered a covenant with David, promising him that there would be a king from his line on the throne forever (2 Sam. 7:12–16). Yet shortly after David died, the golden age began to tarnish under his son Solomon, and when Solomon died, the Davidic kingdom turned to rust with the division between Rehoboam and Jeroboam (1 Kings 12).

Most of the rest of the history of Israel and Judah is a story of corruption and apostasy until both kingdoms were overthrown by foreign powers. But the people yearned for the day when David's fallen house would be set upright again and the golden age would be restored, when one like David would come. In Jesus' day particularly, hope and expectation for the coming of the Messiah was at a fever pitch because the Jewish people were groaning under their subjugation to Rome. During the reign of David, Israel was one of the great and mighty empires of the ancient world. By Jesus' time, Israel was at one of the weakest points in its history, impotent in military strength. The people longed to see the lost glory of their nation renewed.

When we lived in the Netherlands during my graduate studies there, we constantly heard the Dutch people talking about the glory of their country in the seventeenth century. Their tiny nation, about the size of the state of Maryland, was a world power, largely because of its navy and its international trade. It also gave the world great artists, who led the world in aesthetics through their paintings. But now, I'm not sure the Netherlands could win a war with the New York City Police Department. Like Israel in the first century, the Netherlands has fallen from a position of world leadership to a position of little significance on the global stage.

So, the dream of every Jew was that a warrior like David would come, a fierce, strong champion who would lead a revolution against the Roman Empire and throw off the yoke of bondage that was so heavy on their necks. All their hopes were invested in the Son of David, who would do David's exploits again. Therefore, the Pharisees hardly had to think in order to answer the first part of Jesus' question.

The *Adonai* of David

But then Jesus asked a much more difficult question, one that required the Pharisees to reveal their knowledge and understanding of Scripture: **He said to them, "How then does David in the Spirit call Him 'Lord,' saying: 'The Lord said to my Lord, "Sit at My right hand, till I make Your enemies Your footstool"'? If David then calls Him 'Lord,' how is He his Son?"** (vv. 43–45). In this question, Jesus cited the first verse of Psalm 110, a psalm of David in which he speaks of the Messiah as his "Lord." In Jewish categories, the son was never greater than the father. Instead, the descendant was always subordinate to the elder. So, Jesus asked, how could it be possible that David should speak of his Son as his Lord?

It is important to notice the manner in which Jesus referred to David's calling the Messiah his Lord. We get a glimpse here of Jesus' understanding of the transmission of sacred Scripture. Our Lord indicates that when David wrote Psalm 110, he was not merely exercising his poetic gifts, he was writing "in the Spirit," that is, under the supervision and superintendence of the Holy Spirit. The Apostle Paul says of this process, "All Scripture is given by inspiration of

God" (2 Tim. 3:16a). Another translation renders this verse slightly differently: "All Scripture is breathed out by God" (ESV). So, the Scriptures ultimately have God as their Author, even though they are written by human authors. It seems that in this discussion with the Pharisees, Jesus wanted to give them a little jab, reminding them that David did not write the text he wanted to discuss out of his own human insight, but he wrote it under the inspiration of the Holy Spirit of God, who is the Spirit of truth. It was under that inspiration that David referred to the Messiah as his Lord.

In Psalm 110:1, David wrote: "The Lord said to my Lord, 'Sit at My right hand, till I make Your enemies Your footstool.'" There is an important difference between the way the two instances of the word *Lord* are rendered in our English Bibles. The first instance is rendered "Lord," with all capital letters. This is the translator's way of alerting us that the word that is being translated here is the sacred name of God, *Yahweh*. When God spoke to Moses from the burning bush in the Midianite wilderness, Moses asked who he should say had sent him to the Israelites in Egypt. God replied: "I AM WHO I AM" (Ex. 3:14). The Hebrew *Yahweh* means "I am" in Hebrew. But in Psalm 110, *Yahweh* is having a conversation with someone apart from Himself, someone whom David identifies as "my Lord." In this instance, the word *Lord* is rendered with capital and lowercase letters. This tells us that the Hebrew word that is translated here is *Adonai*, which literally means "the sovereign One." So, God is speaking to "the sovereign One."

Psalm 110 depicts two separate individuals, *Yahweh* and the *Adonai*, that is, "the sovereign One." But Psalm 8 gives a different picture. There we read, "O Lord, our Lord, how excellent is Your name in all the earth" (v. 1a). Here again we see the different renderings of the word *Lord*. Keeping this difference in mind, we see that this verse literally reads, "O *Yahweh*, our *Adonai*, how excellent is Your name in all the earth." Both words are here—*Yahweh* and *Adonai*—and both refer to one and the same person, namely, God. The title *Adonai* is perhaps the most significant title that is given to God in the Old Testament. *Yahweh* is His name; *Adonai* is His title. It is the supreme title that belongs exclusively to God. So, the psalmist in Psalm 8 is saying, "O *Yahweh*, our Sovereign One."

Again, Psalm 110 tells of God speaking to David's *Adonai*. This *Adonai* is God Himself, but He is also a different person. This can be only One person—the Lord Jesus Christ. David's Son is David's Lord. David's Son is David's Sovereign. The One who comes forth from the lineage of David is David's King.

Notice that in Psalm 110, the psalm that David wrote under the inspiration of the Spirit, *Yahweh* said to David's *Adonai*, "Sit at My right hand." God the Father was inviting God the Son to sit in the seat of cosmic authority. The Father was promising to install the Son at His right hand as the King of the kings and as the Lord of the lords. David understood that his Son would be King over all things, even David himself.

What was Jesus getting at here? Why did He emphasize this psalm? He completely understood the Pharisees' and Sadducees' expectations for the Messiah, which meant that He understood that their view of the Messiah was far too small. They were looking for a human conqueror rather than a sovereign Lord who would be exalted to the right hand of the Father in the ascension. They needed to get their minds off the Romans and think about the kingdom of God, which they were missing completely.

Matthew tells us, **And no one was able to answer Him a word, nor from that day on did anyone dare question Him anymore** (v. 46). The Pharisees did not know how to explain Psalm 110. They could not even venture an answer to Jesus' searching questions. From that point on, the interrogations ended. The religious leaders were tired of being embarrassed by Jesus' superior wisdom. But their embarrassment only fueled their rage. How tragic that it did not humble and convict them.

104

WOES TO THE PHARISEES, PART 1

Matthew 23:1–12

Then Jesus spoke to the multitudes and to His disciples, saying: "The scribes and the Pharisees sit in Moses' seat. Therefore whatever they tell you to observe, that observe and do, but do not do according to their works; for they say, and do not do. For they bind heavy burdens, hard to bear, and lay them on men's shoulders; but they themselves will not move them with one of their fingers. But all their works they do to be seen by men. They make their phylacteries broad and enlarge the borders of their garments. They love the best places at feasts, the best seats in the synagogues, greetings in the marketplaces, and to be called by men, 'Rabbi, Rabbi.' But you, do not be called 'Rabbi'; for One is your Teacher, the Christ, and you are all brethren. Do not call anyone on earth your father; for One is your Father, He who is in heaven. And do not be called teachers; for One is your Teacher, the Christ. But he who is greatest among you shall be your servant. And whoever exalts himself will be humbled, and he who humbles himself will be exalted."

One of the great concerns of our Puritan forefathers had to do with what they called "an unconverted clergy." A New Jersey pastor named Gilbert Tennent (1703–1764) preached a sermon titled "The Danger of an Unconverted Ministry," and others preached and taught on the same theme. However, this problem is almost absent from the discussions in contemporary evangelical churches. We tend to assume that if a person is ordained to the ministry, surely he must be converted. We wonder why someone would go through the laborious process of college and seminary education, then stand the trials of ordination in order to be set apart for Christian ministry, if he has no desire to obey and please God. But I can assure you that there are a host of reasons why people enter the ministry while having no real affection for the things of God or for Christ.

In my college days, there was a pre-ministerial fraternity for those who were planning to go on to seminary, and while I cannot read anyone's heart, it seemed as if the majority of members of that particular club were quite hostile to all things Christian. I scratched my head and wondered, "What are these men doing preparing for the ministry when they're so hostile to the things of Christ?" In time, it became apparent to me that one of the reasons why people go into the ministry is to refute the truth claims of Christianity. Becoming a pastor is one of the easiest ways to gain a public hearing; the preacher can air his views to a captive audience for an hour each Sunday morning. However, those unbelieving men (and sometimes women) who are ordained to the ministry usually find it difficult to sustain a viable ministry in the local church for any length of time, so they tend to gravitate to administrative positions, and before you know it, the unconverted control entire denominations.

This was the very situation in Israel in Jesus' time. The leading religious figures were the scribes and the Pharisees. The scribes were experts on interpreting the Old Testament law. They were essentially biblical scholars. The Pharisees were theologians. But they also were members of a religious sect that was dedicated to promoting the law of God in the life of the people. This sect originated sometime in the four-hundred-year period between the close of the Old Testament and the opening of the New Testament, what we call the intertestamental period. Following Alexander the Great's program of Hellenization, his effort to spread Greek culture, a serious cultural secularism invaded Israel. The law of God was in disuse and disrespect. In response, a group of pious Jews banded together and committed themselves to try to bring about a renewal of interest in the Old Testament law. These were very devout men—at the beginning. But their zeal for the recovery of the law basically turned to dust as one generation followed another, and they became more and more self-righteous and hypocritical, and more at odds with the law of God as they twisted it to suit their own framework.

These men should have been the ushers for the people, leading them into the kingdom of God. But instead of serving as ushers, the scribes and the Pharisees were barriers between the people and the kingdom, for they were openly hostile to the One whom the Father had appointed to be the King. From the day Jesus walked along the Jordan River and John the Baptist proclaimed Him as the Lamb of God (John 1:29), the leaders in Jerusalem were outraged against John the Baptist and against Jesus Himself. Throughout the original Holy Week, they tried to trap Jesus in words, looking for a way to undermine Him and discredit Him. For His part, Jesus told a number of parables that revealed the hypocrisy of the religious leaders. Finally, Jesus began to expose them openly. In chapter 23 of his Gospel, Matthew records Jesus' denunciations of these charlatans, and it is here that we find what is probably the harshest language that we ever hear from the lips of Jesus. He pronounced a series of woes upon the scribes and Pharisees, but only after directly warning the crowds and His disciples to be very wary of them.

When we studied the Beatitudes in the Sermon on the Mount (5:3–12), we saw that Jesus prefaced each one with the word *blessed*. That is why these pithy teachings are called Beatitudes—the word for "blessed" in the Latin New Testament is *beati*. Jesus was self-consciously using a form of speech that was associated with pronouncements delivered by Old Testament prophets. These pronouncements were known as oracles. Oracles were simply messages from God, and there were two types. There were oracles of weal, which announced prosperity or blessedness, good news of God's blessing. The Beatitudes were oracles of this type. Also, there were oracles of woe, which announced doom from God, declarations of divine judgment. There are many prophetic pronouncements of woe in the Old Testament, but one of the most memorable is found in Isaiah 6, when Isaiah the prophet was given a vision of the heavenly throne room, with God seated in splendor. Seeing this magnificent sight, Isaiah cried: "Woe is me, for I am undone! Because I am a man of unclean lips, and I dwell in the midst of a people of unclean lips; for my eyes have seen the King, the Lord of hosts" (v. 5). This was a pronouncement of doom.

This is precisely what we find in Matthew 23. Here is the record of Jesus' denunciations of the clergy of his day with oracles of doom. But before He spoke to them directly, He spoke to the people and to His disciples about them.

Good Teaching, Bad Examples

Matthew writes: **Then Jesus spoke to the multitudes and to His disciples, saying: "The scribes and the Pharisees sit in Moses' seat"** (vv. 1–2). What did Jesus mean with these words? Contrary to the way in which classes are normally taught today, with the teacher standing in front of the students, a teacher in the ancient world sat in a chair, and the students sat on the floor around him. They literally sat at the feet of their teacher. The teacher's chair was known as the seat of teaching. It was the task of the scribes and the Pharisees to teach and explain the law that had been delivered through Moses, so they figuratively sat in the seat of Moses. It was, really, the chair of theology. This is why, in the university and in the seminary, certain positions are called "the chair of philosophy" or "the chair of theology."

Because the scribes and the Pharisees were vested with this responsibility and position, Jesus acknowledged that a certain respect was due to them. He said, **"Therefore whatever they tell you to observe, that observe and do"** (v. 3a). He was saying that the teachers knew the law of God and the doctrine that flowed out of it. Therefore, the people were to follow the biblical instructions they received from the scribes and Pharisees. However, Jesus added, **"but do not do according to their works; for they say, and do not do"** (v. 3b). The problem with the scribes' and Pharisees' teaching was that they themselves did not follow their own lessons. They taught the law to the people, but they believed they themselves were above the law. Jesus advised the people, "Do as they say, not as they do."

Jesus continued, **"For they bind heavy burdens, hard to bear, and lay them on men's shoulders; but they themselves will not move them with one of their fingers"** (v. 4). Here Jesus borrowed an image from His own culture, which employed beasts of burden to carry goods from one place to another. The people of that time obviously did not have trains, planes, or trucks to deliver items, so they used donkeys, camels, and other animals. They were very careful how they packed these materials, because there was a science to it. However, they also gave consideration to the welfare of the animal, because overburdening an animal could harm it. They had to balance the weight evenly to put the optimum burden on the back of the animal.

So, Jesus was saying that merchants who packed their donkeys and camels with heavy burdens were more compassionate than the scribes and Pharisees. They did not care how heavy was the burden they put on the backs of the people. They not only burdened the people with the details of the law that Moses gave, they added all kinds of rules and regulations that could not be found in the law of Moses. In other words, they bound their people where God had left them free.

Seeking the Applause of Men

Jesus continued: **"But all their works they do to be seen by men. They make their phylacteries broad and enlarge the borders of their garments"** (v. 5). The scribes and Pharisees made ostentatious displays of piety, actively trying to attract the notice of their countrymen, that they might receive the applause of men. Phylacteries were small leather boxes that contained passages of Scripture. They were worn on the forehead or the arm in a literal fulfillment of Deuteronomy 11:18: "Therefore you shall lay up these words of mine in your heart and in your soul, and bind them as a sign on your hand, and they shall be as frontlets between your eyes." The "borders of their garments" was a reference to tassels that were attached to the hems of garments to remind the people to obey the law of God (see Num. 15:37–41). These tassels were legitimate parts of garments in that time period, but the scribes and the Pharisees tried to outdo one another with ever larger tassels. By following these biblical instructions with more ostentation than was necessary, the scribes and Pharisees were seeking the praise of men, not of God. It is this kind of behavior that the Apostle Paul warns against: "If I still pleased men, I would not be a bondservant of Christ" (Gal. 1:10b).

Jesus went on to say, **"They love the best places at feasts, the best seats in the synagogues, greetings in the marketplaces, and to be called by men, 'Rabbi, Rabbi'"** (vv. 6–7). All of these were ways of showing honor—the head tables at dinners, prominent seats in the synagogue, public recognition, and distinguished titles. The word *rabbi* literally meant "my lord," though it was usually applied to teachers of the law. The scribes and Pharisees lived for personal honor in the eyes of men.

Jesus then made application to the people and His disciples, showing them how the godly man ought to live. First He said: **"But you, do not be called 'Rabbi'; for One is your Teacher, the Christ, and you are all brethren. Do not call anyone on earth your father; for One is your Father, He who is in heaven. And do not be called teachers; for One is your Teacher, the Christ"** (vv. 8–10). This is a difficult passage. Was Jesus banning the office of teacher? Was He saying we may not even call our earthly fathers "father"?

We must interpret this passage in the context of Jesus' teaching on the errors of the scribes and Pharisees. He was not literally forbidding the office of teacher or even the use of the title *teacher*; after all, Paul recognized the office of teacher as a spiritual gift (1 Cor. 12:28). He was saying that His disciples should not get caught up in titles and the implied authority they confer. It is futile and ungodly to seek titles and honors that we might be exalted above other men. Furthermore, it is vital to remember that God is our Father and that Christ is our teacher, and we must never give any minister, any preacher, any teacher, any writer, or any conference speaker the same kind of respect and obedience that is to be given to the Father and the Son.

Jesus then reminded His disciples of a lesson He had taught them earlier, when James and John's mother asked Jesus to let them sit on His right and left in His kingdom (20:20–28). He said: **"But he who is greatest among you shall be your servant. And whoever exalts himself will be humbled, and he who humbles himself will be exalted"** (vv. 11–12). The religious leaders did not have servant hearts. They did not want to serve anyone. They wanted to be served by everyone. They were not interested in being humbled, only in being exalted. By contrast, the very essence of the work of Jesus was His voluntary submission to humiliation. His food was to be obedient, to do the will of the Father (John 4:34). He humbled Himself and took on the form of a servant (Phil. 2:5–8). For this reason, "God also has highly exalted Him and given Him the name which is above every name, that at the name of Jesus every knee should bow, of those in heaven, and of those on earth, and of those under the earth, and that every tongue should confess that Jesus Christ is Lord, to the glory of God the Father" (vv. 9–11).

We have a wonderful promise here: If we follow Jesus' example and humble ourselves now, we will be exalted later. However, He also gives a warning: If we exalt ourselves now, we will be humbled later. Because the scribes and Pharisees were so committed to exalting themselves, Jesus had oracles of woe for them, as we will see in the next chapter.

105

WOES TO THE PHARISEES, PART 2

Matthew 23:13–22

> But woe to you, scribes and Pharisees, hypocrites! For you shut up the kingdom of heaven against men; for you neither go in yourselves, nor do you allow those who are entering to go in. Woe to you, scribes and Pharisees, hypocrites! For you devour widows' houses, and for a pretense make long prayers. Therefore you will receive greater condemnation. Woe to you, scribes and Pharisees, hypocrites! For you travel land and sea to win one proselyte, and when he is won, you make him twice as much a son of hell as yourselves. Woe to you, blind guides, who say, "Whoever swears by the temple, it is nothing; but whoever swears by the gold of the temple, he is obliged to perform it." Fools and blind! For which is greater, the gold or the temple that sanctifies the gold? And, "Whoever swears by the altar, it is nothing; but whoever swears by the gift that is on it, he is obliged to perform it." Fools and blind! For which is greater, the gift or the altar that sanctifies the gift? Therefore he who swears by the altar, swears by it and by all things on it. He who swears by the temple, swears by it and by Him who dwells in it. And he who swears by heaven, swears by the throne of God and by Him who sits on it.

The first twelve verses of Matthew 23, which we examined in the previous chapter, are something of a preamble to the real heart of this chapter, wherein Jesus pronounced a series of woes on the scribes and Pharisees. As I mentioned in the previous chapter, this episode features what is probably the harshest language that Jesus ever used during His ministry. It is so harsh that some have said Jesus went over the edge here and actually sinned by insulting these religious leaders so deeply. However, this kind of polemical language has been characteristic of theological disputes for centuries. Moreover, we dare not impute sin to the One who used this language, for the Scriptures are clear that He was the sinless Son of God, and He spoke these words to the scribes and Pharisees out of a posture of true righteous indignation.

Matthew tells us that Jesus began by saying: **"But woe to you, scribes and Pharisees, hypocrites! For you shut up the kingdom of heaven against men; for you neither go in yourselves, nor do you allow those who are entering to go in."** (v. 13). As I noted earlier, the Pharisees should have been ushering people into the kingdom. They should have been, like John the Baptist, heralds of the Messiah. They should have been saying to the multitudes: "Go and listen to Jesus. Learn of Jesus. Jesus is the Messiah, who is preaching the kingdom of God." Instead, they had set themselves up as impediments and barriers to people entering the kingdom. Not only did they refuse to embrace Christ, but in their hostility to Him they did everything in their power to discourage the common people from coming to Him.

Many clergy today are like this. They are too sophisticated to speak about repentance and about coming to Christ for redemption. They want to cast religion more on the level of humanitarianism than the realm of personal redemption involving the reception and worship of Jesus. But Christianity, from start to finish, is about Jesus, the One whom the Father sent into the world to redeem His people from sin and death. A person can earn a PhD in theology and study all kinds of sophisticated and technical points, but none of those things should ever trump the foundational message of the coming of the kingdom of God in the person of Christ. Just as Jesus pronounced an oracle of doom against the scribes and the Pharisees for slamming the door to the kingdom of God and keeping people from entering, so He is angered when pastors today fail to lead His people to His Son.

A Textual Variant

Jesus then said: **"Woe to you, scribes and Pharisees, hypocrites! For you devour widows' houses, and for a pretense make long prayers. Therefore you will receive greater condemnation"** (v. 14). This verse is quoted from the New King James Version of the Bible, the translation I cite throughout this commentary. However, if you read this passage in some other translations, you will not find this verse. The reason for this is simple—there is a textual variant at this point in Matthew's Gospel.

We do not have the original copy of this Gospel. It was lost centuries and centuries ago. But the people in the early church did not simply receive the original manuscript of Matthew, read it once, thank God for it, and then throw it in the garbage can. They went through the painstaking process of making very exact copies for other people and for future generations. For hundreds of years, copies of the original manuscript were very carefully preserved by scribes and monks, who busied themselves with the meticulous work of copying each letter of the ancient texts. But even the most careful copyists from time to time missed a letter here or a verse there, and so we have a small number of discrepancies among the various copies that still exist.

There is a science called textual criticism, by which New Testament scholars and Greek scholars look at the thousands of copies of the ancient texts that still exist, and they weigh and measure them in terms of their accuracy. In most cases, they can come to within 99 percent accuracy of reconstructing the original text. But sometimes there is a passage for which the evidence is not completely overwhelming one way or the other, and so the scholars must make choices. In the case of Matthew's Gospel, 23:14 is absent from the best manuscripts of antiquity. So, if there is a consensus, it is that this verse was not in the original. Therefore, even though it is included in the New King James Version text, I will refrain from commenting on it.

Zeal for Evangelism

Jesus continued: **"Woe to you, scribes and Pharisees, hypocrites! For you travel land and sea to win one proselyte, and when he is won, you make him twice as much a son of hell as yourselves"** (v. 15). Historically, the Jewish people were not all that interested in evangelizing, in winning Gentiles to the Jewish faith. At some point, they largely accepted the idea that they would find salvation by segregation, by making sure they did not come into contact with sinful people. So, they kept to themselves. On the other hand, there was an unprecedented zeal for proselytizing in the first century. The Pharisees wanted to win people to their version of Judaism, to Pharisaism. Jesus remarked on this zeal. He said, "You travel land and sea to win one proselyte."

I receive a number of invitations to speak. People write to me, saying, "We want you to come and speak for such and such a gathering; there will be five thousand people there." However, I have yet to receive an invitation to preach to one person. If I did receive such an invitation, I would say, "Do they think I'm going to get on a plane and fly across the country or the ocean to preach to one person?" Yet, the Pharisees did essentially that. They walked. They rode donkeys. They went on camels. They were zealous to make proselytes.

As we progress through these denunciations of the Pharisees, it is good to keep in mind something Jesus said in the Sermon on the Mount. It is, I believe, one of the scariest statements He ever uttered. He said, "Unless your righteousness exceeds the righteousness of the scribes and Pharisees, you will by no means enter the kingdom of heaven" (5:20). As He pronounced His woes, Jesus made clear that the scribes and the Pharisees did some things right, and Jesus commended them for those things. One of those things they did right was their evangelism. They would do anything to lead someone else to the same commitment to the law of God they had. In light of Matthew 5:20, we need to ask ourselves whether our zeal for evangelism exceeds or comes anywhere close to that of the Pharisees.

Unfortunately, the Pharisees tended to twist the good things they did into bad things, and that was the case with their evangelism. Jesus said that after they made a proselyte through their strenuous efforts, they made him "twice as much a son of hell" as themselves. Do not miss that language—Jesus said the scribes and Pharisees were "sons of hell." They were blind, hypocritical, and foolish, and those they "converted" were in the same condition. This was not "gentle Jesus, meek and mild" talking at this point. He used very tough language to call a spade a spade when he talked to these scribes and Pharisees. He did not mince or varnish His words.

When I read this verse, I am forced to ask myself, "What will Jesus call me?" We want to hear that we are sons and daughters of heaven, not sons and daughters of hell. But the New Testament teaches us that we are sons and daughters of whomever we obey, and we obey whomever we love. If we love God and obey God, it is appropriate for us to be known as children of God, because we have been adopted into the family of God. But if we are indifferent or hostile toward the things of God, we cannot assume that we are in His family. Our secular culture teaches that we are all children of God. That is simply not true. No one is born a child of God. The only way we can become children of God is to be adopted into His family through the work of God's Son, our elder Brother, Jesus Christ.

Proper Oaths and Vows

Jesus then issued an oracle regarding oaths and vows: **"Woe to you, blind guides, who say, 'Whoever swears by the temple, it is nothing; but whoever swears by the gold of the temple, he is obliged to perform it.' Fools and blind! For which is greater, the gold or the temple that sanctifies the gold?"** (vv. 16–17). In this pronouncement, instead of addressing His hearers as "scribes and Pharisees, hypocrites," He called them "blind guides." What good is a guide who is blind? Jesus elsewhere said that if the blind lead the blind, both of them will fall into a ditch (15:14). This was not a criticism of blind people, because blind people can do wonderful things, but one of the things at which they do not usually excel is acting as guides. Jesus said the Pharisees were guides by virtue of their position, but they were blind in the sense of lacking understanding of the true meaning of the law of God.

Jesus then began to explain one very significant way in which the Pharisees had misunderstood, misinterpreted, and twisted the law of God. The Pharisees had devised all sorts of rules and regulations about how to make appropriate vows, and which vows had to be kept and which could be fudged. They gave the people loopholes, ways out of the obligations they entered.

For instance, they taught that if someone swore an oath by the temple, it was not necessary to keep it. However, if he swore by the gold of the temple, that oath had to be kept. In the Pharisees' thinking, the gold of the temple was of greater value than the temple. Jesus turned their thinking on its head with a rhetorical question: "Which is greater, the gold or the temple that sanctifies the gold?" The obvious answer was the temple, the house of God. The temple sanctified the gold, not the other way around.

Jesus gave another example: **"And [you say], 'Whoever swears by the altar, it is nothing; but whoever swears by the gift that is on it, he is obliged to perform it.' Fools and blind! For which is greater, the gift or the altar that sanctifies the gift?"** (vv. 18–19). Again, the Pharisees regarded the sacrifices as greater and more significant than the altar on which the sacrifices were presented to God. So, Jesus pointed out again that the altar sanctified the sacrifice, which clearly made it the more significant object by which to make a vow.

Then Jesus brought His argument to a stunning conclusion: **"Therefore he who swears by the altar, swears by it and by all things on it. He who swears by the temple, swears by it and by Him who dwells in it. And he who swears by heaven, swears by the throne of God and by Him who sits on it"** (vv. 20–22). By swearing by the altar, they were also swearing by the sacrifices. By swearing by the temple, they were also swearing by "Him who dwells in it," namely, God Himself. By swearing by heaven, they were swearing by the throne of God in heaven and by "Him who sits on" the throne, namely, God Himself. Obviously, it was extremely unwise and arrogant of the scribes and the Pharisees to teach that the people could make vows on the altar or on the temple without intending to keep them. The people needed to know the full implications of swearing by those holy objects, but the sad truth is that the Pharisees, the guides of the people, did not know themselves. They were blind.

Theology is involved in the making of vows or the taking of oaths to emphasize promises. Have you ever heard someone say, "I swear by my mother's grave that I will do such and such" or "I swear by my mother's grave that what I'm saying is the truth"? Do you realize how blasphemous that is? If I make such a vow and fail to keep it, what can my mother's grave do about it? My mother's grave is an inanimate object. I can stand in the cemetery all day long and make promises on my mother's grave, but it will never hold me accountable. So, if I break my word, I need not worry about a penalty. But if I take a vow before God, as we do in our marriage vows and in our church membership vows, I am asking the Lord God to bear witness to the promise that I make. I know He can hear my words and can see whether I keep my vow. Not only that, He has the authority and the power to punish me for breaking my vow. That is why, in the Old Testament, vows were made in the name of God. A vow was understood to be an appeal to God. The person taking a vow was saying, "I am exposing myself to God's justice and judgment if I violate the truth in my testimony or in my promise." But the Pharisees trivialized the seriousness of vows with their ridiculous loopholes.

There are yet four more woes to consider, and we will do so in the next two chapters. But we dare not abstract these judgments of Jesus and simply blast the Pharisees for their hypocrisy without feeling the weight of these concerns in our own lives. We need to be very careful that our religion be not showy, counterfeit, and hypocritical, but authentic and from the heart.

106

WOES TO THE PHARISEES, PART 3

Matthew 23:23–28

Woe to you, scribes and Pharisees, hypocrites! For you pay tithe of mint and anise and cummin, and have neglected the weightier matters of the law: justice and mercy and faith. These you ought to have done, without leaving the others undone. Blind guides, who strain out a gnat and swallow a camel! Woe to you, scribes and Pharisees, hypocrites! For you cleanse the outside of the cup and dish, but inside they are full of extortion and self-indulgence. Blind Pharisee, first cleanse the inside of the cup and dish, that the outside of them may be clean also. Woe to you, scribes and Pharisees, hypocrites! For you are like whitewashed tombs which indeed appear beautiful outwardly, but inside are full of dead men's bones and all uncleanness. Even so you also outwardly appear righteous to men, but inside you are full of hypocrisy and lawlessness.

As Jesus continued pronouncing His oracles of doom against the scribes and Pharisees, He chastised them for trivializing religion and for base hypocrisy. These are criticisms we dare not dismiss lightly, inasmuch as they might very well apply to us today.

Matthew tells us that Jesus said: **"Woe to you, scribes and Pharisees, hypocrites! For you pay tithe of mint and anise and cummin, and have neglected the weightier matters of the law: justice and mercy and faith. These you ought to have done, without leaving the others undone"** (v. 23). As I noted in the previous chapter, throughout these pronouncements of woe,

Jesus regularly complimented the scribes and Pharisees for various things they were doing right, and this is another example—they were scrupulous tithers. The last time I saw a study of tithing in the United States, it showed that only about 4 percent of professing Christians tithe. Again, we need to consider Jesus' words about the need for our righteousness to surpass that of the scribes and Pharisees (5:20).

In the Old Testament, God commanded His people to give the tithe—one-tenth of one's produce or one-tenth of the increase in one's livestock (Lev. 27:30–32). Pious Jews religiously gave that 10 percent to the work of God. The scribes and Pharisees, however, were extraordinarily careful to give a tithe on any increase at all. They were so careful that if they had little window gardens of herbs such as mint, anise, and cummin, they would give 10 percent of that. Their attitude would be like someone today finding a dime on the street and saying to himself, "I must remember to add a penny to my next tithe." I do not know anyone who is that careful about tithing. But the scribes and Pharisees were.

However, Jesus went on to say that the religious leaders had "neglected the weightier matters of the law: justice and mercy and faith. These you ought to have done, without leaving the others undone." He did not call them foolish for paying the tithe. His implication is that they did the right thing in tithing so carefully. But there were "weightier matters"—justice, mercy, and faith—to which they had not given scrupulous attention. In other words, the scribes and the Pharisees were majoring in minors—at least, minors by comparison. The proper course for them was to do the minor duties while also striving to fulfill the weightier matters, and we need to do the same. Among these important matters are justice, which involves upholding the law with equity; mercy, which involves compassion, forbearance, and discretion in mitigating punishment; and faith or faithfulness, which involves remaining true to one's calling and responsibilities.

Jesus then uttered one of His most memorable statements: **"Blind guides, who strain out a gnat and swallow a camel!"** (v. 24). For the Jews, gnats were the smallest and camels the largest unclean animals. The scribes and the Pharisees strained wine so that they could avoid consuming gnats. However, in figurative terms, they swallowed camels. Jesus' meaning is clear—in their consuming concern over less weighty matters, they were ignoring major issues. This verse is reminiscent of Jesus' pointed question in the Sermon on the Mount: "And why do you look at the speck in your brother's eye, but do not consider the plank in your own eye?" (7:3).

The Outside and the Inside

In His next two woes, Jesus again called the scribes and Pharisees hypocrites, but He also detailed the nature of their hypocrisy. He asserted that while they were adept at practicing the forms, the externals, the rituals of the Jewish religion, they were bankrupt with respect to the matter that the forms articulated.

If the Old Testament history of God's people teaches us anything, it is that God is not unconcerned with forms. When the people of Israel were enslaved in Egypt, suffering under the tyranny of Pharaoh, they cried out to God, and He heard them and liberated them. But He did not simply crush the power of Pharaoh, free the Israelites, and then tell them to go where they pleased and enjoy their freedom. Rather, He declared that He was redeeming them so that they could come out and worship Him (Ex. 3:12, 18). In time, He gave them detailed instructions on how He was to be worshiped. When we read God's instructions for the building of the tabernacle, we see almost infinitesimal attention to the details of the architecture, the furniture, the clothing, and the rituals, all of which were pointing to spiritual realities of transcendent and eternal importance. Why was there a veil between the Holy Place and the Holy of Holies? Why was it that only the high priest was able to enter into the Holy of Holies to pour the blood on the mercy seat, and then only once a year and only after elaborate rituals of cleansing? Why was there a basin in the outer court for cleansing, an altar for burnt offerings, a table on which bread was displayed, and so on? These were forms, externals, rituals. But these forms, externals, and rituals were designed by God to communicate deeply important truths. Every form is an art form, and every art form communicates something. Each one of these rituals and objects pointed beyond itself, as every decent symbol does, to the reality that would be fulfilled so magnificently in the person and work of Christ, who is the very incarnation of the Old Testament tabernacle.

The scribes and the Pharisees understood that abiding by the forms, paying attention to the externals, and maintaining the rituals was important. But they became so focused on the externals that their religion declined into formalism, externalism, and ritualism. They thought that if they paid attention to the outward things, they were doing what was pleasing to God. But they were completely missing the truth, the reality behind the forms, externals, and rituals.

Soon after the expulsion of Adam and Eve from the garden of Eden, we read of the first act of worship, when Cain and Abel brought sacrifices. The author of Hebrews tells us that Abel brought his offering by faith, but Cain did not (11:4). For this reason, Abel received the praise and acceptance of God, while Cain was rejected for his hypocritical worship (Gen. 4:4–5), for which Cain rose up and murdered his brother (v. 8). Both of them observed the form of worship.

Both of them paid attention to the externals of worship. Both of them followed the rituals of worship. But the worship of Cain was empty because it was *only* formal, *only* external, *only* ritual. The internal dimension, the substance, was missing. The scribes and the Pharisees had the same problem.

This behavior provoked the wrath of Jesus, and He said to them: **"Woe to you, scribes and Pharisees, hypocrites! For you cleanse the outside of the cup and dish, but inside they are full of extortion and self-indulgence. Blind Pharisee, first cleanse the inside of the cup and dish, that the outside of them may be clean also"** (vv. 25–26).

Can you imagine anything more silly, when cleaning your dishes, than carefully wiping the outer surface of a coffee cup but paying no attention to the coffee dregs and such that are on the inner surfaces? The next day, when you pour your coffee, you will pour it into that filthy cup. That night, you carefully polish the outside of the cup once more and pay no attention to what is on the inside. This behavior is foolish because it is backward. It is the inside of the cup that receives the most use and which therefore must be cleansed most carefully.

Jesus was using this picture to unveil the problem in the lives of the scribes and the Pharisees. They were obsessed with getting the externals correct, with doing everything just so. But their inner lives were wastelands. Jesus accused them of "extortion and self-indulgence." I am unsure of exactly what Jesus meant by these terms, but His overall meaning was clear—the scribes and the Pharisees needed to get their hearts right with God. Again, there may have been an implied compliment here—God did not state the forms of His worship with no expectation that they would be followed, and the scribes and the Pharisees were striving to follow them. However, God had said much in the Old Testament about what the heart of a righteous man should look like, and the scribes and the Pharisees had paid only scant attention.

Earlier in Matthew, we saw an incident in which the scribes and Pharisees chided Jesus for letting His disciples eat with unwashed hands. Later, He said: "Not what goes into the mouth defiles a man; but what comes out of the mouth, this defiles a man. . . . Do you not yet understand that whatever enters the mouth goes into the stomach and is eliminated? But those things which proceed out of the mouth come from the heart, and they defile a man. For out of the heart proceed evil thoughts, murders, adulteries, fornications, thefts, false witness, blasphemies. These are the things which defile a man, but to eat with unwashed hands does not defile a man" (15:11, 17–20). Outward practices can never change a man. Only a renewal of his heart will bring real change.

The next woe Jesus pronounced made a similar point: **"Woe to you, scribes and Pharisees, hypocrites! For you are like whitewashed tombs which indeed**

appear beautiful outwardly, but inside are full of dead men's bones and all uncleanness. Even so you also outwardly appear righteous to men, but inside you are full of hypocrisy and lawlessness" (vv. 27–28). The Jews had cemeteries, but many people buried their loved ones in private plots. Of course, God had given the Israelites very strict laws regarding purification and ritual cleanliness, and these laws dictated that the people not come into contact with a burial vault, a gravesite, or a sepulcher. Anyone who did have such contact was ceremonially defiled, and he had to go through several days of cleansing rituals before he could resume worship with the people of God and other activities (Num. 19:11–16). So, those who had private tombs and burial sites regularly applied whitewash to the surfaces of those gravesites so that anyone who happened to be journeying near would see immediately that he was in the vicinity of a grave. No groups in Israel were more judicious in obeying this principle than the scribes and the Pharisees.

But Jesus' point was that the scribes and the Pharisees themselves were like such whitewashed tombs. In their strict observance of Jewish rituals, they appeared to be the very embodiment of men of God. Like whitewashed tombs, they were beautiful on the outside. However, as Jesus noted, even the most beautiful tombs contained dead men's bones and the remains of corpses that would cause defilement if touched. The scribes and the Pharisees were like that. Although they gave the appearance of zeal, faith, and piety, they were spiritually dead inside. As Jesus put it, they were filled with hypocrisy and lawlessness, and John tells us, "Sin is lawlessness" (1 John 3:4b).

The Forms and the Realities

Jesus was not saying to the scribes and Pharisees that we should do away with the forms, the externals, the rituals. However, it is not enough simply to do the outward forms; we must give close attention to the internals, the spiritual realities.

In the Old Testament period, Israel's religion decayed into mere formalism, externalism, and ritualism. People simply went through the motions, making the sacrifices, reciting the prayers, and singing the hymns, with no faith, no passion, no love, and no joy. They gave an external salute to the things of God, but they completely missed the essence of it. So, God thundered to His people through the voice of the prophets, calling them back to love for Him. But never did the prophets say that inasmuch as the people had corrupted the forms, God was going to dispense with them. The forms, externals, and rituals were not the problem; it lay in the hearts of the people.

I constantly hear people saying, "At our church, we have no liturgy." How can a church have no liturgy? Every church has something. The service follows some order; it is not simply chaos. In truth, such churches have just exchanged one form for another, one external for another. We must remember that God Himself designed the worship for His people, and when He did so, He commanded them to worship Him with the forms, the externals, and the rituals He designed. But we do well to remember Cain and Abel. It is not enough to worship by the forms only; we must worship in faith, in spirit, and in truth. We must never neglect the internal realities, beginning with sincere love for God.

107

WOES TO THE PHARISEES, PART 4

Matthew 23:29–39

> Woe to you, scribes and Pharisees, hypocrites! Because you build the tombs of the prophets and adorn the monuments of the righteous, and say, "If we had lived in the days of our fathers, we would not have been partakers with them in the blood of the prophets." Therefore you are witnesses against yourselves that you are sons of those who murdered the prophets. Fill up, then, the measure of your fathers' guilt. Serpents, brood of vipers! How can you escape the condemnation of hell? Therefore, indeed, I send you prophets, wise men, and scribes: some of them you will kill and crucify, and some of them you will scourge in your synagogues and persecute from city to city, that on you may come all the righteous blood shed on the earth, from the blood of righteous Abel to the blood of Zechariah, son of Berechiah, whom you murdered between the temple and the altar. Assuredly, I say to you, all these things will come upon this generation. O Jerusalem, Jerusalem, the one who kills the prophets and stones those who are sent to her! How often I wanted to gather your children together, as a hen gathers her chicks under her wings, but you were not willing! See! Your house is left to you desolate; for I say to you, you shall see Me no more till you say, "Blessed is He who comes in the name of the Lord!

I have said on many occasions that I sometimes wonder whether the man who made the verse and the chapter divisions in the English Bible was perhaps an itinerant preacher who was whiling away the time while headed to the next town on horseback. I ask myself that question because sometimes the verse and chapter divisions seem to make such little sense. We are approaching one of those divisions where I always ask this question—the separation between chapters 23 and 24 of Matthew's Gospel. Chapter 24 contains what is known as the Olivet Discourse, one of the most important discourses recorded by the Gospel writers, one in which Jesus makes some very significant prophecies. It is also one of the most controversial sections of the New Testament, and has been for centuries. But Matthew 23 and 24 fit together like two pieces of a jigsaw puzzle; therefore, I am puzzled as to why a new chapter begins at the start of the discourse.

In any case, as we study the last of Jesus' oracles of woe for the scribes and Pharisees, it is good that we begin to think ahead. Jesus' teaching in the Olivet Discourse about the destruction of the temple, the destruction of Jerusalem, and His coming in glory should not be isolated from the things He taught in the last of His woes to the scribes and Pharisees. These passages are closely related, as we will see in the chapters to come.

Matthew tells us that Jesus concluded His woes by saying: **"Woe to you, scribes and Pharisees, hypocrites! Because you build the tombs of the prophets and adorn the monuments of the righteous, and say, 'If we had lived in the days of our fathers, we would not have been partakers with them in the blood of the prophets'"** (vv. 29–30). In the first century BC, the Jewish people became zealous to honor heroes from the past centuries, especially those who were martyrs for the truth of God. They searched out burial places and built monuments to declare the greatness of the prophets for future ages. Heading this effort to honor the prophets and adorn their resting places were the scribes and Pharisees. Jesus took note of their zeal in this process, saying, "You build the tombs of the prophets and adorn the monuments of the righteous." Again, we see Jesus complimenting something the scribes and Pharisees did.

But, as always, the scribes and the Pharisees were concerned also to draw attention to themselves. Apparently, they made speeches when tombs were erected and dedicated, praising themselves, saying, "If we had lived in the days of our fathers, we would not have been partakers with them in the blood of the prophets." They denied that they would have spurned the prophets and killed them, as their ancestors did. In other words, they claimed that they were more wise, humble, and godly than their forebears. They claimed that if they had been in their ancestors' shoes, they would have received the men sent from God and heeded to their messages.

Jesus added: **"Therefore you are witnesses against yourselves that you are sons of those who murdered the prophets. Fill up, then, the measure of your fathers' guilt. Serpents, brood of vipers! How can you escape the**

condemnation of hell?" (vv. 31–33). Despite their claims, their actions spoke louder. By plotting against Jesus, they were showing that they were exactly like their ancestors who murdered God's prophets. In the end, they were going to prove themselves just as guilty as their forefathers.

Jesus held nothing back, calling the scribes and Pharisees "serpents, brood of vipers." By calling them serpents, Jesus was likening them to Satan, who had snakelike cunning (Gen. 3:1) and a poisonous bite. Another prophet had also called them a brood of vipers—John the Baptist (see 3:7), and Jesus Himself had used the term before (12:34). Given this character, the clear answer to Jesus' rhetorical question—"How can you escape the condemnation of hell?"—is that they cannot. This was indeed an oracle of woe.

A Warning of Judgment

Jesus then prophesied about the next few years and decades to come, saying: **"Therefore, indeed, I send you prophets, wise men, and scribes: some of them you will kill and crucify, and some of them you will scourge in your synagogues and persecute from city to city, that on you may come all the righteous blood shed on the earth, from the blood of righteous Abel to the blood of Zechariah, son of Berechiah, whom you murdered between the temple and the altar"** (vv. 34–35). Jesus promised to send "prophets, wise men, and scribes" during the ministry of the scribes and Pharisees. This seems to be a clear reference to the Apostles and their helpers who would spread the gospel and build the church. Some of them, Jesus said, the scribes and the Pharisees would kill and crucify, while others they would scourge and persecute from city to city. We see most of this prophecy fulfilled in the book of Acts.

Jesus then warned them that "all the righteous blood shed on the earth" would come upon them. He mentioned first "the blood of righteous Abel." The first homicide was really fratricide, when Cain rose up and killed his brother Abel out of jealousy and envy (Gen. 4:8). God came to Cain and said, "Where is Abel your brother?" Cain replied: "I do not know. Am I my brother's keeper?" God then said, "The voice of your brother's blood cries out to Me from the ground" (vv. 9–10). That cry for divine retribution had never been fully satisfied. Neither had the blood of Zechariah. In the Old Testament, the Jews put Genesis at the beginning, and the last of the historical books, 2 Chronicles, at the end. There is recorded the martyrdom of Zechariah, who was killed in the house of God between the porch and the altar (2 Chron. 24:20–22). By mentioning these two martyrdoms, Jesus was encompassing all the ungodly killings in the Hebrew canon. He was saying that from Abel to Zechariah, from A to Z, the history was the same—the Jewish religious authorities killed the people God sent to speak His word, because they did not want to be ruled by Him.

Then came a chilling word: **"Assuredly, I say to you, all these things will come upon this generation"** (v. 36). Divine retribution, Jesus said, was going to fall on that generation. All the evil in all of redemptive history, all of the rejection of God's prophets by God's people, would be brought to judgment in the very near future. The crisis point of all of redemptive history was at hand.

At the beginning of the twentieth century, there was a group of theologians who were known as the "crisis theologians." That moniker was partly derived from the Greek word *krisis*, which is the New Testament word for "judgment." These men understood that the advent of Jesus Christ, that time period when Jesus came into this world, represented the supreme crisis for humanity, because it was a time of judgment. He came to divide and to separate, to bring not peace but a sword (10:34–36). People's eternal destinies would be determined by how they responded to Jesus. That crisis continues to this day. Where we will spend eternity will be determined by how we respond to Him.

As we will see when we examine Matthew 24, there is a great dispute about the specific meaning of the term *generation*, but the overwhelming testimony of Jewish interpretation and language study shows that the word refers to a group of people within a period of about forty years. We talk today about the younger generation or the older generation, and we identify generations as segments of the population that are close in age. So, when Jesus talked about the judgment of God falling on "this generation," He was talking about people who were alive when He spoke. He was not talking about something that would happen two thousand years later. The crisis, the judgment, was coming very soon. John the Baptist had initiated his ministry by declaring to the people of Israel, "Even now the ax is laid to the root of the trees" (3:10), and Jesus was saying virtually the same thing. This was the first foretaste of the prophecies He would give in the Olivet Discourse.

A Lament over Jerusalem

Jesus then directed His words away from the scribes and Pharisees directly to the city of Jerusalem, delivering a lament that is filled with pathos: **"O Jerusalem, Jerusalem, the one who kills the prophets and stones those who are sent to her! How often I wanted to gather your children together, as a hen gathers her chicks under her wings, but you were not willing!"** (v. 37).

When we examined Matthew 7:21–23 (chapter 35), I mentioned that I believe Jesus' statements in that passage are some of the most terrifying words that ever fell from His lips. He announced to those who were listening to His

Sermon on the Mount that at the last day many would come to Him and say, "Lord, Lord, have we not prophesied in Your name, cast out demons in Your name, and done many wonders in Your name?" But Jesus said that He would reply, "I never knew you; depart from Me, you who practice lawlessness." When we looked at that text, I pointed out that Jesus used a literary device that is exceedingly rare in Scripture, the repetition of a personal address. It occurs only about fifteen times: "Abraham! Abraham!" "Jacob! Jacob!" "Moses! Moses!" "Martha, Martha." "Simon, Simon." "My God! My God!" I showed that when we see a name repeated in this fashion, it is a suggestion of intimacy. Jesus was saying that people will come to Him at the last day and address Him as "Lord, Lord," suggesting: "Jesus, I know you, I know You intimately. I have a deep personal relationship with You." Sadly, they will be deceived. They actually will not know Him at all. Rather, He will not know them. That is why His words are so terrifying.

I bring this up because when Jesus gave His lament over Jerusalem, He addressed the city in this intimate fashion: "O Jerusalem, Jerusalem." Of course He was intimate with the city. It was Jerusalem, the Holy City, Zion, the city of the temple, the focal point of divine action in redemptive history. But as Jesus looked at it, His heart was sorrowful, for it had steadfastly rejected the prophets who had brought His Word, stoning them and killing them. Such was His love for the people of Jerusalem that He had longed to gather them as a hen gathers her chicks, but they were unwilling. He desired intimacy with His people, and they spurned His advances.

This rejection would be costly. Jesus said: **"See! Your house is left to you desolate; for I say to you, you shall see Me no more till you say, 'Blessed is He who comes in the name of the Lord!'"** (vv. 38–39). Imagine the scene. Jesus told the people that "your house is left to you desolate." Everyone's heads snapped around. They looked at the massive walls, the temple, and the houses, and all were in fine condition. The temple stood tall. The city over which Jesus wept was filled with the bustling activity of everyday commerce. Nothing looked any different. There was no appearance of desolation. But Jesus said that the desolation was coming soon. This was another preview of the Olivet Discourse, wherein He would foretell the destruction of the temple and the city, and His own coming in judgment.

What did Jesus mean when He said, "You shall see Me no more till you say, 'Blessed is He who comes in the name of the Lord'"? The people of Jerusalem had cried these words as He came into the city only a few days before (21:9). Jesus seems to have been foretelling His future return, when His people truly would be ready to receive Him.

As an aside, I should note that this lament has been used by many to argue against the biblical doctrine of election. The argument goes like this: Jesus wanted to gather the people together as a hen gathers her chicks, they were not willing to come to Him, and He did not force them. However, this verse teaches us nothing about election, only about the natural state of all people, which is unwillingness. Yes, we have wills that are free to do what we want to do. But our wills cannot will obedience to God. We cannot will to come to Christ. Jesus explained this truth when He said, "No one can come to Me unless it has been granted to him by My Father" (John 6:65). The people of Jerusalem refused to come to Jesus because they simply did not want to come. No one comes to Christ unless God in His mercy changes the hardness of that person's heart so as to make him willing and even eager to come. He redeems us from our own corrupt freedom, which is really bondage, because we do what we want to do rather than what God wants us to do.

Christ Himself, knowing all of that, nevertheless wept for those who were unwilling. We should, too.

108

THE DESTRUCTION OF THE TEMPLE

Matthew 24:1–3, 32–35

> Then Jesus went out and departed from the temple, and His disciples came up to show Him the buildings of the temple. And Jesus said to them, "Do you not see all these things? Assuredly, I say to you, not one stone shall be left here upon another, that shall not be thrown down." Now as He sat on the Mount of Olives, the disciples came to Him privately, saying, "Tell us, when will these things be? And what will be the sign of Your coming, and of the end of the age?" . . . [Jesus said:] "Now learn this parable from the fig tree: When its branch has already become tender and puts forth leaves, you know that summer is near. So you also, when you see all these things, know that it is near—at the doors! Assuredly, I say to you, this generation will by no means pass away till all these things take place. Heaven and earth will pass away, but My words will by no means pass away."

Imagine that you are part of my congregation at Saint Andrew's Chapel in Sanford, Florida. One Sunday morning, when I step into the pulpit to deliver my sermon, you hear me give the following statement: "Last night I received a special revelation from God. I was given a vision in which God told me things that will shortly come to pass. Sometime within the next twelve months, the United States of America will fall as a nation. The Capitol Building and the White House will be destroyed. The union of the fifty states will be dissolved. America as an independent nation will be no more. I do not know the exact date. I cannot tell you the day, the week, or even the month. But I know that within the next twelve months, all these things will come to pass."

I suggest this hypothetical scenario as a way to help you put yourself in the place of Jesus' disciples, who heard Him speak the words in the texts of Matthew 24 that we are considering in this chapter, as well as the whole sum and substance of the Olivet Discourse, which is found in all three of the Synoptic Gospels. I cannot think of any prophecy, in either the Old or New Testaments, more astonishing than the one our Lord Jesus gave on the Mount of Olives regarding the temple and Jerusalem. He brought His disciples together and said of the temple, "Not one stone shall be left here upon another," and He told them that Jerusalem itself would be destroyed and "trampled by Gentiles until the times of the Gentiles are fulfilled" (Luke 21:24b). Furthermore, He said the people of Israel would be dispersed throughout the world, "led away captive into all nations" (v. 24a).

Hearing this, the disciples must have been as startled as you would be were I to tell you that the United States is doomed. No Jew in Jesus' time could imagine that the temple would be destroyed. Of course, an earlier temple, Solomon's temple, had been destroyed by the Babylonians, but it was rebuilt following the Babylonian exile toward the end of the sixth century BC. However, that temple never had the same degree of splendor as Solomon's temple, and by the end of the first century BC, it was in disrepair. So, King Herod the Great launched a rebuilding program that lasted some forty-six years. Herod is perhaps most famous for his architectural genius, which included the refurbishing, strengthening, and expansion of the temple. As a result of his efforts, if there was any building on the face of the earth that was deemed impregnable in the first century, it was the temple in Jerusalem. No one could conceive that such a magnificent building could be demolished to such an extent that not one stone of it would be left upon another.

I would venture to say no prophecy that Jesus made during His ministry so thoroughly proves His identity and so completely validates the inspiration of Scripture by the Holy Spirit as this one. We know from history that the things He foretold came to pass in precise detail. We have eyewitness accounts from the Jewish historian Josephus of the siege of Jerusalem by the Romans and its subsequent destruction, including the demolition of the temple itself. This text ought to shut the mouths of the obstreperous and silence the tongues of the skeptics and the cynics about Jesus and the Bible.

Ironically, however, I know of no portion of the New Testament that is used more often as a foil to deny the accuracy of Jesus' prophetic statements and to attack the credibility of sacred Scripture than the Olivet Discourse. For instance,

Bertrand Russell wrote an essay titled "Why I Am Not a Christian" in which he cited the Olivet Discourse as one of the major reasons he was convinced that Christ was not the Son of God and the Bible is not the Word of God. Likewise, when I was in seminary, the higher critical scholars on the faculty often made the same argument against Jesus' identity and the Bible's inspiration, and they, too, cited the Olivet Discourse.

If the prophecy's fulfillment was so dramatic and clear, why all the skepticism? The reason is in verse 34, which is why I want to look at this verse as we begin to consider the Olivet Discourse.

Signs for the Generation

Matthew tells us, **Then Jesus went out and departed from the temple, and His disciples came up to show Him the buildings of the temple** (v. 1). As Jesus was going out of the temple one day during the week leading up to His crucifixion, perhaps headed back out to Bethany for the evening, His disciples remarked to Him about the large, beautiful buildings of the temple complex that Herod had built. But Jesus gave them a surprising response: **And Jesus said to them, "Do you not see all these things? Assuredly, I say to you, not one stone shall be left here upon another, that shall not be thrown down"** (v. 2). Here is the specific prophecy about the temple; Jesus said it would be totally destroyed, every stone cast down, with no ruins left standing.

As we might well expect, this remark piqued the disciples' curiosity. Matthew writes: **Now as He sat on the Mount of Olives, the disciples came to Him privately, saying, "Tell us, when will these things be? And what will be the sign of Your coming, and of the end of the age?"** (v. 3). In a private moment, as Jesus was sitting on the Mount of Olives overlooking Jerusalem, the disciples asked Him to tell them more about what lay ahead. Specifically, they asked Him when the destruction of the temple would happen, and what specific signs would herald His coming and the end of the age. Jesus responded with a long discussion of the signs of the times, then with descriptions of a time of tribulation and finally the coming of the Son of Man.

This discourse has served as fodder for dispensational speculations such as the book *The Late Great Planet Earth* and the *Left Behind* series of books. Certain biblical teachers are very interested in the things Jesus said here and are constantly calling attention to events in Israel and the world that seem to line up with Jesus' prophecy. They want to believe that we are drawing near to the consummation of the kingdom, the time of Jesus' glorious return.

However, the critics zero in on a small section of the discourse, where, Matthew tells us, Jesus said: **"Now learn this parable from the fig tree: When its branch**

has already become tender and puts forth leaves, you know that summer is near. So you also, when you see all these things, know that it is near—at the doors! Assuredly, I say to you, this generation will by no means pass away till all these things take place. Heaven and earth will pass away, but My words will by no means pass away" (vv. 32–35). Here, Jesus told His disciples that the things He had mentioned to that point in the discourse (vv. 4–31) should be signs for them that His coming was imminent. Furthermore, He gave them a promise: "This generation will by no means pass away till all these things take place."

For the Jews, a generation was about forty years. As we saw in the previous chapter, when Jesus concluded His oracles of woe for the scribes and Pharisees, He said justice for all the innocent blood shed by the Jewish religious leaders would come upon "this generation" (23:36). Those leaders of the Jews who were conspiring together to destroy Jesus would experience this judgment. Likewise, in answer to the disciples' question, "When will these things be?" Jesus said it all would happen before the generation then living had passed away. He was saying that everything He was prophesying—the destruction of the temple, the destruction of Jerusalem, and His coming—would take place within forty years.

Do you feel the weight of the problem? The critics focus in on this statement and say: "Jesus said He would come back within forty years. He said the end of the world would happen within a generation. He said the consummation of His kingdom would be complete in just a few decades." They also note that He said similar things elsewhere. As we saw earlier in the Gospel of Matthew, He said, "Assuredly, I say to you, you will not have gone through the cities of Israel before the Son of Man comes" (Matt. 10:23). Likewise, He said, "Assuredly, I say to you, there are some standing here who shall not taste death till they see the Son of Man coming in His kingdom" (16:28). On the basis of these statements, the critics say that Jesus' own prophecies undermine His credibility, because He not only did not come back within one generation, He *still* has not come.

Proposed Solutions

Conservative scholars have said that in the latter prophecy (16:28), Jesus was referring to the coming of the kingdom when the power of the Holy Spirit was poured out on the disciples at the day of Pentecost. I cannot agree with this interpretation. It would have made no sense for Jesus to say that *some* of the disciples would live to see an event that was only a few weeks in the future. History shows that only one of them died before Pentecost, namely, Judas.

Others try to deal with the difficulty presented by these statements by saying Jesus must not have meant a literal generation because later in the discourse He said that no one knew the time of His coming, not even He Himself (v. 36). However, the fact that Jesus did not know the precise day, week, or month of His coming does not prove that He did not know that it would occur within a generation. He had a margin of forty years for His prophecy to be fulfilled.

Still others say that Jesus was completely right in His prophecy and that everything He foretold came to pass in the first century, including His coming. Sometimes my name is linked with this group of scholars, but I do not agree with this interpretation. I believe in a future consummation of the kingdom of God. According to yet another view, the word *generation* refers not to a time frame but to a type of person, a wicked, doubting person such as the scribes and Pharisees. Thus, Jesus was simply saying that wicked, doubting people would still be in the world when He returned. Some believe that when Jesus referred to "all these things," He was speaking about the destruction of the temple and the city, not His return in judgment. Finally, others say that this prophecy had both a preliminary fulfillment and an ultimate fulfillment, as is typical of many prophecies in the Bible. Thus, the destruction of Jerusalem has happened but Jesus' return has not. This idea has merit, but if the Bible is the Word of God and these are Jesus' teachings, there must be a sense in which all of these things came to pass in the forty years after Jesus gave this prophecy.

As we explore this discourse in the next few chapters, I will be writing with the conviction that Jesus was speaking here about a judgment coming on the Jewish nation at the end of the Jewish age, which ended with the destruction of Jerusalem and the dispersion of the Jews, inaugurating what the New Testament calls the time of the Gentiles, which is still going on. I want to interpret the Olivet Discourse in a manner that is consistent with the way Jesus' disciples heard it. They asked him a simple question: "When will these things be?" In reply, He told them that certain things would take place within the next generation.

109

THE SIGNS OF THE END

Matthew 24:3–14

> Now as He sat on the Mount of Olives, the disciples came to Him privately, saying, "Tell us, when will these things be? And what will be the sign of Your coming, and of the end of the age?" And Jesus answered and said to them: "Take heed that no one deceives you. For many will come in My name, saying, 'I am the Christ,' and will deceive many. And you will hear of wars and rumors of wars. See that you are not troubled; for all these things must come to pass, but the end is not yet. For nation will rise against nation, and kingdom against kingdom. And there will be famines, pestilences, and earthquakes in various places. All these are the beginning of sorrows. Then they will deliver you up to tribulation and kill you, and you will be hated by all nations for My name's sake. And then many will be offended, will betray one another, and will hate one another. Then many false prophets will rise up and deceive many. And because lawlessness will abound, the love of many will grow cold. But he who endures to the end shall be saved. And this gospel of the kingdom will be preached in all the world as a witness to all the nations, and then the end will come.

In the previous chapter, as we began considering this astonishing teaching of Jesus known as the Olivet Discourse, I noted that this chapter presents great difficulties for biblical scholars. There is no doubt that the destruction of the temple and Jerusalem took place exactly as Jesus foretold and within the time frame of that generation, but other things He prophesied, such as His coming, do not appear to have happened in that time frame. Did all these things take place within the time Jesus specified? Or was Jesus wrong? How do we unravel these difficulties?

As we seek to answer these questions, we must tread very carefully indeed. When I suggest possible ways to understand this text, I am not standing on Mount Olympus giving a decree that has final authority. I have wrestled with this passage for many years, and some of the views I have taken have had to give way to correction and change along the way. So, I am not yet at the place where I am certain I can dogmatically declare the proper interpretation of this portion of sacred Scripture. Please struggle along with me as we seek to discern the mind of our God on these matters.

Jesus had told the disciples that the temple, which seemed so massive and impregnable, was going to be totally destroyed, to the point not even one stone would be resting upon another (v. 2). That prompted them to come to Him for a fuller explanation: **Now as He sat on the Mount of Olives, the disciples came to Him privately, saying, "Tell us, when will these things be? And what will be the sign of Your coming, and of the end of the age?"** (v. 3).

Before I begin to consider Jesus' answer, I want to think through their questions. Most of what they asked is clear, but what did they mean by "the end of the age"? What age did they have in mind? When people read this text today, they customarily think that "the end of the age" means the conclusion of history at the time of Jesus' ultimate triumphant return, when He will consummate His kingdom. But is there any other possible interpretation?

Many scholars have noted that the New Testament makes a distinction between the age or time of the Jews and the age or time of the Gentiles. One of the places where we find such a distinction is in Luke's version of the Olivet Discourse. We read there:

> But when you see Jerusalem surrounded by armies, then know that its desolation is near. Then let those who are in Judea flee to the mountains, let those who are in the midst of her depart, and let not those who are in the country enter her. For these are the days of vengeance, that all things which are written may be fulfilled. But woe to those who are pregnant and to those who are nursing babies in those days! For there will be great distress in the land and wrath upon this people. And they will fall by the edge of the sword, and be led away captive into all nations. And Jerusalem will be trampled by Gentiles until the times of the Gentiles are fulfilled. (Luke 21:20–24)

Jesus urged His disciples to watch out for armies gathering around Jerusalem.

His instructions as to what they should do in that instance were completely contrary to normal procedures in cases of invasion. Usually, when a nation was invaded, the people would flee from the villages to the city with the biggest walls. The city was the place of refuge, for city walls were built specifically to thwart invaders. The walls of Jerusalem at that time were 150 feet high. Even the Roman army, with all of its implements of war and military ingenuity, had a Herculean task to breach the walls of Jerusalem in AD 70, just as other invaders had in previous centuries. The siege of the city in AD 70 lasted six months. So, the city was usually the place to go when a foreign power invaded. But Jesus told His disciples not to go there. Instead, He told them to flee to the mountains. Why? Because Jerusalem was not going to be a place of safety in AD 70. It was going to be destroyed. The Jewish historian Josephus testifies that when Jerusalem fell and was destroyed by the Romans, more than a million Jews were killed, but very few Christians died. They had followed the advice of Jesus and fled to the mountains rather than the city.

According to Luke's account, Jesus spoke of the destruction of Jerusalem as "the days of vengeance." It was a time in which God poured out His wrath upon His people. We saw earlier that Jesus lamented over Jerusalem and said, "Your house is left to you desolate" (23:38). God punished His people for rejecting His Son. So, the destruction of Jerusalem was the end of an old economy.

Finally, notice that Jesus said, "Jerusalem will be trampled by Gentiles until the times of the Gentiles are fulfilled." He made a distinction between the times of the Gentiles and, by implication, the times of the Jews. Similarly, in the book of Romans, Paul speaks of "the fullness of the Gentiles" (11:25), which seems to indicate an end to the times of the Gentiles.

In June 1967, I was riveted by television news coverage of the Six-Day War as the Israelis were fighting for the city of Jerusalem. When they got to the Temple Mount, even though there was a firefight in progress, the Israeli soldiers threw down their rifles and ran to the Wailing Wall, the last surviving portion of the wall that surrounded the temple courtyard in old Jerusalem, and there they began to pray. As you can imagine, I was very moved as I watched these events. I could not believe what I was seeing, and I could not help wondering whether the "times of the Gentiles" were being "fulfilled" right before my eyes. You see, Jesus' word *until* points to a terminal point. He was saying that Jerusalem would not be left desolate forever. There would be an end to Gentile control of the city. So, biblical scholars in 1967 were reading the Bible in one hand and the newspaper in the other, wondering if that terminal point had arrived. Of course, this question is still being debated.

I mention all of this because I believe it is probable that when Jesus told His disciples what to expect at "the end of the age," He did not have the end of the world in mind. I believe He was thinking about the end of the Jewish age, which end came when Jerusalem fell. That was the beginning of the times of the Gentiles.

The Beginning of Sorrows

Matthew tells us that when the disciples asked these very serious questions, **Jesus answered and said to them: "Take heed that no one deceives you"** (v. 4). He first warned them to be careful that they not be fooled into thinking the end had come when it had not. Then He moved on to list various events that would happen before the end: **"For many will come in My name, saying, 'I am the Christ,' and will deceive many. And you will hear of wars and rumors of wars. See that you are not troubled; for all these things must come to pass, but the end is not yet. For nation will rise against nation, and kingdom against kingdom. And there will be famines, pestilences, and earthquakes in various places. All these are the beginning of sorrows"** (vv. 5–8).

Again, when most people today read this portion of Matthew, they jump to the conclusion that Jesus was describing things that will happen right before the final consummation of His kingdom, so they keep up with the news to see whether these things seem to be happening in the world. However, I think that if we look carefully at this passage, we can see that Jesus was talking about events that had to transpire before the destruction of Jerusalem. In these verses, Jesus told the disciples to watch for five specific signs:

- People falsely claiming to be the Christ
- Wars and rumors of wars
- Famines
- Pestilences
- Earthquakes

As I read this list, I ask myself how these things could be considered signs of anything unusual. In my opinion, these events could serve as signs only if they happened in a significant way and in a significant time frame. Let me explain what I mean.

In our world today, news travels at incredible speed. If there is an earthquake, even if it is on the far side of the globe, we hear about it in minutes. Likewise, famines and pestilences in even remote places are reported in the news. Major wars and minor skirmishes are covered. And because so much information is transmitted, we even hear about people making claims to be Jesus returned in the flesh. So, we now know that these things are commonplace in this large world God made. When are there *not* people claiming to be Jesus? When are there *not* wars and rumors of wars? When are there *not* famines, pestilences, and earthquakes in the world? News travels so quickly in our world, these events, as important as they are in and of themselves, seem insignificant.

But Jesus was talking to a small group of people living in a land the size of the state of Maryland. To say to those people in that time that they could expect a plague of false christs, an unusual number of wars and rumors of wars, and numerous famines, pestilences, and earthquakes was significant. In their time, with their limited ability to get news from afar, it would be very significant to observe all these happenings.

Notice, however, that Jesus said, "All these are the beginning of sorrows." The word translated as "sorrows" here literally means "birth pains." These were not signs that the end was imminent; these were merely the discomforts of the first "contractions" leading to the birth. There was more to come.

Signs before the End

Jesus continued, giving the disciples more personal signs to watch for: **"Then they will deliver you up to tribulation and kill you, and you will be hated by all nations for My name's sake"** (v. 9). The book of Acts shows that the Apostles endured great persecutions from the Jewish religious leaders and later from the Romans. They were indeed seemingly hated nearly everywhere they went, and tradition tells us that all but one of the Twelve (minus Judas, of course) died as martyrs.

Jesus then said: **"And then many will be offended, will betray one another, and will hate one another. Then many false prophets will rise up and deceive many. And because lawlessness will abound, the love of many will grow cold"** (vv. 10–12). These signs seem to concern relationships within the church. Jesus said many "will be offended" (or "will fall away"), and there would be betrayals among the brethren. Love would grow cold and hate would take its place. There would be deception as false prophets rose up. There would even be lawlessness in abundance. Jesus was sketching out a breakdown of body life. However, He said, **"He who endures to the end shall be saved"** (v. 13). Jesus was not saying that endurance would earn salvation, but that endurance would be the marker of true faith. "The end" here can mean either the end of the persecution or the end of life.

Finally, Jesus told His disciples, **"And this gospel of the kingdom will be preached in all the world as a witness to all the nations, and then the end will come"** (v. 14). Here is another verse that seems to indicate a still-to-come understanding of "the end." Surely, we think, the gospel has not yet been preached to all the nations—after all, we are still sending out missionaries—so "the end" must be in the future still. But "nations" here does not mean *countries*; rather, it means *peoples* or *races*.

This portion of Jesus' prophecy was fulfilled in the first century, as Paul testifies: "the word of the truth of the gospel . . . has come to you, as it has also in all the world" (Col. 1:5b–6). Remember, scholars believe Colossians was written around AD 62, eight years before Jerusalem was destroyed. Paul did not mean that the gospel had been preached in every corner of the globe. He was referring to the known world of that time, the lands around the Mediterranean Sea. The gospel was indeed preached in all that world in the first century, even before the fall of Jerusalem.

So, among these preliminary signs, these "beginnings of sorrows," there does not appear to be anything that must be understood as happening after AD 70 or much later in redemptive history. All the signs of which Jesus speaks here could have happened before the destruction of Jerusalem. To this point in the Olivet Discourse, we have not encountered any reason to doubt that "the end" refers to the destruction of the temple.

However, Jesus had much more about which to tell His disciples, including a time of tribulation and His own "coming." We will look at these topics in coming chapters.

110

THE GREAT TRIBULATION

Matthew 24:15–28

"Therefore when you see the 'abomination of desolation,' spoken of by Daniel the prophet, standing in the holy place" (whoever reads, let him understand), "then let those who are in Judea flee to the mountains. Let him who is on the housetop not go down to take anything out of his house. And let him who is in the field not go back to get his clothes. But woe to those who are pregnant and to those who are nursing babies in those days! And pray that your flight may not be in winter or on the Sabbath. For then there will be great tribulation, such as has not been since the beginning of the world until this time, no, nor ever shall be. And unless those days were shortened, no flesh would be saved; but for the elect's sake those days will be shortened. Then if anyone says to you, 'Look, here is the Christ!' or 'There!' do not believe it. For false christs and false prophets will rise and show great signs and wonders to deceive, if possible, even the elect. See, I have told you beforehand. Therefore if they say to you, 'Look, He is in the desert!' do not go out; or 'Look, He is in the inner rooms!' do not believe it. For as the lightning comes from the east and flashes to the west, so also will the coming of the Son of Man be. For wherever the carcass is, there the eagles will be gathered together."

We continue to make our way through the challenging Olivet Discourse, wherein Jesus prophesied about the destruction of Jerusalem and the temple, and about the coming of the Son of Man. As we have noted, Jesus indicated that all the things He foretold in this discourse would happen before "this generation" passed away (Matt. 24:34). This statement has been problematic for many Bible scholars, and some have argued that this passage shows that Jesus was not a true prophet because He did not return in that time frame as He promised. We have not yet addressed that specific question, but as we began working through the specific events that Jesus prophesied in the previous chapter, we saw that all the preliminary events that He called "the "beginning of sorrows" (vv. 4–14) could have happened in the lifetimes of the disciples and prior to AD 70, the year Jerusalem fell and the temple was destroyed.

As we continue forward, we come to a section of the discourse that many English Bibles identify as His teaching on "The Great Tribulation." Many who hold to dispensational theology expect the world to pass through a time of severe tribulation just before the conclusion of history. So, once again, our task in this section of the Olivet Discourse is to seek to discern whether Jesus was speaking of events that happened just before AD 70 or whether these things are still to come.

Matthew tells us that Jesus said, **"Therefore when you see the 'abomination of desolation,' spoken of by Daniel the prophet, standing in the holy place" (whoever reads, let him understand)** (v. 15). Some believe this and other passages point to the future appearance of the Antichrist (see 2 Thess. 2:4; Rev. 13:14). However, it need not be so radically separated from the context of the Olivet Discourse to this point. As I noted, the previous section of Jesus' discourse concerned preliminary events that would herald the destruction of Jerusalem. Here, Jesus spoke of an even more critical sign to come, one that would show the disciples that the full crisis was upon them.

Jesus was referring to a messianic prophecy of the prophet Daniel. This prophecy speaks of the destruction of the temple and Jerusalem. The final two verses say:

> And after the sixty-two weeks Messiah shall be cut off, but not for Himself; and the people of the prince who is to come shall destroy the city and the sanctuary. The end of it shall be with a flood, and till the end of the war desolations are determined. Then he shall confirm a covenant with many for one week; but in the middle of the week He shall bring an end to sacrifice and offering. And on the wing of abominations shall be one who makes desolate, even until the consummation, which is determined, is poured out on the desolate. (9:26–27)

Scholars have many opinions about what exactly the abomination of desolation is, but many agree that Daniel was prophesying some kind of pagan desecration of the temple. A later verse in Daniel supports this conclusion: "And forces shall be mustered by him, and they shall defile the sanctuary fortress; then they shall take away the daily sacrifices, and place there the abomination of desolation" (11:31).

Jewish scholars in the ancient world believed that there was at least a preliminary fulfillment of this prophecy in the year 168 BC, when Antiochus Epiphanes, ruler of the Seleucid Empire, conquered Jerusalem and erected a pagan altar in the temple. Instead of sacrificing bulls, goats, or lambs, he added insult to injury by sacrificing a pig in the Holy Place. This was such a foul desecration of the Holy Place that it provoked one of the most important revolutions of the Jews against foreign invaders. The Jewish people saw the temple as holy and sacred, not because of the materials that were used to build it, but because it was the place where the Holy One of Israel dwelt and met with them. No site in the world was more sacred than the temple. Thus, to defile it with pagan sacrifices was the greatest insult the Seleucids could inflict on Israel.

Clearly, however, Jesus was speaking of something that had not yet happened, and it would be the supreme sign indicating the imminent fulfillment of His prophecy. New Testament scholars have put forward a number of ideas about this. Some point to the year AD 40, when the Roman Emperor Gaius commanded that a statue of himself be built and placed inside the temple. This was a huge provocation to the people of Israel, but by the goodness of God, Gaius died before that profanation took place.

Another possible fulfillment of this prophecy occurred in AD 69. In 66, the Jews rebelled against the Romans, prompting a Roman military response led by General Vespasian and his son Titus. They began invading the country from the north in 67, working toward Jerusalem. In late 68, Emperor Nero committed suicide, and the empire was embroiled in civil war to decide the succession. Vespasian became involved in the political infighting and was distracted from the Judean campaign; he eventually prevailed and became emperor in 69. During that lull in the fighting in Judea, the Jewish Zealots made their way by force into the temple. They expelled the priests and turned the temple into a military camp, where they committed all kinds of atrocities. The Jewish historian Josephus is extremely passionate in his denunciation of the horrible desecration the Zealots committed in the sacred place. It is possible that Jesus had this event in mind.

Still another possible fulfillment involved the conquest of Jerusalem under the leadership of Titus. When the Roman legions marched, they carried banners with eagle figurines on the ends of the poles. In AD 70, when the Romans finally conquered Jerusalem, they entered the temple with these banners. The Jews saw the figurines as idols, so they viewed this incursion as another desecration.

In the end, we cannot be sure precisely what event Jesus was pointing toward, but it seems likely it was associated with the destruction of the temple in 70. We need not see this passage as referring to events in the distant future.

The Need for Urgent Flight

Jesus had firm advice for His disciples when they saw the abomination of desolation: **"Let those who are in Judea flee to the mountains. Let him who is on the housetop not go down to take anything out of his house. And let him who is in the field not go back to get his clothes"** (vv. 16–18). We saw in the previous chapter that the normal course of action when a nation was invaded in the ancient world was for the people to flee to the cities. But Jesus advised just the opposite. If we understand this passage as referring to AD 70, it is easy to see why Jesus advised this course of action—the chief city of Judea, Jerusalem, would be the focus of attack and would not stand.

Furthermore, when the abomination of desolation appeared, flight would be urgent. Jesus said people on the roofs of their houses should not take time to collect any belongings from within. The Jews' homes had flat roofs that they used as patios, as places to relax and socialize in the cool of the day. He was saying: "If you're relaxing some night on your rooftop and you see or hear about this sign coming to pass, get out of town right away! Don't pack any bags. Just go." Likewise, He said that people in the fields should not go home to get a change of clothes. Even if they were dirty because of their agricultural work, they needed to run for it. The appearance of the abomination of desolation would demand instant, urgent flight.

Jesus then added two curious caveats. First He said, **"But woe to those who are pregnant and to those who are nursing babies in those days!"** (v. 19). Expecting mothers and nursing mothers would not be able to go very quickly; perhaps many would be caught in the upheaval. Second He advised, **"And pray that your flight may not be in winter or on the Sabbath"** (v. 20). Again, Jesus seems to have been thinking about hindrances to speedy travel. It is more difficult to move quickly in cold, wintry conditions. Likewise, Jews were permitted to travel only short distances on the Sabbath. Here, then, was a way the disciples could prepare themselves for this disaster—they could pray for ideal circumstances in which to make their escape. With all these words Jesus impressed on the disciples the severity of the coming catastrophe and the need to flee.

He also told them: **"For then there will be great tribulation, such as has not been since the beginning of the world until this time, no, nor ever shall be. And unless those days were shortened, no flesh would be saved; but for the elect's sake those days will be shortened"** (vv. 21–22). History tells us that the siege of Jerusalem created horrible conditions inside the city. Titus allowed

Jewish pilgrims to enter the city for the Passover, but then refused to let them leave. As a result, the city was vastly overcrowded. Supplies soon ran low and many starved. Then, of course, there was a terrible slaughter when the Romans finally breached the walls, according to Josephus. The capture and sack of Jerusalem did indeed bring terrible tribulation upon those in the city.

Yet Josephus reports various events that shortened the length of the siege, probably allowing for more survivors than reasonably could have been expected. His testimony supports Jesus' statement that those days of tribulation had been shortened by God for the sake of His elect.

I believe that those who want to see these words of Jesus as a prophecy of a great tribulation that is still yet to come must grant that there was at least an initial fulfillment in AD 70. Jesus clearly was warning His contemporaries about a disaster that was just around the corner.

No Need to Believe Reports

Jesus continued: **"Then if anyone says to you, 'Look, here is the Christ!' or 'There!' do not believe it. For false christs and false prophets will rise and show great signs and wonders to deceive, if possible, even the elect. See, I have told you beforehand. Therefore if they say to you, 'Look, He is in the desert!' do not go out; or 'Look, He is in the inner rooms!' do not believe it"** (vv. 23–26). Here Jesus returned to the problem of false christs and false prophets, which He had mentioned earlier (v. 5). These men, He said, would display great signs and wonders, so great that the elect might even be taken in were they not guarded by the power of God. But Jesus sternly warned His disciples not to give any credence to claims that He had returned.

The idea is prevalent in the church today that Satan is so powerful he can do miracles as if he were God Himself. I am in a minority on this point, but I do not believe that Satan ever has had or ever will have the ability to perform a bona-fide miracle. His lying signs and wonders are not authentic signs and wonders in the service of lies; rather, they are false signs and wonders, tricks designed to deceive. I tend to become strident about this because the New Testament books appeal to the miracles of Jesus and the miracles of the Apostles as proof that they were true agents of revelation. In other words, the credential God gave to His agents of revelation was the power to work miracles. But if Satan can do miracles, the New Testament's appeal to miracles to authenticate the Apostles is invalid. Someone doing a miracle could be either a representative of God or a representative of Satan.

Recall the classic contest between Moses and the magicians of Pharaoh's court (Ex. 7:8–13). At first glance, it seemed that the magicians were able to match the supernatural power God had given to Moses. When Aaron threw his staff on the floor, it turned into a snake. But Pharaoh's magicians threw their staffs on the floor, and they also turned into snakes. However, Aaron's snake swallowed all of the magicians' snakes. Thus, the magicians' "miracles" were revealed as "enchantments" (v. 11), that is, tricks. But while their tricks ran out, Aaron's miracle did not, because it was empowered by God.

The disciples could safely ignore reports of Jesus' return, He told them, because **"as the lightning comes from the east and flashes to the west, so also will the coming of the Son of Man be"** (v. 27). His coming would be visible and obvious to all, like a streak of lightning across the sky. It would not be secretive, a subject for rumors.

Finally He said, **"For wherever the carcass is, there the eagles will be gathered together"** (v. 28). One of the reasons why prophecy is so difficult to interpret is the use of symbolic imagery. The safest way to interpret images that are used in apocalyptic literature is to explore how those images are used throughout the whole Bible. Unfortunately, that does not always solve the problem, and that is the case here.

I am not sure exactly what Jesus meant by these words. However, some of the finest New Testament scholars understand this verse as a reference to the Jews and the Romans. A carcass, of course, is the body of a dead animal. In the context of Jesus' prophecy, that which was dying was Israel. The nation was being slaughtered by the punitive hand of God, and His instrument of vengeance was the Roman army. The principle symbol of the Roman forces was the eagle, a model of which was mounted on every standard of every legion. Perhaps, some scholars suggest, Jesus was saying that immediately before the climactic moment of judgment, the disciples would see the eagles gathering around the carcass, as the legions of Rome surrounded Jerusalem.

We have now spent two chapters working our way methodically through Jesus' prophecy of a series of terrible events, all of which seem to be connected to the fall of Jerusalem. But in the next section of the Olivet Discourse, Jesus spoke of His appearance, describing it in highly figurative language involving astronomical perturbations. It is easy to see why many are convinced this is a glimpse of His final return to bring down the curtain on history. However, we need to carefully consider His words in the context of the rest of the discourse, and we will take up that task in the next chapter.

111

THE COMING OF THE SON OF MAN

Matthew 24:29–31

Immediately after the tribulation of those days the sun will be darkened, and the moon will not give its light; the stars will fall from heaven, and the powers of the heavens will be shaken. Then the sign of the Son of Man will appear in heaven, and then all the tribes of the earth will mourn, and they will see the Son of Man coming on the clouds of heaven with power and great glory. And He will send His angels with a great sound of a trumpet, and they will gather together His elect from the four winds, from one end of heaven to the other.

When Plato established his Academy on the outskirts of Athens, he was driven by a single passion. He wanted, in his words, to "save the phenomena." What did he mean? He was looking for a foundation of truth that would make it possible for science to make sense of all of the phenomena that we observe in the world. In other words, he was looking for an ultimate theory, a paradigm that would give clarity to all of the mysteries and puzzles of life.

It has been said that the entire history of philosophy is nothing more than a footnote to the theories of Plato and Aristotle, the great thinkers of ancient Greece. We see the truth of that statement in the fact that philosophers and scientists have followed Plato's quest for centuries, seeking ways to explain everything.

Paradigms are put forward, but then anomalies are discovered that do not fit, so new systems of explanation are sought. For instance, Stephen Hawking, the British physicist, recently announced that we do not need God to explain the creation. His way of saving the phenomenon was to affirm spontaneous generation, a process by which the universe created itself. Of course, in order for something to create itself, it would have to be before it was. Nothing violates the law of contradiction more radically than such a concept. Hawking's paradigm will not last long.

What does all this have to do with the Olivet Discourse? In my comments on this chapter, I am trying to save the phenomenon. I began our study of this section of Matthew by saying that no portion of the New Testament more clearly demonstrates the supernatural knowledge of Jesus and the inspiration of the New Testament, because it gives us uncannily accurate descriptions of the destruction of Jerusalem and the temple. However, no portion of the New Testament has been used more frequently by skeptics to deny the prophetic accuracy of Christ and the authority and trustworthiness of the New Testament. The reason, as we have seen, centers on the time frame Jesus mentioned. He told His disciples that the temple would be destroyed, that there would be a time of upheaval and tribulation, and that the Son of Man would come on the clouds of heaven, and He said "this generation will by no means pass away till all these things take place" (v. 34). My task is to find a paradigm that explains all these seemingly contradictory "phenomena."

We have seen that the temple was destroyed in AD 70, and that there were great tribulations just before it happened. But what about the coming of the Son of Man, Jesus Himself? The critics charge that Jesus was not a prophet because He did not come back within that generation.

It must be acknowledged that the description of the coming of the Son of Man in this passage bears similarities to another New Testament passage. Paul writes: "For the Lord Himself will descend from heaven with a shout, with the voice of an archangel, and with the trumpet of God. And the dead in Christ will rise first. Then we who are alive and remain shall be caught up together with them in the clouds to meet the Lord in the air. And thus we shall always be with the Lord" (1 Thess. 4:16–17). It is widely accepted that this passage is speaking of Jesus' climactic return. Yet we need not assume that the coming Jesus mentioned in the Olivet Discourse and the descent of the Lord about which Paul speaks are the same event. We must treat the coming in Matthew 24 in its context and in light of all of Scripture.

We have now come to the portion of Matthew 24 in which Jesus foretold this coming of the Son of Man. I believe this is the most difficult section of the Olivet Discourse. We need to look at it carefully.

Figurative Cosmic Phenomena

Matthew tells us that Jesus said: **"Immediately after the tribulation of those days the sun will be darkened, and the moon will not give its light; the stars will fall from heaven, and the powers of the heavens will be shaken. Then the sign of the Son of Man will appear in heaven, and then all the tribes of the earth will mourn, and they will see the Son of Man coming on the clouds of heaven with power and great glory"** (vv. 29–30). Notice the first word Jesus used here: *immediately*. He had just finished telling His disciples to watch for a series of events that would signal the approach of the destruction of the temple. Then He said that immediately after the tribulation—not a year, not a hundred years, not two thousand years or more—He would come. As we saw in the previous chapter, many of the things Jesus prophesied—false christs, wars, famines, earthquakes, the desecration of the temple, tribulations—are documented to have occurred between the time Jesus spoke and AD 70. Thus, the word *immediately* indicates that this coming of Jesus was also at that time, that this event also happened within this generation. How can that be?

There are basically two solutions. One way to resolve this problem is to treat the time-frame reference in this discourse—"this generation will by no means pass away till all these things take place" (v. 34)—as figurative while seeing the descriptions of Jesus' coming as literal. Some commentators do just that. They say that the word *generation* indicates a certain type of person, not a time frame of roughly forty years. In other words, Jesus was saying that wicked, doubting people such as the scribes and Pharisees would always be around, from the time when He gave this prophecy to the time of His return thousands of years in the future. According to this view, Jesus' return will be accompanied by real astronomical signs, but it has not happened yet.

The other option is to treat the language Jesus used to describe His coming as figurative and the time-frame reference as literal. That is, Jesus actually came back in AD 70, but the sun and moon were not actually darkened, the stars did not fall, and the powers of heaven were not shaken. Those signs did not literally happen; rather, Jesus was speaking figuratively to describe a real event.

In order to decide which option is best, we must use sound principles of biblical interpretation. What does the Bible say? Do we see similar language used elsewhere in Scripture? If so, in what context does it appear?

In Old Testament prophecy, there is a very clear use of cosmic phenomena in descriptions of judgment. In other words, when God promised to send judgment,

He often spoke in highly figurative language. For instance, Isaiah 13 speaks of the divine judgment that was to be visited on Babylon. God said:

> Behold, the day of the LORD comes,
> Cruel, with both wrath and fierce anger,
> To lay the land desolate;
> And He will destroy its sinners from it.
> For the stars of heaven and their constellations
> Will not give their light;
> The sun will be darkened in its going forth,
> And the moon will not cause its light to shine. . . .
>
> "Therefore I will shake the heavens,
> And the earth will move out of her place,
> In the wrath of the LORD of hosts
> And in the day of His fierce anger." (vv. 9–10, 13)

Likewise, Isaiah 34 addresses the judgment to come upon Edom. God said:

> All the host of heaven shall be dissolved,
> And the heavens shall be rolled up like a scroll;
> All their host shall fall down
> As the leaf falls from the vine,
> And as fruit falling from a fig tree. (v. 4)

Here we see language that is very similar to the words Jesus used in Matthew 24: descriptions of the sun, moon, and stars being darkened, the host of heaven being dissolved, and the heavens being rolled up like a scroll. Of course, we know that the sun and moon did not cease to shine, and the heavens were not rolled up like a scroll—but God's judgment certainly happened. Prophecies of this nature were frequently communicated by way of metaphor and figures to communicate their cosmic significance. That was why Jesus employed this language in the Olivet Discourse.

I believe the presence of this language in connection with prophecies of judgment in the Old Testament is a strong indication for us that Jesus' language was figurative, but He was describing a judgment event that literally happened within that generation. When He spoke of "the Son of Man coming on the clouds of heaven with power and great glory," He was telling the disciples that

He would carry out judgment on Jerusalem in AD 70. He was not referring to His final coming. Thus, this coming did indeed happen within that generation.

Literal Cosmic Phenomena

Strangely, however, historical records include some reports of actual astronomical phenomena. Josephus writes that certain signs were observed between the years AD 60 and 70, one of which was a blazing comet. The people in the ancient world were very superstitious about comets. The pagan soothsayers interpreted it as a herald of a radical political upheaval and the replacement of a king. The Emperor Nero was so terrified by it that he had all of his progeny murdered, to make sure that none of them would try to wrest the throne from him. He was deeply paranoid after that and committed suicide in 68.

Josephus reports an even stranger phenomenon. He fought in the Jewish rebellion and was an eyewitness of the destruction of Jerusalem after he was captured. Later, he wrote about that experience in *The Jewish Wars*. In one extraordinary passage, he writes:

> A few days after that feast, on the one and twentieth day of the month Artemisius, a certain prodigious and incredible phenomenon appeared; I suppose the account of it would seem to be a fable, were it not related by those that saw it, and were not the events that followed it of so considerable of a nature as to deserve such signals; for, before sun-setting, chariots and troops of soldiers in their armor were seen running about among the clouds, and surrounding the cities. Moreover, at the feast which we call Pentecost, as the priests were going by night into the inner [court of the temple] as their custom was, to perform their sacred ministrations, they said that, in the first place, they felt a quaking, and heard a great noise, and after that they heard a sound as of a great multitude, saying, "Let us remove hence."[1]

According to this account, around the time of the destruction of Jerusalem, multitudes of people testified to seeing chariots and soldiers surrounding the city in the clouds. Thus, in this case, there may have been actual manifestations of astronomical and heavenly perturbations.

Finally Jesus said: **"And He will send His angels with a great sound of a trumpet, and they will gather together His elect from the four winds, from one end of heaven to the other"** (v. 31). This statement is very reminiscent of Paul's description of the final return of Christ and the rapture of believers (1 Thessalonians 4). We must remember, however, that the Greek word that is translated here as "angel" is *angelos*, and it literally means "messenger." Thus, Jesus

[1] Flavius Josephus, *The Jewish Wars*, 6.5.3.

might have been speaking of the missionary efforts of His disciples following the destruction of Jerusalem, as they gathered the elect by means of the preaching of the gospel.

I acknowledge again that the entire Olivet Discourse is very difficult, and this passage especially so. Yet, I continue to believe that the most natural way to understand this text is to regard everything Jesus said as taking place in that generation, including His coming in judgment upon the nation of Israel.

112

THE DAY AND THE HOUR

Matthew 24:36–44

But of that day and hour no one knows, not even the angels of heaven, but My Father only. But as the days of Noah were, so also will the coming of the Son of Man be. For as in the days before the flood, they were eating and drinking, marrying and giving in marriage, until the day that Noah entered the ark, and did not know until the flood came and took them all away, so also will the coming of the Son of Man be. Then two men will be in the field: one will be taken and the other left. Two women will be grinding at the mill: one will be taken and the other left. Watch therefore, for you do not know what hour your Lord is coming. But know this, that if the master of the house had known what hour the thief would come, he would have watched and not allowed his house to be broken into. Therefore you also be ready, for the Son of Man is coming at an hour you do not expect.

The Olivet Discourse, as we have seen, is a difficult passage to interpret. But in the passage we are considering in this chapter, it becomes, if anything, even more difficult. There seems to be a shift in Jesus' teaching here, and New Testament scholars have differed as to the meaning and purpose of that shift.

Some argue that through verse 28, Jesus was talking about the destruction of Jerusalem and the temple, His judgment against the Jewish nation, but He then shifted and began to speak about matters concerning His ultimate coming at the time of the consummation of His kingdom (vv. 29–31). Others argue that

He was speaking about the events of AD 70 through verse 35, but He began to teach about His ultimate coming in verse 36—the beginning of the passage we have before us in this chapter. I tend to agree with this latter interpretation, but Jesus' words in this passage are applicable to His coming in judgment on Jerusalem in AD 70 and His final coming at the consummation of history.

Remember, this whole discourse was provoked by Jesus' announcement that the temple would be destroyed, which prompted the disciples to ask Him two questions: "When will these things be? And what will be the sign of Your coming, and of the end of the age?" (v. 3b). This passage would be so much easier to understand if only Jesus had answered the first question with all of the indications that He gave—false Christs, wars, famines, earthquakes, tribulations—and finished by saying, "This generation will by no means pass away till all these things take place," after which He had gone on to speak about His coming. Unfortunately for the task of interpretation, He announced the destruction of Jerusalem and the temple, then gave the announcement of the coming of the Son of Man on the clouds of heaven, and only then did He say, "This generation will by no means pass away till all these things take place."

Since He spoke of the destruction of Jerusalem, the destruction of the temple, and His coming, then mentioned "all these things," it would seem that the natural interpretation would be that "all these things" includes all of these events. But as we have seen, that is the issue that has provoked so much skepticism and criticism of Jesus and the Bible. The favorite fodder for the cynics to attack Jesus and Scripture is the apparent failure of "all these things"—specifically, His coming—to have taken place within the framework of that generation, which was roughly forty years.

However, some scholars say we can escape this problem because while Jesus foretold that His coming would happen within the timeframe of that generation, that prediction was negated by what He taught in our text for this chapter. Let us consider what He said.

Jesus' Lack of Knowledge

Matthew tells us that Jesus said, **"But of that day and hour no one knows, not even the angels of heaven, but My Father only"** (v. 36). According to Mark's account, Jesus specifically said "nor the Son" (13:32). So, according to some, Jesus' integrity remains intact and He cannot be accused of false prophecy for saying His coming would take place within that generation. Frankly, that idea amazes me, because I merely hear Jesus saying, "I can tell you all of these things are going to take place within the next forty years, but I don't know the precise year, month, day, and hour." The fact that Jesus qualified His prophecy by saying He did not know the precise time did not negate the time frame He already had mentioned. These words of Jesus did not represent a retreat from His first prediction about the fulfillment of the things He had prophesied.

The fact that Jesus admitted here that there was something He did not know bothers many Christians. They point out that He had to have had supernatural knowledge to predict the destruction of Jerusalem and the temple, along with all the events leading up to it, with such astonishing accuracy. Also, the fact that He knew that His coming would happen within forty years showed that He had supernatural knowledge. Why, then, did He back off and say He could not state the precise day and hour of His coming? How could Jesus have any limitation of His knowledge of what was going to take place in the future?

Even Thomas Aquinas, the great theologian of the Roman Catholic Church, tripped all over this passage. He said Jesus is the Son of God, the second person of the Trinity. Furthermore, God is omniscient; there are no limits to the knowledge of God. So, if God and man are perfectly united in the incarnation, Thomas said, Jesus *had* to know the day and the hour. Why, then, did He say He did not know? To answer this question, Thomas developed what he called the accommodation theory. He said Jesus really did know, but that knowledge was too much for the people to bear; therefore, to accommodate their weakness, He simply told them He did not know. That explanation preserves the omniscience of Jesus at a very high price. It envisions the Son of God speaking a falsehood for expedient reasons. That falsehood might be only the tiniest blemish on Jesus' perfection, but that tiny blemish would disqualify Him from being the Lamb without blemish, the perfect sacrifice for the sins of His people. I would much rather deal with limitations on Jesus' knowledge than with limitations on His sinlessness.

How do we resolve this problem? Actually, there is nothing to resolve if we have an orthodox understanding of the incarnation. At the Council of Chalcedon in AD 451, the church acknowledged the mystery of the incarnation, noting that no man can fully grasp the way in which the two natures of Jesus are united in one person. Chalcedon took a firm stand, saying that Jesus is *vera homo*, *vera Deus*, that is, "truly man and truly God." In Jesus, true humanity is united with the true deity of the second person of the Godhead. But Chalcedon drew a line in the sand, defining the boundaries of speculation about the incarnation by affirming that the union of God and man is without mixture, confusion, separation, or division, each nature retaining its own attributes. All that theological language simply means that the incarnation did not result in a single theanthropic nature, wherein the deity and the humanity are blended together in such a way that the divine is not really divine and the human is not really human. A deified human nature would no longer be human, and a humanized divine nature would no longer be divine. When Chalcedon said each nature retained its own attributes, it meant that in the incarnation, the attributes of deity remained in the divine nature, and the attributes of humanity remained in the human nature.

There were times in Jesus' earthly ministry when His human nature manifested itself. When He was hungry, that was evidence of His humanity, because God never gets hungry. When He sweated in Gethsemane, that was evidence of His humanity, because deity does not perspire. Also, in that human nature, Jesus did not possess omniscience. Of course, the divine nature could and frequently did communicate supernatural knowledge to Jesus' human nature. There were times when Jesus spoke of things that no human being could know in and of himself. But the divine nature did not communicate everything it knew to the human nature. So, when Jesus said He did not know the day and the hour of His coming, He was speaking with regards to His humanity. His divine nature communicated to His human nature that it would be within forty years, but it did not give the precise time. It's very simple. The only people who have a problem with this are those who want to deify the human nature of Jesus. The two natures must be kept separate. Jesus' human nature did not know the day and the hour. However, He did know the general time frame—that generation.

Business as Usual

Jesus then began to describe the circumstances at the time of His coming. Again, we cannot be sure whether He was talking about the situation at the time of the destruction of Jerusalem or at His final appearance. But His description of the times is true for either scenario. He said: **"But as the days of Noah were, so also will the coming of the Son of Man be"** (v. 37). Here, Jesus said the time of His coming would be analogous to the time of Noah. What was going on among the people at the time of the flood that would also be going on at the time of the coming of Christ?

The primary similarity was this—it would be business as usual: **"For as in the days before the flood, they were eating and drinking, marrying and giving in marriage, until the day that Noah entered the ark, and did not know until the flood came and took them all away, so also will the coming of the Son of Man be"** (vv. 38–39). God told Noah to construct an ark, and it took Him many years to do it. People laughed at the lunatic who was building a boat. They gave no heed to the judgment that was coming. They kept on eating and drinking, marrying and giving in marriage, going about business as usual, until the day that Noah entered the ark. That day, it started to rain. It rained all day, and people who were not on the ark were annoyed. Their plans and their work were altered. Even their eating and drinking were disrupted by the storm.

It kept raining, and soon the creeks were rising and the people were beginning to get nervous. Perhaps some tried to get into the ark with Noah and his family, but the door was shut. Eventually, the waters rose so high the ark began to float. The waters continued to rise until they covered the mountains. Noah, his family, and the animals he took on the ark were the only survivors.

The world is filled with people like that. Our Lord has warned each of us that we will be called into judgment at the ends of our lives, and none of us knows the day and the hour when that will be. But people are at ease in Zion. Many mock those who warn of the judgment of God. They say that God does not judge anyone because He loves everyone. They think God will give them a pass. As it was in the days of Noah, so shall it be at the coming of the Son of Man.

Jesus went on to say: **"Then two men will be in the field: one will be taken and the other left. Two women will be grinding at the mill: one will be taken and the other left"** (vv. 40–41). Again, the picture here is of business as usual. Jesus asked the disciples to imagine two men at work in the fields and two women grinding wheat into flour at the mill. In both cases, He said, one would be taken and the other left. He was saying that at the time of His appearing, there would be a separation, just as the door of the ark separated Noah and his family from the rest of the human race.

This idea of separation is politically incorrect and offensive to the pluralistic, relativistic culture in which we live today. Before he died, Francis Schaeffer observed that the biggest problem that afflicts the church is the loss of the sense of antithesis. Schaeffer understood that if we affirm a truth, we automatically deny its opposite, its antithesis. We want it both ways. We want to have faith in Christ and play with the antichrist. We want to say there is one way to the Father, but perhaps other ways are valid also. We delude ourselves to obscure and escape the conflict of division. We need to acknowledge that truth divides. It always has and it always will. The truth of Jesus Christ is the great divide of all history. Jesus said, "He who is not with Me is against Me, and he who does not gather with Me scatters" (Luke 11:23). There is no middle ground.

The Need to Keep Watch

Jesus then added a warning, and like His description of the times, this warning is as applicable for us in our day as it was for the disciples in theirs. Jesus said: **"Watch therefore, for you do not know what hour your Lord is coming. But know this, that if the master of the house had known what hour the thief would come, he would have watched and not allowed his house to be broken into. Therefore you also be ready, for the Son of Man is coming at an hour you do not expect"** (vv. 42–44). Imagine getting a call from someone who said, "I just want to let you know that I'm going to break into your house tomorrow at noon and rob you." If you took the caller seriously, what would you do? You would have the whole police department waiting for the robber. You probably would arm yourself. But there are not too many criminals dumb enough to announce the day and the hour when they are going to break into a home. Likewise, Jesus did not give the day and the hour of His coming. Therefore, He counseled His disciples to keep watch for Him, for He would come at an unexpected time—a time when the world would be going about business as usual.

Every now and then, we read about preachers or prognosticators who predict the day and the hour for the return of Jesus. They have it all figured out. They have their charts. They know all the signs that are going on in the Middle East. So, they tell us that Jesus is coming, and they set a date and time. I do not know how many times in my life I have seen such predictions made, but every last one of them has been wrong. These people presume to have a calendar that even Jesus did not have. He did not give us a precise day and time. He only told us to keep watch and be ready.

Jesus ended His parable of the persistent widow with a poignant question: "When the Son of Man comes, will He really find faith on the earth?" (Luke 18:8b). If He was talking about His final return, and if He comes before I die, I want Him to find faith in me. How about you? Whether He comes during your lifetime or you go to Him at your death, there will be a reckoning that no human being can escape. We need to be ready.

113

THE FAITHFUL AND EVIL SERVANTS

Matthew 24:45–51

Who then is a faithful and wise servant, whom his master made ruler over his household, to give them food in due season? Blessed is that servant whom his master, when he comes, will find so doing. Assuredly, I say to you that he will make him ruler over all his goods. But if that evil servant says in his heart, "My master is delaying his coming," and begins to beat his fellow servants, and to eat and drink with the drunkards, the master of that servant will come on a day when he is not looking for him and at an hour that he is not aware of, and will cut him in two and appoint him his portion with the hypocrites. There shall be weeping and gnashing of teeth.

When I was in seminary in Pittsburgh, one of my professors was Dr. Markus Barth, son of the world-famous Swiss theologian Karl Barth. As a student, I was astonished when Markus Barth produced a two-hundred-page academic paper on one word from the Apostle Paul's epistle to the Romans. Paul begins this epistle by saying, "Paul, a bondservant of Jesus Christ," then goes on to further identify himself and his mission. Professor Barth's manuscript did not focus on the name *Paul.* There would be nothing strange about a two-hundred-page paper on Paul; many volumes could be and have been written about the person, the ministry, and the theology of the Apostle Paul. Neither did Dr. Barth write his paper on the words *Jesus* or *Christ.* Again, hundreds of thousands of weighty tomes have been written about the name *Jesus* and the title *Christ*, so it would not have surprised anyone that a scholar could write a two-hundred-page paper about either. Instead, the whole focus of Professor Barth's manuscript was the single word *bondservant*, which was the word the apostle Paul chose to identify himself with respect to his relationship to Jesus. The Greek word that is translated as "bondservant" in the New King James Version is *doulos*, which does not refer to a hired servant but to a slave.

Dr. John MacArthur has released a book with a very simple title—*Slave*. When I read it, I was reminded of Markus Barth, because in this book, Dr. MacArthur gives exclusive attention to the New Testament meaning of the word *slave*. Near the beginning of the book, he asks why most English translations of the New Testament translate *doulos* as "servant" rather than "slave." He opines that perhaps it is part of a national consciousness of shame for Western participation in the evils of the slave trade, in which slave traders would raid villages in Africa and literally steal men and women from their villages, put them on ships, and carry them to England or to the Colonies, there to be sold in the slave market. Perhaps, Dr. MacArthur suggests, we are embarrassed by the word *slave*.

Whatever the reason may be, we see the phenomenon in the New King James Version translation of Matthew 24:45. The NKJV uses the word *servant* here, but the Greek word is *doulos*. Jesus did not use the word *servant*. He used the word *slave*.

One of the great ironies of the teaching of the New Testament is that it tells us no one ever becomes truly free until he becomes a slave to Jesus Christ. We may never have to experience the indignity of being bought or sold in a slave market in this world, but all of us are slaves of one sort or another. We are either slaves of Christ or slaves of sin. There is no other option for fallen humanity. That is why Paul writes, "You are not your own" (1 Cor. 6:19b). What does he mean? In our culture, we hear people say, "I want to find myself." What foolishness. Paul says Christian do not belong to themselves. We are not autonomous. We cannot do whatever we want to do any time we want to do it. Why? As Paul goes on to explain, "for you were bought at a price" (v. 20a). Someone else owns us. We do not own ourselves. We have been purchased, and the price that was paid for us was the blood of Christ; when He redeemed us, He bought us. So, this is a metaphor with which we should dare not trifle.

A Faithful and Wise Slave

In the previous chapter, we saw that Jesus warned His disciples to be ready for His return, for they would not know the precise day and hour. As He continued His teaching in the Olivet Discourse, He gave another warning, telling the disciples not to grow lazy and inattentive to their duties in His absence. Just as His warning for His followers to keep watch was applicable both for the disciples and for us, so this warning is one we need to heed as much as did the disciples.

Jesus said, **"Who then is a faithful and wise servant, whom his master made ruler over his household, to give them food in due season?"** (v. 45). The first issue Jesus raised was fidelity. He asked, "Who is a faithful slave?" *Faithful* is a strange word to use for a slave, one who is not his own. But a faithful slave, according the simplest meaning of the term, is one who is full of faith, one who can be trusted, one who is consistent in allegiance to his owner. Jesus was asking: "Who is the faithful slave? Who is the slave that can be trusted?" Furthermore, He asked: "Who is the wise slave?" That is, who is the one who works with insight?

Giving a little more information about this hypothetical slave, Jesus added, "whom his master made ruler over his household, to give them food in due season?" The master went on a journey, but before he left, he called one of his slaves and made him the steward of the house. Stewardship is about ruling over the house in the master's absence. This slave was responsible to make sure that all the other slaves were fed and cared for at the appropriate time.

Jesus went on to say, **"Blessed is that servant whom his master, when he comes, will find so doing"** (v. 46). The idea here is that if the master returned and found the slave doing what he had been called to do in service to the one who had bought him, he would be "blessed"—he would enjoy the trust and esteem of his master. The faithful slave and wise slave, the one who did what his master called him to do, would become the blessed slave.

How would he be blessed? Jesus said, **"Assuredly, I say to you that he will make him ruler over all his goods"** (v. 47). The master would give the faithful slave even more responsibility, even more esteem, because he had shown himself to be faithful. There is an echo here of the parable of the talents, which we will study in Matthew 25, where the master said to one of the wise servants, "You were faithful over a few things, I will make you ruler over many things" (v. 21). He who wants to be given more responsibility in the kingdom of God must be faithful in little things before the Lord will make him responsible for the big things.

A Faithless and Foolish Slave

But Jesus then proposed a very different scenario: **"But if that evil servant says in his heart, 'My master is delaying his coming,' and begins to beat his fellow servants, and to eat and drink with the drunkards, the master of that servant will come on a day when he is not looking for him and at an**

hour that he is not aware of, and will cut him in two and appoint him his portion with the hypocrites" (vv. 48–51a).

Here the slave began to think: "My master's gone. Who knows when he's coming back? Who knows whether he's *ever* coming back? I'm free to enjoy my authority over the household." It is interesting that the slave said these things in his heart, that is, in the deepest part of his being. The Bible says, "As he thinks in his heart, so is he" (Prov. 23:7). The Bible is not confusing the heart and the mind. When the Jews spoke of one thinking in his heart, they were not talking about a passing idea that flits through a person's mind but an idea that takes root in the very core of his being. So, this slave began to beat the master's other slaves, and he began to take his ease, spending time with drunkards and neglecting his duties.

Most of you have jobs and employers. With those jobs come certain responsibilities. Ask yourself this question: How do you work when no one is watching? Do you stay on task? Do you fulfill the responsibility that has been given to you and for which you are being compensated? Or do you take advantage of a gap in oversight to do what you want to do? I could tell you horror stories about employee behavior. I have found employees watching Internet pornography on their computers during office hours. I found one employee that was doing day trading on his computer. The computer has given all kinds of opportunities for people to engage in activities other than the things they are called to be doing. How easy it is when the boss is not looking to call up a game on the computer, to go shopping on Amazon, or to simply surf the Web.

Why does our behavior change when no one is watching? Why do businesses, foundries, mills, and the like have clocks where workers have to punch in every day? Why can we not expect people to come to work when they are supposed to come to work and leave when they are supposed to leave, rather than coming late and leaving early? Why do employers have to monitor that? It is because of sin. In our sin, we are naturally lazy and self-centered, and we tend to indulge those tendencies when we are not being watched.

It has always been interesting to me that in the parable of the prodigal son, when the prodigal took his father's inheritance, he did not waste it on riotous living in his hometown. Instead, he went into a far country. No one knew him there. No one was watching his behavior. He was free from all restraint. As a result, he lived so profligately, he ended up with the pigs.

In this scenario, the slave was neither faithful nor wise. He was unfaithful and foolish. He was like the fool of whom the psalmist speaks: "The fool has said in his heart, 'There is no God'" (Ps. 14:1). Probably the most serious and fatal self-delusion of the wicked is the delusion that because God has not brought them to judgment thus far in their lives, the hammer will never fall. I cannot count the number of people I know who never give a thought to the fact that they are going to die and stand before the Judge of heaven and earth. The Bible tells us God is longsuffering and forbearing to give us time to repent, time to come to Christ (2 Peter 3:9). But just the opposite effect often takes place. When God in His mercy is patient, people harden their hearts and stiffen their necks. They think: "I can eat, drink, and be merry. God will not judge me. He gives everyone a free pass." That is the quintessence of foolishness.

Weeping and Gnashing of Teeth

Jesus was talking about people who would behave this way in *His* absence, people who would assume that because He was in a distant place and had delayed His coming, that He was never coming, so they could do whatever they wished to do. Based on this assumption, they would beat the other slaves, and eat and drink with the drunkards.

But Jesus had a warning for them: "the master of that servant will come on a day when he is not looking for him and at an hour that he is not aware of, and will cut him in two and appoint him his portion with the hypocrites." Jesus will be the unexpected visitor. The slave will hear the key turning in the door and wonder who is coming in. Then the door will swing open and Jesus will be standing there.

I mentioned in the previous chapter that Jesus concluded His parable of the persistent widow with a very pointed question: "When the Son of Man comes, will He really find faith on the earth?" (Luke 18:8b). Will He find His people living faithfully? Christ has bought us for Himself and given us duties to perform, whether He is present or not. That is what discipleship is all about. Of course, we know that God is omniscient, and there is nowhere we can hide from Him. He always sees us. So, it is foolish to imagine that we can do anything in private.

Jesus said that He will cut the unfaithful slave in two—not literally but figuratively—and "appoint him his portion with the hypocrites," that is, the place of judgment. Furthermore, Jesus said that in that place, **"There shall be weeping and gnashing of teeth"** (v. 51b). Have you ever seen a person weep and gnash his teeth? I once saw a professing Christian who was involved in very serious sin brought to repentance by the Holy Spirit. When he realized what he had done, he began to wail and to sob. Furthermore, his weeping was joined with gnashing of teeth as he said to himself, "How could I have done this?" That will be the behavior of those who assume the Master would not return.

Let us never make the mistake of the slave in this passage. Jesus *will* return. Until He comes, it is our calling to be faithful to our Master. If we do, we shall be blessed.

114

THE PARABLE OF THE WISE AND FOOLISH VIRGINS

Matthew 25:1–13

Then the kingdom of heaven shall be likened to ten virgins who took their lamps and went out to meet the bridegroom. Now five of them were wise, and five were foolish. Those who were foolish took their lamps and took no oil with them, but the wise took oil in their vessels with their lamps. But while the bridegroom was delayed, they all slumbered and slept. And at midnight a cry was heard: "Behold, the bridegroom is coming; go out to meet him!" Then all those virgins arose and trimmed their lamps. And the foolish said to the wise, "Give us some of your oil, for our lamps are going out." But the wise answered, saying, "No, lest there should not be enough for us and you; but go rather to those who sell, and buy for yourselves." And while they went to buy, the bridegroom came, and those who were ready went in with him to the wedding; and the door was shut. Afterward the other virgins came also, saying, "Lord, Lord, open to us!" But he answered and said, "Assuredly, I say to you, I do not know you." Watch therefore, for you know neither the day nor the hour in which the Son of Man is coming.

When we studied the conclusion of the Sermon on the Mount in Matthew 7, I noted that it contains what I believe to be the most frightening warning that Jesus ever gave to His disciples. He said: "Many will say to Me in that day, 'Lord, Lord, have we not prophesied in Your name, cast out demons in Your name, and done many wonders in Your name?' And then I will declare to them, 'I never knew you; depart from Me, you who practice lawlessness!'" (vv. 22–23). The idea that there will be some who are convinced they belong to Christ but who will find out otherwise at the last day is terrifying. However, if there is a passage that can contend with that warning from Matthew 7 for sheer terrorizing power, it is the parable of the wise and foolish virgins, which we encounter in the first few verses of Matthew 25.

Although we are moving into a new chapter of Matthew's Gospel, we are still in the Olivet Discourse, and the passage we are considering in this chapter is thematically similar to the one we studied in the previous chapter. There, Jesus taught His disciples the need to be vigilant for His return, a lesson that is as valid for us as it was for them. Here, Jesus stresses the need for preparation before His coming, using a very powerful parable to make His point.

Awaiting the Bridegroom

Matthew tells us that Jesus began this parable by saying, **"Then the kingdom of heaven shall be likened to ten virgins who took their lamps and went out to meet the bridegroom"** (v. 1). These virgins were members of a bridal party. They were not guests who had come from here and there for the wedding; they were friends of the bride. According to the parable, the wedding was set. All the preparations had been made, the bridal party had been selected, and these ten virgins were to be the attendants of the bride, to join in the celebration of her marriage and to participate in honoring the bridegroom. In the ancient world, these bridal attendants would come to the home of the bride, and there they would wait for the arrival of the groom. No one knew precisely when the groom would be able to get to the appointed place, but when he came, there would be a glorious procession from the bride's home to the groom's home. It was a great honor and privilege to be a part of the bridal party and to march in procession with the groom to his home, where the feast was to be celebrated. These ten virgins, then, were ready to meet the groom and welcome him.

What is the meaning behind this parable? Obviously the symbolism of the parable is pointing to the great marriage feast of the Lamb at the end of the age (Rev. 19:7, 9), when Christ will come for His bride, the church (Eph. 5:25–32; Rev. 21:2, 9). The more difficult question is this: Who did the virgins represent? On this occasion, Jesus was not speaking to people who had never made a profession of faith in Him. These virgins were a picture of those who, at least outwardly, were His followers. By extension, they are representative of church members, of those who profess to believe in and trust Him, people who consider themselves to be Christians, loyal disciples of Jesus. But as we will see, although all ten virgins were in the bridal party and all ten of them went out to meet the groom, there was a huge difference among them, and so there is a huge distinguishing feature among church members. Jesus spoke of wheat and tares growing in the same field (13:24–30), and there were wheat and tares among these ten virgins, just are there are wheat and tares in every church.

Jesus added: **"Now five of them were wise, and five were foolish"** (v. 2). I think that the translators' selections of the English words here were motivated at least in part by sensitivity, because the other possible translations of the Greek words are "sensible" and "stupid." In my view, we might as well translate it correctly—five of these virgins were stupid. But why were they worthy to be called stupid, and why were the wise virgins worthy to be called sensible? Jesus said, **"Those who were foolish took their lamps and took no oil with them, but the wise took oil in their vessels with their lamps"** (vv. 3–4). Yes, this was stupidity. Can you imagine going to a wedding celebration without making the necessary preparations for the joyous procession?

The Lights and the Oil

Translators have faced a difficulty in this text, one that has divided them about equally. The difficulty concerns the meaning of the word the New King James Version translates as "lamps." In Palestine at the time of Jesus, people used small clay lamps that held a small amount of oil. A wick floated in the oil, and once it was lighted, it would burn until the oil was consumed. Therefore, if a person was going on a long journey in the night and needed to have illumination, he not only made sure to fill his lamp with oil, he brought along another vessel containing extra oil in the event that the first supply ran out. But this Greek word also can be translated as "torches" rather than "lamps." A torch was created by wrapping rags around a pole and then dipping the rags in oil. When the oil-soaked rags were ignited, the torch would provide illumination for about fifteen minutes. Then the rags had to be soaked in oil again so the torch could continue to give light. Personally, I think Jesus had torches in mind because He was speaking about an evening procession.

But in any case, the problem was the same whether it was lamps or torches—the foolish virgins did not bring sufficient oil for their instruments of illumination. It was as if they had gone out with flashlights that had no batteries in them. That would be a true example of stupidity, because a flashlight is of no use whatsoever if it has no batteries.

I have noted in connection with our study of earlier parables in the gospel of Matthew that most of Jesus' parables were not allegorical. That is, there is usually one simple meaning to a parable, and Jesus did not intend His hearers to look for a one-to-one correspondence between each element of a parable and something in real life. This parable of the wise and foolish virgins may or may not have been meant to have allegorical elements. If it does, and if there is a specific symbolic significance to the oil, it is not hard to understand that to which it refers. In biblical categories, the primary referent of the symbol of oil is the Holy Spirit. If the Spirit is indeed in view, the parable must mean that the five foolish virgins came without the Holy Spirit. They had a good standing with the bride, they had their invitations, and they had their wedding garments. They had all of the things that the wise virgins had—except that which was essential to participate in the wedding feast.

The meaning for us is clear—if we do not have the Spirit, who is given to those who trust Jesus with saving faith, we will not be admitted to the marriage supper of the Lamb. I constantly plead with my congregation to distinguish clearly between the possession of saving faith and the mere profession of it. No one has ever been saved by a mere profession of faith. Unless the faith we profess is authentic, unless it has taken root in our hearts, unless it is there by the power of God the Holy Spirit, it will not save us. Clearly Jesus was talking here about the difference between nominal Christians, people who are Christians only in name, and genuine Christians, those who are Christians indeed.

Many preachers in history have been known for a signature sermon they gave. A prime example is "Sinners in the Hands of an Angry God" by Jonathan Edwards. My mentor, Dr. John Gerstner, also had a signature sermon, and it was about this parable. It was a rather terrifying sermon, and probably the scariest part of it was when he turned to 1 Corinthians 13, to Paul's treatment of biblical love, to show all the wonderful things that a person who has no love can do. He can speak with the tongues of men and angels. He can prophesy and understand all mysteries and all knowledge. He might even give away all his worldly goods and submit to a martyr's death. He can do all of these magnificent acts and yet not have saving faith manifested in love. Such were the foolish virgins. They lacked that which was essential.

A Failure to Prepare

Jesus continued, **"But while the bridegroom was delayed, they all slumbered and slept"** (v. 5). The arrival of the groom was delayed for an unstated reason, so all of the virgins grew weary and went to sleep, which was a sensible thing to do, even for the foolish ones. He added: **"And at midnight a cry was heard: 'Behold, the bridegroom is coming; go out to meet him!' Then all those virgins arose and trimmed their lamps"** (vv. 6–7). When the arrival of the groom was imminent, the virgins scrambled to light their lamps or torches so that they could meet him.

That was when the foolish virgins discovered their mistake: **"And the foolish said to the wise, 'Give us some of your oil, for our lamps are going out.' But**

the wise answered, saying, 'No, lest there should not be enough for us and you; but go rather to those who sell, and buy for yourselves'" (vv. 8–9). The wise virgins had no problem; they had plenty of oil, so they lit their torches immediately. But the foolish virgins had no way to light their torches. In their desperation, they turned to their friends and begged them to share some of their excess oil. But this parable is not about sharing. It is about being ready for the coming of the bridegroom, and the wise virgins were ready. So, the wise virgins said they could not share what they had lest their experience of the wedding be ruined. They counseled the foolish virgins to go to the merchants who sold oil in order to buy some.

We cannot share the Holy Spirit with someone who is empty of Him. In other words, no one can get into the kingdom of God on the coattails of one with genuine faith. Everyone must believe on his own; he cannot rely on his father's faith, his mother's faith, his wife's faith, or anyone else's faith.

At this point, this parable becomes very sad. Jesus said, **"And while they went to buy, the bridegroom came, and those who were ready went in with him to the wedding; and the door was shut"** (v. 10). No doubt the foolish virgins hurried to find extra oil, but even so, they missed the arrival of the groom. But those who were ready, including the five wise virgins, joined the groom in the honorable procession to his home, and there they began the celebration. Then, the door was shut.

But there was even more disappointment to come: **"Afterward the other virgins came also, saying, 'Lord, Lord, open to us!' But he answered and said, 'Assuredly, I say to you, I do not know you'"** (vv. 11–12). The foolish virgins presumably got their oil and then hastened to the home of the groom. They were disappointed to have missed his arrival and the procession, but they were still looking forward to the celebration. But when they arrived, they were refused admittance. They addressed the groom respectfully: "Lord, Lord." But the groom pronounced those chilling words Jesus had said that He Himself would speak at the last day: "I do not know you."

The point of this parable is simple. Jesus said the kingdom of God is like this. When He comes, people in the church will be excited. There will be Sunday school teachers, elders, deacons, pastors, missionaries, faithful tithers, and church attenders. Sadly, many of them will have no oil, no Spirit. They will be Christians only in name. They will not be admitted to the celebration. It is vitally important that we be ready for His coming, for like the arrival of the bridegroom, the time of the return of our Lord is uncertain. For this reason, Jesus urged His disciples, **"Watch therefore, for you know neither the day nor the hour in which the Son of Man is coming"** (v. 13).

Every one of the virgins, the foolish and the wise, assumed that she would be welcomed by the groom and would participate fully in the great feast. However, fully half of them were deceived. I do not know why Jesus divided the virgins the way He did, making half foolish and half wise. That is a terrifying percentage. God forbid that 50 percent of those in the pews of our churches should find the time of Christ's return a day of darkness with no light in it. I urge you to examine your heart to make sure the faith you profess is genuine. Do not be a foolish virgin.

115

THE PARABLE OF THE TALENTS

Matthew 25:14–30

For the kingdom of heaven is like a man traveling to a far country, who called his own servants and delivered his goods to them. And to one he gave five talents, to another two, and to another one, to each according to his own ability; and immediately he went on a journey. Then he who had received the five talents went and traded with them, and made another five talents. And likewise he who had received two gained two more also. But he who had received one went and dug in the ground, and hid his lord's money. After a long time the lord of those servants came and settled accounts with them. So he who had received five talents came and brought five other talents, saying, "Lord, you delivered to me five talents; look, I have gained five more talents besides them." His lord said to him, "Well done, good and faithful servant; you were faithful over a few things, I will make you ruler over many things. Enter into the joy of your lord." He also who had received two talents came and said, "Lord, you delivered to me two talents; look, I have gained two more talents besides them." His lord said to him, "Well done, good and faithful servant; you have been faithful over a few things, I will make you ruler over many things. Enter into the joy of your lord." Then he who had received the one talent came and said, "Lord, I knew you to be a hard man, reaping where you have not sown, and gathering where you have not scattered seed. And I was afraid, and went and hid your talent in the ground. Look, there you have what is yours." But his lord answered and said to him, "You wicked and lazy servant, you knew that I reap where I have not sown, and gather where I have not scattered seed. So you ought to have deposited my money with the bankers, and at my coming I would have received back my own with interest. Therefore take the talent

> from him, and give it to him who has ten talents. For to everyone who has, more will be given, and he will have abundance; but from him who does not have, even what he has will be taken away. And cast the unprofitable servant into the outer darkness. There will be weeping and gnashing of teeth."

Right after the parable of the wise and foolish virgins, by which Jesus instructed His disciples to be prepared for His coming, He told them the parable of the talents to teach them to be diligent as they waited for Him. As we have seen time and time again in the Olivet Discourse, this same lesson applies to us, Jesus' disciples in the twenty-first century. Sadly, the basic principles found in this parable fly in the face of everything we hear in contemporary culture. If ever Jesus told a parable that is politically incorrect in contemporary America, it is this one. We need to close our ears to the siren voices of the pagan culture in which we live, and listen carefully to the teaching of our Lord and Savior.

According to Matthew, Jesus told His disciples: **"For the kingdom of heaven is like a man traveling to a far country, who called his own servants and delivered his goods to them. And to one he gave five talents, to another two, and to another one, to each according to his own ability; and immediately he went on a journey. Then he who had received the five talents went and traded with them, and made another five talents. And likewise he who had received two gained two more also. But he who had received one went and dug in the ground, and hid his lord's money"** (vv. 14–18).

Jesus told a story about a wealthy man who went away for a long journey, and before he went he entrusted some of his riches to three of his servants, giving each of them "talents." These talents were not abilities but units of weight. In the ancient world, a talent could be a unit of gold, silver, or bronze. Jesus did not say which kind of precious metal the master entrusted to his servants, but a talent of gold or silver was quite valuable.

The master gave five talents to one servant, two talents to another, and one to a third. He distributed these talents according to his estimation of the ability of each servant to handle them. This is why he did not distribute them equally. Then, after the master's departure, the man to whom the master gave five talents doubled that number. Likewise, the man to whom the master gave two talents also produced a hundred-percent increase. The third servant, however, was concerned that he might lose the one talent he had been given and land in serious trouble with his master, so he played it safe and buried his master's gold or silver in the ground.

Stewardship Capitalism

On the surface, the interpretation of this parable is about as simple as it gets. It focuses on the productivity of the Lord's people, on fruitfulness. That is, Jesus was telling the disciples to engage in productive activity until His return.

What we find initially in this rather simple parable is a lesson about stewardship. A steward was a servant in the ancient world who was given authority to make sure everything functioned properly in the master's household. The Greek word that is translated as "stewardship" in the New Testament is *oikonomia*; we get the English word *economy* from it. The word *oikonomia* is a combination of two other words: *oikos*, which means "house," and *nomos*, which means "law." So, stewardship has to do with the law of the house or the rule of the house—how matters in the house are handled.

However, I think this parable points beyond stewardship to something else. It will be politically incorrect for me to write this, but I believe Jesus was speaking here not just about stewardship but about a particular kind of stewardship, which I call "stewardship capitalism." The term *capitalism* has become a dirty word in Western culture. Of course, capitalism can take all kinds of shapes and faces, and at times it can be ruthless and greedy. But the Bible presents a picture of stewardship capitalism and gives basic principles that are extremely important.

The first of these principles is that we possess nothing. Everything we think we own is really God's, for He owns everything, and all that we have we hold as stewards for Him. Second, God gives us capital not to waste, to horde, or to bury in the ground, but to be productive. If we put our capital to work, it can earn while we sleep. Third, stewardship capitalism includes the principle of delayed gratification. When we receive our paychecks, we do not spend everything we have earned to gratify every desire we have. Instead, we put the brakes on our consumption and invest a portion of what we take home for the future.

I saw the benefits of delayed gratification as I was growing up in Pittsburgh, the largest steel manufacturing city in the world. Pittsburgh and all the towns around it were marked by the billowing smoke from the steel mills of Western Pennsylvania. Sadly, on Friday afternoons, when the whistles would blow at the mills, the men would go to the paymaster's office and get their money, and then most of them would head to the nearest bars. Only about one out of ten would go home and give his wife his pay so she could deposit it in the bank. Guess which of those workers sent their sons to college? The sons of those men who delayed their gratification and invested in the futures of their children became doctors, lawyers, and engineers.

The Bible is also very concerned about the material well-being of human beings. It is not a Gnostic book that is concerned only with our souls. Our Lord

Jesus was profoundly concerned that people should have enough to eat, that they should not be naked, that they should have homes. All of these things cost money. My father-in-law used to say he would rather clothe me than feed me. He said I was eating him out of house and home when I came around to date his daughter. But God is concerned about all human needs.

So, what is the single most important factor for the material well-being of people? The answer to that question is simple—production. Unless food is produced, people starve. Unless clothing is produced, people freeze. Unless houses are built, people are without shelter. So, the most important factor in improving the welfare of human beings is to increase productivity. On an individual basis, it is extremely important that we be productive.

What is the most important factor for increasing productivity? The answer is very simple: tools. Let me give you a simple example. You probably have a lawn outside your home. Having that lawn requires you to balance three factors—labor, time, and money. Your grass needs to be cut. What is the cheapest way to cut it? You could go out, kneel down, and start chewing off each blade of grass one at a time. You probably would never get it done. It would be extremely labor-intensive. However, it would be cheap—so long as you did not need to spend time doing something else to earn money. You can increase your productivity by using a pair of scissors instead of our teeth. It would be a little more expensive to use scissors rather than your teeth, and it still would be labor-intensive, but it would be a little bit more efficient. You can increase your productivity even more by buying a push mower. That would save time, but it would cost more money. If you want to save more time and labor, you can buy a power mower. It will cost you more money, but it will certainly save you time and labor because you will have a better tool. The better the tools, the more productive you can be.

In 1989, right after the fall of Nicolae Ceausescu, I had the privilege of visiting Romania. As we traveled across the landscape by train, I could see thousands of babushkas, "grandmothers," wearing black dresses down to their ankles, out in the fields with wooden hoes and wooden rakes, loading their produce on ox-drawn or donkey-drawn carts. It was very primitive and unproductive agriculture. Why could the Romanian farmers not produce as much as American farmers? Was it because the Romanian men were not as strong physically as American men? No. Was it because they were not as smart? No. Was it because they did not have specific knowledge of agriculture? No, all the best methods for growing things was available in their language. The one thing the Romanian farmers did not have that American farmers had was tools. They did not have tractors and mechanical harvesters. That was the reason American farmers could produce a thousand times more in a month than Romanian farmers. It all came down to tools.

What is the single most important factor for acquiring tools? The answer is a really unpopular word—profit. In order to buy tools, you must have surplus capital. If you do not have the surplus capital, you must use wooden hoes and rakes. Profit is simply what is left over from your revenue after you pay your expenses. Somehow we have come to hate the idea of profit. But if you do not have profit, you will not have tools. And if you do not have tools, you will not have production. And if you do not have production, you will not have a shirt on your back, a loaf of bread to eat, or a house to live in.

So, Jesus wants His people to be productive with the things God has given to them. In other words, He wants us to use those things fruitfully, so that they increase.

Good Servants and a Lazy Servant

Jesus then related what happened when the master returned: **"After a long time the lord of those servants came and settled accounts with them. So he who had received five talents came and brought five other talents, saying, 'Lord, you delivered to me five talents; look, I have gained five more talents besides them.' His lord said to him, 'Well done, good and faithful servant; you were faithful over a few things, I will make you ruler over many things. Enter into the joy of your lord.' He also who had received two talents came and said, 'Lord, you delivered to me two talents; look, I have gained two more talents besides them.' His lord said to him, 'Well done, good and faithful servant; you have been faithful over a few things, I will make you ruler over many things. Enter into the joy of your lord'"** (vv. 19–23). When the master learned how productive the first two servants had been, he said: "Well done. You're a good servant, a faithful servant. Since you've been faithful in little, I'm going to make you responsible for more and more things." He gave the same message to the man who doubled the two talents. He was given fewer talents, but he was just as productive with them.

What of the third servant, the man who was given one talent? Jesus said: **"Then he who had received the one talent came and said, 'Lord, I knew you to be a hard man, reaping where you have not sown, and gathering where you have not scattered seed. And I was afraid, and went and hid your talent in the ground. Look, there you have what is yours'"** (vv. 24–25). This man came not with a report of productivity but with excuses. He said: "Lord, I knew you were a hard man. You're the kind of man who reaps where you haven't sown." What kind of man was the servant talking about? He was describing a capitalist, one who buys a field and hires other people to sow the seed and reap the harvest.

They get a salary but the master gets the largest portion of the profit because his capital was working for him.

That excuse did not curry the master's favor. Jesus told His disciples: **"But his lord answered and said to him, 'You wicked and lazy servant, you knew that I reap where I have not sown, and gather where I have not scattered seed. So you ought to have deposited my money with the bankers, and at my coming I would have received back my own with interest. Therefore take the talent from him, and give it to him who has ten talents'"** (vv. 26–28). The master chided the servant because he was wicked, and that wickedness manifested itself in laziness. Laziness is always problematic, but it is especially so when it affects our management of that which has been given to us by our Lord.

I had an economics professor in college who weighed almost three hundred pounds. On the first day of the economics class, he climbed on top of his desk and said, "Let me tell you the one law of economics—you've got to work!" He was right, of course, but we can work and not be good stewards. However, we cannot be good stewards without work.

Jesus concluded the parable by saying: **"For to everyone who has, more will be given, and he will have abundance; but from him who does not have, even what he has will be taken away. And cast the unprofitable servant into the outer darkness. There will be weeping and gnashing of teeth'"** (vv. 29–30). When He returns and sits in judgment, those who have not served Him will lose everything with which they were entrusted, and they will be cast into the outer darkness—for they are "unprofitable servants." But those who have served Him well will be given very much more—they will enter into the joy of the Lord Jesus.

Jesus was saying that we will be judged by the wisdom and diligence with which we manage what He leaves us. He is going to ask us whether we invested in those things that do the most to benefit people. Of course, that which most improves the well-being of people in this world is the work of the kingdom of God. That is where our chief investment needs to be.

Christians, read what Scripture says about managing what God has given you. Then seek to be productive. Only in this way will we have the inestimable blessing of hearing Him say, "Well done, good and faithful servant."

116

THE JUDGMENT OF CHRIST

Matthew 25:31–46

When the Son of Man comes in His glory, and all the holy angels with Him, then He will sit on the throne of His glory. All the nations will be gathered before Him, and He will separate them one from another, as a shepherd divides his sheep from the goats. And He will set the sheep on His right hand, but the goats on the left. Then the King will say to those on His right hand, "Come, you blessed of My Father, inherit the kingdom prepared for you from the foundation of the world: for I was hungry and you gave Me food; I was thirsty and you gave Me drink; I was a stranger and you took Me in; I was naked and you clothed Me; I was sick and you visited Me; I was in prison and you came to Me." Then the righteous will answer Him, saying, "Lord, when did we see You hungry and feed You, or thirsty and give You drink? When did we see You a stranger and take You in, or naked and clothe You? Or when did we see You sick, or in prison, and come to You?" And the King will answer and say to them, "Assuredly, I say to you, inasmuch as you did it to one of the least of these My brethren, you did it to Me." Then He will also say to those on the left hand, "Depart from Me, you cursed, into the everlasting fire prepared for the devil and his angels: for I was hungry and you gave Me no food; I was thirsty and you gave Me no drink; I was a stranger and you did not take Me in, naked and you did not clothe Me, sick and in prison and you did not visit Me." Then they also will answer Him, saying, "Lord, when did we see You hungry or thirsty or a stranger or naked or sick or in prison, and did not minister to You?" Then He will answer them, saying, "Assuredly, I say to you, inasmuch as you did not do it to one of the least of these, you did not do it to Me." And these will go away into everlasting punishment, but the righteous into eternal life.

If someone were to ask me, concerning all the doctrines taught in the Bible, which three are most hated, I would say that they are the doctrines of hell, predestination, and the last judgment. We can only imagine how odious would be a biblical passage that sets forth all three of these doctrines. However, that is what we find in the passage that is before us in this chapter.

This chapter will complete our study of the Olivet Discourse, which is found in Matthew 24 and 25. In the most recent passages we have examined, Jesus taught His disciples some important lessons about how they should await His coming. First, He counseled them to be vigilant (24:45–51), for, He said, no one knows the day and hour of His coming except God the Father (24:36). Second, by means of the parable of the wise and foolish virgins, Jesus taught them to be prepared for His coming (25:1–13). Third, in the parable of the talents, He told His disciples to be diligent and productive while they waited (25:14–30). Again, we are not sure whether He was instructing them at that point to be ready for His coming in judgment on Jerusalem in AD 70 or His final coming, which is yet to happen. However, it matters little, for just as the disciples needed to be prepared and productive as they waited for the destruction of Jerusalem, so we need to be prepared and productive as we await His climactic return.

As He closed this discourse, Jesus seems to have been addressing His final return, for here He foretold what will happen at the end of the age. All the nations will be gathered before Him, He said, and He will make a separation. That is, He will judge each and every individual. Sadly, He will find some who were not vigilant, who were unprepared, and who were not productive before His return.

Separating Sheep and Goats

Matthew tells us that Jesus said, **"When the Son of Man comes in His glory, and all the holy angels with Him, then He will sit on the throne of His glory"** (v. 31). This is the first time in all of Scripture when Jesus clearly referred to Himself not only as the Son of Man but also as the King, for He said He will sit on "the throne of His glory." He then added, **"All the nations will be gathered before Him, and He will separate them one from another, as a shepherd divides his sheep from the goats. And He will set the sheep on His right hand, but the goats on the left"** (vv. 32–33). Jesus' throne will be a throne of judgment. The first thing He will do when He comes in His glory will be to gather everyone from every nation before His throne. Then that gathering will be followed immediately by a separation.

This kind of teaching is very hard for people in modern Western culture, which embraces pluralism, relativism, and universalism, and which has an incurable allergy to any hint of exclusion. The idea of separation goes completely against the grain of our culture, especially since this particular separation means that some will enter the blessedness of eternal life in heaven and the rest will enter the everlasting misery of judgment in hell. Most Westerners, even in the church, believe it will be easy to pass through the last judgment on their way to heaven. We make jokes about St. Peter at the pearly gates, and he always seems to be blind to any sins that would preclude someone's entrance into heaven. We live in a world and in a nation that believes in salvation by death. All you have to do to go to heaven is to die.

When Jesus spoke of this separation He will make, He used the metaphor of sheep and goats. He also likened His judgment to a shepherd dividing sheep from goats. Vesta and I grew up in a suburb outside of Pittsburgh, very close to the farmlands of the region. If we drove just a mile or two out of our town, we could see pastures where cows grazed in some fields, sheep in others, and goats in still others. We never saw these three types of animals grazing together, so it was not difficult for us to distinguish the sheep from the goats. But we were on a trip in a third-world country a few years ago, and the tour guide pointed out a pasture that held both sheep and goats, and we could not tell the difference, at least not from our vantage point. We would have needed to get much closer and have detailed knowledge of the anatomy of sheep and goats in order to distinguish them.

In ancient Israel, just as in that third-world country, it was common for sheep and goats to be kept together. But the animals had to be separated on a daily basis. As the evening began to fall, the shepherd would go into his fields and draw all of the goats away because they did not have that wonderful wool sweater to protect them as the temperature began to drop. The goats needed more warmth, so the shepherd would go out and make this separation and bring the goats into a warmer place. The shepherd, of course, was intimately familiar with his animals, so he was well able to make that separation.

However, Jesus did not suggest He will separate the figurative sheep and goats for some utilitarian reason, as did the shepherds of Israel. Rather, He will separate them so as to place the sheep on His right and the goats on His left, that is, in the place of honor and dishonor respectively.

Blessed Sheep

Jesus then began to tell His disciples what He will say to these two groups, speaking first to the sheep: **"Then the King will say to those on His right hand, 'Come, you blessed of My Father, inherit the kingdom prepared for you from the foundation of the world: for I was hungry and you gave Me food; I was thirsty and you gave Me drink; I was a stranger and you took**

Me in; I was naked and you clothed Me; I was sick and you visited Me; I was in prison and you came to Me'" (vv. 34–36).

The sheep, He will say, are "blessed of My Father," so they will inherit "the kingdom prepared for [them] from the foundation of the world." The ultimate blessing the Father gives to any human being is the blessing of being His gift to the Son. Elsewhere Jesus said, "All that the Father gives Me will come to Me, and the one who comes to Me I will by no means cast out" (John 6:37). In His High Priestly Prayer on the night when He was betrayed, He said, "Those whom You gave Me I have kept; and none of them is lost except the son of perdition, that the Scripture might be fulfilled" (John 17:12). These individuals whom the Father gave to the Son have been predestined to inherit the kingdom of God from the foundation of the world.

When the Father adopts us into His family, we become, as it were, younger brothers and sisters of Jesus, who is the singular heir of the Father (Gal. 4:5; Eph. 1:5). Thus, we become joint heirs of the Father with Him (Rom. 8:17). At the last judgment, Jesus will say to us: "You're in the will. You were put in the will from the foundation of the world." You were not put into the will because God foresaw with His omniscience what you would do when you heard the gospel. Before you were born, before you ever did any good or bad thing, that the purposes of God's sovereign grace may be established and that the Son of God might be honored for eternity, God ordained you to be His heir and wrote your name in the Lamb's book of life (Rom. 9:10–13).

Whenever my grandchildren do anything that remotely displeases me (yes, it happens occasionally), my standard response is, "You're out of the will." We know how painful it is to be disinherited in this world. But to be excluded from the inheritance of the kingdom of God is the worst calamity that can befall a human being.

This doctrine of predestination causes not just confusion and bewilderment but fury, even among professing Christians. This always baffles me. There is no greater demonstration of grace than this doctrine, because I cannot point to any reason why am I in the kingdom of God and someone else is not. It certainly is not because of something I have done.

At this point, you might be thinking: "This whole text is about works, about feeding the hungry, giving drink to the thirsty, taking in strangers, clothing the naked, and visiting the sick and the prisoners. Doesn't that show that works are involved in salvation?" It might seem so, but we are told over and over again in Scripture that justification is by faith alone. Thus, works play no part in salvation. However, justification is not by a faith that is alone; it is not by a mere profession of faith. Anyone who possesses saving faith immediately begins to do good works. We are not justified *by* our works in any way whatsoever, but we are justified *to* good works. Thus, the ultimate test by which we will be determined to be in Christ or not is the presence or absence of fruit. On the last day, our professions of faith will be judged by the works we have performed. Again, we are not justified by our works, but if we do not have works, that is clear evidence that we do not have saving faith.

Jesus showed that good works come naturally to those who are justified. He said: **"Then the righteous will answer Him, saying, 'Lord, when did we see You hungry and feed You, or thirsty and give You drink? When did we see You a stranger and take You in, or naked and clothe You? Or when did we see You sick, or in prison, and come to You?' And the King will answer and say to them, 'Assuredly, I say to you, inasmuch as you did it to one of the least of these My brethren, you did it to Me'"** (vv. 37–40). The sheep will not be aware that they were serving Jesus when they served their neighbors. They simply did what the Spirit laid upon their hearts to do. But in that service, they were obeying Christ.

Cursed Goats

Jesus told His disciples that He will have a very different message for the goats. He said: **"Then He will also say to those on the left hand, 'Depart from Me, you cursed, into the everlasting fire prepared for the devil and his angels: for I was hungry and you gave Me no food; I was thirsty and you gave Me no drink; I was a stranger and you did not take Me in, naked and you did not clothe Me, sick and in prison and you did not visit Me'"** (vv. 41–43). These will be told to depart from Jesus into everlasting fire, for they are cursed, not blessed. Why? Because they failed to do the very things the righteous did: feed the hungry, give drink to the thirsty, take in strangers, and so on.

Jesus added: **"Then they also will answer Him, saying, 'Lord, when did we see You hungry or thirsty or a stranger or naked or sick or in prison, and did not minister to You?'"** (v. 44). The implication here seems to be that if they had *ever* seen Jesus in such need, they certainly would have ministered to Him. But by committing sins of omission in failing to minister to Jesus' people, to the least of these who belong to Him, they failed Him. As Jesus said, **"Then He will answer them, saying, 'Assuredly, I say to you, inasmuch as you did not do it to one of the least of these, you did not do it to Me'"** (v. 45). The goats will not have the works to show they are justified. So, **"these will go away into everlasting punishment, but the righteous into eternal life"** (v. 46).

There is no purgatory. "It is appointed for men to die once, but after this the judgment" (Heb. 9:27). There is no second chance. There is no reincarnation to a new life on this earth. The only reincarnation is the resurrection of the body for heaven or for hell. That is why it is so perilous to keep evading the issue, dodging the question. A judgment awaits each of us, a judgment according to the standards of God's righteousness. Remember what Paul said to the Athenians: "These times of ignorance God overlooked, but now commands all men everywhere to repent" (Acts 17:30). Why? "Because He has appointed a day on which He will judge the world in righteousness by the Man whom He has ordained" (v. 31a).

Do yourself a favor. Before you go to bed tonight, before you fall asleep, ask yourself: "Am I a sheep? Am I a goat? Is my faith real? What is my destiny?" Jesus is going to return one day, and when He does, judgment will happen. Make sure you are prepared.

117

THE ANOINTING AT BETHANY

Matthew 26:1–13

Now it came to pass, when Jesus had finished all these sayings, that He said to His disciples, "You know that after two days is the Passover, and the Son of Man will be delivered up to be crucified." Then the chief priests, the scribes, and the elders of the people assembled at the palace of the high priest, who was called Caiaphas, and plotted to take Jesus by trickery and kill Him. But they said, "Not during the feast, lest there be an uproar among the people." And when Jesus was in Bethany at the house of Simon the leper, a woman came to Him having an alabaster flask of very costly fragrant oil, and she poured it on His head as He sat at the table. But when His disciples saw it, they were indignant, saying, "Why this waste? For this fragrant oil might have been sold for much and given to the poor." But when Jesus was aware of it, He said to them, "Why do you trouble the woman? For she has done a good work for Me. For you have the poor with you always, but Me you do not have always. For in pouring this fragrant oil on My body, she did it for My burial. Assuredly, I say to you, wherever this gospel is preached in the whole world, what this woman has done will also be told as a memorial to her."

As we move into Matthew 26, we cross a line of demarcation. There is a sense in which everything changes at this point in this Gospel. Matthew tells us, **"Now it came to pass, when Jesus had finished all these sayings . . ."** (v. 1a). This is the end of Matthew's record of Jesus' teachings. When we read the Synoptic Gospels, we note that each of them reports substantially the same accounts, but they sometimes appear at very different points in the narrative. That is, particular sayings of Jesus might appear in one location in Matthew, another in Mark, and still another in Luke. It is the almost universal opinion of biblical scholars that the Gospel writers worked from a set of sayings called the *logia* ("words") of Jesus, which words were maintained by an oral tradition with no efforts to keep them in a sequential context. So, the work of the Gospel writers consisted in setting these teachings down in written form, and they were free to use their literary creativity to put each saying where it was most fitting from the perspective of that author. That is what Matthew has been doing to this point.

Now, however, his focus shifts completely to the narrative of Jesus' passion, the suffering and death of Christ. Matthew is beginning to bring his account to a climax, which is the climax of the redemptive activity of Jesus. The cross was now looming directly ahead.

Plotting on the Eve of the Passover

Appropriately, Jesus Himself set the stage for the final act: **He said to His disciples, "You know that after two days is the Passover, and the Son of Man will be delivered up to be crucified"** (vv. 1a–2).

Jesus knew what was going to happen. He knew His destiny; indeed, He had known it from the beginning and had told His disciples about it several times (16:21; 17:22–23; 20:17–19). He knew that the hour that had been drawing near was about to come to pass (John 13:1; 17:1). He also knew that all of the things that were about to transpire were fully under the sovereign ordination of His Father; no one could take His life from Him. He knew very clearly that all the machinations of the scribes, the Pharisees, the Sadducees, the Sanhedrin, and even His own disciple Judas would not have any power over Him unless He allowed Himself to be taken by the Jewish authorities and delivered to the Romans. He stated that He had the authority and the power to call on legions of angels to stop this drama from working itself out and save Him from the suffering He was about to endure (26:53). But as we have seen, He had set His face like flint to go to Jerusalem (Isa. 50:7) so that He might fulfill the mission He had accepted in the covenant of redemption in eternity past.

Jesus tied the moment of His passion to the Passover, which was two days away. The Passover was the most important festival on the Jewish calendar. It was conjoined with the Feast of Unleavened Bread, and together the festival lasted seven full days. Literally hundreds of thousands of pilgrims would find their way to Jerusalem for this celebration.

In the economy of God's plan, it was absolutely fitting that the Lamb of God should be sacrificed at the time of the Passover. The national identity of the Jewish people was established at that point in antiquity when they were spared from the wrath of God in Egypt and then delivered by the exodus. You remember the story. God had brought nine plagues on Egypt as Pharaoh refused God's direct command that he let the Israelites leave (Exodus 7–10). So God vowed to send one more plague. He said that He would go out into the midst of Egypt and cause all of the firstborn of the mighty ones, the firstborn of the lowliest slaves, and even the firstborn of the animals to die (Ex. 11:4–5). But He promised that if the Israelites would put the blood of a lamb on the doorposts of their homes, their firstborn would be spared (Ex. 12:1–13). So it was. The people of God were delivered from the wrath of God when He struck the Egyptians. Where God saw the blood of the lamb on the doorposts, He passed by. Egypt was subdued and the Israelites were freed, for which reason the Passover became a time of unparalleled celebration. Thus, it was appropriate that this feast should be the time for the ultimate atonement, for the sacrifice of the Lamb of God, whose blood delivers from God's wrath.

Matthew then adds one other brief note as He continues to set the stage for the climax of his account: **Then the chief priests, the scribes, and the elders of the people assembled at the palace of the high priest, who was called Caiaphas, and plotted to take Jesus by trickery and kill Him. But they said, "Not during the feast, lest there be an uproar among the people"** (vv. 3–5). These were not mafia chieftains gathered in a manor house in New Jersey. These were the most consecrated men of the Jews, chief priests, scribes, and elders, and even the reigning high priest, Caiaphas, in whose palace they met. These supposedly godly leaders came together for one purpose—to find a way to trap Jesus so that they might execute Him and be rid of Him once and for all.

Stop and think for a moment about what was going on here. The priests of the land were trying to figure out a way to kill the Son of God. I do not believe we can fully grasp the egregiousness of what they were doing. God Himself had taken a human nature and appeared in human history to redeem His people. He came to give His life as a ransom for many (20:28). But these people hated Him with every fiber of their beings. They were of one mind—Jesus had to go. Was there ever a more literally diabolical conspiracy in the history of the world?

But they said to one another, "Not during the feast, lest there be an uproar among the people." They knew many people from Galilee would be in Jerusalem for the feast, and they knew Jesus had a widespread following and a great reputation there. So they agreed to wait until the Passover feast was over before they set their snare. Of course, God had other plans. It was God's will that the

Lamb of God should die during the Passover. God would decide the time of the death of His Son, not the holy men of Israel.

Jesus Anointed for Burial

Matthew abruptly changes the subject. Instead of telling us more about the plans the religious leaders made and how they set their trap, he instead writes, **And when Jesus was in Bethany at the house of Simon the leper, a woman came to Him having an alabaster flask of very costly fragrant oil, and she poured it on His head as He sat at the table** (vv. 6–7). This event happened in Bethany, a village just outside Jerusalem, across the Kidron Valley and over the Mount of Olives. Matthew tells us Jesus was in the home of a man known as Simon the leper. We do not know who this Simon was. It seems unlikely he had leprosy at this time because he seems to have been actively involved in the social life of the town rather than isolated as lepers were at that time. Perhaps he had been healed by Jesus. Some have speculated that Simon was the father of Mary, Martha, and Lazarus, Jesus' dear friends who lived in Bethany (John 11:3). Jesus had spent many hours in the home of that family, and perhaps it was there that this remarkable event took place. Matthew also does not identify the woman who came to him with costly oil. However, John identifies her as Mary, presumably that Mary who was the sister of Lazarus and Martha.

Matthew adds some interesting details in this account. He tells us that Mary brought "very costly fragrant oil," but the fact that it was in an alabaster flask gives away the fact that this was an extremely precious possession. Alabaster is a mineral, and in this case, it probably was gypsum. Both Mark and John report that the flask and the oil were worth three hundred denarii (Mark 14:5; John 12:5). That was the average person's wages for ten months. Consider how much you make in ten months and then ask yourself whether you would spend that much for one alabaster vial of perfume.

This unidentified woman came to the table where Jesus was reclining with Simon and His disciples, and she poured the flask of oil on His head. She anointed Him with oil. It seems that she recognized Him as the Anointed One, which in Greek is the word *Christos*, from which we derive the word *Christ*. She recognized that the one who was reclining at the table was her Messiah, who was anointed by the Holy Spirit at His baptism (3:16).

This scene is such a stark contrast to what was going on behind closed doors at the palace of Caiaphas. There, the Jewish leaders were conferring together about how they could kill Jesus. In Bethany, an unidentified woman was performing an extravagant act of love, devotion, and adoration for her Messiah.

But her extravagant act was interrupted by the disciples. Matthew tells us: **But**

when His disciples saw it, they were indignant, saying, "Why this waste? For this fragrant oil might have been sold for much and given to the poor" (vv. 8–9). The disciples were appalled to see such valuable oil spilled out so copiously. How dare this woman pour all this perfume on Jesus. Did she not realize how much money she was wasting? Did she not realize how much good could have been accomplished if the perfume had been sold and the proceeds given to the poor? I do not know whether this woman had done all the math, but for her, nothing was too good for Jesus. By her act of devotion and sacrifice, she shamed the disciples. They should have praised her, saying, "What a magnificent thing you have done for our Messiah." Instead, they were indignant.

The disciples' attitude did not escape Jesus' attention: **But when Jesus was aware of it, He said to them, "Why do you trouble the woman? For she has done a good work for Me. For you have the poor with you always, but Me you do not have always. For in pouring this fragrant oil on My body, she did it for My burial"** (vv. 10–12). Jesus defended the woman. He told them she had done "a good work for Me." I think a better translation would be "a beautiful work for Me." What she did, the materials she did it with, and her motive in doing it were all beautiful. And what was that motive? Jesus said she did it to prepare Him for His burial. Bodies were often anointed with valuable perfume to show respect to the deceased. Because Jesus was given a hasty burial after He died on the cross and then rose again on the first day of the week before the women could anoint His body with spices, this was the only anointing for burial He was to receive.

As part of this rebuke of His disciples, Jesus uttered a sentence that has often been misunderstood and misapplied: "You have the poor with you always, but Me you do not have always." Several years ago, I preached at a church in inner-city Cleveland, an area that was afflicted with all the problems of urban blight—drug abuse, crime, and so on. The minister of that church had been there for many years, but he told me that he had had more than fifteen associates during the time he had been the pastor. When I asked him why he had experienced such high turnover, he explained that young ministers would come out of seminary with zeal to do good works, but when they came to inner-city Cleveland, they rarely lasted more than a couple of years because they were defeated by the poverty, the squalor, the crime, and the hopelessness. That made me curious as to how he had been able to stay there so long, so I asked him about it. He said: "Because of what Jesus said: 'You have the poor with you always.' I didn't come here to eliminate poverty, because I knew that wasn't going to happen. I came here to minister to people in the middle of it."

That is precisely what Jesus meant. He was not saying that we are free to ignore the poor. He was giving His disciples a realistic picture of ministry. We are not going to get rid of poverty. We are not going to get rid of pain. We are not going to get rid of suffering. But we are to minister in the middle of it. Thus, selling one alabaster flask of perfume would not have solved the problem of poverty.

Finally Jesus told His disciples, **"Assuredly, I say to you, wherever this gospel is preached in the whole world, what this woman has done will also be told as a memorial to her"** (v. 13). Jesus knew that the gospel was going to be preached in the whole world. He knew that the good news He had proclaimed was not going to be snuffed out on a cross outside of Jerusalem. Rather, it would spread everywhere, and when it did, the woman's act of devotion would be told as a memorial to her. She would be honored for her extravagant gift to honor the Lord Jesus Christ.

The great ones of the Jews were meeting in the high priest's palace to hatch their grand schemes. Most of those men are forgotten and their plots are unknown to history. But the action of a simple woman who loved Jesus has indeed been told all over the world as the gospel has been preached.

118

JUDAS'S BETRAYAL

Matthew 26:14–25

Then one of the twelve, called Judas Iscariot, went to the chief priests and said, "What are you willing to give me if I deliver Him to you?" And they counted out to him thirty pieces of silver. So from that time he sought opportunity to betray Him. Now on the first day of the Feast of Unleavened Bread the disciples came to Jesus, saying to Him, "Where do You want us to prepare for You to eat the Passover?" And He said, "Go into the city to a certain man, and say to him, 'The Teacher says, "My time is at hand; I will keep the Passover at your house with My disciples."'" So the disciples did as Jesus had directed them; and they prepared the Passover. When evening had come, He sat down with the twelve. Now as they were eating, He said, "Assuredly, I say to you, one of you will betray Me." And they were exceedingly sorrowful, and each of them began to say to Him, "Lord, is it I?" He answered and said, "He who dipped his hand with Me in the dish will betray Me. The Son of Man indeed goes just as it is written of Him, but woe to that man by whom the Son of Man is betrayed! It would have been good for that man if he had not been born." Then Judas, who was betraying Him, answered and said, "Rabbi, is it I?" He said to him, "You have said it."

It is said with respect to human relationships that it takes a long time, often years, to develop trust, a deep, profound trust between human beings, but it takes only moments to destroy it. What person has never experienced the pain and shock of being betrayed by a friend, a husband or wife, or a brother or sister? Words simply are inadequate to describe the pain that accompanies betrayal.

We see betrayals on the pages of Scripture. King David betrayed the trust of his faithful soldier Uriah the Hittite, committing adultery with Uriah's wife, Bathsheba, and then plotting Uriah's death (2 Samuel 11). Likewise, Paul was betrayed by a companion. He wrote to Timothy from prison, "Demas has forsaken me, having loved this present world" (2 Tim. 4:10a). The annals of history are filled with reports of such treachery. During my first visit to Westminster Abbey in London, I was amazed to discover that Benedict Arnold had been afforded a hero's burial in that sacred shrine. I could understand that from England's perspective he was a hero, but in American history, his name is synonymous with the word *traitor*. In all of these instances, trust was broken and people were harmed.

Yet all of these incidents pale to insignificance when we think about the betrayal of the Son of God Himself. Matthew provides a brief record of the machinations by which Judas Iscariot, one of the Twelve, the men who were closest to Jesus, moved to betray his Lord. Matthew has told us how the scribes, the Pharisees, the Sadducees, and others conspired to do away with Jesus. But here at the critical hour, as Jesus was about to enter His passion, the specter of betrayal invaded His inner circle. It is for this reason that the night before Jesus was crucified is commonly known as "the same night in which He was betrayed" (1 Cor. 11:23). That is an indication of the significance of this terrible event.

A Betrayer among the Twelve

Matthew writes: **Then one of the twelve, called Judas Iscariot, went to the chief priests and said, "What are you willing to give me if I deliver Him to you?"** (vv. 14–15a). The religious leaders did not come to Judas. He volunteered. He took it upon himself to go to them to see what he stood to gain by betraying Jesus. Basically he asked them, "What is it worth to you for me to betray Him into your hands?" In reply, **they counted out to him thirty pieces of silver** (v. 15b), which happened to be the normal price that was paid to purchase a slave in the marketplace. Then Matthew adds, **So from that time he sought opportunity to betray Him** (v. 16). Judas accepted the financial compensation the chief priests offered and began to watch for his chance.

Some scholars look at this transaction and actually try to make a hero out of Judas, saying that he was trying to force the inauguration of the kingdom of God. He knew that the kingdom would not come until the final confrontation between Jesus and the forces of evil at Jerusalem. So, Judas simply was trying to speed things along by striking this surreptitious agreement to hand Jesus over.

Others say he was frustrated because he had counted on Jesus to deliver his people from the Romans, and when he finally came to an understanding that Jesus was going to be a suffering Savior, not a conquering hero, it was more than he could stomach. All of that is pure speculation. The only motive the Scriptures give us for Judas's act of betrayal is money.

I cannot help noticing all of the planning and conspiring that was going on in the minds of evil men. We know that the chief priests, scribes, and elders were meeting at the palace of the high priest to plot a way to trick Jesus and ultimately kill him (vv. 3–5). Of course, they were concerned not to raise a protest from the people who were visiting Jerusalem from Galilee, who loved Jesus because they had profited from His healing ministry and His teaching. Now we see Judas assuming a role in their plotting. At first glance, it can seem that poor innocent Jesus was the victim of these plots and schemes. But that is not how the New Testament sees it. Peter put that idea to rest in his sermon on the Day of Pentecost:

> Men of Israel, hear these words: Jesus of Nazareth, a Man attested by God to you by miracles, wonders, and signs which God did through Him in your midst, as you yourselves also know—Him, being delivered by the determined purpose and foreknowledge of God, you have taken by lawless hands, have crucified, and put to death; whom God raised up, having loosed the pains of death, because it was not possible that He should be held by it. (Acts 2:22–24)

Peter did not say that Jesus was delivered by the wicked machinations of the high priest and the pernicious betrayal of Judas Iscariot. Instead, He attributed Jesus' arrest, trial, and execution by the Romans to "the determined purpose and foreknowledge of God." Who was sovereign over the betrayal of the Son of Man into the hands of His enemies? It was God the Father, who from all eternity sovereignly decreed that at a particular point in time He would make good use of the evil desires of men to bring about His plan of redemption.

As we noted in the previous chapter, Jesus was not surprised by any of this. He knew it was the will of the Father that He go to the cross. He had told His disciples about it weeks before: "The Son of Man is about to be betrayed into the hands of men, and they will kill Him, and the third day He will be raised up" (17:22b–23a). He was aware of what was going to happen, and He was content with it.

Matthew goes on to note: **Now on the first day of the Feast of Unleavened Bread the disciples came to Jesus, saying to Him, "Where do You want us to prepare for You to eat the Passover?" And He said, "Go into the city to**

a certain man, and say to him, 'The Teacher says, "My time is at hand; I will keep the Passover at your house with My disciples."'" So the disciples did as Jesus had directed them; and they prepared the Passover (vv. 17–19). Sometime on Thursday, the disciples asked Jesus where they should prepare for their celebration of the Passover meal that night. He told them to seek out a certain man in Jerusalem and to tell him that Jesus and His disciples would be keeping the Passover at his home. The disciples did as Jesus instructed them and made ready for the meal. Mark adds the detail that the owner of the home directed them to a furnished upper room (14:15). Therefore, **When evening had come, He sat down with the twelve** (v. 20).

Then Matthew tells us: **Now as they were eating, He said, "Assuredly, I say to you, one of you will betray Me." And they were exceedingly sorrowful, and each of them began to say to Him, "Lord, is it I?"** (vv. 21–22). Can you imagine the shock the disciples must have felt when Jesus made this announcement? He had said earlier, "The Son of Man is about to be betrayed into the hands of men," but He had given no indication who would betray Him. Now He told them that the betrayer would be one of *them*. As Matthew writes, they were "exceedingly sorrowful." One by one, probably with great hesitation, they began to ask Him, "Lord, is it I?" I imagine they asked this question with great fear, but they had to know.

Jesus did not reply directly. Instead, **He answered and said, "He who dipped his hand with Me in the dish will betray Me"** (v. 23). All of the disciples had been dipping morsels of bread and meat in the common bowl of sauce, so this statement gave no identity. However, it was another reminder of the seriousness of the betrayal. Jesus was sharing table fellowship with the man who would betray Him.

Man's Evil Will and God's Divine Will

Jesus then made a very interesting comment: **"The Son of Man indeed goes just as it is written of Him, but woe to that man by whom the Son of Man is betrayed! It would have been good for that man if he had not been born"** (v. 24). He was saying that His course to the cross had been laid out by God and foretold in the prophets. It was God's plan from eternity past. Nevertheless, to betray Him was an act of horrendous sin. The betrayer would not be able to say to God that he was simply helping to bring the divine plan to fruition. I can hear Judas at judgment day, saying to the Father: "Why do you want to punish me, God? If it weren't for me, the atonement wouldn't have happened. If it weren't for me, your plan of redemption would have been ruined. I simply carried out the duty that you assigned to me from the foundation of the world.

How can you yet find fault?" But if Judas does indeed make that argument, it will carry no weight. Jesus pronounced woe on Judas and said it would have been better if he had not been born, for even though great good came about through his act of evil, it was evil nonetheless.

This issue comes up again and again in the Scriptures as the sovereignty of God and the sinful choices of human beings intersect. In the book of Job, we see that everything Job had—his livestock, his children, his health—was taken away by various parties (Job 1–2). For instance, his oxen and donkeys were stolen by the Sabeans (1:14–15). Did Satan force the Sabeans to take his livestock? No. The story begins with the complaint of Satan that the only reason why Job praised God was because God had put a hedge around him and protected him from all the assaults of the enemy. Satan said, "Stretch out Your hand and touch all that he has, and he will surely curse You to Your face!" (1:11), so God gave him permission to afflict Job. What happened? Did Satan possess the Sabeans and force them to take the livestock? No. The Sabeans had nothing but cattle rustling in their hearts. For decades, they had loathed the wealth of Job, but they had to look at him through the hedge. As soon as God removed the hedge, these wicked people did their wickedness, unwittingly serving the righteous purpose of God.

We call this the doctrine of concurrence. We see it most clearly in Genesis 37–50, in the account of Joseph's dealing with his brothers. Filled with jealousy toward Joseph because their father favored him, the brothers sold him to Midianite traders. Then they put animal's blood on his coat of many colors and took it back to Jacob, suggesting that he had been killed by a wild animal. Joseph was then sold into slavery, after which he was falsely accused of attacking a man's wife and was thrown into prison. He endured one injustice after another, all because of the treachery and betrayal of his brothers. However, in the providence of God, Joseph was released from prison and elevated to the rank of prime minister of all of Egypt. When a famine hit, Jacob sent his sons down to Egypt to seek food, so the family would not starve. When they arrived, they met with the prime minister, but they did not recognize him. He was dressed in Egyptian clothes and was speaking the Egyptian language. Eventually Joseph revealed himself to them and forgave them, but the brothers remained nervous that Joseph would bring vengeance on them someday. After their father died, the brothers said: "'Perhaps Joseph will hate us, and may actually repay us for all the evil which we did to him.' So they sent messengers to Joseph, saying, 'Before your father died he commanded, saying, "Thus you shall say to Joseph: 'I beg you, please forgive the trespass of your brothers and their sin; for they did evil to you.'" Now, please, forgive the trespass of the servants of the God of your father'" (50:15–17). What did Joseph say? "Do not be afraid, for am I in the place of

God? But as for you, you meant evil against me; but God meant it for good, in order to bring it about as it is this day, to save many people alive" (vv. 19–20).

At the intersection of the divine will and the human will, two forces were acting with pure intentionality. One of those forces was the evil brothers. Joseph said the things they did to him were from an evil motive. But all the while they were doing evil, they were accomplishing the will of God. In His sovereignty, God used their sin. He used their evil to bring about the salvation of Joseph's family. Were the brothers therefore excused? No. They knew what they were doing. Furthermore, they intended what they were doing. They did what they wanted to do. They were freely involved in a treacherous act, but above them stood the sovereign One, who took their evil and used it for His righteous purpose.

The same thing happened when Judas sold Jesus. Judas did what he wanted to do. He did what his evil intentions directed him to do. But the whole time he was doing it, God trumped him. That is why the Apostle Paul writes, "And we know that all things work together for good to those who love God, to those who are the called according to His purpose" (Rom. 8:28). If God were not sovereign, we would have no hope of the ultimate victory of righteousness. But because He is sovereign, He can use even the evil acts of men to accomplish His will. Thus, it truly would have been better for Judas had he not been born. His betrayal of Jesus was unspeakably evil.

Matthew writes: **Then Judas, who was betraying Him, answered and said, "Rabbi, is it I?" He said to him, "You have said it"** (v. 25). Judas followed the other disciples in asking whether he was the betrayer, but he was not asking an honest question. Perhaps he hoped to hide his plans by seeming to be as distressed as the other disciples. But Jesus' reply to his question was different: "You have said it." This was a Greek expression that put responsibility back onto the questioner. So, Jesus essentially identified Judas as His betrayer. In John's Gospel, we are told that Jesus specifically gave him a piece of bread to make the identification. At that point, Satan entered him, whereupon Jesus said, "What you do, do quickly" (13:26–27). As we will see, Judas did just that, betraying His Lord later that night.

119

THE LORD'S SUPPER

Matthew 26:26–35

And as they were eating, Jesus took bread, blessed and broke it, and gave it to the disciples and said, "Take, eat; this is My body." Then He took the cup, and gave thanks, and gave it to them, saying, "Drink from it, all of you. For this is My blood of the new covenant, which is shed for many for the remission of sins. But I say to you, I will not drink of this fruit of the vine from now on until that day when I drink it new with you in My Father's kingdom." And when they had sung a hymn, they went out to the Mount of Olives. Then Jesus said to them, "All of you will be made to stumble because of Me this night, for it is written:

> 'I will strike the Shepherd,
> And the sheep of the flock will be scattered.'

But after I have been raised, I will go before you to Galilee." Peter answered and said to Him, "Even if all are made to stumble because of You, I will never be made to stumble." Jesus said to him, "Assuredly, I say to you that this night, before the rooster crows, you will deny Me three times." Peter said to Him, "Even if I have to die with You, I will not deny You!" And so said all the disciples.

I like to think of the event that we witness in this passage from Matthew's Gospel as the birthday of the New Testament church. Of course, it is not the ultimate birthday of the church, as that happened far back into the days of the Old Testament, when God established His covenant with a particular people. Still, the New Testament church, the new-covenant church, began at a particular point in time, though not all scholars agree as to when that point was. Some believe it began with the earthly ministry of Jesus. More believe it began on the day of Pentecost, when the Holy Spirit was poured out in power. But I am convinced that the church was born in the upper room during the celebration of the Passover, because it was at that time that the Lord Jesus Christ, the Mediator of the new covenant, instituted that covenant, which He ratified with His blood the following day. So, when we read of the celebration in the upper room and the institution of the Lord's Supper, it is important for us to understand that this was not just another moment in the lives of Jesus and His disciples. Rather, it was a moment of tremendous significance in their lives and in the history of redemption.

The obvious context of the institution of the Lord's Supper was the Passover, the Jews' annual celebration of their deliverance from Egypt thousands of years before. On the night when God Himself passed through the land of Egypt and slew all the firstborn in the tenth and last of the terrible plagues He brought on Pharaoh, He passed over the homes of the Israelites where He saw lambs' blood on the doorposts. Every year afterward, the Jews celebrated this wonderful deliverance by divine command. God told them that when they celebrated the Passover, they should tell their sons, "This is done because of what the Lord did for me when I came up from Egypt" (Ex. 13:8).

As a boy, Jesus certainly was involved in the celebration of the Passover, and He no doubt had a growing awareness that it was His destiny to be the absolute fulfillment of the significance of the Passover. He was the Lamb of God, who would be slain and whose blood would set apart everyone who embraced Him, that they might not suffer judgment at the hands of God for their sin.

Jesus Institutes the Lord's Supper

Matthew begins this important account by writing, **And as they were eating, Jesus took bread, blessed and broke it, and gave it to the disciples and said, "Take, eat; this is My body"** (v. 26). Jesus and His disciples were celebrating the ritual Passover meal when Jesus introduced a radical change in the liturgy. Following the normal course of the celebration, He took the bread, blessed it, and broke it. But then He departed from the liturgy and said, "This is My body."

Luke adds a little more to this statement of Jesus: "This is My body which is given for you; do this in remembrance of Me" (22:19). Interestingly, when the Apostle Paul discusses the Lord's Supper, he renders this line slightly differently: "This is My body which is *broken* for you; do this in remembrance of Me" (1 Cor. 11:24, emphasis added). Some scholars fuss about whether He said His body was "given" for the disciples or "broken" for them. Those who disapprove of the use of the word *broken* do so on the grounds that John's Gospel tells us that, in fulfillment of prophecy, not a bone of Jesus' body was broken (19:31–36). It is true His bones were not broken, but His body was broken. It was broken by the thorns in the crown that was pressed on His head. It was broken by the scourge that ripped apart the skin of His back. It was broken by the nails that pierced His hands and feet, and by the spear that pierced His side. They broke Him when they killed Him, just as He tore the bread apart in the upper room.

Matthew continues: **Then He took the cup, and gave thanks, and gave it to them, saying, "Drink from it, all of you. For this is My blood of the new covenant, which is shed for many for the remission of sins"** (vv. 27–28). Once again Jesus gave the prayer of thanksgiving, but then He changed this portion of the liturgy, too. He told the disciples the cup would no longer represent the blood of the lamb that was spread on the doorposts by the Israelites enslaved in Egypt; it would represent His blood. Specifically, it would represent His blood "of the new covenant, which is shed for many for the remission of sins." It was at this moment, I believe, that the church of Jesus Christ was born, because it was at this moment that He instituted the new covenant. In one sense, what Jesus did here mirrored an establishment of a covenant in the Old Testament. But it also completely fulfilled the old covenant and instituted the full measure of the covenant relationship that we have with God in Jesus Christ.

It would be helpful for us to review the establishment of God's covenant with Israel at Sinai. We read in the book of Exodus:

> Now He said to Moses, "Come up to the Lord, you and Aaron, Nadab and Abihu, and seventy of the elders of Israel, and worship from afar. And Moses alone shall come near the Lord, but they shall not come near; nor shall the people go up with him." So Moses came and told the people all the words of the Lord and all the judgments. And all the people answered with one voice and said, "All the words which the Lord has said we will do." And Moses wrote all the words of the Lord. And he rose early in the morning, and built an altar at the foot of the mountain, and twelve pillars according to the twelve tribes of Israel. Then he sent young men of the children of Israel, who offered burnt offerings and sacrificed peace offerings of oxen to the Lord. And Moses took half the blood and put it in basins, and half the blood he sprinkled on the altar. Then he took the Book

> of the Covenant and read in the hearing of the people. And they said, "All that the LORD has said we will do, and be obedient." And Moses took the blood, sprinkled it on the people, and said, "This is the blood of the covenant which the LORD has made with you according to all these words." (24:1–8)

In this ceremony, Moses, the mediator of the old covenant, ratified the covenant God had made with His people. First, he sprinkled the blood on the altar. Then he sprinkled it on the people. This signified the cutting of the covenant, the solemn consecration of the people whom God had chosen to redeem to Himself, set apart in a bloody rite.

In the upper room on the night when He was betrayed, Jesus said His blood was being poured out "for the remission of sins." When sins are remitted, they go away. They are removed. Do you understand how fundamental this is? The basic problem of the human race is that God is holy and we are not. We all sin. We violate the rule of God. Is there any deliverance from it? How do we deal with sin?

Years ago, I was involved in a seminar on apologetics and the rational defense of the truth claims of Christianity on a college campus. After the meeting, I spoke with a young man who brought up one rational argument against Christianity after another. I was praying that God would give me patience to deal with his hostility, cynicism, and skepticism. He would ask a question and I would endeavor to answer it, but instead of sticking to that question and pursuing it, he would jump to the next question, and when I answered that, he would jump to the next question. There was no end to it. After a while, I began to question the honesty of his objections. I finally interrupted the process and said: "Before we jump to the next question, let me ask you a question. What do you do with your guilt?" I did not ask him, "Do you have guilt?" because I knew he did, and I knew that he knew that he had guilt. There was no necessity to debate it. So, I was not surprised that when I asked this question, he fell silent.

What do you do with your guilt? The normal responses are to deny it, to rationalize it, to hide it, or perhaps to admit a little bit of it but not the full weight. But none of these techniques can get rid of it. We are all like Lady Macbeth, screaming, "Out, out, damn spot!" We cannot get our hands clean. There's only one remedy for guilt under heaven—forgiveness. Sin can be remitted only if it is forgiven. Christians are simply a fellowship of forgiven people. Every time we celebrate the Lord's Supper, we celebrate the birth of the New Testament church, the institution of the new covenant, and the day in which our Savior announced that He was going to pour out His blood to remove our sins.

Jesus then said, **"But I say to you, I will not drink of this fruit of the vine from now on until that day when I drink it new with you in My Father's**

kingdom" (v. 29). Jesus apparently was referring to the marriage supper of the Lamb (Rev. 19:9), but it is unclear why He planned to refrain from wine until that time.

Jesus Foretells Peter's Denials

Matthew writes, **And when they had sung a hymn, they went out to the Mount of Olives** (v. 30). Jesus and His disciples completed the Passover liturgy with the singing of a hymn, perhaps the Hallel (Psalms 113–118). Then they left the upper room and went out of the city to the Mount of Olives. As we will see in the next chapter, Jesus was seeking communion with His Father in Gethsemane as the hour of His arrest drew near.

Jesus had delivered bad news to the disciples during their Passover celebration when He told them that one of them would betray Him (v. 21), and there on the Mount of Olives He gave them more bad news: **Then Jesus said to them, "All of you will be made to stumble because of Me this night, for it is written: 'I will strike the Shepherd, and the sheep of the flock will be scattered.' But after I have been raised, I will go before you to Galilee"** (vv. 31–32). Jesus told them that not only would one of them betray Him, *all* of them would stumble because of Him that night. Just as sheep wander about if their shepherd is struck down, so the disciples would "wander" off when Jesus was arrested. But He also promised to lead them north to Galilee when He rose again.

Ever-impetuous Peter had no use for that kind of talk: **Peter answered and said to Him, "Even if all are made to stumble because of You, I will never be made to stumble"** (v. 33). He was certain he was made of sterner stuff than the other disciples and would stand by Jesus no matter what. But Jesus refused to leave him in that self-confidence. Matthew writes, **Jesus said to him, "Assuredly, I say to you that this night, before the rooster crows, you will deny Me three times"** (v. 34). Can you imagine how this prophecy must have hit Peter? Not only would he "stumble," he would deny his Lord, and not once but three times. Yet Peter somehow found the strength to deny what Jesus was saying: **Peter said to Him, "Even if I have to die with You, I will not deny You!" And so said all the disciples** (v. 35). Peter emphatically rejected Jesus' prophetic word, and all of the disciples said the same thing. I do not doubt they loved Jesus and wanted to stand by Him. But the pressures of the night to come would be too much for their feeble faith.

We must never overestimate our courage and devotion to Christ. None of us knows how we will behave when the moment of crisis comes. We need to pray for strength to stand strong when the pressure is on. We can rejoice that the One who gives us the faith by which we believe will strengthen that faith when the time comes.

120

THE GARDEN OF GETHSEMANE

Matthew 26:36–46

Then Jesus came with them to a place called Gethsemane, and said to the disciples, "Sit here while I go and pray over there." And He took with Him Peter and the two sons of Zebedee, and He began to be sorrowful and deeply distressed. Then He said to them, "My soul is exceedingly sorrowful, even to death. Stay here and watch with Me." He went a little farther and fell on His face, and prayed, saying, "O My Father, if it is possible, let this cup pass from Me; nevertheless, not as I will, but as You will." Then He came to the disciples and found them sleeping, and said to Peter, "What! Could you not watch with Me one hour? Watch and pray, lest you enter into temptation. The spirit indeed is willing, but the flesh is weak." Again, a second time, He went away and prayed, saying, "O My Father, if this cup cannot pass away from Me unless I drink it, Your will be done." And He came and found them asleep again, for their eyes were heavy. So He left them, went away again, and prayed the third time, saying the same words. Then He came to His disciples and said to them, "Are you still sleeping and resting? Behold, the hour is at hand, and the Son of Man is being betrayed into the hands of sinners. Rise, let us be going. See, My betrayer is at hand."

One of the first heresies that plagued the infant church was docetism. It derived its name from the Greek verb *dokeō*, which means "to seem, to think, or to appear." Docetists were heavily influenced by the ideas of the Greeks, for whom it was unthinkable that the eternal could come into union with anything physical, material, or temporal. The great scandal to the Greeks was not the resurrection of Christ but His incarnation. The idea that God would take upon Himself a human body, uniting with flesh, was utterly repugnant to them. Under the influence of this viewpoint, the docetists taught that Jesus did not really have a human body and a human nature. He merely appeared to have a body, but Jesus was really a phantom, as it were. In short, this heresy denied and obscured the real humanity of Jesus.

Although the church repudiated this heretical movement in the early centuries, it has never completely disappeared. Elements of docetism still infect our thinking about Jesus. We have a tendency to deify His human nature and to deny the full reality of His humanity. Thankfully, we have passages such as the one before us in this chapter, which displays the authenticity of Jesus' humanity like few others.

I have preached on this episode in Jesus' life many times. Every time I approach it, I come in a spirit of fear and trembling. As I look at this text, I feel as if I am standing over a chasm, and if I make a wrong step, I will fall to my utter destruction. I simply cannot adequately understand what is going on here. As we read this passage, we are, as it were, eavesdropping on the most intense, literally excruciating, prayer ever uttered by mortal lips.

Sometimes in theology we ask frivolous questions. For instance, when I consider the humanity of Jesus, questions such as these come to my mind: Did Jesus ever have a headache? Did Jesus ever have the flu? Did He experience other maladies? Why would questions like these come to my mind? I wonder about these things because our Lord was born without original sin, as a result of which He never committed actual sin. If, in His perfect humanity, He was outside the realm of the impulses of sin, how could He have been affected by the results of sin? We are told in Scripture that diseases and other physical maladies came into this world as a direct result of human sinfulness, but Jesus was without sin. Does that mean He was without headaches? I do not know the answer to that question. My guess, however, is that He *did* suffer headaches and such. Why? Even though He was born without sin, He entered into the fallenness of the human situation. We have seen that during His temptation in the wilderness He felt the pangs of hunger (4:2). While on the cross He said, "I thirst" (John 19:28). If pain is totally incompatible with sinless humanity, how could Jesus have experienced hunger or thirst? I think that even in His sinlessness He was exposed to all of the pain, grief, sorrow, and suffering that accompany humanity's fallen condition, and I believe we see a glimpse of that in this passage.

The Sorrowful Savior

We have already seen that after the Last Supper, Jesus and His disciples went out to the Mount of Olives (v. 30), where Jesus told the disciples that they would all "stumble" that night (v. 31) and told Peter that he would deny Him three times before the morning was out (v. 34). Then, Matthew tells us: **Jesus came with them to a place called Gethsemane, and said to the disciples, "Sit here while I go and pray over there." And He took with Him Peter and the two sons of Zebedee, and He began to be sorrowful and deeply distressed. Then He said to them, "My soul is exceedingly sorrowful, even to death. Stay here and watch with Me"** (vv. 36–38).

They arrived at a garden known as Gethsemane, where the olives that grew on ancient trees there were pressed and the oil was collected for use and for sale. Jesus told most of the disciples to wait while He went apart a short distance to pray, but He asked Peter, James, and John to accompany Him. When the four of them drew apart from the others, Jesus began to show Himself to be "sorrowful and deeply distressed." It was as if He felt more freedom to let down His guard with these three men than the whole group. He described His feelings to them as "exceedingly sorrowful, even to death." Clearly, He was very, very upset and troubled. This was not simply mental anguish. It was grief, a tempest of pain that pierced His soul.

However, Jesus did not ask the three disciples to pray with Him. He did not initiate a prayer meeting. No one else could join with Him; that which was before Him was a solo task for which He was the only human being in all of human history who was qualified. He needed to pray alone, to express His inmost struggles to His Father. He had already moved away from the rest of the group, and now He needed to move away from the inner circle, though He seems to have wanted them to stay close to Him. He asked them to stay and to watch.

I am certain that no prayer in human history was uttered with greater intensity, greater agony, greater poignancy, or greater pathos than the prayer Jesus prayed when He went apart from His disciples. Luke tells us that as He prayed, "His sweat became like great drops of blood falling down to the ground" (22:44). The intensity of His prayer was such that the capillaries in His forehead burst. Before the crown of thorns was ever put on His brow, rivulets of blood cascaded down His cheeks as He wrestled with His sorrow over the suffering He faced.

Do you see why I feel a sense of despair in trying to comprehend what was going on here? I do not know how many times I have read the prayer that Marin Luther wrote in his cell on the night before he had to face the powerful men of church and state at the Imperial Diet (the general assembly) at Worms, Germany, where his life was on the line. I can relate to Luther's agony, but Jesus' torment is another thing entirely. He was not simply another man facing death. If the only thing that lay before Jesus on the morrow was the experience of death, He would have faced it with a greater serenity than Socrates displayed before he drank the hemlock. Multitudes of courageous men and women through history have faced death calmly. But it was not the prospect of death that provoked this sorrow of Jesus' soul. It was the experience He would have to pass through before death came, when He would be forsaken by His Father.

"If It Is Possible, Let This Cup Pass"

Matthew tells us: **He went a little farther and fell on His face, and prayed** (v. 39a). From time to time in the Gospel narratives, we see people who ran to Jesus, imploring Him or thanking Him, and they fell on their faces before Him in subjection to honor Him (Luke 5:12; 17:6). Peter, James, and John fell on their faces when the Father spoke from heaven at the transfiguration (Matt. 17:6). However, this is the only time in all of Scripture when we read of Jesus falling on His face, prostrating Himself in the lowest form of humility before His Father.

In that posture, He prayed, **"O My Father, if it is possible, let this cup pass from Me; nevertheless, not as I will, but as You will"** (v. 39b). Every word He uttered was vital. He began with a heartfelt address: "O My Father." Then He asked, "If it is possible . . ." This plea came from Jesus' human nature. His divine nature is omniscient, for it shares all of the attributes of deity. God knows all things as well as all possibilities, all contingencies. He does not have to wait to see what transpires on earth in order to learn an outcome. There is no *if* in the vocabulary of God. But this was Jesus' human nature speaking. The human nature does not have omniscience. It does not know everything that is possible and not possible. Jesus' human nature was staggering in the face of what was coming, so He asked: "O My Father, is it possible? Is there another way We can do this?"

His hope, if it was possible, was that the Father would "let this cup pass from Me." He was not referring to the cup of sadness, sorrow, and distress. The image of the cup in biblical terms, in Old Testament terms, has to do with the wrath of God. The cup of God's judgment on human sin was being set before the Son of God. Jesus was crying: "O Father, is there any other way? I'll go to the cross. I'll lay down My life. I'll pour out My blood. I can handle the cross. I can take the wrath of the Romans. I can take the wrath of the leaders of the Sanhedrin. But do I have to be utterly exposed to Your unmitigated wrath against the sin of Your people?"

But Jesus was not finished. He prayed, "nevertheless, not as I will, but as You will." He was saying: "Father, with every fiber of My being, I shrink away from that cup. I do not want to drink it. But there is one thing that would be even worse, and that would be to fail to do Your will. If it is Your will that I drink this cup, if there is no other way to do it, then give Me the cup, and I'll drink it to the last drop."

Willing Spirits, Weak Flesh

Matthew continues: **Then He came to the disciples and found them sleeping** (v. 40a). It was as if Jesus was too agitated to stay still. He needed to pace, as it were, or perhaps He needed companionship at that moment. In any case, He went back to where He had left Peter, James, and John, but instead of watching as He had asked, they were sleeping. Despite seeing how distressed Jesus was, which surely was not customary for Him, they were unconcerned enough to doze off. Obviously the Last Supper went late that night, and this episode in Gethsemane, which took place just before the arrest of Jesus, happened in the early morning hours. Nevertheless, it is difficult for me to understand how they could sleep when the moment of crisis seemed so close at hand. I think we can safely guess that Jesus would have to drink the cup that was before Him within the next twelve hours. He was in the final hours of his life, pre-resurrection, and the last minutes of His freedom as a Man on this planet before He was taken into custody, and His closest friends had fallen asleep on their watch.

This prompted Jesus to deliver a mild rebuke. He said to Peter: **"What! Could you not watch with Me one hour? Watch and pray, lest you enter into temptation. The spirit indeed is willing, but the flesh is weak"** (vv. 40b–41). Jesus expressed surprise that the disciples could not stay awake with Him for an hour. He counseled them to "watch and pray," so that they might be delivered from the temptation to fall asleep and thus fail to stand by their Lord. Jesus acknowledged that "the spirit indeed is willing, but the flesh is weak." He was saying that He knew the disciples wanted to support Him, follow Him, and stand with Him, but in the weakness of their flesh, they were tired and sad, and they could not watch with Him even for an hour.

Matthew then tells us, **Again, a second time, He went away and prayed, saying, "O My Father, if this cup cannot pass away from Me unless I drink it, Your will be done"** (v. 42). Reading between the lines here, I get the sense that God had already answered His first prayer, that already God had said to Him, "No! I'm not taking away the cup."

I often hear people say, "Sometimes I feel so frustrated in my prayer life because it seems like God doesn't answer my prayers." They are wrong; God *always* answers our prayers, every one of them. Sometimes He says yes, but many times the answer is no. Our problem is that when He says no, when He chooses in His wisdom not to grant what we have asked of Him, we think He has not answered. But praying to God is not like putting in an order at a restaurant, where we have the right to be upset if the meal is not brought to our table. God is free to answer as He pleases, but we have the assurance that no matter how He answers, it is for His glory and our good. He certainly heard the prayer of His Son, but He said no, and that was most certainly a great good.

But Jesus did not stop praying. He said, "O My Father, if this cup cannot pass away from Me unless I drink it, Your will be done." He was saying: "Father, it is clear this is Your will, and I need Your help to do it. I can do this only if You help Me."

Continuing His pacing, **He came and found them asleep again, for their eyes were heavy** (v. 43). Jesus' earlier rebuke had not induced them to find some way to stay awake, but Jesus said no more to them. Instead, **He left them, went away again, and prayed the third time, saying the same words** (v. 44). Finally, when He had poured out all His agony to His Father, **He came to His disciples and said to them, "Are you still sleeping and resting? Behold, the hour is at hand, and the Son of Man is being betrayed into the hands of sinners. Rise, let us be going. See, My betrayer is at hand"** (vv. 45–46).

This episode teaches us much about Jesus, especially about the authenticity of His humanity. This was no phantom praying in Gethsemane. This was a man of flesh and bone, uniquely indwelt by the divine nature, who was in agony before a single nail pierced His flesh. That with which He was wrestling and pleading with the Father is of the very essence of the gospel. This struggle gives us a glimpse into our salvation. If He had refused to drink that cup to its dregs, there would be no salvation for us. All that would be left for us is wrath, for we would have to drink the cup ourselves.

I must note that while Jesus agreed to drink the cup, He did not agree to drink it for everyone. He drank the cup only for the ones for whom the Father had appointed Him to drink it. If He drank the cup of God's wrath for everyone in the world indiscriminately, everyone would be saved. But the Bible makes it clear that not everyone is saved. All the wrath God had stored up for those who need atonement was taken by Jesus in that cup. He had just told His disciples that He was going to shed His blood of the new covenant for the remission of sins. If you are a Christian, your sins were in that cup. The wrath of God for your disobedience was in that cup.

I wonder whether I would have been able to stay awake that night. Probably not. I find it hard staying awake in the service of the kingdom of God every day. I find it hard to stand with Him. I find it hard to watch with Him even for one hour. Thankfully, while Jesus wanted his friends there, He did not really need them. He does not need us either. Yet, He loved us enough to die for us, drinking the cup to the bottom all alone.

121

JESUS' ARREST

Matthew 26:47–56

And while He was still speaking, behold, Judas, one of the twelve, with a great multitude with swords and clubs, came from the chief priests and elders of the people. Now His betrayer had given them a sign, saying, "Whomever I kiss, He is the One; seize Him." Immediately he went up to Jesus and said, "Greetings, Rabbi!" and kissed Him. But Jesus said to him, "Friend, why have you come?" Then they came and laid hands on Jesus and took Him. And suddenly, one of those who were with Jesus stretched out his hand and drew his sword, struck the servant of the high priest, and cut off his ear. But Jesus said to him, "Put your sword in its place, for all who take the sword will perish by the sword. Or do you think that I cannot now pray to My Father, and He will provide Me with more than twelve legions of angels? How then could the Scriptures be fulfilled, that it must happen thus?" In that hour Jesus said to the multitudes, "Have you come out, as against a robber, with swords and clubs to take Me? I sat daily with you, teaching in the temple, and you did not seize Me. But all this was done that the Scriptures of the prophets might be fulfilled." Then all the disciples forsook Him and fled.

I have noted that the placement of verses and chapters in Scripture frequently makes little sense, as narratives are sometimes divided at crucial points where there is no pause in the action. I am perhaps now guilty of the same practice I have criticized, having ended the previous chapter and begun this one at a point where there is no cessation whatsoever in Matthew's account. Matthew writes,

And while He was still speaking (v. 47a), referring to the words of Jesus that we examined at the end of the previous chapter: "Rise, let us be going. See, My betrayer is at hand" (v. 46). Even as Jesus spoke those words, Judas appeared. So, please understand that even though we are beginning a new chapter, the events of Jesus' passion were rushing forward, and there was virtually no temporal lapse between the conclusion of His anguished prayer in the garden of Gethsemane and the arrival of those sent to arrest Him.

Matthew tells us, **behold, Judas, one of the twelve, with a great multitude with swords and clubs, came from the chief priests and elders of the people** (v. 47b). Judas came to the garden. We know Judas had been looking for an opportunity to betray Jesus (v. 16), and we know that he was familiar with Gethsemane, for John writes, "Judas . . . also knew the place; for Jesus often met there with His disciples" (18:2). Thus, Gethsemane was a likely place for Judas to look.

Judas did not come alone. Neither did he appear with a small committee or a couple of officers sent out from the Sanhedrin to place Jesus under arrest. Rather, he came with a huge multitude of people bearing swords and clubs. It appears that the entire temple guard came to the garden of Gethsemane to arrest one person. The religious leaders of the Jews were not taking any chances. They wanted to make sure Jesus would not escape. This concern to make no mistake was why they had been willing to pay Judas thirty pieces of silver. They wanted someone who could identify Jesus in the darkness, even in the deep shadows under the olive groves, so that they would not arrest the wrong person when the time came.

Of course, they were also acutely aware of the extraordinary power Jesus had manifested on more than one occasion. Perhaps they recalled that occasion when an angry mob in Nazareth was prepared to throw Jesus off a cliff, but "passing through the midst of them, He went His way" (Luke 4:30). Even more likely they had in mind the time when they themselves were prepared to stone him, but "Jesus hid Himself and went out of the temple, going through the midst of them, and so passed by" (John 8:59). From the perspective of the authorities in Jerusalem, sending a mob to arrest Jesus was not overkill.

The Kiss of Death

Matthew continues: **Now His betrayer had given them a sign, saying, "Whomever I kiss, He is the One; seize Him." Immediately he went up to Jesus and said, "Greetings, Rabbi!" and kissed Him** (vv. 48–49).

So much is wrong with this picture. First, Judas came up to Jesus, saying, "Greetings, Rabbi!" then kissed him. In the ancient Jewish world, there were certain protocols that were observed in the rabbi-student relationship, and these rules were never to be disobeyed. One of those rules was this: If ever a rabbi met one of his students on the street, the rabbi was to speak first, extending his greetings to his student, because the student was not above the master. It was considered exceedingly rude, presumptuous, and arrogant for a student to speak to his rabbi before the rabbi spoke to him. The rabbi was supposed to initiate the greeting. In the midst of his treachery, Judas violated this fundamental rule of courtesy.

Second, Judas made a show of affection for Jesus by kissing Him. But Matthew tells us there was no affection involved; the kiss was merely Judas's prearranged sign by which he identified Jesus for those in the mob who were not familiar with His appearance. It is from this episode that we have the expression "the kiss of death," by which someone's recommendation or praise for another actually works to that person's destruction. If ever there was an occasion when love was faked, it was in this episode when our Lord was greeted with the kiss of death.

We see this practice all the way through sacred Scripture. The greatest and most damaging enemies of the righteous are often the ones closest to them—friends, relatives, or disciples. The same is true in church history. The heroes of Christendom have often been killed by arrows in their backs, struck down by those they least suspected.

Of course, I am not counseling an attitude of distrust of family members and of brothers and sisters in Christ. But we do have to be on our guard in a sense. For instance, we all know that the Bible tells us to speak the truth to one another in love (Eph. 4:15), but I have often observed that when one Christian goes to another and says, "I'd like to tell you something in love," what he has to say is not really meant in love. Rather, while he is smiling and extending a sugarcoated greeting, hidden are the unkind words he will soon extend. So, if someone comes to you and says, "Let me tell you something in love," hear him out, but be on your guard.

Of course, Jesus was not deceived by Judas's expressions of love. He already knew what Judas was going to do and had told him so (Matt. 26:25). He had announced at the Last Supper that He was going to be betrayed (v. 21), and he had dismissed Judas to carry out the deed (John 13:27, 30). In the shadows of Gethsemane, when Jesus saw Judas and his horde of soldiers, he knew exactly what was happening. The kiss that Judas put on His cheek did not fool Him.

We see Jesus' awareness of Judas's purpose in the words He spoke to him. Matthew goes on, **But Jesus said to him, "Friend, why have you come?"** (v. 50a). The word that is translated here as "friend" does not carry the meaning of closeness and affection, but merely acquaintance. Even though Judas had been with Him for three years, Jesus knew there was no affection in his heart. Furthermore, the fact that the New King James Version renders these words of Jesus as a question does not mean Jesus did not know why Judas had come. Other versions translate this statement along these lines: "Friend, do what you came to do" (ESV). Do you see the irony in Jesus' words? He knew Judas was no friend and He knew why he had come.

The Arrest of Jesus

Then Matthew tells us: **Then they came and laid hands on Jesus and took Him. And suddenly, one of those who were with Jesus stretched out his hand and drew his sword, struck the servant of the high priest, and cut off his ear** (vv. 50b–51). No doubt this exchange between Judas and Jesus occurred very quickly. As soon as Judas kissed Jesus, the mob surged forward and seized Jesus. He was placed under arrest.

At that moment, one of the disciples took action. He drew His sword and prepared to fight for his master. Matthew does not tell us who it was, but John states that it was the ever-impetuous Peter. He was ready to stand for Jesus all by himself against the temple guard. Of course, he was a fisherman and not a soldier. He swung his sword in the direction of the high priest's servant, whose name was Malchus (John 18:10), but it was a poorly guided thrust. He missed the servant's vital parts, and the blow glanced off the side of his head and cut off one of his ears.

So, Jesus had to rebuke Peter once again: **But Jesus said to him, "Put your sword in its place, for all who take the sword will perish by the sword"** (v. 52). There was no point in Peter's resisting; besides the fact that the odds were overwhelming, resistance was counterproductive. As we have seen, and as Jesus was to reiterate shortly, what was happening *had* to happen, for it was the Father's will and Jesus' destiny. He told Peter that His disciples were not to fight for Him and His kingdom with the sword. Then, according to Luke, Jesus touched Malchus's wound and healed him (22:51). This was His last act of healing before His incarceration.

Jesus went on to say: **"Or do you think that I cannot now pray to My Father, and He will provide Me with more than twelve legions of angels?"** (v. 53). Jesus was telling Peter that if He wanted to escape, it would be simplicity itself. He needed only to ask the Father to send help, and more than twelve legions of angels would be there in a moment. A legion was the basic unit of the Roman army, composed of several thousand men. All Jesus had to do was call to His Father in the silence of His heart, and thousands upon thousands of mighty angels would be at His command, far more than enough to overcome the motley crew that had been sent to arrest Him.

This comment from Jesus reminds me of Elisha and his servant at Dothan. The king of Syria was attempting to capture Elisha because he was warning the king of Israel about Syrian troop movements. One morning, Elisha's servant went out and discovered that a Syrian army had surrounded the city in the night. In a panic, he woke Elisha and cried: "Alas, my master! What shall we do?" Elisha calmly prayed, "Lord, I pray, open his eyes that he may see." When the servant looked again, we read, "Behold, the mountain was full of horses and chariots of fire all around Elisha" (2 Kings 6:8–17). Myriads of angels were there to guard the Lord's prophet. If such a heavenly host was available for Elisha, how much more were the angels available to defend Jesus.

I am also reminded of Jesus' experience of temptation at the hands of Satan. The devil took Him to the pinnacle of the temple in Jerusalem and said to Him, "If You are the Son of God, throw Yourself down. For it is written: 'He shall give His angels charge over you,' and, 'In their hands they shall bear you up, lest you dash your foot against a stone'" (Matt. 4:6). However, Jesus knew He did not have to jump off the temple to discover that angels were watching over Him. He would not yield to the devil's temptations. In frustration, Satan departed from Him. Then what happened? "And behold, angels came and ministered to Him" (v. 11). They were there all the time. Likewise, the angels were with Him in Gethsemane, and He could have called to the Father to send them to His aid.

But Jesus chose not to call for a very important reason: **"How then could the Scriptures be fulfilled, that it must happen thus?"** (v. 54). Time and time again throughout Matthew's Gospel, we have seen him emphasizing how Jesus' words and actions fulfilled Old Testament prophecies. We have even seen Jesus consciously acting to fulfill prophecies, especially when He insisted on riding a donkey into Jerusalem at His triumphal entry (21:1–5). Now we see Him preventing Peter from taking a course of action that would have gone against the Old Testament prophecies that said the Messiah must suffer and die. Jesus knew that the cross *must* happen. God had decreed it and made it known through His prophets, and those prophecies had to be fulfilled lest God be found to be a liar. When God in His sovereignty decrees that something will come to pass, not only will it come to pass, it must come to pass.

This is a wonderful thing, because it is true not only for the bad news that the prophets give us, but also true for every promise that God gives to His people. The Lord's promises will be fulfilled without fail. For instance, Jesus is in heaven right now, preparing a place for us, if our faith is in Him, so that when we die, we will be there with Him (John 14:2–3). This *must* happen. Jesus promised it, which means that God has decreed it.

Before He was led away by the mob, Jesus spoke to them. Matthew writes: **In that hour Jesus said to the multitudes, "Have you come out, as against a robber, with swords and clubs to take Me? I sat daily with you, teaching in the temple, and you did not seize Me. But all this was done that the Scriptures of the prophets might be fulfilled"** (vv. 55–56a). What He said was perfectly obvious. He had not been trying to elude the authorities; He had been out and about in public places. He could have been arrested anytime. Now, however, He was being arrested under cover of night. Why the stealth? As Jesus noted once again, things were progressing just as Scripture had foretold (see Psalm 22; Isaiah 53; Zechariah 12–13). It was almost as if He was reminding the temple guards that they were only playing a part in a great drama that had been written out ages before.

At that point, **all the disciples forsook Him and fled** (v. 56b). Here, yet another prophecy was fulfilled, just as Jesus had said it would be (v. 31). Though the events recorded in this passage are sad in and of themselves, we are given glimpses of God's hand at work behind the scenes, guiding all things toward His desired end—the atonement of His people.

122

JESUS BEFORE CAIAPHAS

Matthew 26:57–68

And those who had laid hold of Jesus led Him away to Caiaphas the high priest, where the scribes and the elders were assembled. But Peter followed Him at a distance to the high priest's courtyard. And he went in and sat with the servants to see the end. Now the chief priests, the elders, and all the council sought false testimony against Jesus to put Him to death, but found none. Even though many false witnesses came forward, they found none. But at last two false witnesses came forward and said, "This fellow said, 'I am able to destroy the temple of God and to build it in three days.'" And the high priest arose and said to Him, "Do You answer nothing? What is it these men testify against You?" But Jesus kept silent. And the high priest answered and said to Him, "I put You under oath by the living God: Tell us if You are the Christ, the Son of God!" Jesus said to him, "It is as you said. Nevertheless, I say to you, hereafter you will see the Son of Man sitting at the right hand of the Power, and coming on the clouds of heaven." Then the high priest tore his clothes, saying, "He has spoken blasphemy! What further need do we have of witnesses? Look, now you have heard His blasphemy! What do you think?" They answered and said, "He is deserving of death." Then they spat in His face and beat Him; and others struck Him with the palms of their hands, saying, "Prophesy to us, Christ! Who is the one who struck You?"

After the arrest of Jesus in the darkness of the garden of Gethsemane, the Jewish authorities found themselves in a serious quandary. Under Roman rule, they had the authority to tend to most of their affairs, particularly religious ones, but the Romans did not give the authorities in their vassal states the freedom to execute criminals. That could be accomplished only with the consent of the Roman authorities. So, the Jewish authorities were limited in what they could actually do to rid themselves of Jesus.

Their first step was to hold a kangaroo court, a quasi-trial. Some have argued that this was merely a preliminary hearing, because it violated virtually every law that governed the judicial system of the Jewish people. For instance, it was against Jewish law to hold a trial at night. Likewise, it was against Jewish law to reach a guilty verdict on the same day as the trial; the law required at least twenty-four hours of contemplation before a guilty verdict could be rendered. Perhaps this was simply a preliminary hearing, but such was the antipathy of the Sanhedrin that I see no reason to conclude that this was not a true trial, conducted without regard for the established procedures. For this reason, I believe this is the record of one of the lowest moments in the history of humanity, when the highest officials of the Old Testament church of God repudiated the Son of God.

Matthew writes: **And those who had laid hold of Jesus led Him away to Caiaphas the high priest, where the scribes and the elders were assembled** (v. 57). The other Gospels tell us Jesus was taken to the house of the high priest. There, the scribes and elders were waiting, for they had been informed that Judas and his mob had gone off to make the arrest.

The fact that Caiaphas is identified as the high priest presents a bit of a problem. In the Old Testament, the high priest was appointed for life, but at this time the former high priest, Annas, the father-in-law of Caiaphas (John 18:13), was still living. Under Jewish tradition, Annas should have been hearing the case, not Caiaphas. However, the Romans apparently had deposed Annas for unknown reasons and allowed Caiaphas to take his place. Even so, the fact that John tells us the temple guard took Jesus to Annas before taking him to Caiaphas shows that Annas was still pulling the strings even though he was no longer officially high priest.

Matthew gives us an interesting footnote: **But Peter followed Him at a distance to the high priest's courtyard. And he went in and sat with the servants to see the end** (v. 58). Obviously the Sanhedrin was not concerned at this moment to arrest all of the followers of Jesus and put them on trial. If they had been, they could have taken them all along with Jesus at Gethsemane. Nevertheless, for safety's sake, Peter kept his distance, though he was compelled to learn how things would turn out.

When we read these texts, we are not interested only in history lessons, as important as they may be. When we read the Word of God, we always should be looking for ways in which the text of Scripture applies to us today. It was—and is—typical of the followers of Jesus to put distance between themselves and their Lord when the moment of crisis comes. When our well-being is threatened, it is easy to retreat. So, we have to ask ourselves: Had we been a part of Jesus' band of followers when He was arrested, would we have fled? Would we have kept a safe distance from Him?

The Savior on Trial

Matthew tells us: **Now the chief priests, the elders, and all the council sought false testimony against Jesus to put Him to death, but found none. Even though many false witnesses came forward, they found none** (vv. 59–60a). Matthew makes no bones about it—the Jewish religious authorities sought people who would be willing to commit perjury against Jesus, to make false accusations, in order to give the Sanhedrin the necessary fodder to justify their judgment against Him. Initially, however, they could not find anyone whose false testimony would work. Many false witnesses came forward, but their testimony was so unworthy it could not be used. **But at last two false witnesses came forward and said, "This fellow said, 'I am able to destroy the temple of God and to build it in three days'"** (vv. 60b–61). This obviously was a distortion of Jesus' actual statement about destroying and rebuilding the temple, though that statement admittedly was cryptic. John alone among the Gospel writers records the actual statement, and he also gives the interpretation, telling us that Jesus was speaking of the temple of His body and foretelling His resurrection (John 2:19–21).

Apparently Jesus was given an opportunity to respond to this false accusation and the others that were put forth but refused to say anything. For this reason, Matthew tells us, **the high priest arose and said to Him, "Do You answer nothing? What is it these men testify against You?" But Jesus kept silent** (vv. 62–63a). Lie upon lie, perjury upon perjury, false charge upon false charge was made against Jesus within His hearing, but He said nothing to defend Himself, fulfilling prophecies about Him: "He was led as a lamb to the slaughter, and as a sheep before its shearers is silent, so He opened not His mouth" (Isa. 53:7b). Jesus knew His destiny. He knew it was utterly futile to offer any defense of Himself in those circumstances. Furthermore, He knew that by defending Himself He would actually be opposing His Father's will. So, He allowed the slander to go unchallenged, knowing that He must suffer and die, but that He would be vindicated on resurrection morning.

Finally, Caiaphas could stand it no more. He rose and asked Jesus why He would not defend Himself, goading Him, as it were. Even then, Jesus remained mute. So, Caiaphas tried a different tactic: **And the high priest answered and said to Him, "I put You under oath by the living God: Tell us if You are the Christ, the Son of God!"** (v. 63b). Finally, Caiaphas came to the point. He wanted to know whether Jesus was the Christ, the Messiah, and He wanted to hear it from Jesus' own mouth. So he put Jesus under oath. This was his strongest judicial tool to compel Jesus to speak to the crucial issue—His identity.

At that point, in obedience to God's law regarding oaths, Jesus did speak: **Jesus said to him, "It is as you said"** (v. 64a). The Greek in this text is awkward and has given itself to various translations. One translation simply has Jesus saying, "Well, you say so," as if He were saying, "You're the one who said it; I didn't say it." Or perhaps Jesus was saying, "I'm not going to say that I am the Messiah because you have no concept of what the Messiah is to be and you do not understand what it means to be the Son of God, so I might as well not use that kind of language among you."

Authority and Power

But then Jesus added, **"Nevertheless, I say to you, hereafter you will see the Son of Man sitting at the right hand of the Power, and coming on the clouds of heaven"** (v. 64b). This statement was as good as a straightforward confession that He was the Messiah. Jesus was acknowledging that the Jewish religious leaders had authority and power in this world, but their authority and power were secondary to His. As soon as Jesus took His seat at the right hand of God, all power in heaven and on earth would be given to Him, and the chief priests and scribes would be subject to His judgment. In short, He was claiming to be not only the Messiah but the King, God Himself.

That was more than Caiaphas could bear. Matthew tells us: **Then the high priest tore his clothes, saying, "He has spoken blasphemy! What further need do we have of witnesses? Look, now you have heard His blasphemy! What do you think?" They answered and said, "He is deserving of death"** (vv. 65–66). When a priest tore his garment, it was a declaration of horror over something terrible that had just been said or had taken place. In this case, Caiaphas was exercised over Jesus' words, which he labeled as blasphemy. Actually, Jesus had not committed blasphemy. Under Jewish law, blasphemy involved using the name of God in a blasphemous way. Jesus had not done that. He had spoken nothing but the truth. The Jewish religious leaders simply chose not to believe what He said. So, even this charge was false; the high priest himself committed perjury.

Of course, Caiaphas and the other religious leaders were not deeply concerned about whether Jesus had committed blasphemy or not. They wanted to get rid of Him, and a charge of blasphemy was not going to do it, because blasphemy was not a crime under the Roman law. The Jews could not convince the Romans to execute Jesus for blasphemy. They simply wanted to make sure they had sufficient ground to deliver Jesus to the Romans. In other words, their first problem was to satisfy Jewish law. Once that was decided, they had to figure out a different way to show that Jesus had violated Roman law. Caiaphas was simply proposing a way to satisfy Jewish law.

So, the high priest made his accusation and called for a verdict. The other religious leaders followed along and said, "He is deserving of death." At last, they had Jesus in their power and had pronounced the sentence of death on Him.

Mistreating the Son of God

As if their kangaroo court, false testimony, and illicit verdict were not bad enough, the leaders of the Jews stooped to gloating over Jesus and mistreating Him. Matthew writes: **Then they spat in His face and beat Him; and others struck Him with the palms of their hands, saying, "Prophesy to us, Christ! Who is the one who struck You?"** (vv. 67–68). This mockery was designed to humiliate Him.

The action that grips me most in this text is the first one that Matthew records—they spat in His face. Can you imagine that? Just as it is today, so it was then—spitting in someone's face was the ultimate gesture of insult and contempt. By spitting in Jesus' face, the Jewish religious leaders completely repudiated His authority. This was an insult to His person and to His office as the Christ and the Son of God. They spat in the face of the God-man.

I can imagine just about any sin that we are prone to as fallen human beings, even as converted Christians. However, to spit in the face of Christ is unthinkable. Yet, I think that we do so, at least in a figurative way. Every time we sin against God, we are, in effect, spitting in His face.

We will never be without sin as long as we are in the flesh. But we are charged with fighting the good fight all our days, striving after holiness. We must see our sin for the heinous crime it is, and I believe the mistreatment that the Jewish religious leaders heaped upon Jesus is a good picture of our iniquity. We should shrink in horror from what they did—and from what we do every day. Then, seeing our despicable hearts, we should pray for help to bow to Him and obey His commands, acknowledging Him as our rightful King.

123

PETER'S DENIAL

Matthew 26:69–75

Now Peter sat outside in the courtyard. And a servant girl came to him, saying, "You also were with Jesus of Galilee." But he denied it before them all, saying, "I do not know what you are saying." And when he had gone out to the gateway, another girl saw him and said to those who were there, "This fellow also was with Jesus of Nazareth." But again he denied with an oath, "I do not know the Man!" And a little later those who stood by came up and said to Peter, "Surely you also are one of them, for your speech betrays you." Then he began to curse and swear, saying, "I do not know the Man!" Immediately a rooster crowed. And Peter remembered the word of Jesus who had said to him, "Before the rooster crows, you will deny Me three times." So he went out and wept bitterly.

After the Jewish religious authorities had reached their verdict and condemned Jesus to death, they spent a few minutes beating, mocking, and insulting Him, as we saw in the previous chapter. One of the insulting things they did was to hit Him in the face and then say: "Prophesy to us, Christ! Who is the one who struck You?" (v. 68). They were mocking the idea that Jesus had the supernatural ability, as the Son of God, to speak prophetically.

In a supreme irony, however, even while these men were taunting Jesus, one of His prophecies was being fulfilled. It was the prophecy Jesus had uttered in the upper room concerning Peter, who, Jesus foretold, would deny Him three times before the rooster crowed that night (v. 34). Peter, of course, had protested that he would never deny his Lord (v. 35), but it happened just as Jesus said it would, and Matthew records this sad moment in the Apostle's life.

In fact, this denial is recorded in all four Gospels. These Gospels were written at a time when Peter had risen to become the leader of the Christian church in Jerusalem, if not in the whole world. Yet the Gospel writers did not shrink from recording this shameful behavior of the Apostle. Mark probably learned of it from the lips of Peter himself. Why would Peter let it be known? We know he felt ashamed when he realized what he had done (v. 75). We also know that Jesus forgave Peter, restored him, and made him the leader of the Apostles (John 21:15–19). Thus, this story of Peter's denial shows us how prone we are to deny our Lord, but that even the most heinous sin does not spell the end of our Christian journey or of our usefulness for the kingdom of God.

Three Denials

As Matthew noted earlier, all the disciples fled when Jesus was arrested (v. 56), but Peter followed the temple guards as they took Jesus to the home of Caiaphas, the high priest, in order that he might "see the end" (v. 58). Matthew notes, **Now Peter sat outside in the courtyard** (v. 69a). He was hoping to follow the proceedings as best he could and to be nearby when word of the verdict against Jesus spread. But there were other people in the courtyard, too, and that soon created a problem for Peter.

Matthew tells us: **And a servant girl came to him, saying, "You also were with Jesus of Galilee." But he denied it before them all, saying, "I do not know what you are saying"** (vv. 69b–70). As Peter sat in the courtyard, a servant girl approached him and stated that he had been with Jesus. Perhaps she had seen Peter with Jesus as He moved about Jerusalem or taught in the temple. In any case, she was sure of the connection; she did not ask whether Peter was with Jesus; she simply stated that he was. We cannot even be sure that she was accusing Peter of wrongdoing. Perhaps she simply wanted to talk to him about Jesus. But Peter was wary, and he immediately blurted out, "I do not know what you are saying." In this way, he denied what the girl had stated as fact—that he was "with" Jesus, that he was a disciple of Jesus.

We must remember that this episode occurred in the ancient world, at a time when women had very little authority and very few rights. Certainly women were not to be feared. Furthermore, this was a young woman; she was just a girl. Not only was she just a girl; she was a slave. Of all the people who may have been milling around that courtyard in Jerusalem that night, the last person Peter had to fear was this little slave girl. Yet, just an hour or so after drawing his sword and cutting off the ear of the servant of the high priest in a bold, dramatic, defiant act against the temple guard, he cowered in fear in front of a slave girl.

Matthew continues: **And when he had gone out to the gateway, another girl saw him and said to those who were there, "This fellow also was with Jesus of Nazareth." But again he denied with an oath, "I do not know the Man!"** (vv. 71–72). Sometime after his encounter with the first servant girl, Peter wandered out to the gateway to the courtyard. There, nearly the same thing happened. Another girl saw him and recognized him as one of Jesus' followers. This time, however, Matthew notes that she stated the connection in the hearing of others, and perhaps some of them were more powerful than a mere servant girl. Therefore, Peter did not merely pretend that he did not understand what the girl was saying. Instead, he straightforwardly denied that he knew Jesus.

Furthermore, Peter denied Jesus with an oath. What was the role of oaths in the culture of the Jews? The Bible says all men are liars (Ps. 116:11). We cannot trust everything people say to us. Even when we marry, we make a promise to our spouse, but we seal our promise with a vow. Basically, we take sacred oaths to underline emphatically that we are speaking the truth, and they were used for the same purpose in Israel. So, when Peter denied Jesus with an oath, it was as if he were saying, "As God is my witness, I do not know the Man!" In other words, he appealed to God to bear witness to his lie. In Jewish courts, this was regarded as perjury. Here we see how far the human heart will go to disguise a lie.

But Peter's shameful behavior was not yet complete. Matthew writes: **And a little later those who stood by came up and said to Peter, "Surely you also are one of them, for your speech betrays you." Then he began to curse and swear, saying, "I do not know the Man!"** (vv. 73–74a). Peter's accent revealed that he was a Galilean. Of course, not every Galilean who was in Jerusalem that night was a follower of Jesus, but Jesus' ministry had focused on Galilee, so that connection was enough to bring Peter into suspicion. But when his connection to Jesus was pointed out for this third time, Peter became angry—or at least he feigned anger. Matthew tells us that he "began to curse and swear," insisting vehemently that he did not know Jesus. The Greek verb that is translated here as "curse" is related to the Greek word *anathema*, which means "damnation." Peter essentially was pronouncing a curse on those who associated him with Jesus, saying that his accusers deserved to be damned. He unleashed a torrent of verbal abuse at the suggestion that he was a follower of Jesus, insisting that he did not know his Lord.

No sooner was this vehement denial out of Peter's mouth than two things happened. First, as Matthew tells us, **Immediately a rooster crowed** (v. 74b). It seems morning was approaching, and, as commonly happens, a rooster crowed somewhere in the courtyard or nearby in the city. Jesus had said Peter would deny Him three times before the rooster crowed, and it happened that way almost to the second.

Second, as Luke tells us, at the moment when the rooster crowed, "the Lord turned and looked at Peter" (22:61a). Their eyes met. I would venture to guess that that was the most horrible moment Peter ever experienced. Remember, at Caesarea Philippi, when Jesus asked the disciples, "Who do you say that I am?" Peter replied, "You are the Christ, the Son of the living God" (Matt. 16:15–16). He knew who Jesus was; as Jesus explained, the Father had revealed Jesus' identity to him (v. 17). Now he was saying, "I do not know the Man." So, Jesus turned and looked at him. There is no record that Jesus said anything to him, but He did not need to speak. Would you like to have been in Peter's skin, looking up, just after denying Jesus, and seeing Him turn His head, beaten and bruised, to look into your eyes and into your soul? I cannot imagine how horrible that moment must have been.

Matthew tells us that that was when it hit Peter: **And Peter remembered the word of Jesus who had said to him, "Before the rooster crows, you will deny Me three times." So he went out and wept bitterly** (v. 75). Suddenly it all came back to him, and he thought: "This is exactly what He said I would do. I swore it would never happen, but I have done just what He said." Peter was filled with shame. His curses stopped and the bitter tears began to fall.

Our Turn to Stand

I believe we all can relate to Peter's experience. It is easy to acknowledge Jesus in the church, when we are among our brothers and sisters in the Lord. But to confess Him before a world that is hostile to Him, to declare that we are followers of Jesus before those who hate God and His Son, is another matter. We tend to go undercover; we become Secret Service Christians. It seems easier to let no one know that we are believers. However, we are called to confess Jesus openly. Somehow, we must get past our fears. We are to affirm with the Apostle Paul, "I am not ashamed of the gospel of Christ, for it is the power of God to salvation for everyone who believes" (Rom. 1:16a).

Before I was converted to Christianity as a college freshman, I basically held Christians in contempt. I thought that any man who was a Christian could not be completely virile; he had to be a loser, certainly a wimp, if he was living his life under the cloak of religion. I figured he just did not have what it took to deal with the difficulties of life in this world. Then I became a Christian and began looking at things from the other side of the aisle.

When I was born again, I was exceedingly hungry for Christian fellowship. I learned that there was a group that met for prayer on our college campus, and I was invited to go. When I went, I discovered that the students who gathered for prayer were not among the most popular people on campus. These were the base, the lowly, and the foolish in the opinion of the campus culture. However, I drew close to some of the students in that group. I can remember, sometime later, walking across campus and thinking, "My friends back home should see me now—my two best friends here are probably the two wimpiest guys in the school." That may have been true, but they were strong for Christ. They were not ashamed of the gospel, and I was completely honored to be in their presence.

In the office, at parties, and at other events, do you hide your Christianity? When someone asks you whether you are a Christian, do you say to them, "I don't know what you're talking about"? Do you want to say "I don't know the Man"? We need to remember the words of Jesus: "Whoever is ashamed of Me and My words, of him the Son of Man will be ashamed when He comes in His own glory, and in His Father's, and of the holy angels" (Luke 9:26).

The Christian church has been built on the shoulders of heroic men and women who were not ashamed to be identified with the Lord Jesus Christ. Now it is our turn to stand for Him in our generation. I urge you never to shrink from your identity with Jesus. Be willing to be called a fool for Christ. Be willing to be humiliated in the social strata in which you live. That's the cost of being a Christian, but it is infinitesimal compared to the cost He paid for our redemption.

124

THE REMORSE OF JUDAS

Matthew 27:1–10

When morning came, all the chief priests and elders of the people plotted against Jesus to put Him to death. And when they had bound Him, they led Him away and delivered Him to Pontius Pilate the governor. Then Judas, His betrayer, seeing that He had been condemned, was remorseful and brought back the thirty pieces of silver to the chief priests and elders, saying, "I have sinned by betraying innocent blood." And they said, "What is that to us? You see to it!" Then he threw down the pieces of silver in the temple and departed, and went and hanged himself. But the chief priests took the silver pieces and said, "It is not lawful to put them into the treasury, because they are the price of blood." And they consulted together and bought with them the potter's field, to bury strangers in. Therefore that field has been called the Field of Blood to this day. Then was fulfilled what was spoken by Jeremiah the prophet, saying, "And they took the thirty pieces of silver, the value of Him who was priced, whom they of the children of Israel priced, and gave them for the potter's field, as the Lord directed me."

As the long night of Jesus' betrayal, arrest, trial, and condemnation came to an end, the Jewish religious leaders prepared to take Him to the Roman governor to secure a formal death penalty. Matthew relates this small detail in the passage before us, but then, before telling us what happened at Pontius Pilate's palace, he completes the sad tale of Judas Iscariot.

Matthew writes: **When morning came, all the chief priests and elders of the**

people plotted against Jesus to put Him to death. And when they had bound Him, they led Him away and delivered Him to Pontius Pilate the governor (vv. 1–2). As we have seen, the chief priests and elders had satisfied themselves that Jesus was deserving of death, condemning Him as a blasphemer for claiming to be the Son of God. But they could not execute Him; the Romans did not grant them that right, and the Romans would not execute Him for committing blasphemy in the eyes of the Jews. Therefore, the priests and elders plotted how they might convince the Roman governor to sign Jesus' death warrant.

In order to move Jesus from the home of the high priest, Caiaphas, to the governor's palace, the priests and elders found it necessary to bind Him. Matthew does not tell us how they bound him, but chains normally were used. After spitting on Him, mocking Him, and slapping Him, the Jewish authorities added this indignity—they led Jesus through the streets in chains. At the moment of His arrest in Gethsemane, Jesus had offered no resistance and made no attempt to flee. He even chided Peter for striking the high priest's servant with a sword (26:52). There was no reason for Jesus' captors to fear that He would try to escape. Yet they could not resist one more opportunity to humiliate Him and remind Him that they at last had the upper hand.

Then we are told that they "delivered Him" to the governor. This simple statement is not just a historical detail; it is very significant. As we have examined this drama of the final day before the crucifixion, we have seen that Jesus foretold Judas's betrayal and Peter's denial, which was a type of betrayal. Now we see yet another betrayal of Christ. In a sense, the worst act of betrayal was committed by the highest spiritual leaders of the Jews, by the priests and elders of the Sanhedrin. The Greek word that is translated as "delivered" here is *paradidōmi*, and this word is often translated in the New Testament as "betrayed." These men, to whom God had given the responsibility of maintaining the integrity of the spiritual life of His people, took it upon themselves to hand Jesus over, fulfilling Old Testament prophecies and Jesus' own prophecies. It is nearly unthinkable that these men could stoop to betray the Son of God into the hands of pagans. But that is how Matthew describes their action in taking Jesus to Pontius Pilate.

Remorse, Not Repentance

Matthew then changes direction and writes, **Then Judas, His betrayer, seeing that He had been condemned, was remorseful and brought back the thirty pieces of silver to the chief priests and elders, saying, "I have sinned by betraying innocent blood." And they said, "What is that to us? You see to it!"** (vv. 3–4). We do not know where Judas was during Jesus' trial. Perhaps he was there in the high priest's home, observing the mockery of justice firsthand.

I cannot fathom what outcome he hoped his betrayal of Jesus would bring about, but apparently he had not foreseen Jesus' condemnation. Thus, Matthew tells us that when he saw that the priests and elders had condemned Jesus, he suddenly was filled with remorse. I believe he was overcome by a sense of guilt.

However, we must not confuse this remorse with godly repentance. The thirty pieces of silver in his pocket condemned him, but he did not choose to flee to God for His mercy, to come in repentance before the Lord, as David had (Psalm 51). Instead, Judas took the money back to the priests and elders, and confessed, "I have sinned by betraying innocent blood." He knew he had sinned, but he did not go to God for forgiveness. He sought a way by which he could free himself from his guilt.

Judas could have found mercy with God if he had sincerely repented, but he found no mercy at all with the religious leaders. They said: "What is that to us? You see to it!" They basically told him that his remorse and guilt were his own problems. They could not care less. This is what happens when betrayers join with betrayers; they are prone to turn on one another in the end.

Matthew tells us, **Then he threw down the pieces of silver in the temple and departed, and went and hanged himself** (v. 5). Judas did not quietly hand over the money. With the fiercest movement he could muster, he threw it down in the temple and left. Then, in a concluding postscript, Matthew tells us he went out from there "and hanged himself." He not only hated the silver, he hated himself. So, he decided not only to get rid of the silver but to get rid of Judas.

Matthew's is the only Gospel that describes Judas's death, but Matthew gives us no details about the hanging. Some scholars make a big deal about an apparent discrepancy between Matthew's account of Judas's death and Luke's in the book of Acts. We read there:

> And in those days Peter stood up in the midst of the disciples (altogether the number of names was about a hundred and twenty), and said, "Men and brethren, this Scripture had to be fulfilled, which the Holy Spirit spoke before by the mouth of David concerning Judas, who became a guide to those who arrested Jesus; for he was numbered with us and obtained a part in this ministry." (Now this man purchased a field with the wages of iniquity; and falling headlong, he burst open in the middle and all his entrails gushed out. And it became known to all those dwelling in Jerusalem; so that field is called in their own language, Akel Dama, that is, Field of Blood.) "For it is written in the Book of Psalms: 'Let his dwelling place be desolate, and let no one live in it.'" (Acts 1:15–20a)

The critics ask whether we are to understand that Judas died by hanging himself or by falling headlong, so that his entrails burst open? However, these two outcomes are not incompatible. Judas may have put a noose around his neck, tied it to a tree, jumped, and strangled, after which the rope broke and his body fell some distance, smashing into the ground. It may also have been the case that he hanged himself and no one took his body down, so that it hung for some length of time and eventually burst open as it decomposed. But in either case, his death was ignominious. His end was total desolation.

God forbid that any of us should be like Judas. Of course, we all fall into sin, and sometimes we remain in it for a time, hostile to the things of God. But if we are truly in Christ, in time, the Holy Spirit melts our hearts and brings us to repentance. For this reason, our destinies are not those of Judas. Our ends will not be desolation but glory.

Him Who Was Priced

Matthew writes, **But the chief priests took the silver pieces and said, "It is not lawful to put them into the treasury, because they are the price of blood"** (v. 6). Suddenly, the priests were concerned about keeping the law. Some scholars believe the priests must have concluded it would be unlawful to put the money back into the treasury based on Deuteronomy 23:18, which states: "You shall not bring the wages of a harlot or the price of a dog to the house of the Lord your God for any vowed offering, for both of these are an abomination to the Lord your God." The thirty pieces of silver had secured Jesus' death; therefore, they were "the price of blood." Actually, the blood was on their hands, not on the money, for they had given the money to buy Jesus' death.

Nevertheless, Judas's return of the thirty pieces of silver was a small windfall for the priests, so they came up with a way to use it: **And they consulted together and bought with them the potter's field, to bury strangers in. Therefore that field has been called the Field of Blood to this day** (vv. 7–8). They bought a field to serve as a cemetery for foreigners. It was given the nickname "the Field of Blood" because it had been purchased with Judas's blood money. This may indicate that the treachery of the priests in hiring Judas to betray Jesus was known by at least some of the people.

This seemingly insignificant incident constituted a remarkable fulfillment of prophecy. Matthew explains: **Then was fulfilled what was spoken by Jeremiah the prophet, saying, "And they took the thirty pieces of silver, the value of Him who was priced, whom they of the children of Israel priced, and gave them for the potter's field, as the Lord directed me"** (vv. 9–10). Matthew attributes this prophecy to the prophet Jeremiah, but what Matthew cites here is actually a mosaic of references to both Jeremiah and Zechariah (Jer. 32:6–9; Zech. 11:12, 13). That has caused some people to choke a little. However, this kind of citation from the Old Testament was not uncommon in biblical times. There is evidence that the Jews maintained their copies of the Old Testament in several scrolls, and each of the scrolls contained several books of prophecy, of both the major prophets and the minor prophets, with the scroll being identified by the name of the prophet whose book was first in the scroll. In this case, the scroll of Jeremiah might have contained not only Jeremiah's prophecies but also Zechariah's. There is no textual problem here.

We need to note Matthew's subtle but significant charge against the religious leaders here. He says that the thirty pieces of silver were "the value of Him who was priced, whom they of the children of Israel priced." Thirty pieces of silver was the value the priests and elders put on Jesus' life. He, the pearl of great price, stood in their midst, and they esteemed Him as next to worthless. How badly skewed was their value system.

As we read this episode, we need to ask ourselves about our own value systems. How valuable is Jesus to us? He is what Christianity is all about. He is the beloved Son of the Father. He is the Alpha and the Omega, the first and the last. He is everything. We ought to esteem Him above all else and therefore serve Him, obey Him, and adore Him.

125

JESUS BEFORE PILATE

Matthew 27:11–26

Now Jesus stood before the governor. And the governor asked Him, saying, "Are You the King of the Jews?" Jesus said to him, "It is as you say." And while He was being accused by the chief priests and elders, He answered nothing. Then Pilate said to Him, "Do You not hear how many things they testify against You?" But He answered him not one word, so that the governor marveled greatly. Now at the feast the governor was accustomed to releasing to the multitude one prisoner whom they wished. And at that time they had a notorious prisoner called Barabbas. Therefore, when they had gathered together, Pilate said to them, "Whom do you want me to release to you? Barabbas, or Jesus who is called Christ?" For he knew that they had handed Him over because of envy. While he was sitting on the judgment seat, his wife sent to him, saying, "Have nothing to do with that just Man, for I have suffered many things today in a dream because of Him." But the chief priests and elders persuaded the multitudes that they should ask for Barabbas and destroy Jesus. The governor answered and said to them, "Which of the two do you want me to release to you?" They said, "Barabbas!" Pilate said to them, "What then shall I do with Jesus who is called Christ?" They all said to him, "Let Him be crucified!" Then the governor said, "Why, what evil has He done?" But they cried out all the more, saying, "Let Him be crucified!" When Pilate saw that he could not prevail at all, but rather that a tumult was rising, he took water and washed his hands before the multitude, saying, "I am innocent of the blood of this just Person. You see to it." And all the people answered and said, "His blood be on us and on our children." Then he released Barabbas to them; and when he had scourged Jesus, he delivered Him to be crucified.

All four of the Gospel writers tell us some things about Jesus' appearance before the Roman governor of Judea, Pontius Pilate. However, none of the four gives us a comprehensive record of the interchange that took place that day. We get some information from Mark, some from Luke, some from John, and some here from Matthew. When we consider all of these accounts, one fact becomes clear—Pilate was concerned that Jesus might really be a ruler of some kind.

Try to put yourself in Pilate's sandals. He had been appointed by the Emperor Tiberius as the fifth Roman governor of Judea, and his administration lasted from AD 26 to 37. Within the Roman government, it was common knowledge that Judea was one of the most difficult provinces in which to maintain peace and order. In other words, the Jews were unusually restive and rebellious. For this reason, Judea was not a plum assignment for an ambitious Roman official. Indeed, assignment to Judea was almost a punishment. By the time of Jesus' trial, Pilate's tenure in Judea had stretched longer than was commonplace, and it seemed his career had plateaued. He had already irritated the emperor by dealing too harshly with the people. In the near future, he would be recalled to Rome in disgrace for his harsh response to a rebellion of Samaritans. So, at this point in time, he was in a tenuous position and did not want to be too offensive to the Jewish authorities. Neither did he want to antagonize the people into a popular revolution. On the other hand, he was unwilling that it should be said in Rome that he was soft on someone who claimed to be a king. Thus, from a political standpoint, Pilate was in a very difficult position.

This might at least partly explain Pilate's first question to Jesus. Matthew tells us: **Now Jesus stood before the governor. And the governor asked Him, saying, "Are You the King of the Jews?" Jesus said to him, "It is as you say"** (v. 11). This question was fraught with peril for Jesus. If He said yes, He would surrender to the Jewish leaders' accusations that He was involved in sedition, and therefore was an enemy of the Roman Empire. If He said no, He would deny the mission His Father had given Him to be the Messiah and the King in the line of David. But Jesus cleverly evaded both of these problems by simply saying, "It is as you say," by which He meant that it was up to Pilate to decide, in his official capacity, who and what Jesus was.

Matthew continues, **And while He was being accused by the chief priests and elders, He answered nothing** (v. 12). The priests and elders presented the false civil charges they had devised, but Jesus raised no protest. This silence finally began to irritate Pilate: **Then Pilate said to Him, "Do You not hear how many things they testify against You?" But He answered him not one word, so that the governor marveled greatly** (vv. 13–14). Jesus would not even speak when the governor encouraged Him to make some defense. At that point, Pilate was astonished. Clearly he knew nothing of Isaiah's prophecy: "He was oppressed and He was afflicted, yet He opened not His mouth; He was led as a lamb to the slaughter, and as a sheep before its shearers is silent, so He opened not His mouth" (53:7).

In John's Gospel, we are told that after this initial examination, Pilate brought Jesus out to the assembled crowd and cried: "Behold the Man! . . . I find no fault in him" (19:5–6). Why was that? It was because there was no fault in Jesus for Pilate to find. Pilate spoke the truth. At this point, he was functioning not merely as the governor of Judea but as the *persona publica*, the "public person" who pronounced judgment on Jesus. Unwittingly and unknowingly, in a very real sense, Pilate proclaimed the truth of God.

Jesus and Barabbas

Pilate had a plan to extricate himself from this political tight spot. Matthew writes, **Now at the feast the governor was accustomed to releasing to the multitude one prisoner whom they wished** (v. 15). It seems that Pilate or one of his predecessors had instituted the custom of releasing a prisoner chosen by the crowds each year at the Passover feast, probably as a way of currying popular favor. Pilate decided to offer Jesus to the crowds as a candidate for release. Perhaps he knew of Jesus' immense popularity and counted on the people to jump at the opportunity to see Him freed. Thus, Pilate could get out of his difficult position and even look good in the eyes of the Jewish masses.

But there was another well-known prisoner, too. Matthew continues: **And at that time they had a notorious prisoner called Barabbas** (v. 16). The Greek New Testament tells us that Barabbas was really this prisoner's last name. His first name was actually Jesus. "Barabbas" means "son of the father." So, there was Barabbas, son of the father, and Jesus, the Son of the Father. We are told that Barabbas was a robber (John 18:40) and that he had committed murder in an uprising (Mark 15:7; Luke 23:19). Given that he had been involved in a rebellion, perhaps he was a popular hero. Pilate's willingness to release a man who had defied the imperial power indicates how desperate he was to keep the populace mollified.

Continuing, Matthew tells us: **Therefore, when they had gathered together, Pilate said to them, "Whom do you want me to release to you? Barabbas, or Jesus who is called Christ?" For he knew that they had handed Him over because of envy** (vv. 17–18). Pilate offered the crowd the choice of Jesus or Barabbas. Matthew provides a small but significant detail—the governor was trying to set Jesus free because he knew the chief priests were merely envious of

Jesus. He was an astute politician and realized what was going on to a certain degree. He knew Jesus had done nothing wrong, but he did not have enough courage or political wiggle room to set Him free outright. Instead, he gave the crowd a chance to make things right by offering this choice.

Matthew then relates a strange twist to this episode: **While he was sitting on the judgment seat, his wife sent to him, saying, "Have nothing to do with that just Man, for I have suffered many things today in a dream because of Him"** (v. 19). Did God give this dream to Pilate's wife? We cannot be sure, but she apparently was convinced, on the basis of her dream, that Jesus was a just Man, and she urged her husband to have nothing to do with Him, which seems to have been an encouragement for Pilate to take no action against Him.

Meanwhile, **the chief priests and elders persuaded the multitudes that they should ask for Barabbas and destroy Jesus. The governor answered and said to them, "Which of the two do you want me to release to you?" They said, "Barabbas!" Pilate said to them, "What then shall I do with Jesus who is called Christ?" They all said to him, "Let Him be crucified!"** (vv. 20–22). I imagine the priest and the elders feverishly circulating through the crowd, murmuring, "Ask him to release Barabbas and destroy Jesus." I do not know what threats or promises they used to motivate the people, but when Pilate offered the two prisoners and invited the crowed to pick, the people obediently asked for Barabbas.

It is clear that Pilate was shocked: **Then the governor said, "Why, what evil has He done?" But they cried out all the more, saying, "Let Him be crucified!"** (v. 23). The governor had never expected the people to demand Jesus' death. I cannot imagine that Pilate was not aware of the tremendous uproar during Jesus' triumphal entry only a few days before—Matthew tells us that "all the city was moved" (21:10)—and the reason for it. He could only have expected the people to implore him to free Jesus. Instead, they asked him to put Jesus to death in grisly fashion. When Pilate asked them to explain their choice by pointing out what evil Jesus had done, they simply cried all the more, "Let Him be crucified!"

At that point, Pilate was losing control of the situation—that which he feared most. Therefore, Matthew tells us: **When Pilate saw that he could not prevail at all, but rather that a tumult was rising, he took water and washed his hands before the multitude, saying, "I am innocent of the blood of this just Person. You see to it"** (v. 24). Pilate made a dramatic symbolic gesture, washing his hands in the sight of the crowd to show that he regarded himself as free of the responsibility for Jesus' death. Rather, he said, it would lie on the people who had called for Jesus to be crucified.

Incredibly, **all the people answered and said, "His blood be on us and on**

our children" (v. 25). If ever the cries of a riotous crowd included more deadly, destructive language than this, I cannot imagine when it was. These people had the audacity to take full responsibility for the condemnation of the Savior, and also to put the responsibility on their children. Did they not know what they were saying? Did they not believe they would be responsible for condemning an innocent man? I cannot grasp how these people could willingly assume this responsibility and even place this guilt on their children. Sadly, God heard them and did indeed require payment for the blood of Christ from them and their children, for, as we have seen, more than a million Jews died in Jerusalem when the city fell to the Romans in AD 70.

Finally, Matthew writes, **Then he released Barabbas to them; and when he had scourged Jesus, he delivered Him to be crucified** (v. 26). Pilate relented to all they asked. He freed Barabbas and set the execution process in motion for Jesus. The first step was to have Him scourged, which was customary before crucifixion. Many prisoners who were scourged died in the process, as they were lashed with cords that had pieces of metal at the ends, and large portions of their skin was flayed from their bodies in this process. This torture both humiliated the prisoner and weakened him to speed his death on the cross. Jesus went through this agony, then Pilate "delivered Him to be crucified."

Exchanging the Son of God

In the first chapter of his epistle to the Romans, the Apostle Paul speaks of the wrath of God being revealed from heaven against all ungodliness and unrighteousness of men (v. 18). The principal act of evil that the Apostle has in view is the suppression of the truth of God. Paul goes on to say that God has revealed Himself clearly through the things He has made, so that everyone on this planet knows that He exists and knows His eternal power and deity, which leaves them without excuse (v. 20). No one will ever be able to say, "We weren't atheists, O God; we were just agnostic, without knowledge." The plea of ignorance will not stand at the last judgment.

But Paul goes on to say that God is angry not only because people have rejected this manifestation of Him, but "because, although they knew God, they did not glorify Him as God, nor were thankful, but became futile in their thoughts, and their foolish hearts were darkened" (v. 21). The primary sin of the human race is the refusal to give glory to God. It is, in other words, a refusal to worship Him. Secondary to that sin is ingratitude. Every good thing we have received in our lives has come from the hands of the benevolent God, yet no person is adequately grateful, because our fallen nature induces us to think that we have a cosmic entitlement, that God owes us the gifts we receive from Him.

We fail to see the things that God gives us as utterly gracious. Because of these twin sins of refusing to glorify God and be thankful to Him, people's thinking is futile and their foolish hearts are darkened.

It gets even worse: "Professing to be wise, they became fools, and changed the glory of the incorruptible God into an image made like corruptible man—and birds and four-footed animals and creeping things" (vv. 22–23). The ultimate insult to God is idolatry. In our fallen condition, we are mass producers of idols, because idolatry is not atheism; it is false religion, a swap. We trade the glory of the true God for the corruption of that which is creaturely. As Paul puts it, we exchange the truth of God for the lie (v. 25). That is our nature.

I do not believe this picture of humanity was ever more clearly displayed than that day in Jerusalem in front of the governor's place, when the people had an opportunity to make an exchange. Tragically, they swapped the Son of God for a hardened criminal. They traded the only begotten of the Father for a pretender, the Son of the Father for the son of the father.

Many people have said to me: "If you believe in Christ, that's fine for you. I respect your views. However, I don't feel the need for Jesus." Here is a clear case of the mind being darkened into foolishness. I do not think any human being could ever make a more foolish statement. There is nothing people need more than Jesus. Every human being without Jesus is destined to face the full measure of the wrath of the Creator, and apart from Jesus and His saving work, they will have no plea.

When someone says, "I don't feel the need for Jesus," he really is saying, "I don't want Jesus." That is why such a person refuses to believe in Jesus and follow Him. And why does he not want Jesus? It is because he does not like Him. Sinful creatures do not like the holy God. Nothing is more repugnant to fallen humanity than a sinless Redeemer.

Given these truths, it is much less shocking that the people chose Barabbas. It would have been foolish to waste time taking a poll before that election was decided, because Barabbas was the people's choice. But what we need to understand is that in our natural condition, our unregenerate state, their choice is our choice. I can see myself standing in that crowd, screaming at the top of my lungs: "Give us Barabbas! Give us anyone except Jesus."

May that not be the choice of your heart. May you cry with all of your strength, "Give me Jesus, lest I die!"

126

THE CRUCIFIXION

Matthew 27:27–44

Then the soldiers of the governor took Jesus into the Praetorium and gathered the whole garrison around Him. And they stripped Him and put a scarlet robe on Him. When they had twisted a crown of thorns, they put it on His head, and a reed in His right hand. And they bowed the knee before Him and mocked Him, saying, "Hail, King of the Jews!" Then they spat on Him, and took the reed and struck Him on the head. And when they had mocked Him, they took the robe off Him, put His own clothes on Him, and led Him away to be crucified. Now as they came out, they found a man of Cyrene, Simon by name. Him they compelled to bear His cross. And when they had come to a place called Golgotha, that is to say, Place of a Skull, they gave Him sour wine mingled with gall to drink. But when He had tasted it, He would not drink. Then they crucified Him, and divided His garments, casting lots, that it might be fulfilled which was spoken by the prophet: "They divided My garments among them, and for My clothing they cast lots." Sitting down, they kept watch over Him there. And they put up over His head the accusation written against Him: THIS IS JESUS THE KING OF THE JEWS. Then two robbers were crucified with Him, one on the right and another on the left. And those who passed by blasphemed Him, wagging their heads and saying, "You who destroy the temple and build it in three days, save Yourself! If You are the Son of God, come down from the cross." Likewise the chief priests also, mocking with the scribes and elders, said, "He saved others; Himself He cannot save. If He is the King of Israel, let Him now come down from the cross, and we will believe Him. He trusted in God; let Him deliver Him now if He will have Him; for He said, 'I am the Son of God.'" Even the robbers who were crucified with Him reviled Him with the same thing.

Saint Andrew's Chapel, the church where I serve as minister of preaching and teaching, holds a service each year on Good Friday. In my sermons on those occasions, I consider aspects of the narrative of the crucifixion and death of Jesus. Yet even if I had a lifetime of Good Fridays on which to consider these matters, I could not even begin to scratch the surface of the significance of these events. In this chapter, I will consider the events that surrounded the crucifixion of Jesus, as recorded by Matthew. In the next chapter, we will look at the episode of Jesus' death.

The Gospel writers give very little interpretation of the meaning of the crucifixion, focusing instead on recording what actually happened. The interpretation is found in the Epistles. The Apostle Paul, for example, says, "I determined not to know anything among you except Jesus Christ and Him crucified" (1 Cor. 2:2). This is apostolic hyperbole, to be sure, but the Apostle is communicating to his readers how vastly important the death of Christ was in terms of defining His person and work. The ministry of Mohammed is symbolized everywhere by the scimitar, the sword. The universal symbol of Christianity is the cross, because it was while He hung on that Roman tool for execution that our Savior paid the price for our sin.

Matthew begins by telling us, **Then the soldiers of the governor took Jesus into the Praetorium and gathered the whole garrison around Him** (v. 27). Matthew already has showed us how the priests and elders abused and mocked Jesus after they had condemned Him (26:67–68). Once Pilate had ordered that Jesus be put to death, He received similar treatment from the Roman soldiers who were tasked with crucifying Him. There were probably between two hundred and six hundred soldiers gathered around Jesus at this point.

First, Matthew says, **they stripped Him and put a scarlet robe on Him** (v. 28). In an act of extreme humiliation, they removed His own clothes and redressed Him in a red or scarlet robe. This garment was meant to be mockingly symbolic of royalty. He then adds: **When they had twisted a crown of thorns, they put it on His head, and a reed in His right hand. And they bowed the knee before Him and mocked Him, saying, "Hail, King of the Jews!"** (v. 29). They gave Him a mock crown, one made of thorns that would have been very painful, and a reed to symbolize a scepter. They pretended to bow before Him, and they hailed Him as the King of the Jews, the title Pilate had heard used to describe Him (27:11). I imagine they were rolling on the ground in laughter at this skit they had invented. But the One they mocked as a king was the King. They were doing this to the Son of God, to God incarnate, the King eternal, the One who would sit at the right hand of God with authority over every one of those soldiers.

After this mockery, their treatment of Jesus turned more savage. Matthew writes, **Then they spat on Him, and took the reed and struck Him on the head** (v. 30). In these actions, they were insulting and abusing Him. Finally, however, they tired of their fun: **And when they had mocked Him, they took the robe off Him, put His own clothes on Him, and led Him away to be crucified** (v. 31). It was time to get on with the job.

To the Place of a Skull

Matthew goes on to say: **Now as they came out, they found a man of Cyrene, Simon by name. Him they compelled to bear His cross** (v. 32). It was customary for prisoners who were being led to the place of crucifixion to be forced to bear the crosses on which they would die, or at least the horizontal beams. Therefore, the fact that the soldiers compelled a man named Simon, a native of Cyrene (an area in North Africa with a significant population of Jews), to bear the cross for Jesus suggests that He was too weak to manage this task. Jesus already had been scourged and may have lost much blood because of it.

Mark adds an interesting detail to this episode. He writes, "Then they compelled a certain man, Simon a Cyrenian, the father of Alexander and Rufus, as he was coming out of the country and passing by, to bear His cross" (15:21). Mark mentions that Simon had two sons, Alexander and Rufus, and he writes as if the readers of his Gospel were familiar with them. That suggests that Simon later came to faith in Jesus and raised his sons in the church. If so, it is interesting to reflect on how God's providence interrupted whatever errand Simon was running that day and caused his path to cross that of Jesus as He walked to Golgotha. We can only wonder what part Simon's role as the bearer of Jesus' cross played in his eternal destiny.

Then Matthew tells us: **And when they had come to a place called Golgotha, that is to say, Place of a Skull, they gave Him sour wine mingled with gall to drink. But when He had tasted it, He would not drink** (vv. 33–34). There are various theories as to why the Place of a Skull was so named. Some believe it was a rocky outcropping that resembled a skull. Others have posited it was because there were tombs in the area. Perhaps the likeliest explanation is simply that it was the place where people were put to death.

When Jesus arrived there, the soldiers gave Him "sour wine mingled with gall." Gall was a reference to bitter herbs. While some commentators believe this mixture was intended as a kind of anesthetic to help the prisoner endure the initial pain of crucifixion, it is possible this was simply another humiliation. Jesus would have been thirsty, but the gall would have made the wine undrinkable; it would have had a "galling" taste. In any case, Jesus refused to drink it.

Next, with eloquent simplicity, Matthew writes, **Then they crucified Him** (v. 35a). Nails were driven through His hands or wrists and into the wood of the crossbeam. More nails pierced His feet. When the cross was stood vertically, the weight of His body tugged on His impaled hands. When He involuntarily tried to ease that pain, He put pressure on His feet. This method of execution was exceedingly painful.

Moreover, it was terribly humiliating. Matthew tells us that the soldiers **divided His garments, casting lots, that it might be fulfilled which was spoken by the prophet: "They divided My garments among them, and for My clothing they cast lots"** (v. 35b). The soldiers already had stripped Jesus temporarily when they had their fun with Him back in the Praetorium (v. 27), but when they reached Golgotha, they stripped Him again. Criminals were executed naked. Classical paintings of the crucifixion always seem to show Jesus in a loincloth, but He almost certainly had no clothing on as He hung on the cross. That was intentional; the Romans wanted the prisoner to feel humiliated and disgraced.

I once talked with the late Charles Colson about his first day in prison. He told me that the first thing prisoners must go through is a strip search, after which they are given their prison clothing. One of the most difficult aspects of this portion of the process is receiving undergarments that have been worn by other prisoners. Colson explained to me that this is done not for economic reasons but to break the spirits of the men coming into the prison. It is a way of shaming them, of embarrassing them. This same sort of thing was done to Jesus.

Matthew is astute enough to recognize that even this act of humiliation was foretold in an Old Testament prophecy. He tells us that the soldiers did not simply discard Jesus' garments. It was one of their prerogatives to take what they wanted from among a prisoner's possessions. In this case, they cast lots to determine who should get which articles of Jesus' clothing. This had been prophesied in Psalm 22:18.

Matthew adds, **Sitting down, they kept watch over Him there** (v. 36). Having crucified Him, the soldiers' primary task was to stand guard until He died. But they did have at least one other task to perform: **And they put up over His head the accusation written against Him: THIS IS JESUS THE KING OF THE JEWS** (v. 37). It was customary to place a placard on the cross over the head of the condemned man stating the crime for which he was dying. This was for the benefit of passers-by, so they might know what was going on and be warned against committing a similar crime. John tells us that Pilate himself wrote this inscription, and it bothered the priests and elders, who asked him to change it to say "*He said*, 'I am the King of the Jews,'" but Pilate refused (19:19–21, emphasis added). Matthew also notes, **Then two robbers were crucified with Him, one on the right and another on the left** (v. 38). Two robbers were executed at the same time. Oddly, Matthew, who is usually so attuned to prophetic fulfillments, says nothing about this aspect of Jesus' crucifixion, but Mark notes that this too fulfilled a prophecy, Isaiah 53:12 (see Mark 15:28).

A Storm of Mockery

Matthew then returns to his account of the mockery Jesus endured, which seems to have made a deep impression on him. Jesus was given no respite from it even as He hung before the world in the shame of nakedness. First, He had to endure the taunts of passers-by: **And those who passed by blasphemed Him, wagging their heads and saying, "You who destroy the temple and build it in three days, save Yourself! If You are the Son of God, come down from the cross"** (vv. 39–40). Those whose daily business took them past Golgotha were not content to gawk. They could not resist the opportunity of blaspheming Jesus, bringing up the old slander about His comment regarding the destruction of the temple and challenging Him to prove He was the Son of God by coming down from the cross. Essentially they were asking Him to do the same thing Satan challenged Him to do, to which Jesus replied, "It is written again, 'You shall not tempt the LORD your God'" (4:7). Just as Jesus refused to submit to Satan's temptation, He rejected the taunting suggestions of the gawkers at Golgotha.

Second, the priests, scribes, and elders could not stop gloating over Him: **Likewise the chief priests also, mocking with the scribes and elders, said, "He saved others; Himself He cannot save. If He is the King of Israel, let Him now come down from the cross, and we will believe Him. He trusted in God; let Him deliver Him now if He will have Him; for He said, 'I am the Son of God'"** (vv. 41–43). They insinuated that Jesus did not have the power He had claimed to have, and like the passers-by, they challenged Him to come down from the cross, promising to believe in Him if He would. I do not know how many times I have heard people talk like these men, saying, "If only God would do such and such, I would believe in Him." If you are reading this book and you are not a believer in Jesus Christ, what more does God have to do before you will bow before Him? God has thoroughly verified the identity of His Son. He has done all He needs to do, but many people choose to mock and blaspheme just as these religious leaders did.

Third, Matthew reports, **the robbers who were crucified with Him reviled Him with the same thing** (v. 44). Though they themselves were dying, they joined in the mockery. Thankfully, we know that one of the two changed his tune and expressed belief in Jesus before his death (Luke 23:39–43).

This passage is a record of ceaseless torment and pain of various kinds—mockery, abuse, embarrassment, terrible physical pain, taunting, and gloating. This was a terrible ordeal for Jesus—but much worse was yet to come.

127

JESUS' DEATH AND BURIAL

Matthew 27:45–66

Now from the sixth hour until the ninth hour there was darkness over all the land. And about the ninth hour Jesus cried out with a loud voice, saying, "Eli, Eli, lama sabachthani?" that is, "My God, My God, why have You forsaken Me?" Some of those who stood there, when they heard that, said, "This Man is calling for Elijah!" Immediately one of them ran and took a sponge, filled it with sour wine and put it on a reed, and offered it to Him to drink. The rest said, "Let Him alone; let us see if Elijah will come to save Him." And Jesus cried out again with a loud voice, and yielded up His spirit. Then, behold, the veil of the temple was torn in two from top to bottom; and the earth quaked, and the rocks were split, and the graves were opened; and many bodies of the saints who had fallen asleep were raised; and coming out of the graves after His resurrection, they went into the holy city and appeared to many. So when the centurion and those with him, who were guarding Jesus, saw the earthquake and the things that had happened, they feared greatly, saying, "Truly this was the Son of God!" And many women who followed Jesus from Galilee, ministering to Him, were there looking on from afar, among whom were Mary Magdalene, Mary the mother of James and Joses, and the mother of Zebedee's sons. Now when evening had come, there came a rich man from Arimathea, named Joseph, who himself had also become a disciple of Jesus. This man went to Pilate and asked for the body of Jesus. Then Pilate commanded the body to be given to him. When Joseph had taken the body, he wrapped it in a clean linen cloth, and laid it in his new tomb which he had hewn out of the rock; and he rolled a large stone against the door of the tomb, and departed. And Mary Magdalene was there, and the other Mary, sitting opposite the tomb.

> On the next day, which followed the Day of Preparation, the chief priests and Pharisees gathered together to Pilate, saying, "Sir, we remember, while He was still alive, how that deceiver said, 'After three days I will rise.' Therefore command that the tomb be made secure until the third day, lest His disciples come by night and steal Him away, and say to the people, 'He has risen from the dead.' So the last deception will be worse than the first." Pilate said to them, "You have a guard; go your way, make it as secure as you know how." So they went and made the tomb secure, sealing the stone and setting the guard.

The four Gospels, as we noted in the previous chapter, mainly give us a straightforward record of the events that surrounded the crucifixion and death of our Lord Jesus Christ. It is mainly in the Epistles, the New Testament letters that were written by some of the Apostles and their associates, that we find explanations of the meaning and significance of these events, and those men were able to provide these explanations only because of the inspiration of the Holy Spirit. So, anyone who was there at Golgotha on that first Good Friday and observed the crucifixion of Christ would not have understood that he or she was watching an event of supreme importance, a cosmic transaction, as the Man on the cross offered a perfect, once-for-all sacrifice, a propitiation of the wrath of God, an atonement for the sins of His people. They needed—and we need—the teachings of the Apostles to grasp these truths.

Nevertheless, Matthew offers some very interesting details about that day that are absent from the other Synoptic Gospels, and these details at least provide clues to the significance of the death of Jesus. As we will see in this chapter, these events made deep impressions on numerous people that day, and they have much to teach us as we read of these things twenty centuries later.

The Death of the Savior

First, Matthew reports the details of Jesus' final moments. He writes: **Now from the sixth hour until the ninth hour there was darkness over all the land** (v. 45). In the heart of the day, from noon until 3 p.m., there was darkness. It was not just gloomy, as might be the case on a cloudy day, but dark as in the deepest night. Some people speculate that a solar eclipse took place at the same time Jesus was being crucified. Personally, I think this was a supernatural darkness, a "divine eclipse," if you will. I believe it was in this time period that God the Father imputed the sins of His people to His Son, and the sight of Jesus bearing all these iniquities was so repugnant, the Father turned away from Him. In order for Jesus to pay for the sin of His people, He had to be cursed, and to be cursed meant that He had to be sent into the darkness, the darkness outside the camp, outside the holy city. The darkness was a sign of divine judgment on the sin Jesus was carrying, for God is too holy to even look at sin. The One who had come into the world as the incarnation of light was now the incarnation of darkness.

This explains what happened next. Matthew tells us, **And about the ninth hour Jesus cried out with a loud voice, saying, "Eli, Eli, lama sabachthani?" that is, "My God, My God, why have You forsaken Me?"** (v. 46). These are the only words of Jesus from the cross that Matthew records. He was at the end of His life. He had almost no breath left in Him. Death was only moments away. We would expect that whatever He might say at this point would be murmured or whispered. Not so. Lest anyone miss His words, our Lord used every ounce of energy in His being and cried with a loud voice, "Eli, Eli, lama sabachthani?" which is a mixture of Hebrew and Aramaic that means, "My God, My God, why have You forsaken Me?"

Why did He say this? Some say he was quoting Psalm 22:1, where this statement appears, but I doubt that. Others say He was feeling forsaken. I believe this is true, but He was not simply *feeling* forsaken, He *was* forsaken. He was forsaken not by His best friends, not by His mother, and not by His brothers and sisters, but by His heavenly Father. God had forsaken Him because He must forsake sin. If He had not forsaken Jesus, He would have to forsake every human being who is not covered by the blood of Christ. It is only by His forsakenness that we can be received into His family. It is only through His rejection that we can be adopted into the household of God.

Matthew writes that some who were there misunderstood what Jesus said: **Some of those who stood there, when they heard that, said, "This Man is calling for Elijah!"** (v. 47). They thought He was appealing for the help of Elijah, though there is no biblical reason to expect that He would have done so. When this happened, **Immediately one of them ran and took a sponge, filled it with sour wine and put it on a reed, and offered it to Him to drink. The rest said, "Let Him alone; let us see if Elijah will come to save Him"** (vv. 48–49). It seems that at least one of the bystanders felt some compassion for Jesus and offered Him a drink, or perhaps he simply wanted to keep Jesus talking. However, others urged him to desist so they could watch to see whether Elijah would come.

While they were waiting, **Jesus cried out again with a loud voice** (v. 50a). Matthew does not tell us what He said; He may have simply uttered a guttural cry. Luke reports that Jesus said, "Father, 'into Your hands I commit My spirit'" just before He died (23:46), and John tells us that He said, "It is finished!" at the moment of death (19:30). Matthew simply writes that Jesus **yielded up His spirit** (v. 50b).

What was finished? The forsakenness. If the time of forsakenness had not been complete, it would have been a futile thing for Jesus to commit His soul into the hands of the Father. At that point, however, He knew He could do so. The atonement was final. He had done the work the Father had sent Him to do. The work of redemption was complete. He would entrust Himself to the Father and wait for Sunday morning.

Significant Manifestations

Matthew then reports on a number of strange manifestations that accompanied Jesus' death. He writes: **Then, behold, the veil of the temple was torn in two from top to bottom** (v. 51a). The New King James Version speaks of a "veil," but Matthew was referring to a heavy, thick curtain that hung in the temple, not a thin, gauzy veil. It was the curtain that formed the Holy of Holies, the most sacred place in all of Judaism, in the interior of the temple. Originally, the ark of the covenant had been kept in the Holy of Holies in the tabernacle and in Solomon's temple, but it was lost around the time of the Babylonian conquest of Jerusalem. Only the high priest could enter the Holy of Holies, and then only once each year on the Day of Atonement. After several acts of purification, he would take the blood of the offered sacrifice into the Holy of Holies and sprinkle it on the mercy seat, the lid of the ark, which was regarded as the throne of God. This ritual was established by divine command immediately after the exodus from Egypt in the days of Moses, and it continued every year for fifteen hundred years.

Of course, the sprinkling of the blood of sacrificial bulls and goats on the mercy seat had no spiritual efficacy. It could not take away sin (Heb. 10:4). This ritual was designed to foreshadow the coming of the One who would offer Himself as a perfect sacrifice once and for all, giving His people access into the presence of God.

When sin first intruded into the creation in the garden of Eden, God banished the human race from fellowship with Him, and He placed an angel with a flaming sword at the entrance to the garden lest His fallen creatures should come again into the garden and into His immediate presence (Gen. 3:23–24). So, after sin came the barrier that blocked man's direct access into the presence of God. That barrier was symbolized by this massive curtain that blocked off the throne room of the holy God.

Finally, after fifteen hundred years of symbolic sacrifices, that which was symbolized actually took place on the cross, when the Lamb of God was offered once and for all as an atonement for the sins of His people. Immediately upon His death, God caused the eighty-foot-tall curtain that separated the people from the presence of God to be torn asunder, ripped from top to bottom, which indicated a divine action. This was a symbolic statement that the barrier was now removed. Therefore, when we come to church to worship God, there is no curtain that separates us from the presence of God. We gather in His presence each Lord's Day morning. We enjoy personal fellowship with Him. Jesus ended the separation by His sacrifice of Himself.

Matthew adds, **and the earth quaked, and the rocks were split** (v. 51b). Just as darkness had fallen over the land as Jesus hung on the cross (v. 45), there was another natural phenomenon at the moment of His death—a rock-splitting earthquake. Earthquakes are not uncommon in Palestine, but the timing of this quake reveals that it was of supernatural origin.

Finally, Matthew relates an even stranger occurrence: **and the graves were opened; and many bodies of the saints who had fallen asleep were raised; and coming out of the graves after His resurrection, they went into the holy city and appeared to many** (vv. 52–53). Matthew is the only Gospel writer who gives us this detail, and this is the only mention of it in the entire New Testament, for which reason some skeptics dismiss it as pure mythology. But we are dealing with the Word of God, so we must treat this account as factual and true. What are we to make of it?

The Jews did not bury people in the ground. They buried them in tombs similar to the one in which Jesus was buried, usually hollowed-out spaces in the rock. Perhaps as a consequence of the earthquake, many of these tombs around Jerusalem were broken open, exposing the bodies of those who had been buried in them. But not only were the tombs opened on Good Friday, but also, on Sunday, along with the resurrection of Jesus, several of those who were in these tombs were raised from the dead, and they came into Jerusalem and were seen by many people.

We do not know whether this resurrection was like that of Jesus', who rose with a glorified body (such as we will experience in the final resurrection), or more like the resurrection of Lazarus, who was given a second term of life on this planet but who ultimately died once more, to await the final resurrection. But no matter which it was, why did God cause this event to happen?

One of the classic works of Christian theology is titled *The Death of Death in the Death of Christ*. It was written by John Owen, the Puritan. The title expresses the biblical truth that one of the dimensions of the atoning death of Christ was His conquest over the last enemy, death itself (1 Cor. 15:21, 26; 2 Tim. 1:10; Heb. 2:14). In His death, Jesus removed the sting from the grave, so that death now is not punishment for sin but a transition to a better dimension.

The Apostle Paul said he was torn between two things—to stay among his people for their well-being or to depart and to be with Christ, which the apostle said was far better (Phil. 1:23–24). I do not think that the church has really understood that. We cling to life on this planet as if there is nothing else beyond it. But the message of the gospel is that Jesus is risen and has conquered this enemy, so that now our deaths are mere transitions and we have a continuity of personal existence, a continuity of consciousness. When we die, we do not go to sleep, but our spirits immediately go into the presence of Christ, which existence is far better than what we have in this world (Luke 23:43; 2 Cor. 5:8).

In this incident, we see, as it were, an earnest, a down payment, a promise that in the death and resurrection of Christ, death is defeated. The graves are opened and people come forth alive. That's the message of the Christian faith.

These incidents were not easily overlooked, and Matthew tells us, **So when the centurion and those with him, who were guarding Jesus, saw the earthquake and the things that had happened, they feared greatly, saying, "Truly this was the Son of God!"** (v. 54). The centurion and the Roman soldiers who had carried out Jesus' crucifixion noticed what happened. They had mocked Jesus when He was condemned and then had carried out His crucifixion. It was just another day on death-penalty duty for them—until the moment Jesus died. When the curtain was split, the earth was shaken, and the graves were opened, the centurion and his men were overcome with fear. I would venture to guess that they had seen hundreds of crucifixions, but they had never seen a prisoner's death bring about such manifestations. It all prompted them to say, "Truly this was the Son of God!" Jesus was rejected by His own people, but a Roman pagan observed the manner in which He died and made a profession of faith about the character and the nature of the crucified One.

Matthew also notes that quite a few others observed these manifestations: **And many women who followed Jesus from Galilee, ministering to Him, were there looking on from afar, among whom were Mary Magdalene, Mary the mother of James and Joses, and the mother of Zebedee's sons** (vv. 55–56). These women were present at the crucifixion and saw everything that happened.

The Beginning of Exaltation

As we study the life of Christ, we observe a general progression from exaltation to humiliation. There is a downward spiral that reaches the nadir of shame, suffering, torment, and humiliation at the cross. But then comes exaltation again. I used to ask my students in the seminary, "Where is the transition between humiliation and exaltation in the ministry of Jesus?" They all gave the same answer: the resurrection. Actually, however, the change from humiliation to exaltation began with the burial of Jesus.

This burial was foretold in the Old Testament prophecy of the Suffering Servant in Isaiah 53. The prophet wrote:

> He was oppressed and He was afflicted,
> Yet He opened not His mouth;
> He was led as a lamb to the slaughter,
> And as a sheep before its shearers is silent,
> So He opened not His mouth.
> He was taken from prison and from judgment,
> And who will declare His generation?
> For He was cut off from the land of the living;
> For the transgressions of My people He was stricken.
> And they made His grave with the wicked—
> But with the rich at His death,
> Because He had done no violence,
> Nor was any deceit in His mouth. (vv. 7–9)

This prophecy declares that the fact that the Suffering Servant's grave would be with the rich would be an indication of His vindication. It would be an honor that would be accorded to Him because He had done no violence. Normally, the bodies of criminals who were executed under Roman law in Jerusalem were carted off and thrown unceremoniously into the city garbage dump. This was part of the disgrace of being executed by crucifixion. But as the prophecy foretold, Jesus was spared this ignominy and was buried "with the rich."

Matthew writes: **Now when evening had come, there came a rich man from Arimathea, named Joseph, who himself had also become a disciple of Jesus. This man went to Pilate and asked for the body of Jesus. Then Pilate commanded the body to be given to him. When Joseph had taken the body, he wrapped it in a clean linen cloth, and laid it in his new tomb which he had hewn out of the rock; and he rolled a large stone against the door of the tomb, and departed. And Mary Magdalene was there, and the other Mary, sitting opposite the tomb** (vv. 57–61).

Joseph of Arimathea was not only a rich man; he was a "prominent council member" (Mark 15:43), probably a member of the Sanhedrin, the ruling body of the Jews. But not only that, he was a disciple of Jesus, but secretly because he feared the other Jewish leaders (John 19:38). His wealth and position gave him access to the governor, and he used that access to go to Pilate to ask for Jesus' body, which request Pilate granted. Joseph then wrapped Jesus' body in a clean linen shroud and laid it in his own tomb, which was newly hewn out of the rock in a nearby garden (John 19:41). Mary Magdalene and "the other Mary" (possibly Jesus' mother) observed His burial, having followed the body from the site of His crucifixion.

Jesus was given a burial in style, in a private tomb owned by one of the wealthiest men in the city. Some believe that His burial is recorded in the Gospels merely to cause people to understand that Jesus was really dead. That may have had something to do with it. But I think it had to do with the beginning of His exaltation. He had said on the cross, at the end of His ordeal of being forsaken by the Father, "It is finished!" (John 19:30). He had completed the work and paid the price. The humiliation was finished. From that moment on, God was determined that His only Son should be exalted forever and ever.

Finally, Matthew tells us of one other small but significant event that occurred: **On the next day, which followed the Day of Preparation, the chief priests and Pharisees gathered together to Pilate, saying, "Sir, we remember, while He was still alive, how that deceiver said, 'After three days I will rise.' Therefore command that the tomb be made secure until the third day, lest His disciples come by night and steal Him away, and say to the people, 'He has risen from the dead.' So the last deception will be worse than the first." Pilate said to them, "You have a guard; go your way, make it as secure as you know how." So they went and made the tomb secure, sealing the stone and setting the guard** (vv. 62–66).

The priests and Pharisees wanted to be sure the disciples had no opportunity to claim that Jesus had risen from death. They understood that He had said He would return to life in three days, so they knew if they could keep the body locked away in the tomb that long, they would be able to refute any claim that Jesus had risen. Therefore, they asked Pilate to station Roman guards at the tomb until the third day passed. Pilate granted this request, and the Jewish authorities and Roman soldiers inspected the stone that sealed the entrance to the tomb, sealed it, and set a guard. They believed they had prepared for every contingency, but they were dealing with a power they could not contain.

128

THE RESURRECTION

Matthew 28:1–15

Now after the Sabbath, as the first day of the week began to dawn, Mary Magdalene and the other Mary came to see the tomb. And behold, there was a great earthquake; for an angel of the Lord descended from heaven, and came and rolled back the stone from the door, and sat on it. His countenance was like lightning, and his clothing as white as snow. And the guards shook for fear of him, and became like dead men. But the angel answered and said to the women, "Do not be afraid, for I know that you seek Jesus who was crucified. He is not here; for He is risen, as He said. Come, see the place where the Lord lay. And go quickly and tell His disciples that He is risen from the dead, and indeed He is going before you into Galilee; there you will see Him. Behold, I have told you." So they went out quickly from the tomb with fear and great joy, and ran to bring His disciples word. And as they went to tell His disciples, behold, Jesus met them, saying, "Rejoice!" So they came and held Him by the feet and worshiped Him. Then Jesus said to them, "Do not be afraid. Go and tell My brethren to go to Galilee, and there they will see Me." Now while they were going, behold, some of the guard came into the city and reported to the chief priests all the things that had happened. When they had assembled with the elders and consulted together, they gave a large sum of money to the soldiers, saying, "Tell them, 'His disciples came at night and stole Him away while we slept.' And if this comes to the governor's ears, we will appease him and make you secure." So they took the money and did as they were instructed; and this saying is commonly reported among the Jews until this day.

In early 2011, I found myself giving rapt attention to television news coverage of a series of demonstrations and uprisings in Cairo, Egypt. I watched as the thronging multitude first was completely shocked and dejected when their wishes did not come true, then was overcome with delirious joy when the president of Egypt resigned and left Cairo. It was also interesting to listen to the news commentators and pundits reflecting on the significance of these events. As they pondered what was happening and guessed about what would follow the aftermath of this activity, one after another of the commentators said: "We're watching history unfold here. The consequences of this revolution could reverberate not only through the Middle East but through the whole world as more and more people who live under the oppression of dictators will take heart from this example and launch their own movements to oust those who oppress them."

The sanguine views of these commentators made me think back for a moment to the resurrection of Jesus. *There* was a watershed moment in history, because the resurrection was earthshaking not just for a week, a year, or a generation, but for the whole scope of human history. Christ's resurrection is celebrated not simply on an annual basis on Easter Sunday but every Lord's Day, every Sunday. What else could have convinced the early church to change its day of corporate worship from the seventh day of the week to the first day of the week except an event as momentous as Jesus' return from death? All that was celebrated and forecast by millennia of Sabbath celebrations was fulfilled in a significant way on the first day of the week. All of God's promises that His people would someday enter into rest were validated and vindicated by the resurrection of the Messiah. There is no way to overestimate the importance and significance of this event for us. It is something we need to think about all the time.

I get annoyed when people want to bring all religions of the world together and make them of equal validity and truth. In America, all religions have equal protection under the law, but equal protection under the law does not mean equal validity or equal truth. So, I am offended when people mention the name of Muhammad, Confucius, Buddha, or any other founders of the world's religions in the same breath as the name of Jesus. This I know: Mohammed died and stayed dead. So did Confucius. Buddha, as enlightened as he may have been, died and stayed dead. None of these other leaders provided an atonement for the sins of the people who put their trust in them. All of them are dead, save One, the Lord Jesus Christ, who alone made atonement for our sins and was raised for our justification.

So, we come to the passage in Matthew's Gospel wherein he records the resurrection of Jesus. This record is brief, as are so many of Matthew's accounts, but it is powerful in its simplicity.

Fear and Great Joy

Matthew tells us, **Now after the Sabbath, as the first day of the week began to dawn, Mary Magdalene and the other Mary came to see the tomb** (v. 1). The other Gospel writers tell us that the women went to the tomb with spices to anoint the body of Jesus (see Mark 16:1). At the time of His death and burial, the day was moving toward sunset and the beginning of the Jewish Sabbath. Joseph of Arimathea did everything he could to give Jesus a proper burial, but a complete anointing of the corpse was not possible under Jewish law. These woman wanted to show honor and devotion to Jesus by preparing His body for burial. So, they came to the tomb at their earliest opportunity, just as dawn was breaking on Sunday morning.

Mark records that as the women approached the tomb, they conversed with each other about a problem they might face: "Who will roll away the stone from the door of the tomb for us?" (16:3). They did not know whether they would be able to gain access to the body, but acting in faith that they would be able to find someone to move the heavy stone, they came to the tomb.

Their faith was rewarded, though in a way they never anticipated: **And behold, there was a great earthquake; for an angel of the Lord descended from heaven, and came and rolled back the stone from the door, and sat on it** (v. 2). As we saw in the previous chapter, there was an earthquake at the moment of Jesus' death (27:51). Here another earthquake occurred as an angel rolled back the stone and opened Jesus' tomb. It is interesting that Matthew and Mark speak of one angel, while Luke and John tell of two. We need not be bothered by this apparent contradiction; if there were two angels, there was certainly one, and the fact that two of the Gospel writers chose to report the actions and words of only one angel does not mean he was the only angel present.

Having rolled back the stone to open the tomb, the angel sat on the stone. Matthew describes him this way: **His countenance was like lightning, and his clothing as white as snow** (v. 3). The distinctive feature of this heavenly being was his brightness; his face was as bright as lightning and his clothing as white as snow, as befits an angel who might enter the presence of God. Not surprisingly, his appearance was a shock to the soldiers guarding the tomb. They were not asleep. They were on duty and prepared to repel anyone who would dare to try to steal the body of Jesus. They were armed and ready for anything—except an angel from heaven. Thus, Matthew writes, **And the guards shook for fear of**

him, and became like dead men (v. 4). They simply fainted with fear when they saw this resplendent sight.

Not the women. They endured the sight of the angel without fainting, though they were very fearful. Matthew tells us: **But the angel answered and said to the women, "Do not be afraid, for I know that you seek Jesus who was crucified"** (v. 5). Notice that Matthew says the angel *answered* them. They must have said something to him; perhaps they asked: "Who are you? Are you going to make us like these guards?" In his reply, the angel reassured the women. He told them they had no reason to fear, for he knew they had come to the tomb because they were looking for Jesus, not to keep people away from Jesus, as was the purpose of the guards.

Then the angel delivered astonishing, wonderful news to the women: **"He is not here; for He is risen, as He said. Come, see the place where the Lord lay"** (v. 6). Their errand to the tomb to anoint the body of Jesus had failed because the body of Jesus was not there. However, it was not because someone had stolen His body away. He was not in the tomb because living men do not belong in tombs. Jesus had risen from death, although the term here is in the passive voice, which means not that He had risen, as if it had happened under His own power, but that He had been raised. Jesus was raised by the Holy Spirit under the authority of the Father.

That the women might be convinced that Jesus was alive again, the angel invited them to look at the spot where His body had lain, for they were familiar with how the body had been arranged, having watched as Joseph of Arimathea placed it there (27:61). So, the women gazed into the empty tomb, probably filled with wonder and growing joy.

At this point, let me pause to say that our faith is not based on an empty tomb. There could be a thousand reasons why the tomb was empty, most of them having nothing to do with a resurrection or anything supernatural at all. Our faith is based on the resurrection appearances of the risen Jesus, on the testimony of the hundreds and hundreds of people who saw Him in His resurrected state. The empty tomb is a powerful and significant symbol of Jesus' victory over the grave, but it receives that power and significance because He was seen alive.

When the women had seen the tomb, the angel gave them a commandment: **"And go quickly and tell His disciples that He is risen from the dead, and indeed He is going before you into Galilee; there you will see Him. Behold, I have told you"** (v. 7). The angel charged the women to take word of the resurrection to the eleven disciples, who were hiding for fear that they too would be arrested (see John 20:19). He wanted them to go to Galilee, the focus of so much of Jesus' ministry. There, the angel promised, the disciples would see Him.

The women obeyed the angel without hesitation: **So they went out quickly from the tomb with fear and great joy, and ran to bring His disciples word** (v. 8). What an interesting combination of emotions—fear and great joy. They did not know whether to cry or laugh. They wanted to both tremble and leap with joy. It was terrifying to see an angel, but it was thrilling to hear such an announcement. Nothing could give them more joy than to hear that their beloved Lord was alive again, not dead as they had known Him to be. Such news could not be kept, so they hastened to tell the disciples.

A Reason for Rejoicing

However, their joy soon became even more surpassing. Matthew writes: **And as they went to tell His disciples, behold, Jesus met them, saying, "Rejoice!"** (v. 9a). Jesus said one word to them, and if Jesus ever uttered a word that did not need to be uttered, it was here. He did not formally greet them. He did not say, "It is I," or some such words to identify Himself, for apparently they knew Him. He simply said, "Rejoice!" and I imagine that at that moment joy completely took over their hearts and all their fear was forgotten.

Why did Jesus say, "Rejoice"? He had overcome death. He had conquered the great and last enemy that scares us all. No matter what happens in this world, no matter what pain and suffering may befall us, those things are not worthy to be compared to the joy that is set before the people of God (Rom. 8:18), because He lives. God raised Him from the dead, not only to vindicate Him but to make Him the firstborn of many brothers (Rom. 8:29). He has been raised for us with the promise that if we believe in Him we too will be raised. Christians have reason to rejoice exceedingly (2 Cor. 7:4, 13).

Notice what the women did: **So they came and held Him by the feet and worshiped Him** (v. 9b). His feet were on the ground. So, in order to hold Him by the feet, they had to get down on the ground. They fell to the ground on their faces and took hold of His feet. This was the kind of thing that people in antiquity did only for kings. But the women went even further. They recognized Him first as their King and then as their God. They knew that while great homage was due to a king, they must never worship a king, because the highest king in the world is still a creature, and to worship him would be an act of idolatry. But the women did not hold back their worship from Jesus. They acknowledged Him as their God.

Matthew then tells us: **Jesus said to them, "Do not be afraid. Go and tell My brethren to go to Galilee, and there they will see Me"** (v. 10). Jesus encouraged the women not to be afraid—again, I can only imagine that this exhortation was largely unnecessary—and then repeated the command the angel had given them, to tell the disciples to go to Galilee, where they would see Him. So, the women left Him, running to tell the disciples the wonderful, glorious news that their Lord and Savior was alive once more.

Matthew adds a postscript to this account to explain what happened to the stricken guards at the tomb and to account for one of the main lies about the resurrection. He writes: **Now while they were going, behold, some of the guard came into the city and reported to the chief priests all the things that had happened. When they had assembled with the elders and consulted together, they gave a large sum of money to the soldiers, saying, "Tell them, 'His disciples came at night and stole Him away while we slept.' And if this comes to the governor's ears, we will appease him and make you secure." So they took the money and did as they were instructed; and this saying is commonly reported among the Jews until this day** (vv. 11–15).

It seems the guards came to their senses after fainting at the sight of the angel while the women were on their way to the disciples. They could see that the tomb was empty, so there was nothing they could do except report to the priests. When the guards told what had happened, the priests and elders bribed them to spread the false story that they had been sleeping on the job at the tomb and the disciples had stolen the body of Jesus in the night. The problem was that sleeping while on guard represented a major dereliction of duty, one for which the soldiers could be put to death. To appease the guards' concerns about this possibility, the priests and elders promised to smooth things over if the governor should happen to hear the false story. So, the guards took the bribe and spread the false story, and Matthew tells us it was still going around at the time he wrote his Gospel years later.

Actually, this story is still repeated today. However, the idea that the disciples stole Jesus' body and proclaimed that He was alive is plausible only if the evidence for the resurrection consists of nothing more than an empty tomb. But the Jewish religious leaders did not have enough money to cover up the fact that Jesus was risen. Furthermore, they could not keep Him from appearing to hundreds of His followers, many of whom were willing to die for Him. The story of the resurrection is not a lie but the truth, and it is a cause for exceeding joy among those who love the risen Christ.

129

THE GREAT COMMISSION

Matthew 28:16–20

Then the eleven disciples went away into Galilee, to the mountain which Jesus had appointed for them. When they saw Him, they worshiped Him; but some doubted. And Jesus came and spoke to them, saying, "All authority has been given to Me in heaven and on earth. Go therefore and make disciples of all the nations, baptizing them in the name of the Father and of the Son and of the Holy Spirit, teaching them to observe all things that I have commanded you; and lo, I am with you always, even to the end of the age." Amen.

We have come to the final verses of the Gospel of Matthew, and here, in a sense, the book comes full circle. Matthew began by presenting a genealogy of Jesus, but unlike Luke, who traced Jesus' ancestry all the way back to Adam (Luke 3:23–38), Matthew traces it back to Abraham (1:1–17). As we have seen, Matthew was writing to Jews, and he was very concerned about Jesus' ancestry and genealogical credentials, for these were important matters for the Jews. Thus, it was perfectly natural for him to trace Jesus' ancestry back to Abraham, the father of the Jewish nation, whom God called out of a pagan land and with whom He made a covenant, which was fulfilled at last in the coming of Christ.

Consider again the great promise that God made to Abraham:

> Now the Lord had said to Abram:
> "Get out of your country,

> From your family
> And from your father's house,
> To a land that I will show you.
> I will make you a great nation;
> I will bless you
> And make your name great;
> And you shall be a blessing.
> I will bless those who bless you,
> And I will curse him who curses you;
> And in you all the families of the earth shall be blessed." (Gen. 12:1–3)

In this promise, God pledged that He would bless Abraham and all those who would bless him. But notice that God also said Abraham would "be a blessing," and that "in you all the families of the earth shall be blessed." God was saying that He would make Abraham a nation, and that from that nation the whole world would be blessed.

Matthew's account of the life and ministry of Jesus reveals that He spent nearly His whole lifetime within a hundred miles of the place where He was born. Except for a period of time when He was taken to Egypt as an infant to escape the wrath of King Herod (2:13–15) and a couple of days when He crossed over the northern border of Israel (15:21), He never left that tiny country, which is no bigger than the state of Maryland. His focus was very narrow, principally to the Jews. Where, then, was the universal blessing that was promised to Abraham?

Jesus did not take the gospel to all the nations of the world personally. He left that task for His bride, the church. We see this in the passage that is before us in this chapter, but also in the parallel account in Acts 1:4–8. Just before Jesus ascended to heaven, the disciples asked, "Lord, will You at this time restore the kingdom to Israel?" (v. 6b). I would not have been surprised to see Jesus become frustrated at this point and say, "How many times do I have to tell you I'm not going to do that?" But He did not respond in that way. He simply said, "It is not for you to know times or seasons which the Father has put in His own authority" (v. 7). In other words, they were asking about something that was none of their business. But then He went on to explain the task with which they needed to concern themselves: "But you shall receive power when the Holy Spirit has come upon you; and you shall be witnesses to Me in Jerusalem, and in all Judea and Samaria, and to the end of the earth" (v. 8).

This was Jesus' blueprint for the building of His church, the spread of the gospel. Notice how it works outward from Jerusalem. The disciples were to wait in Jerusalem until the Holy Spirit came upon them. Then they were to begin preaching about Him there. Next, they were to reach out to all of Judea. But they were to keep going, even to Samaria, that region of mixed-race people whom the Jews so despised. And yet, Samaria was not the limit either—they were to go to the ends of the earth. They were to preach everywhere.

The book of Acts shows that the disciples followed this pattern. They began in Jerusalem on the Day of Pentecost. They moved outward into Judea. They went among the Samaritans with the good news. Then the Apostle Paul began striving to take the gospel to the entire Mediterranean world—to Asia Minor, to Greece, to Rome, and beyond. With that, the promise God had made to Abraham began to be fulfilled, and it is still being fulfilled today as the church carries on its mission.

The Supreme Apostle

With that background, let us now look at Matthew's account of this final interaction of Jesus and His disciples. He writes: **Then the eleven disciples went away into Galilee, to the mountain which Jesus had appointed for them** (v. 16). Matthew does not specify which mountain Jesus had appointed or when He appointed it. All we know is that Jesus told the disciples to go to Galilee (vv. 7, 10), but no doubt He specified the place well before He died or in a post-resurrection conversation that is not recorded for us. The disciples did as they were instructed and made the journey north to meet Him at this mountain.

Matthew goes on to say, **When they saw Him, they worshiped Him; but some doubted** (v. 17). The fact that they worshiped Him is so important. They did not simply greet Him and listen to Him. Like the women who sought Him at the tomb, they worshiped Him. The deity of Christ was not a doctrine that was invented in the fourth century at the Council of Nicea. It is clearly established in the New Testament, and the behavior of His followers confirms the propriety of it. If Jesus was not God incarnate, their act of worshiping Him would have been the epitome of idolatry. They would have been worshiping the creature rather than the Creator. But they readily worshiped Him, and Jesus received their worship without rebuke.

Notice, however, that Matthew also says "some doubted." Other translations read "some hesitated." Scholars argue about whether it was some of the eleven who doubted or whether others were present at this meeting, and it was some of them who had doubts. We know that on one occasion, the risen Jesus appeared to more than five hundred people at once (1 Cor. 15:6), although we cannot be sure this was that occasion. In any case, there was an initial hesitation by some in the band of the disciples, even though they were seeing Him with their own eyes. This doubt is reminiscent of the skepticism of Thomas, who said, "Unless

I see in His hands the print of the nails, and put my finger into the print of the nails, and put my hand into His side, I will not believe" (John 20:25b).

Do you have any hesitation about embracing Jesus as God? Are you teetering back and forth, hoping He is the Son of God, but not entirely sure? There's an old adage in our culture, a proverbial statement that certainly applies in this case: He who hesitates is lost. Jesus came to a people who were lost. He comes to us when we are lost. When He comes, that is not the time to hesitate. That is the time to fall on your face and embrace Him as your Lord and your God. That is what Thomas did. His hesitation vanished when Christ appeared to him. He said, "My Lord and my God!" (v. 28). He immediately began to worship Jesus. I encourage you to do the same.

Matthew then tells us, **And Jesus came and spoke to them, saying, "All authority has been given to Me in heaven and on earth"** (v. 18). Jesus pronounced that He is the supreme Apostle of the Christian faith. I used to ask my students in seminary, "Who was the greatest Apostle in the New Testament?" They would start arguing over Peter, Paul, and the rest, until finally I would jump in and say, "No, no, no, Peter, Paul, John, and all the others are not worthy to be mentioned in the same breath as the supreme Apostle in the New Testament." The Greek word *apostolos*, from which we get the English word *apostle*, means "one who is sent." An apostle is one who is sent by a king and given the king's authority to speak in behalf of the king. So, the supreme Apostle in the New Testament is Jesus, to whom the Father gave all authority in heaven and on earth. There is no limit to Jesus' authority as Lord. He, in turn, said to His disciples, "As the Father has sent Me, I also send you" (John 20:21b). The disciples became Apostles of the supreme Apostle.

We have to understand that when we speak of the Great Commission, it is not the great suggestion. It is not the grand idea. It is not an essay on manifest destiny. It is a mandate from the King of kings, who possesses all authority in heaven and on earth. We say that Jesus is the Lord of the church and that we believe in Him, and that means we must obey this mandate He has given us.

The Great Commission

According to Matthew, Jesus told His disciples: **"Go therefore and make disciples of all the nations, baptizing them in the name of the Father and of the Son and of the Holy Spirit, teaching them to observe all things that I have commanded you"** (vv. 19–20a). There are four imperatives in this commission: (1) go, (2) make disciples, (3) baptize, and (4) teach.

From time to time in the Gospel records, we see Jesus inviting people to come to Him. In one of His best-known invitations, He said, "Come to Me, all you who labor and are heavy laden, and I will give you rest" (Matt. 11:28). He welcomed people to come to Him for rest, for life, for provision, for comfort, for help of any kind. But we also see that when people came to Him, He often sent them away with a mission. So it was with the disciples. He sent them out. The first command in the great commission is "Go."

In early 2010, a devastating earthquake struck near Port-au-Prince, Haiti. An acquaintance of mine told me that he knew a doctor that was putting together a team to go down to give medical care to the Haitian people who were dying and severely injured. I brought that need to Saint Andrew's, and in one Sunday morning we raised more than $10,000 for that relief mission to Haiti. I talked to that doctor recently, and he said, "R.C., I went back to Haiti last week, and I saw so many people who I thought had little chance of making it." Then he gave me pictures of some of the people he had worked with, and he began to tell me about them. As he spoke, he started to weep. He said: "I can't believe what God has done in this—and your church is such an important part of that." That is the kind of thing that happens when we go.

But not only are we to go, we are to make disciples. I have found that it is relatively easy to raise funds to support missions work that is focused on evangelism. People see the importance of converting people to Christ. Likewise, it is easy to raise money to help starving children or for other kinds of mercy ministries because those needs are so glaring. But it is never easy to raise money for missions involving Christian education. People do not really think Christian education is all that important. However, when a person is converted, he may be ten years old, fifty years old, or ninety years old, but spiritually he is only a newborn. He needs to be nurtured spiritually and brought up to maturity in the faith.

I remember reading a biography of Billy Graham in which he remarked that he often laid awake at night wondering about the people who made decisions for Christ at his rallies. He wondered whether anyone was following up with them, teaching them, helping them become grounded in the faith. I am thankful he had that concern, which is a biblical concern. The Great Commission calls us to do more than work to convert people. It calls us to teach them, to ground them, to help them grow in conformity to Christ. That is our mission.

Jesus also commissioned His church to baptize. Why did He see fit to include this ritual in the Great Commission? Just as the covenant that God made with Abraham was sealed by the covenant sign of circumcision, so the new covenant that Christ has given to the church is sealed by the sign of baptism. Baptism communicates that we have been united to Jesus Christ. It shows that we have been cleansed from sin, regenerated by the Holy Spirit, and buried and raised again with Jesus Christ, just to mention a few of its significations. God promises that all who have faith in His Son, Jesus Christ, will participate in all of the promises, all of the benefits, that Christ has secured. Baptism is not a sign of one's faith; it is a sign of the faithfulness of God to give all of His Son to all who believe. That is why the Apostles not only preached, but also they baptized individuals and entire households, all who came into the body of Christ in the first-century church. It is also very important that baptism is to be in the Trinitarian formula—Father, Son, and Holy Spirit.

Finally, we are to teach. Jesus commanded the disciples to teach others to "observe"—that is, to obey—"all things" He had commanded. We are to make known the whole counsel of God, pressing it home to people's hearts and minds.

The Presence of Christ

Jesus did not end the Great Commission with this final admonition. Instead, He ended it with one of the most incredible promises He ever pronounced: **"And lo, I am with you always, even to the end of the age"** (v. 20b). He assured the disciples that wherever they went to fulfill their mission, whatever borders they might cross—physical, cultural, racial, socioeconomic, and so forth—He would be with them. Though He returned to heaven, He remained with them, in a real sense. In regard to His human nature, Jesus is no longer present with us. He is in heaven at the right hand of God. But regarding His divine nature, which is perfectly united at every second to His human nature, He is never absent from us.

Knowing that Jesus is always with us, there should be no place on this globe we are afraid to go. If He were standing beside us and said, "Come; go with Me," we would go wherever He led us. However, since we cannot see Him, we do not always live as if He is with us. But this is His promise. If He broke it, it would be the first one He ever broke, because Jesus does not know how to fail to keep His word. He is not merely present in our hearts, in our consciousness, or in our memories. He is really present. He is always with us.

This is the Great Commission. Any church that accepts the commission and works to fulfill it, trusting in the promise it contains, will be a blessed body of believers.

Finally, Matthew closes his Gospel with one simple word: **Amen** (v. 20c). Just as we use this simple word to conclude our prayers, Matthew uses it to conclude his Gospel. It means essentially, "It is so." This is Matthew's closing declaration that all he has written is faithful, and we do well to receive it as such.

INDEX OF NAMES

ABOUT THE AUTHOR

Dr. R.C. Sproul was founder of Ligonier Ministries, founding pastor of Saint Andrew's Chapel in Sanford, Fla., first president of Reformation Bible College, and executive editor of *Tabletalk* magazine. His radio program, *Renewing Your Mind*, is still broadcast daily on hundreds of radio stations around the world and can also be heard online. He was author of more than one hundred books, including *The Holiness of God*, *Chosen by God*, and *Everyone's a Theologian*. He was recognized throughout the world for his articulate defense of the inerrancy of Scripture and the need for God's people to stand with conviction upon His Word.